Filiation and the Protection of Parentless Children

Nadjma Yassari · Lena-Maria Möller ·
Marie-Claude Najm
Editors

Filiation and the Protection of Parentless Children

Towards a Social Definition of the Family in Muslim Jurisdictions

ASSER PRESS

Springer

Editors
Nadjma Yassari
Research Group "Changes in God's Law—An Inner Islamic Comparison of Family and Succession Laws"
Max Planck Institute for Comparative and International Private Law
Hamburg, Germany

Lena-Maria Möller
Research Group "Changes in God's Law—An Inner Islamic Comparison of Family and Succession Laws"
Max Planck Institute for Comparative and International Private Law
Hamburg, Germany

Marie-Claude Najm
Centre of Legal Studies and Research for the Arab World
Faculty of Law and Political Science
Saint Joseph University of Beirut
Beirut, Lebanon

ISBN 978-94-6265-313-9 ISBN 978-94-6265-311-5 (eBook)
https://doi.org/10.1007/978-94-6265-311-5

Published by T.M.C. ASSER PRESS, The Hague, The Netherlands www.asserpress.nl
Produced and distributed for T.M.C. ASSER PRESS by Springer-Verlag Berlin Heidelberg

This T.M.C. ASSER PRESS imprint is published by the registered company Springer-Verlag GmbH, DE part of Springer Nature
The registered company address is: Heidelberger Platz 3, 14197 Berlin, Germany

Preface

This volume marks the completion of the second project of the Max Planck Working Group on Child Law in Muslim Countries. It compiles selected contributions presented at the workshop "Establishing filiation: Towards a social definition of the family in Islamic and Middle Eastern Law?", which, under the auspices of the Research Group "Changes in God's Law—An Inner Islamic Comparison of Family and Succession Law", was convened in cooperation with the German Orient-Institut and the Centre of Legal Studies and Research for the Arab World (CEDROMA) at the Saint Joseph University in Beirut, Lebanon, from 8 to 11 November 2017.

While the Working Group's first project focused on the principle of the best interests of the child and parental care, the second project phase explores existing social and legal structures providing for the care and protection of "parentless" children. Parentless children, in this context, are defined as either children of unknown filiation, such as foundlings, children who lack permanent caretakers due to their parents' death or inability to provide care, and, finally, children who lack paternal filiation due to the oftentimes strict rules regarding the legal status of children born out of wedlock in contemporary Muslim jurisdictions.

In order to understand how different concepts of alternative care and protection of parentless children function, it is crucial to first explore how filiation operates so as to identify those children potentially facing difficulties in instances where their legal filiation is somehow flawed, or where their biological parents are absent. Accordingly, the eleven country reports collected herein engage in an initial analysis examining (i) how maternal and paternal filiation is established (either by operation of law or by an autonomous party act, e.g. acknowledgement) and (ii) the legal and social status of children that are not covered by these legal schemes. In a second step, structures in place for the care and protection of parentless children are presented and discussed with a view to identifying their legal implications and their potential to recreate a full parent–child relationship.

In addition to the country-specific analyses collected here, the contributions authored by Robert Gleave and Ahmed Fekry Ibrahim explore the subject matter from the perspective of pre-modern Shiite and Sunni legal doctrine, respectively.

Further, Béligh Elbalti discusses questions of filiation in the private international law regimes of contemporary Arab countries. Finally, a synopsis at the end of the volume provides a comparative analysis of the encompassed themes.

The editors wish to thank the former Orient-Institut director Stefan Leder, the current director Birgit Schäbler and the former deputy director Astrid Meier as well as Olaf Dufey, Hussein Hussein and Caroline Kinj for hosting the Working Group's day-one session at the German Orient-Institut Beirut and Zeina Risha and Hiba El Ahmadié for their support in organizing the day-two workshop session, as well as a public lecture programme, at the Saint Joseph University of Beirut. We also would like to express our deep gratitude to Tess Chemnitzer, Michael Friedman, and Jane Yager for their continuous assistance in editing and formatting this volume.

Hamburg, Germany — Nadjma Yassari
Hamburg, Germany — Lena-Maria Möller
Beirut, Lebanon — Marie-Claude Najm
January 2019

Contents

Editors and Contributors

About the Editors

Nadjma Yassari is a senior research fellow at the Max Planck Institute for Comparative and International Private Law in Hamburg, Germany, where she heads the Department for the Laws of Islamic Countries. Since April 2009, she has led the Research Group "Changes in God's Law—An Inner Islamic Comparison of Family and Succession Laws". Her main fields of research are national and private international law of Islamic countries, particularly the Arab Middle East, Iran, Afghanistan and Pakistan, with a special focus on family and successions law. In her monograph *Die Brautgabe im Familienvermögensrecht—Innerislamischer Rechtsvergleich und Integration in das deutsche Recht* (Mohr Siebeck, 2014), she considers the function of the dower within the marital property law regimes of pre-modern Islamic law, contemporary Muslim jurisdictions and German law. Born on 6 March 1971 in Tehran, Iran, she studied law in Vienna, Paris and London. She holds an LL.M. from the School of Oriental and African Studies at the University of London and an LL.D. from the University of Innsbruck in Austria. In 2000/2001, she spent a year at the faculty of languages of the University of Damascus in Syria. In 2016, she was awarded a postdoctoral degree (Habilitation) from the University of Hamburg.

Lena-Maria Möller is a senior research fellow at the Max Planck Institute for Comparative and International Private Law in Hamburg, Germany. Holding an M.A. in Middle East studies and a Ph.D. in law, she has taught and researched in the area of Islamic law, with a particular focus on Muslim family law, as well as in comparative and private international law. She has held teaching positions at the University of Hamburg, the University of Augsburg and, most recently, the University of Münster, where she served as visiting professor of Islamic law. She is the author of *Die Golfstaaten auf dem Weg zu einem modernen Recht für die Familie?* (Mohr Siebeck, 2015) and a co-editor of *Parental Care and the Best Interests of the Child in Muslim Countries* (T.M.C. Asser Press 2017). Her articles have been published in journals including Hawwa (Journal of Women of the

Middle East and the Islamic World), Journal of Private International Law and The American Journal of Comparative Law, and she is a contributor to *Brill's Encyclopedia of Law and Religion* and the *Encyclopedia of Women and Islamic Cultures*.

Marie-Claude Najm is a professor at the Faculty of Law and Political Science of Saint Joseph University of Beirut, Lebanon, where she is president of the Department of Private Law and director of the Centre of Legal Studies and Research for the Arab World (CEDROMA) and a visiting professor at Panthéon-Sorbonne University (Paris I) and Panthéon-Assas University (Paris II). Her focal field of research is private international law, specifically concentrating on family and successions law. Born in Beirut, she studied law in Paris and Beirut and holds a Ph.D. from Panthéon-Assas University (Paris II), and she is an Agrégée des Facultés françaises de droit. Her main publications include *Principes directeurs du droit international privé et conflit de civilisations: Relations entre systèmes laïques et systèmes religieux* (Dalloz, 2005); "La Cour de cassation française et la répudiation musulmane, une décennie après l'entrée en vigueur des réformes du droit de la famille au Maroc et en Algérie", Journal de droit international, 2015; "The Enforcement of Foreign Judgments in Lebanese Private International Law", Yearbook of Private International Law 2015/2016; "Lebanon", in Basedow/Rühl/Ferrari/De Miguel (eds.), *Encyclopedia of Private International Law* (Edward Elgar Publishing, 2017).

Contributors

Souhayma Ben Achour Faculté de Droit et des Sciences Politiques, Université de Tunis El Manar, Tunis, Tunisia

Harith Al-Dabbagh Faculty of Law, University of Montreal, Montreal, QC, Canada

Béligh Elbalti Graduate School of Law and Politics, Osaka University, Toyonaka, Osaka, Japan

Dörthe Engelcke Max Planck Institute for Comparative and International Private Law, Hamburg, Germany

Robert Gleave Institute of Arab and Islamic Studies, University of Exeter, Exeter, UK

Melanie Guénon Asien-Afrika-Institut, Universität Hamburg, Hamburg, Germany

Katherine E. Hoffman Department of Anthropology, Northwestern University, Evanston, IL, USA

Ahmed Fekry Ibrahim Institute of Islamic Studies, McGill University, Montreal, QC, Canada

Lama Karamé The Legal Agenda, Badaro, Beirut, Lebanon

Isfandyar Ali Khan S&K Partnership, Peshawar, Pakistan

Dominik Krell Max Planck Institute for Comparative and International Private Law, Hamburg, Germany

Myriam Mehanna The Legal Agenda, Badaro, Beirut, Lebanon

Azizah Mohd Ahmad Ibrahim Kulliyyah of Laws, International Islamic University Malaysia, Kuala Lumpur, Malaysia

Lena-Maria Möller Max Planck Institute for Comparative and International Private Law, Hamburg, Germany

Marie-Claude Najm Faculty of Law and Political Science, Saint Joseph University, Ashrafieh, Beirut, Lebanon

Ayesha Shahid Coventry University, Coventry, UK

Nadjma Yassari Max Planck Institute for Comparative and International Private Law, Hamburg, Germany

Chapter 1
Care of Abandoned Children in Sunni Islamic Law: Early Modern Egypt in Theory and Practice

Ahmed Fekry Ibrahim

Contents

Abstract The concept of the *best interests of the child* comes into tension with premodern Islamic law with respect to the issue of adoption because Islamic law does not allow a child to take the name or inheritance of her or his non-biological parents. Many scholars and policymakers have considered premodern Islamic

Ahmed Fekry Ibrahim is assistant professor at the Institute of Islamic Studies at McGill University, Montreal.

I am indebted to Dr. Walter Edward Young for his help with the final drafts of this chapter and to my students, Ahmad Munir and Omar Edaibat, for their research help. I am grateful to the Social Sciences and Humanities Research Council (SSHRC) for their research grant, which enabled me to conduct the research for this article.

A. F. Ibrahim (✉)
Institute of Islamic Studies, McGill University, 3485 McTavish Street, Montreal, QC H3A 0E1, Canada
e-mail: ahmed.f.ibrahim@mcgill.ca

N. Yassari et al. (eds.), *Filiation and the Protection of Parentless Children*, https://doi.org/10.1007/978-94-6265-311-5_1

juristic discourse to violate the child's best interests as it creates a number of disadvantaged legal categories of children in Islamic law, all while prohibiting adoption. In this chapter, I show the ways in which premodern Muslim jurists and judges (with focus on early modern Egypt) were able to circumvent the prohibition of adoption through discursive moves and practices, which helped create a family life for many parentless and non-biological children. I discuss the institutional care of children to show that most premodern children were indeed given a family life rather than left to the care of orphanages. The premodern jurists' permissive attitude toward the acknowledgement of children without the presentation of evidence of paternity was one of the ways in which they were able to provide a family life for foundlings and abandoned children more broadly.

Keywords Adoption · *kafāla* · Paternity · Foundlings · Acknowledgement · Medieval charities

> Since the Islamic Sharia is one of the fundamental sources of legislation in Egyptian positive law and because the Sharia, in enjoining the provision of every means of protection and care for children by numerous ways and means, does not include among those ways and means the system of adoption existing in other bodies of positive law, the government of the Arab Republic of Egypt expresses its reservation with respect to all clauses and provisions relating to adoption in the said convention, and in particular with respect to the provisions governing adoption in Articles 20 and 21 of the Convention.[1]

1.1 Introduction

The above quote expresses Egypt's reservation regarding certain articles of the Convention on the Rights of the Child (CRC), which was signed by Egypt in 1990. It is based on the assumption that adoption (*al-tabannī*) – in which a child takes the name of the adoptive parent and whereby she is treated as a biological child with respect to inheritance and kinship ties – is strictly forbidden in Islamic law.[2] Some policymakers and scholars have interpreted the prohibition of adoption as reflecting a lack of concern for the best interests of the child in premodern Islamic law. This assumption has been recently challenged by scholars who have argued that there were sites of 'quasi-adoptive relationships,' 'functional equivalents,' or 'alternatives' to adoption in Islamic juristic discourse.[3]

In this chapter, I aim to build on the revisionist historiography of Islamic adoptive practices by exploring the ways in which Sunni jurists writing treatises of law and Sunni judges adjudicating on matters of family law in early modern Egypt

[1] Paradelle 1999, pp 105–6; United Nations 2005, p 325.

[2] For more on *al-tabannī* see Al-Mawsūʿa al-Fiqhiyya 1990, s.v. *tabannī*, vol 10, pp 120–22; Powers 2008; Chaumont 2012; Mattson 2009.

[3] Yassari 2015, pp 927–62; Landau-Tasseron 2003, pp 169–92; Pollack et al. 2004, p 693.

(1517–1820s) found loopholes around the prohibition of adoption to provide private care – and even filiation – for Egyptian children without challenging the *theoretical* prohibition of adoption head-on. The strategies that Ottoman Egyptian judges utilized to circumvent the prohibition of adoption provided avenues for care of non-biological children that were functionally identical to adoption under the fiction of biological parenthood, which jurists knowingly facilitated for the welfare of children. The situation of adoption in early modern Egypt thus resembles the situation regarding the charging of interest, which, while prohibited *in theory*, was practiced in early modern Egypt through legal stratagems (*ḥiyal*).

The idea of childhood, the rights of the child, and the place of the child in society are all questions that have undergone radical transformations in Muslim countries in the modern period in the same way that gender underwent much contestation throughout the nineteenth and twentieth centuries. These changes were the result of the encounter with colonialism, rapid urbanization, industrialization, and massive improvements in healthcare – especially with respect to infant mortality rates. The Swedish reformer Allen Key predicted in 1900 that the twentieth century would be the 'century of the child.' Despite the varying ways in which childhood was conceptualized and children's rights were theorized in different cultural and legal traditions, the twentieth century witnessed a slow convergence of conceptions of childhood and children's rights, a phenomenon that some historians have dubbed the 'globalization of childhood.'[4] This convergence resulted from both the promotion of Euro-American ideas about childhood across the world through international conventions and the influence of popular culture both locally and transnationally. Despite the Euro-American origins of the children's rights discourses prevalent in international law, such discourses have also been claimed by many nation-states in the global south that have signed international conventions such as the Convention on the Rights of the Child (CRC), which was promulgated by the United Nations in 1989. It states:

> In all actions concerning the child, whether undertaken by public or private social welfare institutions, courts of law, administrative authorities or legislative bodies, the best interests of the child shall be a primary consideration. (Article 3, para 1)

In the realm of care of non-biological children, international conventions contain a number of assumptions about what is best for children, which are themselves driven by non-neutral cultural assumptions as well as the legal legacy of Euro-America, including the following: (1) it is better for the child to be raised by private citizens, rather than by the state in an orphanage; (2) it is better for a child to be raised in an environment that replicates a biological nuclear family, wherein the child takes the name of the adoptive parents and whereby she has a right to inheritance as if she were a biological child. Despite international conventions' general acceptance of alternative methods of care of non-biological children such as Islamic fosterage (*kafāla*), these assumptions implicitly privilege adoption over

[4] Thelen and Haukanes 2010, pp 1–4.

other types of care, creating sites of incompatibility with premodern Islamic jurisprudence, which is what this article seeks to disentangle.[5]

Islamic juristic discourse runs into serious tension or incompatibility with modern conceptions of the child's best interests in the following ways: (1) Islamic law does not allow for a family name to be given to a non-biological child; (2) inheritance is a right of biological children, and therefore non-biological children have no right of inheritance to an adoptive parent's estate; (3) even biological children who are born outside of wedlock are treated as non-biological children in that they have no right to paternity, nor to inheritance from the biological father. Marriage and biology are essential to a child receiving full rights, including a family name and inheritance rights – both of which are often considered part of the child's best interests in Euro-American adoption practices.[6] In light of these tensions, some children are placed at a disadvantage by virtue of the circumstances of their birth. There are therefore five main categories of children with respect to their legal status, the first of which represents the normative Muslim family:

(1) Children born in a valid marriage without any challenge to paternity levelled by the husband against his wife and where the parents are in charge of the children
(2) Children born in a valid marriage wherein the husband engages in the procedure of swearing on the wife's (unproven) unfaithfulness (*liʿān*), which has the consequence of establishing a divorce
(3) Children born too early (less than six months after the consummation of a marriage) or too late (more than a few years after the end of a marriage, death, or absence of a husband)
(4) Children born outside of wedlock
(5) Foundlings whose parents are unknown

Categories 2, 3, 4 and 5 are placed at a disadvantage in Islamic law; therefore, it is important to discuss the rules of paternity in precolonial Islamic law that inform these categories.

The remainder of this chapter will explore the pragmatic ways in which the law, both in discourse and in practice, allowed for the private care and paternity of children despite clear out-of-wedlock restrictions and in the absence of an alternative to adoption. In what follows, I address the areas of perceived incompatibility between premodern Islamic legal doctrine on the care of parentless children and the legal principles that animated the jurists' pursuit of alternative non-institutional forms of care. In Sect. 1.2, I discuss the different categories of children in juristic discourse, based on circumstances of birth, paying attention to legally disadvantaged children. In Sect. 1.3, after a brief exposé on the nature of premodern Islamic orphanages and *institutional* care, I discuss the ways in which jurists sought to provide for *private* care for these children in their discourse. And in Sect. 1.4, I offer some remarks on *kafāla* fosterage and court practice.

[5] Ishaque 2008, pp 393–420; Liefaard and Doek 2015.
[6] Ishaque 2008; Liefaard and Doek 2015.

1.2 Legally Disadvantaged Children

1.2.1 The Conjugal Bed and Fatherless li'ān *Children*

As already noted, only children born in a marriage (or concubinage in the precolonial period) enjoy full rights. It is therefore important to first discuss the rules of paternity in precolonial Islamic law. Instead of trying to establish paternity through physiognomy (*qiyāfa/qāfa*), a pre-Islamic practice through which paternity disputes were often settled, Muslim jurists opted for a system that privileged legal presumptions rather than biological investigations. The legal maxim that 'the child belongs to the "conjugal bed" (*al-walad li-l-firāsh*)' emerged early in Islamic law and was considered superior to physiognomy.[7] Although the Ḥanafīs reject physiognomy, the other schools of Sunni jurisprudence accept it in theory. Yet most jurists from all the Sunni schools have consistently ignored physiognomy in their discussions of disputes over paternity, despite a Prophetic precedent with respect to the paternity of Usāma b. Zayd b. Ḥāritha.[8] According to Ibn Qayyim, physiognomy could be resorted to only in the absence of stronger evidence or applicability of the *firāsh* principle.[9]

That choice of *firāsh* over physiognomy meant that the husband was the presumptive father so long as the child was born no less than six months after the consummation of the marriage and no more than two (or four) years after the end of the marriage (more on the permissible gestation period below). This solution was pragmatic because it ensured that contestation of paternity was limited. Otherwise, any suspicion of infidelity would have been subjected to the test of physiognomy. Interestingly, it is this desire for family stability that was to be mobilized by contemporary jurists who strongly oppose DNA testing in paternity disputes, which they fear would open a Pandora's box, as Ron Shaham has argued.[10]

Maternity is of course easier to establish, being linked directly to the (presumably witnessed) birth of the child. In situations of dispute, in which more than one woman claimed to have given birth to a child, the testimony of the midwife (*qābila*) was used in court to settle the matter. The midwife's testimony was also used to determine whether a child belonged to the husband in the event of his denial of his wife's maternity of a child.[11]

The husband, however, also had an alternative way to deny paternity of a child born in a valid marriage, against the *firāsh* presumption: He could formally challenge the assumption of paternity via a mutual oath-swearing procedure known as

---

[7] For more on *qiyāfa* and the *walad li-l-firāsh* maxim see Al-Mawsū'a al-Fiqhiyya 1990, s.v. *firāsh*, vol 32, pp 80–82, and s.v. *qiyāfa*, vol 34, pp 92–105; Ibn Rushd 1995, vol 4, pp 214ff, 217–20 [transl. Nyazee 1999, vol 2, pp 431ff, 434–36]; Al-Jazīrī 2003, vol 4, pp 461ff, and vol 5, pp 108–9.

[8] Al-Balādhurī 1997, vol 5, pp 197–204.

[9] Shaham 2010, pp 154–94.

[10] Shaham 2010, pp 154–94.

[11] Al-Miṣrī et al. 1997, vol 4, p 273.

liʿān, leading to a divorce without establishing the child's filiation. According to this procedure, the husband, having claimed his wife is adulterous, swears four times that he is telling the truth, and a fifth time calling down God's curse on himself if he is lying, while the wife responds by swearing four times that he is lying, and a fifth time calling down God's curse on herself if he is telling the truth. The resultant type of divorce ends the marriage while allowing the husband to prevail in his denial of paternity. The mother has no recourse to forcing the husband to accept paternity of the child, much less to receiving child maintenance. Not even a test of physiognomy can help her in this case. According to Ibn Nujaym al-Miṣrī (d. 970/1563), the *liʿān* child inherits from the mother and vice versa but no inheritance rights exist between the child and the *liʿān* husband.[12]

Jurists generally assumed that having filiation was a privilege and therefore, in ambiguous circumstances, they often erred on the side of caution by granting the child filiation. According to Ibn Nujaym al-Miṣrī, 'if two apparent signs (*ẓāhirān*) contradict each other in questions of paternity, the one attributing paternity is given priority because caution (*iḥtiyāṭ*) is exercised in filiation.'[13] The same is true for freedom. If there was doubt, for instance, over whether a child was a slave or a free person, jurists often opted for freedom. This was part of the jurists' general emphasis on the interests of the child (*maṣlaḥat al-ṣaghīr*). Consider the following example: according to al-Shaybānī (d. 189/805), if a slave owner married his female slave to his male slave and the owner then claimed that her child belonged to him, the mother would be considered an *umm walad* (meaning that the child would be automatically free upon birth, and the mother free upon death of the owner).[14] Yet the child's filiation would be to the slave husband, not the owner, because children belong to the '*firāsh*' (conjugal bed). There is tension in this case between the *firāsh* principle and doing what is best for the child, but many jurists chose freedom in case the child was biologically the owner's, while maintaining the *firāsh* rule by granting filiation to the slave husband.[15]

The normative Muslim family consisted of two scenarios: (1) a man and a woman having children in monogamous or polygynous marriages in which a child is born within no less than six months of the beginning of a marriage and no more than a few years of a divorce or separation;[16] (2) a male master and his female slave

---

[12] Al-Miṣrī et al. 1997, vol 4, p 200. For more on *liʿān* see Al-Mawsūʿa al-Fiqhiyya 1990, s.v. *liʿān*, vol 35, pp 246–67, and s.v. *walad al-liʿān*, vol 45, pp 224–27; Ibn Rushd 1995, vol 3, pp 213–29 [transl. Nyazee 1999, vol 2, pp 140–49]; Al-Jazīrī 2003, vol 5, pp 95–110; Schacht 2012a.

[13] Al-Miṣrī et al. 1997, vol 4, p 274.

[14] For more on the *umm walad* see Al-Mawsūʿa al-Fiqhiyya 1990, s.v. *istīlād*, vol 4, pp 164–69; Ibn Rushd 1995, vol 4, pp 283–88 [transl. Nyazee 1999, vol 2, pp 475–77]; Al-Jazīrī 2003, vol 4, p 237; Schacht 2012b.

[15] Al-Shaybānī 2012, vol 5, pp 163–64.

[16] According to Ḥanafīs, the marriage contract is sufficient to establish paternity even if the husband can prove no contact for years. Most non-Ḥanafī jurists treat lack of contact due to long absence as grounds for denying paternity. See Shaham 2010, pp 154–59.

with similar restrictions relating to the period of gestation. Children falling outside of these norms were placed at a disadvantage. The rules of *firāsh*, *liʿān* divorce and the period of gestation were designed to settle paternity disputes without recourse to physiognomy.

1.2.2 Children Born Outside the Gestation Period

The *firāsh* principle pushed jurists to decide what constituted conception of a child in a marriage. In their attempt to ascertain that a given child was conceived in a marriage ('a conjugal bed'), they had to discuss the period of gestation. Premodern Sunni jurists agreed that the minimum period of gestation was six months, but they disagreed over the maximum period, which varied from two years to four years among the different schools.[17] In the modern period, there has been a drive to limit the gestation period in order to make Islamic law more closely compatible with modern scientific knowledge. Many Muslim states have thus limited the maximum gestation period to one year.[18]

According to the Ḥanafīs, if a wife gives birth within less than six months of the beginning of a marriage even by a day, paternity is not attributed to the husband (this trumps the *firāsh* principle) and the marriage itself becomes invalid (*fāsid*). If the wife claims that they have been married for six months and the husband claims that it has been less than six months, her testimony prevails over his and the child is attributed to the husband unless there is evidence to the contrary.[19] The maximum gestation period is two years according to the Ḥanafīs.[20] Ibn Nujaym al-Miṣrī contended that the logic of the law is a logic of caution about lineage (*nasab*), and therefore the longest possible gestation period is permitted due to the need (*ḥāja*) to prove paternity.[21]

1.2.3 Fatherless Children: awlād al-zinā

Children born outside of legal wedlock (*awlād al-zinā*) present another category of disadvantaged children, since they enjoy neither paternity nor inheritance or maintenance rights from their biological father.[22] In this case, the mother and her

---

17 Shaham 2010, pp 154–59.

18 Welchman 2007, pp 142–55.

19 Al-Miṣrī et al. 1997, vol 4, p 274.

20 Al-Miṣrī et al. 1997, vol 4, p 264.

21 Al-Miṣrī et al. 1997, vol 4, p 265.

22 For more on the *awlād al-zinā*, or 'children of fornication/adultery', see Al-Mawsūʿa al-Fiqhiyya 1990, s.v. *walad al-zinā*, vol 45, pp 215–24; Ibn Rushd 1995, vol 4, p 217 [transl. Nyazee 1999, vol 2, pp 433–34].

family are expected to bear the responsibility of maintaining the child. The situation of these 'illegitimate' children is particularly precarious given the Qur'ānic prohibition of adoption, creating a difficult situation for both mothers and children. According to Welchman, biological paternity alone does not impose legal and financial responsibilities on the father, but biological maternity determines the mother's duties to her child, since the financial burdens are borne by the mother and her family when paternity is denied.[23]

An anecdote conveyed by Ibn Nujaym al-Miṣrī suggests the social consequences of this imbalance: It was reported that a baby was found in Baghdad, with money. On the child's chest, there was a parchment note that read: 'This is the daughter of a wretched man and a wretched woman.' The parchment explained that the accompanying thousand Jaʿfarī dinars should be used to buy an Indian slave to serve the child, and then concluded: 'This is a punishment to those who do not marry off their adult daughters!' This episode suggests that jurists were well aware that pregnancies occurring outside of wedlock were the main cause of foundlings.[24] They nevertheless found ways to circumvent the prohibition of granting paternity for these children, as we shall now see.

1.3 Protection of Children Without Filiation

1.3.1 Overview of Juristic Bases and Discursive Aims[25]

Full adoption (*al-tabannī*) is proscribed by the Qur'ān, particularly in parts of verses Q.33:4 'Nor has He made those whom you claim [as sons] your sons,' and Q.33:5 'Call them after their fathers, and if you do not know their fathers, then they are your brethren in religion and your clients.'[26] Although this prohibits fictive filiation, it in no way bars the means to private or institutional foster care for parentless and non-biological children; indeed, both the Qur'ān and the Sunna repeatedly exhort believers to provide for such, especially orphans (*aytām* or *yatāmā*, s. *yatīm*).[27] A famous example of a Sunnaic appeal (and the evident basis for the legal category of *kafāla* as a type of fosterage) is recorded in the *Ṣaḥīḥ* of al-Bukhārī: 'The Prophet said, "I and the person who looks after an orphan and

---

23 Welchman 2007, pp 142–55.

24 Al-Miṣrī et al. 1997, vol 5, p 249.

25 The default position for substantive rulings reviewed in the following sections will be the majority Ḥanafī opinion. Divergent Ḥanafī opinions, as well as those of other Sunnī *madhhabs*, may be found in the general reference works cited for specific legal terms and categories.

26 Nasr et al. 2015, pp 1019–20.

27 For more on the *yatīm* see Al-Mawsūʿa al-Fiqhiyya 1990, s.v. *yatīm*, vol 45, pp 254–59; Chaumont and Shaham 2012.

provides for him (*kāfil al-yatīm*) will be in Paradise like this," putting his index and middle fingers together.'[28]

Jurists analyzed and expanded upon these and other Qur'ānic and Sunnaic bases, developing a number of legal categories and strategies in their discourses on the care of parentless and non-biological children, whether legally disadvantaged or otherwise. Along with asserting paternity through the *walad li-l-firāsh* principle, these include expansive rulings for care of the foundling (*laqīṭ*), acknowledgement of filiation (*al-iqrār bi-l-nasab*), and *kafāla* fosterage. But before surveying these, a brief discussion of Islamic orphanages and institutional care is in order.

1.3.2 Institutional Care of Parentless Children

Despite the prohibition of adoption, Muslim jurists implicitly and sometimes explicitly agreed that the state is less capable of taking care of children than private citizens. In reality, the majority of parentless premodern Muslim children did not receive their care in orphanages, but rather in private homes. In this sense, this premodern Islamic assumption about the superiority of private care is similar to modern conceptions in Euro-America. Two pieces of evidence suggest that jurists assumed that it is better if private citizens care for abandoned children: (1) juristic discourse shows that the judge played a role in finding members of the community to care for children, rather than locating an appropriate orphanage; (2) the rules that jurists made with respect to neglected children, such as foundling laws or laws pertaining to children born out of wedlock, exhibit a clear preference for private care. In fact, the intervention of the state was a last resort because, as one early modern Egyptian Shāfiʿī jurist explained, relatives have 'more time and kindness than the Sultan' (*ashfaq wa-akthar farāghan min al-sulṭān*).[29]

Muslim jurists' reliance on private care contrasts sharply with charity in premodern Europe, where for a host of historical reasons, orphanages and foundling homes were indispensable to the care of children.[30] When we compare early Byzantium to medieval Islam, we are struck by the absence of public institutions for the poor and disabled in medieval Islam. The legal reforms of the Christian Roman emperors from Constantine to Theodosius had the unintended consequence of making orphanages indispensable. According to Timothy Miller, in their attempt to protect orphans against unscrupulous guardians, Christian Roman emperors imposed many restrictions on guardians, including the placement of a lien on the guardian's property until the child reached the age of twenty-five. They also took strict punitive measures against guardians, making it difficult for children to find guardians willing to take on these increasingly stringent financial and legal

---

[28] Al-Bukhārī 1997, vol 8, pp 33–34, no 6005.

[29] Al-Shirbīnī 1997, vol 3, p 597.

[30] Boswell 1990; Dols and Immisch 1992; Heywood 2001; Miller 2003.

responsibilities.[31] Byzantine orphanages also gave rise to the orphan school, where orphans were taught Greek grammar, music, and Christian doctrine.[32] In Western Europe, another institution that cared for abandoned children was the foundling home, which existed in Europe beginning in the Middle Ages and was mostly run by the Catholic Church.[33]

According to Yaacov Lev, the situation in medieval Islam was different. While there were hospitals, Lev argues that there is no evidence of institutions such as orphanages on the Byzantine model.[34] Adam Sabra makes a similar observation about Mamluk Cairo, assuming rightly that the care of children must have fallen to their immediate and extended families.[35] I would add, however, that this assumption should be qualified in two ways. First, it appears to be driven by the lack of references in primary sources to specific institutions tied to the housing and care of orphans in the same way that Sufis, for example, had Sufi lodges known as *zāwiya*s, *khānqāh*s, and *ribāṭ*s. Second, the fact that there is no technical term for orphanages in the sources is misleading, because endowment deeds often cited the care of orphans – including their housing – regardless of the primary function of the institution in question. In reality, orphans were housed and cared for in institutions with other primary functions. Consider that in one Mamluk Egyptian endowment deed, the Mamluk Sultan, Qaytbay, established a Qur'ānic school (*kuttāb*) wherein orphans were both housed and educated, according to the wording of the deed.[36]

In fact, Lev rightly points out that the absence of a specialized terminology for charitable institutions 'does not necessarily mean that there was an institutional void, since charitable institutions and services were attested to in connection with the most common institutions that served other goals.' He goes on to examine the ways in which institutions such as the *ribāṭ*, *zāwiya*, and *khānqāh* had varying functions that went beyond the nomenclature.[37] According to Ibn Khallikān, for instance, Muẓaffar al-Din established four *khānqāh*s for the chronically ill, the blind, widows, young orphans, and foundlings in twelfth-century Irbil, suggesting that the *khānqāh*, a term which usually refers to a Sufi lodge, was used to serve the

---

[31] In order to partially relieve the problem of lack of willing guardians, Theodosius I and Valentinian II broke with Classical Roman law by removing the traditional legal barrier against women serving as guardians in 390 AD – but only when there was no testamentary guardian. See Lev 2005, pp 113–15; Dols and Immisch 1992; Miller 2003, pp 49–77.

[32] According to Miller, the Constantinople Orphanotropheion had an educational program as early as the fifth century and many sources attest to the existence of an orphan choir that, according to some accounts, greeted the emperor with songs as he entered the Hagia Sophia. See Miller 2003, pp 49–77.

[33] Boswell 1990; Pullan 1994; Heywood 2001; Lester 2007, pp 1–17; Gardner 1998, pp 114–208.

[34] See Lev 2005, pp 113–15.

[35] Sabra 2000, p 84.

[36] The endowment deed establishes a Qur'ānic school where the orphans and their teacher also stayed (*kuttāb al-sabīl al-madhkūr a'lāh al-mu'add li-iqāmat al-aytāmi wa-mu'addibihim*). Mayer 1938, p 9.

[37] Lev 2005, pp 113–14. Baron also shows that certain terms such as *malja'* (refuge) were used in the nineteenth century. See Baron 2008, p 33.

larger population. Some *ribāṭ*s were built for women, especially widows. Other *ribāṭ*s and *zāwiya*s that primarily served mystics also offered food and shelter for the wider population, while others were dedicated to the education of women. Some endowments had no clear beneficiaries, stipulating that their revenues be spent on 'charitable causes' (*wujūh al-birr*). This vague, albeit common, reference gave the endowment supervisor wide discretionary powers in determining the beneficiaries, who must have included orphans and other abandoned children.[38]

The fact that Qur'ānic schools served different functions not suggested by the nomenclature (including orphanages) is not surprising. We know that *kuttāb*s were established throughout Muslim lands to educate, feed, and provide clothing for orphans. For example, both the Ayyubids and Umayyad caliphs in Cordova established Qur'ānic schools to educate orphan boys. Saladin established schools for orphans in Cairo, Damascus, and Jerusalem. The school in Jerusalem was maintained with a pious endowment, which included orphans' clothing needs. The Ayyubid emir, Fakhr al-Dīn 'Uthmān Ibn Qizzil, established a law school and a Qur'ānic school for orphans in Fayyoum.[39] It would be hard to imagine that orphans who did not have extended families were provided with food, clothing, and an education but no place to sleep. It is therefore fair to assume, based on the evidence available to us, that the provision of housing in some *kuttāb*s was common for orphans who did not have extended families to house them. The transition from Mamluk to Ottoman rule had little effect on the management of the education of orphans.[40] These educational institutions were normally designed for boys, although there are some references to Qur'ānic schools for girls, which were run by women teachers.[41]

Places serving the functions of orphanages were established by both the ruling elite and wealthy citizens, which is why Goitein described charity in premodern Islamic polities as 'semi-public.'[42] The state played a larger role in the administration of the funds of orphans than feeding them or providing them with housing. It had complete oversight over the appointment of guardians through its judiciary, which regularly audited the orphans' estates.[43] It was a responsibility that pertained to the establishment of justice, an essential obligation of the ruler.[44] Yet it left other

[38] Lev 2005, pp 113–18; Fernandes 1983, p 14.

[39] Lev 2005, pp 85–90; Behrens-Abouseif 1994; Raymond 1979, pp 235–91.

[40] Lev 2005, pp 85–90; Behrens-Abouseif 1994; Raymond 1979; Sabra 2000, pp 80–94.

[41] Giladi 1995, pp 291–308.

[42] Goitein 1988, vol 2, p 91.

[43] Sabra 2000, pp 62–63.

[44] The administration of justice was essential to the very success of the state, as has been argued by Wael Hallaq in his exposition on the 'Circle of Justice' (Hallaq 2009, pp 197–200). An expression of the Circle of Justice is found in the 14th-century Mamluk chief judge who quoted sayings attributed to pre-Islamic Persian kings in a treatise written for the Turkish Sultans: 'There is no kingship without an army, there is no army without money, there is no money without justice and cultivation of the land, there is no cultivation without subjects, there are no subjects without justice.' Winter 2001, p 201.

areas of poverty relief to the community. There were no regular distributions of food by the state in Mamluk Cairo, for instance, as was the case in ancient Rome. Few premodern Muslim states took charge of collecting *zakāt* and distributing it to the poor.[45]

The Church and the clergy were often the center of charity in Christendom, and the absence of a Church-like institution in Islam meant that the state and society were together the sources of charity. It was not the *zakāt* taxes collected by the state that cared for orphans and other abandoned children, though the state may have played a limited role, but rather the semi-public religious endowments of the military and mercantile elite, and more importantly the orphans' extended families or other members of the community.[46]

To sum up, in caring for abandoned Muslim children, the state and jurists could either establish large-scale orphanages or allow private citizens to take over the responsibility of caring for non-biological children. And what the Ottoman state and society did was a mix of both, with a strong preference for the private care of children.

I am therefore in agreement with the tenor of Sabra's argument that orphans received most of their support through their extended families, rather than state poverty relief efforts. The majority of children were not to be found in these semi-public orphanages, but rather in private homes. As mentioned earlier, this is clear from two pieces of evidence: (1) juristic discourse showing the judge's preference for community-member childcare over orphanages; and (2) the clear preference for private care found in relevant rules for foundlings and children born out of wedlock. In fact, this preference was even explicitly stated by some jurists, such as al-Shirbīnī. In the remainder of this section, I will briefly address the first category of evidence, the role of the judge as the arm of the state, while the remainder of the essay will address the second category of evidence, as well as the ways in which disadvantaged children were cared for by the premodern ecology of Islamic law.

Judges were the guardians of foundlings and other parentless children, but they passed on this responsibility to members of the community after investigating their reliability. The Islamic court had the communal and legal knowledge to find guardians for abandoned children. The court had witnesses and scribes who were members of the society they served. The court's local knowledge was mobilized to deliver abandoned children to new homes and to ascertain that children were properly cared for. Some jurists, for instance, required that the judge find a neighbor to oversee the upbringing of children raised by a non-Muslim mother to ascertain that they were raised according to Islamic values. Juristic discourse is replete with

---

[45] The absence of the state from the business of poverty relief led to the prevalence of begging (i.e., the direct appeal to the community for help) in medieval Cairo. In the case of the Mamluk state, see Sabra 2000, pp 32–40.

[46] On inadequate handling of the *zakāt* and its limited role in caring for the underprivileged, see Lev 2005, p 157.

references to situations in which the judge is required to place a foundling with a Muslim family to care for her on the public purse.[47]

*1.3.3 Parenting a Foundling (*laqīṭ*)*

In order to solve the problem of children born out of wedlock, jurists devised ingenious solutions in foundling (*laqīṭ*) laws going as far back as the earliest extant (eighth-century) texts of Islamic law.[48] According to al-Shaybānī, the Prophet's son-in-law ʿAlī (fourth Sunni Caliph and first Shīʿī Imam) was reported to have held that foundlings are free, and that he and the second Caliph, ʿUmar b. al-Khaṭṭāb, placed the burden of their maintenance on the public purse. Al-Shaybānī nonetheless reports that a woman who spent money on a foundling was given nothing by the famous early judge Shurayḥ when she asked him for compensation. This presents two very early positions on the role of the state vis-à-vis foundlings. One obligates the state to pay maintenance, while the other gives the judge discretion in determining whether to pass the responsibility to the public purse, the private 'finder' (*multaqiṭ*), or the child herself.[49]

Al-Shaybānī himself opts for granting the judge greater discretion. According to him, if a man comes across a foundling and brings her to the judge to assign her a salary, it is the judge's prerogative to decide whether or not to accept the child. The judge can also rule that the finder must maintain the child while establishing that maintenance as a debt on the child. This approach, which does not obligate the judge to care for the child on the public purse, must have been driven by the practical realities of Islamic charities, which, as we discussed, were community-centered. Using his discretion, the premodern judge often handed the child over to a person in the community to care for her without burdening state finances.[50]

According to the Ḥanafī Ibn al-Humām (d. 861/1457), however, the foundling is to be maintained on the public purse. This is based on a report that ʿUmar b. al-Khaṭṭāb told a finder to keep the child, promising that the state would pay for maintenance of the child. Ibn al-Humām claimed that there was no disagreement over the state's obligation to care for the foundling. If the finder wanted to be reimbursed for costs, they had to prove that the child was a foundling. The reason for this precaution was to ascertain that parents were not falsely claiming their biological children to be foundlings in order to avoid paying the costs of their

---

47 Ibn Qudāma 2004, vol 2, p 2008.

48 For more on the *laqīṭ* see Al-Mawsūʿa al-Fiqhiyya 1990, s.v. *laqīṭ*, vol 35, pp 310–25; Fadel 2013; Delcambre 2012; Ibn Rushd 1995, vol 4, p 124 [transl. Nyazee 1999, vol 2, p 374].

49 Al-Shaybānī 2012, vol 5, pp 241–42.

50 Al-Shaybānī 2012, vol 5, p 243. For more on this type of care see our discussion of *kafāla*, below.

maintenance. According to another report, whenever foundlings were discovered, ʿUmar sent their maintenance to the guardian (*walī*) every month.[51]

If the finder handed over a foundling due to insolvency, the judge could transfer the foundling to a volunteer. If the finder later requested the foundling's return, the judge had the discretion to either keep the child with the volunteer or return the child to the original finder.[52] Given the jurists' attentiveness to the child's welfare, it is safe to assume that the judge's discretion was also guided by this principle.

If someone claimed a foundling as their child, they were not to be believed unless they produced evidence. This ruling applied analogical reasoning (*qiyās*) on the basis of the case of the finder of an object or animal. In this case, the claimant of ownership had to produce evidence in order to be granted possession of the object or animal. Al-Shaybānī stated, however, that he would use 'juristic preference' (*istiḥsān*) over analogical reasoning to grant paternity to the claimant without evidence, thus breaking with the analogy to a finder of an object or animal in favor of *istiḥsān*.[53] His pragmatic reasoning (*istiḥsān*) was driven by the welfare of the child. Paternity was granted 'because the child needs it' (*istiḥsānan li-iḥtiyājihi ilayhi*), which contradicts a simple reading of the first half of Qur'ān 33:5. According to Ibn Nujaym al-Miṣrī, having a lineage is a source of pride and its absence a source of shame for a child. Such a justification suggests that jurists understood clearly that this claim was based not on biology but rather on the welfare of the child. No proof of paternity had to be presented except in cases of conflict. Moreover, this applied to a living child; were she already dead, no claim of paternity would be accepted without proof. This also makes it clear that care for the child was the reason for a less strict approach to granting paternity (especially among Ḥanafīs), which was unnecessary if the child was deceased.[54]

The act of finding a child also established legal rights. No one could take the child from the finder without their consent, except for just cause; if a person found a child, then another took possession of that child, the child would be returned to the finder.[55] If, on the other hand, an outsider (that is, someone other than the finder) claimed paternity of the child, he was given paternity without proof – even if he was a non-Muslim living in a Muslim polity (*dhimmī*). If both the finder and an outsider claimed paternity of the child, whoever claimed her first was given priority. If they claimed the child simultaneously, the finder had priority even if the finder was a *dhimmī*. Some jurists, however, supported the finder against evidence from an outsider. Ibn Nujaym al-Miṣrī explained that 'possession' (*yad*) was given priority for the benefit of the child (*manfaʿat al-walad*). If two claimants had equal evidence

---

51 Ibn al-Humām and al-Marghīnānī 2003, vol 6, pp 103–5.

52 Al-Miṣrī et al. 1997, vol 5, pp 241–43.

53 Al-Shaybānī 2012, vol 5, p 243. On the requirement for objects and animals found in public spaces, see Ibn al-Humām and al-Marghīnānī 2003, vol 6, p 121.

54 Al-Miṣrī et al. 1997, vol 5, pp 243–44.

55 Al-Shaybānī 2012, vol 5, p 243.

or neither had any evidence, on the other hand, they were both given paternity according to some jurists.[56]

Ibn al-Humām argued that if a *dhimmī* claimed a child found in a Muslim village, the *dhimmī* had paternity but the child was a Muslim. In this case, the child was presumptively Muslim owing to the child's birth in a Muslim village but paternity was granted to the *dhimmī* for the welfare of the child.[57] In other words, jurists once again privileged private care. But this was only the case so long as the child's religion was not in danger. If the *dhimmī* dressed the child in non-Muslim accoutrements such as a cross, jurists reasoned that the child should be taken away from the *dhimmī* once she reached the age of discernment (*ya'qil fīhi al-adyān*) on the basis of analogy with the custody of a non-Muslim mother.[58]

Of course, unless the finder claimed the child as their own, they did not enjoy the same privileges as a parent or guardian. There were no impediments to marriage between a finder and child unless a milk relationship had been established through breastfeeding. Finders were allowed neither to marry off a foundling nor to sell her property, because the finder only had authority in terms of protecting the child. This being the case, the finder who did not claim paternity was made analogous to a mother who did not have the power of *taṣarruf*, that is, managing the child's assets. In order for a caregiver to be allowed to manage the property of the child, it was reasoned, they needed to have both kindness and sound opinion (*ra'y*). According to Ibn al-Humām, however, the mother had kindness but no sound opinion, while the *multaqiṭ* (presumably a male) did not have kindness, but might have sound opinion.[59] In other words, the legal capacity of the finder was more similar to the custody of a mother than to guardianship. This must have created an incentive for finders to claim paternity in order to have full rights of guardianship over the person and property of the child.

As for cases in which someone claimed paternity of a foundling who had reached maturity, the foundling's consent was sought before paternity was granted.[60] And if a foundling died with an estate, no claim of paternity was accepted after the foundling's death.[61] One would assume the reason for this rejection was to forestall illicit attempts to access the child's wealth, which would otherwise go to the state. Interestingly, if a Muslim and a non-Muslim both claimed to have discovered a Muslim foundling, the judge would choose the Muslim claimant. Ḥanafī law, however, did not prioritize a woman over a man, and the judge would draw lots in such cases. Nevertheless, it prioritized a well-off person over a poor person

[56] Al-Miṣrī et al. 1997, vol 5, p 247.

[57] Ibn al-Humām and al-Marghīnānī 2003, vol 6, pp 103–5.

[58] Ibn al-Humām and al-Marghīnānī 2003, vol 6, pp 103–5.

[59] Ibn al-Humām and al-Marghīnānī 2003, vol 6, pp 109–10.

[60] Al-Shaybānī 2012, vol 5, p 243.

[61] Al-Shaybānī 2012, vol 5, p 243.

and a person known to be honest over a person whose honesty was not established (*mastūr*).[62]

Finally, it should be noted that if two people claimed paternity of a child, they were both granted paternity if there was no preponderance of evidence privileging one claim over the other. Some jurists allowed for up to five parents, while others restricted the number to three or two. And if two women claimed maternity of a child and they both had equal evidence, some jurists granted them shared maternity.[63]

*1.3.4 Acknowledgement (*iqrār*)*

Acknowledgement of paternity (*iqrār bi-l-nasab*) or paternity claims as outlined in the previous section could also be exercised with respect to children who were not foundlings.[64] This situation must have arisen in the premodern period when children were born out of wedlock. In this case, parents commonly claimed they were married, albeit without providing evidence. At the very least, they might have avoided discussing how the child came about at all, given that most jurists (except for Mālikīs) did not consider pregnancy itself as evidence of fornication out of wedlock. This leniency was driven by the concept of *shubha* (doubt), whereby mitigating considerations of doubt are introduced due to an illicit case's semblance to a licit one.

If someone claimed he was the father of a child of unknown filiation, Ḥanafī jurists granted paternity so long as the claimant's fathering of the child was not

[62] Al-Miṣrī et al. 1997, vol 5, p 241–43.

[63] Al-Miṣrī et al. 1997, vol 5, p 244. This is of particular interest, in that such a juristic opinion may be mobilized in modern times to allow for adoptions by same-sex couples. Should one follow a pragmatic approach treating juristic rulings in the same way legal transplants are conceptualized – as opposed to a *maqāṣid* approach concerned with the coherence of the entire system of Islamic law – one could mobilize individual rules to solve contemporary problems (see Ibrahim 2015, pp 157–220, for the historical evolution of this pragmatic approach in Islamic law). Such a method is consistent with the *taqlīd* approach to lawmaking (see Jackson 1996, pp 165–92; Fadel 1996, pp 193–233; Ibrahim 2016a, pp 801–16; Ibrahim 2016b, pp 285–303). Drawing upon the rules allowing co-acknowledgement of two or more mothers or fathers as legal stratagems which can be mobilized to legitimize the same-sex parenting of Muslim children would constitute a poignant example. Combined with the rules for non-Muslim acknowledgement of filiation, the 2013 case of a lesbian couple who adopted a Muslim child in the Netherlands would become a possibility; and the overall tactic would not be dissimilar to many widely practised *ḥiyal* strategies in Islamic banking today (Note that this case of adoption led to a diplomatic row between Turkey and the Netherlands in 2013. See Roberts 2013.).

[64] For more on *iqrār* as it relates to paternity claims (*iqrār bi-l-nasab*), see Al-Mawsūʿa al-Fiqhiyya 1990, s.v. *al-iqrār*, vol 6, pp 46–79, esp. s.v. *al-iqrār bi-l-nasab*, pp 75–79; Linant de Bellefonds 2012a, esp. section III.

patently impossible. This often meant that the age difference between putative parent and child had to allow for the possibility of parenthood.[65]

As for acknowledgement of maternity, however, Ḥanafīs were split according to Ibn al-Humām. Some jurists were concerned that if the mother acknowledged a child without her husband's acknowledgement, it would be tantamount to forcing the husband to assume paternity against his will (*taḥmīl al-nasab ʿalā al-ghayr*). This is why the majority of Ḥanafīs did not allow a mother or a child to exercise acknowledgement without the husband's/claimed father's approval.[66] This position assumed the absence of evidence. In the presence of evidence, such as the testimony of a midwife, the husband had no way to deny paternity – which belonged to the *firāsh* – except through the process of *liʿān*.[67]

Ibn al-Humām found this position deeply problematic because it denied women maternity rights without justification, whereas the clear analogy (*qiyās jalī*) was that the mother should be treated like the father. Ibn al-Humām argued that the majority view must have been supported by a textual source, consensus, or hidden analogy (*qiyās khafī*), that is, as Ibn al-Humām explained, via *istiḥsān*. He did not know the source of the majority view that did not allow the mother the same right by analogy, but reasoned that 'just because we do not know the evidence behind this position does not mean that it is not valid according to *mujtahid*s' (those capable of exercising personal reasoning). He further explained that if the reason was to protect a husband from paternity that he might not acknowledge, then this rule would not apply to an unmarried mother, whose acknowledgement should be accepted like that of a man.[68] Finally, Ḥanafī jurists were sure to emphasize that once paternity was established it could not be retracted (*al-nasab lā yaḥtamilu al-naqd baʿda thubūtihi*).[69]

1.4 Court Practice and *kafāla*

Perhaps the most common way in which private citizens bound themselves before the judge to care for children was through *kafāla*. Not to be confused with the contract of guarantee or surety-bond, also called *kafāla*, this *kafāla*-qua-fosterage is contracted by a foster parent or guardian (*kāfil*, or *walī*) on the one side, and the child's mother, legal guardian, or the state on the other, binding the former to care for the child without conferring lineage.[70]

---

65 Ibn al-Humām and al-Marghīnānī 2003, vol 8, pp 412–13.

66 Ibn al-Humām and al-Marghīnānī 2003, vol 8, pp 413–14.

67 Ibn al-Humām and al-Marghīnānī 2003, vol 8, p 415.

68 Ibn al-Humām and al-Marghīnānī 2003, vol 8, p 414.

69 Ibn al-Humām and al-Marghīnānī 2003, vol 8, p 419.

70 Welchman 2007, pp 142–55. For more on *kafāla*-qua-surety/guarantee see Al-Mawsūʿa al-Fiqhiyya 1990, s.v. *al-kafāla*, vol 34, pp 287–320; Linant de Bellefonds 2012b; Peters 2013;

In the courts, judges also appointed guardians to manage orphans' estates. These guardians were either relatives of the child, which was more common, or pious members of the community. Guardians were sometimes unrelated to the child due to the child having no relatives, or due to such relatives being ineligible or unwilling. In these situations, Ottoman Egyptian judges often appointed religious figures, who were considered both trustworthy and knowledgeable about the responsibilities of guardianship.[71] They also did not hesitate to fire guardians when they realized that it was in the best interests of the wards to remove them. They explained that their decisions were motivated by the 'welfare and good fortune' (*al-ḥaẓẓ wa-l-maṣlaḥa*) of the child.[72]

Children often resided with relatives or, in the absence of relatives, with a Muslim family that the judge found. If the child had assets, maintenance was deducted from her money. Otherwise, the child's maintenance was paid for by the state or by the community in line with the wide judicial discretion already noted in juristic discourse, especially in the Ḥanafī school.

There are very few references to filiation and foundlings in the court records. This might suggest that most foundlings and children born out of wedlock were dealt with outside the very public space of the court. Determinations of filiation and foundlings might have more commonly been kept a private affair and dealt with according to custom rather than according to the rigid rules of the Islamic law of filiation. One may even assume that the legal fictions that jurists accepted in their discourse represented a general social ethos that informed communal solutions to questions of filiation and care for non-biological children. Unfortunately, we do not have references to customary adoptive and filiation practices in premodern Muslim societies. Unlike child custody, which was often discussed at the time of divorce, adoption and filiation practices rarely show up in Ottoman Egyptian courts.[73]

Yet there are many references to *kafāla*,[74] which was often assumed by a relative. The most common form of *kafāla* was performed by a stepfather. This was often a condition imposed by mothers on their would-be husbands. In Ottoman Egypt, for instance, there were many marriage contracts in which the husband obligated himself to provide for all of the financial needs of the children of his would-be wife. In one case from the Cairo court of al-Ṣāliḥiyya al-Najmiyya in 951/1544, a woman inserted two conditions into her marriage contract. One of them stated that her future husband would be responsible for the maintenance of her son,

---

Ibn Rushd 1995, vol 4, pp 93–98 [transl. Nyazee 1999, vol 2, pp 355–59]; Al-Jazīrī 2003, vol 3, pp 210–18; Hallaq 2009, pp 258–60.

71 Court of Qisma ʿArabiyya, Sijill 2 (970-1/1562-3), Archival Code 1004-000002, Dār al-Wathāʾiq al-Qawmiyya, Cairo, doc 19, 13.

72 Court of Qisma ʿAskariyya, Sijill 26 (1019/1610), Archival Code 1003-000105, Dār al-Wathāʾiq al-Qawmiyya, Cairo, doc 160, 77; Court of Qisma ʿArabiyya, Sijill 3 (973/1566), Archival Code 1004-000003, Dār al-Wathāʾiq al-Qawmiyya, Cairo, doc 176, 104.

73 Ibrahim 2018.

74 Usually expressions of the verb forms *kafala* and *takaffala*.

Muhammad, whom she had begotten in a previous marriage.[75] This condition was quite common in Ottoman Egyptian courts and offered a solution to the father's death or insolvency by transferring the financial care of children to the new husband. Notably, there are also other situations in the court records in which a relative volunteered to provide financial support to a child who was being cared for by the mother.[76]

1.5 Conclusion

Two types of care of non-biological children have been discussed in this article: one is tied to institutions similar to orphanages in Europe and the other is private, and I have argued that unlike in medieval Europe, premodern Sunni jurists privileged private care over institutional care. The medieval European reliance on institutional care would change in the modern period, leading to the contemporary Euro-American assumption that private care is generally preferred over institutional care because it enables the child to have a more normal family life. I have argued that most premodern, Muslim, parentless children were given a family life by their extended families or members of the community. The judge played a central role in finding members of the community to care for these non-biological children, whether their paternity was known or not.

The normative Islamic family in the premodern period has also been discussed, as have children stigmatized by the circumstances of their birth. This stigma could not be removed through open adoption, but was rather relieved through 'functional equivalents.' The categories of legally disadvantaged children included children born to a *liʿān* divorcée and children born out of wedlock, and jurists found ways to grant these disadvantaged children a private family life via rules for foundlings and lax restrictions on acknowledgement of paternity (*iqrār*). In the same way that the Islamic legal tradition developed a system of legal stratagems (*ḥiyal*) enabling interest to be charged in legally acceptable forms, it also indirectly allowed adoption-like forms of care for non-biological children. Jurists allowed both biological parents and strangers to claim out-of-wedlock children as their legitimate progeny through the rules of foundlings and acknowledgement. The objective of these laws was to ensure that children were cared for by private individuals rather than by the state, since the latter was considered a less attractive, and perhaps a less efficient, model of care.

These functional equivalents could only address children of unknown filiation; they did not apply to children of known filiation, except in some cases of

[75] Court of Ṣāliḥiyya al-Najmiyya, Sijill 3 (951/1544), Archival Code 1012-000003, Dār al-Wathāʾiq al-Qawmiyya, Cairo, doc 125, 39.

[76] Court of Qisma ʿArabiyya, Sijill 2 (970-1/1562-3), Archival Code 1004-000002, Dār al-Wathāʾiq al-Qawmiyya, Cairo, doc 86, 57.

acknowledgement of children born out of wedlock since their filiation was known at least to the biological parents. However, for most children with known filiation, *kafāla* was the only option. Not surprisingly, *kafāla*, a common way for premodern Muslim children to receive private care (whether their filiation was known or not), remains in tension with certain conceptions of the best interests of the child in modern, Euro-American legal discourses. The reason is that it does not map well onto European conceptions of adoption in which the child receives the full rights that biological children enjoy, including a family name and inheritance rights.

References

Al-Balādhurī ABY (1997) (Zakkār S, Ziriklī R (eds)) Kitāb Jumal min Ansāb al-Ashrāf, Dār al-Fikr, Beirut.

Al-Bukhārī MBI (1997) (Khan MM (transl)) Ṣaḥīḥ al-Bukhārī: the Translation of the Meanings of Sahih al-Bukhari: Arabic-English, Darussalam Pub. & Distr., Riyadh.

Al-Ḥalabī IBMBI et al (1998) Multaqā al-Abḥur, Majma' al-Anhur: al-Durr al-Muntaqā fī Sharḥ al-Multaqā, Dār al-Kutub al-'Ilmiyya, Beirut.

Al-Jazīrī 'A al-R (2003) Kitāb al-Fiqh 'alā al-Madhāhib al-Arba'a, 5 vols, Dār al-Kutub al-'Ilmiyya, Beirut.

Al-Mawsū'a al-Fiqhiyya (1990) 45 vols, Wizārat al-Awqāf wa'l-Shu'ūn al-Islāmiyya, Kuwait.

Al-Miṣrī Z al-D IN et al (1997) ('Umayrāt Z (ed)) Al-Baḥr al-Rā'iq Sharḥ Kanz al-Daqā'iq wa-ma'ahu al-Ḥawāshī al-Musammā Minḥat al-Khāliq 'alā al-Baḥr al-Rā'iq, Dār al-Kutub al-'Ilmiyya, Beirut.

Al-Shaybānī MB al-Ḥ (2012) (Boynukalın M (ed)) Al-Aṣl, Dār Ibn Ḥazm, Beirut.

Al-Shirbīnī Sh al-D MB al-Kh (1997) ('Aytānī M Kh (ed)) Mughnī al-Muḥtāj ilā Ma'rifat Ma'ānī Alfāẓ al-Minhāj, Dār al-Ma'ārif, Beirut.

Baron B (2008) Orphans and Abandoned Children in Modern Egypt. In: Naguib N, Okkenhaug IM (eds) Interpreting Welfare and Relief in the Middle East. Brill, Leiden, pp 13–34.

Behrens-Abouseif D (1994) Egypt's Adjustment to Ottoman Rule: Institutions, Waqf and Architecture in Cairo, 16th and 17th Centuries. E.J. Brill, Leiden and New York.

Boswell J (1990) The Kindness of Strangers: The Abandonment of Children in Western Europe from Late Antiquity to the Renaissance. Vintage Books, New York.

Chaumont E (2012) Tabannin. In: Bearman P et al (eds) Encyclopaedia of Islam, 2nd edn. http://dx.doi.org/10.1163/1573-3912_islam_SIM_8913. Accessed 1 March 2018.

Chaumont E, Shaham R (2012) Yatīm. In: Bearman P et al (eds) Encyclopaedia of Islam, 2nd edn. http://dx.doi.org/10.1163/1573-3912_islam_COM_1362. Accessed 1 March 2018.

Delcambre A-M (2012) Laḳīṭ. In: Bearman P et al (eds) Encyclopaedia of Islam, 2nd edn. http://dx.doi.org/10.1163/1573-3912_islam_SIM_4620. Accessed 1 March 2018.

Dols MW, Immisch DE (1992) Majnūn: The Madman in Medieval Islamic Society. Clarendon Press and Oxford University Press, Oxford and New York.

Fadel M (1996) The Social Logic of *Taqlīd* and the Rise of the *Mukhtaṣar*. Islamic Law and Society 3(2):193–233.

Fadel M (2013) Foundling (laqīṭ). In: Fleet K et al (eds) Encyclopaedia of Islam, 3rd edn. http://dx.doi.org/10.1163/1573-3912_ei3_COM_27175. Accessed 1 March 2018.

Fernandes L (1983) Some Aspects of the *Zāwiya* in Egypt on the Eve of the Ottoman Conquest. Annales Islamologiques 19:9–17.

Gardner JF (1998) Family and Familia in Roman Law and Life. Clarendon Press and Oxford University Press, Oxford and New York.

Giladi A (1995) Gender Differences in Child Rearing and Education: Some Preliminary Observations with Reference to Medieval Muslim Thought. Al-Qantara 16(2):291–308.

Goitein SD (1988) A Mediterranean Society: The Jewish Communities of the Arab World as Portrayed in the Documents of the Cairo Geniza. University of California Press, Berkeley.

Hallaq WB (2009) Sharīʿa: Theory, Practice, Transformations. Cambridge University Press, Cambridge and New York.

Heywood C (2001) A History of Childhood: Children and Childhood in the West from Medieval to Modern Times. Polity Press, Cambridge and Malden, MA.

Ibn al-Humām K al-D, al-Marghīnānī B al-D (2003) Sharḥ Fatḥ al-Qadīr. Dār al-Kutub al-ʿIlmiyya, Beirut.

Ibn Qudāma M al-D al-M (2004) (Edited by Ibn Abī ʿAlafa RBṢ) Al-Mughnī. Bayt al-Afkār al-Dawliyya, Beirut.

Ibn Rushd A al-W M (1995) (Edited by Ḥallāq MṢḤ) Bidāyat al-Mujtahid wa-Nihāyat al-Muqtaṣid. Maktabat Ibn Taymiyya, Cairo (Nyazee 1999 transl)).

Ibrahim AF (2015) The Codification Episteme in Islamic Juristic Discourse between Inertia and Change. Islamic Law and Society 22(3):157–220.

Ibrahim AF (2016a) Rethinking the *Taqlīd* Hegemony: An Institutional, Longue-Durée Approach. Journal of the American Oriental Society 136(4):801–816.

Ibrahim AF (2016b) Rethinking the *Taqlīd-Ijtihād* Dichotomy: A Conceptual-Historical Approach. Journal of the American Oriental Society 136(2):285–303.

Ibrahim AF (2018) Child Custody in Islamic Law: Theory and Practice in Egypt since the Sixteenth Century. Cambridge University Press, Cambridge.

Ishaque S (2008) Islamic Principles on Adoption: Examining the Impact of Illegitimacy and Inheritance Related Concerns in Context of a Child's Right to an Identity. International Journal of Law, Policy and the Family 22(3):393–420.

Jackson SA (1996) *Taqlīd*, Legal Scaffolding and the Scope of Legal Injunctions in Post-Formative Theory: *Muṭlaq* and *ʿĀmm* in the Jurisprudence of Shihāb al-Dīn al-Qarāfī. Islamic Law and Society 3(2):165–192.

Landau-Tasseron E (2003) Adoption, Acknowledgement of Paternity and False Genealogical Claims in Arabian and Islamic Societies. Bulletin of the School of Oriental and African Studies 66:169–192.

Lester AE (2007) Lost but Not yet Found: Medieval Foundlings and Their Care in Northern France, 1200–1500. Proceedings of the Western Society for French History 35:1–17.

Lev Y (2005) Charity, Endowments, and Charitable Institutions in Medieval Islam. University Press of Florida, Gainesville.

Liefaard T, Doek JE (eds) (2015) Litigating the Rights of the Child: The UN Convention on the Rights of the Child in Domestic and International Jurisprudence. Springer, Dordrecht.

Linant de Bellefonds Y (2012a) Iḳrār. In: Bearman P et al (eds) Encyclopaedia of Islam, 2nd edn. http://dx.doi.org/10.1163/1573-3912_islam_COM_0357. Accessed 2 March 2018.

Linant de Bellefonds Y (2012b) Kafāla. In: Bearman P et al (eds) Encyclopaedia of Islam, 2nd edn. http://dx.doi.org/10.1163/1573-3912_islam_COM_0415. Accessed 2 March 2018.

Mattson I (2009) Adoption and Fostering: Overview. In: Joseph S (ed) Encyclopedia of Women & Islamic Cultures. http://dx.doi.org/10.1163/1872-5309_ewic_EWICCOM_0064a. Accessed 2 March 2018.

Mayer LA (1938) The Buildings of Qāytbāy as Described in His Endowment Deed. A. Probsthain, London.

Miller TS (2003) The Orphans of Byzantium: Child Welfare in the Christian Empire. Catholic University of America Press, Washington, D.C.

Nasr SH et al (eds) (2015) The Study Quran: A New Translation and Commentary. HarperOne, New York.

Nyazee IK (transl) (1999) The Distinguished Jurist's Primer: a Translation of Bidāyat al-Mujtahid. Garnet Publishing, Reading.
Paradelle M (1999) Legal Pluralism and Public International Law: An Analysis Based on the International Convention on the Rights of the Child. In: Dupret B et al (eds) Legal Pluralism in the Arab World. Kluwer Law International, The Hague and Boston, pp 97–112.
Peters R (2013) Guarantee. In: Fleet K et al (eds) Encyclopaedia of Islam, 3rd edn. http://dx.doi.org/10.1163/1573-3912_ei3_COM_27527. Accessed 2 March 2018.
Pollack D et al (2004) Classical Religious Perspectives of Adoption Law. The Notre Dame Law Review 79(2):693–753.
Powers DS (2008) Adoption. In: Fleet K et al (eds) Encyclopaedia of Islam, 3rd edn. http://dx.doi.org/10.1163/1573-3912_ei3_SIM_0304. Accessed 2 March 2018.
Pullan BS (1994) Poverty and Charity: Europe, Italy, Venice, 1400–1700. Variorum, Aldershot and Brookfield, VT.
Raymond A (1979) Les fontaines publiques (sabīl) du Caire à l'époque ottomane (1517-1798). Annales Islamologiques 15:235–291.
Roberts S (2013) Row between Netherlands and Turkey over Lesbian Foster Couple Overshadows Prime Ministerial Visit. PinkNews, 21 March 2013. www.pinknews.co.uk/2013/03/21/row-between-netherlands-and-turkey-over-lesbian-foster-couple-overshadows-prime-ministerial-visit. Accessed 2 March 2018.
Sabra AA (2000) Poverty and Charity in Medieval Islam: Mamluk Egypt, 1250–1517. Cambridge University Press, Cambridge and New York.
Schacht J (2012a) Liʿān. In: Bearman P et al (eds) Encyclopaedia of Islam, 2nd edn. http://dx.doi.org/10.1163/1573-3912_islam_SIM_4665. Accessed 2 March 2018.
Schacht J (2012b) Umm al-Walad. In: Bearman P et al (eds) Encyclopaedia of Islam, 2nd edn. http://dx.doi.org/10.1163/1573-3912_islam_COM_1290. Accessed 2 March 2018.
Shaham R (2010) The Expert Witness in Islamic Courts: Medicine and Crafts in the Service of Law. University of Chicago Press, Chicago.
Thelen T, Haukanes H (2010) Parenting after the Century of the Child: Travelling Ideals, Institutional Negotiations and Individual Responses. Ashgate, Farnham and Burlington, VT.
United Nations (2005) Multilateral Treaties Deposited with the Secretary-General: Status as at 31 December 2004, vol. I:1. United Nations Publications, New York.
Welchman L (2007) Women and Muslim Family Laws in Arab States: A Comparative Overview of Textual Development and Advocacy. Amsterdam University Press, Amsterdam.
Winter M (2001) Inter-*Madhhab* Competition in Mamlūk Damascus: Al-Ṭarsūsī's Counsel for the Turkish Sultans. Jerusalem Studies in Arabic and Islam 25:195–211.
Yassari N (2015) Adding by Choice: Adoption and Functional Equivalents in Islamic and Middle Eastern Law. American Journal of Comparative Law 63(4):927–962.

Ahmed Fekry Ibrahim is assistant professor of Islamic law at McGill University's Institute of Islamic Studies in Montréal. He holds a B.A. from al-Azhar University, an M.A. from the American University in Cairo, and a Ph.D. in Islamic studies from Georgetown University (2011). His research interests cover juristic discourse and court practice in both the formative period of Islamic law and the post-classical Mamluk and Ottoman periods. He has recently completed a book manuscript on the theory and practice of child custody in Ottoman Egypt and the role of social perceptions of the family and the child's best interests, which influenced judicial practice, bringing it in tension with jurisprudence of author-jurists. He is currently working on two book manuscripts entitled "Judicial Custom in Islamic Law: A Theory of Practice," and "Child Adoption in Early Modern Egypt". His last two projects have been supported with research grants from the Fonds de recherche du Québec – Société et culture (FRQSC) and the Social Sciences and

Humanities Research Council of Canada (SSHRC). He is the author of *Pragmatism in Islamic Law: A Social and Intellectual History* (Syracuse University Press 2017) and *Child Custody in Islamic Law: Theory and Practice in Egypt since the Sixteenth Century* (Cambridge University Press 2018).

Chapter 2
Filiation/*nasab* and Family Values in Pre-modern Shiʿi Law

Robert Gleave

Contents

Abstract In this chapter, I explore the various rules concerning familial relationships, particularly the rules around filiation/*nasab* in the classical Imami Shiʿi school of Islamic law. The Imami school shares many legal doctrines with the other Muslim legal schools, but it also has a number of distinctive legal doctrines. Here I outline these distinctive doctrines and discern a common pattern – namely that close kin family relations are particularly prized to the exclusion of more distant family relations, making the family unit (as understood in legal terms) smaller; also, there is a general suspicion of legal stratagems which create fictional filiation relationships. What mattered for Imami jurists was, on the whole, that the law reflect

---

Robert Gleave is professor of Arabic studies at the Institute of Arab and Islamic Studies at the University of Exeter.

Research for this chapter was partially funded by European Research Council award: 'Law, Learning and Authority in Imami Shi'ite Islam' (project no. 695245).

R. Gleave (✉)
Institute of Arab and Islamic Studies, University of Exeter, Stocker Road,
Exeter EX4 4ND, UK
e-mail: r.gleave@exeter.ac.uk

N. Yassari et al. (eds.), *Filiation and the Protection of Parentless Children*, https://doi.org/10.1007/978-94-6265-311-5_2

commonly accepted notions of the roles of parents and children. In the conclusion, I offer an interpretation of these particular doctrines, and propose a linkage between them and the fundamental notion of the family of the Prophet Muhammad and its authority, a founding element of Shiʿi doctrine.

Keywords Filiation · Islamic law · Shiʿi law · Shiʿism · Muhammad ibn Hasan al-Tusi · Family of the Prophet

2.1 Introduction

Shiʿism generally, and Imami (or 'Twelver' – *ithnā ʿasharī*) Shiʿism, in particular, developed out of a specific early Muslim devotion to the family and descendants of the Prophet Muhammad. Proper community leadership and religious authority is to be found within the members of this family, and for the so-called Twelvers this leadership was to be found in twelve descendants of the Prophet, beginning with the Prophet's cousin and son-in-law ʿAli b. Abi Talib (d. 661) and ending with the Twelfth Imam, who did not die, but in 941, went into hiding, to return at some future date. The qualifications for leadership (Imamate) of the community is, in Twelver Shiʿi thought, traced first to descent from the Prophet through his daughter Fatima's marriage to ʿAli, and designation (*naṣṣ*) by the previous Imam. One might think that filiation (*nasab*) is a particular concern for Shiʿi thinkers, given the claim that the rightful Imam must be a descendent from the Prophet through his daughter's marriage to Imam ʿAli, and the focus on designation by the living Imam of a preferred success from amongst his heirs. Family is clearly of central importance in the way Shiʿi thinkers conceptualize their religious thinking, since the Prophet's family is seen as (potentially) paradigmatic for legal purposes. Hence, one does find in the secondary literature the notion that the distinctive Shiʿi succession regulations are, in one way or another, derived from the dispute around the leadership succession to the Prophet.[1] Similarly, some of the distinctive rules around post-manumission master-slave ties (*walāʾ*) in Imami Shiʿi legal thought might be linked to notions of the strength of blood ties and the importance of manumitted slaves within the Shiʿi movement.[2] In this chapter, my aim is, first, to trace the development of the legal doctrine of *nasab* in Imami law and then to indicate whether this Shiʿi notion of the importance of family bonds is a credible explanation for the distinctive Shiʿi rulings on *nasab*.

In reference to the rules of *nasab*, there is no clear and incontestable evidence that distinctive Imami Shiʿi doctrines are formed by anything more than specific

---

1 Schacht 2012 makes this argument; Coulson 1971, p 108 argues Imami inheritance laws are not sectarian but Qur'anic – see also Kimber 1998, pp 291–293.

2 Gleave 2005.

readings of sources and internally consistent legal logic. The possibility that these distinctive doctrines are formed by the unique and specific Imami Shiʿi theological perspective concerning the importance of the Prophet's family remains, but it is the result of a triangulation of evidence rather than direct, explicit statement amongst the authors, particularly al-Tusi, examined below. The most one can claim at this stage is that Shiʿi views generally on the importance of the Prophet's family may have combined with the distinctive notions of lineage and legitimate leadership found in Imami Shiʿism to create a space in which certain types of legal argument (which promote a particular conception of *nasab*) flourished. How closely related these elements might be is one area of future research. We are used to thinking that the distinctive legal doctrines of this or that Sunni school are explicable by their adoption of particular hermeneutic principles, or more specifically the reading of particular texts; or it may be due to a prevalent theological commitment within the school (Maturidism, Ashʿarism, Traditionalism, Literalism etc.). How useful these models are for explaining Shiʿi doctrines is yet to be fully explored in the secondary literature, but one of the findings of my presentation below is that the theological commitment to the Prophet's family had some legal repercussions in the conception of the family in Shiʿi law.

2.2 *Nasab* in Imami Shiʿi Hadith

As in many areas of Islamic law, there are idiosyncratic features of Imami Shiʿi legal doctrine on *nasab*, and there are elements which the Imami Shiʿi jurists share with other Muslim legal traditions. Imami Shiʿi conceptions of *nasab* are, in many ways, unremarkable when compared with those prevalent in the other schools of thought. Hence, the maxim (formulated as a Prophetic hadith) that 'the child belongs to the marriage bed' (*al-walad li-l-firāsh*) is the bedrock of the Shiʿi notions of *nasab*, as it is in Sunni jurisprudence. In hadith reports found in Shiʿi collections, the phrase is placed in the mouths of both the Prophet and the Imams. For example, in reference to the Prophet, we have the following report:

> ʿAli b. Ibrahim from his father, from Ibn Abi ʿUmayr, from Hammad, from al-Halabi, from Abu ʿAbdallah (Imam Jaʿfar al-Sadiq): Whenever a man has sex with a female slave illegally, sells her and then claims her child as his own, then he [the child] does not inherit anything from him – for the Prophet said, 'the child belongs to the marriage bed…'[3]

In reference to one of the Imams, we have the report:

> Muhammad b. Yahya relates from Ahmad b. Muhammad, from ʿAli b. al-Hakam, from Aban b. ʿUthman, from al-Hasan al-Sayqal from Abu ʿAbdallah (Jaʿfar al-Sadiq):
>
> [al-Hasan al-Sayqal] heard [Jaʿfar al-Sadiq] speaking, and he was asked about a man who buys a female slave, and then has sexual intercourse with her before waiting the allotted

---

3 Al-Kulayni 1998, vol 7, p 163.

> time.[4] [Ja'far said], 'What an evil thing he has done – May God be forgiving and he must not return to her.' [al-Hasan al-Sayqal] said, 'Say he sells her to another, and she does not wait the allotted time, and the second person sells her to a third person, who has sex with her when she has not observed the allotted time. She gets pregnant whilst with [i.e. under the ownership of] this third person. [What is to be done?] Abu 'Abdallah said, 'the child belongs to the marriage bed…'[5]

It is likely that Imam Ja'far al-Sadiq, the sixth Imam of the Imami Shi'ites, is to be understood as simply quoting the Prophet here, or citing the maxim in order to answer the question. There is no difference, in terms of legal evidence, between the statements of the Prophet or those of the Imams for Imami jurisprudence: both are considered impeccable sources of legal rules and therefore have probative force (*ḥujjiyya*). However, the use of the Prophet's maxim by Imam Ja'far al-Sadiq confirms it as a fully acceptable principle on which to determine *nasab*.

In each case, the famous phrase 'the child belongs to the marriage bed' is used to clinch the argument. In both cases, the phrase is used to demonstrate that *nasab* belongs to the current (and most recent) owner, and the fact that illicit sexual intercourse took place such that there is a doubt over paternity does not affect the legal situation: the child is treated as the offspring of the one who currently has the legal right to have sexual intercourse with the mother and who could possibly be the father of the child given the timing of pregnancy and child birth.

The Imami Shi'i hadith corpus explores issues of *nasab* quite extensively, with many cases being put to one or other of the Imams and with answers provided. These reports predate, of course, the earliest Imami Shi'i *fiqh* works, and are theoretically the raw material out of which Imami *fiqh* was constructed. That, at least, is the theory; regularly though we find the *fiqh* works to be an elaboration of the hadith material (and occasionally directly opposing rulings found within it).

2.3 *Nasab* in Imami Shi'i Jurisprudence

In the areas where the rules of *nasab* are shared between Sunni and Shi'i jurisprudence, I make only occasional comment in what follows. My aim is to highlight the distinctive areas of Shi'i legal discussions around *nasab*. I do this through exploring the legal rules found in a principal text – the six-volume *Kitāb al-Khilāf* of Muhammad b. Hasan al-Tusi (d. 1067), supplemented by references to other legal works where appropriate. Al-Tusi's work is not, necessarily, '*madhhab*-defining'. Al-Tusi's views are just one amongst a number in the Imami Shi'i tradition. However, the *Kitāb al-Khilāf* contains, in perhaps the most convenient

---

[4] Literally, 'before it has been demonstrated that her womb is free (of a child)' (*yastabri' raḥimahā*). *Al-istibrā'* is the time a female slave should wait before her new owner can have sexual intercourse with her. It is, then, the rough equivalent of the *'idda* (waiting time) of a divorced woman. See Linant de Bellefonds 2012.

[5] Al-Kulayni 1998, vol 5, p 491.

form in Imami Shiʿi legal literature, the distinctive Shiʿi opinions and how they could be contrasted with the schools of the Sunni legal authorities (with a particular focus on the four *madhāhib*, but with mention of other non-Shiʿi legal authorities).

The *Khilāf* of al-Tusi, which forms the base text for my exploration, has a common, repetitive structure. It is not a comprehensive work of *fiqh*, but like most works of 'juristic differences' (*khilāfiyyāt*), the aim is to explain the author's doctrines as against those of other schools. Al-Tusi's practice is then to identify an issue (*masʾala*) in which his (and the Imami) view contrasts with Sunni schools; list their opinions; and then demonstrate the reasoning which leads to the Imami view. You will see this repeated regularly in the citations below. Of course, the views of the other schools are al-Tusi's understanding of those positions – they are not always how an adherent of that *madhhab* might present them. Nonetheless, the editor of the modern edition has kindly searched through the other works of *fiqh* of the other *madhāhib* and referenced where these views are laid out. The existence of these views in an Imami work of law and the fact that al-Tusi is more than often accurate in his description of the opponents' views reveal his learning beyond the Imami Shiʿi tradition and the need to define the Imamiyya against the other groups.

2.3.1 Parents' Duties and Children's Rights in the **Khilāf**

There is a very useful summary of the rights of a parent over his children in an early work of Imami jurisprudence attributed to the 8th Imam Abu al-Hasan al-Rida (d. 819). The work is extremely unlikely to be by the Imam himself, and the Imami tradition recognizes this – it is usually identified as the *Kitāb al-Taklīf* of Muhammad b. ʿAli al-Shalmaghani (d. 943), repackaged as the work of ʿAli al-Rida in the later Safavid period.[6] It is, though, certainly a Shiʿi legal work from at least the tenth century, and it therefore preserves at least one element of Imami legal thinking in the early period:

> Chapter on the rights of the Parent over his child:
>
> One must obey and respect one's father; [one must show] humility, submission, recognition of superiority and respect to him. One should lower one's voice in his presence. The father is the source of the son, and the son is a branch from him. Without him, he would not be; by the power of God, grant them wealth, and rank, and life.
>
> Respect them with the greatest respect in this work; and after their death, pray for them and be merciful to them.
>
> It is related that anyone who respects his father during his life, but does not pray for him after death will be declared disobedient by God.
>
> The Teacher of all Good and Religion [i.e. the Lawgiver] stands in the role of a father. Obligation to him is like obligation to him; so recognise this right.

[6] Ess 1991–97.

> Know that the rights of the mother bring about duties which obligate you to her, for she carried you when no one else did. She looked out for you with her hearing, sight and all her limbs, happy and delighting in that. She carried him over what is displeasing when no one else would have the patience to do so...[7]

Such sentiments, establishing the duty of a son to his parents, and the importance of parents as sources of authority, are common in works of morality (*akhlāq*); and are made elements in legal discourse as well in the later tradition. Respect, honour and gratitude are, of course, difficult to regulate, and hence such sentiments, when they appear in *fiqh*, remain exhortations rather than legal rules as such.

The role of parents can also be found in the description of legal duties in al-Tusi's *Khilāf*, and here there are minor differences with some Sunni schools:

> Issue: It is obligatory for the parents to teach the child when he reached seven or eight; and his *walī* must teach him prayer and fasting, and when he is ten he should beat him for not doing this, even though it is only obligatory for the *walī* not the child. This is the view of Shafiʿi. Ahmad says it is necessary for the youth to do this.
>
> Our proof of this is what is related from the Prophet: 'Order them to pray when they are seven, beat them for it when they are ten and separate them in their beds.' Also, the youth is not able to discriminate [i.e. he is not *ʿāqil*], so how can he be subject to (*mukallaf*) the law?[8]

The Hanbali position is viewed as covering any young person (without the age progression), whilst the Imami Shiʿi and Shafiʿi view sets specific ages for specific measures in the tutoring of the child. The legal problems created by this are obvious. The child is not required to pray – but the child's legal guardian (usually the father) is permitted to perform corporal punishment on the child for failure to fulfil ritual duties. Where can the permission for the father to harm another individual for failure to perform certain actions come from if the actions themselves are not obligatory? Since the child is not legally 'of age', he or she is not charged with religious duties; so there can be no rational justification for the permission to beat the child for failure to perform prayer. The answer is in a Prophetic report which, according to al-Tusi, places a duty on the guardian to tutor the child in these duties and to beat the child on failure (the 'separate them in their beds' phrase is a reference to the need to keep the sexes separate from the age of ten onwards).

For some religious duties, such as the payment of *zakāt al-fiṭra*, the father has a responsibility to ensure his children's duty is fulfilled. *Zakāt al-fiṭra*, the alms tax required marking the end of the month of Ramadan, differs from other forms of religious taxation because all Muslims, regardless of age or monetary wealth, are required to make a contribution. Children, therefore, are liable, under the Shari'a, for *zakāt al-fiṭra* payments, and the guardian is responsible for ensuring payment:

> Issue: If a young child cannot afford it, then his father should pay his *fiṭra*. This is also the view of Abu Hanifa and al-Shafiʿi, except that Abu Hanifa says, 'He is obligated to pay [the child's] *fiṭra* tax because he has the power of guardianship (*wilāya*).'

[7] Al-Shalmaghani and al-Rida 1986, p 334.

[8] Al-Tusi 1998–99, vol 1, p 306.

> For us (i.e. the Imami Shiʿa) [the father] must pay because [the child] is part of the family. This falls under a general ruling; it is explicitly stated in the transmissions [from the Prophet and Imams] that [the father] must pay *fiṭra* for himself and his children. Al-Shafiʿi says this is because [the father] provides maintenance (*nafaqa*) for [the child].

To explain the differences here: all agree that the father must pay for the children's *fiṭra* tax. For the Hanafis, the father should do it because of his *wilāya* over the child. For the Shafiʿis because he provides maintenance for the child (the child is not legally the holder of any wealth until he becomes mature), and therefore the father must fulfil the child's obligations in addition to his own. These reasons for the guardian's responsibility are too 'contractual' for al-Tusi. For him, as for the Imamiyya generally, the duty of a father to pay for the child is the result of the close family bonds, which mean the father is responsible for the religious observance of his children. This is extended, when necessary, into adulthood for the Imamis (as we shall see in the case of the poor adult child and their *fiṭra* tax payment). For the Imamis the payment of the *fiṭra* tax is a *familial* duty, and it falls on the father to ensure the payment of the child. Here the importance of the family unit (rather than the individual) could reflect a less individualistic notion within Imami *fiqh*. This, possibly, is derived from a more highly developed notion of a single family unit in the Imami legal tradition, derived perhaps from the theological notion that the Imams form a single line of continuous authority within a single family. In legal terms, the Imams and the Prophet's family form a single unit of analysis in theology and in the *fiqh*.

The *fiṭra* tax responsibilities provide a useful window into how al-Tusi envisages the family unit operating; even if the child in question can afford to pay for their *fiṭra* themselves, the father still has the responsibility:

> Issue: (Even) if the young child is rich, then the father should pay maintenance and *fiṭra*. This is the view of Muhammad b. al-Hasan, Abu Hanifa and Malik and Abu Yusuf; al-Shafiʿi says that the maintenance and the *fiṭra* should come from [the child's] own wealth.
>
> Our proof is that it is reported that [the father] must do his *fiṭra* for himself and his children, and this applies to this situation. Anyone who wants to make such a rule specific [i.e. that the rule that the father should pay for the children can be subject to exceptions, such as in the case of wealthy children] should provide evidence.

Here – even more evident than in the previous discussion – the child's ability to pay does not affect the father's duty. As with the Sunni schools, the father's duty to pay for the *fiṭra* and the maintenance does not lapse. Al-Tusi examines a whole series of issues, rejecting potential reasons for the father to be exempt from paying for his child's *fiṭra* tax:

> Issue: If the son is young, the maintenance and *fiṭra* is a duty on his father, whether he is well or sick…

> Issue: The adult child, if he is wealthy, should look after himself and his *fiṭra* tax is his responsibility, but if he is poor, then his maintenance and *fiṭra* is on his father, whether he is well or sick....[9]

The father's duty, then, even extends into adulthood, making the responsibility of the father more long-lasting in Shiʿi *fiqh*, being a legal reflection of the strength of the paternal bond.

However, it should be noted that fulfilment of religious duties takes precedence over respect for parents when necessary:

> Both parents, or only one of them cannot prevent a child from going on pilgrimage – there is no dispute on this. It is better (*afḍal*) that he does not take on *iḥrām* [i.e. the ritual state of being prepared to make pilgrimage] except with the parents' approval given voluntarily. But if he does it, and takes on *iḥrām*, they are not permitted to, either individually or together, prevent him.
>
> Al-Shafiʿi says they can prevent him from taking on *iḥrām* in a single statement; if he wishes and puts on *iḥrām*, then one or other of them can prevent him by two declarations.
>
> Our proof is that to bar him from taking on *iḥrām*, and to bar him [from going on pilgrimage] after the commitment to do so require evidence, and there is no evidence to bar him. The principle here is that his duty should be fulfilled.[10]

Whilst all schools say a parent cannot prevent a child from going on *ḥajj*, it is, by common agreement, better to get their permission. However, for the Shafiʿis, the parents can object after the child has taken on *iḥrām*, and the child will pay no penalty for failing to complete a religious duty he has begun. For the Imamis, the child cannot abandon his pilgrimage simply because his parents object after having taken on *iḥrām*.

The Imamis are keen also to emphasise how female and male children are equal in the largesse of the parents:

> Issue: When a man gives his offspring presents, it is recommended that he not give more to one than the other, whether they are male or female, and whatever the circumstances. This is the view of Abu Hanifa, Malik, al-Shafiʿi and Abu Yusuf. Ahmad, Ishaq (al-Rahwayh) and Muhammad b. al-Hasan say you should favour boys over girls in the same way they get more in inheritance. Shurayh says this also.
>
> Our proof is what is related from the Prophet and the Imams...
>
> Issue: If he doesn't perform the recommended distribution and he prefers one over another, the gift stays where it is, but it is permitted for him to claim it back and give it to them equally when they are older...

Here the Imamis are with the Hanafis, Malikis and the Shafiʿis in saying gifts should not be given disproportionately to boys. The Hanbalis say the boys should be favoured. The Imamis go further than the simple equality of gifts. They argue that favouritism in the early years can (and morally should) be rectified in later life when the father realizes he has not acted properly. Whilst the other schools say such gifts cannot be reclaimed, the Imamis provide a legal remedy for the intra-familial

[9] Al-Tusi 1998–99, vol 2, pp 133–136.

[10] Al-Tusi 1998–99, vol 2, p 433.

injustice which may have taken place earlier in life. The rules and regulations set out by al-Tusi on the distribution of gifts (which could surely be the source of potential internal family strife) are based on a principle of equal giving to both the sexes; though this principle is recommended, al-Tusi recognizes it may not take place. For that reason, he argues that ownership can be reversed for moral reasons. That is, the discriminatory gift is not necessarily legally invalid, but it is immoral, and because of this it can be a justifiable legal cause to break a contract. Equity, and most likely internal family unity, are moral goods which can provide a reason to adjust existing, discriminatory but legal, distributions of wealth.

2.3.2 Filiation Regulations in Imami **fiqh**

If the maxim 'the child belongs to the marriage bed' is to be translated into legal terms, the generally recognized rule is that for there to be a legitimate parental relationship, and therefore *nasab*, the relationship between the father and mother must have been such that sexual intercourse between them was legitimate. In a collection of legal questions supposedly answered by the seventh Imam Musa b. Jaʿfar, the Imam is asked:

> Question: a man has sexual intercourse with his slave-girl. Then he sells her before she has a menstrual period. The one who bought her has sexual intercourse during this period before her next menstrual period. She gives birth to a child – to whom belongs the child?

The point of the question being that either of the two successive owners could be the father of the child.

> He said: The child belongs to the one who with whom she is at present. It is so, for the Prophet said, 'The child belongs to the bed.'[11]

In one sense, both men are equally likely to be the father of the child, but legally speaking, the current owner of the slave-girl has the legal sexual relationship with her. Even though his act of sexual intercourse with her was irregular (perhaps even illegal) since he should have waited until she had her menstrual period (her *istibrāʾ*, mentioned earlier), nonetheless it is he who is awarded the paternity of the child. It is he who has the legitimate sexual relationship with her at this moment and therefore is the legal father. In the Imami hadith literature, the prerequisite of a legal relationship which permits sexual intercourse is worked through questions posed to the Imams. For example:

> Zurara asked Abu Jaʿfar (Imam Muhammad al-Baqir) about a man who divorces his wife; she remarries, performs her waiting period. She gives birth in her fifth month. The son is for the first husband. If it is a child of less than 6 months, then it goes to the mother and the first father; and if it is more than 6 months it is for the other.[12]

---

[11] Ibn Jaʿfar (attrib.) 1988, p 110.

[12] Al-Tusi 1970, vol 8, p 167.

> I asked [the Imam] about a woman who marries during her waiting period. [The Imam] said, 'Separate them, then she completes a single waiting period. If she has a child in the next 6 months or more, then this belongs to the second husband; and if she gives birth to a child in less than 6 months, it belongs to the first husband.'[13]

> One of the companions wrote to Abu Jaʿfar the second ... he asked him about a man who commits an indecency with a woman, and then marries her after she becomes pregnant. She brings forth a child, and he looks more like him than all of God's creation. He replied in his own handwriting and with his own seal, 'the child is due to sin and he does not inherit.'[14]

In these examples, and the many others like them, the principle of 'the child belongs to the marital bed' is observed in a manner not at all dissimilar to that found in Sunni works, demonstrating that at least up to a certain point, the legal systems are operating on common assumptions.

In other areas, the Imami Shiʿi doctrine shows a more distinctive set of issues. One issue which reveals the complexities of filiation in pre-modern Islamic jurisprudence is the famous case of marrying one's bastard daughter. This is, of course, a test case – a most likely hypothetical instance used to illustrate the limits of the law. I will not go into great detail about the precarious position of the *walad al-zinā* in Imami legal discussions. The *walad al-zinā* in Shiʿism has been researched by Kohlberg in an important article.[15] Being a *walad al-zinā* is clearly a more serious predicament in religious terms for the Imamiyya than for their Sunni counterparts. On a host of questions, the *walad al-zinā* is treated with a set of regulations which seem harsher and more punitive than in Sunni literature. Their purity status, whether they can ever be full believers, and their inheritance rights are all examples elicited by Kohlberg. He traces this back to the notion of the Shiʿa being pure of birth and a 'race' apart from the rest of the (Sunni and non-Muslim) world. This may be part of the truth, but I would argue that the strict rules concerning *walad al-zinā* may also reflect the Shiʿi conception of the family, influenced in some way by their commitment to the special status of the family of the Prophet. The *walad al-zinā* represents a threat to the family unit so prized in early Shiʿi history. In the legal system, one can see traces of the prioritizing of familial linkages. As one observes in the examples below, actual lineage (and not just the legal definitions of it) become more important for the Imamis, and this may be because of the leadership doctrine at the heart of their identity.

In the Shiʿi tradition the question of marrying one's illegitimate daughter became a mechanism with which to explore the limits of *nasab* and, in turn, to ridicule other schools. Al-ʿAllama al-Hilli (d. 726/1325) describes the issues at stake nicely in his own *khilāf* work *Tadhkirat al-Fuqahāʾ*. This work is similar to al-Tusi's *Khilāf*, though it benefits from al-ʿAllama al-Hilli having access to a wider variety of Sunni literature for his comparative survey. It is worth citing in full the passage where al-ʿAllama al-Hilli discusses this issue, as it illuminates the underlying presumptions

---

[13] Ibn Babawayh 1992, vol 3, p 301.

[14] Al-Kulayni 1998, vol 7, p 163.

[15] Kohlberg 1985.

of the Imami position and where this differs from the presumptions within the various Sunni systems:

> Issue: The daughter is created from illicit sexual intercourse (*zinā*). It is prohibited for the fornicating father to have sex with her, as it is for his son, his father, and his grandfather. In short, the rule concerning her in terms of who is prohibited from having sex with her is the same as a daughter from a sound contract in the view of our scholars – they all agree on this.
>
> Abu Hanifa agrees with this, on the basis of God's words: '[forbidden to you] are your daughters' (Qur'an Sura al-Nisāʾ 23). The proof here is that the true meaning of the word ('your daughters') applies to her. A daughter is the one created from the seed of man. That she is the object of the prohibition legally speaking, does not [necessarily] mean she is actually [a daughter] because the thing forbidden in the law is related to legal rules – such as inheritance and the like [as opposed to actual, biological relationships]. However, since she has come about from his seed apparently, it is not permitted for him to marry her, as he might have sex with someone who he thinks is [permitted] to him.
>
> Al-Shafiʿi says that it is not forbidden [to marry her], merely discouraged. This is the view of Malik also. This is because [the legally recognized daughter] is certainly and definitely the object of the prohibition; but between the two of them in this case, there is no prohibition based on birth, just as would be the case with someone unknown to him. The prohibition, as we have said, is only related to legal rules, not to linguistic meanings.
>
> The Shafiʿis have disagreed over why it is discouraged.
>
> Some say that the reason is because in this they are differing from the accepted variety of opinion amongst the scholars. Some forbid her completely. And piety demands one court her. Therefore it is prohibited from marrying her.
>
> Others say the reason is the *possibility* that she is created from his seed [is the reason for it being discouraged].
>
> On this second opinion, if he is certain that she is made from his seed, then it is prohibited to marry her – and this is the opinion of some Shafiʿis.
>
> Regarding the first opinion, it is not prohibited even if he is certain.
>
> However the more sound view, in their opinion, is that she is not forbidden.
>
> It is amazing that they all agree that if she gives birth to a child [by another man], that [child] is forbidden to him in marriage – but what is the difference?[16]

The case, discussed here at great length, reveals the legal principles of the different schools:

1. For the Hanafis, the term 'daughters' in the Qur'an includes both legitimate and illegitimate daughters – because that is the linguistic meaning of the word.
2. For the Shafiʿis, only the legal definition of daughter is to count in the Qur'anic prohibition, and an illegitimate daughter is not, legally speaking, a daughter. They clearly feel uncomfortable about this, as they move it to the discouraged category, and for some, even the prohibited category when the father 'knows' he is the father.
3. For the Shi'a, according to al-ʿAllama al-Hilli, marriage prohibitions are not based on the 'soundness' of marriage contract in law, but on actual biological relationships.

[16] Al-ʿAllama al-Hilli 1968–69, vol 2, p 614 (lithograph); see also al-Tusi 1998–99, vol 4, p 310; al-Tusi 1995–96, vol 7, p 84; Ibn Idris 1997, vol 2, p 526; Al-Bahrani 1957–58, vol 23, p 312.

> Therefore he says 'the rule concerning her in terms of who is prohibited from having sex with her is the same as a daughter from a sound contract in the view of our scholars'. Biology is more important for *nasab* than strict legal definitions of sons or daughter.

In the contemporary period, the famous Lebanese jurist Mohammad Jawad Mughniyyah (d. 1979) expresses this nicely when he says, in relation to Sunni opinions on *nasab* related questions:

> These arguments, if they prove anything, indicate that these jurists were pious and their intentions were good – but that most of the time, the logic of piety has conquered the logic of reality.[17]

The reality of biological lineage means that the Imamis have little time for the scholastic discussions over gestation time. In al-Tusi's *Khilāf* we have the issue of the minimum and maximum gestation time discussed:

> Issue: the shortest gestation time is six months – with no disagreement. The most is, in our view, nine months. Some reports say a year.
>
> Al-Shafiʿi says no more than four years. Al-Zuhri and al-Layth b. Saʿd say the maximum is seven years.
>
> From Malik there are different transmissions, the best known of which are three separate views: the first is like the position of Shafiʿi – four years; the second is five years; and the third is seven years. Al-Thawri and Abu Hanifa and his followers all say two years, and this is the preferred choice of Muzani also.
>
> Our proof [for nine months] is the consensus (*ijmāʿ*) of the [Imami] Sect and custom (*ʿāda*). I have never seen or heard of, now or in the past, a gestation period of two years, or four or seven. What they report is based on isolated stories which one should not rely on as they are uncertain. What we rely on is, however, something one can be certain about, without any dispute (*maqṭūʿ bihi bi-lā khilāf*).[18]

The Imamis discuss whether it should be nine months or one year as the minimum gestation period – and although al-Tusi here says nine months, elsewhere he accepts a year, a choice available to most other Imami jurists. There is a famous statement of the Imam Jaʿfar al-Sadiq:

> Al-Husayn b. Muhammad from Muʿalla b. Muhammad from al-Hasan b. ʿAli from Aban from Ibn Hakim from Abu Ibrahim [Imam Musa al-Kazim] or his father [Jaʿfar al-Sadiq] (upon them be peace): he discussed the woman divorced by her husband who says, 'I am pregnant', and then stays [with the man] for a year. He said, 'If she brings him [the child] in more than one year, she is not believed in her claim [it is from the husband], even if it is by an hour.'[19]

As mentioned above, in many areas relating to *nasab*, the Imamis have not developed a distinctive doctrine. For example, al-Tusi's work does not discuss in any detail differences regarding the foundling (*laqīṭ*) between Sunni and Shiʿi

---

[17] Mughniyya 1982, vol 2, p 362.

[18] Al-Tusi 1998–99, vol 5, p 89.

[19] Al-Kulayni 1998, vol 6, p 101.

doctrine. In the case of maintenance for the child, the Imamis almost always have the most demanding doctrine:

> Issue: The father must pay maintenance for the child if he is wealthy. If he has passed away, or if he is too poor, then it is a duty placed on the child's grandfather; and if he is not there, or he is poor, then on his father and so on. This is the view of Abu Hanifa and al-Shafi'i also.
>
> Malik says that the father must provide maintenance, but if he is not there or he is poor, then the grandfather does not have to, because the *nasab* has gone too far.[20]

The Maliki doctrine that the *nasab* has 'gone too far' (*li-anna al-nasab qad baʿuda*) reveals a more limited notion of family responsibility; something which the Imamis refuse to accept. The reasoning for al-Tusi is partly linguistic here – the grandfather is often referred to with the Arabic word which literally means 'father' (namely, *ab*). The grandfather has the right to say he is the *ab* of his grandchildren; and the Prophet referred to his grandchildren, Hasan and Husayn (the second and third Imams of the Imami Shiʿites) as 'sons' (using the term *walad*). All of this indicates that the sources (namely, the Qur'an and reports from the Prophet and Imams) which indicate the father must provide maintenance should also apply to the grandfather.

In a similar vein, al-Tusi writes:

> If the grandfather – the father's father however high he may be – and the mother are alive, then the maintenance is for the grandfather not the mother. This is what Abu Yusuf, Muhammad [al-Shaybani] and al-Shafiʿi all say. Abu Hanifa says they should share the responsibility for the maintenance – to the mother a third and the grandfather two thirds – in line with inheritance.
>
> Our proof is as we have already shown: the grandfather shares in the name '*ab*' – and the father is always preferred for maintenance over the mother by agreement.[21]

Time and again in the *Khilāf*, al-Tusi's version of Shiʿi rules represents a greater burden on family members compared with the other schools. Here are some examples:

> Issue: the father is capable of carrying out the law (i.e. he is of the age of discrimination – *ʿāqil*), and he is able to do it (i.e. he is not disabled), but he is poor and in need. In such instances, it is obligatory for the son to provide maintenance for him. For Shafiʿi there are two opinions – the first is like ours; the second is that he is not obligated to do so…
>
> Issue: The son, if he is capable of carrying out the law and is able but poor, then it is obligatory on the father to provide for him. For Shafiʿi there are two opinions which follow the two views concerning the father…[22]

There is also a strong emphasis on the equal maintenance due to the mother and father in such circumstances, in contrast to other opinions:

---

[20] Al-Tusi 1998–99, vol 5, p 120.

[21] Al-Tusi 1998–99, vol 5, pp 122–123.

[22] Al-Tusi 1998–99, vol 5, p 125.

> Issue: If a son has himself an adolescent son, who is fully able but negligent in his fulfilment of the law, and a father who is observant in the law, but has a health issue, and he has surplus wealth such that he can provide full maintenance for one of them, then he should divide it between them equally. Al-Shafiʿi has two opinions: the first is that the son gets preference, because his maintenance is established by a text [i.e. from a textual source of the law], whilst the father's is established through juristic reasoning (*ijtihād*). The second is that the father has preference because his piety has a preferential status, and because he cannot be ordered around by his son…
>
> If he is poor, and he has a rich father and a rich son, then the maintenance is a duty for both of them equally. For al-Shafiʿi there are two opinions: one is like ours, and the other is that it is the father's duty…[23]

Finally there is the issue of custody (*ḥaḍāna*). As is well known the Imamis generally have rather more stringent rules concerning the ages at which the divorced mother's right to custody ends (the main opinions being two years for boys, seven years for girls; and at fifteen years old they can choose – al-Tusi seems to hold the view of seven for both boys and girls). There is clearly more to lose for the mother in a divorce in terms of custody, and this (it might be argued) is true generally for Imami law – the separated mother for Imamis continues to have some rights over the child's upbringing, but they are generally more restricted compared to the other schools. For example:

> Issue: When the mother remarries, the right to look after the child (*ḥaḍānat al-walad*) is lost. This is the view of Abu Hanifa, Malik and al-Shafiʿi…
>
> Issue: If her [second] husband divorces her, then her right to *ḥaḍāna* returns. This is the view of Abu Hanifa and al-Shafiʿi. Malik says it does not return, because the marriage cancelled her right…
>
> Issue: If her [second] husband divorces her with a revocable divorce, then her right does not return, only if it is irrevocable. This is the view of Abu Hanifa and al-Muzani. Al-Shafiʿi says it returns under all circumstances.[24]

Of the schools which permit her to regain custody rights, the Imamis are the more restrictive.[25]

In terms of the custody rights on the death of the mother, the Imamis consistently favour the father's side of the family in cases of an orphan child – the Sunni schools, at least initially, favour the mother's side:

> Issue: The sister of the father has more custody rights than the sister of the mother… [the Shafiʿis agree; the Hanafis say the opposite]…[26]
>
> Issue: If the mother passes away, but there is the mother of the mother, or the grandmother of the mother, and there is a father – then the father takes priority…[27]

---

[23] Al-Tusi 1998–99, vol 5, p 126.

[24] Al-Tusi 1998–99, vol 5, p 134.

[25] They are not as harsh as the Malikis, who entertain no circumstances, making the divorcee stay unmarried permanently if she wishes to maintain custody.

[26] Al-Tusi 1998–99, vol 5, p 134.

[27] Al-Tusi 1998–99, vol 5, p 136.

Within the father's family there is a preference for vertical relatives, and male ones:

> Issue: The mother of the father has preferences over the paternal aunt…

Following the Imami rules of inheritance, though, the male agnatic heirs (*ʿaṣaba* – so crucial to the Sunni systems of inheritance group) are given no special favours: 'there is no *ḥaḍāna* for any of the *ʿaṣaba* when there is a mother'.[28] For the Shafiʿis, on the other hand, they 'stand in place of the father' (*yaqūmūna maqām al-ab*). The rules here are quite complex and could receive a greater examination than that offered here, but the inter-relationship of these rules of preference and the inheritance laws (and the rules of patronage following manumission – *walāʾ*)[29] seems to be usually (but not always) one of equivalence.

Two areas of controversy within the Sunni schools can also be seen as points of debate amongst Imami jurists: the legal status of paternal acknowledgement (*iqrār*) and, second, the thorny issue of adoption (*tabannī*). On paternal acknowledgement, this is recognized as valid amongst the Imami jurists generally, and they claim justification for this based on various statements from the Imams:

> From Imam Ali: If someone acknowledges a child (*aqarr al-rajul bi-l-walad*) for an hour, he can never deny him [viz. the child being his].[30]
>
> From Jaʿfar al-Sadiq: When a man acknowledges a child, and then denies it, then this denial means nothing, and is degrading; his son is associated with him.[31]

There are conditions for the validity of this acknowledgement, and these are the same conditions for the validity of any other form of legal acknowledgement (or confession). These are succinctly put in the influential work of al-Muhaqqiq al-Hilli (d.1277), titled *al-Mukhtaṣar al-Nāfiʿ*:

> To acknowledge filiation of a young child is conditional on [1] it being possible that there is a relationship, and [2] that the child be of unknown lineage, and [3] that there are no contesting claims [of lineage].[32]

In the *Khilāf*, al-Tusi deals with a number of questions related to paternal acknowledgment, which indicates the distinctive Imami position on this form of filiation, for example:

> If a man acknowledges that a child is his, this does not mean that he is also acknowledging that the mother was his wife, whether she was known to be a free woman or not. This is al-Shafiʿi's opinion. Abu Hanifa says that if she was known to be free, then this is an acknowledgement of marriage. If she was not known to be free, then her marriage to him is not established…

---

[28] Al-Tusi 1998–99, vol 5, p 138.

[29] See Gleave 2005.

[30] Al-Tusi 1970, vol 8, p 184.

[31] Al-Tusi 1970, vol 9, p 346.

[32] Al-Muhaqqiq al-Hilli 1989, p 234.

> Our reasoning here is that it is possible that the child came from a sound marriage, as he says; but it is also possible that it came from an irregular marriage, or from sexual intercourse which only appeared to be legitimate [but was not]. Whenever there are elements of uncertainty, one cannot interpret this as a sound contract over and above any other [type of contract].[33]

There is, then, a refusal by the Imamis in this case to presume the validity of contracts which are only implied by the acknowledgement of the father. The potential legal ramifications beyond acknowledgement (such as inheritance for the mother as a supposed wife) are not to be entertained. With the acknowledgement itself though, the presumption is that it is sound unless there is reason to doubt it:

> Say a woman enters the land of Islam from the land of the unbelievers (*dār al-ḥarb*, literally, the 'land of war'), and she has a child with her. A man in the land of Islam acknowledges that he is his son, and it is possible that this is the case, because he has been in the land of the unbelievers, or the woman had previously been in the land of Islam – then [the child] is attached to him.
>
> If it is known that he did not go to the land of the unbelievers, and the woman had not previously been to the land of Islam, then he is not associated with the [child].
>
> Al-Shafi'i says he is attached to him if it is possible [that he is the child], even if is clear that he has never been to the land of unbelief (*dār al-kufr*), and it appears as if the woman has never previously been to the land of Islam, because it is possible that he sent to her his seed in a vial, and she inserted this into herself, and the boy was born thus. This, though, is a bit far-fetched.[34]

Here the Imami reasoning continues some of the operative presumptions in the earlier examples: whilst it might be possible for a man to put his semen in a vial and send it to a woman and that she insert it in herself, this is rather far-fetched, and this possibility cannot be part of the usual basis on which paternal filiation is attributed. Rather, the impossibility of intercourse means the denial of paternity, and far-fetched examples do not provide a legal mechanism for establishing something as important as *nasab*.

On the issue of adoption, the full adoption of an individual – using the term *tabannī* – according to all the sources I have consulted, is not permitted. Succession rights and marriage prohibitions are not transferable for Shiʿi jurists, as they are for Sunni jurists. This is, perhaps, not surprising, given the emphasis already noted on actual lineage (and the refusal to countenance any legal stratagems or assumptions). The famous case is that of the Prophet's supposed 'adoption' (*tabannī*) of his freed slave Zayd bin Haritha; Zayd's marriage to Zaynab b. Jahsh would have made her unavailable to the Prophet (as one cannot marry the ex-wives of one's sons). However, as al-Tusi points out, the 'adoption' was not a literal one – and Zayd did not have a blood relationship with the Prophet – and hence the Prophet could marry Zaynab after Zayd has divorced her. In the course of the discussion al-Tusi repeats the oft cited argument that even though the Prophet stated that he had adopted

33 Al-Tusi 1998–99, vol 3, p 380.

34 Al-Tusi 1998–99, vol 3, pp 380–381.

Zayd, 'God has prohibited adoption', and hence the rule prohibiting marriage with one's own sons remains.[35] The ruling is maintained up until the contemporary period, with Mohammad Jawad Mughniyyah stating:

> *Al-tabannī* is when a man takes a child whose lineage is known, and gives him his own lineage. The Islamic Sharia does not recognise *tabannī* as a cause of inheritance, because it cannot change the reality from its true state (*lā yaghayyir al-wāqiʿ ʿan ḥaqīqatihi*).[36]

The emphasis on how adoption cannot change the reality of lineage, once again demonstrates the emphasis placed by the Imami jurists, right up until the modern day, on real, actual lineage relations, and their impatience with assumptions and legal constructions when discussing familial relations.

2.4 Theological and Political Elements of the Imami Regulations on *Nasab*

The rules on *nasab* as found in *fiqh* literature are based on particular conceptions of the family unit – its membership and the responsibilities of the various members. In the above analysis I have presented how the rules proposed by Imami jurists in the formative period of Imami Shiʿi law reveal a particular version of the family. There is an emphasis on common experience to delimit, say, the period of pregnancy to between six months and one year (or even more usually, nine months). This, it might be argued, prevents fantastical claims to parentage, with the Maliki claim of seven-year pregnancies being the example ridiculed by Imami jurists. For the Imamis, these extended periods are clearly a legal stratagem, aimed at creating non-real, but legally valid relationships. The Imami system aims to recognize real relationships, as far as possible within the legal and textual limitations; one might be tempted to say Imamis have a 'biological' notion of filiation rather than the strictly legal one of the other schools – this would, however, presume that they understood biology as a science in the contemporary sense of the term. Rather, their argument is based on customary understandings – it is simply not credible given the custom of pregnancy and childbirth to extend the period beyond a year. The link between what is customary and what is scientific in the medieval Islamic texts has, of course, already been recognized within scholarship on the period. Here we have it worked out in the ideas of the Imami jurists.

This applies also to the regulations on a man marrying his daughter born of an illicit sexual relationship. The legal links of parenthood may be missing for some Sunni schools in this circumstance, and therefore there is no impediment to marriage. For Imamis, though, there is no escaping the fact that the individual is the

[35] Al-Tusi 2009, vol 6, p 51 (in the context of manumission; one can marry one's manumitted slave's ex-wife).

[36] Mughniyya 2000, p 296.

father of the girl, even if there is no legal filiation relationship between them. Once again, the argument here is not strictly scientific, but develops out of customary usage of the term 'daughter'. The legal definition of daughter is not the one meant in the Qur'anic injunction 'Forbidden to you are your daughters'.[37] Instead, it is the customary understanding of 'daughter', which is what is meant by God in the Qur'an.

There is, one suspects, at root in both these cases a fundamental rejection of unlikely and far-fetched legal argumentations of the opponents which fly in the face of common sense and usual practice. The Imami jurists are attempting to make the rules more reflective of their customary reality. Whether this is replicated throughout Imami *fiqh* requires further study.

What is clear, though, is that behind these rules is a strong notion of family as understood in the customary sense (or even the 'scientific'/'biological' sense, as far as these modern notions are comprehensible in the medieval milieu). This conception of the family is, I would argue, likely to come from the original impetus of the Imami Shiʿi movement – namely that a direct biological relationship to the Prophet (through the offspring of ʿAli to Fatima) qualifies an individual for possible selection as religious and political leader of the community. In the rules concerning *nasab* one has an echo of this political position, not dissimilar to how the Shiʿi inheritance laws have been portrayed in some secondary literature.

Other examples of how *nasab* and other family responsibilities and relationships play out in practice elaborate yet further the underlying dynamics used by Imami jurists. The family operating as a unit for *zakāt al-fiṭra* payment, for example, reveals the importance of these relationships for certain legal duties in the Imami system; the strict rules concerning the loss of the mother's rights of custody (*ḥaḍāna*) following divorce demonstrate how responsibilities for upbringing and maintenance are more closely tied to each other in Imami jurisprudence, strengthening the father-child bond of duties and responsibilities. All this, one could argue, springs from a particular notion of the family unit drawn from the founding myth of Shiʿism. For Shiʿites generally, and Imamis in particular, the Prophet's familial relations created a unit which shared in the Prophet's charismatic authority.

2.5 Conclusion

Whilst there remain comparative elements not examined here, the general tendency in Imami thinking around filiation appears to be one element of a larger nexus of relationships which promote a certain vision of how the family unit is constructed. The importance given to tight-knit familial relationships, and the restrictive regulations on family membership, are indications that, for Imami Shiʿite jurists, the

[37] On customary and legal understandings of words, see Gleave 2016.

individual locates him- or herself primarily within a family structure; other affiliations become less important, perhaps even secondary. Imami Shiʿi inheritance regulations also reflect an emphasis on the immediate family, and this overrides more traditional, more extended family relationships (including the rejection of the male agnatic relatives in favour of more closely related female relatives). That emphasis, when taken in conjunction with the tendencies identified here in relation to *nasab*, is not due to any promotion of female rights within Imami law; rather it is the conception of the family (which remains, on the whole, patriarchal) which is the root of these regulations. This distinctive characteristic of Imami Shiʿi law could be explained by many factors. It seems, though, quite plausible (at this stage, I would not want to go further than this) that the notions of the family implicit in the founding myths of Shiʿism, linked to the political and religious authority given to the Prophet's family, play themselves out in a legal context through regulations which preserve a particular notion of the family.

References

Al-ʿAllama al-Hilli al-Hasan Bin Yusuf (1968–69) Tadhkirat al-Fuqahaʾ. Al-Maktaba al-Murtadawiyya, n.p.

Al-Bahrani Yusuf (1957–58) Al-Hadaʾiq al-Nadira fi Ahkam al-ʿItra al-Tahira. Muʾassasat al-Nashr al-Islami, Qom.

Al-Kulayni Muhammad (1998) Al-Kafi fi ʿIlm al-Din. Dar al-Taʿaruf, Beirut.

Al-Muhaqqiq al-Hilli (1989) Al-Mukhtasar al-Nafiʿ. Muʾassasat al-Biʿtha, Tehran.

Al-Shalmaghani ʿAli, al-Rida ʿAli (1986) ʿUyun Akhbar al-Rida. Muʾassasat al-Nashr al-Islami, Qom.

Al-Tusi Muhammad (1970) Tahdhib al-Ahkam fi Sharh al-Muqniʿa li-l-Shaykh al-Mufid. Dar al-Kutub al-Islamiyya, Tehran.

Al-Tusi Muhammad (1995–96) Mukhtalaf al-Shiʿa. Muʾassasat al-Nashr al-Islami, Qom.

Al-Tusi Muhammad (1998–99) Kitab al-Khilaf. Muʾassasat al-Nashr al-Islami, Qom.

Al-Tusi Muhammad (2009) Al-Mabsut fi Fiqh al-Imamiyya. Al-Maktaba al-Murtadawiyya, Tehran.

Coulson NJ (1971) Succession in the Muslim Family. Cambridge University Press, Cambridge.

Ess J van (1991–97) Theologie und Gesellschaft im 2. und 3. Jahrhundert Hidschra: Eine Geschichte des religiösen Denkens im frühen Islam. Walter de Gruyter, Berlin.

Gleave R (2005) Patronate in Early Shīʿite Law. In: Bernards M, Nawas J (eds) Patronate and Patronage in Early and Classical Islam. Brill, Leiden, pp 134–166.

Gleave R (2016) Modern Shiʿite Legal Theory and the Classical Tradition. In: Kendall E, Khan A (eds) Reclaiming Islamic Tradition: Modern Interpretations of the Classical Heritage. Edinburgh University Press, Edinburgh, pp 12–32.

Ibn Babawayh (1992) Man la Yahduruhu al-Faqih. Dar al-Adwaʾ, Beirut.

Ibn Idris Muhammad (1997) Saraʾir al-Hawi li-Tahrir al-Fatawi. Muʾassasat al-Nashr al-Islami, Qom.

Ibn Jaʿfar ʿAli (1988) Masaʾil ʿAli Bin Jaʿfar. Muʾassasat Al al-Bayt, Qom.

Kimber R (1998) The Qurʾanic Law of Inheritance. Islamic Law and Society 5(3):291–325.

Kohlberg E (1985) The Position of the walad zinā in Imāmī Shīʿism. Bulletin of the School of Oriental and African Studies 48:237–266.

Linant de Bellefonds Y (2012) Istibrā'. In: Bearman P et al. (eds) Encyclopaedia of Islam, 2nd edn. http://dx.doi.org/10.1163/1573-3912_islam_COM_0394. Accessed 31 January 2019.
Mughniyya Muhammad Jawad (1982) Al-Fiqh ʿala al-Madhahib al-Khamsa. Dar al-Taʿaruf, Beirut.
Mughniyya Muhammad Jawad (2000) Fiqh al-Imam Jaʿfar al-Sadiq. Ansariyan, Qom.
Schacht J (2012) Mīrāth. In: Bearman P et al. (eds) Encyclopaedia of Islam, 2nd edn. http://dx.doi.org/10.1163/1573-3912_islam_COM_0747. Accessed 31 January 2019.

Robert Gleave is professor of Arabic studies at the Institute of Arab and Islamic Studies at the University of Exeter. His primary research interests include hermeneutics and scriptural exegesis in Islam; Islamic law and works of Islamic legal theory (usul al-fiqh); violence and its justification in Islamic thought; and Shiʿism, in particular Shiʿi legal and political theory. He has organized a number of funded research projects including Islamic Reformulations: Belief, Governance and Violence (www.islamicreformulations.net) and Legitimate and Illegitimate Violence in Islamic Thought (www.livitproject.net). He is author of *Islam and Literalism: Literal Meaning and Interpretation in Islamic legal theory* (EUP 2011) and *Scripturalist Islam: The History and Doctrines of the Akhbari Shii School of Thought* (Brill 2007). His current projects are Understanding Shari'a (www.usppip.eu) and Law and Learning in Imami Shiite Islam (funded by the European Research Council).

Chapter 3
Algeria

Melanie Guénon

Contents

Abstract Filiation (*nasab*) in Algeria is established through valid, defective or erroneously assumed marriage as well as acknowledgement (*iqrār*) and proof (*bayyina*). The new Family Code of 2005 also puts scientific means (*ṭuruq* *ᶜilmiyya*) at the judge's disposal for establishing filiation. Thus, Algerian law provides a variety of methods to establish a child's filiation. However, children born out of wedlock have no legal connection to their biological father, being affiliated instead to their mother only. Nevertheless, there is evidence that fathers of these children regularly use acknowledgement to establish filiation and hence bypass the law. A legal relationship to a child can also be constituted by *kafāla*, which has been introduced to care for children without filiation or with an unfit caretaker. Implemented in 1976, the *kafāla* has far reaching legal consequences. Even though

Melanie Guénon is a research assistant in the ERC project COBHUNI (Contemporary Bioethics and the History of the Unborn in Islam) at the University of Hamburg.

M. Guénon (✉)
Asien-Afrika-Institut, Universität Hamburg, Edmund-Siemers-Allee 1, 20146 Hamburg, Germany
e-mail: melanie.guenon@uni-hamburg.de

N. Yassari et al. (eds.), *Filiation and the Protection of Parentless Children*, https://doi.org/10.1007/978-94-6265-311-5_3

no filiation arises from a *kafāla* arrangement, the person undertaking *kafāla* becomes the legal guardian of the child and since 1992 may also transfer his or her name to the child under *kafāla*.

Keywords Algeria · Family law · *nasab* · DNA test · Acknowledgement · Paternity · *kafāla* · Children born out of wedlock · Best interest of the child

3.1 Introduction

The history of Algerian family law since the country's independence in 1962 has been affected by divergent political positions that have impacted the legislative process. Establishing Islam as the state religion[1] of an independent Algeria is the most noticeable legal and political delimitation to the former French colonial power. However, the influence of the *sharīᶜa* is mainly limited to family and inheritance law; French-inspired law has been maintained for most other legal fields.[2] It was, and still is, also family law in which the conflicting political interests of the so-called modernists and traditionalists became apparent.[3]

In 1984, Algeria enacted for the first time a family code (code de la famille/ *qānūn al-usra*).[4] The Algerian Family Code (FC) clearly preserves the model of the 'legitimate family'[5] that is built on the notion of a licit sexual relationship, i.e. marriage. According to Islamic jurisprudence (*fiqh*), legal paternity and thus filiation (*nasab*) is established only by marriage and the *sharīᶜa*-based techniques of acknowledgement (*iqrār*) and proof (*bayyina*).[6] Children born out of wedlock have no legal connection to their biological father. The primary legal precept of filiation is the *firāsh* principle,[7] meaning that the husband of the mother is considered the (legal) father of the child. For a long time, Algerian law has neglected children born from an illicit relationship as well as foundlings. Eventually, it was the dramatic

[1] Article 2 of the Constitution of the People's Democratic Republic of Algeria of 28 November 1996 [Constitution de la République algerienne démocratique et populaire/*Dustūr al-Jumhūriyya al-Jazāʾiriyya al-Dīmuqrāṭiyya al-Shaᶜbiyya*], Al-Jarīda al-Rasmiyya no. 76 of 8 December 1996, as amended by Law no. 02-03 of 10 April 2002, Law no. 08-19 of 15 November 2008 and Law no. 16-01 of 6 March 2016, Al-Jarīda al-Rasmiyya no. 14 of 7 March 2016, pp 3–38. Due to the official use of both Arabic and French for law titles and official names in Algeria, this bilingual approach will also be followed throughout this article.

[2] Dennerlein 1998, p 46.

[3] See Bras 2007; Marzouki 2010.

[4] Law no. 84-11 of 9 June 1984 on the Family Code [Loi portant code de la famille/*Qānūn Yataḍamman Qānūn al-Usra*], Al-Jarīda al-Rasmiyya no. 24 of 12 June 1984, pp 910–924.

[5] Dennerlein 2001, p 254.

[6] For a detailed overview of the premodern Sunni and Shiite law on filiation see Ibrahim and Gleave, respectively, in this volume.

[7] It is derived from a statement of the prophet Muhammad that reads '*al-walad li-ṣāḥib al-firāsh*', literally meaning 'the child belongs to the owner of the bed'.

increase in abandoned children that led the Algerian government to address the problems of filiation and care of children born out of wedlock.[8] Consequently, the Algerian legislature has introduced several legal means aiming at protecting children's rights by ensuring the care of children of unknown filiation or parents. Initially, the *kafāla* ('sponsorship' or 'fosterage') was introduced in the Code of Public Health in 1976 to encourage Algerians to care for children other than their own.[9] In 1992, Algeria passed a law that enabled the person undertaking *kafāla* (*kāfil*) to transfer his or her name to the minor under *kafāla* (*makfūl*).[10] The Algerian state also ratified the UN Convention on the Rights of the Child (UNCRC) in December 1992.[11] Taking into consideration the prohibition of adoption (*tabannī*) in Algerian law as well as the importance of *nasab* in Islamic law in general, the Algerian *kafāla* has had profound effects on the legal status of children with unknown filiation and it is a measure that only few Muslim-majority countries have implemented. Additionally, in the course of the 2005 family law reform, scientific means were included in the FC as a way to establish filiation.[12] Hence, the reformed FC adopts new approaches regarding *nasab*. However, the exact application of the different methods to establish filiation remains vague and sometimes contradictory. This also applies to the regulations concerning the *kafāla*. Thus, it can be concluded that the most important principle for the Algerian legislature is to avoid confusion regarding *nasab* whilst taking into account the best interest of the child. The importance of the latter is emphasized by the 2005 FC.[13] Moreover, the latest version of the Algerian constitution not only pronounces that the state has a duty alongside the family and society to protect children's rights; it also expressly declares the state's responsibility towards abandoned children and children without filiation.[14] Despite the proscription against establishing filiation of children born out of wedlock, Algeria grants protection to these children.

---

[8] Exact figures of abandoned children are not available. The average number of children who are handed over to public institutions since the 1970s is estimated at 3,000 per year. See Moutassem-Mimouni 2008, para 21.

[9] Decree no. 76-79 of 23 October 1976 on the Public Health Code [Ordonnance portant code de la santé publique/*Amr Yataḍamman Qānūn al-Ṣiḥḥa al-ᶜUmūmiyya*], Al-Jarīda al-Rasmiyya no. 101 of 19 December 1976, pp 1116–1141.

[10] Decree no. 92-24 of 13 January 1992, Al-Jarīda al-Rasmiyya no. 5 of 22 January 1992, p 113, amending Decree no. 71-157 of 3 June 1971 Regarding the Change of Name [Décret relatif au changement de nom/*Marsūm Yataᶜallaq bi-Taghyīr al-Laqab*], Al-Jarīda al-Rasmiyya no. 47 of 11 June 1971, p 758.

[11] Decree no. 92-461 of 19 December 1992, Al-Jarīda al-Rasmiyya no. 91 of 23 December 1992, pp 1885–1894.

[12] Article 40 para 2 FC. Algerian Family Code Law no. 84-11 of 9 June 1984 [Code de la Famille/*Qānūn al-Usra*], Al-Jarīda Al-Rasmiyya no. 24 of 12 June 1984, pp 910–924, as amended by Decree no. 05-02 of 27 February 2005, Al-Jarīda al-Rasmiyya no. 15 of 27 February 2005, pp 18–22.

[13] Especially in Articles 65–69 FC.

[14] Article 72 Constitution 2016.

In what follows, we will see that the abovementioned reforms and the associated legal practice follow the general endeavours by Islamic *fiqh* to establish *nasab* whenever possible and thereby preserve the interests of the child. The Algerian legislature clearly attempts to strike balance between the perceived religious precepts and socio-political demands, although this balancing approach has sometimes led to the enactment of unclear regulations concerning paternity tests and acknowledgement.

3.2 Establishment of Filiation

Filiation (*nasab*) in Algeria is regulated by Articles 40–46 of the FC. Pursuant to Article 40 of the Algerian FC, paternity is established through marriage (whether the marriage is valid, defective or erroneously assumed) as well as acknowledgement (*iqrār*) or proof (*bayyina*). In addition, scientific means for establishing *nasab* were introduced by the 2005 family law reform in a new para 2 of Article 40; however, the use of these new means depends on the judge's discretion. In any event, *nasab* produces the same legal consequences regardless of the legal means by which it was established. This section first analyses the different kinds of marriages which establish *nasab* before then discussing acknowledgement, proof and scientific means.

3.2.1 Marriage

The simplest manner of establishing *nasab* in Algerian family law is by marriage, following the *firāsh* principle illustrated by Ibrahim in this volume. Marriage, parentage and *nasab* build a coherent concept. A child born into a valid marriage is automatically affiliated to the husband of the mother. In other words, *nasab* is the outcome of a birth resulting from a licit sexual relationship. Legal effects emanating from *nasab* in Algeria are, as in premodern Sunni law, impediments to marriage and the reciprocal rights of maintenance (*nafaqa*) and inheritance; also included are rights to guardianship (*wilāya*), custody (*ḥaḍāna*) and the right of the child to the father's family name.

Alongside a valid marriage, and in accordance with the aforementioned Article 40, *nasab* is also established by a defective (*bāṭil*) or an erroneously assumed marriage (*nikāḥ shubha*).[15] A marriage is invalid if one of the requirements stated in Article 9 FC is not fulfilled. These include: the age of consent, dower (*maḥr*),

[15] In premodern Islamic law, the concept of *nikāḥ shubha* primarily intends to avoid *ḥadd* punishments for the consummation of invalid marriages. Accordingly, it is assumed that the parties had sexual intercourse under the belief of being legally married. Thus, the conditions for the crime of adultery (*zinā*) are not fulfilled. See Nasir 2009, p 76.

presence of a custodian (*walī*), presence of two witnesses and an absence of impediments to marriage.[16]

Furthermore, the Algerian FC lists *nikāḥ shubha* in Article 40. The official French version of the FC translates the term as 'mariage apparent', i.e. an 'obvious marriage'. Regarding the *nasab* of a child, it is pointed out that *nikāḥ shubha* falls under the category of invalid marriages. Therefore, as specified in Article 34 FC, a child resulting from an invalid marriage is assumed legitimate. Although different types of *nikāḥ shubha*, as discussed by the *fuqahā'*, are presented in commentaries, a discussion of its significance in Algerian case law is lacking.[17] Nevertheless, a case from 2011 illustrates an interesting application of the *nikāḥ shubha* notion. In that case, an allegedly raped woman, striving for the *nasab* of her daughter, interpreted the alleged rape as a *nikāḥ shubha* in order to establish the paternity of the defendant.[18] This argument was probably based on the fact that the claimant was not able to prove a valid marriage between the parties. Whether the categorization of rape as *nikāḥ shubha*[19] is a prevailing view in the Algerian law or rather a bold interpretation of the attorney on behalf of his client is not clear from court documents. Since the Supreme Court remanded the case to the lower court, the final judgment from the lawsuit is not available. Thus, the likelihood of the strategy's success remains speculative. It is obvious, however, that all feasible means are used to prove a marriage in order to establish the child's *nasab*.

Another type of marriage that leads to establishing *nasab*, although not explicitly mentioned in the FC, is the *ᶜurfī* marriage, i.e. an unregistered traditional or religious marriage. Registration of marriages is prescribed by Article 22 FC. Yet the same article specifies that marriages may be registered at a later stage.[20] The legal obligation of registering the marriage is therefore not constitutive but only declaratory. This means that the registration has no effect on the marriage's validity,

16 Articles 34 and 40 FC. For the grounds of invalidity, see Articles 32–34 FC.

17 Dhiyābī 2010, pp 55–58; Ṣaqr 2006, pp 74–86; Laᶜwar and Ṣaqr 2007, pp 32–35; Qamrāwī and Ṣaqr 2008, pp 40–43.

18 Decision of the Supreme Court no. 617374 of 12 May 2011, Majallat al-Maḥkama al-ᶜUlyā no. 1 of 2012, pp 294–298. In this case, the first instance court ruled for the withdrawal of the child's *nasab* (*isqāṭ al-nasab*) at the alleged father's request on the basis that the child was born only one month after the marriage. The mother initially argued that the alleged father had registered the child under his name and that this action has to be interpreted as *iqrār* – and therefore would establish *nasab*. During the appeals procedure, the mother additionally raised the allegation of rape. After the decision of the first instance court to withdraw *nasab* was confirmed by the court of appeal, the mother appealed again. Finally, the Supreme Court decided to set aside the judgment and remanded the case to the lower court. Since the mother's attorney has used different strategies and arguments and presented various facts at different times during the lawsuit, I will refer to this case again in the upcoming section on acknowledgement, where the focus is on the matters of registration and *iqrār*.

19 For the practice and function of this argument in Ottoman Syria see Tucker 1998, pp 159–163.

20 In addition, Article 6 FC states that if the parties recite the first sura of the Quran, the *fātiḥa*, in mutual agreement and if all legal requirements in accord with Article 9bis are met, their marriage is constituted.

which allows in particular the validation of unregistered *ᶜurfī* marriages within the rural population. This is not only because the legislation wishes to grant protection to women and their children but also because parts of the vast southern territories lack the necessary legal infrastructure. Problems concerning the *nasab* of a child born in an *ᶜurfī* marriage occur if the suspected father denies his parentage. If the claimant cannot provide documents proving the religious marriage or stating an acknowledgement of the parentage, no legal basis for *nasab* is given. In such cases, mothers and children concerned have no options to claim the establishment of *nasab* by marriage. Similar difficulties appear if a longer period of time has passed between the marriage and its registration. As a consequence, the date of birth may be less than six month[21] after the registration, i.e. the official marriage date. Likewise, the husband could deny the traditional marriage and consequently his parentage. Although informal marriages are valid, only the registration document serves as full evidence. The sole way to circumvent the described scenario is to record an official note of the date the *ᶜurfī* marriage was concluded in the marriage registration document. Dennerlein, who studied family court cases before the reform in 2005, indicates that relying on the judge's sense of justice in the case of a known or assumed biological parentage has little prospect of success.[22] Instead, a child born out of wedlock is affiliated only to his or her mother even if the biological father is known.

3.2.2 Acknowledgement

Besides marriage, Article 40 FC recognizes the acknowledgement of paternity (*iqrār*) as a means for establishing *nasab*.[23] Regarding this *shariᶜa*-based proof of *iqrār*, the Algerian legislature follows the majority view of Islamic *fiqh*. Hence, under Article 44 FC, *iqrār* requires that the acknowledged child's *nasab* is unknown (*majhūl al-nasab*). Legal commentaries on the Family Code stress further prerequisites – namely, that no doubts exist as the legitimacy of the *iqrār*, such as a small age difference that proves parentage impossible or evidence that the acknowledged child was born out of a non-marital relationship (*walad al-zinā*).[24] This last point is especially emphasized by the observation that the acknowledging person may not acknowledge his child born out of wedlock because adultery (*zinā*) is a crime that cannot lead to establishing *nasab*.[25] This view is underlined by a

---

[21] The minimum duration of pregnancy of six months and the maximum duration of ten months is defined in Article 42 FC. Accordingly, Article 43 specifies that a child is affiliated to her father if born within ten months after separation or decease of the latter.

[22] Dennerlein 2001, pp 248–250.

[23] Pursuant to Articles 44 and 45 FC the child's mother can also acknowledge her maternity.

[24] Dhiyābī 2010, pp 61–63.

[25] Dhiyābī 2010, p 62.

decision of the Algerian Supreme Court (cour suprême/*al-maḥkama al-ᶜulyā*) ruling that establishing *nasab* for the concerned child would be impermissible because she was born only few days after the marriage, which means that the minimum duration of pregnancy was not met.[26] Hence, *iqrār* in the Algerian Family Code is, like *firāsh*, based on the assumption that the acknowledging man is the biological father. It is the possible fraud, however, that leads commentators to strongly emphasize that *iqrār* must not be equated with adoption, which is forbidden.[27]

Still, the contradictory interpretation in commentaries reveals the complex nature of *iqrār*. In some decisions, it is indicated that a *walad al-zinā* may be acknowledged by *iqrār*, namely in the case where either the offender (of *zinā*) acknowledges the child or the acknowledgement is imposed as part of a judgment; whereas other decisions considered that *zinā* cannot establish *nasab*.[28] The first view is supported by the abovementioned case heard by the Supreme Court.[29] In that case, the claimant appealed the decisions of the first instance court as well as the appeal court, which both ruled in favour of the withdrawal of her daughter's *nasab* after the alleged father applied for this withdrawal (*isqāṭ al-nasab*) on the basis that the child was born only one month after the marriage. However, the defendant had registered the child under his name at the relevant registry office, and the registration document issued by the registry office was presented to the judge. It is not stated in the Algerian FC whether the registration document is considered as *iqrār* or not. However, since the alleged father went to court in order to withdraw his previous acknowledgement and thus the *nasab* of the child, there must have been an established *nasab* he asked the court to revoke. After the court of appeal also dismissed the claim for *nasab*, the mother took her case to the Supreme Court. There, the mother contested the courts' taking of evidence, stating that the child's having been born outside the legally fixed duration of pregnancy was not a sufficient proof for *zinā* or for the non-existence of a marriage. Moreover, the mother argued that the popular *ᶜurfī* marriage should have been taken into consideration by

---

[26] Quoted in Dhiyābī 2010, pp 62–63. No file number nor date is given. Decisions of the Supreme Court analysed by Dennerlein come to the same conclusion: a child conceived before marriage is a *walad al-zinā* and *nasab* cannot be established. Dennerlein 1998, pp 163–166.

[27] Dhiyābī 2010, pp 69–76. The issue also being discussed by an Algerian master thesis in family law, in which the author describes *iqrār* as a possible 'perversion of justice' (*al-taḥāyul ᶜalā al-qānūn*), suggests that *iqrār* is used to acknowledge children born from an illicit relationship. Moreover, it reveals the possibility of 'secret adoptions', in other words, using *iqrār* as an alternative to adoption. In order to underline the unlawfulness of such action, the author points to the penalty for a false statement in front of a public official under Article 217 of the Penal Code. The thesis is available at: http://dspace.univ-biskra.dz:8080/jspui/handle/123456789/6306. Accessed 6 July 2017.

[28] Laᶜwar and Ṣaqr 2007, pp 37–39. The initial assertion contradicts other commentaries which emphasize that the acknowledging person must not declare that he is acknowledging his illegitimate child because *zinā* is a crime that cannot establish *nasab*. See for example Dhiyābī 2010, pp 62–63.

[29] Decision of the Supreme Court no. 617374 of 12 May 2011.

the court of appeal. Registration and birth dates do not imply an illicit sexual relationship; given the fact that the child had been registered by the defendant himself, the court should have considered all possible manners of proof listed in Article 40 of the Family Code. According to the attorney, the child's registration was considered as *iqrār* and therefore established *nasab* as defined by Article 40. Since *nasab* is a right of the child, a personally conducted acknowledgement would be irreversible. Taking these arguments into consideration, the Supreme Court granted the appeal and remanded the case for further consideration as there was a strong possibility that the acknowledgement of the defendant would serve as sufficient proof of his parentage. Hence, even though the *ᶜurfī* or any other marriage between the parties could not be proven, *zinā* could not be proven either. With regard to the Supreme Court's favourable view of the appeal, it can be assumed that, firstly, the duration of pregnancy is not sufficient evidence for *zinā* and therefore does not prevent *iqrār* or the establishment of *nasab*. Secondly, the registration of the child at the registry office is characterized as *iqrār*. What remains unclear is whether the registration was either possible without a marriage certificate or whether the parties were actually married. Whatever the circumstances of the relationship may have been, the case implies that official bodies do not (always) check marriage certificates before acknowledgements are undertaken.

The second view has been expressed in decisions issued by various first instance courts and appellate courts during the 1980s and 1990s, in which the duration of pregnancy subsequent to the official date of the marriage was less than six months. It is thus, according to the decisions cited by the commentaries, obvious that the child was born as a result of *zinā*. Consequently, the courts repeatedly stressed that *zinā* cannot establish *nasab*, although the judges have ruled differently in other cases described in the literature. These latter instances are usually followed by a remark from the commentators that the respective court has violated the law by recognizing the *iqrār* of a child born less than six month after the official marriage.[30]

Taken together, these somehow contradictory decisions suggest that the court's ruling on the *nasab* of a child born out of wedlock depends on the (suspected) father's attitude towards the child. Namely, it appears that if a *nasab* case is brought to court and the alleged father does not want to acknowledge the child, the court refers to the duration of pregnancy or to the lack of a marriage certificate and thus refuses to establish of *nasab*. However, if the father voluntarily acknowledges the child, the latter's *nasab* will not be questioned. This specific approach gives the impression of legislation whose primary objective is to establish paternity whenever possible and, more importantly, not to negate it once established. Assuming this, the Algerian case law follows the general effort of *fiqh*, namely to establish *nasab* rather than negating it. This supposition is bolstered by several decisions on the application of DNA tests in paternity disputes, which will be discussed below.

[30] Laᶜwar and Ṣaqr 2007, pp 37–39.

3.2.3 Proof

Another way of establishing *nasab* stated in Article 40 FC is proof (*bayyina*). The definition of *bayyina* is not given in the code itself but in the legal commentaries. The majority of lawyers and *fuqahā'* define *bayyina* as testimony (*shahāda*).[31] However, the official French version of the Family Code uses the term 'preuve', which is a rather general term that could also include written or circumstantial evidence. According to one of the legal commentaries, in the case of *nasab* the probative value of *bayyina* is stronger than *iqrār*. That is due to two reasons: Firstly, not only the applicant (as in the case of *iqrār*) but at least two people are involved in *bayyina*, giving their testimony. Secondly, it is once again stated that *iqrār* is susceptible of false claims.[32]

According to the Ḥanbalī scholar Ibn Qayyim al-Jawziyya (d. 1350), *bayyina* may refer to all kinds of proof.[33] This opinion is especially relevant when it comes to scientific proof.[34] Interestingly, performing blood tests in order to prove paternity had already been an issue in the late 1990s. In a case from 1999, the first instance court (tribunal/*maḥkama*) as well as the court of appeal (cour/*majlis al-qaḍā'iyya*) authorized a blood test (*taḥlīl al-damm*) as *bayyina* to establish a child's *nasab*. However, the Supreme Court rejected the decisions, reasoning that (the then) Article 40 of the Family Code does not allow for such a conclusion and that the courts exceeded their competence in developing the law independently.[35] Hence, under Algerian law, *bayyina* cannot be interpreted as scientific proof.

Accordingly, the legal literature as well as court practice imply that *bayyina* was included in the FC for the sake of completeness given that it is a *sharī*ᶜ*a*-based method for establishing *nasab*. Yet in contemporary Algeria there is no indication of *bayyina* being a relevant option for establishing filiation.

3.2.4 Scientific Means

Since Algeria's family law reform in February 2005, the means for establishing *nasab* have been broadened. Now, scientific means (*ṭuruq* ᶜ*ilmiyya*) are at the judge's disposal for establishing *nasab*. Accepting that scientific means cover all medical examinations based on genetic analysis, including DNA tests,[36] Algerian

---

31 Brunschvig 2009, p 215.

32 Dhiyābī 2010, p 83.

33 For the discussion on contemporary interpretations of the term, see Shabana 2014, pp 13–26.

34 This view has also been taken by some medical and legal experts in bioethical debates concerning the use of DNA tests to establish paternity. See Shabana 2014, pp 25–26.

35 Decision of the Supreme Court no. 222674 of 15 June 1999, quoted in Dhiyābī 2010, pp 80–81.

36 Due to the fact that DNA analysis became the primary genetic testing technique in paternity cases to determine genetic genealogy, this method is representatively used in this article when writing about genetic testing. The terms 'DNA test' and 'DNA analysis' are used interchangeably.

positive law acknowledges filiation on the basis of biological paternity. Using the vaguely defined term 'scientific means' opens, at least in theory, the door for all available and future technology.

Barraud considers the possibility that the reformed Article 40 is implicitly addressed to single mothers having children born out of wedlock. Given this, such women have the opportunity to sue the suspected biological father so that he is legally forced to acknowledge the child.[37] This view is supported by a statement of the former minister for employment and national solidarity (Ministère de la solidarité nationale et de l'emploi/*wizārat al-taḍāmun al-waṭanī wa-l-tashghīl*)[38] Djamel Ould Abbès (2003–2007), who said in 2006 that scientific means could possibly be a way of determining parentage. Specifically, such means could be considered as 'threats' ('menaces'[39]) to biological fathers who do not take responsibility for their children. Hence, this remark implies the intention of improving the legal and social status of children born out of wedlock.[40]

The judge of the family court can either order a DNA test on its own motion or accept an applicant's request for DNA testing. It is up to the judge to determine whether the test is admissible or not. Furthermore, the judge also evaluates the test results: In doing so, he is not bound by the opinion of a medical expert.[41] However, the FC does not specify which circumstances allow the implementation of a DNA test for establishing *nasab*. It defines neither which of the involved individuals has to give permission nor whether DNA testing is permissible if one the concerned persons has already died. Instead, the process of standardizing norms is left to the judges. In addition, the law does not point out how to address a person's refusal to undertake the test. In accordance with the right to physical integrity, recognized by Article 34, para 2 of the Algerian Constitution, each individual may reject the procedure of DNA testing. Since the Constitution prevails over the ordinary law, the judge could never oblige a person to undergo DNA testing.

Indeed, Algerian court practice reveals some restraint in authorizing DNA testing. Instead, judges give priority to the established methods of premodern Islamic law, especially the *firāsh* principle and *iqrār*, this despite the legal integration of DNA testing into the scope of legal methods establishing paternity. In the available decisions dealing with biological and legal paternity, the implementation

[37] Barraud 2010, paras 10–11.

[38] Today, these two realms are covered by separated ministries, namely the Ministry for Labour, Employment and Social Security (Ministère du Travail, de l'Emploi et de la Sécurité Sociale/ *Wizārat al-ᶜAmal wa-l-Tashghīl wa-l-Ḍamān al-Ijtimāᶜī*) and the Ministry for National Solidarity, Family and the Status of Women (Ministère de la Solidarité Nationale, de la Famille et de la Condition de la Femme/*Wizārat al-Taḍāmun al-Waṭanī wa-l-Usra wa-Qaḍāyā al-Mar'a*).

[39] Quoted in Barraud 2010, para 11.

[40] Barraud 2010, paras 10–11.

[41] Mahieddin 2007, p 111. Mahieddin refers to Articles 43 and 54 Code of Civil Procedure, Law no. 08-09 of 25 February 2008 on the Code of Civil Procedure [Loi portant code de procédure civile et administrative/*Qānūn Yataḍamman Qānūn al-Ijrā'āt al-Madaniyya wa-l-Idāriyya*], Al-Jarīda al-Rasmiyya no. 21 of 23 April 2008, pp 2–83.

of a DNA test has been judicially prevented. The Supreme Court decisions[42] suggest that the Algerian jurisdiction rather adheres to premodern Islamic law and the official consensus of the international *fiqh* boards.[43] Accordingly, DNA analysis is not considered as an equivalent means of proving *nasab* compared to the *sharīᶜa*-based methods. Obviously, the legal rationale of the Supreme Court is aimed less at the determination of biological parentage than on the enforcement of the right of the child to *nasab*. Above all, the court does not refer to genetic testing if parentage can be established by other means, i.e. the verification of a marriage or *iqrār*.

Similarly to the FC, the majority of the legal commentaries do not go into detail about the possibility of genetic testing in paternity disputes and do not discuss the term '*al-ṭuruq al-ᶜilmiyya*'.[44] Only Ṣaqr in his commentary explicitly refers to the 2001 final statement of the Islamic Organization of Medical Science (IOMS), which states that there is no general prohibition on using genetic testing. According to Ṣaqr, this opens various fields of application: dispute over an unknown filiation (*majhūl al-nasab*), refusal of the suspected father to acknowledge the child, negation of *nasab*, inheritance disputes and determining maternity if no witnesses to the birth are available.[45] However, the author does not explain whether he is only discussing theoretical applications or is actually identifying its relevance for Algerian court practice. Indeed, Ṣaqr continues to express significant constraints on DNA usage in family law. He argues that genetic testing is not proof of *firāsh* because marriage is determined by other means.[46] Other commentaries imply a similar opinion towards DNA analysis. Of particular note is that commentators repeatedly distinguish between establishing filiation (*ithbāt al-nasab*) by a valid marriage and 'adding' filiation (*ilḥāq al-nasab*) in the case of non-marital sexual relations.[47] In the repeatedly cited decision of the Supreme Court on the subject,[48] the court stressed that *ithbāt al-nasab* and *ilḥāq al-nasab* must not be confused. In that case, the child's *nasab* was initially rejected by the first instance court on the ground that the parents were not married, although biological parentage was proven by DNA test. Based on the established biological paternity, the child could not have been affiliated to the mother's present husband. Ultimately, the Supreme Court

---

[42] Decision of the Supreme Court no. 617374 of 12 May 2011; decision of the Supreme Court no. 605592 of 15 October 2009, Majallat al-Maḥkama al-ᶜUlyā no. 1 of 2010, pp 245–248; decision of the Supreme Court no. 439265 of 27 May 2009, Majallat al-Maḥkama al-ᶜUlyā no. 2 of 2009, pp 370–373.

[43] The most influential *fiqh* boards are the Islamic Fiqh Council associated with the Islamic World League, the International Islamic Fiqh Academy associated with the Organization of Islamic Cooperation (IOC) and the Islamic Organization of Medical Science (IOMS).

[44] Bi-l-Khayr 2009; Laᶜwar and Ṣaqr 2007; Ṭāhirī 2009.

[45] Ṣaqr 2006, p 91, fn 1. Dhiyābī also mentions the discussions of IOMS and the Islamic Fiqh Council on DNA testing. Dhiyābī 2010, pp 87–94.

[46] Ṣaqr 2006, p 91, fn 1.

[47] Qamrāwī and Ṣaqr 2008, p 45; Dhiyābī 2010, pp 74–76.

[48] Decision no. 355180 of 5 March 2006, Majallat al-Qaḍā'iyya no. 1 of 2006, p 460, quoted by Dhiyābī 2010 and by Qamrāwī and Ṣaqr 2008.

decided that the child should be affiliated (*laḥiqa*) to the biological father. Even though the difference between *ithbāt* and *ilḥāq* was emphasized, the distinct legal effects to be expected remain undefined. In fact, the expression *ilḥāq al-nasab* cannot be found in the FC. The judges gave the impression of creating a new but second-class category of *nasab* that acknowledges biological parenthood without establishing legal parentage. However, neither the concept of *ilḥāq al-nasab* nor the alleged legal differences between *ithbāt* and *ilḥāq* are explained in more detail.

Additionally, the decision demonstrates that Algerian courts differentiate between *sharīᶜa*-based proof and modern methods for the establishment of *nasab*. *Sharīᶜa*-based proof establishing *nasab* is prioritized by highlighting its effect of *ithbāt al-nasab*, using *fiqh* terminology. By comparison, genetic testing is demarcated as unequal, leading to *ilḥāq al-nasab*. However, the Algerian FC itself does not draw any distinctions, instead clearly referring to *ithbāt al-nasab* through scientific means.

3.3 Status of Children of Defective or Unknown Filiation

Children born from an illicit sexual relationship have no legal connection to their biological father. Therefore, *nasab* and all rights deriving from it will not be established. However, the child will be affiliated to his or her mother. Accordingly, only the name of the mother will be mentioned in the birth certificate of a child lacking a legal father.[49] Hence, she will assume guardianship and custody for her child. Additionally, inheritance rights arise between the child and her mother's family. An Algerian mother also transfers her citizenship to her child.[50]

A child with an unknown father born in Algeria obtains Algerian citizenship unless filiation with a non-Algerian parent is established during her minority, thus establishing non-Algerian citizenship. Likewise, a foundling is considered Algerian.[51] Apart from citizenship, the legal status of a foundling is not explicitly defined. According to the Civil Status Law, a state official will give to a child with unknown parents at least two first names, of which the last one serves as her family name.[52] This regulation is criticized as being stigmatizing because children without

[49] Article 7, para 2 Algerian Code of Citizenship, Decree no. 70-86 of 15 December 1970 on the Code of Citizenship [Ordonnance portant code de la nationalité algérienne/*Amr Yataḍamman Qānūn al-Jinsiyya al-Jazāʾiriyya*], Al-Jarīda al-Rasmiyya no. 105 of 18 December 1970, pp 1570–1574, amended by Decree no. 05-01 of 27 February 2005, Al-Jarīda al-Rasmiyya no. 15 of 27 February 2005, pp 15–18.

[50] Articles 6 and 7, para 2 Code of Citizenship.

[51] Article 7, para 1 Code of Citizenship.

[52] Article 64 Decree no. 70-20 of 19 February 1970 Bearing Civil Status Law [Ordonnance relative à l'état civil/*Amr Yataᶜallaq al-Ḥāla al-Madaniyya*], Al-Jarīda al-Rasmiyya no. 21 of 27 February 1970, pp 233–241.

filiation are thus easily identified and hence exposed to social discrimination.[53] Regarding the welfare of abandoned children, a 1980 decree concerning the care of foster children regulates the broad organization of children's homes. In these institutions, which are under the control of the Ministry of Health, foster children are housed and educated until they reach majority. Their guardianship is taken over by the respective province (*wilāya*).[54] Political measures to prevent the abandonment of children were promised in a law in 1985,[55] although not further defined. Similarly, the state's self-imposed obligation to protect children without filiation, as expressed in the Constitution, has not been specified.

An additional aspect in the Algerian debate on children of unknown filiation is anonymous birthing. Inspired by French law, Algerian hospitals allow anonymous births so that the mother can give birth without her data being recorded. Activists demand mandatory paternity tests for all children born out of wedlock to combat discrimination against them and to preserve their right to know their natural parents. Moreover, some groups call for the abolition of anonymous births. Alternatively, they advocate that mothers leave reference information that is stored in a database which permits children to later identify them.[56] Since Algerian women abandon their children primarily because they face social stigmatization, the latter proposal would improve the situation neither of the children nor of their mothers.[57] Even though an abandoned child is legally presumed to be born within a licit sexual relationship, he or she is socially perceived as an illegitimate child. The social problem of stigmatization may only be lessened if DNA tests become obligatory for all respective parties and especially if biological paternity is accordingly acknowledged as legal paternity.

3.4 Protection of Children Without Filiation or Permanent Caretakers

As in the regulations on *nasab*, the Algerian attempt to reconcile *fiqh* with modern social demands is evident in the measures concerning the protection of children without permanent caretakers. Algeria is one of the Muslim countries which

[53] Barraud 2010, paras 48–55; Aït Zaï 1996, para 26.

[54] Decree no. 80-83 of 15 March 1980 on the Establishment, Organization and Functioning of Children's Homes [Décret portant création, organisation et fonctionnement des foyers pour enfants assistés/*Marsūm Yataḍamman Iḥdāth Dūr al-Aṭfāl al-Mus^c^afīn wa-Tanẓīmuhā wa-Sayruhā*], Al-Jarīda al-Rasmiyya no. 12 of 18 March 1980, pp 318–320. For the living conditions in these institutions and psychological effects on Algerian children see Moutassem-Mimouni 2001.

[55] Article 73 Law no. 85-05 of 16 February 1985 on the Protection and the Promotion of Health [Loi relative à la protection et à la promotion de la santé/*Qānūn Yata^c^allaq bi-Ḥimāyat al-Ṣiḥḥa wa-Tarqiyatuhā*], Al-Jarīda al-Rasmiyya no. 8 of 17 February 1985, p 176.

[56] A 2014; B 2013; Larbi 2016.

[57] Tagzout 2011.

explicitly prohibit adoption (*tabannī*). However, due to the French colonization (1830–1962), the concept of adoption has not always been neglected by Algerian courts. In fact, different family law provisions co-existed during the French colonial rule in Algeria. From 1944 until the country's independence, Muslim Algerians had the option to be governed by either French or Muslim family and inheritance law.[58] Thus, in accord with French family law, Muslim couples were allowed to adopt children.[59] In 1965, three years after independence, the Algerian legislation precluded *tabannī*. Similar to other family law regulations under discussion, the prohibition of adoption was a matter of heated debates between the so-called modernists and traditionalists.[60] Finally, the Algerian FC codified in 1984 states that adoption is prohibited under both statutory and religious law.[61]

Since the number of abandoned children increased dramatically during the 1970s and 1980s, the government was impelled to react.[62] Therefore, in 1976 Algeria introduced the *kafāla* in the Code of Public Health.[63] Especially in the Maghreb, the term *kafāla* denotes the guardianship and caretaking of children in a family other than the biological parents.[64] Initially, pursuant to the 1976 law, the *kafāla*'s legal effects included mainly custody and personal affairs, i.e. decisions concerning education. The 1984 Algerian FC clarified these regulations by dedicating to the *kafāla* ten articles of the Code, namely Articles 116–125. *Kafāla* is defined as a legal act by virtue of which the *kāfil* undertakes to provide maintenance, education and protection for the *makfūl* as a father would do for his child,[65] in other words, as if the child was the *kāfil*'s biological child.[66] The *kāfil* must be Muslim, sane, respectable and able to provide for and protect the child.[67] The child can be of either known or unknown filiation (*majhūl al-nasab*).[68] If the child has an established *nasab*, this *nasab* must be preserved.[69] Additionally, if the parents are known, they

58 Mitchell 1997, pp 194–195.

59 Aït Zaï 1996, para 4.

60 Aït Zaï 1996, para 4.

61 Article 46 FC.

62 On the socio-economic reasons driving women to abandon their children, see Zemmour-Khorsi 1994 and Moutassem-Mimouni 2001.

63 Decree no. 76-79 of 23 October 1976. Between the preclusion of adoption in 1965 and the introduction of *kafāla* in 1976, regulations on the protection of children without permanent caretakers remained vague. Due to the lack of a codified family code, the family law reforms adopted under French colonization remained in force until 1975. After 1975 family law affairs were subject to premodern Islamic law. See Dennerlein 1998, pp 60–61.

64 Yassari 2015, p 950. For an overview of the term see Linant de Bellefonds 1978.

65 Even though the official wording reads: 'as a father would do for his son' ('au même titre que le ferait un père pour son fils'/'*qiyām al-ab bi-ibnihi*'), both boys and girls can be taken into *kafāla*.

66 Article 116 FC.

67 Article 118 FC.

68 Article 119 FC.

69 Article 120 FC.

must agree that their child is to be taken care of under the *kafāla*.[70] Since 1992, the Decree Regarding the Change of Name[71] allows the *kāfil* to transfer his family name (*laqab*) to the *makfūl* if the father of the child is verifiably unknown and the mother, provided that she is known, agrees. Considering that the prerequisite for the right to bear one's father's name is *nasab*, the Algerian legislator has taken a major step to integrate children without filiation into society. For this reason, some voices raise the concern that due to this provision the *kafāla* strongly resembles prohibited adoption.[72] Parallels to adoption also occur in legal representation. Once a *kafāla* agreement is enacted, the *kāfil* holds parental responsibilities. Not only the custody (*ḥaḍāna*)[73] but also the guardianship (*wilāya*)[74] of the *makfūl* will be transferred to him. Thus, he becomes the legal representative of the child and is therefore in charge of the child's financial means[75] and all personal affairs. This also covers the right of the guardian to determine the place of residence.[76] However, no inheritance rights derive from the *kafāla*. Nonetheless, the *kāfil* may pass up to one-third of his assets to the *makfūl*. If the stipulated amount exceeds one-third, the disposition is void, unless the legal heirs consent to the will.

Consequently, the legal effects *kafāla* unfolds do not equal filiation. Unlike the latter, *kafāla* does not constitute *nasab*, so that neither legal paternity nor inheritance rights derive from it. Nevertheless, due to its far-reaching legal implications, the Algerian *kafāla* is often characterized as an 'alternative' to adoption,[77] 'quasi-adoption'[78] or even as 'mini-adoption'.[79] The same notion was implied by the Algerian government representative introducing the *kafāla*, who declared: 'Comme il est interdit d'adopter, la *kafāla* remplace légalement l'adoption.'[80] Furthermore, the fosterage agreements which were reached before the *kafāla* was enacted contained the notation 'en vue d'adoption'.[81] Thus, the socio-political context indicates that the Algerian *kafāla* was introduced as a substitute for adoption.

An even more pronounced analogy between *kafāla* and adoption has been drawn by Yassari. She has argued that the Algerian *kafāla* may be defined as a functional

[70] Article 117 FC.

[71] Decree no. 71-157 of 3 June 1971 as amended by decree no. 92-24 of 13 January 1992.

[72] In Dhiyābī's opinion, the 1992 decree already violates the prohibition of adoption, see Dhiyābī 2010, pp 71–72.

[73] Article 116 FC.

[74] Article 121 FC.

[75] Article 122 FC.

[76] Article 38 Civil Code, Decree no. 75-58 of 26 September 1975 on the Civil Code [Ordonnance portant code civil/*Amr Yataḍamman al-Qānūn al-Madanī*], Al-Jarīda al-Rasmiyya no. 78 of 30 September 1975, pp 990–1059, as amended by Law no. 07-05 of 13 May 2007, Al-Jarīda al-Rasmiyya no. 31 of 13 May 2007, pp 3–5. This ruling does not exclude the guardian's expatriation.

[77] E.g. Barraud 2008b; Aït Zaï 1996, para 5.

[78] Barraud 2008b, p 135.

[79] Pruvost 1996, p 169.

[80] Quoted from Aït Zaï 1996, para 5.

[81] Aït Zaï 1996, paras 14–15: 'With the purpose of adoption'.

equivalent of adoption.[82] There are two main arguments for this claim. The first is the fact that both the *ḥaḍāna* as well as the *wilāya* pass to the *kāfil*, so that he is in charge of all the *makfūl*'s legal affairs without state interference. The second argument touches on the termination of a *kafāla* arrangement. The FC outlines two potential grounds by which the *kafāla* may end. Firstly, according to Article 124 one or both parents may reclaim the *wilāya* of their child. In this regard, children who have reached the decision-making age of thirteen years[83] must be asked for their opinion and may refuse to return to their biological parents. As for children who have not yet reached the age of thirteen, the judge must give his approval to the return by taking into consideration the child's best interest.[84] Secondly, the subsequent article states that in terminating a *kafāla* the public prosecutor's office must be informed prior to submitting the proposal before the same court which authorized the *kafāla*.[85] Although this provision has sometimes been recognized as the *kāfil*'s opportunity to end *kafāla* at will, Yassari advocates another interpretation, namely that the Algerian *kafāla* was built to establish a permanent bond between the *kāfil* and the *makfūl*; here, the giving of notice to the public prosecutor serves as check against indiscriminate termination. In fact, the law neither declares whether the *kafāla* ends with the *makfūl* reaching majority nor does it further define the circumstances which justify its termination.[86] Moreover, the law does not provide that a testamentary disposition in favour of the *makfūl* expires when he attains full age. In the event of the death of the *kāfil*, the right to perform the *kafāla* passes to the *kāfil*'s heirs, provided that they accept the responsibility. Otherwise, the judge will transfer the guardianship to a public institution.[87]

Besides this, families or couples entering a *kafāla* agreement usually perceive it as an adoption. Yet, due to unclear regulations on the revocation of the arrangement, they view the current legislation as an obstacle. As a result, fraud affecting personal data occurs in the form of secret adoptions, that is, an agreement between two parties arranging the handing over of a newborn baby to an adopting family; the latter would then pass the baby off as its own, sometimes even simulating a pregnancy beforehand.[88] To my knowledge, neither figures nor further in-depth research is available on this phenomenon. However, it points not only to the gap between individual desires and the law but also to the social stigma of children without filiation; it highlights as well as those childless couples who would sometimes even break the law to comply with social norms, and of course it demonstrates the desire to have

[82] Yassari 2015, pp 952–954.

[83] Article 42 Civil Code.

[84] Article 124 FC.

[85] See also Articles 492–497 Code of Civil Procedure.

[86] Yassari 2015, pp 953–954.

[87] However, according to the Algerian lawyer and women's rights activist Nadia Aït Zaï, the *kafāla* is not transmitted to the *kāfil*'s spouse. Unfortunately, Aït Zaï does not cite her sources. Aït Zaï 2005, pp 24–25.

[88] Barraud 2008b, p 136; Barraud 2008a, para 8; Barraud 2011, p 159.

children.[89] The aspiration of couples to be perceived as a 'proper family' is also reflected in the numbers on *kafāla*. Even though accessible figures and statistics are incomplete and often deficient, it can be said that following its introduction, the *kafāla* did not appeal to many Algerians. An explanation given for this is the 'double honte',[90] the 'twofold shame' of being unfertile and taking on an illegitimate child. This view has changed considerably, very likely as a consequence of the 1992 Decree Regarding the Change of Name.[91] The relevance of this Decree is underlined by the institutions engaged in drafting it, namely, the Association Algérienne Enfance et Famille d'Accueil Bénévole (AAEFAB), the Ministry of Social Affairs and the Supreme Islamic Council. The involvement of the latter shows the legislature's attempt to reduce the social stigma of children born out of wedlock without compromising the Islamic principles of *nasab*. The difficulty of maintaining the unstable balance between religious precepts and social demands is also reflected by Shaykh Ḥamānī, then president of the Supreme Islamic Council. In a fatwa of 1991 he approved the name transfer from *kāfil* to *makfūl*, although he also expressed his reluctance as to the possible similarity between filiation and *kafāla* in the public perception.[92]

Since the possibility of transferring the family name was enacted, the *kafāla* became more common among Algerians. According to official numbers, 9,080 *kafāla* agreements were concluded between 2001 and 2005, of which 8,182 were national and 898 international agreements. Especially among Algerians living in France or Italy, the *kafāla* has become more popular during this period, increasing from 4.2 to 17.1% of the total amount.[93] Other official figures indicate that more than 50% of the abandoned children who were initially taken care of in the associated institutions between 1999 and 2009 were eventually taken into *kafāla*.[94]

In order to conclude a *kafāla* contract, the applicant applies to the competent office of the Public Welfare Ministry. An inquiry by the authorities then determines the applicant's eligibility. The respective consulate is responsible for the applications by Muslim Algerians living abroad.[95] Two modes of the *kafāla* exist: the *kafāla judiciaire*, which is ordered by the judge for children of unknown filiation; and the *kafāla notariale*, which is attested by a notary and covers children with known filiation. Except for the differing competence in handling the application, there are no differences between the two.

By enacting the *kafāla* for children of unknown filiation, i.e. with either both parents or the father unknown, the legislature acknowledged the existence of

---

[89] Barraud 2008a, para 8.

[90] Barraud 2011, p 155.

[91] Barraud 2011, pp 155–156; Moutassem-Mimouni 2008, para 24.

[92] Bettahar 2005/2006, para 33; Pruvost 1996, pp 158–174.

[93] Figures of the Algerian Ministry of Employment and National Solidarity of 2006 and 2007, cited from Barraud 2008a, para 19.

[94] Official figures cited from Barraud 2011, p 156.

[95] Barraud 2008b, para 135, fn 11.

unmarried mothers and their children who had been legally negated until then. Especially during the 1990s, the *kafāla* was used by unmarried mothers to care for their children as *kāfila* so that less stigmatization occurred.[96]

Another point that requires consideration is the social aspects of the *kafāla*. Besides foundlings, children of unknown filiation, children born out of wedlock and children whose parents are not able to take care of them, the transfer of children within their greater family must not be ignored. According to Barraud, the introduction of the *kafāla* institutionalized the intra-family transfer of children. Two common scenarios exist. First, a child of a nuclear family already having many children is 'given' to a childless couple of the greater family. It regularly occurs that the accepting family lives in France, so that the biological parents have little personal contact with their child. In these instances, the *kafāla* can indeed be described as a 'quasi-adoption'. In the second possible scenario, a child between five and seventeen years old is given into the *kafāla* of relatives living in France. That is done either to send the child to school abroad and/or to lessen the financial burden on the biological parents.[97]

Interestingly, Algerian commentaries do not deal with the *kafāla* in detail.[98] Accordingly, this gives room for two different deductions: either contemporary lawyers do not assess the *kafāla* as being worthy of discussion because legal practice is unambiguous or they do not want to highlight possible equivalents to adoption.

3.5 Conclusion

Under Algerian family law, filiation can be established by marriage, acknowledgment, *bayyina* and scientific means. Since legal practice indicates that judges are guided by the Islamic objective of establishing or maintaining *nasab* whenever possible, lawyers usually try to prove a marriage between the parties involved. Accordingly, the law acknowledges a variety of marriage types, namely valid, defective or erroneously assumed marriages. Additionally, *ᶜurfī* marriages are considered valid, although problems may arise if the religious marriage cannot be verified. Apart from marriage, acknowledgement is the second most relevant method in Algerian court practice to establish filiation. While legal commentaries emphasize that a child born out of wedlock must not be acknowledged, the same commentaries as well as court decisions (also) show a different picture. Hence, *iqrār* is commonly used to establish constitute the filiation of children born out of

---

[96] Barraud 2008b, p 136.

[97] Barraud 2008a, paras 16–17; Barraud 2008b, p 137. On the legal problems concerning the Algerian *kafāla* in France see Barraud 2008a. See also Oubrou 2013, para 27, who refers to the French region of Haute-Vienne, where all Algerian children under *kafāla* come from the Algerian region of Mostaganem. This may lead to a suspicion of some kind of '*kafāla* traffic'.

[98] Ṣaqr 2006, pp 313–315; Laᶜwar and Ṣaqr 2007, pp 109–110; Qamrāwī and Ṣaqr 2008, pp 184–187.

wedlock. This approach may be in the best interest of the child since children without *nasab* face not only social stigmatization but also legal discrimination. Considering the best interest of the child has also been the target of the 2005 FC reform. Since then, scientific means are at the judge's disposal to establish the *nasab* of a child. Yet the Algerian legislature has hesitated in solving the conflict between genetic technology and the recognized types of evidence under Islamic jurisprudence. Given the lack of precise regulations regarding the implementation of DNA tests, it remains unclear whether it is permitted to determine the biological paternity of children born out of wedlock and to establish *nasab* on this basis. Consequently, the present FC curtails the right of husbands and children to know the biological truth.

Since adoption is prohibited in Algeria, the *kafāla* was introduced in 1976 in order to improve the social status of children with unknown filiation. The *kāfil* assumes responsibility for both the *ḥaḍāna* and the *wilāya* of the *makfūl*, and since 1992 may also transfer his name to the child. It was precisely the 1992 Decree Regarding the Change of Name that made the *kafāla* more popular in Algeria as children under *kafāla* were no longer easily recognized by their name. However, despite the *kāfil* also being allowed to pass on up to one-third of his or her assets to the *makfūl*, the *kafāla* does not establish filiation. Moreover, *kafāla* regulations remain unclear regarding the termination of the agreement. While the FC states that the biological parents may reclaim their child and also that the *kāfil* may propose its termination before the court, it does not define any further detailed conditions for such action. It thus remains unclear if the *kāfil* may end the *kafāla* at will and also if the *kafāla* ends with the child reaching majority. Given the legal effects of *kafāla*, it can be assumed that it is supposed to create a permanent bond between the *kāfil* and the *makfūl*. In conclusion, it may be said that, keeping the best interests of the child in mind, the Algerian legislation attempts to react to changing social and technological developments and to grant legal protection to children without filiation while also adhering to the principles derived from Islamic jurisprudence.

References

A S (2014) Actualités: enfants nés sous X. Même si le secret de la filiation est révélé, le droit à la paternité est refusé. www.lesoirdalgerie.com/articles/2014/02/18/article.php?sid=160617&cid=2. Accessed 11 July 2017.

Aït Zaï N (1996) La kafāla en droit algérien. In: Bleuchot H (ed) Les institutions traditionelles dans le monde arabe. Karthala and Iremam, Paris and Aix-en-Provence, pp 95–105.

Aït Zaï N (2005) Les droits de l'enfant en Algérie: Rapport alternatif. www.crin.org/en/docs/resources/treaties/crc.40/Algeria_ngo_report.pdf. Accessed 11 July 2017.

B A (2013) L'obstacle du test ADN. www.djazairess.com/fr/infosoir/155677. Accessed 11 July 2017.

Barraud E (2008a) Adoption et kafala dans l'espace migratoire franco-maghrébin. L'Année du Maghreb 4:459–468.

Barraud E (2008b) Les multiples usages sociaux de la Kafala en situation de migration: protection et non protection des mineurs recueillis. E-Migrinter 2:133–142.

Barraud E (2010) La filiation légitime à l'épreuve des mutations sociales au Maghreb. Droit et Cultures 59:255–282.
Barraud E (2011) L'adoption au prisme du genre: l'exemple du Maghreb. Clio 34:153–165.
Bettahar Y (2005/2006) La construction sociale de la parentalité: l'exemple de l'Algérie. L'Année du Maghreb 2:155–167.
Bi-l-Khayr S (2009) Al-Usra wa-Ḥimāyatuhā fī al-Fiqh al-Islāmī wa-l-Qānūn al-Jazāʾirī [The Family and its Protection in *Fiqh* and in Algerian Law]. Dār al-Khaldūniyya, Algiers.
Bras J-P (2007) La réforme du code de la famille au Maroc et en Algérie: quelles avancées pour la démocratie? Presses de Sciences Po 37:93–125.
Brunschvig R (2009) Bayyina. In: Ergene B (ed) Judicial Practice: Institutions and Agents in the Islamic World. Brill, Leiden and Boston, pp 215–217.
Dennerlein B (1998) Islamisches Recht und sozialer Wandel in Algerien: Zur Entwicklung des Personalstatuts seit 1962. Klaus Schwarz, Berlin.
Dennerlein B (2001) 'Legalizing' the family: disputes about marriage, paternity and divorce in Algerian courts (1963–1990). Continuity and Change 16:243–261.
Dhiyābī B (2010) Ḥujjiyyat al-Ṭuruq al-Sharʿiyya wa-l-ʿIlmiyya fī Daʿāwā al-Nasab ʿalā Ḍawʾ Qānūn al-Usra al-Jazāʾirī [The Probative Force of *Sharīʿa*-Based Methods and Scientific Means in Paternity Cases under the Algerian Family Code]. Dār al-Hudā, Aïn M'lila.
Laʿwar A, Ṣaqr N (2007) Al-Dalīl al-Qānūnī li-l-Usra [Guide to the Family Code]. Dār al-Hudā, Aïn M'lila.
Larbi F (2016) Les droits des enfants né sous 'X' dans la constitution: une avancée considerable. www.elmoudjahid.com/fr/actualites/90583. Accessed 11 July 2017.
Linant de Bellefonds Y (1978) Kafāla. In: Donzel E van et al. (eds) Encyclopaedia of Islam, 2nd edn. Brill, Leiden, pp 404–405.
Mahieddin N (2007) L'évolution du droit de la famille en Algérie: nouveautés et modifications apportées par la loi du 4 mai 2005 au Code algérien de la famille. L'Année du Maghreb 2:97–137.
Marzouki N (2010) Algeria. In: Breslin J, Kelly S (eds) Women's Rights in the Middle East and North Africa: Progress Amid Resistance. Freedom House/Rowman and Littlefield, New York, pp 29–58.
Mitchell R (1997) Family Law in Algeria before and after the 1404/1984 Family Code. In: Gleave R, Kermeli E (eds) Islamic Law: Theory and Practice. Tauris, London and New York, pp 194–204.
Moutassem-Mimouni B (2001) Naissances et abandons en Algérie. Karthala, Paris.
Moutassem-Mimouni B (2008) Les enfants privés de famille en Algérie. Revue algérienne d'anthropologie et de sciences sociales 41:67–81.
Nasir J (2009) The Islamic Law of Personal Status, 3rd edn. Brill, Leiden and Boston.
Oubrou T (2013) La Kafala et la Sharia: lecture contemporaine du droit islamique. https://tareqoubrou.com/la-kafala-et-la-sharia-lectures-contemporaines-du-droit-islamique. Accessed 18 September 2018.
Pruvost L (1996) Intégration familiale de l'enfant sans généalogie en Algérie et en Tunisie: *kafāla* ou adoption. In: Recueil d'articles offert à Maurice Borrmans par ses collègues et amis, Collection. P.I.S.A.I., Rome, pp 155–180.
Qamrāwī A, Ṣaqr N (2008) Qānūn al-Usra: Naṣṣ wa-Taṭbīq [The Family Code: Text und Practice]. Dār al-Hudā, Aïn M'lila.
Ṣaqr N (2006) Qānūn al-Usra: Naṣṣ wa-Fiqh wa-Taṭbīq [The Family Code: Text, *Fiqh* and Practice]. Dār al-Hudā, Aïn M'lila.
Shabana A (2014) Islamic Law of Paternity Between Classical Legal Texts and Modern Contexts: From Physiognomy to DNA Analysis. Journal of Islamic Studies 25:1–32.
Tagzout L (2011) L'enfant, prisonnier entre test ADN et religion. www.djazairess.com/fr/elwatan/329014. Accessed 11 July 2017.
Ṭāhirī H (2009) Al-Awsaṭ fī Sharḥ Qānūn al-Usra al-Jazāʾirī [Commentary on the Algerian Family Code]. Dār al-Khaldūniyya, Algiers.

Tucker J (1998) In the House of the Law: Gender and Islamic Law in Ottoman Syria and Palestine. University of California Press, Berkeley.
Yassari N (2015) Adding by Choice: Adoption and Functional Equivalents in Islamic and Middle Eastern Law. The American Journal of Comparative Law 63:927–962.
Zemmour-Khorsi N (1994) Mères célibataires et enfants abandonnés en Algérie. Journal de Pédiatrie et de Puériculture 7:359–366.

Melanie Guénon is a research associate at the University of Hamburg. She holds an M.A. in Islamic Studies from the University of Hamburg, and has also studied in Oran, Algeria, and Odense, Denmark. During her graduate studies, she joined the Max Planck Research Group on Family and Succession Law in Islamic Countries, where she focused on Algeria. Her recent article examines the Algerian family law regulations concerning paternity and the use of DNA tests in Algerian paternity disputes. Currently, she is a doctoral candidate within the ERC research project "Contemporary Bioethics and the History of the Unborn in Islam (COBHUNI)." Her dissertation will analyze the role of Muslim non-ᶜulamāʾ in contemporary bioethical debates on embryological development and the beginning of human life. Her research deals with the interplay of religious knowledge and modern medicine as well as different approaches to scientific exegesis.

Chapter 4
Iran

Nadjma Yassari

Contents

Abstract Filiation arises under one of several schemes under Iranian law. Primarily, it results from a child being conceived in a marriage and born within a certain time frame, which is the only approved legal framework for establishing a parent-child relationship. At the same time, however, the law concedes the establishment of filiation as a legal fiction in situations where the marriage of the parents

Nadjma Yassari is director of the Research Group 'Changes in God's Law – An Inner Islamic Comparison of Family and Succession Law' at the Max Planck Institute for Comparative and International Private Law, Hamburg.

N. Yassari (✉)
Max Planck Institute for Comparative and International Private Law, Mittelweg 187, 20148 Hamburg, Germany
e-mail: yassari@mpipriv.de

N. Yassari et al. (eds.), *Filiation and the Protection of Parentless Children*, https://doi.org/10.1007/978-94-6265-311-5_4

cannot be proven or where the circumstances under which it took place are uncertain. Furthermore, filiation can be established through the acknowledgment of a child's parentage, which creates a full-fledged parent-child relationship. Where those mechanisms do not apply, parentless children are not left entirely without protection. In fact, Iranian law has conceived different schemes to provide for a minimum of legal security and financial support for children of defective, unknown or illegitimate parentage. In particular, the legislature passed the Act on the Protection of Children without a Guardian in 1975, with the aim of integrating parentless children into new families on a permanent basis. In 2013, this Act was repealed and replaced by the Act on the Protection of Children without a Guardian or with an Unfit Guardian in order to provide for both permanent and temporary placements of children in new homes.

Keywords *sarparastī* · Shiite legal doctrine · Temporary marriage · Marriage obstacle · Single women as caretakers · Fictional parent-child relationship · Foundling · Name of a child

4.1 Introduction

4.1.1 Sources of Law

Regulations regarding children can be found in various pieces of legislation. The bulk of the relevant provisions is codified in the Iranian Civil Code of 1928/1935 (CC),[1] which regulates filiation (*nasab*), parental care including custody (*ḥiżānat*) and guardianship (*vilāyat*), maintenance (*nafaqih*), and various forms of appointed guardianship (Articles 1158–1256 CC). These provisions are mainly based on Shiite *fiqh* and have survived the Iranian Revolution of 1979 without significant changes. The Iranian legislature has also enacted a series of bylaws, decrees and other pieces of legislation regarding specific aspects of child law, particularly on the protection and care of children without proper caretakers. Some of these were passed before the revolution, namely the Act on the Protection of Children without a Guardian (*sarparast*) (CPA 1975)[2] and the Family Protection Act of 1975,[3] which

[1] Civil Code [*qānūn-i madanī*] of May 8, 1928, in Rūznāmih-i Rasmī-i Kishvar-i Shāhanshāhī-i Īrān (ed) Majmūᶜih-i Qavānīn-i Sāl-i 1307 [Annual Compilation of Laws 1928/29], and of February 17 and March 12, 1935, in Rūznāmih-i Rasmī-i Kishvar-i Shāhanshāhī-i Īrān (ed) Majmūᶜih-i Qavānīn-i Sāl-i 1313 [Annual Compilation of Laws 1934/35].

[2] Act on the Protection of Children without a Guardian [*qānūn-i ḥimāyat az kūdakān bidūn-i sarparast*] of March 20, 1975, Official Gazette no. 8819 of April 20, 1975 (CPA 1975).

[3] Family Protection Act [*qānūn-i ḥimāyat-i khānivādih*] of February 4, 1975, Official Gazette no. 8785 of March 3, 1975 (FPA 1975).

both remained in force after the revolution.[4] Other laws followed after 1979, such as the Act on the Protection of Women and Children without a Guardian of 1992.[5] In addition, in 1994 Iran ratified the United Nations Convention on the Rights of the Child.[6]

In 2013, the Iranian legislature enacted two further laws considerably impacting child law. The first of these was a new Family Protection Act[7] (FPA 2013), which contains procedural regulations in litigation involving children and some substantive norms on custody and the best interests of the child. This new Family Protection Act, it was said, was necessary to consolidate and clarify the legal situation, as it was meant to replace the FPA 1975 and ensure legal certainty.[8] The uncertainty remains, however, as the list of legislation that became obsolete with the new FPA does not in fact include the FPA 1975.[9] Second and also in 2013, the CPA 1975 was repealed and replaced by a new law, the Act on the Protection of Children without a Guardian (*bī sarparast*) or with an Unfit Guardian (*bad sarparast*) (CPA 2013).[10] All these laws will be examined in more detail below.

4.1.2 Jurisdiction of the Courts

The courts competent to hear family law cases are the family courts, established as specialized courts headed by a male judge. The judge must be married and must have been employed in the judiciary for at least four years.[11] In 1992, the judges

---

[4] The FPA 1975 has never been officially repealed. Only Article 15 FPA 1975, which provided that a divorced mother of a child could be appointed as the child's *valī*, was abolished in 1979, see Official Gazette no. 10094 of October 18, 1979.

[5] Act on the Protection of Women and Children without a Guardian [*qānūn-i ta'mīn-i zanān va kūdakān bī sarparast*] of November 15, 1992, in Rūznāmih-i Rasmī-i Jumhūrī-i Islāmī-i Īrān (ed) Majmūᶜih-i Qavānīn-i Sāl-i 1371 [Annual Compilation of Laws 1992/93], pp 466–468.

[6] Upon ratification, Iran made the following reservation to the Convention: 'The Government of the Islamic Republic of Iran reserves the right not to apply any provisions or articles of the Convention that are incompatible with Islamic Laws and the international legislation in effect.' See http://indicators.ohchr.org (accessed January 1, 2017).

[7] Family Protection Act [*qānūn-i ḥimāyat-i khānivādih*] of February 19, 2013, Official Gazette no. 19835 of April 11, 2013, pp 1–5 (FPA 2013).

[8] Draft Law No. 36780/68357 of July 23, 2007, http://rc.majlis.ir/fa/legal_draft/states/720519 (accessed May 1, 2012).

[9] Article 58 FPA 2013.

[10] Act on the Protection of Children without a Guardian or with an Unfit Guardian [*qānūn-i ḥimāyat az kūdakān va nūjavānān bī sarparast va bad sarparast*] of October 2, 2013, Official Gazette no. 19997 of October 28, 2013, pp 6–8 (CPA 2013).

[11] Article 3 FPA 2013.

were given the option to appoint a female consultant to the family court.[12] These female consultants have similar obligations to their male counterparts but cannot issue judgments independently. As of summer 2003, thirty percent of the judges of the main Tehran family court complex had appointed a female legal consultant in their departments.[13] In 2013, this option was made mandatory under the new Family Protection Act. Pursuant to Article 2 FPA 2013, family courts must be staffed with a female associate judge.[14] She must submit her written viewpoint on each case to the male judge within three days of the closing of the procedure; the male judge, in turn, must refer to her opinion in his decision and must justify any divergence from it in his ruling.[15]

The parties can initiate legal proceedings by lodging a petition; the procedural formalities of the Code of Civil Procedure do not apply in family cases.[16] The law gives the court a broad margin of discretion to conduct the proceedings. This includes the authority of the court to admit all kinds of evidence and means of proof to clarify the case.[17] The parties have to bear the costs of the proceedings; they can, however, be exempted in the case of financial inability.[18]

Until 2000, just one family court in Tehran was qualified to hear the family law cases of its 12 million inhabitants. Today six courts operate throughout the city.[19] The FPA 2013 provided for the establishment of family court departments in all ordinary court complexes within three years of its enactment so as to ensure nationwide access to family courts.[20] Tehran's main family law court complex is organized into 60 departments; each department is responsible for approximately 400 cases per month, and the judge has an average of nine hearings each day. There is no obligation to be represented by a lawyer, and indeed most parties attend court without legal representation. Children under the age of fifteen are not allowed to attend a court hearing unless the judge deems this necessary;[21] in practice, however, it is very common that children are present, as are a rather large number of family members who appear in support of their relative's case.

---

[12] Article 1, note 5 of the former Act on the Amendment of the Divorce Provisions [*qānūn-i iṣlāḥ-i muqarrarāt-i marbūṭ bih ṭalāq*] of November 19, 1992, Official Gazette no. 13914 of December 10, 1992, p 1.

[13] Author's 2003 field research in Tehran.

[14] Article 2 FPA 2013.

[15] Article 2 FPA 2013.

[16] Article 8 FPA 2013.

[17] Madanī Kirmānī 2002, p 30.

[18] Article 5 FPA 2013.

[19] See www.mizanonline.ir/fa/news/65148 (accessed January 1, 2017).

[20] Article 1 FPA 2013.

[21] Article 46 FPA 2013.

4.2 The Establishment of Filiation

4.2.1 Establishing Filiation by Law

4.2.1.1 Children Born into a Valid Marriage

Under Iranian law, filiation (*nasab*) is established as a rule by blood relation between the wedded parents and the child. *Nasab* operates on the basis of the principle of the 'child of the marital bed' (*qāᶜidih-i firāsh*), that is, a child resulting from a valid marriage. This principle is concretized in Articles 1158–1167 CC. Accordingly, a child conceived during marriage will be linked to the mother's husband if the child is born at least six months after the conclusion of the marriage (i.e. the date of the first legally permissible intercourse) and not more than ten months after the last incident of intercourse.[22] The legal presumption in Article 1158 CC rests on two facts: (i) the conception of the child during marriage and (ii) the child's birth within a certain time frame after intercourse.[23] Iranian scholarly writings discuss the question of whether the intercourse must actually be proven or whether the existence of the marriage itself proves its occurrence.[24] Generally, and with due consideration of the best interests of the child, the majority view accepts that whenever parents live in a marital community (*zindigī-i mushtarak*), they are understood to engage in sexual relations.[25] Thus, the presumption of Article 1158 CC applies without the actual intercourse having to be proven.[26] If, however, such a marital community was not established at the time of the child's conception, for example because the husband was provably absent, the presumption does not apply. It is therefore not sufficient for the child to be born into the marriage; the actual possibility of conception is equally relevant.[27]

If the child is born after the dissolution of the marriage, the child will be linked to the mother's ex-husband, under the conditions that the mother has not remarried and no more than ten months elapsed between the dissolution of the marriage and the birth of the child.[28]

---

22 The reference to months in the Iranian Civil Code relates to lunar months.

23 Ṣafā'ī and Imāmī 2011, p 52.

24 See for this discussion Ṣafā'ī and Imāmī 2011, p 53.

25 Shīravī 2016, p 235.

26 Kātūziyān 1999, vol II, p 54.

27 Ṣafā'ī and Imāmī 2011, p 54; Kātūziyān 1999, vol II, p 61. The Iranian Supreme Court considers spousal intercourse to be a condition for the presumption of paternity (Article 1158 CC). If the non-occurrence of sexual intercourse is proven, the presumption does not apply; judgment of the 33rd Chamber of the Supreme Court no. 33/5321 of February 23, 1995, quoted in Bāzgīr 1999, pp 229–230.

28 Article 1157 CC. This does not apply if it is proven that the period between (the last) intercourse between the (ex-)spouses and the birth of the child is less than six months or more than ten months; cf. Ṣafā'ī and Imāmī 2011, pp 56–57.

The presumption of filiation in Iranian law is thus based on both the conception of the child in the marriage and a time limit within which the child must be born. Here Iranian law follows the rules of Shiite *fiqh*, which adhere to biological realities. This contrasts with Sunni legal doctrine, in which a woman's gestation period may fictionally be extended to anywhere from six months to seven years under the notion of the *sleeping embryo* (*al-rāqid*).[29]

While paternity is presumed under the above-mentioned rules, the filiation of the child to the mother is established by her giving birth to the child. It must, however, be emphasized that Shiite views on the legal mother of a child are being reconsidered in light of new reproductive technologies. Discussing legal motherhood in the case of egg donation, contemporary Shiite authorities[30] have argued that maternity is established at conception. Consequently, some argue that motherhood is to be conferred on the contributor of the egg (i.e. of the genetic material). Some Grand Ayatollahs such as Ali al-Sistani, however, adhere to the Sunni view, according to which the gestational carrier (i.e. the woman giving birth) is the legal mother of the child.[31] These discussions may have an impact on the concept of *nasab* in the future, but for the time being the majority of Shiite scholars (as well as statutory Iranian law) adhere to the principle of the 'child of the marital bed' (*firāsh*) as the general principle establishing *nasab*. This is not to say, however, that there are no other means to establish *nasab* under Shiite and Iranian law in instances where the status of the child is uncertain or where the circumstances surrounding the parents' marriage or the child's birth are dubious.

4.2.1.2 Children Born into Temporary or Informal Marriages

Iranian law recognizes two types of marriages that differ as specifically regards their duration. Generally, marriages are meant to be of indeterminate duration, but the spouses may agree to limit the period of their marriage to a period of between one hour and ninety-nine years and conclude a so-called temporary marriage (*ṣīghih*, *mut^{c}ih*, *izdivāj-i muvaqqat*). Thus, *mut^{c}ih* is a marriage between a man and an unmarried woman for a stipulated period of time. Under the concept of temporary marriage, the couple is religiously and legally permitted to live as husband and wife

[29] Al-^{c}Āmilī 2008, p 468. The theory of the sleeping embryo has no basis in the Qur'an or the Sunna and was mainly devised by the Maliki school of law, whose founder Malik ibn Anas appears to have himself been a 'sleeping embryo,' Gilson Miller 2006, p 421. The other Sunni schools of law envisage female gestation periods from two to four years, with the Maliki school extending the period up to even seven years, Maghniyyih 2001, pp 92–93.

[30] Those include Ayatollahs Ali Khamenei and Muhammad Husayn Fadallah, the late Imam Khomeini, Yousef Saanei, Mohammad Mo'men Qomi, Safi Golpayegani, Naser Makarem Shirazi, see Clarke 2009, pp 116–140.

[31] Some Shiite scholars designate two mothers, the contributor of the egg and the carrying mother, see Mahmoud 2012, p 83. The differences between Sunni and Shiite perspectives mainly stem from a different weighting of the Qur'anic verses 2:76 and 2:58.

and to have licit sexual relations without necessarily binding themselves to a life-long commitment. *Mutᶜih*, literally meaning 'marriage of pleasure,' was a pre-Islamic tradition of the Arabian Peninsula and has retained legitimacy only in the Shiite school of law, while it has been outlawed by the Sunni school of Islamic jurisprudence. Sunni authorities agree that temporary marriage was permitted at the time of the prophet Mohammad,[32] but they maintain that it was prohibited under the second Caliph Omar in the seventh century A.D.[33] In contrast, the Shiites argue that since the Prophet did not ban it, it is not permissible to forbid it, and they cite numerous hadiths[34] from Sunni as well as Shiite sources to prove their point of view.[35] As far as codification of temporary marriage is concerned, the Iranian Civil Code regulates it explicitly,[36] whereas Sunni Islamic countries do not accept temporary marriage as a valid form of marriage.[37]

Children born into a temporary marriage are considered the legitimate children of both parents, with all rights bestowed on them, including inheritance rights.[38] The parents owe them care and maintenance, regardless of whether they are temporary or permanent spouses. At the end of the marital union, the same regulations on parental care apply as at the dissolution of a permanent marriage. In this respect the idea has prevailed that the children should not be disadvantaged if their parents have decided to live together on a temporary basis. Thus, children born within the legal presumption of Article 1158f CC will have an established *nasab* to both parents.

---

[32] The source of temporary marriages is the Qur'anic verse 4:24: 'Also (prohibited are) women already married, except those whom your right hands possess: Thus hath [God] ordained (prohibitions) against you: Except for these, all others are lawful, provided ye seek (them in marriage) with gifts from your property,– desiring chastity, not fornication. Give them their [dowers] for the enjoyment you have of them as a duty; but if, after a dower is prescribed, ye agree mutually (to vary it), there is no blame on you, and [God] is All-knowing, All-wise.' All translations of the Qur'an are taken from The Holy Qur-ān: English translation of the meanings and Commentary (1990) (Translated by Ali Y) King Fahd Holy Qur-ān Printing Complex, Medina.

[33] See Haeri 1989, p 1.

[34] A hadith is a narrative about the life, deeds and actions of the prophet Mohammad. They are to be followed as an example by the Islamic community and are considered the second source of law after the Qur'an.

[35] See for the hadith on *mutᶜih* ᶜAllāmih-Ḥā'irī 2001, pp 71–80.

[36] Articles 1075–1077, 1085, 1113, 1139 CC. The Afghan Personal Status Code for Shiite Afghans also refers to the possibility of a *mutᶜih* marriage, albeit implicitly (see Article 124 para 4 of the Personal Status Code for Shiite Afghans [*qānūn-i aḥvāl-i shakhṣiyyih-i ahl-i tashayyuᶜ*], Official Gazette no. 988 of July 27, 2009, pp 1–250). *Mutᶜih* or *mutᶜa* (in Arabic) is also available to Bahraini Shiites, although the Bahraini draft code on the personal status of Shiite Bahrainis does not explicitly include regulations on *mutᶜa*; on the Bahraini draft code, see Al-Ittiḥād al-Nisā'ī al-Baḥraynī 2009, pp 93–111. Iraqi Shiites are subject to the unified Iraqi Personal Status Code applicable to all Iraqi Muslims, which does not allow *mutᶜa*. The Iraqi draft code on the personal status of Iraqi Shiites also does not encompass regulations on *mutᶜa*, see Hamoudi 2016.

[37] Bakhtiar 1996, p 461.

[38] Rajabī and Muḥammadiyān 2002, p 6; Bakhtiar 1996, p 462; Articles 1158–1163 CC on children also apply to children resulting from a temporary marital bond.

Although temporary marriage has been incorporated into statutory law, in practice problems may arise in the event of legal disputes with regards to the existence of such a marriage. It must be borne in mind that the conclusion of any marriage under Iranian law, be it temporary or permanent, does not require any form of state ratification for its validity, although it is legally required to be registered.[39] In fact, marriage is a contract that is concluded without state involvement and solely requires the parties' consent and their ability to marry. Also under Shiite *fiqh*, the presence of witnesses is not a requirement for the validity of the marriage.[40] While the permission of the bride's guardian (*valī*) is required for her first marriage, the judge can provide such permission if the *valī* refuses to give his consent without a valid reason.[41]

Thus, marriages may be validly concluded by the spouses (and the *valī*) in private. It is true that state law requires the parties to register all marriages,[42] but non-compliance with these rules does not vitiate the marriage. In practice, it seems, a majority of Iranians do register their first marriage. This is widely due to the fact that the marriage certificate needs to be presented to authorities in many instances, from renting a house together to enrolling children in school. However, temporary marriages are generally not contracted as a first marriage; very often they are used in polygynous marriages that, although legally valid, are not met with broad social acceptance. Thus, notwithstanding the legal obligation to register marriages, more often than not temporary marriages are not registered. This may pose substantial problems when one spouse, generally the wife, claims a marital right and the other spouse denies the existence of the marriage. Moreover, this may jeopardize not only the ground for marital claims between temporary (or informally married permanent) spouses, but also the legal status of their children. Consequently, although children born to temporary spouses are perfectly legitimate, they might face obstacles to proving their parents' marriage and therefore their filiation. Children born into a permanent but unregistered marriage may also face such problems.

4.2.1.3 Children Born into a Presumed Marriage

Iranian law recognizes the notion of '*waṭ' bi-shubhih*', which is also based on *fiqh*. Accordingly, children born to parents who mistakenly believed themselves to be married at the time of sexual intercourse are legitimate.[43] Article 1165 CC states that

[39] Imāmī 2005, p 326.

[40] Muḥaqqiq Dāmād 2002, p 170.

[41] See Article 1043 CC. The marriage of a widowed or divorced woman does not require the permission of her father, see judgment of the Iranian Supreme Court no. 1-29/1/1363 of April 18, 1984, registration no. 62/62, in Riyāsat-i Jumhūrī (2011) Majmūᶜih-i Qānūn-i Madanī, 8th edn, Muᶜāvinat-i Tadvīn-i Tanqīḥ va Intishār-i Qavānīn va Muqarrarāt, Tehran, Article 1043 CC, p 302.

[42] This including temporary marriages, cf. Article 943 CC and Article 20 FPA 2013 (for permanent marriage) and Article 21 FPA 2013 (for temporary marriage).

[43] Maghniyyih 2001, pp 96–98; Khan 2010, pp 212–213.

a child born as a result of *shubhih* will have *nasab* to any of the parents that were mistaken about the existence of the marriage.[44] Likewise, the child will have *nasab* to any of her parents who were unaware that their marriage was null and void because, for example, of the unknown existence of a marriage obstacle (Article 1166 CC). The mistake may thus be *de jure* or *de facto*.[45] As such, it can relate to the identity of the person, such as intercourse with a woman other than one's spouse, or it can be based on the supposition that intercourse was permissible, when in fact it was not. Examples include the case of a defective re-marriage or intercourse with a divorced woman during her waiting period from her last divorce.[46] The law attaches importance to the parents' beliefs about their behavior. This emphasis on the good faith of the parents is an indication of the endeavors of Islamic scholars and, by extension, the Iranian legislature to uphold the *nasab* of the child. Likewise, a child resulting from forced sexual intercourse outside wedlock (rape) will have *nasab* to the person that has been forced (usually the mother) but not to the other party.

4.2.1.4 Filiation Based on Other Presumptions

While the Civil Code is silent on other situations of doubtful filiation, Ayatollah Khomeini took a child-friendly position in his writings on children born under dubious circumstances. While children resulting from the adulterous sexual activities of a married woman face rather harsh consequences in terms of filiation, children born as a result of an unmarried woman's sexual activities are treated differently. According to Khomeini, if the parents of the latter children marry subsequent to their sexual relationship and are in doubt about whether the child born into the marriage was conceived before it, the child will be considered legitimate.[47]

4.2.2 Establishing Filiation by Private Autonomy: Acknowledgement of Filiation

Another means of establishing a parent-child relationship is the acknowledgement of filiation (*iqrār bih nasab*). *Iqrār* under Iranian law operates as a means of evidence, and confers upon the acknowledged child the same legal status as that of

---

[44] This was explicitly confirmed by the Legal Department of the Iranian Ministry of Justice, statement no. 7/13311 of September 27, 1993, in Riyāsat-i Jumhūrī (2011) Majmūᶜih-i Qānūn-i Madanī, 8th edn, Muᶜāvinat-i Tadvīn-i Tanqīḥ va Intishār-i Qavānīn va Muqarrarāt, Tehran, Article 1158 CC, p 375.

[45] Ansari-Pour 2001, p 144; Shīravī 2016, p 237.

[46] See Shabana 2014, p 7, note 11.

[47] Al-Khumaynī (n.d.), Q. no. 2454, p 497; see also Ansari-Pour 2001, p 144.

a legal child, including reciprocal inheritance rights.[48] The articles of the Civil Code relating to *iqrār* are based on the majority view of Shiite *fiqh*.[49] Pursuant to Article 1273 CC, *iqrār bih nasab* is valid (and *nasab* established) if said kinship is possible under custom (*ᶜādat*) and law (*qānūn*). The person that is being acknowledged must confirm the acknowledgement, unless the person is a minor and no other person disputes the filiation. *Iqrār* can also be made implicitly. Accordingly, *nasab* is understood to have been acknowledged tacitly by a father, for instance, when he takes all necessary administrative steps to provide the child with an ID (*shināsnāmih*), treats the child as his own, cares for her and acts as her father.[50] Also, according to Article 1161 CC a person who has tacitly or explicitly acknowledged a child is barred from later taking any action for the denial of filiation. Finally, it must also be noted that under Iranian law both a woman and a man can acknowledge the filiation of a child.[51]

A child can thus be acknowledged under three conditions: first, *nasab* must be possible according to custom. This condition is understood to relate to biological aspects such as the age difference between the parties. Second, *nasab* must be legally possible. This means that *iqrār bih nasab* is not allowed regarding a child whose filiation with another person is legally presumed.[52] Third, *nasab* must not be claimed by another person. Generally, the Islamic schools of law are unanimous that for a child to be validly acknowledged, her filiation must be unknown.[53] This status is, however, often presumed, as the designation of the *causa* for the acknowledgement is not required.[54] What matters is the 'conclusiveness of the declaration of acknowledgement.'[55] Thus, a biological child can be acknowledged as long as her illegitimate status is not widely known. Conversely, the existence of a biological genetic relationship to the child is not a condition for *iqrār*.

In practice, the scope of application of *iqrār bih nasab* specifically extends to situations where the marriage of the parents is doubtful or the parents have only presumed they were married and where legal certainty is sought for subsequent legal claims, such as inheritance rights. The literature suggests, however, that courts will often ask for additional proof to accompany *iqrār*.[56]

Besides these constellations, acknowledgement of filiation has also been used to establish a legal relationship between persons that have no biological link with each

---

48 Ṣafā'ī and Imāmī 2011, p 90.

49 Cf. Al-ᶜĀmilī 2008, p 570f.

50 Cf. Legal Department of the Iranian Ministry of Justice, statement no. 1/7/94 of March 28, 2015, as quoted in Karīmī 2015.

51 Ṣafā'ī and Imāmī 2011, p 88.

52 Al-ᶜĀmilī 2008, p 570.

53 On the conditions for a valid acknowledgement of paternity in the different Islamic schools of law, see Al-ᶜĀmilī 2008, p 469; Khan 2010, p 219.

54 Al-Dasūqī 1980, p 413; Al-Marghīnānī (n.d.), p 393.

55 Kohler 1976, p 111.

56 ᶜĀmirī and Yāsīnī Niyā 2016/2017, p 70, point to the use of medical tests, such as blood and DNA tests. See also below Sect. 4.2.3.

other, in particular between a married couple and a child of unknown *nasab*. Because of the very lenient conditions of acknowledgement, foundlings in particular can be brought into a legal scheme of filiation (see below).

Whereas *iqrār* is deemed acceptable as long as the possibly illegitimate status of the child is not widely known, the law does not address explicitly the question of whether a child that is knowingly the result of prohibited non-marital intercourse can be acknowledged by her biological parents. At first glance, this would seem impossible, as established unlawful sexual intercourse outside marriage is illegal under Iranian law and subject to penal sanctions.[57] Additionally, the Civil Code prohibits the subsequent marriage of persons who previously had sexual relations while they were married to other persons.[58] Therefore, it seems that the status of such a child cannot be remedied by either subsequent *iqrār bih nasab* or the marriage of her biological parents (if they were married previously to other persons).[59] However, that does not preclude the existence of a legal relationship between them. In fact, any parent may acknowledge a biological child, with the consequence of creating certain reciprocal rights and duties, even though this does not establish *nasab*. As will be seen below in more detail, a child born out of wedlock can claim rights vis-à-vis her biological parents, and her non-married parents likewise may acknowledge their parenthood.[60] Such acknowledgement may be socially and personally a difficult step to take; however, one has to bear in mind that while an established *zinā* is liable to punishment under Iranian penal law,[61] acknowledging someone as one's child does not represent sufficient evidence for *zinā*.[62] In other words, acknowledging a child born out of wedlock does not equate with the acknowledgement of *zinā* itself.

4.2.3 DNA Screening: A Valid Way to Establish or Deny Filiation?

Iranian statutory law does not take up the question of whether DNA tests may be resorted to in *nasab* cases. In fact, the law makes no reference to any kind of

---

[57] See Article 222ff Iranian Penal Code [*qānūn-i mujāzāt-i islāmī*] of April 21, 2013, Official Gazette no. 19873 of May 27, 2013, pp 1–32.

[58] Cf. Articles 1050–1051 CC. The subsequent marriage of persons that had non-marital intercourse while not married to other persons is, however, permissible; cf. Al-Khumaynī (n.d.), Q. 2399, p 488.

[59] Ansari-Pour 2001, p 144.

[60] See Kātūziyān 2006, p 214; see Legal Department of the Iran. Ministry of Justice, statement no. 7/5114 of October 12, 1998, in Riyāsat-i Jumhūrī (2011) Majmūᶜih-i Qānūn-i Madanī, 8th edn, Muᶜāvinat-i Tadvīn-i Tanqīḥ va Intishār-i Qavānīn va Muqarrarāt, Tehran, Article 1166 CC, p 377, referring to the acknowledgement of filiation by a mother of her child born out of wedlock.

[61] Cf. Articles 221–232 Iranian Penal Code.

[62] Cf. fatwa by Khamenei and others, www.islamquest.net/fa/archive/question/fa19638# (accessed October 9, 2018); see Article 172 and 232 Iranian Penal Code.

medical assistance for the proof or denial of *nasab*. The question, however, of whether medical tests (including blood and DNA screening) hold or should hold evidentiary powers, and if so, which powers, is the subject of lively discussion in the media, on fatwa platforms[63] and in scholarly writings.[64] The main question is whether DNA screening can set aside the presumption of paternity in accord with the principle of *firāsh*. With few exceptions, the contributions do rebut the admissibility of DNA screening for such purpose.

In 2009, the Legal Department of the Iranian Ministry of Justice, which issues non-binding commentaries on and interpretations of statutory law on request, took up the question and stated that DNA tests could not overrule the principle of *firāsh*.[65] In 2013, the Iranian Supreme Court (*dīvān-i* *ᶜālī*) had to state its view on the evidentiary value of DNA tests for establishing *nasab* in a succession case.[66] In that case the plaintiffs had rejected the defendant's right to succeed to their late father's estate on the grounds that the defendant was not their half-sister (i.e. the daughter of their deceased father and his first wife) but rather had been 'adopted' (i.e. taken into *sarparastī*) by their father. She was thus not entitled to inherit. To prove their case, the plaintiffs had presented a DNA test according to which the defendant and the deceased did not match genetically. The courts of first and second instance followed the plaintiffs' arguments and denied the defendant the right to inherit. The Supreme Court, however, rejected both decisions. It argued that the father had been married to the mother of the defendant, his first wife, and that the child's date of birth indicated that she had been born into this marriage within the limits of Article 1158 CC. She was thus a child of the marital bed. Furthermore, the Court held that the deceased had always acted as the father of the girl, and had referred to her as his 'daughter.' These facts allowed the court to establish a judicial presumption (*imārih-i qażā'ī*) of paternity in addition to the presumption of paternity in Article 1158 CC.[67] DNA tests, the court continued, have neither legal nor religious evidentiary power for the denial of *nasab* and therefore could not be taken into consideration. The daughter was thus permitted to succeed to her late father's estate. In 2015, the Legal

[63] The author contacted several Shiite clerics via their online fatwa platforms, including some Shia *marjaᶜ* (title given to the highest level of Shia authority) such as Grand Ayatollah Naser Makarem Shirazi, Grand Ayatollah Sayyid Mohammad Taqi al-Modarresi, and Grand Ayatollah Yousef Saanei. All rebutted the admissibility of DNA tests as a means to undo filiation in cases where the principle of *firāsh* applied. Ayatollah Ali Khamenei, the religious leader of the Islamic Republic of Iran, was the only one not to answer the question with reference to the fact that only questions related to general question of *fiqh* could be answered, but not those that had a judicial aspect (*janbih-i qażā'ī*) (all on file with author).

[64] Yazdānī Pūr et al. 2015/2016, pp 85–98; Pīlih et al. 2013, pp 139–158; ᶜĀmirī and Yāsīnī Niyā 2016/2017, pp 55–82; Sādāt Ṭabā'ī 2012, pp 49–74; Bāqirī and Āyatullāh Shīrāzī 2015, pp 79–95.

[65] Legal Department of the Iranian Ministry of Justice, statement no. 7/1156 of May 16, 2009, in Riyāsat-i Jumhūrī (2011) Majmūᶜih-i Qānūn-i Madanī, 8th edn, Muᶜāvinat-i Tadvīn-i Tanqīḥ va Intishār-i Qavānīn va Muqarrarāt, Tehran, Article 1158 CC, p 375.

[66] Iranian Supreme Court, chamber 1, decision no. 9209970906100634 of October 12, 2013 (on file with author).

[67] On judicial presumption, see in more details Ṣafā'ī and Imāmī 2011, pp 59–60.

Department of the Iranian Ministry of Justice reiterated this finding, stating that DNA tests are not acceptable means of evidence in *nasab* cases to set aside the principle of *firāsh*.[68] Other similar judgements have followed.[69]

These rulings are in line with religious and statutory Iranian law. In fact, the only way for a legal father to be exempted from *nasab* established by *firāsh* is to initiate a process called '*li*ᶜ*ān*'. This procedure is regulated neither in the Civil Code nor in the Code of Civil Procedure, but follows Islamic prescriptions.[70] *Li*ᶜ*ān*, which literally means 'imprecation' or 'curse,' is a process whereby the husband swears four times that the child is not his and the fifth time implores the curse of God should he be lying. The wife then swears four times that her husband is lying and then implores the wrath of God if he has spoken the truth.[71] According to Article 882 CC, through this process succession rights such as those between the spouses and between the father and his child are extinguished. This does not, however, strip the child of her legitimate status, as the filiation between the mother (and her relatives) and the child remains in place. It is the link between the father (and his relatives) and the child that is terminated. Article 883 CC further regulates the revocation of *li*ᶜ*ān*. Thus, if the father reverses his action and revokes *li*ᶜ*ān*, the child will inherit from him, but the father may not inherit from the child. Systematically, these articles are located in the section on obstacles to inheritance (Articles 875–885 CC). This would *prima facie* suggest that the effects of *li*ᶜ*ān* are confined to inheritance. The literature is, however, unanimous that *li*ᶜ*ān* dissolves the marriage between the parents as well as the filiation link between the father and the child *ipso jure*.[72] The confinement of the effects of *li*ᶜ*ān* to inheritance rights in Articles 882–883 CC is merely exemplary, as is the reinstatement of the child's inheritance rights vis-à-vis her father in the event that he revokes the *li*ᶜ*ān*. In fact, the revocation of *li*ᶜ*ān* by the father re-establishes not only succession rights but also *nasab*. This re-establishment, however, only works in one direction: it is only the rights of the child towards her father that are resurrected; the father, on the other

---

[68] Legal Department of the Iranian Ministry of Justice, statement no. 1/7/94 of March 28, 2015, as quoted in Karīmī 2015.

[69] Cf. decision of the Court of second instance Tehran of January 17, 2015, http://judgements.ijri.ir/SubSystems/Jpri2/Showjudgement.aspx?id=YzdPR0M1M1JDWUE9.

[70] Legal Department of the Iranian Ministry of Justice, statement no. 7/5723 of September 18, 2001, in Riyāsat-i Jumhūrī (2011) Majmūᶜih-i Qānūn-i Madanī, 8th edn, Muᶜāvinat-i Tadvīn-i Tanqīḥ va Intishār-i Qavānīn va Muqarrarāt, Tehran, Article 882 CC, p 252; Kātūziyān 1999, vol I, p 127, writes that *li*ᶜ*ān* has to take place before the court. The Legal Department of the Iranian Ministry of Justice issued a statement (no. 7/4328 of October 17, 1985, in Riyāsat-i Jumhūrī (2011) Majmūᶜih-i Qānūn-i Madanī, 8th edn, Muᶜāvinat-i Tadvīn-i Tanqīḥ va Intishār-i Qavānīn va Muqarrarāt, Tehran, Article 1052 CC, p 308) in which it declared that only judges with a specific (religious) authorization could perform *li*ᶜ*ān*. The spouses have to use specific formulas in Arabic. At the same time, *li*ᶜ*ān* can only be initiated within two months after the father has learned about the birth of the child (Article 1162 CC); otherwise the courts are barred from hearing such a case.

[71] See Schacht 2012.

[72] See Kātūziyān 1999, vol I, p 127.

hand, does not wield any powers over the child. The occurrence of *li^cān* is, however, very rarely reported and no case law could be found on it. It seems that it hardly ever happens and that Articles 882–883 CC must be considered dead law.[73] It follows that once *firāsh* is lawfully established, it can scarcely be undone.

Where the principle of *firāsh* does not apply, medical tests (including DNA screening) may be used to establish *nasab*. Although this rule has no statutory basis, the literature suggests that courts are willing to admit such evidence for the sake of establishing *nasab* in the best interests of the child.[74] If, for instance, the child is born within the time limits of Article 1158 CC, but the man denies the consummation of the marriage, medical tests, including blood and DNA tests, can be produced to prove the mother's husband's paternity.[75]

4.3 Status of Children of Defective or Unknown Filiation

4.3.1 Children Born Out of Wedlock

Generally, children with an established *nasab* enjoy all rights emanating from filiation. They have a right to maintenance, custody and guardianship,[76] and inheritance;[77] they also have the right to take their father's name.[78] Conversely, pursuant to Article 1167 CC, a child born from a non-marital relationship (*zinā*) will have no legal connections to the 'fornicator' (*zānī*). Article 222 of the Iranian Penal Code defines *zinā* as intercourse between a man and a woman who are not married to each other and who have not based their intercourse on a false assumption of the existence of a marriage between them (*waṭ' bi-shubhih*).[79]

The use of the Arabic word *zānī* in its singular masculine form in Article 1167 CC seems to indicate that the nonexistence of a legal relationship refers only to the father. But one has to bear in mind that in Shiite doctrine, no distinction is drawn between the mother and the father as regards their relationship to their illegitimate child.[80] Thus, Article 1167 CC generally applies to both the mother and the father.[81]

73 Ṣafā'ī and Imāmī 2011, p 70.

74 Ṣafā'ī and Imāmī 2011, pp 60–61; ^cĀmirī and Yāsīnī Niyā 2016/2017, p 68.

75 ^cĀmirī and Yāsīnī Niyā 2016/2017, p 68.

76 Article 1168 CC.

77 Articles 862–863 CC.

78 Pursuant to Article 41 note 1 of the Act on the Registration of Matters of Personal Status [*qānūn-i s̱abt-i aḥvāl*] of July 7, 1976, Official Gazette no. 9212 of August 14, 1976, the child takes the surname of her father.

79 Shiite jurisprudence defines *zinā* as sexual intercourse between persons not married to each other who are of age and maturity and who know that their intercourse is prohibited, see Al-^cĀmilī 2008, p 647. For an analysis of Articles 221ff see Kamalipour Ravari and Taram 2016, p 89f.

80 Maghniyyih 2001, p 530; Kohlberg 1985, p 249.

81 Ṣafā'ī and Imāmī 2011, p 128.

As a general rule, in traditional Shiite *fiqh* there are no means to establish a legal connection between a child born out of wedlock and her biological parents.[82] However, Article 1167 CC and its consequences, i.e. the lack of any legal connection of the child to her biological parents, have been subject to wide public debate in Iran.[83] This is mainly due to the fact that Ayatollah Khomeini had drawn a distinction between legitimate and illegitimate kinship relations in his *fiqh* book *taḥrīr al-vasīlih*. According to him, even a child born outside the acceptable frame will have certain legal rights towards her biological parents, even though *nasab* could never be established.[84] The debates in Iranian academic writings were split: while some argued that the child herself was innocent and should not be deprived of protection, the dominant view was that such a child had no rights whatsoever towards her parents and that it fell upon the impacted society to take care of the child.[85] It was argued that giving legal protection to children born out of wedlock would encourage illicit non-marital relationships.[86] Even though these commentators insisted that this rule was meant to punish not the child but the parents who had disturbed the social order and violated good morals, the negative effects for the child remained: the biological parents did not have a legal duty to protect the child; no action could be taken for maintenance or support; the child had neither a name nor a lineage. The law basically negated the child's existence.

A clarification of the situation was thus desperately needed. In 1997, the Plenary Assembly of the Iranian Supreme Court had to consider this matter to reconcile conflicting judgments given by two different chambers of the Supreme Court.[87] In its plenary judgment,[88] the Supreme Court declared that a child born out of wedlock as a result of *zinā* had to be considered the child of her biological parents and be afforded the associated legal benefits, with the key exception of reciprocal intestate inheritance rights.[89] This view was mainly based on Khomeini's opinion and was backed by the Iranian Civil Code, which – alongside Article 1167 CC – contains only two other explicit provisions on children born out of wedlock, namely Articles 884 and 1045 CC. Article 884 CC states that a child born from *zinā* (*valad-ul-zinā*)

---

[82] See for a discussion of the consequences of the absence of a kinship relation between the parent and their illegitimate child, Kohlberg 1985, p 245, referring to the question of marriage.

[83] Kātūziyān 1999, vol II, p 25; Ṣafā'ī and Imāmī 2011, p 126ff; see also the detailed account of the various opinions in ᶜAẓīmzādih Ardibīlī and Ṭūqānīpūr 2011.

[84] Quoted in Ansari-Pour 2001, p 148.

[85] To this end the Iranian legislature enacted several acts, e.g. the Act on the Protection of Women and Children without a Guardian providing that children without caretakers had to be taken care of by the Juvenile Welfare Centers.

[86] Ṣafā'ī and Imāmī 2011, p 123.

[87] Decision of the 22nd Chamber of the Supreme Court and decision of the 30th Chamber of the Supreme Court (on file with author).

[88] Decision of the Plenary Assembly of the Iranian Supreme Court no. 617 of July 24, 1997, in Riyāsat-i Jumhūrī (2011) Majmūᶜih-i Qānūn-i Madanī, 8th edn, Muᶜāvinat-i Tadvīn-i Tanqīḥ va Intishār-i Qavānīn va Muqarrarāt, Tehran, Article 884 CC, p 252.

[89] For a detailed account of the Supreme Court's judgment, see Ansari-Pour 2001, 151ff.

may not inherit from her biological parents, nor from their kin. Article 1045 CC states that marriage hindrances apply also where the kinship of the parties is established by *shubhih* or *zinā*. Against this background and in the context of the ongoing debates, the Court held that the parents of the child born out of wedlock owed the child maintenance and had to care for her.[90] The Supreme Court further held that the father was obligated to register the child and request an identity card for her. While the registration of the child would provide her with a name and an identity card, it was particularly emphasized that this did not establish *nasab* between the child and her biological parents.[91] Also, the rights bestowed on the child had no impact on the non-marital nature of her parents' relationship: that relationship remained illegitimate.[92]

4.3.2 Children of Unknown Filiation/Foundlings

The legal status of foundlings is not explicitly regulated in the Civil Code. Their status must therefore be derived from Shiite *fiqh*.[93] A foundling (*laqīṭ*) is a child found in a public space who is unable to care for herself and whose filiation is unknown.[94] Generally, such a child has to be taken care of by the finder. Taking a foundling into one's care imposes a duty of continuity on the finder; she may not refrain from taking care of the child once she has started to do so.[95] She may only refrain from exercising that duty if it can be taken up by another suitable person. This care is limited to custody and personal care, and in the event that the foundling has some wealth, the finder has to involve the state for the management of those assets. The finder has no right of guardianship (*vilāyat*) over the child because a child found in a Muslim territory will be considered free and a power relationship cannot be imposed upon her by the sheer fact that she has been found. Rather, it is the state's duty to take charge of the financial interests of the child. The costs for the upbringing of the foundling are to be covered by the foundling if she has her own assets, or by the state through social welfare transfers. The finder herself is under no obligation to provide financially for the foundling, although this is strongly recommended by Islamic scholars. In any case, the finder must seek the permission of the state (court) for the management of the child's assets. Also, the state acts as guardian as regards the authority to consent to the first marriage of a female foundling. Shiite *fiqh* seems unanimous that the finder of a child may acknowledge

---

90 See also decision of the Iranian Supreme Court no. 71/69/30, file no. 10/30/636, quoted in Bāzgīr 1997, p 195.

91 Decision of the Iranian Supreme Court no. 71/1021/7, quoted in Bāzgīr 1997, pp 195–196.

92 Ṣafā'ī and Imāmī 2011, p 129.

93 See Article 3 of the Iranian Code of Civil Procedure [*qānūn-i āyīn-i dādrasī-i dādgāhhā-i ᶜumūmī va inqilāb*] of April 9, 2000, Official Gazette no. 16070 of April 30, 2000, pp 28–50.

94 Naẓarī Tavakkulī 2012, p 344.

95 See Anṣārī (n.d.), p 346.

filiation under the general conditions of *iqrār*. The acknowledgement will be valid if the relation is factually and legally possible; the actual (biological) reality of the claim is irrelevant. Also, the acknowledgement may not be withdrawn subsequently by the acknowledging person.[96]

A foundling must be differentiated from an orphan. The term 'orphan' (*yatīm*) denotes a child who has lost her parents. In some contexts the term is also used to indicate a child who has lost only her father.[97] Generally, the filiation of such children is known. As in the case of foundlings, legal regulations with regard to orphans are mainly aimed at their protection within the social welfare system and state institutions. Those children generally have no legal problems as regards their *nasab*, but face social problems and are in need of care and safeguarding by the state.

In practice, foundlings (and orphans whose family and relatives are not available to care for them) are given into the care of the Juvenile Welfare Centers as regulated in the Act on the Protection of Women and Children without a Guardian of 1992 and are placed in children's homes.

4.4 Protection of Children without Filiation or Permanent Caretakers

4.4.1 General Legal Schemes of Protection and Care

Iranian law devotes a large number of rules to the protection and care of children. Generally, childcare is the right and duty of the parents, with custody being generally the common right and duty of both parents, whereas guardianship, i.e. the right and obligation to manage the child's assets, is the duty of the *valī*, i.e the father and the paternal grandfather. In some cases (separation of the parents, inability of the parents to assume childcare responsibilities, death of the father/grandfather, or the child's partial lack of legal capacity), the court appoints a person to take care of specific tasks related to the well-being, upbringing, or finances of a child. These judicially established 'guardianships' can take different forms, depending on the matter at hand. The main structures existing in Iranian law are *qaymūmat* (with the *qayyim* as the bearer of that duty) and *amānat* (*amīn*). Whenever the *valī* is not capable or needs assistance in the management of the child's assets, an *amīn* will be appointed.[98] In the event that the father (and grandfather) or both parents of the child are deceased, a

[96] See Anṣārī (n.d.), pp 349–350.

[97] On the use of the term orphan, see Yazbak 2001, p 124.

[98] Article 1184 sentence 2 CC: This provision will be applicable in cases where the guardian of the child is unable to administer the estate of his ward owing to his advanced age, sickness or similar reasons.

qayyim[99] will be nominated by the court. A *qayyim* has duties of care and management that are generally wider than those of the *amīn*, who is generally given a rather isolated duty on a specific matter. A *qayyim* must also be appointed for a child born out of wedlock whose father cannot be ascertained.[100] Besides managing the child's assets and being her legal representative, the *qayyim* may also have to assume responsibility for the educational care and upbringing of the child. The authority of the *qayyim* is thus determined by the court and can range from managing very specific matters to a broad general authority to care for the child and handle her affairs, potentially bringing it very close to the authority of the *valī*.[101]

The authority, rights and duties of these persons are determined by the court on a case-by-case basis. The *amīn* (and the *qayyim* insofar as the authority is limited by the court) must coordinate all matters related to the financial management of the child with the court, and both are accountable to the court for their actions.[102] Generally, these two types of guardians are remunerated for their efforts.[103] Children under *amānat* or *qaymūmat* keep their surnames and generally do not live with their *qayyim* or *amīn*.

Generally, these schemes do not entail the placement of the child into the home of the nominated guardian. Foundlings and orphans that came under the protection of the state were generally cared for in state institutions such as children's homes. It was only in 1975, four years before the Islamic revolution, that the Iranian legislature passed the Act on the Protection of Children without a Guardian (*sarparast*) (CPA 1975) in order to provide for a legal structure to place parentless children in new homes. This law was subsequently amended and replaced in 2013 by the Act on the Protection of Children without a Guardian (*bī sarparast*) or with an Unfit Guardian (*bad sarparast*) (CPA 2013).

4.4.2 *Act on the Protection of Children without a Guardian* (sarparast) *(CPA 1975)*

4.4.2.1 Terminology

The CPA 1975 was enacted to close the legal gap that existed in Iranian law, which until that point had not provided a legal mechanism for integrating a child fully into

---

99 Article 1218ff CC; Article 48ff of the Code of Non-Contentious Proceedings [*qānūn-i umūr-i ḥisbī*] of June 23, 1940, in Rūznāmih-i Rasmī-i Kishvar-i Shāhanshāhī-i Īrān (ed) Majmūᶜih-i Qavānīn-i Sāl-i 1319 [Annual Compilation of Laws 1940/41], pp 59–138.

100 See Legal Department of the Iranian Ministry of Justice, statement no. 7/3332 of July 31, 1975, in Riyāsat-i Jumhūrī (2011) Majmūᶜih-i Qānūn-i Madanī, 8th edn, Muᶜāvinat-i Tadvīn-i Tanqīḥ va Intishār-i Qavānīn va Muqarrarāt, Tehran, Article 1167 CC, p 377; Shīravī 2016, p 237.

101 Kātūziyān 1999, vol II, p 260.

102 Beevers and Ebrahimi 2002, p 170.

103 Article 1246 CC.

a new family. According to Article 2 CPA 1975, the aim of the Act was to safeguard the physical and mental needs of a child placed in a new home. The term literally denoting adoption in Farsi is *farzand khāndigī*. This term was, however, not used in the CPA 1975. The terminology chosen by the Iranian legislature in connection with this new legal scheme was *sarparast*, denoting the person who takes a child into her care, and *sarparastī* as the label for the legal institution itself. This latter term had already been used in legal writings as an umbrella term denoting childcare,[104] and it had appeared in statutory law denoting the duties of the state to care for parentless children.[105] Furthermore, it has no roots in religious law. The CPA 1975 did not define the term *sarparastī* explicitly, but the Iranian legislature's terminological choice points to the deliberate introduction of a new legal concept into Iranian law,[106] distinct from existing forms of guardianship. The specific connotation of *sarparastī* as a distinct legal institution was also confirmed by a 1981 decision of the Iranian Supreme Court in which it explicitly held that *sarparastī* did not equate to *qaymūmat*.[107]

4.4.2.2 Regulations of the CPA 1975

According to the CPA 1975, children whose parents were deceased or had abandoned them without any recourse for at least three years and who therefore had been placed under the supervision of the Juvenile Welfare Center were eligible for *sarparastī*. The children had to be under the age of twelve; the potential parents had to have been married for at least five years and must have remained childless. After a thorough check of the prospective parents (financial capacity, social environment) and extensive interviews, the child was given into the care of the new parents for a trial period of six months under the supervision of the Juvenile Welfare Center. After the end of this period, a court decree on final *sarparastī* would be issued.[108]

The rights and duties between the new parents and the child corresponded to the rights and duties of a legal parent-child relationship in terms of custody, the management of the child's assets, maintenance and mutual respect. Furthermore, the child would take the surname of her new father.

Thus, *sarparastī* came close to the concept of adoption but stopped short of entailing all the effects of a plenary adoption: the parent-child relationship only extended to the child and her new parents and did not establish a kinship relationship with other relatives of the parents. Additionally, *sarparastī* did not create intestate inheritance rights between the child and her new parents. The prospective

---

[104] Beevers and Ebrahimi 2002, p 172.

[105] Specifically, in the Act on the Protection of Women and Children without a Guardian.

[106] Kātūziyān 1999, p 404ff; Tavasulī Nā'īnī 2010, p 103.

[107] Judgment of the Iranian Court of Cassation no. 22-6/4/1360 of June 27, 1981, Official Gazette no. 10735 of January 2, 1982, cited in Kātūziyān 1999, vol II, p 407.

[108] Beevers and Ebrahimi 2002, p 174.

parents were, however, obligated to make sure the costs of the child's upbringing were secured in the event of their death. In practice, the new parents would either transfer some property to the child or otherwise make an irrevocable testamentary disposition in which the child was bequeathed one-third of the estate of each parent.[109] Also, the relationship of *sarparastī* would be a permanent one. It could be cancelled only in the best interests of the child in instances where the behavior of either party would make the continuation of the *sarparastī* unbearable and detrimental to the child. If the child under *sarparastī* was an abandoned child and the biological parents of the child reappeared, *sarparastī* could be revoked by agreement between the new parents and the biological parents.

The CPA 1975 did not regulate, however, the taking into care of children that had only *temporarily* come under the supervision of the Juvenile Welfare Center, because, for instance, their biological parents lacked the ability to raise them appropriately. Legal mechanisms such as a foster care arrangement, whereby the child lived for a limited period of time with a new family, did not yet exist in Iran.[110] The existing schemes, i.e. *qaymūmat* and *amānat*, provided for measures to satisfy specific needs of a child, but they generally did not encompass the placement of the child into a new family. Statistics from the early 2000s showed that most children under the supervision of the Juvenile Welfare Center were not children whose parents were unknown or deceased, but rather children whose parents had abandoned them or were temporarily unable to take care of them and whose custody rights had been revoked.[111] These children had to wait three years pursuant to the CPA 1975 before any kind of placement with a new family was possible. Furthermore, as the placements were of a permanent nature, the biological parents had no possibility of retrieving their children if the reasons for their inability to provide care ceased to exist, other than through an agreement with the new parents with due consideration of the best interests of the child.

Against this background, in 2004 the Juvenile Welfare Center addressed the office of the judiciary to inquire about possible legal amendments to the CPA 1975 in order to facilitate foster family placements for children whose parents' identity was known but whose parents' ability to raise the child was impaired. The first draft of a new CPA was prepared in October 2009. However, it took another four years until the Act on the Protection of Children without a Guardian (*bī sarparast*) or with an Unfit Guardian (*bad sarparast*) was passed in 2013.

[109] Beevers and Ebrahimi 2002, p 174.

[110] Beevers and Ebrahimi 2002, p 171.

[111] See interview with Hamid Reza Alvand, the president of the Organisation for the Welfare of Children and Youth, from November 18, 2013, www.mehrkhane.com/fa/print/9058 (accessed August 23, 2016); see also interview with the vice-president of the organization, Habibollah Mas'udi, from December 16, 2016, www.mehrkhane.com/fa/print/30420 (accessed August 23, 2016), in which he points to the fact that 78% of the children under the supervision of the welfare centers do have either a living mother or father.

4.4.3 Act on the Protection of Children without a Guardian (bī sarparast) *or with an Unfit Guardian* (bad sarparast) *(CPA 2013)*

4.4.3.1 Terminology and Scope of Application

The CPA 2013, which repealed the CPA 1975, came into force in October 2013. It consists of 36 articles, and its scope of application is broader than that of its predecessor.[112] This is reflected in the title of the law: whereas the CPA 1975 referred to children without a *sarparast*, the new Act encompasses regulations on children without a *sarparast* as well as children with an unfit *sarparast*. The initiators of the new law wanted to create schemes for both the permanent and temporary integration of a child into a new family.[113] Unfortunately, the legislature's good intentions were not matched by good legal drafting. A main deficiency is – again – the lack of a definition for the term *sarparastī*. Article 1 CPA 2013 only states that the '*sarparastī* of children and youth without *sarparast* aims at safeguarding their physical and mental needs and can be established in accordance with the permission of the leader of the Islamic Republic (*rahbar*) and according to the following provisions.' In fact, the Act uses the term *sarparastī* both in its broad meaning of caretaking in general[114] and as a specific term to denote the placement of children into new homes. Interestingly, however, in contrast to the CPA 1975, the CPA 2013 not only uses the term *sarparastī* but also synonymously uses the Farsi term for adoption, '*farzand khāndigī*'.[115] This terminology is also reflected in the court judgments issued since the enactment of the law that refer to *farzand khāndigī* as the subject matter of the case in the heading of the decision, whereas the actual text of the decision sticks to the word '*sarparastī*'.[116]

The Act also does not differentiate explicitly between temporary and permanent placements. The articles of the Act, however, can be assigned to the one or other kind of *sarparastī* and in some cases – with reference to the wording of the articles and the aim of the legislature to create two legal structures for the placement of children – it is apparent that the articles are meant to be applicable to both schemes, as will be shown subsequently.

---

[112] For an account of the parliamentary debates on the conception and enactment of the Acts, Yassari 2015, pp 957–959.

[113] See first legislative proposal dated February 23, 2009, http://rc.majlis.ir/fa/legal_draft/state_popup/737637?fk_legal_draft_oid=720687&a=download&sub=h (accessed August 23, 2016); see also the statement of the parliamentarian expert group dated March 7, 2009, http://rc.majlis.ir/fa/legal_draft/state_popup/737945?fk_legal_draft_oid=720687&a=download&sub=p (accessed August 23, 2016).

[114] As for example in Article 8 note 1 and Article 10 CPA 2013.

[115] Articles 26 and 35 CPA 2013.

[116] Decisions on file with author.

The lacunae and inconsistent terminology make the Act ambiguous. A meaningful interpretation of the Act thus requires taking into account the evolution and background of the law, its aims and purposes, and the parliamentary discussions during the lengthy law-making process. Also, its interpretation must be situated within the larger legal framework of Iranian family law, in particular the provisions of the new Act on the Protection of the Family of 2013. A major novelty of that law is the general introduction of the principle of the best interests of the child as the paramount criterion in all (court) decisions and matters related to children and youth (Articles 40–47 FPA 2013). The application of this principle is not confined to parental care, instead extending to all court decisions relating to children and youth.[117]

4.4.3.2 The Procedure for the Award of *sarparastī*

The competent state organs for dealing with applications for *sarparastī* are the Juvenile Welfare Centers (*sāzmān-i behzīstī*) (JWC) and the family courts. The application for *sarparastī* must be lodged at the local JWC, which then transfers the application to the court after having checked the conditions for *sarparastī*.[118] These preliminary checks encompass extensive interviews and an inquiry into the financial and mental status of the applicants, including medical tests (alcohol and drug tests). Subsequently, the application will be forwarded to the court, which examines the criminal record of the applicant and decides on the approval or rejection of the application after hearing the opinion of the JWC and with due application of the CPA 2013 regulations.[119] The court first issues an order of *sarparastī* for a trial period of six months.[120] In that period, the child lives with her potential *sarparast* under the regular supervision of the JWC. If, after that period, the conditions are still fulfilled and the JWC issues a positive statement, the final decree on *sarparastī* will be issued by the court and the child will be permanently placed with her new caretakers.[121] It is clear from these provisions that *sarparastī* does not have a contractual nature and does not come into existence because of the will of the parties. Rather, it is created by the decision of the court, with the court having the sole authority to establish this relationship.[122]

---

[117] Article 45 FPA 2013.

[118] For the procedure see Decree for the Implementation of the CPA [*āyīn-nāmih-i ijrāyī-i qānūn-i ḥimāyat az kūdakān va nūjavānān bī sarparast va bad sarparast*] of July 11, 2015, Official Gazette no. 20492 of July 14, 2015, pp 7–8.

[119] Articles 1, 11 CPA 2013.

[120] Article 11 CPA 2013.

[121] Article 13 CPA 2013.

[122] Sharīᶜatī Nasab 2011, pp 88–89. This book evaluates the provisions of the CPA 1975, but the analysis is also applicable to the new Act as far as the procedure is concerned since no changes have been introduced in this respect.

In practice, a *sarparastī* procedure can take between one-and-a-half and six years. According to statistics of the Juvenile Welfare Centers, 800 to 1,200 *sarparastī* procedures are performed every year in Iran, while over 22,000 children live in children's homes.[123] The actual number of parentless and abandoned children in Iran that are not registered and are not under the supervision of any state organization is, however, alarming. It is estimated that more than 200,000 children are homeless and living mostly without identity cards or birth certificates in abandoned houses and public parks.[124]

4.4.3.3 The Revocation of *sarparastī*

As far as the revocation of *sarparastī* is concerned, the Act provides for different grounds with regard to the status of the children. For children with living but unfit parents, Article 25 lit. d CPA 2013 states that the child's *sarparastī* can be revoked by the court and parental care re-established whenever the biological parents prove and convince the court that they have overcome their deficiencies. This rule obviously does not apply to orphans, who fall under the general grounds for revoking *sarparastī*. Accordingly, *sarparastı* can only be revoked by court order, first, when the behavior of either the child or the caregiver(s) makes the continuation of the *sarparastī* unbearable and detrimental to the child; and, second, whenever the *sarparast* and a child who has reached the age of majority agree to terminate their relationship. It is evident from these regulations that children with unfit parents are meant to be provided for on a temporary care basis with the possibility of being returned to their parents, whereas orphans are meant to stay permanently with their new families. Their relationship will only be terminated when severe circumstances demand so, with due consideration of the best interests of the child, or where the adult child and the caretakers decide to end their relationship. Also, it must be emphasized that the revocation of *sarparastī* always requires a court decision following a petition by one of the parties. As with its

[123] See www.khabaronline.ir/print/316561/society/social-damage? of October 8, 2013 (accessed August 23, 2016); see also mehrkhane.com/fa/print/30515 of December 24, 2016 (accessed August 23, 2016).

[124] See report of Al Arabiya (June 15, 2015) Inside Iran: The industry of child trafficking, english.alarabiya.net/en/perspective/features/2015/06/15/Inside-Iran-The-industry-of-Child-trafficking.html (accessed August 23, 2016). According to a 2012 report by Humanium, an international child sponsorship NGO dedicated to stopping violations of children's rights throughout the world, '[m]ost of these children are not orphans, but usually have drug-addicted [or unemployed and refugee] parents, which forces them [to live in the streets and] to work to help support their families', see Humanium (March 15, 2012) Children of the [sic] Iran – Realizing Children's Rights in the Islamic Republic of Iran, www.humanium.org/en/middle-east-north-africa/iran (accessed August 23, 2016).

establishment, *sarparastī* may not be cancelled by the involved parties alone but needs a court decree to this end. Therefore, *sarparastī* does not have a contractual nature regarding either its inception or its revocation.[125]

4.4.3.4 Eligibility of the *sarparast* and the Child

Articles 3–6 CPA 2013 define the conditions under which a person may be a *sarparast*. Accordingly, Iranian nationals (with a domicile in Iran or abroad) who have been married for over five years and who have remained childless are eligible to be *sarparasts* provided one of the spouses is over thirty years old. Furthermore, married couples with children are now eligible, provided again that one of the spouses has reached the age of thirty. Another interesting novelty has been introduced in the same article as regards single women: pursuant to Article 5 lit. c CPA 2013, single women – a category including never-married women as well as widows and divorcees[126] – who have reached the age of thirty are eligible to be a *sarparast*, albeit only for a female child. The article also sets an order of priority for the processing of applications for *sarparastī*, progressing from (i) married childless couples to (ii) unmarried, childless women and finally to (iii) married couples with children. Furthermore, in addition to having no criminal record, applicants must be of good reputation and morality, financially capable, mature, physically and mentally fit, and factually capable of caring for and educating a child or youth.[127] Finally, the law specifies that drug addicts and alcoholics are disqualified from *sarparastī*, as are people with contagious or difficult-to-cure diseases.

The law also makes reference to religion by specifying that only persons belonging to one of the official state-recognized religions under the Iranian constitution may become *sarparasts*. Furthermore, the child and the *sarparast* must belong to the same religion, although the legislation does make an exception for Muslims becoming the *sarparast* of a non-Muslim child with due consideration of the best interests of the child.[128] These two last provisions are interesting insofar as Iranian family law is inter-religiously divided, with each religious community falling under the ambit of its own religious provisions. Thus, family and inheritance matters of a non-Shiite Iranian fall under the religious laws of that person, not under the law applicable to Shiite Iranians. This is true for adoption in particular, as the 1933 Act on the Observance of the Personal Status of Non-Shiite Iranians in the Courts[129] explicitly enumerates adoption (*farzand khāndigī*) as one of the fields that

---

[125] Sharīᶜatī Nasab 2011, p 92.

[126] As to previously unmarried women, the article uses the word *dukhtar*, which translates to 'maiden;' the term '*zan*' denotes women who are divorced or widowed.

[127] Article 6 CPA 2013.

[128] Article 6 CPA 2013.

[129] Act on the Observance of the Personal Status of Non-Shiite Iranians in the Courts [*qānūn-i ijāzih-i raᶜāyat-i aḥvāl-i shakhṣiyyih-i īrāniyān-i ghayr-i shīᶜih dar maḥākim*] of July 22, 1933, Official Gazette no. 3157 of August 1, 1933.

is governed by communitarian religious law. The provision that Muslims can become the *sarparasts* of non-Muslims must therefore be seen as an internal public order clause, deviating from the interreligious rule so as to favor Muslims.

What group of children may come under *sarparastī*? First, the Act sets an age limit. Accordingly, children that have not reached the age of puberty[130] may come under *sarparastī*; children that have reached the age of puberty but are under the age of sixteen are also eligible if the court finds them lacking mental maturity (*ᶜadam-i rushd*); and finally, also very broadly, 'children that are in need of a *sarparast*.'[131] Second, the Act is only applicable if these children also fulfil the following conditions:[132] their parents or paternal ascendants must be indeterminable or dead,[133] or, if known and alive, must be unfit or unable to raise them.[134] The responsibility of caring for these children is initially transferred to the Juvenile Welfare Center before an appropriate *sarparast* is sought.

Media coverage on *sarparastī* reveals that most couples are primarily interested in taking a very young child into their care, preferably a baby under the age of six months.[135] The main reason given is that older children have already experienced situations and circumstances that might have harmed them, and the interviewees very often felt that they would not be able to raise them properly or deal with their potential problems adequately. Also, most interviewees said they would not want to take into their care a child that still has living albeit unfit parents, for fear that at some point they would have to return the child. In practice, it therefore seems that the legislature's aim of providing temporary placement for neglected children is not being embraced by a broad majority of the public.

4.4.3.5 The Rights and Duties of the *sarparast*

Parental Care and Maintenance

According to Article 17 CPA 2013, the rights and duties of the *sarparasts* as regards care, education, maintenance and respect are the same as between parents

---

[130] That is, nine lunar years for girls and fifteen lunar years for boys, Article 1210 note 1 CC.

[131] Article 9 CPA 2013.

[132] Article 8 CPA 2013.

[133] Article 8 lit. a and b CPA 2013. Furthermore, lit. b points to the fact that the *vaṣī* of the child must also be deceased for the child to be eligible for permanent *sarparastī*. Under Iranian law the *vaṣī* is a person chosen by the *valī* by testamentary disposition to take over *vilāyat* after his death.

[134] According to Article 8 lit. c and d CPA 2013, the biological parents, the parental ascendants and the *vaṣī* are to be given priority for *sarparastī* even if they are only able to assume *sarparastī* with the assistance of a court-nominated supervisor (*nāẓir*).

[135] Parsnews.com; according to the online newspaper *mehrkhane*, although the number of families taking on a child is rather high (seven applicants per child), most of them want to care for a baby under six months, see www.mehrkhane.com/fa/print/30420 of December 19, 2016 (accessed August 23, 2016).

and their children. Thus, the *sarparasts* are under the same duty to care for, educate, and maintain the child as are parents for their legal children.[136] The article, however, fails to state the reciprocity of this rule and merely states that the child is subject to the duty to respect her *sarparasts*. The omission of the rule of reciprocity casts doubt on whether the child – upon reaching the age of majority – would also have a duty of maintenance vis-à-vis her *sarparasts*. Relying on the differentiation between temporary and permanent *sarparastī*, Article 17 CPA 2013 could, however, be interpreted as specifying only the minimum duties of the child, applying to both forms of *sarparastī*. Furthermore, as we will see in the next section, the financial rights and duties created under Articles 14, 15 and 19 CPA 2013 – obliging the *sarparast* to safeguard the child's financial independence – could support the inference that the child will *in casu* be under an implied legal obligation to maintain her new parents if they become needy. This, however, remains speculative at present, as thus far no court cases have arisen in which the *sarparast* has petitioned for maintenance.

Financial Duties of the *sarparast*

Pursuant to Article 14 CPA 2013, in order for the final decree on *sarparastī* to be issued, the potential *sarparast* must transfer a certain amount of property to the child. This rule, which also existed in the CPA 1975, is fulfilled in practice by the *sarparast* transferring some property to the child or executing an irrevocable last will in which the child will be bequeathed up to one-third of the estate.[137] Furthermore, Article 15 CPA 2013 requires the *sarparast* to acquire life insurance with the child as beneficiary to ensure that all costs of the child's upbringing are secured in the event of the *sarparast*'s death. The financial security duties of the *sarparast* can exceptionally be waived if – notwithstanding the financial needs of the child – the court considers the *sarparastī* nonetheless to be in the best interests of the child.[138] Finally, the child is also included in the group of beneficiaries that are entitled to a share in any pension rights of the *sarparasts* in the event of their death.[139] These articles do not state to which group of children they refer (those without parents or those with unfit parents). Their scope of application is, however, naturally contained by the status of the children and, correspondingly, the financial rights and duties afforded to the *sarparast* for each group of children, as will be shown next.

Generally, the parental authority to manage a child's financial affairs (*vilāyat*) rests with the father or grandfather, who are both considered to be the child's

---

[136] Article 17 CPA 2013.

[137] See Beevers and Ebrahimi 2002, p 174.

[138] Article 14 note 1 and Article 15 note 1 CPA 2013.

[139] Article 19 CPA 2013.

valī.[140] The father may designate in his last will another person to exercise this authority after his death, the so-called *vaṣī*.[141] Therefore, if the child has a *valī* or a *vaṣī* – even if they are unfit – the *sarparast* cannot exercise *vilāyat*. Instead, the court may grant the *sarparast* the right to act on behalf of the child as the child's judicially nominated guardian, either as a *qayyim* or an *amīn*,[142] while the general authority of *vilāyat* as such will nominally remain with the child's *valī* or *vaṣī*. For these specific tasks, the *sarparast* (i) has to coordinate her activities with the court, (ii) is accountable for her actions to the court,[143] and (iii) will be remunerated for her services.[144] If, on the other hand, the child has no *valī* or *vaṣī*, the court will award the *sarparast* of such a child a general mandate under the scheme of *qaymūmat* to act as the guardian of the child in the management of the child's financial matters.[145] In accordance with this wider authority, the *sarparast* of a child without a *valī* or *vaṣī* will correspondingly be assigned greater financial responsibility.

It thus can be argued that the legislature conceived two schemes: one for children without a *valī* or *vaṣī*, whose *sarparast* is vested with full financial authority in the management of the child's assets and therefore is obliged to commit to providing financially for the child as a precondition for the awarding of *sarparastī* (Articles 14 and 15 CPA 2013); and another for children with an (unfit) *valī*/*vaṣī*, where the *sarparast* will be granted certain financial rights but where the heavy financial burdens under Articles 14 and 15 CPA 2013 may be waived. As in this last scheme of *sarparastī* the possibility remains that the exercise of the *vilāyat* will be (re)claimed by the *valī*, the *sarparast* will not be vested with full parental financial authority and responsibility.

While these rules are meant to protect the child financially, media coverage of *sarparastī* in Iran points to the difficulties this can create for couples who consider *sarparastī* as an option. According to such media reports, some potential applicants perceive the transfer of a significant amount of assets to the child at the beginning of *sarparastī* to be rather burdensome, causing them to reconsider their capability and willingness to apply in the first place.[146]

---

[140] See Articles 1180–1181 CC.

[141] See Article 1188 CC.

[142] Article 10 CPA 2013. The awarding of that position is further conditional on the approval of the Juvenile Welfare Center and is subject to Articles 1184 and 1187 CC. On the *qayyim* and the *amīn*, see above Sect. 4.4.1.

[143] Articles 1184, 1218ff CC; Article 48ff Code of Non-Contentious Proceedings; see also Beevers and Ebrahimi 2002, p 170.

[144] See Article 95 Code of Non-Contentious Proceedings.

[145] Article 16 CPA 2013.

[146] Parsnews.com.

4.4.3.6 Other Legal Issues Concerning *sarparastī*

Marriage Between the *sarparast* and the Child

A further contentious issue is the question of whether *sarparastī* creates a marriage obstacle between the child and her *sarparasts*. The CPA 1975 had left that question unregulated. Academic literature occasionally raised the question, answering it negatively, largely with social and moral arguments. The problem remains that the list of marriage obstacles under Islamic law is exhaustive and does not mention *sarparastī*. The drafters of the CPA 2013, however, were determined to regulate this issue explicitly. Representatives of the Juvenile Welfare Centers had specifically raised that issue, as there had been three (official) cases where the *sarparast* father had asked to marry the child under his *sarparastī*.[147]

Therefore, the first draft of 2009 tentatively stated that the marriage of a child under *sarparastī* with her *sarparast* or, alternatively, of a child previously under *sarparastī* with her former *sarparast* was conditioned on the approval of the family court, with the court being obliged to hear the view of the Juvenile Welfare Center.[148] One parliamentary committee objected to this rule. It argued that as the occurrence of such marriages was close to nil and as they infringed upon Iranian morality, such an article should be omitted on the whole.[149] The Parliament's group of legal experts, however, opposed this omission. The experts remarked that even if such marriages occurred very rarely,[150] the silence of the law would not suffice; rather an explicit prohibition of such marriages needed to be included in the Act.[151] The Council of Guardians[152] replied that such a straightforward prohibition would in its strictness infringe upon Islamic *fiqh* (as no such marriage obstacle existed in Shiite *fiqh*) and such a marriage could not take place even if the parties consented to it.[153] Nonetheless, Parliament continued to insist on incorporating the prohibition,

---

147 See www.khabaronline.ir/print/316561/society/social-damage? of October 8, 2013 (accessed August 23, 2016).

148 See the first draft of the Act of February 22, 2009, first lecture in the Parliament (1st year, 8th session), registration no. 288 (on file with author).

149 Parliamentary Committee Statement of July 29, 2009 (on file with author).

150 Statement of the Expert Committee of the Parliament of March 7, 2009, registration no. 288, p 15 (on file with author).

151 See Article 26 note 1 of the second draft of the Act of October 13, 2009, registration no. 288/34852 (on file with author).

152 The Council of Guardians is an appointed and constitutionally mandated twelve-member organ that is charged under Articles 94 and 96 of the Iranian Constitution with interpreting the Constitution and ensuring the compatibility of legislation passed by the Parliament with the criteria of Islam and the Constitution. All draft laws must therefore be presented to the Council, and its approval is necessary for any law to come into force.

153 See Statement of the Council of Guardians no. 91/35/47840 of August 15, 2012, p 2 (on file with author), see also interview with Prof. Hosseyn Mehrpour, Dean of the Law Faculty of the Shahid Beheshti University, from November 18, 2013, www.mehrkhane.com/fa/print/9058 (accessed August 23, 2016).

and advanced an interesting line of argument in order to heed the requirement of the Council. It conceded that no religious grounds for prohibiting such marriages existed but maintained that it was allowed to set certain conditions for *sarparastī*, among which is a prohibition against marrying a child put under *sarparastī*.[154] The prohibition of marrying the child had therefore to be considered as an underlying condition in a *sarparastī* arrangement. This line of argument was then concretized in Article 26, with the prohibition of marriage established as the general rule alongside an exceptional right of the courts to permit such a marriage if it was considered to be in the best interests of the child. The Council of Guardians saw this amendment as sufficient to meet its demands and allowed the enactment of Article 26 note 1 CPA 2013 as follows: 'The marriage of the child to the *sarparast*, be it during the period of custody, be it after that, is prohibited unless the family court considers the marriage, after consultation with the Juvenile Welfare Centers, to be in the best interests of the child.'

Despite embodying a general rule prohibiting marriage of the child with the *sarparast*, the article was nonetheless widely criticized among the public for so much as raising the possibility of marriage: it was argued that such a potentiality not only was contrary to the spirit of the CPA as legislation aiming to protect children and provide them with a new secure home, but also ran afoul of morality in Iranian society.[155]

Islamic scholars also participated in this debate and proposed solving the issue (i.e. establishing a marriage obstacle) through genuinely Islamic tools.[156] One of these proposed tools was the establishment of milk-kinship (*riżāᶜ*) between the child and her new parents.[157] Milk-kinship is created by the nursing of a child over a certain period of time or on several consecutive occasions by a woman who is not the biological mother of the child. The legal consequence of this kind of nursing is the creation of a fictional kinship prohibiting marriage: the nursed boy may not marry the nursing woman and the nursed girl may not marry the husband of the nursing woman. The marriage impediment also extends to the biological children of the nursing woman, who may not marry the nursed child, as these children are considered to be siblings.[158] Interestingly, Grand Ayatollah Makarem Shirazi, who is known for his conservative views, recommended solving the marriage issue in *sarparastī* by establishing a milk-relationship between the child and the *sarparast* mother or other female relatives of the parents.

---

154 See Statement of the Expert Committee of the Parliament of November 3, 2012, registration no. 24012435-1 (on file with author).

155 See interview with Iranian lawyer Mohamad Maqsud from October 6, 2013, www.yjc.ir/fa/print/4581909 (accessed August 23, 2016); see also www.salamatnews.com/news/85571 of October 29, 2013 (accessed August 23, 2016).

156 See for example the proposal of Ayatollah Makarem Shirazi, www.khabaronline.ir/print/316561/society/social-damage? of October 8, 2013 (accessed August 23, 2016).

157 Al-ᶜĀmilī 2008, pp 392–398.

158 Al-ᶜĀmilī 2008, p 397. The marriage must be valid at the time of nursing, Altorki 1980, pp 233, 234; Fortier 2007, pp 18–19.

The other tool for creating a marriage obstacle that was debated amongst religious scholars was the conclusion of a non-sexual temporary marriage. As discussed above, Shiite *fiqh* recognizes the institution of temporary marriage. Although the bulk of Shiite writing on temporary marriage relates to a sexual marital union, Shiite scholars acknowledge non-sexual *ṣīghih* as well, which is also called *ṣīghih-i maḥramiyat.*[159] This term refers to the creation of a *maḥramiyat* relationship, i.e. a bond that prohibits marriage but does not involve sexual relations. The concept of *maḥramiyat* revolves around the idea of an inner and outer sphere of the family. As such, the inner core of the family means the immediate family, this extending to persons related to each other by close blood relationship (in direct line, i.e. parents and children, and on the lateral lines, i.e. uncles, aunts, sisters and brothers, nieces and nephews) and also to relations created by affinity (in-laws and spouses of the parents). Persons outside this group are generally treated as alien to the family, i.e. not *maḥram*, and are thus eligible for marriage. Interactions with such alien persons therefore imply a different code of behavior as regards openness in clothing, intimacy, and trust.

Such a bond of *maḥramiyat* between unrelated persons can also be obtained through a non-sexual *ṣīghih*. Such a union creates a 'fictive' marital relationship between the wedded persons and an affinal relationship between them and their respective immediate families. As a result, the legal distance between those persons is eliminated and marriage impediments are installed. Historically, such unions were performed, for example, between an adult man (often the grandfather) and girls who would work in the household of that family, thus enabling the family to interact more freely and giving the girls protection from any possible offers of marriage from the father.[160] Today, such unions are not uncommon in Iran and are often used in traditional settings to enable the persons involved to interact and move more freely.[161] In *sarparastī* arrangements, the child could then be wedded on the basis of a non-sexual fictive temporary marriage to, for example, the father (or widowed mother) of the *sarparast*, by which the *sarparast* would be barred from marrying the child, even after the end of the temporary marriage. There are no reliable data on whether these kinds of arrangements are actually practiced with regard to *sarparastī*.

The Single *sarparast* Mother

Another novelty in the CPA 2013 is the right of single women to take on a girl child as a *sarparast*. That rule had been contested by various expert commissions of the

[159] See Haeri 1989, p 89ff.

[160] Under Shiite law, a man may not under any condition marry any of his biological father's wives, see also Article 1048ff CC.

[161] See Haeri 1989, pp 89–96 for examples of non-sexual *ṣīghih*.

Parliament,[162] which claimed that this would undermine the institution of marriage and deter women from marrying. The drafter of that rule, by contrast, argued with statistics showing that couples generally preferred to choose a boy for *sarparastī* and that children's homes housed more girls, who lived under very bad conditions.[163] The eligibility of single women for *sarparastī* was not only meant to help fulfil those women's desire for motherhood but also to better the situation of girls in those homes.[164]

Also, in order to address potential legal problems for a single female *sarparast* parent, the law regulates the situation where the single female *sarparast* subsequently wishes to marry. The main legal obstacle for such a marriage is the legal rule regarding parental care in the case of (re)marriage. Pursuant to Article 1170 CC, a divorced mother who has custody of her children will lose this right when she marries a person that is not *maḥram* to her child. The rationale behind this rule is threefold: first, it is believed that a stepfather has no natural inclination to care for a child with whom he is not genetically linked. Second, as no bond of *maḥramiyat* exists between the child and her stepfather, there is the danger of abuse; the welfare of the child is believed to be better preserved if the child is not obliged to live with a stranger. The third assumption is that a remarrying mother will be busy with her new marital duties and will thus be distracted from her parental duties and not able to care properly for her children.[165] To anticipate such problems, the CPA 2013 states that in the case of a prospective marriage, the single female *sarparast* has to inform the court and the Juvenile Welfare Center. The court then has to decide whether to award common *sarparastī* to the couple or to withdraw it in the best interests of the child. Interestingly, in the several opinions given by the Council of Guardians, no mention was made of these articles, and they passed the Council's control untouched.

Inheritance

Children under *sarparastī* are exempted from intestate succession. While the CPA 1975 explicitly mentioned this,[166] the CPA 2013 adopts this position implicitly. However, both laws demanded that the child be ensured financial security upon the

---

162 See first opinion of the Expert Committee of the Parliament (*daftar-i muṭālaᶜāt-i ḥuqūqī*) of August 25, 2009, serial no. 9667-1 (on file with author).

163 See interview with Prof. Mozaheri, Dean of the Psychology Faculty of the Shahid Beheshti University, from November 18, 2013, www.mehrkhane.com/fa/print/9058 (accessed August 23, 2016).

164 See www.salamatnews.com/news/85571 of October 29, 2013 (accessed August 23, 2016); see interview with Prof. Fereshte Motavi, member of the research group on family law at the Shahid Beheshti University, from November 18, 2013, www.mehrkhane.com/fa/print/9058 (accessed August 23, 2016).

165 See Yassari et al. 2017, pp 340–341.

166 See Article 2 CPA 1975.

death of her *sarparasts*. Pursuant to Article 19 CPA 2013, the child is regarded as one of the beneficiaries of any pension rights that the *sarparast* was entitled to. Also, in accordance with their financial commitment in Articles 14 and 15 CPA 2013, the new parents in practice generally bequest the child a certain portion of the free third of their estate. Thus, notwithstanding the exclusion of the child from intestate succession, the law foresees very strong schemes for ensuring the financial security of the child following the *sarparasts*' death, thereby making up for this legal gap.

Name

The transfer of name as regulated in the CPA 2013 is a very interesting issue. Generally, a legal child takes the surname of her father. Children taken into *sarparastī* will similarly take the surname of their *sarparast*: the court has to serve the *sarparastī* order to the registration office, which in turn must enter the (new) name and surname of the child as well as the *sarparastī* arrangement into both the register (*asnād-i sijillī*) and the identity cards (*shināsnāmih*) of the child's *sarparasts*.[167] The registration office must also issue a new identity card for the child, which is to incorporate the new first name (if any) chosen by the child's new caretakers and the surname of her *sarparasts*. If the child is taken on by a married couple, the child will take the husband's surname;[168] if the child is taken on by an unmarried woman, the child takes the woman's surname and a fictive male first name is inscribed as the name of the child's father in the documents.[169] With this rule, the CPA 2013 has reiterated the rule in the former law. The CPA 2013, however, also introduced new regulations: not only the *sarparastī* arrangement itself must be inscribed in the child's identity document, but also the names of the child's biological parents (where known).[170] Under the CPA 1975, the identity card of the child would only bear her new name and surname, and nowhere could an outsider see that the child was not the biological child of the named parents. The *sarparastī* arrangement as well as the names of the biological parents of the child were included in the register entry of the child, but they would not appear on the identity card.

The new regulations came under harsh criticism. Many MPs objected to the inscription of the *sarparastī* arrangement on the identity card of the child as potentially creating a social stigma for the child. They argued in particular that in Iranian society *sarparastī* is still frowned upon, and very often the children are not

---

[167] See Decree for the Implementation of Article 22 CPA 2013 [*āyīn-nāmih-i ijrāyī-i māddih-i 22 qānūn-i ḥimāyat az kūdakān va nūjavānān bī sarparast va bad sarparast*] of July 12, 2015, Official Gazette no. 20494 of July 16, 2015, p 3.

[168] Article 6 Decree for the Implementation of Article 22 CPA 2013.

[169] Article 5 Decree for the Implementation of Article 22 CPA 2013.

[170] Article 22 CPA 2013.

informed about their origins by their *sarparast*. Whereas critics agreed that the truth about the origins of the child must be preserved and acknowledged the right of children to know their origins and be informed of their genetic identity,[171] they argued that this issue should not be made public on the identity document; instead, they favored leaving it to the *sarparast* to sort out the right time and circumstances for advising the child of this reality. Thus, in their view it would have sufficed if this information were deposited with the registration office without specifying it on the child's identity card. This position is indeed defensible. The general view on *sarparastī* in Iranian society is rather ambivalent, and there is a strong tendency to keep the matter secret. It therefore seems very probable that a child under *sarparastī* will be subject to discrimination and suffer from the public accessibility of her status.

4.5 Conclusion

Filiation arises under one of two schemes under Iranian law. Primarily, it results from a child being born into a marriage within certain timeframes. At the same time, however, the law acknowledges the establishment of filiation as a legal fiction in situations where the parents' marriage cannot be proven or where the circumstances under which it took place are uncertain. The only conditions for these exceptions are the good faith of the parents and their subjective belief that such a marriage existed at the time the child was conceived. This emphasizes the principle of *ḥusn-i niyyat*, or good faith, as a remedy for legal deficiencies. What these exceptions have in common is that they operate within the given scheme of *nasab*, the religiously based requirement for the establishment of filiation and the attribution of the children to their biological parents.

Yet where those presumptions do not apply, parentless children are not left without protection. In fact, Iranian law has conceived different schemes to provide for a minimum of legal security and financial support for children of defective, unknown or illegitimate parentage. This is reflected, for example, in the rulings of the Iranian Supreme Court according various rights to children born out of wedlock, including parental care and the right to carry the father's name. Another illustration is the Act on the Protection of Children without a Guardian of 1975 and its 2013 successor, in which the legislature aimed to find legal means to integrate children into new families. The shortcomings of the CPA 2013, namely its vague scope of application and the lack of a clear statement as to the temporary or permanent nature of *sarparastī* arrangements, can be accounted for by the difficult process of enacting the law; in order to have the law enacted at all, the various stakeholders

[171] See interview with Prof. Fereshte Motavi, member of the research group on family law at the Shahid Beheshti University, from November 18, 2013, www.mehrkhane.com/fa/print/9058 (accessed August 23, 2016).

were compelled to make a number of significant compromises. This tightrope walk can also be seen in other aspects of the Act, in particular as regards the creation of a marriage obstacle in connection with *sarparastī* and in the quest to balance the dual interests of safeguarding the child's real identity and transferring the *sarparast*'s name to the child. The endeavors of the legislature, however, illustrate its awareness and willingness to afford legal protection to parentless children and to venture beyond the traditional reasoning of Islamic *fiqh*.

References

Al-cĀmilī Z al-D al-J (2008) (Translated into Persian by Luṭfī A) Tarjumih-i Mabāḥis̱-i Ḥuqūqī-i Sharḥ-i Lumcih [Translation of the Legal Part of the *Sharḥ al-Lumca*], 5th edn. Majmac-i cIlmī va Farhangī-i Majd, Tehran.

Al-Dasūqī MIAIcA et al (1980) Ḥāshiyat al-Dasūqī calā al-Sharḥ al-Kabīr [Al-Dasūqī's Commentary on the *Sharḥ al-Kabīr*], vol III. Dār Iḥyā' al-Kutub al-cArabiyya, Cairo.

Al-Ittiḥād al-Nisā'ī al-Baḥraynī (2009) Al-Mar'a al-Baḥrayniyya fī al-Maḥākim al-Sharciyya [Bahraini Women in the Sharia Family Courts]. Mu'assasat al-Ayyām li-l-Nashr (n.p.).

Al-Khumaynī R Al-M (n.d.) Risālih-i Tawżīḥ al-Masā'il [A Clarification of Questions]. Kitābfurūshī-i Islāmiyyih, Tehran.

Al-Marghīnānī B al-D al-F (n.d.) Al-Hidāya maca Takmilat Sharḥ Fatḥ al-Qadīr [The *Hidāya* (Guide) with Commentary], vol VIII (n.p.).

cAllāmih-Ḥā'irī cA (2001) Izdivāj-i Muvaqqat dar Ḥuqūq-i Īrān [Temporary Marriage in Iran]. Intishārāt-i Khāqānī, Tehran.

Altorki S (1980) Milk-Kinship in Arab Society: An Unexplored Problem in the Ethnography of Marriage. Ethnology 19:233–244.

cĀmirī P, Yāsīnī Niyā H (2016/2017) Naqsh-i Dalāyil-i Zhintīkī dar Dacāvī-i Is̱bāt-i Nasab [The Role of Genetic Evidence in Filiation Disputes]. Fiqh va Ḥuqūq-i Khānivādih 65:55–82.

Anṣārī Q (n.d.) Aḥkām va Ḥuqūq-i Kūdakān dar Islām [Child Law in Islam], vol I. Markaz-i Fiqhī A'immih Iṭhār. www.markazfeqhi.com/main/books/5906-9. Accessed August 23, 2016.

Ansari-Pour MA (2001) The Legal Relationship of a Father with his Illegitimate Child under Islamic and Iranian Law. YIMEL (1999–2000) 6:140–155.

cAẓīmzādih Ardibīlī F, Ṭūqānīpūr F (2011) Ḥuqūq-i Khānivādigī-i Kūdakān khārij az Nikāḥ bā Muṭālicih-i Taṭbīqī [The Legal Status of Children Born out of Wedlock]. http://familylawandjurisprudence.isuw.ac.ir/article_1754_0.html. Accessed August 23, 2016.

Bakhtiar L (1996) Encyclopedia of Islamic Law – A Compendium of the Views of the Major Schools. ABC International Group, Chicago.

Bāqirī A, Āyatullāh Shīrāzī R (2015) Bāzpazhūhī-i Qācidih-yi Firāsh bā Rūykardī Intiqādī bih Ravishhā-yi Nuvīn-i Is̱bāt-i Nasab [Research on the Principle of *firāsh* with a Critical View on Modern Methods to Establish Filiation]. Faṣlnāmih-i Qażāvat 82:79–95.

Bāzgīr Y (1997) cIlal-i Naqż-i Ārā'-i Maḥākim dar Mawżūcāt-i Aḥvāl-i Shakhṣiyyih va Madanī dar Dīvān-i cĀlī-i Kishvar [Reasons for the Reversal of Judgments Regarding Personal and Civil Status by the Supreme Court]. Intishārāt-i Qaqnūs, Tehran.

Bāzgīr Y (1999) Ārā'-i Dīvān-i cĀlī-i Kishvar dar Umūr-i Ḥuqūqī [Judicature of the Supreme Court in Civil Law Matters], vol III. Intishārāt-i Qaqnūs, Tehran.

Beevers K, Ebrahimi SN (2002) Iranian Child Protection Law – Towards a Concept of Adoption. IFL, pp 166–177.

Clarke M (2009) Islam and New Kinship – Reproductive Technology and the Shariah in Lebanon. Berghahn Books, New York and Oxford.

Fortier C (2007) Blood, Sperm and the Embryo in Sunni Islam and in Mauritania: Milk Kinship, Descent and Medically Assisted Procreation. Body & Society 13(3):15–36.
Gilson Miller S (2006) Sleeping Fetus. In: Joseph S (ed) Encyclopedia of Women & Islamic Cultures: Family, Body, Sexuality and Health, vol III. Brill, Leiden and Boston, pp 421–424.
Haeri S (1989) Law of Desire – Temporary Marriage in Shi'i Iran. Syracuse University Press, Syracuse.
Hamoudi HA (2016) Resurrecting Islam or Cementing Social Hierarchy? Reexamining the Codification of 'Islamic' Personal Status Law. Arizona Journal of International and Comparative Law 33(2):329–382. http://ssrn.com/abstract=2603811. Accessed August 23, 2016.
Imāmī SḤ (2005) Ḥuqūq-i Madanī [Civil Law], vol IV, 18th edn. Intishārāt-i Islāmiyyih, Tehran.
Kamalipour Ravari E, Taram M (2016) Comparative Study of Duress in Certain Religious Penalties in Imami Jurisprudence and Islamic Penal Code. Journal of Politics and Law 9(5):88–94.
Karīmī ᶜA (2015) Āyā Istinād bih DNA barā-yi Inkār-i Farzand Muvajjih Ast? [Are DNA Tests Acceptable for the Denial of Filiation?]. Rūznāmih-i Īrān (Iranian newspaper), September 5, 2015. www.magiran.com/npview.asp?ID=3221876. Accessed October 10, 2018.
Kātūziyān N (1999) Ḥuqūq-i Madanī, Khānivādih [Family Law], vol I and II, 5th edn. Shirkat-i Sihāmī-i Intishār, Tehran.
Kātūziyān N (2006) Is̱bāt va Dalīl-i Is̱bāt [Law of Evidence], vol I, 4th edn. Nashr-i Mīzān, Tehran.
Khan MM (2010) Encyclopaedia of Islamic Law and Jurisprudence: Islamic Law and Family, vol IV. Discovery Publishing House, New Delhi.
Kohlberg E (1985) The Position of the *walad zinā* in Imāmī Shī'ism. BSOAS 48(2):237–266.
Kohler C (1976) Das Vaterschaftsanerkenntnis im Islamrecht und seine Bedeutung für das deutsche internationale Privatrecht. Schöningh, Paderborn.
Madanī Kirmānī ᶜĀ (2002) Daᶜāvī-i Khānivādigī [Family Law Litigation], 2nd edn. Majmaᶜ-i ᶜIlmī va Farhangī-i Majd, Tehran.
Maghniyyih MJ (2001) (Translated into Persian by Jabbārī M, Sarā'ī ḤM) Aḥvāl-i Shakhṣiyyih – Juz'-i Duvum-i al-Fiqh ᶜalā al-Madhāhib al-Khamsa [Personal Status – Part Two of the *Fiqh* According to the Five Schools of Law]. Intishārāt-i Qaqnūs, Tehran.
Mahmoud F (2012) Controversies in Islamic Evaluation of Assisted Reproductive Technologies. In: Inhorn MC, Tremayne S (eds) Islam and Assisted Reproductive Technologies – Sunni and Shia Perspectives. Berghahn Books, New York and Oxford, pp 70–97.
Muḥaqqiq Dāmād SM (2002) Barrisī-i Fiqhī-i Ḥuqūq-i Khānivādih [Studies of Islamic Family Law], 9th edn. Markaz-i Nashr-i ᶜUlūm-i Islāmī, Tehran.
Naẓarī Tavakkulī S (2012) Ḥiżānat-i Kūdakān dar Fiqh-i Islāmī [Custody in Islamic Fiqh], 2nd edn. Sāzmān-i Muṭālaᶜih va Tadvīn-i Kutub-i ᶜUlūm-i Insānī Dānishgāhhā, Tehran.
Pīlih A et al (2013) Barrisī-i Ḥujiyyat-i Āzmāyish-i DNA dar Nafy-i Nasab [DNA Tests as a Means to Deny Filiation]. Majallih-i ᶜIlmī-Pazhūhishī-i Ḥuqūq-i Khuṣūṣī 1:139–158.
Rajabī M, Muḥammadiyān D (2002) Izdivāj-i Muvaqqat va Daghdaghihhā-i Zanān [Temporary Marriage and Troubles Caused to Women]. Ḥuqūq-i Zanān 22:5–9.
Sādāt ṭabā'ī M (2012) Naqsh-i Āzmāyishhā-yi DNA dar Is̱bāt-i Nasab [The Role of DNA Screening in Establishing Filiation]. Dū Faṣl-Nāmih-i Fiqh va Ḥuqūq-i Khānivādih 56:49–74.
Ṣafā'ī SḤ, Imāmī A (2011) Ḥuqūq-i Khānivādih [Family Law], vol II, 5th edn. Intishārāt-i Dānishgāh-i Tihrān, Tehran.
Schacht J (2012) Liᶜān. In: Bearman P et al (eds) Encyclopaedia of Islam, 2nd edn. http://dx.doi.org/10.1163/1573-3912_islam_SIM_4665. Accessed June 15, 2018.
Shabana A (2014) Islamic Law of Paternity Between Classical Legal Texts and Modern Contexts: From Physiognomy to DNA Analysis. Journal of Islamic Studies 25(1):1–32.
Sharīᶜatī Nasab Ṣ (2011) Farzand-Khāndigī [Adoption]. Mu'assasih-i Muṭālaᶜāt va Pažūhishhāy-i Ḥuqūqī-i Shahr-i Dānish (S.D.I.L.), Tehran.
Shīravī ᶜA (2016) Ḥuqūq-i Khānivādih [Family Law]. Sāzmān-i Muṭālaᶜih va Tadvīn-i Kutub-i ᶜUlūm-i Insānī Dānishgāhhā, Tehran.

Tavasulī Nā'īnī M (2010) Farzand-Khāndigī dar Kunvānsiyyūn-i Ḥuqūq-i Kūdak 1989 va Muqāyisih-i ān bā Ḥuqūq-i Īrān [Adoption in the CRC 1989 as Compared to Iranian Law]. Faṣlnāmih-i Ḥuqūq 39(4):89–109.
Yassari N (2015) Adding by Choice: Adoption and Functional Equivalents in Islamic and Middle Eastern Law. The American Journal of Comparative Law 63:927–962.
Yassari N et al (2017) Synopsis. In: Yassari N et al (eds) Parental Care and the Best Interests of the Child in Muslim Countries. T.M.C. Asser Press, The Hague, pp 325–353.
Yazbak M (2001) Muslim Orphans and the *Sharīʿa* in Ottoman Palestine According to *Sijill* Records. JESHO 44(2):123–140.
Yazdānī Pūr N et al (2015/2016) Barrisī va Taḥlīl-i Fiqhī-Ḥuqūqī-i Ḥujiyyat-i Āzmāyish-i DNA dar Is̱bāt-i Nasab [Legal Study and Analysis of DNA Tests as Evidence for the Proof of Filiation]. Mabānī-i Fiqhī-i Ḥuqūq-i Islāmī 16:85–98.

Nadjma Yassari is a senior research fellow at the Max Planck Institute for Comparative and International Private Law in Hamburg, Germany, where she heads the Department for the Laws of Islamic Countries. Since April 2009, she has led the Research Group "Changes in God's Law – An Inner Islamic Comparison of Family and Succession Laws." Her main fields of research are national and private international law of Islamic countries, particularly the Arab Middle East, Iran, Afghanistan and Pakistan, with a special focus on family and successions law. In her monograph *Die Brautgabe im Familienvermögensrecht – Innerislamischer Rechtsvergleich und Integration in das deutsche Recht* (Mohr Siebeck, 2014), she considers the function of the dower within the marital property law regimes of pre-modern Islamic law, contemporary Muslim jurisdictions and German law. Born on March 6, 1971 in Tehran, Iran, she studied law in Vienna, Paris and London. She holds an LL.M. from the School of Oriental and African Studies at the University of London and an LL.D. from the University of Innsbruck in Austria. In 2000/2001, she spent a year at the faculty of languages of the University of Damascus in Syria. In 2016, she was awarded a post-doctoral degree (Habilitation) from the University of Hamburg.

Chapter 5
Iraq

Harith Al-Dabbagh

Contents

Abstract The Iraqi legal corpus on filiation consists of a set of rules that are a mix of traditional law and modern law. Inspired by Islamic law in general, the Personal Status Code of 1959 expressly recognizes two grounds for establishing filiation, namely valid marriage (*firash*) and acknowledgment of filiation (*iqrar*). The Code of Evidence of 1979 is more modern, allowing the court to expand its investigations

Harith Al-Dabbagh is an associate professor of comparative and private international law at the University of Montreal in Canada.

H. Al-Dabbagh (✉)
Faculty of Law, University of Montreal, P.O. Box 6128, Montreal
QC H3C 3J7, Canada
e-mail: harith.al-dabbagh@umontreal.ca
URL: https://aldabbagh.openum.ca

N. Yassari et al. (eds.), *Filiation and the Protection of Parentless Children*, https://doi.org/10.1007/978-94-6265-311-5_5

by resorting to DNA tests and testimony (*bayyina*). In this respect, the lenient conditions under which case law admits the existence of a valid marriage significantly facilitate the establishment of filiation. The child who does not enjoy legal filiation under the conditions mentioned previously, designated as *majhul al-nasab*, is nonetheless entitled to a certain degree of protection with regard to civil status and nationality. Furthermore, the Iraqi legislature has created an institution called affiliation (*damm*), which allows an orphan or a child of unknown filiation to be linked to a family in a definitive manner, even though adoption is formally prohibited. This institution can create a filiation link that is similar to that which results from an adoption, and can therefore be considered a true functional equivalent of adoption.

Keywords Iraq · Legitimate filiation (*nasab*) · Foundling (*laqit*) · Child of unknown filiation (*majhul al-nasab*) · DNA test · Adoption (*tabanni*) · Affiliation (*damm*)

5.1 Introduction

Being fragile and vulnerable, a child is in need of protection, attention and affection. For their harmonious development, children should grow up in a family environment, in an atmosphere of happiness, love and understanding.[1] This environment is usually secured within the child's biological family. However, children can be left without family care in various situations; this is the case for orphaned children and for those who are deprived or abandoned, as well as for children of unknown filiation. Providing a home for these children seems to have been a major concern of humanity throughout history.[2] Nowadays, children's protection has become a key challenge for national policies, and states feel compelled to provide parentless children with alternative forms of care.

In international law, it is acknowledged that children deprived of family care are entitled to some alternative form of protection. Article 20 of the UN Convention on the Rights of the Child recognizes four alternative modes of protection: placement in a foster family, *kafala* of Islamic law, adoption or, if necessary, placement in an appropriate public institution. When the family environment is not able, or is no longer able, to ensure adequate care of the child or when the child is considered abandoned, such care can be public (placement in a foster family or in an institution) or private by nature (care by close relatives).

In Iraq, which is the scene of many armed conflicts, thousands of children are growing up without one or both of their parents. In the past quarter of a century, the country has experienced three major wars and twelve years of economic embargo,

---

[1] Preamble of the Hague Convention of 29 May 1993 on Protection of Children and Co-operation in Respect of Intercountry Adoption. Full text available at www.hcch.net/en/instruments/conventions/full-text/?cid=69 (accessed February 5, 2019).

[2] See Ancel and Molines 1980, passim.

leaving a serious aftermath in their wake. With half of Iraq's population under the age of 18, children have been hit the hardest by violence, insecurity and the devastation of the country's economic and social infrastructure.[3] An estimated two and a half million children are orphaned, abandoned or living in deprivation.[4] Worse yet, the recent war against the Islamic State group (Daesh) has resulted in approximately two and a half million internally displaced people (IDP), 30% of whom are children,[5] in addition to the children born from rape and forced marriages with terrorist group combatants.[6] The number of abandoned children is continually growing.[7] Without parental care, these children are exposed to discrimination, abuse and exploitation.

This context raises the urgent issue of children whose filiation is not known or is not established. It is therefore important to evaluate the effectiveness of the alternative care systems in place in the context of the current crisis. What is the fate of these children in the Iraqi legal system? What are the measures taken to guarantee their protection? In order to grasp this complex issue, it is essential first to examine the very concept of filiation in Iraqi law, which is largely inspired by Islamic law. In this respect, the Iraqi family model remains, like in Islamic societies in general, that of the patriarchal family based on marriage. The establishment of filiation usually takes place in the context of marriage. Children born outside of marriage cannot establish their paternal filiation (*nasab*) a priori, and thus cannot benefit from the consequences of *nasab* in terms of care, maintenance or inheritance, which places them in a precarious situation that adds to their social stigmatization. Furthermore, the Islamic prohibition of adoption is often seen as aggravating the unfavorable status of illegitimate children.[8] However, such a picture results from a literal and theoretical reading of the law and deserves to be presented in greater nuance, especially in the light of the evolution of the Iraqi legal system in recent decades. Without formally breaking with its Islamic conception, Iraqi law on filiation has experienced significant mutations. Torn between deference to religious teachings and aspirations of modernity, the Iraqi legislature has adopted a pragmatic approach that reflects this ambivalence. Furthermore, a careful reading of the case law reveals an evolution towards a liberal system of filiation.

---

[3] Combined second to fourth periodic reports of States parties due in 2011, submitted by Iraq to the Committee on the Rights of the Child, December 2, 2013, doc. CRC/C/IRQ/2-4, para 58.

[4] According to statistics from the Ministry of Planning and Cooperation in 2016, reported by Radio Rudaw, www.rudaw.net/arabic/middleeast/iraq/270720166 (accessed February 5, 2019).

[5] Draft Statement of H. E. Minister of Human Rights to discuss the Child's Reports in Geneva (Iraq), http://tbinternet.ohchr.org/Treaties/CRC/Shared%20Documents/IRQ/INT_CRC_STA_IRQ_19299_E.pdf (accessed February 5, 2019).

[6] Concluding observations on the combined second to fourth periodic reports of Iraq, March 3, 2015, doc. CRC/C/IRQ/CO/2-4, para 52.

[7] Local media often report children or newborns found in public places, on sidewalks or in front of mosques. See, for the case of an infant girl abandoned in a vacant lot, www.hjc.iq/view.4030/ (accessed February 5, 2019).

[8] Such a presentation is quite common in foreign-language (English and French) works on Islamic law. See, for example, Abu-Sahlieh 2008, esp. pp 178 et seq.

5.2 Sources of Law

5.2.1 Written Sources

At the inception of modern Iraq in 1921, following the dissolution of the Ottoman Empire, the status of Iraqi children was unclear and ill-defined. Falling under personal status matters, children's legal status was typically governed by Sharia according to the interpretations of Sunni and Shiite schools. Non-Muslim Iraqis were, similarly, governed by their respective religious laws in matters of personal status.[9]

In the aftermath of the country's independence in 1932, at the end of the British mandate, Iraq had a pressing need for legislative unity. The legal uncertainty caused by the lack of official codification and the recourse to medieval *fiqh* treaties and *fatwas* had to be addressed. The heterogeneity of sources of law gave rise to divergent judgments on similar issues. This resulted in instability in family status, and the first victims of this instability were women and children.[10]

However, it was not until the 1958 coup d'état and the end of the monarchy that the religious authorities' reluctance to undertake state codification was overcome. The unification of laws and the establishment of a stable society in its rights and duties was among the objectives of the Revolution,[11] and the country could no longer maintain the fragmentation of the law applicable to family and inheritance matters. The Personal Status Code (PSC) was finally promulgated, and entered into force on the day of its publication in the Official Gazette, December 30, 1959.[12] The Code, which was rather concise,[13] drew its sources from the generally accepted Islamic prescriptions, without following one specific school or doctrine. It also made reference to the legislation of Muslim countries and to consistent Iraqi case law.[14] Article 1 of the Code is quite indicative of this eclecticism, stating that in the absence of a written provision of the law, the judge will rule 'according to the

[9] This statutory pluralism reflects the well-known tradition of the personality of the laws that goes back to the founding of the Islamic city.

[10] See the Explanatory Memorandum (*al-asbab al-mujiba*) annexed to Personal Status Code No. 188-1959.

[11] Explanatory Memorandum of the Personal Status Code, para 1. The objective was to put an end to the existence of separate Sunni and Shiite courts applying distinct rules.

[12] On the process of elaboration of the Code, see Al-Dabbagh 2007, pp 1510–1511; Anderson 1960, pp 542 et seq.

[13] The Code contains ninety-four articles. Its relative brevity, in comparison with the previous 1947 draft (177 Articles), is justified by the following remark in the Explanatory Memorandum: 'The committee has tried to bring together in this Code the most important general principles governing personal status, leaving it up to the judge to refer to the Sharia treatises in order to extract the specific rules that are the most compatible with the provisions of this law, since the committee found it impossible to integrate into this corpus all issues of personal status.'

[14] This is the selection method known as *talfiq*, which consists in creating a kind of synthesis of various solutions. On this technique, Sourdel 1997, p 48.

principles of Islamic Sharia that are most appropriate to the provisions of this Code,' without being confined to a predetermined school or doctrine.

Along with this synthetic approach, the Personal Status Code of 1959 governs all Muslim Iraqis, whether Sunni or Shiite.[15] For the first time, the Iraqi courts have had a *corpus juris* allowing them to standardize solutions in a field that had previously given rise to significantly divergent interpretations. This unification is, however, partial, as it does not include non-Muslim communities. Yet the Personal Status Code remains the ordinary law and would therefore be called upon to fill the lacunae in any of the non-Islamic derogatory laws.[16]

The rules regarding filiation are set out in Articles 51–54 of the Personal Status Code. Many modern laws have been enacted since, and have contributed to better defining children's status and improving their protection. In the wake of the socialist reforms of the 1970s–1980s,[17] two important laws related to childhood were promulgated: the first, the Care of Minors Act No. 78-1980 (*qanun ri'ayat al-qasirin*), is a civil law regulating the guardianship and management of the property of minor children,[18] whereas the second, the Juvenile Protection Act No. 76-1983 (*qanun ri'ayat al-ahdath*), is rather of a criminal nature and addresses the situation of delinquent children by establishing preventive and curative mechanisms, especially specialized institutions for minors. In addition, the Civil Status Act No. 65-1972 contains specific regulations concerning the status of the abandoned newborn child (*laqit*) and the child of unknown filiation (*majhul al-nasab*).[19] The latter, as well as all children deprived of parental care (orphans, indigents, homeless children, etc.), are eligible for social assistance and placement in state children's homes, which were instituted by the Social Welfare Act No. 126-1980.[20] Other rules concerning the child can also be found in a variety of laws such as the Civil Code, the Labor Code, the Public Education Act and the Criminal Code.[21]

In short, child-related provisions in Iraq are scattered among various laws, depending on their nature. Promulgated at different times, these laws reflect a variety

[15] The desire to restore Shiite personal status reappeared after the US invasion in 2003. A draft law on Ja'fari (Shiite) personal status was written in 2011, but remained unsuccessful.

[16] There are seventeen non-Islamic religious communities officially recognized in Iraq, and thus theoretically seventeen confessional sets of laws that are applicable in the field of personal status. For further details, see Al-Dabbagh 2013–2014, pp 319 et seq.

[17] This set of reforms was triggered by Law No. 35-1977 on the Reform of the Legal System, which is a framework law aimed at laying down guidelines for reforming the legal system in a way that is consistent with the building of a modern socialist state.

[18] The law introduces significant restrictions on the powers of guardians and imposes a supervisory regime to protect the rights of protected persons (minors, incapable adults, absent and missing persons).

[19] Articles 32–33 of Civil Status Act No. 65-1972 and Articles 25–29 of its Implementing Decree No. 32-1974 (*nizam*).

[20] Articles 29–41 of Social Welfare Act No. 126-1980.

[21] For example, Articles 381–388 of Criminal Code No. 111-1969 deal with crimes relating to filiation, the protection of minors, family abandonment and the endangerment of children and the elderly.

of concerns, and therefore need to be harmonized and interpreted in a way that prevents contradictions and guarantees optimal child protection, which is a constitutional objective.[22] From this point of view, the law governing children in Iraq can be qualified as mixed or hybrid law, given its multiplicity of sources of inspiration and guidance. Whereas the Personal Status Code – which mainly regulates, with regard to children, matters related to birth, filiation, custody, breastfeeding, child maintenance and inheritance – remains largely dependent on religious principles, the other legal provisions of an economic, social or criminal nature are more modern and are in many cases inspired by Western, particularly French, laws.[23]

5.2.2 Case Law

The organization and functioning of courts in Iraq is largely inspired by the French model. Litigation between individuals is brought before the ordinary courts, with the Court of Cassation as the highest instance. The mission of the Court of Cassation is to ensure that legal rules have been correctly interpreted and applied by the trial judge; it thus contributes to the harmonization of case law throughout the country.[24]

From this perspective, Iraqi law falls within the civil law family. It is a written law, which is codified and is therefore characterized by the absence of the key common-law concept of 'judicial precedent.' The role of the courts is to apply the rules of law, interpret them and supplement them as needed. The courts are not bound by prior rulings, and the effect of a judgment is limited to the case that has been ruled on, without influencing future litigation. However, Court of Cassation decisions that establish a long-term solution have strong persuasive value in similar cases; the matter is then referred to as consistent case law, *qada' mustaqirr*.[25] Such consistent case law is of great importance in the field of the law of filiation, given the concise nature of the Personal Status Code. Thus, in the absence of applicable legal provisions, judges are required to refer to the body of Sharia by choosing the prescriptions that fit the provisions of the Code the best.[26] Guided by established case law, they are generally inclined to look for solutions that fit the best interests of

---

[22] Article 29(1) of the 2005 Constitution states that 'the State shall guarantee the protection of motherhood, childhood and old age, shall care for children and youth, and shall provide them with the appropriate conditions to develop their talents and abilities.'

[23] For more details, see Al Dabbagh 2005, pp 265 et seq.

[24] With the exception of the Kurdistan region, which has had its own Court of Cassation with similar functions since 2007.

[25] See, for example, for a statement of reasons referring to 'constant case law:' Court of Cassation, December 13, 1987, case no. 573/civ./1987, www.hjc.iq/qview.10/ (accessed February 27, 2019).

[26] Article 1(2) PSC. The whole of Islamic law, and not a determined school, thus constitutes the common pool from which it is necessary to draw where there are gaps. This can be seen as a sign of the legislature's desire to free the judge from the yoke of rites (*madhahib*).

the child and the needs of society. Moreover, Article 3 of the 1979 Code of Evidence calls upon the courts 'to follow the dynamic interpretation (*al-tafsir al-mutatawwir*) of the law and adhere to the spirit of the law when applying it.' On the basis of these interpretative guidelines, Iraqi courts have been able to play a crucial role in filling the gaps left by the legislature.

With regard to the child, two courts deserve special attention, namely the personal status courts (specialized in family matters) and the criminal courts for children (juvenile courts). The personal status court settles disputes involving at least one Muslim person, and rules on all matters relating to the parent-child relationship: filiation, guardianship, custody, maintenance, breastfeeding, etc. It is composed of a single judge, who is necessarily Muslim,[27] and it applies the Personal Status Code of 1959. Disputes between non-Muslim parties are brought before the personal matters court, which is to rule according to the law of the religious community to which the persons concerned belong. In order to take judicial notice of the applicable law, the personal matters court usually calls upon the relevant religious authorities through a process called referral (*ihala*). The juvenile courts deal with misconduct by minor children. The preliminary investigation is entrusted to a juvenile investigative judge.[28] A juvenile trial judge then orders the appropriate measures.[29] The coexistence of these modern courts with the personal status courts applying religious laws is a specific feature of the Iraqi judicial system. However, although the personal status judge is necessarily Muslim as indicated above, he is no longer a cleric trained in a Sharia school. The personal status courts are indeed now composed of professional judges trained in law schools, and are organized in the same way as civil courts.[30]

5.3 Establishment of Filiation (*nasab*)

Filiation is generally defined as the kinship between the child and his or her father (paternal filiation) or mother (maternal filiation).[31] However, in Islamic literature, the term *nasab* usually refers to paternal or agnatic filiation: in a patrilineal society, it is paternal filiation that gives the child an identity and a status.[32] Paternal filiation

---

[27] Article 28 Code of Judicial Organization No. 160-1979 (COJ). The personal status court is the only court in the country where such a condition is required.

[28] Article 49 Juvenile Protection Act No. 76-1983.

[29] Article 33 COJ.

[30] Article 36 COJ prohibits the recruitment of judges or public prosecutors who did not graduate from the Judicial Institute.

[31] Filiation 2007.

[32] Qur'an Sura 25, verse 54: 'It is He Who has created man from water: then has He established relationships of lineage and marriage: for thy Lord has power (over all things).' (The Holy Qur-ān: English translation of the meanings and Commentary (1990) (Translated by Ali Y) King Fahd Holy Qur-ān Printing Complex, Medina).

entails multiple legal consequences both patrimonial (maintenance obligation, inheritance rights) and extra-patrimonial (transmission of the surname, guardianship rights and obligations). Maternal filiation is considered less important and is barely addressed by Islamic jurists (*fuqaha'*), with the child being related to his or her mother through the tangible evidence of the pregnancy and the child's birth.

Paternal filiation (*nasab*) is regulated by Articles 51–54 of the Personal Status Code as one of the 'consequences of birth.' According to these provisions, the establishment of filiation takes place under a legal presumption established either by the law or by a voluntary recognition of filiation, referred to as acknowledgment (*iqrar*).

5.3.1 Legal Presumption of Paternity

The model of filiation set up by the Personal Status Code tends to protect agnatic filiation and to prevent its loss or confusion, which is a priority of family legislation in Islam.[33] While the relationship between the child and his or her mother is established by the mere fact of childbirth, the relationship between the child and his or her father (*a patre* filiation, or *nasab* in the Islamic meaning) is in principle established only if the filiation results from marriage. In this regard, Article 51 of the PSC reflects the well-known Islamic principle of *al-walad li-l-firash* (the child belongs to the marital bed). Accordingly, a child born to a married woman will be linked to this woman's husband. This legal presumption of paternity is based on two conditions stated in the same article: first, that the child's birth occurred within a certain timeframe in accordance with the legal period of conception based on the duration of pregnancy; second, that the physical meeting (*talaqi*) of the spouses was possible at the time of conception.

The Code did not fix the duration of pregnancy. All *fiqh* schools generally accept the minimum duration of six months.[34] A child born six months after the date of the marriage therefore has filiation established with his or her mother's husband.[35] The maximum duration of pregnancy varies among the *fiqh* schools: it ranges from nine months to one year among the Ja'faris,[36] and is extended to two years according to the Hanafis.[37] The practice of Iraqi courts goes in the latter direction. Today, this lengthy duration is widely discussed in the scholarship: while recognizing that the objective of the rule is to provide the child with legal filiation, contemporary Iraqi

[33] Khallaf 1990, p 176.

[34] This unanimity results from the combination of two verses in the Qur'an (Sura 46, verse 15 and Sura 31, verse 14). Linant de Bellefonds 1973, p 34.

[35] Court of Cassation, September 11, 1971, appeal no. 261/plen. ass./1971, Al-Nashra al-Qada'iyya no. 3 of 1971, p 72.

[36] Mughaniyya 1998, p 363.

[37] Article 332 Qadri Pasha Code (unofficial codification of Muslim law on family and inheritance according to the Hanafi school, written by Muhammad Qadri Pasha in Egypt in 1875).

authors advocate a maximum duration of one year, based on more reasonable scientific data.[38]

Iraqi courts have adopted a lenient and liberal application of the aforementioned rules. In order to locate the birth of the child within the minimum and maximum durations of pregnancy, the Council of State, which is the supreme court of the administrative judicial order, has decided that courts should take into account the date when the marriage occurred according to the rules of Sharia and not the date when the marriage was officially registered.[39] It follows that a child born from an unregistered marriage[40] – a customary, religious or private marriage – is deemed to be a legitimate child conceived in the marital bed if the parents acknowledge that they were married at least six months before the birth, regardless of the date of the marriage's registration. Thus, the filiation of a child born in 1984 was established in a case where his parents' marriage was only registered in 2014: after having noted that the couple was married in Iran in 1982, the Court found that the child had been conceived in the marital bed.[41] Knowing that marriage in Islamic law is a mere civil contract with minimal formal requirements,[42] it is possible to measure the wide scope of such a solution. It is sufficient for the father and mother of the child to state that they were married on a specific date, and to let the legal presumption operate.

As for the second condition, it refers to the material possibility of conception. The presumption of paternity cannot operate if conception was impossible because of the husband's absence, his impotence, or the non-consummation of the marriage. This is the case when it is established that the mother did not cohabitate with her husband and had not met with him since the marriage. However, it is important to emphasize that such a condition does not imply effective cohabitation, but the mere possibility of having intercourse (*imkaniyyat al-dukhul*), or the lack of obstacles to such intercourse. In other words, for the presumption of paternity to operate, it must not be ascertained that intercourse was impossible between the spouses.[43]

The presumption of paternity does not only function within a valid marriage. It also operates in invalid marriages (*zawaj fasid*[44]) and in marital relationships by

[38] Al-Khatib et al. 1980, p 201.

[39] Opinion of the Council of State, June 5, 1961, no. 85/8, Majallat Diwan al-Tadwin al-Qanuni no. 1 of 1961, p 40.

[40] Article 10 PSC requires, under criminal penalty, the registration of marriages in a special register kept by the personal status court. However, Article 11 of the same Code allows for the marriage that has not abided by the legally required forms to be proven by acknowledgment (*iqrar*) made by one of the spouses with the consent of the other.

[41] Federal Court of Appeal of Dhi Qar, January 8, 2015, appeal no. 3/perso/2015, http://iraqld.hjc.iq/ (accessed February 27, 2019).

[42] In Islam, marriage is a consensual and private contract concluded by the consent of the parties in the presence of two witnesses. Linant de Bellefonds 1965, pp 39 et seq.

[43] Al-Khatib et al. 1980, p 203.

[44] In contrast with the Hanafi *fiqh*, the Iraqi Personal Status Code makes no distinction between a void marriage (*zawaj batil*) and a defective marriage (*zawaj fasid*). The two terms are therefore synonymous and refer to marriages in which one of the conditions for validity is absent (Article 6 PSC).

mistake (*wat' bi-shubha*). The Court of Cassation has ruled that, when the remarriage of a woman who was still married to her missing first husband is declared null and void, the filiation to the second husband of the child born out of the annulled second marriage remains established, by *shubha*.[45] In such cases, the six-month period begins from the time of consummation, since the origin of filiation is not the marriage contract (annulled), but the fact of coitus.[46]

5.3.2 Acknowledgment

Children who have not been able to benefit from the presumption of paternity can still access filiation through the mechanism of acknowledgment, in accordance with the Islamic tradition allowing the establishment of filiation through the *iqrar bi-l-nasab*, also called *istilhaq*. A person – man or woman – can recognize a child as his or her own. Articles 52–54 of the PSC regulate the different types of acknowledgment allowed by the *fiqh*.

Iqrar consists of a declaration, made before a judge, by which an individual acknowledges a child of unknown descent to be his child. Article 52 of the PSC makes it possible to recognize the filiation of a child of unknown filiation, provided that there is a sufficient age difference between the acknowledger and the acknowledged child, making filiation possible. If the child to be acknowledged has already reached the age of discernment, that is, seven years old,[47] the commentators consider his or her consent to be required[48] although the law is silent on this matter. Finally, the courts do not require that acknowledgment has to be made in a particular form. In a case in which the defendant did not oppose the action brought by the plaintiff to claim alimony (*nafaqa*) for her and her daughter, the Court of Cassation granted the claim by considering the defendant to have acknowledged both the marital relationship and the daughter's paternity.[49] When validly done, acknowledgment establishes filiation with respect to the acknowledger since the birth of the child. The child acquires the quality of a legitimate child with all the consequences resulting from *nasab*. Acknowledgment may even occur, according to Article 52(1) of the PSC, during the final illness preceding the death of the acknowledger (*marad al-mawt*).

A woman can acknowledge a child under the same conditions. However, Article 52(2) states that if the acknowledgment is made by a married woman, its effects are limited to the acknowledging woman and her lineage, and do not extend to her

---

[45] Court of Cassation, February 23, 2010, appeal no. 22/enlarged chamber/2010, www.hjc.iq/qview.1649/ (accessed February 27, 2019).

[46] Al-Khatib et al. 1980, p 202.

[47] Article 97(2) Civil Code.

[48] Al-Khatib et al. 1980, p 204.

[49] Court of Cassation, July 20, 2009, appeal no. 2979/perso/2009, cited by Alwan 2011, pp 38–39.

husband, unless the husband consents or there is complete testimonial evidence (*bayyina*).[50]

Finally, according to Article 53 of the PSC, the acknowledger may be the child himself or herself, attesting that such a man is his or her father or that such a woman is his or her mother. The validity of such acknowledgment is subject to three conditions: the filiation of the child must be unknown; the parent concerned must consent to this acknowledgment; and the age difference with the child must make paternity or maternity plausible. In such circumstances, as the child is most often not registered in the civil registry, a difficulty may arise as to the assessment of the age difference;[51] the courts' practice is usually to refer the child for medical examination to determine his or her approximate age.[52]

It is important to emphasize that filiation is established by *iqrar* regardless of any requirement to prove the existence of a marriage. *Iqrar* is not simply a declarative act for filiation previously established by the legal presumption of paternity, but also an act constitutive of filiation.[53] Iraqi courts do not seem to require it to be established that the birth took place during the marriage. In a case where an Iraqi person admitted to being the father of a child born to a German woman a few months before their marriage, the Council of State considered this acknowledgment to be valid so long as the conditions of Article 52(1) of the PSC had been fulfilled, notwithstanding the birth of the child outside marriage. This acknowledgment implies that the child will enjoy all of the rights of a legitimate child.[54] Similarly, the filiation of the child will be assigned to the acknowledging mother, even though she was neither married nor in the waiting period after a divorce (*'idda*) at the time when the child was born.[55]

This lenient approach is in line with traditional *fiqh*, which teaches that the acknowledgment of paternity by which a man attaches a child to himself is valid without the need to prove the marriage with the mother of the child. The only condition is that the acknowledger refrain from declaring that the child is born from *zina*, or fornication: 'he is being asked, in short, to remain silent on this point.'[56]

---

[50] By the testimony of two men, or one man and two women, attesting to the birth of this child from the union with her husband (the judge, however, having the power to freely asses the probative force of the testimonial evidence).

[51] 'That such a child could be born to such a father,' to quote the exact words of the text.

[52] See, for example, Federal Court of Appeal of Dhi Qar, December 27, 2016, appeal no. 275/perso/2016, http://iraqld.hjc.iq/ (accessed February 27, 2019).

[53] Linant de Bellefonds 1973, p 25, who notes that acknowledgment of filiation 'is not, in Islamic law, simply declarative of right, the husband does not confine himself to confessing the circumstances of the birth, which will, in turn, entail the legal presumption. He assigns to himself the paternity of a child without having to establish the existence of a marriage at the time of the birth, and without even having to prove that this birth is legitimate.'

[54] Opinion of the Council of State, July 6, 1977, no. 83/1977, quoted by Al-Karbasi 1989, pp 104–105.

[55] Article 351 Qadri Pasha Code. In this case, only maternal filiation will be established.

[56] Linant de Bellefonds 1973, p 52.

Thus, theoretically, a man who has never been married (which is rather rare in Muslim countries) may nevertheless acknowledge an individual as his or her legitimate child. However, Iraqi cases on this point are still rare, as this situation is negatively perceived in society. Filiation claims tend to place the birth in the context of a marriage, even if the marriage was later dissolved or annulled. The claimants usually seek to establish, even artificially, the existence of a legitimate relationship in which the conception took place. Thus, where the defendant acknowledges the paternity of the plaintiff's child by admitting that the child was conceived in the marital bed of a customary marriage, the courts tend to establish filiation on the bases of both Article 51 (presumption of paternity) and Article 52 (*iqrar*),[57] while one of the two mechanisms would have been sufficient to achieve the same result.

5.4 Contestation of Filiation

A duly established filiation is sometimes challenged in court. The Personal Status Code contains no provision in this regard. The judge will then have to rule, according to Articles 1–2 of the PSC, by applying the Sharia principles that are more appropriate to the provisions of the Code.

5.4.1 Contestation Through Traditional Means

In classical Islamic law, filiation established in the context of marriage can only be challenged through the formal process of *li'an*. The accusation of a woman's adultery and the subsequent disavowal result from the husband swearing an oath of anathema five times before the judge. The Qur'anic text allows the husband who accuses his wife of adultery (*zina*) and who is not able to produce witnesses of such to swear four times before God that he speaks the truth. The fifth time invokes upon him the curse of God if he has lied.[58] Once the sacramental formula is sworn, the judge has to pronounce the divorce of the spouses and exclude paternal filiation by attaching the child exclusively to the mother.[59] This action must also be taken as soon as possible, either before delivery or at the latest a few days after birth.[60]

Disavowal by *li'an* has in practice been obsolete for centuries. The Iraqi Personal Status Code remains silent on the procedure and no trace of it is found in

[57] See Personal Status Court of al-Kahla' district, June 24, 1992, case no. 71/perso/1992, http://iraqld.hjc.iq/ (accessed February 27, 2019).

[58] Sura 24, verses 6 and 7.

[59] Article 335 Qadri Pasha Code.

[60] Article 336 Qadri Pasha Code.

judicial records. Some authors[61] even consider recourse to *li'an* to be impossible in practice under Iraqi contemporary law since the legislature has not adopted the shariatic conception of the crimes of adultery (*zina*) and false accusation of adultery (*qadhf*).[62] Therefore, it is impossible to inflict the punishment provided by the Qur'an (*hadd al-qadhf*) on the husband who accuses his wife of adultery but refrains from taking the oath of anathema, or to inflict the punishment for adultery (*hadd al-zina*) on the wife who refuses to deny it by contrary oath.

5.4.2 Contestation on the Basis of Genetic Evidence

Although the only means of challenging paternity that is admitted under Islamic law is thus inhibited, it would be wrong, however, to conclude that no challenge of filiation is possible under Iraqi law in its current state. Scientific and technological advances over the past two decades have opened the door to new litigation in filiation. As genetic analysis can prove or deny filiation with a high degree of certainty, parties are increasingly using it as evidence in claims brought before the court to establish or challenge filiation. It is, therefore, necessary to determine the admissibility and probative force of this new evidence. No specific provision of Iraqi law deals with the issue. However, Article 3 of the Code of Evidence No. 107-1979 obliges the judge to follow the dynamic interpretation of the law and to take the spirit of the legislation (*ratio legis*) into account not only when the law is promulgated, but also when it is being implemented. In addition, Article 104 allows the judge to rely on the means provided by scientific progress in order to make judicial presumptions applicable. The personal status judges can thus use scientific evidence to reach their ruling.

In the silence of the law, Iraqi case law has witnessed an uneven development as to the admissibility and probative force of genetic testing regarding filiation. In a first phase, the Court of Cassation decided, in a case in which the defendant (alleged father) denied the filiation claim,[63] that the court could refer the parties to a health facility to perform all the relevant analyses (blood, tissues, etc.) in order to assess the likelihood that the defendant was the plaintiff's father.[64] In this decision, the Court overruled the decision of the first judge, who had rejected the alleged daughter's request for genetic expertise, by considering that in cases relating to *nasab*, judges are obliged to broaden their investigations, in particular by using technical means. Similarly, when a mother summons the brother of her deceased

[61] Al-Salim and al-Nu'aymi 2010, pp 71–72.

[62] Being a modern and secularist code, Iraqi Criminal Code No. 111-1969 completely deviated from the notion of *hudud*, the cornerstone of Islamic criminal law.

[63] As we have observed, when the child makes the *iqrar*, it is valid only with the assent (*tasdiq*) of the person concerned (father or mother).

[64] Court of Cassation, June 9, 1988, appeal no. 4940/perso/1988, www.hjc.iq/qview.52/ (accessed February 27, 2019).

husband in order to have her religious marriage recognized by the court, the court shall, in the absence of the defendant's assent, refer the children to medical expertise to inquire whether the parties share a common ascendant and to consider the result as evidence establishing a marital union. The Court emphasizes that this is 'scientific evidence settling the dispute and guaranteeing the rights of the children as a consequence of the valid marriage,' in accordance with Article 1 of the Code of Evidence, which expands the judge's powers in case management and related evidence.[65]

Such a solution based on scientific evidence does not seem, however, to prevail when the action is aimed at challenging or breaking up filiation that had been previously established and recorded in the official registers. As several authors point out, the Iraqi case law does not take into account the results of genetic analysis in the context of denial of filiation (*nafi al-nasab*).[66] Several judgments have reached this conclusion. In order to preserve vested rights and to ensure stability and legal certainty, the Court of Cassation has considered the register of civil status to be an official register kept by a public officer and, consequently, its content is deemed authentic until a claim of forgery is filed, in accordance with Article 22 of the Code of Evidence. Therefore, the claim that a girl had been falsely declared the daughter of the deceased in the civil register cannot be accepted.[67] Similarly, the child whose filiation has been established by *iqrar* cannot be disavowed later. Thus, a claim by which the father of a girl born from a customary marriage sought to deny paternity of his daughter was rejected on the grounds that he had recognized that the daughter was born from his marital bed during the procedure brought by his wife to request the approval of the marriage.[68] This solution is therefore intended to make filiation unquestionable once established, notwithstanding scientific proof that could establish its lack of conformity to biological truth.

However, more recent decisions of the Court of Cassation seem to indicate an evolution towards the admissibility of such proof. A DNA test was accepted in a case in which the plaintiff claimed to be the biological father of a girl who had been registered under the name of his brother and sister-in-law, a sterile couple, when she was born. The Court of Cassation approved the approach of the judge who, after collecting all the relevant information, referred the parties to a forensic institute, which made a report that revealed corresponding 'genetic profiles' between the claimant and the girl.[69] This judgment seems to indicate that a filiation claim can succeed on the basis of a DNA test supported by testimony, notwithstanding a contrary entry in the official register. Such a solution has been also extended to cases

---

[65] Court of Cassation, April 7, 2016, appeal no. 2316/perso/2016, http://iraqld.hjc.iq/ (accessed February 27, 2019).

[66] Al-Salim and al-Nu'aymi 2010, pp 71–72, who criticize this position.

[67] Court of Cassation, November 11, 2008, appeal no. 1992/perso1/2008, Al-Nashra al-Qada'iyya no. 6 of 2009, pp 10–11.

[68] Personal Status Court of Kadhimiya, March 14, 2006 (unpublished).

[69] Court of Cassation, February 10, 2009, appeal no. 124/plen. ass./2008, Majallat al-Tashri' wa-l-Qada', www.tqmag.net/body.asp?field=news_arabic&id=896 (accessed February 5, 2019).

in which the father whose paternity is being challenged is dead. The Court of Cassation has decided that the use of scientific means of evidence does not contradict Sharia or the law, as long as such means lead to establishing the truth, according to the Qur'anic verse 'Call them by [the names of] their fathers: that is juster in the sight of Allah.'[70] Therefore, the claim for paternity of a girl who had been falsely registered under the name of another man in the civil status registers was deemed admissible.[71] The Court of Cassation appears to have made a reversal by deciding that the principles of legal certainty and the stability of the person's status no longer oppose the rectification of official registers that do not reflect legal and Sharia reality.[72] Therefore, legal reality would clearly correspond to biological reality.

Nevertheless, a recent decision has cast a shadow over this position.[73] In this case, the trial judge had decided to break the filiation relationship between a daughter and her father, a deceased soldier, on the basis of the genetic tests requested by the sisters of the deceased; the enlarged Civil Chamber,[74] ruling following a second cassation appeal, considered this solution to violate a well-established Sharia rule according to which the child belongs to the marital bed (*al-walad li-l-firash*) and which has to be enforced under Article 1 of the Personal Status Code. In fact, the child's mother remained married to the deceased until his death. In this context, the evidence resulting from the genetic analysis would be superfluous and inoperative. The high authority of the Court of Cassation thus ended up making the legal presumption of paternity prevail over scientific evidence.

In short, it can be concluded that proof established by technical means (DNA testing or other means) cannot destroy filiation resulting from the presumption of paternity. The case law is thus reluctant to accept genetic tests that tend to exclude filiation (*nafi al-nasab*). However, it is difficult to determine from reading the judgment whether such reasoning will also prevail when challenging paternity arising from an acknowledgment of filiation (*iqrar*). It must be noted, in this respect, that contestation of filiation is often used for inheritance purposes, particularly by collateral heirs (brothers and sisters of the deceased), to prevent the child from receiving any part in the estate. It is probably to prevent the multiplication of this kind of litigation that the Court of Cassation, after having been extremely open to genetic expertise, now seems to be bending its position in order to prevent a child's vested rights from being permanently challenged after the death of his ascendant.

---

[70] Sura 33, verse 5.

[71] Court of Cassation, June 30, 2011, appeal no. 2901/1st perso/2010, Majallat al-Tashri' wa-l-Qada', www.tqmag.net/body.asp?field=news_arabic&id=1335 (accessed February 5, 2019).

[72] Court of Cassation, May 29, 2011, appeal no. 159/plen. ass./2010, Majallat al-Tashri' wa-l-Qada', www.tqmag.net/body.asp?field=news_arabic&id=1315 (accessed February 5, 2019).

[73] Court of Cassation, February 25, 2013, appeal no. 329/enlarged chamber/2012 (unpublished). The final judgment by the Personal Status Court of al-Adhamiyah issued after cassation is available on the Facebook page https://ar-ar.facebook.com/permalink.php?story_fbid=1621057334792749&id=1492673717631112.

[74] *Al-hay'a al-madaniyya al-muwassa'a*, which corresponds to the mixed chamber in the French system.

5.5 Legal Status of Children Without Filiation

5.5.1 The Notion of 'Children Without Filiation'

The child without filiation is one whose filiation could not be established by any of the means described in Sect. 5.3 above. Islamic jurists have dealt with the situation of the child born of unknown parents under the term *al-laqit*,[75] which refers to a newborn found alive and whose parents' identity is unknown. This is usually a child who has been abandoned shortly after birth due to poverty, or to escape social stigmatization or the accusation of adultery. Abandonment can also occur due to uncontrollable events such as natural disaster or war.[76] Such a child can be discovered by someone on the street or on the doorstep of a mosque or a charitable institution. The *fiqh* teaches that anyone who discovers an abandoned child must take him or her in and offer the necessary help. It is a recommended act (*mandub*), which is transformed into individual duty (*fard 'ayn*) when the child is in conditions where one could fear for his or her life, such as if the child is found hungry, in a desert or on a cold night.[77] The person who has found the child has the right to keep and take care of him[78] or her. As the young child is of unknown filiation, it is in his or her interest to assign filiation to him or her, and the Islamic jurists have always admitted the child's filiative attachment to any person who claims him or her, without further proof.[79] The filiation of the *laqit* is established with respect to the person who claims him or her as soon as this person recognizes the child.[80] The child thus recognized will be treated as a legitimate child of the acknowledger. If many individuals claim paternity, priority will be given to the one who found the child.[81]

The 1959 Personal Status Code is silent on the situation of the *laqit* child and does not even use this term. However, the courts consider the precepts of Sharia law to be applicable. These precepts imply that 'the person who has taken in the child has priority over others to keep him or her unless this person is unable to look after the child. The court must therefore verify whether the claimant is fit to take care of and educate the child, and must decide in the light of these investigations.'[82] The term '*laqit*,' though absent from the Personal Status Code, appears in various texts in conjunction with '*majhul al-nasab*,' the child of unknown filiation. The latter

[75] Etymologically, the root of the term *laqata* means picking up, recovering, grasping or taking something that has fallen to the ground. The abandoned newborn is considered as such because his or her rescue is required from a religious point of view. Al-Razi 1986, p 251.

[76] Al-Kubaysi 2010, p 204.

[77] Sujimon 2002, pp 359–360.

[78] See Articles 356–358 Qadri Pasha Code.

[79] Al-Kubaysi 2010, p 205.

[80] Article 361 Qadri Pasha Code.

[81] Article 362 Qadri Pasha Code.

[82] Court of Cassation, August 24, 1978, appeal no. 1556/perso/1978, Majmu'at al-Ahkam al-'Adliyya no. 3 of 1978, p 69.

term, however, takes on a wider meaning because it includes, in addition to the abandoned newborn, any person whose affiliation is not legally established, regardless of his or her age and the circumstances of his or her discovery. But the distinction seems obviously theoretical insofar as the two categories are subject to the same legal regime. The Iraqi legislature has indeed reserved the same fate for persons without known filiation and for foundling children. This is probably the reason why the reform of the Juvenile Protection Act in 1979 definitively replaced the pejorative term '*laqit*' with '*majhul al-nasab*.'[83] Only the new terminology is used in the legal provisions currently in force.[84]

However, the exact signification of the concept of the 'child of unknown filiation' (*majhul al-nasab*) in the current legal context remains to be determined. This term covers all cases in which the filiation between the child and one of his or her parents has not been legally established by one of the modes of establishment mentioned above. However, the term seems to designate *sensu stricto* the failure of paternal filiation, given that filiation in Islamically inspired law refers to the paternal lineage.[85] The term *majhul al-nasab* therefore refers, more specifically, to the child whose father is unknown.

Consequently, a child born less than six months after the marriage or more than two years after its dissolution is considered to be of unknown filiation, as the presumption of paternity is inoperative.[86] Thus, it was held that, when a marriage took place on January 24, 2008, and the child was born on June 30, 2008, *nasab* could not be established unless the date of the marriage was rectified at the request of one of the parents.[87] The child born out of wedlock is also considered to be of unknown filiation, on the condition that the relationship could be described as fornication (*zina*): according to the Sharia rules, the child of *zina* cannot establish paternal filiation.[88] In principle, 'illegitimate filiation' produces none of the effects of legitimate filiation with the father.[89] Nevertheless, such a strict rule is used only in very rare cases. In fact, the child born to unmarried parents is hardly free of filiation. An illegitimate but ambiguous relationship (*shubha*) does not prevent the assigning of paternal filiation, as we have noted. In addition, Iraqi case law tends to consider that marriage will be presumed from the moment of *de facto* marital cohabitation. Thus, it

[83] Law No. 123-1979 on the First Reform of the Juvenile Act No. 64-1972.

[84] Juvenile Protection Act No. 76-1983.

[85] Khallaf 1990, p 176.

[86] Even though the Iraqi scholarship advocates a one-year delay, the court practice still seems to be aligned with the maximum duration of pregnancy of two years as adopted by the Hanafi school. See Al-Kubaysi 2010, p 198.

[87] Court of Cassation, February 15, 2012, appeal no. 7/interest of the law/2012, Majallat al-Tashri' wa-l-Qada', www.tqmag.net/body.asp?field=news_arabic&id=2215 (accessed February 5, 2019).

[88] Court of Cassation of the Kurdistan Region, April 7, 2010, appeal no. 99/perso/2010. For critical commentary, see al-'Agayli RH, www.tqmag.net/body.asp?field=news_arabic&id=1833 (accessed February 5, 2019).

[89] On the other hand, with regard to the mother, filiation is established by birth alone, regardless of the nature of the relationship between the child's parents.

has been held that if the defendant had intercourse with the claimant in marital relations '*mu'asharat al-azwaj*' and cohabited with her under the same roof, the children born during this period will be attached to him.[90] In this context, a judgment that established filiation only with respect to the mother would be overruled.[91]

Another situation to be considered is that of the child born within a marriage but later disavowed by his father. However, such a situation seems improbable given that the procedure of *li'an* is impeded in Iraqi law, as we have already pointed out.[92] While some recent decisions admit the rectification of incorrect filiation declared at birth, this does not mean that the child is considered 'of unknown filiation'. The judgment of rectification implies that the child is attached to his or her true genealogy, as stated by the Court of Cassation.[93] If the court grants the request, it will concomitantly order the registrar of civil status to rectify the records and register the new filiation.

In the light of the foregoing considerations, it must be concluded that the courts adopt an extensive interpretation allowing for a significant reduction in the number of cases in which the child is deprived of filiation. Through various means, courts are willing to admit the establishment of filiation more easily than its rupture. Claims tending to break filiation are generally treated with rigor and circumspection. In some judgments, one can even find the statement that '*nasab* is established by the slightest evidence and can be dismissed only by the strongest evidence.'[94] As such, legal filiation does not always follow the biological truth. Nevertheless, the presence of children without filiation is a social reality that the law cannot ignore. It is therefore important to address the legal status of these children.

5.5.2 The Rights of Children Without Filiation

The establishment of filiation is a prerequisite on which other rights are based, such as rights to custody, maintenance, education, inheritance, etc. In order to protect the *majhul al-nasab* child, the law attempts to remedy the harmful effects of the absence of filiation. In this respect, the rights to a name and a nationality seem particularly important. Article 24 of the International Covenant on Civil and Political Rights, which has been ratified by Iraq,[95] provides that '2. Every child

---

[90] Court of Cassation, March 16, 1976, appeal no. 239/perso/1976, Majmu'at al-Ahkam al-'Adliyya no. 1 of 1977, p 91.

[91] Court of Cassation, September 17, 1985, appeal no. 2309/perso/1984-1985, cited by Al-Mashahadi 1989, pp 259–260.

[92] See Sect. 5.4.1.

[93] Court of Cassation, September 19, 2012, appeal no. 197/perso/2012, www.hjc.iq/qview.1831/ (accessed February 27, 2019).

[94] Personal Status Court of Kadhimiya, March 14, 2006 (unpublished).

[95] Law No. 193-1970.

shall be registered immediately after birth and shall have a name. 3. Every child has the right to acquire a nationality.'

With regard to nationality, Article 3 of Iraqi Nationality Law No. 26-2006 confers Iraqi citizenship on any individual 'born to an Iraqi father or an Iraqi mother.' The nationality therefore results from paternal or maternal *jus sanguinis*.[96] However, the law also confers Iraqi citizenship upon any person born in Iraq of unknown parents and considers that 'every child found in Iraq is presumed to be born in Iraq, unless proven otherwise.' The child born on Iraqi soil of unknown parents is therefore automatically granted Iraqi citizenship (*jus soli*).

As to the patronymic name (surname), it extends *de plano* from a father to his children under Iraqi law.[97] According to Article 15 of Civil Status Act No. 65-1972, children of the same family receive their father's patronymic name at birth, and are automatically registered under this name. When a newborn of unknown filiation is discovered, a report is drafted by the police and sent to the Juvenile Court, which assigns the child a surname and a given name and fixes the date and place of his or her birth. Under Section 32(1) of the Civil Status Act, the Juvenile Court then confidentially forwards to the Registrar of Civil Status a copy of its decision to name the foundling or child of unknown filiation, as well as other relevant information: the date and place of birth, the date of the child's discovery and the name of the home that hosted the child. A copy is also sent to the Ministry of Health for the issuance of the birth certificate.[98] The child's full name therefore includes the fictitious first names of his or her father and grandfather, who are registered as deceased.[99] The information is kept confidential and the identity document issued accordingly contains no indication of the unknown origin.[100]

A child of unknown filiation who has not been taken into care by social welfare agencies may, once he or she has reached the age of fifteen, apply to the competent court[101] to obtain identity documents. The judge then has to conduct all the necessary verifications to trace the person's origins (police, civil registry, city council, etc.). If the search is unsuccessful, the court will issue a confidential order containing the name, place of birth, religion and age, which will be set following a medical examination.[102] This judgment serves as a birth certificate.

---

96 The law was amended in 2005 to allow Iraqi mothers to pass on their nationality to their children, thereby lifting Iraq's reservation to Article 9(2) of the Convention on the Elimination of All Forms of Discrimination against Women.

97 Article 40(1) Civil Code.

98 Article 19 of the Births and Deaths Registration Act No. 148-1971.

99 Article 28 of the Decree (*nizam*) on Civil Status No. 32-1974.

100 Al-Musawi 2016.

101 Personal Status Court (for Muslims) or Personal Property Court (for non-Muslims), depending on the case.

102 Article 32bis Civil Status Act and Articles 300–301 of the Code of Civil Procedure No. 83-1969.

It is important to note, finally, that a foundling or a child of unknown parents is presumed to be Muslim unless proven otherwise.[103] This presumption is based on probability, given that the population of the country is predominantly Muslim. However, this presumption is not irrefutable. For example, the child will be considered a Christian if he or she has been discovered in a predominantly Christian neighborhood and raised in a Christian family, and if there are indications of his or her religion of origin.[104] This rule seems to be in line with the liberal position of the Hanafi School regarding the *laqit* child: a child found by a non-Muslim in a place reserved for non-Muslims (such as a church or a synagogue) follows the religion of whoever found the child and cares for him or her.[105]

It is clear that all of the above provisions, particularly with regard to confidentiality of information, seek to ensure the social integration of the child without filiation by facilitating his or her relationships with public and private institutions (school, hospital, town hall, etc.). Nevertheless, the sad fate of children born of rape, slavery or forced marriages in the liberated territories formerly controlled by Daesh currently remains a source of major concern for local authorities and civil society organizations.[106]

5.6 Protection of Children Deprived of Parental Care

5.6.1 General Legal Framework

The term 'children deprived of parental care' encompasses both children without filiation and children orphaned or abandoned by their parents. These children are commonly referred to as 'street children' or homeless people (*musharrad*). The regulations in this area aim to provide shelter for these children and prevent any abuse, violence or harm to them.

The protection of parentless children is not recent. Ancient Mesopotamia offers early examples of such protection – for example, the principle that an adopted child should be treated equally with legitimate children. Article 190 of the Code of Hammurabi (circa 1750 BC) provides that '[i]f a man has adopted an infant as a son, and brought him up, but has not reckoned him with his children; then that adopted son shall return to his father's house.' Furthermore, Article 191 of the Code establishes a guarantee for the child taken and then abandoned by his new family by stating that '[i]f a man has adopted an infant as a son, and brought him up, and has

[103] Article 32(2) Civil Status Act and Article 45 Juvenile Protection Act No. 76-1983.

[104] For a judicial application concerning a 47-year-old woman of unknown parentage, see Al-Musawi 2016.

[105] For more details, see Al-Dabbagh 2013–2014, p 356.

[106] The terrorist organization forced women in the conquered territories to marry its fighters. As these marriages are not recognized, the children who are born to these unions are at risk of being deprived of their rights and subjected to stigmatization. See UN Human Rights 2017.

founded a household, and afterwards has had children, and if he has set his face to disown the adopted son; then that child shall not go his way. His foster father shall give him out of his possessions one-third of the portion of a son, and then he shall go. Of field, or garden, or house, he shall not give him.'[107] Adoption was also a common practice in pre-Islamic Arabia, where it served a variety of purposes such as ensuring descendants or a large family, freeing a slave, or gaining skilled labor.[108] This ancestral institution was maintained at the dawn of Islam before being abolished in the fifth year of the Hegira (627).[109] The Qur'an, however, ensures God's compassion for those who take care of children in need, especially if the children are poor or orphaned.[110] In this perspective, *kafala* is regarded as a highly meritorious act of benevolence for believers.

Kafala as such is not regulated in the Iraqi legal system. It is a private act of beneficence, often practiced in a family or a community context.[111] The law, however, regulates the care of the child in public institutions. An abandoned child will be placed in a host institution by decision of the court or other competent authority. Social Welfare Act No. 126-1980[112] established state houses (*dur al-dawla*) to provide children of unknown filiation, as well as orphaned or abandoned children and children with dysfunctional families, with a safe and healthy environment to meet their emotional and material needs and ensure their education. The state houses are an effective alternative from a social point of view, but their number remains highly insufficient.[113]

In parallel, Article 27(2) of the Juvenile Protection Act allows the Juvenile Court to entrust the child who is at risk of delinquency[114] to a person of trust for the purposes of his education and training (temporary placement). This person must have sufficient resources, be of good character and enjoy a good reputation, and be of the same nationality and religion as the child. This procedure can only be ordered in the light of a psychosocial examination report. The court must ensure through a probation officer or social worker that the person concerned is properly performing the assigned task for the period of time that is deemed appropriate. This is usually a time-limited preventive measure that is taken in the best interests of the child.[115]

[107] The Hammurabi Code and the Sinaitic Legislation (1904) (Translated by Edwards C) Watts & Co., London, pp 60–61.

[108] Sulayman 1987, pp 262 et seq.

[109] Sura 33, verse 40.

[110] The word orphan (*yatim*) and its derivatives are quoted in twenty-three Qur'anic verses, e.g. Sura 2, verse 220; Sura 4, verses 2, 10, 36; Sura 93, verse 9.

[111] Such care being not regulated by law but part of social practices of charity, no statistics are available on the number of children living in their extended families or religious communities.

[112] Articles 29–42 Social Welfare Act No. 126-1980.

[113] There are only 23 state houses, 4 in Baghdad and 19 in the governorates.

[114] Vagrant child, homeless, with no means of support or who has run away and has no guardian. Articles 24–25 Juvenile Protection Act.

[115] Article 28 Juvenile Protection Act.

Finally, it goes without saying that the phenomenon of 'street children' is linked to economic, social and political factors that have been aggravated in recent years.[116] These children are more likely to fall into vagrancy and delinquency or exploitation networks. The above measures are struggling to remedy this problem. We will see that a third solution, called *damm*, which is closer to adoption, offers more promising prospects.

*5.6.2 Affiliation (***'damm'***)*

5.6.2.1 Definition and Objectives of *damm*

'Affiliation' (*damm*) is a process established by Iraqi law to allow a married couple to host on a permanent basis a minor child who is an orphan or of unknown filiation, in order to take care of him exactly as parents would do for their own children. The aim is to provide a home for a child who does not have a family. The 1983 Juvenile Protection Act deals with this particular institution in Articles 39–46 as a preventive measure against the risk of delinquency and misconduct.

Often presented as an alternative to adoption, this institution aims to fully or partially fulfill the functions of adoption. As in other Islamic countries,[117] the Iraqi legal system prohibits adoption, at least as an institution creating a filiation link. In fact, Iraqi law is silent on this point, but the prohibition of adoption results from the general reference made by Article 1 of the PSC to traditional Islamic law *fiqh* to fill the gaps in the law. Thus, we can read in an opinion of the Council of State of Iraq: 'If we mean by adoption (*tabanni*) the attachment of the child to the filiation of the one who supports him or her, this is prohibited as long as the child's filiation is known. However, when it entails the care of the child who has lost his or her guardian and responsibility for the management of his or her affairs, without any change of filiation, this is not prohibited by Sharia or the law.'[118] Therefore, the adoption has no legal effect. It is not considered to constitute kinship within the meaning of the Civil Code,[119] nor is it considered by the Personal Status Code to be a cause of an impediment to marriage or a source of maintenance obligations or inheritance rights.[120]

[116] These causes include war, forced displacement, poverty, rural depopulation and unemployment. Hasan 2014, pp 1113 et seq.

[117] With the exception of Tunisia, the only Arab country that expressly allows adoption (Law No. 58-27 of 1958 on Public Tutorship, Unofficial Tutorship and Adoption).

[118] Opinion of the Council of State, September 23, 1962, no. 94/9, Majallat Diwan al-Tadwin al-Qanuni no. 1 of 1963, p 104.

[119] Articles 38 and 39 Civil Code.

[120] Al-Dawudi 1983, p 30.

To compensate for this prohibition, the legislature intervened in 1955[121] to provide a solution that, while not contrary to Islamic prescriptions, would allow individuals (a married couple specifically) to take care of an abandoned child and to exercise the rights of custody and education over him or her. Originally called '*tarbib*' (initiation), then '*ilhaq*' (annexation), the institution was eventually renamed '*damm*' in 1979,[122] a term that can be translated as 'affiliation.' Juvenile Protection Act No. 76-1983, while maintaining this new terminology, provides more guarantees to ensure the rights of the child who is taken care of through this scheme.[123]

5.6.2.2 Conditions and Procedure of *damm*

According to Article 39 of the Juvenile Protection Act No. 76-1983, a married couple may submit a joint application to the Juvenile Court to be affiliated (*damm*) with a young child (*saghir*), who must be an orphan or a child of unknown filiation according to the definition above, and must be less than nine years old at the time of the application.[124] Therefore, children who are over nine years of age, or whose parents are known or alive but incapable of taking care of them, are not eligible for this scheme, but are entrusted to state houses. The applicants, who are necessarily married spouses, must be Iraqis, of good standing, of sound mind, of good faith, free of contagious diseases, and able to raise and provide for the child.[125] Along these lines, the court would reject any '*damm*' application that is not in the best interests of the child. Thus, a person who has been convicted of a crime or an offense with respect to honor is considered not to meet the requirements.[126] Furthermore, the Court of Cassation approved the decision of a judge of first instance who rejected a request on the grounds that the applicants were itinerant gypsies (Roma), which cast doubts on their ability to provide the child with an adequate education.[127] Courts generally seem to favor civil servants over other candidates, given their fixed domicile and stable income.[128]

---

[121] Juvenile Delinquents Act No. 44-1955.

[122] Act No. 132-1979 Amending the Juvenile Act No. 64-1972.

[123] For more details on this evolution, see Al-Dawudi 1983, pp 28 et seq.

[124] The term young child (*saghir*) is defined by Article 3(1) of the Juvenile Protection Act No. 76-1983 as being one who has not reached the age of nine. The age of civil majority is, however, 18 years old (Article 106 Civil Code).

[125] Article 39 of the Juvenile Protection Act No. 76-1983.

[126] Al-Dawudi 1983, p 38.

[127] Court of Cassation, July 22, 1990, appeal no. 80/enlarged chamber/1990, quoted by Al-Mashahadi 1998, pp 9–10.

[128] Interview with Judge Sayma' Na'im, Al-Qada' no. 7 of May 2016, p 2, www.hjc.iq/upload/pdf/no_7.pdf (accessed February 27, 2019).

It is worth noting that under the current law married couples can apply for '*damm*' without further restrictions, whereas the previous regulation limited this option to couples who had been married for at least seven years without having children.[129] This evolution has been criticized by some authors, who argue that permitting affiliation in this case can harm the rights of the (legitimate) children, particularly in matters of inheritance, and is not in line with the spirit of the law, which is to give a child to sterile couples.[130] Such an argument is hardly convincing for several reasons. First, it is the interest of the child that must be the paramount consideration in this matter, in accordance with the Convention on the Rights of the Child, which has been ratified by Iraq.[131] Secondly, the current context, which is marked by an increase in the number of children in distress, requires widening the admissibility of affiliation cases, all the more so since public assistance can never replace the warmth of a home. Finally, the infringement of the rights of potential heirs would be insignificant insofar as the financial capacity of the applicants must be proven and the affiliate's share will be allocated from the disposable portion by will, as we shall see below.[132]

In addition, although the law requires the applicants to hold the same nationality as the child (Iraqi), it remains silent on their religious affiliation.[133] In traditional Islamic law, the *kafil* is also a custodian of the child, and the right of custody (*hadana*) implies 'the education of the child in the religion of his father,'[134] which should prohibit non-Muslims from taking in Muslim children and vice versa. Therefore, the question arises as to whether the silence of the law on this point could be interpreted as renouncing such a condition. Some authors argue that the court must ensure that the child and the applicants share the same faith because this is required under Article 27(2) of the Act to temporarily assign a delinquent child or a homeless child to a volunteer guardian; it should thus be all the more so in the scheme of affiliation.[135] We believe, however, that the omission in the law, far from being an oversight, may be indicative of its willingness to override this condition. One should recall that, unlike the Personal Status Code, the Juvenile Protection Act is a law that applies to all Iraqis regardless of their religious affiliation. The general terms of such provisions should not allow for a distinction based on religion. To date, no decision seems to have been issued on this matter.

---

129 Article 55 Juvenile Act No. 64-1972 (repealed).

130 In this sense, Al-Dawudi 1983, p 52.

131 Law No. 3-1994 Ratifying the Convention on the Rights of the Child. For more details, see Al-Dabbagh 2017a, pp 86–89.

132 In this sense too, see 'Abd al-Latif 2008, p 64.

133 The previous laws (No. 44-1955 and No. 11-1963 (repealed)) provided for shared religious identity between the child and the applicants. This condition was no longer mentioned in the law in force.

134 Al-Dabbagh 2017a, p 111.

135 'Abd al-Latif 2008, p 65. In the same vein, Mahmud 2002, p 32.

Once it has verified that the conditions set out above are met, the Juvenile Court is to pronounce the affiliation and decide on the temporary placement of the child at the applicants' home for a trial period of six months, which may be extended only once for the same duration. During the initial or extended period, the court sends a social worker to the couple's home at least once a month to ensure that the spouses wish to receive the child and that the process of integration is running smoothly. A detailed report is submitted to the court.[136] If, during the probationary period, one or both of the spouses do not wish to continue the proceedings, or if it appears that the affiliation is not in the best interests of the child, the court cancels the placement and, at the same time, entrusts the child to one of the social institutions set up for that purpose.[137] At the end of the probation period, the court pronounces the definitive affiliation if it observes that the applicants' desire for *damm* has been ascertained and that it serves the best interests of the child.[138] Thus, the implementation of the *damm* scheme is subject to a two-stage control mechanism to ensure that the child's interests are taken into consideration.[139]

5.6.2.3 Effects of *damm*

The effects of the affiliation judgment are significant. First, the affiliant parents are required, according to Article 43(1), to provide for the needs of the child (maintenance). In this respect, affiliant fathers and mothers receive the same welfare benefits as those usually available to parents. For example, it has been decided that a female civil servant may be granted maternity leave to care for her 'adopted' child who has not yet reached the age of four.[140]

In addition, the affiliant parents undertake to bequeath to the affiliated child an inheritance share that is equivalent to the smallest share received by any other heir and that does not exceed one-third of the total inheritance.[141] This mandatory and irrevocable legacy (*al-wasiyya al-wajiba*) had previously been used to allow grandchildren to inherit in the place of their predeceased father, along with the latter's brothers and sisters.[142] The use of this concept in favor of the affiliated child is therefore new. The current practice is to establish the child as the universal legatee of one third of the inheritance, regardless of the smaller share of an heir.[143] The legacy is, moreover, irrevocable, unlike an ordinary will governed by the Personal

---

136 Article 40 of the Juvenile Protection Act.

137 Article 41 of the Juvenile Protection Act.

138 Article 42 of the Juvenile Protection Act.

139 Mahmud 2002, p 31.

140 Circular of the Ministry of Finance No. 21519 of November 1, 1981, quoted by Al-Dawudi 1983, p 42.

141 Article 43 of the Juvenile Protection Act.

142 Article 74 PSC.

143 See al-Iftayhat 1998, p 52.

Status Code.[144] The law clearly seeks to remedy the lack of inheritance resulting from the lack of filiation. This obligation breaks with the classical rule according to which *kafala* creates no filiation and thus no inheritance rights.[145]

With regard to the name of the child, it is necessary to distinguish, in the light of Articles 43 and 44 of the Act, between the child of unknown filiation (*majhul al-nasab*) and the orphaned child who has lost both parents (*yatim al-abawayn*). The latter, being born of known but deceased parents, will keep his or her name and filiation of origin. No change will be introduced in this regard, given that *nasab* is irrevocable and is not subject to limitation periods.[146] Although Article 46 of the Act requires the court to send a copy of the affiliation decision to the Registrar of Civil Status, the purpose of recording it is only to institute the affiliants as guardians of the child and to meet their obligations arising from the law.[147] For the child of unknown filiation, the affiliation leads to changing his or her name. In this respect, the applicant spouses are to acknowledge paternal and maternal affiliation by *iqrar* in accordance with Article 52 of the PSC.[148] Specifically, the husband is obliged to acknowledge his paternity of the child, who is then given the affiliant father's name.[149] The Juvenile Court sends a copy of its decision to the Directorate of Civil Status for recording in its registers.[150] On the basis of this judgment, the registration of the acknowledged child is joined to the new parents' booklet, without any mention of the circumstances of the birth. It follows that (1) the child who is initially of unknown filiation becomes of known filiation; (2) the civil status registers cannot allow the tracing of the child's origin; and (3) moreover, this acknowledgment produces all the effects of legitimate filiation. Simply put, the child will retroactively have a regular family status. In addition, 'any claim to challenge this filiation, on any ground, brought after the death of the acknowledging person is deemed inadmissible.'[151] It should be noted, with respect to the consequences of '*damm*,' that assigning the name of the affiliant acknowledging 'father'

---

[144] Article 72(1) PSC allows the testator to revoke his will in writing.

[145] See, for a recognition of this rule, Article 2 of Moroccan Law No. 15-01 of 2002 Relating to the Care (*kafala*) of Abandoned Children (Dahir No. 1-02-172 of 2002), stating that '*kafala does not give rights to filiation or succession.*'

[146] Mughaniyya 1998, p 370.

[147] 'Abd al-Latif 2008, p 68.

[148] The conditions for validity of recognition, as we have already mentioned, are unknown filiation, a sufficient age difference and the approval of the beneficiary, if he is of the age of discernment.

[149] Article 44 of the Juvenile Protection Act provides that 'recognition of the filiation of a child of unknown parentage shall be done before the Juvenile Court, in accordance with the Personal Status Code.'

[150] Article 24(2) Decree on Civil Status No. 32-1974.

[151] Court of Cassation, December 27, 1979, appeal no. 663/plen. ass./1979, Majmu'at al-Ahkam al-'Adliyya no. 1 of 1980, p 37.

to the child seriously departs from traditional Islamic law on *kafala*, under which any concordance of name between *kafil* and *makful* is absolutely refused.[152] Such a solution also appears to be surprising beyond the borders of Iraq.[153]

In light of the above, the Iraqi regime of affiliation '*damm*' appears, from a functional perspective, to be nothing other than adoption. How can this be explained in view of the prohibition of adoption? Authors argue that the institution does not contradict traditional Islamic law on this point. The filiation between the child and the person who claims the child is established on the grounds of *istihsan*,[154] because it benefits the child by allowing a defective filiation to be remedied and by ensuring his or her care.[155] As we have previously observed, classical *fiqh* admits the *iqrar* in favor of the *laqit* child who becomes *de jure* the legitimate child of the acknowledger. Whereas the initial objective of acknowledgment is to give legal existence to a pre-existing filiation, the mechanism is used in the Iraqi law on *damm* to create a fictitious filiation. This explains why the earlier version of the law uses the term *ilhaq* (annexation), as the child is attached and attributed to the person who takes him or her into her care. We believe therefore that *damm* is, more or less,

---

[152] The child keeps the name of his biological parents, but if these parents are unknown, as in the case of a foundling, the Qur'anic verse (Sura 33, verse 5) orders that he be treated as a brother in faith or as a friend. He must be given a name that does not deceive society into believing he is the biological child of the *kafil*.

[153] Federal Supreme Court (UAE), April 5, 2010, appeal no. 79/pen./2010, www.eastlaws.com (accessed February 5, 2019). In this case brought before the United Arab Emirates courts, two underage Iraqi girls were arrested in front of a hotel and suspected of prostitution. Their mother was interrogated. A DNA test revealed that this mother was not the biological mother of the two girls. She was therefore arrested and charged with using a falsified Iraqi passport bearing the names of the minor girls to enter the UAE with the children. While admitting that she was not the girls' biological mother, she stated during her interrogation that she had adopted the two girls in Iraq after having taken them from an orphans' home with her husband, and therefore that she held a regular passport issued in Baghdad. Before the court, she categorically denied any fraud or falsification of documents to enter the country. On the question of how her passport identified the children as her own daughters, the woman claimed that she had attached the girls to her filiation by 'adoption' and therefore that they were named after her deceased husband under Iraqi law. Following the trial, the Emirati Federal Supreme Court released the woman. The Court was not called upon to recognize the Iraqi adoption in the UAE or to pronounce on its validity, but to rule on the existence of a criminal offense relating to the use of forgery. To this end, it stated that 'although adoption (*tabanni*) is illegal (*muharram*) in Sharia, it is nevertheless practiced under conditions in some Muslim countries. It follows that the adoptee is affiliated to the adopter and enjoys all the rights and duties of the legitimate [biological] child such as inheritance and patronymic name …'

[154] *Istihsan*, or the principle of preference, is a process of rational reasoning used in particular by the Hanafis. Inasmuch as the child found is of unknown filiation and it is in his or her interest to have an established parentage, the *fuqaha'* then alter the legal principles.

[155] Fityan 1986, p 187; Karim 2004, p 256; Al-Kubaysi 2010, p 205.

a disguised adoption, because it entails a filiation change in the child's civil status.[156] Some judgments even use the terms *tabanni* (adoption) and *mutabanna* (adopted child).[157]

Moreover, the bonds that are formed between the child and his or her new family in the context of an affiliation are not as precarious as they might appear at first glance. Some effects, such as name change and inheritance rights, are long-lasting; maintenance also extends well beyond the child's attainment of the age of majority. All such effects are irrevocable.[158] This is clearly a significant break with the traditional concept of *kafala*: 'the institution established by Iraqi law is in this sense closer to Western adoption than to the original Islamic *kafala*.'[159]

Some authors have praised this new approach. For 'Abd al-Latif, 'the path taken by the Iraqi legislature in the Juvenile Protection Act is the translation of a policy aimed at protecting the orphan and the child born of unknown parents from the misdeeds of delinquency, by providing them, without infringing on the rights of other parties, with stability and legal certainty through a resolutely modern legislative style, but at the same time in accordance with the essence of Sharia.'[160] However, other authors are critical and see in the law a subterfuge prohibited by Sharia because it leads to the confusion of lineages and to infringement upon the legitimate heirs' rights.[161] To dispel the suspicions surrounding the lawfulness of the process, other authors seek to correctly distinguish the institution established by Iraqi law from the adoption prohibited by the Qur'an. According to Karim, unlike *iqrar*, the adoption prohibited in Islam is that of a child whose filiation is known. On closer examination, Iraqi law does not permit such adoption since *iqrar* is only valid for children of unknown filiation.[162] Several authors share this view, arguing that the Qur'anic prescriptions only prohibit changing the filiation of the child whose affiliation is already established, which in any event excludes the *majhul al-nasab* child.[163] This is the opinion we personally subscribe to. Indeed, the Qur'anic verse

[156] Article 46 Juvenile Protection Act.

[157] See e.g. Testamentary Act No. 295-1298 issued on July 8, 1998, by the Personal Status Court of Mosul, quoted by Al-Iftayhat 1998, p 52. This is the will approved by the court to institute an affiliated child as heir for one-third of the estate.

[158] According to the previous law (Juvenile Act No. 64-1972), if the biological father of the child appeared, he had the possibility of claiming the child before the court, which had then to cancel the affiliation and order the child's reintegration with his father (Article 60). The new law discards this solution, which placed the child in a precarious and unpredictable situation and was a source of litigation.

[159] Al-Dabbagh 2017b, p 213.

[160] 'Abd al-Latif 2008, p 71.

[161] In this sense, Al-Iftayhat 1998, pp 51–52; Al-Fatlawi 2009, pp 266 and 301.

[162] Karim 2004, pp 257–258.

[163] In this sense, Al-Karbasi 1989, p 101; Al-Khatib et al. 1980, p 208; Al-Dabbagh 2017b, pp 208 et seq.

orders 'Call them by [the names of] their fathers … but if ye know not their father's names, (then they are) your Brothers in faith, or your friends'.[164] Therefore, when filiation is unknown, the Qur'anic prescriptions impose no solution.

5.7 Conclusion

This paper has highlighted the different mechanisms for establishing filiation and the protection of children who are deprived of filiation or parental care. In the light of the description and analysis made above, two dynamics seem to emerge in Iraqi law.

Firstly, the logic of the law of filiation is directed towards reducing the number of cases in which filiation cannot be established or can be successfully challenged. The ambivalence of the *fiqh* in this regard has allowed Iraqi case law, on the one hand, to restrict substantially the number of cases in which duly established filiation can be broken and, on the other hand, to favor its establishment whenever any cause gives it an appearance of lawfulness. We have noticed, for example, that even if relations outside marriage are hardly tolerated in society, the child who is born out of wedlock will not be systematically deprived of filiation. The lenient conditions under which marriage is allowed have largely facilitated the regularization (and legitimization) of such births. At the same time, by its simple and abstract character, the acknowledgment of filiation (*iqrar*) also entails all the effects of legitimate filiation regardless of any proof of marriage. By tackling the root causes, the law and the way it is implemented attempt to preserve the interest of the child with respect to the establishment of the filiation.

Secondly, the status of the child deprived of filiation has improved significantly in situations where such rules or remedies are not available. Children who do not have legal filiation are nevertheless given a name and a nationality. The confidentiality of their origins aims at facilitating their integration into society. Modern child protection legislation has ensured state care for children without families. Government programs are put into place to protect them. Moreover, the Islamic prohibition of adoption seems, in practice, more formal than real. The regime of affiliation (*damm*) is indeed very close to the effects that would result from an adoption. Certain loopholes admitted by traditional *fiqh*, such as the *iqrar* and the mandatory bequest, have experienced a surprising resurgence designed to establish a fictional filiation link and to give it maximum strength. Living law does not seek to make the legal and the biological coincide, but, on the contrary, to reconstruct reality according to values that are accepted by society.

Finally, our analysis of the evolution of law and case law in Iraq highlights the very specific nature of the construction of filiation (*nasab*) in Islamic law. The theoretical rigor of the system is giving way to a surprising flexibility of practice.

[164] Sura 33, verse 5.

References

'Abd al-Latif BM (2008) Al-Siyasa al-Jina'iyya fi Qanun Ri'ayat al-Ahdath [Criminal Policy in the Juvenile Protection Act]. Dar al-Hamid li-l-Nashr, Amman.

Al-Dabbagh H (2005) La réception du modèle juridique français par le Code civil irakien. Revue internationale de droit comparé 2:263–290.

Al-Dabbagh H (2007) Droit de la famille et nouvelle Constitution irakienne. Revue de la recherche juridique - Droit prospectif 3:1507–1542.

Al-Dabbagh H (2013–2014) Le statut juridique des minorités non-musulmanes en Irak: Heurs et malheurs du pluralisme juridique. Annuaire Droit et Religions 7:319–376.

Al-Dabbagh H (2017a) Iraq. In: Yassari N, Möller L-M, Gallala-Arndt I (eds) Parental Care and the Best Interests of the Child in Muslim Countries. T.M.C. Asser Press, The Hague, pp 81–119.

Al-Dabbagh H (2017b) La réception de la *kafala* dans l'ordre juridique québécois: vers un renversement du paradigme conflictuel? Revue générale de droit 47(1):165–226.

Al-Dawudi Gh'A (1983) Al-Athar al-Qanuniyya li-l-Tabanni wa-l-Damm fi Qawanin al-Ahdath wa-l-Ahwal al-Shakhsiyya wa-l-Jinsiyya al-'Iraqiyya [The Legal Effects of Adoption and Affiliation in Iraq's Juvenile Laws and Personal Status Laws]. Majallat al-Qanun al-Muqaran 15:7–56.

Aldeeb Abu-Sahlieh SA (2008) Religion et droit dans les pays arabes: Domaines influencés par la religion. Presses universitaires de Bordeaux, Bordeaux.

Al-Fatlawi S (2009) Al-Madkhal li-Dirasat 'Ilm al-Qanun [Introduction to Legal Sciences], 2nd edn. Maktabat al-Dhakira, Baghdad.

Al-Iftayhat Y (1998) Al-Wasiyya al-Wajiba [The Mandatory Bequest]. Unpublished Master's Thesis, Faculty of Law, University of Mosul.

Al-Karbasi 'AM (1989) Sharh Qanun al-Ahwal al-Shakhsiyya Raqm 188-1959 [Commentary on the Personal Status Code No. 188-1959]. Dar al-Hurriyya, Baghdad.

Al-Khatib A'A, al-Kubaysi H'U, al-Samarra'i M'A (1980) Sharh Qanun al-Ahwal al-Shakhsiyya [Commentary on Personal Status Law]. Jami'at al-Mawsil, Mosul.

Al-Kubaysi AA (2010) Al-Wajiz fi Sharh Qanun al-Ahwal al-Shakhsiyya wa-Ta'dilatuhu [Short Commentary on the Personal Status Code and its Amendments], 3rd edn. Al-Maktaba al-Qanuniyya, Baghdad.

Al-Mashahadi I (1989) Al-Mabadi' al-Qanuniyya fi Qada' Mahkamat al-Tamyiz fi Qism al-Ahwal al-Shakhsiyya [The Legal Principles in the Jurisprudence of the Court of Cassation, Personal Status Section]. Matba'at As'ad, Baghdad.

Al-Mashahadi I (1998) Al-Mukhtar min Qada' Mahkamat al-Tamyiz, al-Qism al-Jina'i [Selected Case Law of the Court of Cassation in Criminal Matters], vol IV. Matba'at al-Zaman, Baghdad.

Al-Musawi SR (2016) Al-Ahkam al-Tanzimiyya li-Majhul al-Nasab fi al-Qanun al-'Iraqi [The Provisions Governing the Child of Unknown Filiation Under Iraqi Law]. Al-Hiwar al-Mutamaddin, August 20, 2016. http://m.ahewar.org/s.asp?aid=528528&r=0&cid=0&u=&i=842&q. Accessed February 5, 2019.

Al-Razi MBAB (1986) Mukhtar al-Sihah [Dictionary of the Arabic Language]. Maktabat Lubnan, Beirut.

Al-Salim ShMD, al-Nu'aymi AHS (2010) Al-Ahkam al-Shar'iyya wa-l-Qanuniyya li-Ithbat al-Nasab bi-l-Basma al-Wirathiyya [The Legal Regime of Establishing Filiation by DNA]. Majallat al-Rafidayn li-l-Huquq 43:47–79.

Alwan RJ (2011) Al-Mukhtar min Qada' Mahkamat al-Tamyiz al-Ittihadiyya: Qism al-Ahwal al-Shakhsiyya [Selected Decisions of the Federal Court of Cassation: Personal Status Part]. Maktabat Sabah, Baghdad.

Ancel M, Molines H (eds) (1980) La protection judiciaire de l'enfant en fonction de l'évolution du droit et des institutions judiciaires. A. Pedone, Paris.

Anderson JND (1960) A Law of Personal Status for Iraq. The International and Comparative Law Quarterly 9(4):542–563.

Filiation (2007). In: Cornu G (ed) Vocabulaire juridique, 8th edn. Presses Universitaires de France, Paris.
Fityan F (1986) Sharh Qanun al-Ahwal al-Shakhsiyya ma'a Ta'dilat al-Qanun wa-Ahkam Mahkamat al-Tamyiz [Commentary on the Personal Status Code with Its Amendments and the Judgments of the Court of Cassation], 2nd edn. Dar Wasit, London.
Hasan WM (2014) Zahirat Tasharrud al-Inath bayna al-Tahmish wa-l-Indimaj [The Phenomenon of Vagrancy Among Women: Between Marginalization and Integration: Field Study]. Majallat Kulliyyat al-Tarbiya li-l-Banat 25:1112–1124.
Karim FA (2004) Al-Wasit fi Sharh Qanun al-Ahwal al-Shakhsiyya al-'Iraqi [Commentary on the Iraqi Personal Status Code]. Jami'at al-Sulaymaniyya, Sulaymaniyya.
Khallaf A (1990) Ahkam al-Ahwal al-Shakhsiyya fi al-Shari'a al-Islamiyya 'ala Wafq Madhhab Abi Hanifa wa-ma 'alayhi al-'Amal bi-l-Mahakim [The Personal Status in Islamic Sharia According to the Hanafi School and Jurisprudential Practice], 2nd edn. Dar al-Qalam li-l-Nashr, Kuwait.
Linant de Bellefonds Y (1965) Traité de droit musulman comparé, vol II: Mariage, dissolution du mariage. Mouton & Co., Paris and The Hague.
Linant de Bellefonds Y (1973) Traité de droit musulman comparé, vol III: Filiation – incapacités-libéralités entre vifs. Mouton & Co., Paris and The Hague.
Mahmud DhK (2002) Mabda' Masalih al-Tifl al-Fudla fi-l-Qanun al-Dawli wa-l-Qanun al-'Iraqi [The Principle of the Best Interests of the Child in International Law and in Iraqi Law]. Majallat al-'Adala 1:19–44.
Mughaniyya MJ (1998) Al-Fiqh 'ala al-Madhahib al-Khamsa [The *fiqh* According to the Five Schools], 4th edn. Mu'assasa al-Sadiq li-l-Tiba'a wa-l-Nashr, Tehran.
Sourdel D (1997) Droit musulman et codification. Droits 26:27–50.
Sujimon MS (2002) The Treatment of the Foundling (*al-Laqīṭ*) According to the Ḥanafīs. Islamic Law and Society 9(3):358–385.
Sulayman A (1987) Al-Qanun fi al-'Iraq al-Qadim: Dirasa Tarikhiyya Qanuniyya Muqarana [Law in Ancient Iraq]. Manshurat Wizarat al-Thaqafa wa-l-I'lam, Baghdad.
UN Human Rights (United Nations Office of the High Commissioner for Human Rights) (2017) Justice essential to help Iraqi victims of ISIL's sexual violence rebuild lives – UN report, August 22, 2017. www.ohchr.org/EN/NewsEvents/Pages/DisplayNews.aspx?NewsID=21986&LangID=E. Accessed February 5, 2019.

Harith Al-Dabbagh is an associate professor of comparative and private international law at the University of Montreal in Canada. He holds an LL.B. (1996) and an LL.M. (1998) from his native country Iraq. He completed his DEA in private law (2003) and comparative law (2006) and his Doctorat en droit (2009) in France. He was previously a lawyer and assistant professor at the Faculty of Law of the University of Mosul in Iraq. He also served as a half-time professor at the University of St.-Etienne in France, where he taught various foundational courses in private law. Trained in civil and comparative law, he has focused his recent work on the study of legal pluralism, legal hybridity, mixtures and movements, especially the interaction between secular and religious rules. He is the author of numerous publications in French, English and Arabic on legal systems in the Middle East.

Chapter 6
Jordan

Dörthe Engelcke

Contents

Abstract According to the 2010 Jordanian Personal Status Law, filiation (*nasab*) to the mother is established by giving birth. By contrast, *nasab* to the father can be established in four cases: in the case of the existence of a valid marriage (*firāsh zawjiyya*), by acknowledgement (*iqrār*), by means of evidence (*bayyina*), and through conclusive scientific methods coupled with a valid marriage. The 2010 law for the first time allows the use of DNA tests as one way to establish *nasab*. The introduction of DNA tests has brought tensions between biological filiation and the concept of *nasab*, which primarily emphasizes the existence of *firāsh zawjiyya,* to

Dörthe Engelcke is a Senior Research Fellow within the Research Group 'Changes in God's Law – An Inner Islamic Comparison of Family and Succession Law' at the Max Planck Institute for Comparative and International Private Law, Hamburg.

D. Engelcke (✉)
Max Planck Institute for Comparative and International Private Law, Mittelweg 187, 20148 Hamburg, Germany
e-mail: engelcke@mpipriv.de

N. Yassari et al. (eds.), *Filiation and the Protection of Parentless Children*, https://doi.org/10.1007/978-94-6265-311-5_6

the forefront. Since *nasab* remains linked to the existence of a valid marriage, single mothers continue to find it difficult to establish *nasab* for their children. Jordan has established a number of legal schemes, including *iḥtiḍān* to integrate children from defective families as well as orphans, children of unknown affiliation (*majhūl al-nasab*), and foundlings (sing. *laqīṭ*) into foster families. However, these schemes do not create a full child-parent relationship. They do not establish either the right to inheritance or the right to carry the name of the foster parents. Foster parents can only assume the role of custodian (*ḥāḍin*) and the role of *waṣī*. Foster families do not have the right to guardianship (*wilāya*).

Keywords Jordan · *iḥtiḍān* · Name of a child · *majhūl al-nasab* · DNA tests · Children born out of wedlock · *al-waṭ' bi-shubha* · Rape · Honour crimes

6.1 Introduction

6.1.1 Applicable Law

Filiation of children and general provisions regarding children are regulated by the Jordanian Personal Status Law of 2010 which includes provisions regulating parental care, maintenance, guardianship, and filiation (*nasab*).[1] Since the early 2000s, family law has undergone a significant reform process. In 2001 the Jordanian Personal Status Law of 1976 was reformed for the first time when six amendments were issued. In 2010 Jordan issued a completely new family law.[2] While the 1976 law only contained three articles on *nasab*, the 2010 law considerably expanded the provisions regulating it.[3]

The 1976 law was primarily based on Hanafi *fiqh*. In cases not regulated by the 1976 code, judges were obliged to resort to the Hanafi school.[4] By contrast, the preamble of the 2010 family law stipulates that the 2010 law is derived from the Quran, the Sunnah, and *ijtihād* (independent reasoning) based on the four Sunni legal schools. The 2010 Jordanian family law stipulates that in cases not regulated

[1] Temporary Personal Status Law no. 36 of 2010, 17 October 2010, *Al-Jarīda al-Rasmiyya* [Official Gazette] no. 5061, pp 5809–5888 (hereinafter: 2010 law or the Jordanian Personal Status Law of 2010). In April 2019 a number of amendments to the 2010 law were adopted. At the time of writing these amendments had not been published in the Official Gazette.

[2] Temporary Personal Status Law no. 82 of 2001 amending the Personal Status Law no. 61 of 1976, 31 December 2001, *Al-Jarīda al-Rasmiyya* no. 4524, pp 5998–6001, and Temporary Personal Status Law no. 61 of 1976, 12 January 1976, *Al-Jarīda al-Rasmiyya* no. 2668, pp 2756–2758 (hereinafter: 1976 law or the Jordanian Personal Status Law of 1976). For a detailed analysis of the reform process see Dörthe Engelcke, *Reforming Family Law: Social and Political Change in Jordan and Morocco* (Cambridge: Cambridge University Press, 2019).

[3] Articles 147–149 of the 1976 law regulate *nasab*. By comparison, 14 Articles (Articles 156–169) of the 2010 law regulate *nasab*.

[4] Article 183 Jordanian Personal Status Law of 1976.

by the law, the judge turns to the Hanafi school. If he cannot find any appropriate provisions in the Hanafi school, he is allowed to resort to any of the other Islamic legal schools.[5] Opening the code up to other legal schools than the Hanafi has increased the judge's ability to exercise judicial discretion. According to a Jordanian shariʿa judge, the judge's *ijtihād* could become important to determine *nasab* on the mother's side, especially in cases of surrogate motherhood which are not regulated by the 2010 family law.[6]

The Jordanian legislature has also issued different pieces of legislation that allow the permanent or temporary placement of children who lack caretakers or have unfit caretakers new families. The legal basis for foster care is the 1972 Childhood Protection Order (*niẓām riʿāyat al-ṭufūla*).[7] The 1972 law contains only broad provisions regarding the temporary or permanent placement of children in foster families. In order to regulate foster care in greater detail, the 2013 *iḥtiḍān* instructions (*taʿlīmāt al-iḥtiḍān*) were issued in accordance with Article 3 of the Childhood Protection Order.[8] The 2013 instructions outline the conditions foster parents and children have to meet, the process of awarding and revoking *iḥtiḍān*, and the rights and responsibilities of foster parents. The *iḥtiḍān* programme has been in existence since the 1960s, but has for most of the time been only loosely regulated.

Iḥtiḍān, which literally translates to 'embracing', is presented in the Jordanian media as the Islamic alternative to adoption.[9] Despite the fact that the *iḥtiḍān* programme has existed since the 1960s, between 1967 and 2015 only 1193 children were integrated into foster families through the programme.[10] The low number can be explained by the fact that few children and families meet the strict criteria of the *iḥtiḍān* programme, which include that only children of unknown filiation (*majhūl al-nasab*) are eligible. The potential foster parents, among other things, need to have been married for no less than five years and at least one of them needs to be infertile.[11]

To widen the pool of eligible children and foster parents, the Ministry of Social Development launched the Program of Alternative Foster Families (*barnāmaj*

---

[5] Article 325 Jordanian Personal Status Law of 2010. The four main Sunni legal schools are meant.

[6] The Jordanian shariʿa courts have not yet adjudicated such a case. Interview with Ashraf Omari, chancellor of the *dāʾirat qāḍī al-quḍāt*, the Supreme Justice Department (SJD), 27 July 2017, Amman. To increase subject protection most interviewees are identified only in terms of their position.

[7] Childhood Protection Order no. 34 of 1972, 1 June 1972, *Al-Jarīda al-Rasmiyya* no. 2360, p 1004ff. (hereinafter: 1972 law). The 1972 law does not mention '*iḥtiḍān*', but refers to the term *riʿāya* (care).

[8] The *iḥtiḍān* instructions were issued by the Minister of Social Development. They are available on the Ministry's website: www.mosd.gov.jo/index.php?option=com_content&view=article&id=2088:2015-11-09-12-50-28&catid=15:15 (accessed 20 August 2017).

[9] Nimri 2016.

[10] Nimri 2016. This figure was cited in the media. However, during an interview, the director of the family section at the Ministry of Social Development said the total number was 1557. Interview with the director of the family section at the Ministry of Social Development, 25 July 2017, Amman.

[11] Article 4 *iḥtiḍān* instructions.

al-usar al-ri'āya al-badīla) in 2011. The aim of the programme is to make foster families an alternative to institutional care facilities where the psychological needs of children are often insufficiently met. The programme is probably also motivated by financial considerations, since foster families effectively become the providers for these children, which takes pressure off the state's budget. It is therefore in the state's interest to broaden the pool of eligible children.

The Alternative Family Care Programme primarily addresses children of unfit guardians. Children up to the age of six are eligible. The foster period is not fixed. It depends on the state of the biological family and is determined in accordance with the best interests of the child. In contrast to the *iḥtiḍān* programme, marriage is not one of the pre-conditions and even single women can become caretakers.[12] The programme operates informally under the umbrella of the Ministry of Social Development and currently no law regulates it.

6.1.2 *Jurisdiction of the Courts*

According to the constitution, the Jordanian legal system is divided into religious, regular, and special courts (Article 99). Regular courts have jurisdiction over all people in civil and criminal matters (Article 102), while family law is adjudicated by religious courts, either shari'a courts or courts of other religious communities (Article 104). Shari'a courts have jurisdiction over all Muslims with respect to personal status matters (Article 105).[13] Thus, all cases related to *nasab* are adjudicated by the shari'a courts. Many of these cases are regarding proof of filiation (*ithbāt al-nasab*). Cases relating to proof of filiation normally enter the courts together with a demand for proof of marriage (*ithbāt al-zawāj*). The registration of a customary marriage is often the first step for mothers who want to establish *nasab* for their children (see below). According to the official fee list for shari'a courts (*niẓām rusūm al-maḥākim al-shar'iyya*), a claim for proof or denial of filiation (*ithbāt al-nasab aw nafīhi*) costs 30 Jordanian Dinars (JD) (around 42 US dollars).[14] A proof of marriage (*ithbāt al-zawāj*) costs 25 JD (around 35 US dollars).[15]

The shari'a courts are supervised by the *dā'irat qāḍī al-quḍāt*, the Supreme Justice Department (SJD), which organizes the recruitment, training, and disciplining of shari'a court judges.[16] To date, all of the judges of the shari'a court have been male. In 2008 a female shari'a court lawyer, Abir al-Tamimi, applied to sit the

[12] Nimri 2016.

[13] For a brief overview of the Jordanian legal system, see Engelcke 2016, pp 180–186.

[14] Article 6 of the *niẓām rusūm al-maḥākim al-shar'iyya* no. 61 of 2015, 7 June 2015, *Al-Jarīda al-Rasmiyya* no. 5349, pp 6782–6795 (hereinafter: 2015 law).

[15] Article 5 of the 2015 law.

[16] See Article 105 Jordanian Constitution. See also Article 18 of the '*qānūn tashkīl al-maḥākim al-shar'īyya*', law no. 19 of 1972, 1 January 1972, *Al-Jarīda al-Rasmiyya* no. 2357 (hereinafter: 1972 law).

entry exam organized by the SJD to become a shariʿa judge. The SJD rejected her application. Thus, shariʿa judges continue to be exclusively male in Jordan.[17]

The shariʿa courts are courts of first instance. Their decisions can be appealed before the shariʿa court of appeal.[18] In 2015 a Shariʿa Supreme Court was created.[19] Since then, decisions issued by the shariʿa court of appeal have been able to be appealed in front of the Shariʿa Supreme Court.[20] The court has in the meantime issued a number of rulings on *nasab* (see below). Shariʿa courts do not have jurisdiction in cases of *iḥtiḍān* or the Program of Alternative Foster Families. In these cases the Ministry of Social Development requires foster families to obtain a court ruling from the juvenile court (*maḥkamat al-aḥdāth*) that formalizes the allocation of foster care.[21] The role of the juvenile court is not specified in the 2013 *iḥtiḍān* instructions. This indicates that this process is not formalized, but is merely the practice of the Ministry of Social Development.

The shariʿa courts only get involved in the foster care process in two kinds of cases. First, foster families can ask the shariʿa courts to issue a guardianship document for abandoned children (*ḥujjat wiṣāya ʿalā mahjūr ʿalayhi*). Foster families normally require a guardianship document for abandoned children to handle the financial affairs of the foster child, to travel with the child, and for administrative procedures like enrolling the child in school and receiving medical treatment. However, according to a shariʿa judge, sometimes the obligatory court ruling from the juvenile court is considered sufficient for these purposes.[22] The guardianship document for abandoned children confirms that the abandoned child does not have a father and has no grandfather on the father's side and that no *waṣī* has been appointed for the child. The document makes the foster parent the *waṣī* of the child. It specifies that the *waṣī* cannot sell, mortgage, or rent any property belonging to the abandoned child. The *waṣī* is not allowed to exercise power of attorney with respect to the minor's property or to take any amount of money above 25 JD (around 35 US dollars) belonging to the minor per month except with the written permission of the shariʿa court. The *waṣī* is obliged to submit a written report of his actions every six months.[23]

---

[17] For an analysis of the case and the overall role of women in the Jordanian judiciary, see Engelcke 2018.

[18] The conditions and procedures of appeal are outlined in Articles 135–152 of the 1959 law (*qānūn uṣūl al-muḥākamāt al-sharʿiyya*) [Shariʿa Courts Procedure Law], law no. 31 of 1959.

[19] See Article 3 '*qānūn muʿaddal li-qānūn tashkīl al-maḥākim al-sharʿiyya*', law no. 20 of 2015, 23 April 2015, *Al-Jarīda al-Rasmiyya* no. 5316, pp 5316–5323 (hereinafter: amendment to the Shariʿa Court Formation Law of 2015). The law stipulates that it enters into force 90 days after the publication date in the Official Gazette.

[20] See Article 21(3)(e) of the amendment to the Shariʿa Court Formation Law of 2015.

[21] Interview with an employee at the family section of the Ministry of Social Development, 25 July 2017, Amman.

[22] Interview with the chancellor of the *dāʾirat qāḍī al-quḍāt*, the Supreme Justice Department (SJD), 27 July 2017, Amman.

[23] I obtained a sample form from the SJD.

The document helps to guarantee state control over the financial affairs of the abandoned child.

Shari'a courts also play a role in the foster care process in the event that the biological family reappears and wants to reassume the role of caretaker of a child who has been integrated into a foster family. These cases are very rare.[24] In that case the biological parents or one of them need to obtain a document from the shari'a courts that confirms *nasab*. However, even if *nasab* is established, this does not create an automatic right to take the child back. Whether the child will remain with the foster family or be returned to the biological family is decided in accordance with the best interests of the child.[25] Depending on the age of a child, a child could be questioned by the judge in such a case. Children are generally not present during court hearings when they are below the age of 15. If the children are between the age of 15 and 18, they can attend court hearings and can be questioned by the judge.[26]

6.2 The Establishment of Filiation

6.2.1 Establishing Filiation by Law

6.2.1.1 Children Born into a Valid Marriage

The 2010 Personal Status Law considerably expands the provisions on *nasab* of the previous 1976 law, which only contained three articles on *nasab*.[27] However, despite the introduction of new means to establish filiation, such as DNA tests, the 2010 family code remains true to Islamic legal doctrine that stipulates that *nasab* is established within a valid marriage. The concept of the best interests of the child is not considered in these cases even though it is the paramount principle of the Convention on the Rights of the Child (CRC), which Jordan ratified on 24 May 1991.[28] The CRC stipulates that in all actions concerning children, the best interests of the child should be the primary consideration.[29] While the concept of the best interests of the child has been integrated into the provisions of the 2010 Personal Status Law that regulate custody and visitation rights, it is not explicitly stipulated in the provisions regulating *nasab*.

---

[24] An employee at the Ministry of Social Development said that she only knew of two cases in which the biological mother reclaimed her child. Interview with anonymous, 25 July 2017.

[25] Interview with the chancellor of the *dā'irat qāḍī al-quḍāt*, the Supreme Justice Department (SJD), 23 September 2017, Amman.

[26] Interview with the chancellor of the *dā'irat qāḍī al-quḍāt*, the Supreme Justice Department (SJD), 27 July 2017.

[27] Articles 147–149 Jordanian Personal Status Law of 1976.

[28] The CRC was published in the Official Gazette in 2006. See *qānūn al-taṣdīq 'alā ittifāqiyyat ḥuqūq al-ṭifl* no. 50 of 2006, 16 October 2006, *Al-Jarīda al-Rasmiyya* no. 4787, pp 3991–4024.

[29] Article 3 CRC.

According to the 2010 Personal Status Law, filiation of a child to its mother is established through the mother giving birth to the child.[30] Future cases on assisted reproductive technologies and in particular surrogate motherhood could challenge this general rule (see introduction). By contrast, filiation between the child and the father is subject to conditions. It is established in four cases: through the existence of a valid marriage, i.e. the marital bed (*firāsh zawjiyya*); by acknowledgement (*iqrār*); by evidence (*bayyina*); or by scientific means coupled with the existence of a marital bed (*firāsh zawjiyya*).[31] The law does not specify what is meant by 'evidence' or 'scientific means' or what kind of 'evidence' is admissible. However, interviews with judges and legal practitioners reveal that evidence often refers to the testimony of witnesses.[32] Zeid al-Kilani, a prominent shariʿa judge, argued that evidence (*bayyina*) can also refer to a DNA test.[33] Scientific means refers to DNA tests. It is interesting to note that DNA tests are only permissible in the context of a valid marriage, whereas most of these claims likely arise when women who have children out of wedlock try to establish *nasab* for their children.[34] It remains unclear whether any of the four stipulated means to establish *nasab* are valid on their own.

The 2010 Personal Status Law preserves the provisions of the 1976 law which stipulate that if the father denies paternity, a demand to establish *nasab* is not heard if it is proven that there has been no physical contact between the couple since the signing of the marriage contract.[35] Like the 1976 law, the 2010 Personal Status Law stipulates that the shortest period of pregnancy is six months and the longest is one year.[36] A demand for establishment of paternity is therefore not heard when the woman gives birth one year or more after the absence of the husband. The same applies to women who give birth one year or more after a divorce and to women

[30] Article 157(1) Jordanian Personal Status Law of 2010.

[31] Article 157 Jordanian Personal Status Law of 2010.

[32] Interview with the chancellor of the *dāʾirat qāḍī al-quḍāt*, the Supreme Justice Department (SJD), 27 September 2017, Amman.

[33] Interview with lawyer and executive director of the Mizan Law Group for Human Rights, 27 July 2017, Amman.

[34] In April 2019, an amendment of Article 157 was adopted. It stipulates that *nasab* can be proven by scientific means not only in the context of a valid marriage, but also in cases of *shubha al-waṭʾ* (erroneous sexual intercourse). The JNCW proposed to add scientific means as one of the four means of evidence without specifying in what context it can be applied – thereby opening up the possibility of conducting DNA tests in cases of *zināʾ*. The JNCW specified that even in the case of *zināʾ* a man should not be able to escape his responsibilities and that *nasab* is the right of the child, see JNCW (no date). A shariʿa judge at the SJD explained that when the SJD prepared the current amendment to Article 157, the question of whether the opinion of Ibn al-Qayyim should be adopted, according to whom *nasab* can be established even in cases of *zināʾ*, was discussed. However, this opinion was subsequently dismissed because of fear that it would weaken the importance of marriage. Interview with the chancellor of the *dāʾirat qāḍī al-quḍāt*, the Supreme Justice Department (SJD), 23 September 2017. The latter argument also features in other contexts. See Eich 2012, p 47.

[35] Article 157(3) Jordanian Personal Status Law of 2010.

[36] Article 156 Jordanian Personal Status Law of 2010.

who give birth more than one year after the husband passes away.[37] The 2010 law adds that in the event that scientific means establish that the husband is the child's father, the court hears the claim to establish paternity.[38] Sometimes a woman can establish *nasab* for her child even when she gave birth one year or longer after the separation occurred. If the woman claims that she thought that the repudiation (*ṭalāq*) was not final and she and her husband continued to cohabitate, this can be regarded as a case of *al-waṭ' bi-shubha* (erroneous sexual intercourse). The shariʿa court can order a DNA test in such cases.[39]

The definition of the maximum and minimum duration of pregnancy gives rise to situations in which a child could be entitled to *nasab* from both the previous and the current husband. In one case the plaintiff had filed for denial (*nafī*) of *nasab*, because he claimed that the previous husband was the biological father of the child. The wife had given birth within one year of the divorce and seven months and 18 days after her marriage to her current husband, the plaintiff. The Shariʿa Supreme Court stated that the fear of mixing filiations (*khashyat ikhtilāṭ al-ansāb*) was a valid concern in this case. The court reasoned that on the one hand, the child is attributed to the husband if the birth occurs at least six months after the conclusion of a valid marriage contract in accordance with Article 158 of the 2010 law. On the other hand, the child is attributed to the previous husband if the woman gives birth within one year of the divorce in accordance with Article 159 of the 2010 law. The court therefore ordered a DNA test to clarify whether *nasab* should be attributed to the previous or the current husband. The court based itself on Article 157, which permits the use of DNA tests within the context of a marriage to establish *nasab*. The test revealed that the previous husband was the biological father and *nasab* was subsequently attributed to him. The fact that the court of first instance and the court of appeal had both rejected the husband's claim for denial of *nasab* demonstrates how difficult it is for men to renounce filiation within the context of a valid marriage.[40]

Legal practice shows that DNA tests are often ordered at the appeal stage and that they serve to establish *nasab* in conjunction with other forms of evidence rather than as the sole proof. In 2015 the shariʿa court of appeal in Amman reviewed a judgment on *nasab* issued by the shariʿa court of first instance in Alrusayfah.[41] The plaintiff Imane had filed for acknowledgment of filiation for her minor daughter Zaina by her husband Muhammad. The court confirmed that Imane was the wife of Muhammad, the defendant, based on a marriage contract issued by the shariʿa court in Alrusayfah, and that the marriage had been consummated. However, at the time when the marriage contract was drawn up, Imane was already pregnant with Zaina.

---

[37] Article 157(4) Jordanian Personal Status Law of 2010.

[38] Article 157(3), Jordanian Personal Status Law of 2010.

[39] Interview with the chancellor of the *dā'irat qāḍī al-quḍāt*, the Supreme Justice Department (SJD), 27 September 2017.

[40] See decision of the Shariʿa Supreme Court, no. 11/2018-60, 12 February 2018 (on file with author).

[41] All names mentioned in court rulings have been changed throughout the text.

Imane's previous husband, Ahmed, had repudiated her, which was documented by a repudiation document (*wathīqat ṭalāq*). Ahmed, who denied *nasab* to Zaina, entered the lawsuit as a third party, because Imane gave birth less than a year from the date of the divorce from Ahmed. Given that Zaina was born less than a year after the divorce from Ahmed, Imane could have claimed *nasab* for Zaina from Ahmed based on Article 159 of the 2010 law. The shariʿa court of first instance of Alrusayfah issued a ruling that established *nasab* between Zaina and Muhammad, the current husband. The fact that the defendant Muhammad confirmed the facts of the case and did not deny paternity in combination with a valid marriage contract was seen as sufficient proof to establish *nasab*. When the case was reviewed by the shariʿa court of appeal, the court ordered a DNA test, which confirmed that Imane and Muhammad were the biological parents of Zaina. The appeals court therefore confirmed the judgment of the first instance court that had established *nasab* between Zaina and Muhammad.[42] Since Imane became pregnant before the conclusion of a marriage contract, her pregnancy was a case of *zinā'* (illicit sexual relations). The ruling states that Ahmed, her previous husband, had pronounced the *liʿān* (curse or oath) accusing Imane of *zinā'*, which is one of the established ways to deny paternity. However, according to the judgment Imane had not confirmed that she had engaged in *zinā'*. The 2010 Personal Status Law stipulates that the *liʿān* of the husband alone is only valid when the wife admits that she has engaged in *zinā'*.[43] Since this was not the case, the case of *zinā'* was left open, which likely meant that it was not followed by a criminal prosecution. The 1960 Jordanian Penal Code stipulates that illicit sexual relations (*zinā'*) are punished by a one- to three-year prison sentence. If the act of *zinā'* is committed in the marital home of one of the two parties, the maximum penalty of three years is imposed.[44]

The provisions of the 2010 Personal Status Law make it almost impossible for the husband to use the *liʿān* to deny *nasab*. The filiation that is established by the marital bed cannot be denied by the two spouses except if both the husband and the wife complete the *liʿān*. If the filiation of a child is proven by the marital bed or as a result of consummation of a defective (*fāsid*) marriage or through *al-waṭ' bi-shubha*, it is possible for the husband to deny the pregnancy or the child through *liʿān*. However, the husband can only do the *liʿān* alone if the woman has acknowledged that she engaged in *zinā'* as explained above. The husband is forbidden to utter the *liʿān* to deny filiation of the child in a number of cases: after one month has passed after the birth of a child or the knowledge of the birth, if he has explicitly or implicitly acknowledged the filiation, or if scientific means (a DNA test) have proven that he is

[42] Decision of the shariʿa court of appeal in Amman, no. 309 of 2015, appeal number 96749-309/2015 (on file with author). It is interesting to note that the ruling does not contain any references to articles of the Jordanian Personal Status Law.

[43] Article 163(2) Jordanian Personal Status Law of 2010.

[44] Article 282 Jordanian Penal Code Law no. 16 of 1960, 1 May 1960, *Al-Jarīda al-Rasmiyya* no. 1487, pp 374 ff.

the father.[45] In cases of *li'ān*, the wife can also ask for a DNA test.[46] In the event that the *li'ān* is pronounced, the marriage contract is annulled. If the *li'ān* occurred to deny *nasab* and the judge rules in favour of the denial of paternity for the child, then the father does not have to pay *nafaqa* (maintenance), and father and child do not inherit from each other. Even in this rare case, the law leaves a backdoor open. If the husband admits that he lied, *nasab* between him and the child is established even if there is a ruling regarding denial of paternity.[47]

The introduction of DNA testing has, however, allowed for more deviation from the dominant rule that links *nasab* to a valid marriage. In one case, a man requested a retrial of a filiation case. The plaintiff, Ahmed, argued that after the ruling was issued he had obtained new scientific evidence – in the form of a DNA test – that would change the outcome of the case. The plaintiff stated that the first defendant, Muhammad, his alleged son, had agreed to a DNA test being conducted and had accepted the outcome of the test, which proved that the plaintiff was not Muhammad's biological father. The DNA test had been conducted in Lebanon, but the plaintiff and the defendant both declared that they did not object to a second DNA test being carried out in Jordan. The court of first instance then granted a retrial. During the retrial, Ahmed presented a written endorsement in which the second defendant, Fatima, the mother of Muhammad, stated that Muhammad was not the plaintiff's biological son. The court heard the testimony of the lawyer who had registered Fatima's acknowledgement (*iqrār*) as well as the testimony of a witness who had witnessed her acknowledgment. Muhammad stated that he was present when his mother had declared that he was not the plaintiff's son and that he did not know who his father was. Ahmed then performed the *li'ān*, swearing that he was not the biological father of Muhammad. The court then ordered the plaintiff and the defendant to do another DNA test, which confirmed the plaintiff's claim. The court of first instance therefore ruled in favour of denial of *nasab*.[48] The ruling does not mention the marital status of the parties, but it can be assumed that Ahmed and Fatima had been married. The case demonstrates to what extent DNA tests have undermined the concept of *firāsh zawjiyya* since without a DNA test it would have been (nearly) impossible to contest a *nasab* relationship that had already been established, presumably within the context of a valid marriage. It would have been interesting to see to what extent the outcome of the case would have been altered had the second defendant, Fatima, not corroborated the claims of the plaintiff.

---

[45] Article 163 Jordanian Personal Status Law of 2010.

[46] Interview with the chancellor of the *dā'irat qāḍī al-quḍāt*, the Supreme Justice Department (SJD), 23 September 2017.

[47] Article 165 Jordanian Personal Status Law of 2010.

[48] The court of first instance forwarded the case to the court of appeal in accordance with Article 138 of the 1959 Shari'a Courts Procedure Law. The court of appeal then annulled the judgment on procedural grounds; judgments issued by the court of first instance can only be appealed; a retrial is not permissible. The Shari'a Supreme Court then confirmed the decision of the court of appeal. See decision no. 19/2017-25, 14 June 2017 (on file with author).

6.2.1.2 Children Born into Informal Marriages

ʿUrfī (customary) marriages are a widespread phenomenon in the MENA region. Customary marriages are concluded for a variety of reasons. Some men want to hide a second marriage from their first wife. At other times, a couple wants to legalize a sexual relationship when an extra-marital pregnancy has occurred.[49] In her book about customary marriage in Egypt and the United Arab Emirates, Frances Hasso observes that customary marriages usually receive state attention when legal challenges emerge: a woman demanding *nafaqa* (maintenance) for her child after the husband has deserted her, the husband denying the marriage, or a woman wanting to enrol the child in school.[50]

These marriages are often concluded simply by pronouncing the *fātiḥa*, the first Surah of the Quran. They are not officially registered and thereby do not meet the legal registration requirements. The Personal Status Law obliges parties to register their marriage. However, failure to register the marriage does not automatically render the marriage invalid. Should the marriage meet all the legal requirements, it can belatedly be registered, and full marital rights, including *nasab*, materialize. A fine is imposed for belated registration of the marriage. All of the contracting parties, including the witnesses, are fined 200 JD (around 281 US dollars) each.[51]

Women who have children within the context of a customary marriage face a number of forms of discrimination. Since there is no proof of registration of the marriage, these women are considered unmarried. The line between children who are born into an informal marriage and children who are born out of wedlock is very blurry. When a woman, Muslim or Christian, gives birth at a hospital and is unable to present a marriage contract, the hospital informs the local authorities. Once she has delivered the baby, the woman will be taken into administrative detention (*tawqīf idārī*) and the baby is sent to the Al Hussein Social Foundation for Orphans, which was founded in 1953 to provide care for orphans, foundlings, and children from disjoined families – that is, children who are born out of wedlock. The foundation has a section specifically dedicated to new-borns. The ties between the biological mother and the child are normally severed at that point.[52]

The Jordanian authorities claim that administrative detention protects women whose extra-marital pregnancy has tarnished their family's honour from becoming victims of honour crimes. The women are held under the 1954 Crime Prevention Law.[53] The law allows the governor to arrest without charge people who are suspected of being about to commit a crime or assist others in committing a crime, as

[49] Frances Hasso describes reasons why couples conclude customary marriages. See Hasso 2011, p 83.

[50] Hasso 2011, p 82.

[51] Article 36(2) and (3) Jordanian Personal Status Law of 2010.

[52] Ibrahim 2016, p 128.

[53] Crime Prevention Law no. 7 of 1954, 1 March 1954, *Al-Jarīda al-Rasmiyya* no. 1173.

well as people who, if free, would present a danger to others.[54] Although the law does not provide any legal basis for protective custody, the scope of application has been widened to include placing women in administrative detention. Human Rights Watch has documented cases of women who have been held in administrative detention for over ten years. Only the local governor has the authority to release the woman. This only happens if the woman's family is no longer considered a threat to her and has provided guarantees that they will not harm her.[55] In July 2018, a shelter called the Amneh House was inaugurated by the Ministry of Social Development. The shelter houses women who are in danger of becoming victims of so-called honour crimes. Women who are being held in administrative detention at the Jweideh Correctional and Rehabilitation Centre will be transferred to the Amneh House.[56] The new shelter mainly aims to improve the living conditions of these women while providing health care, recreational facilities, legal assistance and educational opportunities.[57]

When a woman is released from administrative detention, she can turn to the Al Hussein Social Foundation for Orphans or the Ministry of Social Development to file a demand to reclaim her child. According to an employee of the Ministry of Social Development, the Ministry then gets in touch with the foster family if the child has entered the foster care system. However, the woman will only be reunited with her child if she has officially legalized her customary marriage – that is, if she has married the biological father in the meantime. She needs to provide a marriage contract and proof of *nasab* issued by a shariʿa court. Otherwise, she will be unable to reclaim her child.[58]

Female migrant workers also become victims of administrative detention when they give birth at a hospital and are unable to present a valid marriage contract. Their babies are then also sent to the Al Hussein Social Foundation for Orphans. Unmarried or informally married migrant workers therefore often choose to deliver their children at home.[59] However, the argument that women need to be put in 'protective' custody to prevent them from becoming victims of honour crimes does not apply in these cases since the families of these female migrant workers (normally) do not live in the country.[60]

A child born within the context of a *ʿurfī* marriage is thus not automatically considered a child of the marital bed and therefore does not have a right to *nasab*.

---

[54] Article 3 Crime Prevention Law, as cited in Human Rights Watch 2009, p 7.

[55] Human Rights Watch 2009, pp 10–12.

[56] Husseini 2018.

[57] The shelter is regulated by Order no. 171 of 2016 about the role of shelters for women in danger issued in accordance with Article 4 of the law about the Ministry of Social Development and Work no. 14/1956 [*niẓām dawr īwāʾ al-muʿarraḍāt li-l-khaṭar ṣādir bi-muqtaḍā al-mādda 4 min qānūn wizārat al-shuʾūn al-ijtimāʿiyya wa-l-ʿamal raqm 14 li-sanat 1956*], 20 November 2016, *Al-Jarīda al-Rasmiyya* no. 5432, pp 6709–6715.

[58] Interview with anonymous, 25 July 2017.

[59] Tamkeen Fields for Aid 2015, p 109.

[60] Interview with the director of Tamkeen Fields for Aid, 26 July 2017, Amman.

Informal marriages only automatically establish *nasab* on the mother's side. To claim *nasab* from the father, the marriage needs to be officially confirmed. A first step to claiming *nasab* for a child that has been born into an informal marriage is therefore to turn to the shariʿa court to ask for a ruling that verifies the marriage contract (*tathbīt ʿaqd zawāj*). The court then examines whether the informal marriage meets the legal requirements of a valid (*ṣaḥīḥ*) marriage. Only if the marriage meets the conditions of a valid marriage do the full rights related to *nasab* emerge. The aforementioned fine then needs to be paid.

Marriage contracts can be valid (*ṣaḥīḥ*), defective (*fāsid*), or void (*bāṭil*).[61] A marriage contract that is void (*bāṭil*) does not establish *nasab* regardless of whether the marriage has been consummated or not. Moreover, there is no right to *nafaqa* (maintenance) or inheritance, and no obligation for the wife to undergo the *ʿidda* (waiting period).[62] A marriage contract that is considered defective (*fāsid*) establishes *nasab,* but not all rights that are associated with *nasab* (see below).[63] For a contract to be valid, both parties need to express their consent.[64] The conclusion of the contract needs to be witnessed by two men or one man and two women. All witnesses need to be Muslim if the couple is Muslim.[65] The *mahr* (dower) needs to be paid to the wife at the time of the conclusion of the contract.[66]

If a customary marriage meets all of the legal requirements of a valid marriage and the husband acknowledges the marriage, it is relatively easy to belatedly register the marriage contract. In 2010 the shariʿa court of first instance of Sweileh issued such a judgment regarding the verification of a marriage contract (*tathbīt ʿaqd zawāj*). In October 2009 the plaintiff Nur filed a lawsuit against the defendant Ahmed. She asked for the verification of her marriage contract, which met all of the legal requirements. The two parties had expressed their consent. The contract had been concluded at the home of the defendant's father, the immediate *mahr* had been stipulated at 50 JD (about 70 US dollars), and the delayed *mahr* at 1000 JD (about 1406 US dollars). The contract had been concluded in the presence of witnesses. The judgment lists the names of the witnesses. The judgement states that the woman had been a virgin, Muslim, and not previously married. The religion is likely listed because the woman was a migrant worker and it was thus not evident that she was Muslim. The ruling stipulates that the defendant was fully in possession of his mental capacities and almost 32 years old. He was capable of paying the immediate *mahr* as well as *nafaqa* during the marriage. The defendant Ahmed and the testimony of the witnesses confirmed all of the facts of the case. Based on

---

[61] For the conditions under which a marriage contract is considered void (*bāṭil*) see Article 30 Jordanian Personal Status Law of 2010.

[62] Article 33 Jordanian Personal Status Law of 2010.

[63] For the conditions under which a marriage contract is considered defective (*fāsid*) see Article 31 Jordanian Personal Status Law of 2010.

[64] Article 6 Jordanian Personal Status Law of 2010.

[65] Article 8(1) Jordanian Personal Status Law of 2010.

[66] Article 40 Jordanian Personal Status Law of 2010.

the verification (*taṣāduq*) of the facts, the acknowledgment (*iqrār*), and the means of personal evidence (*bayyina shakhṣiyya*), the court ruled that the marriage had been proven.[67]

Difficulties arise when the *'urfī* marriage does not meet the legal requirements of a valid marriage. In 2011 the shari'a court of appeal in Amman reviewed a judgment from the shari'a court of first instance of south Amman regarding the establishment of *nasab* and the validity of a marriage contract. The plaintiff Malika had filed a request for the recognition of her customary marriage (*zawāj 'urfī*) to the defendant Nadim. The customary marriage happened in October 2008. The couple then consummated the marriage and their daughter Nadia was born in June 2009. Since they had no valid marriage contract, Nadia was designated of unknown filiation (*majhūl al-nasab*) upon birth and was delivered to the Al Hussein Social Foundation for Orphans. The ruling specifies that both parties had expressed their consent to the marriage, but that they had no witnesses and no *mahr* had been stipulated at the time of the conclusion of the contract.[68] The first instance court of south Amman had ruled the marriage contract of Rania and Nadim valid and subsequently established *nasab* between Nadia and Nadim. The court also ordered the two parties to pay a fine of 200 JD for failing to register their marriage contract.[69]

When the shari'a court of appeal reviewed the ruling, it ordered a DNA test. The DNA test confirmed Malika and Nadim as the biological parents of Nadia. The court then confirmed the ruling of the shari'a court of first instance that had established *nasab* between Nadia and Nadim, The judgment states that the defendant Nadim confirmed the facts of the case and that *nasab* was therefore also established by *iqrār*. Thus the DNA test was again used in conjunction with other means of proof (*iqrār*) to establish *nasab*. However, the shari'a court of appeal rejected the shari'a court of first instance's ruling that had declared the marriage contract of Malika and Nadim valid. According to the court, the customary marriage did not meet the conditions of a valid marriage contract since no witnesses had assisted during the conclusion of the contract and no *mahr* had been stipulated. The court therefore ruled the 200 JD fine for failing to register a (valid) marriage contract invalid. The court of appeal also stated that *nasab* for the minor girl would have been established even without ruling the customary marriage contract valid. The court referred to Article 34 of the Personal Status Law in its ruling, which stipulates that in the case of a defective (*fāsid*) marriage contract which is followed by consummation (*dukhūl*), *nasab* is established.[70]

The reference to Article 34 of the Personal Status Law has important implications for the rights of the child. Article 34 stipulates that in the case of a defective

---

[67] Decision of the shari'a court of first instance of Sweileh, no. 230 of 2010, case number 160/137/68 (on file with author).

[68] Article 6 Jordanian Personal Status Law of 2010.

[69] Article 36(7) Jordanian Personal Status Law of 2010.

[70] Decision of the shari'a court of appeal in Amman, no. 2431 of 2011, appeal number 80960-2431/2011 (on file with author).

(*fāsid*) marriage contract that has been consummated, the *mahr* and the *ʿidda* (waiting period) become obligatory and *nasab* is established. Article 34 uses the term '*nasab*'. However, the Jordanian legislature has hollowed out the meaning of the concept, because despite '*nasab*' being established within the context of a defective marriage, the child does not have the right to inheritance or *nafaqa* (maintenance).[71] This is thus not 'full' *nasab*. In practice this means that the child will be able to carry the father's name, but it will not be entitled to any other rights that normally follow the establishment of *nasab*. This demonstrates that children who are born into an informal marriage do not possess the same rights as children who are born in wedlock if the *ʿurfī* marriage cannot belatedly be registered as a valid marriage. Whereas the court of first instance had more loosely applied the family law, which worked in favour of the plaintiff, the court of appeal was more legalistic in its interpretation and subsequently only established a weaker version of *nasab*. In this case, greater legal security was not an advantage for the plaintiff.

6.2.1.3 Children Born into a Presumed Marriage

The 2010 Personal Status Law introduces the term *al-waṭʾ bi-shubha* (erroneous sexual intercourse), which was not present in the provisions regulating *nasab* of the 1976 law. These marriages are often *ʿurfī* marriages. In accordance with the legal minimum and maximum period of pregnancy, the child is considered a child of the marital bed when the wife gives birth at least six months after the conclusion of a valid marriage contract. In the case of a defective (*fāsid*) marriage contract or a situation of erroneous sexual intercourse (*al-waṭʾ bi-shubha*), the child needs to be born at least six months after the consummation of the marriage or the erroneous sexual intercourse occurred.[72] If the child is born after the dissolution of the marriage, *nasab* to the ex-husband can be established up to one year after the dissolution of the marriage.[73] According to a shariʿa judge, in cases of *al-waṭʾ bi-shubha,* a DNA test can be ordered to establish *nasab*.[74]

The 2010 law thereby puts greater emphasis on couples' intentions. It continues to link *nasab* to marriage, but it gives greater leeway to couples who have *erroneously* engaged in sexual intercourse without the existence of a valid marriage contract. Since they acted in good faith and there was no intention to violate the law or societal norms, their behaviour should not be punished. The introduction of *al-waṭʾ bi-shubha* is a way to integrate extra-marital relationships into the socially accepted framework. The introduction of the concept into the 2010 law has arguably made it easier to establish *nasab* in such cases. It remains unclear, however,

---

71 Article 34 Jordanian Personal Status Law of 2010.

72 Article 158 Jordanian Personal Status Law of 2010.

73 Article 159 Jordanian Personal Status Law of 2010.

74 Interview with the chancellor of the *dāʾirat qāḍī al-quḍāt*, the Supreme Justice Department (SJD), 23 September 2017.

whether 'full' *nasab* – entitling the child to the right to carry the father's name and to maintenance and inheritance rights – is established for children born within the context of *al-waṭ' bi-shubha* once such a marriage is registered. Presumably, like in the case of *'urfī* marriages, the judge will establish whether all of the conditions that give rise to a valid marriage contract were in place. If that is the case, the child receives 'full' *nasab*. This would put children who are born within the context of *al-waṭ' bi-shubha* at an advantage vis-à-vis children who are born within the context of a defective marriage (see above).

The doctrine of the sleeping embryo (*rāqid*) is not acknowledged by Jordanian law. A shariʿa judge at the SJD explained that the SJD generally follows the latest medical scientific evidence. He admitted that one year was an exceptionally long period for pregnancy and six months an extremely short period, but said that according to medical expertise this was still within the limits of what is possible. The law thereby acknowledges these exceptional cases.[75] The legislature probably intended to legalize the status of children who could normally not be considered of the marital bed while at the same time reframing extra-marital relationships as presumed marriages in order to avoid an official violation of social norms.

6.2.2 Establishing Filiation by Private Autonomy: Acknowledgement of Filiation

Filiation of a child to his or her father can also be established by acknowledgement (*iqrār*). For this purpose, a document for the acknowledgment of filiation (*ḥujjat iqrār bi-nasab*) is drawn up by the shariʿa courts. Acknowledgement is subject to conditions. The child needs to be alive and of unknown filiation (*majhūl al-nasab*). The law further stipulates that the father cannot lie about the true circumstances of the case. This latter provision was not present in the 1976 law. It implies that people might have previously abused this right in some way. The person who wants to acknowledge the child needs to have reached puberty and needs to be of sound mind. The age difference between the person who is acknowledging the child and the child needs to be feasible. Like in the 1976 law, the possibility of conception is thereby considered. Should the child in question have reached puberty and be of sound mind, the child needs to consent to the *iqrār*.[76] Once established, *iqrār* creates a full parent-child relationship between the child and the person who has acknowledged the child.

The 2010 Personal Status Law specifies that the acknowledgement of filiation can be explicit or implicit.[77] A shariʿa judge at the SJD explained that explicit in

75 Interview with the chancellor of the *dāʾirat qāḍī al-quḍāt*, the Supreme Justice Department (SJD), 23 September 2017.

76 Article 160 Jordanian Personal Status Law of 2010.

77 Article 161 Jordanian Personal Status Law of 2010.

this case means that the man comes to court in person to acknowledge the child. Implicit refers to certain types of behaviour that indicate fatherhood. Those include paying the bill of the hospital where the woman gave birth, visiting the woman, and bringing flowers and chocolate to the hospital.[78] Court practice demonstrates that these types of behaviour are commonly seen as implicit acknowledgements of *nasab*. In one case a husband claimed that he suffered from impotence – literally inadequacy (*ḍaʿf*) – and therefore denied *nasab*. The lawyer of the wife stated that the man is the defendant's husband and that they consummated the marriage. His client therefore gave birth on the marital bed. According to the wife, the husband knew about the pregnancy and was happy about it. According to the defendant, he distributed sweets and accompanied her to the hospital. He also covered the costs for the hospital and received congratulations from family and friends. The court of first instance and the court of appeal both rejected the claim for denial of *nasab*. The plaintiff then appealed in front of the Shariʿa Supreme Court, which rejected the case on procedural grounds.[79]

However, it remains unclear whether or not *iqrār* on its own establishes *nasab*. Legal practice seems to suggest that, like DNA tests, *iqrār* establishes *nasab* in conjunction with other means of proof. In 2013 the shariʿa court of appeal reviewed a judgment issued by the shariʿa court of first instance in Zarqa. The shariʿa court of first instance had established *nasab* for Ali from his parents, the plaintiff Zahar and the first defendant Muhammad. The marriage had been concluded in 2002 in Amman. The ruling states that Ali had been born in a correct marital bed in Iraq in 2004. Zahar had brought Ali to Jordan as the son of her brother Majid. Majid had a son who had passed away. For this reason, *nasab* was first established between Ali and Majid. After considering the facts, the shariʿa court of first instance annulled Ali's *nasab* to Majid, the second defendant, and Intisar, his wife. When the shariʿa court of appeal reviewed the case, it ordered a DNA test, which confirmed Zahra and Muhammad as the biological parents of Ali. The ruling explicitly states that the establishment of *nasab* is based on Zahra and Muhammad corroborating the facts, the *iqrār* of the defendant Muhammad, and the testimony of a biological expert (*khabīr biyūlūjī*) who had conducted the DNA test, as well as the existence of a proven valid marriage.[80] The emphasis on the existence of a valid marriage, DNA evidence and witness testimony indicates that in the context of a marital dispute, *iqrār* functions more in conjunction with other types of proof for the establishment of *nasab* rather than as the sole type of proof.

[78] Article 161 Jordanian Personal Status Law of 2010.

[79] The court stated that the ruling of the court of appeal had been issued before the issuing of the 2016 law that allowed the appeal of decisions issued by the court of appeal in front of the Shariʿa Supreme Court. See decision of the Shariʿa Supreme Court, no. 1/2017-7, 3 January 2017 (on file with author).

[80] Decision of the shariʿa court of appeal in Amman, no. 1861 of 2013, appeal number 88731-1861/2013 (on file with author).

By contrast, it also seems possible that a man could simply acknowledge a child through *iqrār* to 'claim' a child as his own. In one case, the brother of a deceased man filed for denial of *nasab*. The plaintiff claimed that the two children of his deceased brother were not his biological children and therefore had no right to inheritance. The plaintiff claimed that his brother was infertile and had adopted (*tabannī*) the children 25 years ago, added them to his family booklet (*daftar ʿāʾila*), and registered them at the civil registry. Thus, he claimed, the children did not have *nasab* through the deceased and they were not from the marital bed, nor could their *nasab* be established through scientific means. The two defendants had inherited the movable and immovable property of the deceased, thus depriving the plaintiff and his brother of what they claimed were their legitimate inheritance rights. The court of first instance dismissed the case and claimed that the acknowledgement (*iqrār*) of the deceased through the registration of the children in the civil registry was correct. The court of appeal then confirmed the ruling of the court of first instance.[81]

In 2017 the shariʿa court of appeal in Amman upheld a judgment issued by the shariʿa court of first instance of Amman. The court of first instance had established *nasab* for two minors, Yazan and Laith, from their late father Ahmed. The judgment stated that *nasab* had not been established to anyone else but Ahmed. The court based its decision on the fact that Ahmed had confirmed the facts of the case – Ahmed's acknowledgment (*iqrār*) happened before he died – and two types of evidence: convincing personal testimony and official written evidence. This was a revised ruling. The first ruling by the court of first instance had been annulled by the shariʿa court of appeal. The reason for the annulment is not stated in the judgement, but it is clear from the context that the appeal court had annulled the ruling because the court of first instance had failed to order a DNA test. The court of first instance then revised its ruling, ordered a DNA test, and issued the aforementioned ruling. The DNA test was carried out by the laboratories of the security service and it confirmed that the defendant Ahmed was the biological father of the two minors.[82] It seems that in this case *iqrār* on its own had not been sufficient to establish *nasab*. Only when a DNA test confirmed *nasab* did the court confirm the ruling. Once again *iqrār* established *nasab* in conjunction with other means of proof.

---

[81] The Shariʿa Supreme Court annulled the decision of the court of appeal. According to the court, the case was mysterious (*ghāmiḍa*) because no inheritance inventory had been registered with a shariʿa court, but the court did not directly question the *nasab* of the children. See decision of the Shariʿa Supreme Court, no. 5/2017-11, 22 February 2017 (on file with author).

[82] Decision of the shariʿa court of appeal in Amman, no. 679 of 2017, appeal number 107409-679/2017 (on file with author).

6.3 Status of Children of Defective or Unknown Filiation

6.3.1 Children Born Out of Wedlock

The Personal Status Law does not address the status of children who are born out of wedlock. A child born out of wedlock is the result of *zinā'* (illicit sexual relations). The child does not have any legal relationship with the biological father. He or she is not entitled to carry the father's name, to receive *nafaqa* or to inherit from the father.

A woman who gives birth out of wedlock can only establish *nasab* for her child if she proves that the child was born within the context of an informal marriage or that she had engaged in *al-wat' bi-shubha*. Thus, she has to establish that there was some form of marriage in the first place. If she cannot prove such a relationship, the child will not get *nasab*.

Children are expected to carry the name of the father. According to the Jordanian Civil Code (*al-qānūn al-madanī*), every person has a name (*ism*) and a surname (*laqab*) and the father's surname is added to the names of his children.[83] This does not apply to children who are born out of wedlock. The 2001 Civil Status Law (*qānūn al-aḥwāl al-madaniyya*) regulates the name allocation of illegitimate (*ghayr shar'ī*) children – that is, children who are born out of wedlock. If the child is born out of wedlock, the names of the father and the mother are not mentioned in the birth registry (*sijill al-wilāda*) except if one or both of them obtains a favourable and final court ruling. The responsible employee at the Department of Civil Status and Passports (*dā'irat al-aḥwāl al-madaniyya wa-l-jawāzāt*) chooses a fictional name for the parents of the child.[84] The people who are eligible to report the birth of a child include an adult relative (to at least the fourth degree), a medical doctor, a hospital director, a birth house, a prison or a midwife.[85] If the birth of a child out of wedlock happens in the presence of one of those parties, the name of the mother is mentioned and the responsible employee at the Department of Civil Status and Passports chooses a father's name.[86] There are, however, two exceptions to this rule. If the child is the result of an incestuous relationship or the mother is married and her husband is not the father of the child, the responsible employee is not allowed to register the name of the mother and the father.[87] Only once *nasab* has been officially established can the names of the parents and subsequently the child be changed. The parents or one of them have to appear in front of the responsible employee at the Department of Civil Status and Passports and declare the acknowledgment (*iqrār*) of *nasab*. The acknowledgment needs to be supported by a final court decision.[88]

---

[83] Article 38 Jordanian Civil Code, law no. 43 of 1976.

[84] Article 20 Civil Status Law no. 9 of 2001.

[85] Article 14(1) Civil Status Law no. 9 of 2001.

[86] Article 20(2) Civil Status Law no. 9 of 2001.

[87] Article 22 Civil Status Law no. 9 of 2001.

[88] Article 21 Civil Status Law no. 9 of 2001.

In August 2017 the Jordanian parliament voted in favour of the abrogation of Article 308 of the 1960 Jordanian Penal Code. Article 308 stipulated that if a valid marriage is concluded between a victim and a perpetrator, the charges against the perpetrator are dropped.[89] This article was also applied in cases of rape and thereby enabled a rapist to avoid a prison sentence. A coalition of women's groups and lawyer activists had fought for the repeal of Article 308. The reasoning behind the article is that the law is supposed to help the woman restore her honour by legalizing an illegitimate relationship. As in the case of administrative detention, it is supposed to protect the woman from becoming the victim of an honour crime. Rape in this sense is not primarily regarded as a crime against an individual, but as a violation of the community's honour. Defending the importance of Article 308, the government had argued that the law helps women to establish *nasab* for their children by forcing the rapist to marry the victim and thereby acknowledge the child. This argument is echoed by a shariʿa judge: 'Very often there is no rape but it is simply the case that the two parties have a relationship. If the man then marries her, he is exempted from a penalty. The child of such a relationship is then legalized. This is a way to force a man to recognize a child and to prevent him from escaping his responsibility. If he prefers to go to jail, then the child does not get *nasab*.'[90] The president of the legal committee of the lower house of parliament had asked the *dāʾirat al-iftāʾ* (Fatwa Department) whether DNA tests can establish *nasab* in cases of rape between the rapist and the child born as a result of rape. The Fatwa Department did not directly answer the question but instead recommended the amendment of Article 157 of the 2010 law stating that *nasab* to the father is established through the marital bed, erroneous sexual intercourse, acknowledgement or evidence. The fatwa further states that the court can prove *nasab* through scientific means, taking into account the rules that *nasab* is established through the marital bed.[91]

The abrogation of Article 308 does not help to solve the problem of children who are born as a result of rape. The fundamental problem remains that filiation is not understood as a mere biological concept, but depends on the existence of a valid marriage. Women's groups and activists have been pushing to turn *nasab* into a biological concept, but these efforts have so far not succeeded.[92]

6.3.2 Children with Unknown Filiation and Foundlings

Children whose mother and father are unknown are considered of unknown filiation (*majhūl al-nasab*). Foundlings (sing. *laqīṭ*) normally fall into this category.

89 Article 308 Jordanian Penal Code.

90 Interview with the chancellor of the *dāʾirat qāḍī al-quḍāt*, the Supreme Justice Department (SJD), 23 September 2017.

91 Fatwa Department, decision no. 255/8/2018, 19 April 2018 (on file with author).

92 Interview with lawyer and executive director of the Mizan Law Group for Human Rights, 27 July 2017.

Foundlings are children who have been abandoned. Reasons for abandonment are often linked to poverty and the marital status of the woman; some children who are born out of wedlock become foundlings. Incest is another reason to abandon a child.[93] The Civil Status Law stipulates that 'the religion of the foundling is the religion of the state.' Thus, foundlings are considered Muslim. Some foundlings are orphans. The term orphan is also commonly used for children who have lost their father, even when the mother is still alive.

It is difficult to establish how many children are abandoned in Jordan. According to a government report, between 2007 and 2010 an average of 27 foundlings were delivered to the Al Hussein Social Foundation for Orphans annually.[94] On average, between 800 and 1100 children live in the 33 care homes throughout Jordan.[95] A study for which 42 Jordanians were interviewed who had spent at least two consecutive years in one of the residential care facilities found that 43% of them were of unknown filiation.[96]

There are a number of RNGOs (royal NGOs) that provide services to orphans. The Al Aman Fund for the Future of Orphans was established by Queen Rania and began operating in 2006. It provides vocational training, scholarships, health insurance, and psychological support to orphans above the age of 18 when they are obliged to leave the care facilities. According to the director, 579 orphans have benefitted from the scholarship programme since the foundation began operating.[97]

Overall, social attitudes to these children are ambiguous. On the one hand, caring for orphans is seen as admirable. Many affluent families are involved in charity work that focuses on orphans, and people often donate to orphanages, especially during Ramadan. Queen Rania tends to share an *ifṭār* meal with orphans during Ramadan.[98] Orphan children can be treated kindly because they lack family support. On the other hand, they can be stigmatised and seen as representative of immoral social behaviour.[99] This is also reflected by the derogatory terms that are at times used for foundlings and orphans, such as '*ibn ḥarām*' or '*ibn zinā*'', which both translate to 'bastard'.[100]

---

93 It seems that women in the Ottoman Empire abandoned their children for similar reasons. Maksudyan in her study on orphans and destitute children states that births out of wedlock, poverty, migration, and hardship during wartime were the most common reasons for abandonment. See Maksudyan 2014, p 18.

94 UN Committee on the Rights of the Child (CRC) Fourth and Fifth Periodic Report of States Parties, Jordan (1 March 2013), CRC/C/JOR/4-5, p 9.

95 Ibrahim 2016, p 129.

96 Ibrahim 2016, p 127.

97 Interview with the director of the Al Aman Fund For the Future of Orphans, 25 July 2017, Amman.

98 Jordan Times 2016.

99 Ibrahim 2016, p 128.

100 Maksudyan remarks that the terms 'foundling' and 'bastard' were used interchangeably in the Ottoman Empire. See Maksudyan 2014, p 22.

Taking care of orphans is often seen as a religious duty, which might also explain why caring for orphans is seen as commendable. A *fatwā* (judicial opinion) issued by the Fatwa Department (*dāʾirat al-iftāʾ*) declared taking care of orphans to be a *farḍ al-kifāya*, which, according to the Jordanian media, has increased popular support for foster care.[101] In contrast to *farḍ al-ʿayn* (individual duty), which refers to a religious obligation the individual Muslim has to perform like daily prayer or pilgrimage, *farḍ al-kifāya* (sufficiency duty) refers to communal obligations of the Muslim community as a whole. As long as enough members of the community carry out this obligation, the others remain free to focus on their individual duties. If the communal obligation is not sufficiently fulfilled, it becomes an obligation for all Muslims.

6.4 Protection of Children Without Filiation or Permanent Caretakers

6.4.1 General Legal Schemes of Protection and Care

The legal basis for foster care is the 1972 Childhood Protection Order (*niẓām riʿāyat al-ṭufūla*). Article 3 of the 1972 law stipulates that the caretaker or the alternative family (*al-usra al-badīla aw al-ḥāḍina*) assumes the regular responsibilities of the biological family under the supervision of the Ministry of Social Development.[102] The 1972 law only contains broad guidelines. The 2013 *iḥtiḍān* instructions (*taʿlīmāt al-iḥtiḍān*) were issued in accordance with Article 3 of the Childhood Protection Order. The instructions regulate how *iḥtiḍān* is awarded and revoked, as well as the rights and responsibilities of foster families, in greater detail. However, instructions (*taʿlīmāt*) do not have the same status as laws and it remains unclear to what extent rights stipulated in instructions can be enforced. To date, there is no *iḥtiḍān* law.

The *iḥtiḍān* instructions do not use the term adoption (*tabannī*). The Personal Status Law only stipulates that *tabannī* does not create *nasab* even if the adopted child is of unknown filiation (*majhūl al-nasab*).[103] Jordan has stipulated reservations against certain articles of the CRC, including Articles 20 and 21, which concern adoption. The Jordanian government justified its reservations with reference to Islamic law that does not permit the practice of adoption.[104] It is partly due to the fact that adoption is seen as contrary to Islamic law that foster care and in particular *iḥtiḍān* remain a sensitive topic in Jordan. This also explains why, despite several visits, I was unable to obtain the relevant statistics about *iḥtiḍān* from the

---

[101] Nimri 2016.

[102] Article 3 of the 1972 law.

[103] Article 162 Personal Status Law of 2010.

[104] UN Committee on the Rights of the Child (CRC) Initial Report of State Parties, Jordan (26 November 1993), CRC/C/8/Add. 4, p 23.

Ministry of Social Development with respect to the nationality of the foster parents, their place of residence, and the age and sex of the children.[105]

In 2011 the Ministry of Social Development launched the Program of Alternative Foster Families (*barnāmaj al-usar al-riʿāya al-badīla*). Previously, children in care facilities only had two options: to remain in institutional care or to find a family through *iḥtiḍān*. The Ministry of Social Development launched the programme in cooperation with partners including Columbia University's Amman Center, Columbia University's School of Social Work, and UNICEF.[106]

The *iḥtiḍān* programme creates a permanent relationship between the caretaker and the child, whereas the Alternative Family Care Programme gives children living in poor conditions an opportunity to live in a foster family for a specific period of time. The period is not fixed from the beginning, and depends on the state of the biological family of the child in accordance with the best interests of the child. Thus the possibility remains that the children will leave the foster family when the situation of the biological family improves. This is why many families prefer the *iḥtiḍān* programme. The Program of Alternative Foster Families can be an alternative for families who have been on the waiting list of the *iḥtiḍān* programme for a long time.[107]

Potential foster families have to meet a number of conditions. The foster family needs to be socially and psychologically stable, be financially capable, and have no criminal record, and their place of residence needs to be appropriate for foster care. The family is also obliged to attend training sessions carried out by the Ministry of Social Development, and to undergo a social inquiry by the Ministry. If the child is Muslim, the foster family has to be Muslim. Children who are non-Muslim will be placed into a family of their religion. Since in general all foundlings are assumed to be Muslim, Christian Jordanians are only eligible to become foster parents in a limited number of cases. In contrast to the *iḥtiḍān* programme, the Program of Alternative Foster Families allows single women to become foster parents. The child also has to fulfil a number of conditions. He or she needs to be below the age of seven and should not have any contagious diseases.[108]

The children who get integrated into foster families through the Alternative Family Care Programme are not of unknown filiation. In most of the cases, the biological mother is known and the father is unknown. In this case, the biological mother must sign a document indicating that she has no objection to her child being taken into a foster family. The foster family signs a pledge to return the child if the biological mother asks for it.[109] There is currently no law that regulates the Family

[105] The director of the Al Aman Fund for the Future of Orphans also complained that it was difficult to obtain any detailed information from the Ministry of Social Development. Interview with the director of the Al Aman Fund for the Future of Orphans, 25 July 2017.

[106] Nimri 2014.

[107] Nimri 2016.

[108] Nimri 2014.

[109] Interview with anonymous, 25 July 2017.

Alternative Care Programme. The process depends entirely on the practice of the Ministry of Social Development. The analysis below will therefore focus on the *iḥtiḍān* instructions.

6.4.2 Iḥtiḍān *Instructions*

6.4.2.1 Terminology

The instructions define the child of unknown filiation (*al-ṭifl al-majhūl al-nasab*) as a child who does not know his mother or father. This suggests that the child is already considered to be of unknown filiation when one parent is unknown. However, the director of the family section at the Ministry of Social Development has stated that both parents have to be unknown.[110] The foster family is called the custodian family (*al-usra al-ḥāḍina*). It is defined as the family that has been assigned the *iḥtiḍān* for a child of unknown affiliation by the Minister of Social Development or by the competent court. The foster family needs to be Muslim. If they have converted to Islam, the conversion needs to date back at least three years. The conversion needs to be proven by a conversion document (*bi-ḥujjat islām*).[111]

6.4.2.2 The Procedure for the Award of *iḥtiḍān*

The family that wants to foster a child needs to file a written demand addressing the Ministry of Social Development of their place of residence. A family that lives outside of Jordan has to submit a written demand either to the Jordanian embassy or the consulate in their country of residence or fax their demand directly to the Ministry of Social Development.[112] The law is silent on nationality, but interviews with employees at the Ministry of Social Development confirm that the foster parents need to be Jordanian, or at least the husband needs to be Jordanian.[113]

Families who live outside of Jordan are obliged to cover the costs of the social inquiry, which is carried out either by an employee of the Ministry of Social Development or by an employee of the embassy or the general consulate in the family's country of residence.[114] The social inquiry (*al-dirāsa al-ijtimāʿiyya*) needs to be supported by a number of documents: a photocopy of the civil status card (*biṭāqat al-aḥwāl al-madaniyya*); the identity card; a photocopy of the family

[110] Interview with the director of the family section at the Ministry of Social Development, 25 July 2017, Amman.

[111] Article 2 *iḥtiḍān* instructions.

[112] Article 6(1) *iḥtiḍān* instructions.

[113] Interview with anonymous, 25 July 2017.

[114] Article 6(2) *iḥtiḍān* instructions.

booklet (*daftar al-ʿāʾila*); a certified copy of the marriage contract; a copy of the health certificate issued by one of the clinics that belong to the Ministry of Health; and a report that confirms the inability of the husband or one of the spouses to reproduce, which needs to be issued by a medical doctor specialized in reproduction. Families who have converted to Islam needs to present a conversion document. Further documents that need to be submitted include a document that establishes the husband's type of work, the monthly income, or any other source of income (land, rents, assets in the bank, businesses, etc.), a criminal record certificate for both spouses, two photographs of the spouses, and any other document that provides information about the family's situation.[115]

Once written approval is issued, the Department of Social Development informs the family about their place on the waiting list. When their turn comes on the waiting list, the family is put in touch with a care centre to choose a child. The family has the right to see the health certificate of the child and can choose to have the child examined by a medical doctor of their choice at their own expense. The spouses are then referred to the Department of Civil Status and Passports (*dāʾirat al-aḥwāl al-madaniyya wa-l-jawāẓāt*) where they obtain a birth certificate (*shahādat al-milād*), a family booklet (*daftar al-ʿāʾila*), and a passport for the child. The provisions explicitly state that these documents do not establish *nasab*. The family needs to give the department at the Ministry of Social Development a copy of the child's birth certificate which was issued by the Department of Civil Status and Passports in order to receive the child. Families who live abroad have the right to obtain an official note to make it easier for the child to obtain a visa and to leave the country together with the child. Families who live outside the country need to pay the costs of travel for the employee of the Jordanian embassy in their country of residence in order for the employee to conduct the social inquiry.[116] According to the regulations, the period of *iḥtiḍān* is permanent. It begins when the foster family takes the child and continues for the duration of the child's life except if reasons occur that forbid the continuation of the arrangement.[117] In that case *iḥtiḍān* is revoked.

6.4.2.3 The Revocation of *iḥtiḍān*

The right to *iḥtiḍān* can be withdrawn by the Minister of Social Development or the responsible court in the following cases: if one of the conditions of *iḥtiḍān* is no longer met or *nasab* of the child is established by a court decision, *iḥtiḍān* can be revoked. If one or both of the spouses have a health or a psychological problem or display poor morals *iḥtiḍān* can also be revoked. (Physical) abuse and neglect of supervisory duties also lead to *iḥtiḍān* being revoked. The right to *iḥtiḍān* is also withdrawn if one of the spouses is no longer Muslim. If the couple gets divorced, it

[115] Article 7 *iḥtiḍān* instructions.

[116] Article 8 *iḥtiḍān* instructions.

[117] Article 2 *iḥtiḍān* instructions.

is possible for one of the spouses to keep the child. However, this requires a new social inquiry. The demand is only granted if it is in accordance with the best interests of the child.[118]

6.4.2.4 Eligibility of the Care Giver and the Child

The law defines the conditions the caregiver has to meet. The foster family needs to be composed of two spouses[119] who live in shared accommodation[120] and have been married for at least five years.[121] The instructions specify that the relationship has to be based on love, strong bonds, and understanding.[122] The monthly income of the family needs to be at least 500 JD (about 703 US dollars).[123] The spouses or one of them need to be unable to reproduce.[124] Thus, they cannot have any biological children. The law also regulates the age range during which spouses can foster a child as well as the age of the child. The husband cannot be younger than 35 years old or older than 55 years old. The wife cannot be younger than 30 years old or older than 50 years old.[125] The child needs to be at least five years old if a wife married at the age of 45 or a husband married at the age of 50.[126] A foster family who has fostered a child for at least two years is eligible to file a claim to foster a second child. The second child needs to be of the same sex as the first child. The family is not allowed to foster a third child.[127]

The family has the right to foster a different child if the foster child dies a natural death. If it is shown that the selected child has a disability or a permanent illness, the family has the right to give the child back and to ask to foster a different child, but a foster family cannot arbitrarily return the child. The Minister of Social Development needs to be convinced that the reasons are in the best interests of the child. It is not possible to return the child after the child has turned 18.[128]

The 1972 law stipulates that the foster family needs to be of the same religion as the child. In cases in which there is no proof of the child's religion, the child is

---

118 Article 10 *iḥtiḍān* instructions.

119 Article 4(1) *iḥtiḍān* instructions.

120 Article 4(5) *iḥtiḍān* instructions.

121 Article 6 *iḥtiḍān* instructions.

122 Article 4(11) *iḥtiḍān* instructions.

123 Article 4(7) *iḥtiḍān* instructions. The minimum wage in Jordan is set at 190 JD (around 267 US dollars).

124 Article 4(3) *iḥtiḍān* instructions.

125 Article 4(4) *iḥtiḍān* instructions.

126 Article 4(8) *iḥtiḍān* instructions.

127 Article 5 *iḥtiḍān* instructions.

128 Article 10 *iḥtiḍān* instructions.

considered Muslim.[129] In accordance with the 1972 law, the *iḥtiḍān* instructions require the foster parents to be Muslim.[130] Thus non-Muslims are unable to foster a child under the *iḥtiḍān* program.

6.4.3 The Rights and Duties of the Caretaker

6.4.3.1 Parental Care and Maintenance

The family has a number of obligations. The family needs to provide for the child and they need to meet all of the needs of the child, including needs related to medical treatments and education.[131] The regulations do not stipulate whether children have an obligation to maintain their parents. The well-being of the child is verified through follow-up visits and social inquiries that are to be conducted one year after the beginning of the foster care arrangement and then once a year or as the need emerges. The foster parents are obliged to bring the child up in such a way that the child is able to face the challenges of life and become self-sufficient.[132]

The family needs to tell the child that he is not their biological offspring when the child turns five years old. They need to inform the Ministry in the event of any changes of their place of residence or their relationship with the child.[133] The foster family can assume the role of *wasī*. In order to do so they turn to the shariʿa courts to request a guardianship document for abandoned children (*ḥujjat wiṣāya ʿalā mahjūr ʿalayhi*) (see above). Foster parents are not given the right of guardianship (*wilāya*). The foster father thus cannot act as the *walī* of a foster daughter during a marriage. In such a case the shariʿa judge acts as the *walī* of the girl.[134]

6.4.3.2 Marriage between the Foster Parent and the Child

It is not explicitly stipulated whether or not *iḥtiḍān* creates an impediment to marriage between the child and the foster parents. An employee at the Ministry of Justice who has been overseeing the *iḥtiḍān* process for the past 17 years explained that if the

[129] Article 5 of the 1972 law.

[130] Article 4(2) *iḥtiḍān* instructions.

[131] The 1972 law stipulates that the foster family can obtain a monthly fee between 2 and 5 JD from the Ministry (Article 7). It is unclear how such a small amount of money should help to sustain the upbringing of a child. It follows that foster families were expected to pay for the maintenance of the child. The 2013 provisions do not stipulate that the family is entitled to any payments.

[132] Article 9 *iḥtiḍān* instructions.

[133] Article 9 *iḥtiḍān* instructions.

[134] Interview with shariʿa judge and chancellor of the *dāʾirat qāḍī al-quḍāt*, the Supreme Justice Department (SJD), 27 July 2017.

mother breastfeeds the child, then that constitutes a case of milk kinship and thereby an impediment to marriage. In general, she stated that it 'would not be normal' for foster parents to marry their foster child. She did not know of any such cases.[135]

6.4.3.3 Inheritance

The *iḥtiḍān instructions* are silent on inheritance. *Iḥtiḍān* does not create a right to inheritance and foster parents are not obliged to set up a pension fund for the child. However, the child is not automatically excluded from intestate succession. An employee at the Ministry of Social Development stated that some more affluent families sometimes register a piece of land in the name of the child, but that this was not common and most families were reluctant to do so.[136] The *iḥtiḍān instructions* do not provide for any legal mechanisms to ensure the financial security of the child in the event that the foster parents pass away.

6.4.3.4 Name

The Jordanian government's 2011 CRC report states that 'children have a natural right to a name.'[137] However, this does not seem to imply a right to a family name. Like children who are born out of wedlock, foundlings and orphans do not have a family name, but are given two first names (for example: Ahmed Muhammad) by the Department of Civil Status and Passports. They get a family booklet (*daftar al-ʿāʾila*) for themselves and are not listed in their foster parents' family booklets. According to the director of the Al Aman Fund for the Future of Orphans, orphans or foundlings cannot be given a random family name, because Jordanian society is tribal and family-oriented. A family would complain if their name was assigned to a child that is not a real member of the family.[138]

When a foundling is brought to a police station, the police deliver the baby to an orphanage or the Ministry of Social Development. The Ministry or the orphanage has to report the birth to the Department of Civil Status and Passports. The Department then chooses an appropriate name for the child and its parents and registers the birth in the official registry. Somebody who wants to establish *nasab* for the child after the birth has been recorded needs to present a proof of *nasab* supported by a court ruling. In that case, the name of the child can be altered accordingly.[139]

---

[135] The director of the family section at the Ministry of Social Development was offended by the question. Interview with the director of the family section at the Ministry of Social Development, 25 July 2017.

[136] Interview with an employee at the Ministry of Social Development, 25 July 2017.

[137] UN Committee on the Rights of the Child (CRC) Fourth and Fifth Periodic Report of States Parties, Jordan (1 March 2013), CRC/C/JOR/4-5, p 8.

[138] Interview with the director of the Al Aman Fund for the Future of Orphans, 25 July 2017.

[139] Article 19(2) Civil Status Law no. 9 of 2001.

6.5 Conclusion

According to the 2010 Jordanian Personal Status Law, filiation (*nasab*) to the father can be established in four cases: if a valid marriage exists (*firāsh zawjiyya*), by acknowledgement (*iqrār*), by means of evidence (*bayyina*) and by conclusive scientific methods coupled with a valid marriage. The 2010 law has considerably expanded the provisions on *nasab* of the previous 1976 law. The 2010 law for the first time introduces DNA tests as a way to establish *nasab*. The introduction of *al-waṭ' bi-shubha* emphasizes the parents' intentions and presents a way to integrate extra-marital relationships into the socially accepted framework. The introduction of the concept and DNA tests have arguably made it easier for women to establish *nasab*.

While DNA tests have strengthened claims that emphasise the biological dimension of *nasab*, these claims are not absolute. At least in theory, *nasab* can be established without biological filiation. *Nasab* remains a concept that is closely linked to the existence of a valid marriage. This is why women who have children out of wedlock or in the context of an informal marriage continue to face challenges when they try to establish *nasab* for their children. DNA tests are often ordered at the appeals court stage when the shariʿa court of first instance has failed to request a DNA test.[140] Legal practice demonstrates that the four legal ways to establish *nasab* are normally not regarded as valid on their own. Acknowledgment (*iqrār*) or DNA tests often function in conjunction with other means of proof like a valid marriage contract and the testimony of witnesses, rather than as the sole proof.

Jordan has put in place legal schemes to organize foster care. The *iḥtiḍān* programme has been better regulated since the issuing of the 2013 *iḥtiḍān* instructions (*taʿlīmāt al-iḥtiḍān*), whereas there are no legal regulations that organize the 2011 Program of Alternative Foster Families (*barnāmaj al-usar al-riʿāya al-badīla*). Overall, the foster care process remains under-regulated and heavily dependent on the practice of the Ministry of Social Development. Whereas historically, shariʿa courts have been the primary courts when it comes to the protection of orphans, in contemporary Jordan they are only marginally involved in the foster care process.

References

Eich T (2012) Constructing Kinship in Sunni Islamic Legal Texts. In: Inhorn MC, Tremayne S (eds) Islam and Assisted Reproductive Technologies: Sunni and Shia Perspectives. Berghahn Books, New York, pp 27–52.

Engelcke D (2016) Jordan. In: Robbers G, Durham WC, Thayer D (eds) Encyclopedia of Law and Religion, vol III: Asia. Brill Nijhoff, Leiden et al, pp 180–186.

[140] Interview with the chancellor of the *dāʾirat qāḍī al-quḍāt*, the Supreme Justice Department (SJD), 23 September 2017.

Engelcke D (2018) Law-making in Jordan: Family Law Reform and the Supreme Justice Department. Islamic Law and Society 25(3):274–309.

Engelcke D (2019) Reforming Family Law: Social and Political Change in Jordan and Morocco. Cambridge University Press, Cambridge.

Hasso FS (2011) Consuming Desires: Family Crisis and the State in the Middle East. Stanford University Press, Stanford/California.

Human Rights Watch (2009) Guests of the Governor: Administrative Detention Undermines the Rule of Law in Jordan. Human Rights Watch, 26 May 2009. www.hrw.org/report/2009/05/26/guests-governor/administrative-detention-undermines-rule-law-jordan. Accessed 20 August 2017.

Husseini R (2018) Safety, Security of Abused Women Top Priority — Lattouf. Jordan Times, 31 July 2018. www.jordantimes.com/news/local/safety-security-abused-women-top-priority-%E2%80%94-lattouf. Accessed 10 September 2018.

Ibrahim RW (2016) Care Leavers Looking Back on Residential Care Experiences in Jordan. In: Islam T, Fulcher L (eds) Residential Child and Youth Care in a Developing World: Global Perspectives. CYC-Net Press, Cape Town, pp 125–140.

Jordanian National Commission For Women (JNCW) (no date) Mulāḥaẓāt al-Lajnat al-Waṭaniyya al-Urdunniyya li-Shuʾūn al-Marʾa wa-Shurakāʾihā ʿalā Qānūn al-Aḥwāl al-Shakhṣiyya al-Muʾaqqat Raqm 36 li-Sanat 2010 (on file with author).

Jordan Times (2016) Queen joins orphans at Al Hussein Social Foundation for iftar. Jordan Times, 21 June 2016. www.jordantimes.com/news/local/queen-joins-orphans-al-hussein-social-foundation-iftar. Accessed 20 August 2017.

Maksudyan N (2014) Orphans and Destitute Children in the Late Ottoman Empire. Syracuse University Press, Syracuse/New York.

Nimri N (2014) 'Al-Tanmiya al-Ijtimāʿiyya' Taṭluqu al-Barnāmaj mundhu 2011 wa-Taḥḍīn 32 Ṭiflan Ḥattā al-Ān: 'al-Usar al-Riʿāya al-Badīla' Bāriqa Amal Jadīda. Al-Ghad, 16 March 2014.

Nimri N (2016) 1193 Ṭiflan Iltaḥaqū bi-Usra Badīla bayna al-Iḥtiḍān wa-l-Riʿāya al-Badīla: ʿĀʾilāt Yuʿtaṣaruhā al-Intiẓār al-Ṭawīl. Al-Ghad, 8 February 2016.

Tamkeen Fields for Aid (2015) Invisible Women: The Working and Living Conditions of Irregular Migrant Domestic Workers in Jordan. http://tamkeen-jo.org/download/Invisible%20Women%20English%20.pdf. Accessed 20 August 2017.

Dörthe Engelcke is a senior research fellow at the Max Planck Institute for Comparative and International Private Law. She received her Ph.D. from St Antony's College, University of Oxford, in 2015. She is the co-winner of the 2016 BRISMES Leigh Douglas Memorial Prize for the best Ph.D. dissertation on a Middle Eastern topic in the Social Sciences or Humanities awarded by a British University. She has held fellowships at the Islamic Legal Studies Program at Harvard Law School and the Lichtenberg-Kolleg at the Göttingen Institute of Advanced Study. Her research focuses on the interaction of law and society in the MENA region as well as questions of legal pluralism, Islamic law, and legal politics. She is the author of Reforming Family Law: Social and Political Change in Jordan and Morocco (CUP, 2019) and a contributor to the *Brill Encyclopedia of Law and Religion*. Her work has appeared in Law & Social Inquiry and in Islamic Law and Society.

Chapter 7
Lebanon

Marie-Claude Najm, Myriam Mehanna and Lama Karamé

Contents

Marie-Claude Najm is a professor at the Faculty of Law and Political Science of Saint Joseph University of Beirut and director of the Centre of Legal Studies and Research for the Arab World (Centre d'études des droits du monde arabe (CEDROMA)).

Myriam Mehanna is attorney-at-law at the Beirut Bar, researcher at the Legal Agenda (Beirut) and lecturer at the Faculty of Law and Political Science of Saint Joseph University of Beirut.

Lama Karamé is attorney-at-law at the Beirut Bar and researcher at the Legal Agenda (Beirut).

M.-C. Najm (✉)
Faculty of Law and Political Science, Saint Joseph University, Huvelin street, Ashrafieh, Beirut, Lebanon
e-mail: marieclaude.najm@usj.edu.lb

M. Mehanna (✉) · L. Karamé (✉)
The Legal Agenda, Moughayzel Street, Al-Nakheel Bldg, Badaro, Beirut, Lebanon
e-mail: myriam.mehanna@gmail.com; lamakarame@gmail.com

N. Yassari et al. (eds.), *Filiation and the Protection of Parentless Children*, https://doi.org/10.1007/978-94-6265-311-5_7

Abstract Filiation (*nasab*) of Muslim and Druze children in Lebanon arises primarily from the blood relationship between a child and his or her validly wedded parents (*firāsh*). In parallel, legal rules and court practice offer other means to establish filiation, such as acknowledgment (*iqrār*). Children of illegitimate or unknown descent hold an unfavourable status, but are not left without any protection. The main characteristic of the Lebanese system is, however, the lack of a proper state law or policies regulating alternative care for parentless children. In the absence of family members or caretakers, and given the Islamic prohibition of adoption, none of the alternative care schemes entail the placement of the child into a foster family, save for very rare and limited circumstances such as for newborn children. Furthermore, the lack of a national inclusive law addressing children's alternative care, and the lack of religious laws regulating *kafāla* arrangements, have allowed the implementation of informal practices that are decided within the family or the private sphere. These practices, which include placing the child directly within his or her extended family or in residential care institutions, occur out of court and lack governmental oversight. This is all the more regrettable given that the family's poverty has been clearly identified as one of the main grounds for children's admission to residential care institutions. Unjustified institutionalisation of children from poor families is an indicator of the failure of the alternative care system, which is merely financed instead of being properly regulated by the state.

Keywords Lebanon · Muslim and Druze children · *nasab* (filiation) · *iqrār* · DNA test · Defective filiation · Unknown filiation · Foundling (*laqīṭ*) · *riʿāyat al-aṭfāl al-majhūlī al-nasab* · *riʿāya badīla* · Best interests of the child (CRC) · Juvenile protection · Adoption *tabannī* (no) · Residential care institutions · Foster care · *kafāla*

7.1 Introduction

7.1.1 Muslim Jurisdiction(s) in the Lebanese Legal System

Unlike most Middle Eastern states, Lebanon is not a Muslim state and does not adopt any state religion. However, the Lebanese Constitution and statutory laws[1] entitle the religious communities to exercise authority over matters pertaining to the personal status of their members.[2] The eighteen religious groups that enjoy such jurisdiction in Lebanon are the 'historically recognized communities' designated by law,[3] i.e. the twelve Christian sects,[4] the four Muslim sects,[5] the Druze sect (also referred to as '*al-muwaḥḥidīn*') and the Israelite (Jewish) sect.

It is important, in this respect, to point out a specific feature of Muslim authorities in Lebanon, which exists for historical reasons that date back to Ottoman times. While the non-Muslim religious authorities in Lebanon are not part of the state apparatus, and directly establish their own laws as well as the organisation and functioning of their courts, the Islamic judicial and legislative corpus is incorporated into the state's structure.[6] Hence, Muslim and Druze court members are appointed and remunerated by the state and their statutes are defined by Lebanese state laws.[7]

As a result of this state-organisation feature, the laws governing the personal status of Muslim and Druze communities in Lebanon offer fertile ground for interference by the Lebanese legislature, and demonstrate the possibility for the state to adapt long-established regulations to new needs and arising challenges. However, observing the current situation, one can only join the author who noted that 'under its communitarian legal and political system and the sensitivities involved in any adjustments to it, the codification and reform of Muslim family law

---

[1] See Article 9 of the Lebanese Constitution and Article 10 of Legislative Decree No. 60/1936 of 13 March 1936 (amended by Legislative Decree No. 146/1938 of 11 November 1938) on the 'Status of the religious communities'.

[2] On the religious prerogatives in matters of personal status, see Al-Bīlānī (1997), pp 17–39.

[3] Annex I of above-cited Legislative Decree No. 60/1936; Article 1 of the Law of 2 April 1951 on the 'Jurisdiction of religious courts for Christian and Israelite communities'.

[4] The Christian sects are the Maronite, Greek-Orthodox, Greek-Catholic (Melkite), Armenian-Orthodox (Gregorian), Armenian-Catholic, Syriac-Orthodox (Jacobite), Syriac-Catholic, Assyrian (Nestorian), Chaldean, Latin (Roman Catholic) and Evangelical, to which the Coptic sect was added by Law No. 553/1996 of 24 July 1996.

[5] The two main Islamic sects are the Sunni and the Shi^ci (Ja^cfari-Twelver or Imami Shi^ci). The Alawite and the Isma^cili (Sevener Shi^ci) are the smallest Muslim Shi^ci sects. The Alawite sect was only recently organized in Lebanon, by virtue of Law No. 448/1995 of 17 August 1995; Alawite courts have therefore been established and they are to apply Ja^cfari law and customs (Article 32 of Law No. 448/1995). The Isma^cili sect does not yet enjoy any legal organisation.

[6] Bilani 1963, p 53.

[7] Law of 16 July 1962 on the Regulation of the Shar^ci (Sunni and Ja^cfari) Courts; Legislative Decree No. 3473/1960 of 5 March 1960 for the Druze courts.

found across most of the Islamic world has been comparatively limited with regards to Lebanon's Sunni and Ja^{c}fari (i.e. Twelver Shi^{c}i) shari^{c}a courts'.[8]

This state inaction is all the more regrettable given that the Lebanese civil courts do not exercise any control over the way religious law is made applicable before religious courts, even for those courts whose organisation and function are set by the state as mentioned above. Yet decisions issued by the religious courts can be challenged before the Plenary Assembly of the Court of Cassation – which is the highest civil court in Lebanon – in the following two cases: (i) lack of jurisdiction and (ii) violation of a substantial formality pertaining to public order, i.e. a formality that is critical to due process. Such review cannot, however, extend to the merits of the case.

7.1.2 The Law Applicable Before Muslim and Druze Courts

Islamic law in Lebanese law can be defined as the set of rules in force that are based on the *fiqh* and vary depending on the Muslim sect concerned.[9] Key in this matter is Article 242 of the Law of 16 July 1962 on the Regulation of the Shar^{c}i (Sunni and Ja^{c}fari) Courts (hereafter referred to as the 'Law on Shar^{c}i Courts'), referring to the preponderant schools of law (*madhāhib*) in the Sunni and Ja^{c}fari sects.

Pursuant to Article 242 of this law, the personal status of Sunni community members is governed by the Law of 25 October 1917 (Ottoman Family Code),[10] still in force, and, in the absence of any other provision, by the rules of the *fiqh* in the Hanafi school. The main reference for such Hanafi rules before Shar^{c}i Sunni judges is the Qadri Pasha Code,[11] as well as its commentary by al-Ibiyānī.[12]

In 2011, Article 242 of the Law on Shar^{c}i Courts was amended[13] in order to make the resolutions of the Supreme Islamic Council – headed by the Mufti of the Republic – the main source of reference for Sunni courts, which raised legitimate criticism of the Parliament's renouncement of its right to legislate in the field of

[8] Clarke 2014, p 32.

[9] The laws applicable in matters of personal status in Lebanon can be consulted in their Arabic version, featuring a French translation, in Mahmassani and Messarra 1970. The reforms or amendments made to these laws in recent decades are only available in the official Arabic version.

[10] Also referred to as Ottoman Law of Family Rights.

[11] In 1875, in order to facilitate the tasks of the courts, Qadri Pasha drafted the traditional rules of the Hanafi doctrine on personal status and inheritance in Egypt in a book titled 'Al-Aḥkām al-Shar^{c}iyya fī al-Aḥwāl al-Shakhṣiyya ^{c}alā Madhhab al-Imām Abī Ḥanīfa' [Shar^{c}ī Rules in Matters of Personal Status according to the Doctrine of Imām Abī Ḥanīfa]. This book – known as the Qadri Pasha Code – has not been promulgated as a law; it is, however, still taken into consideration by the courts in the absence of any other provision. For an Arabic version with a French translation, see Mahmassani and Messarra 1970. For an English translation, see Sterry and Abcarius 1914.

[12] Al-Ibiyānī 1911 (2 volumes, filiation issues are addressed in vol. II).

[13] Law No. 177/2011 of 29 August 2011 amending Article 242 of the Law of 16 July 1962.

personal status law. On the basis of this amendment, the Supreme Islamic Council issued a new Family Law in 2011 (Sunni Family Law).[14] The new law, which addresses cases related to the care of children, visitation and spousal maintenance, is applicable to all ongoing proceedings before Sharᶜi Sunni courts in Lebanon[15] and abrogates all previous conflicting provisions.[16]

As for the members of the Shiᶜi community, their personal status is governed, pursuant to the same Article 242 of the Law on Sharᶜi Courts, by the rules of the Jaᶜfari school, and by the 1917 Ottoman Family Code when the latter is not contrary to the Jaᶜfari rules. However, the Jaᶜfari rules enforced in the Lebanese legal system are not formally codified, which makes it difficult for researchers to identify the rules applicable before the courts.[17] Hence, the *Guide to Jaᶜfari Justice*[18] drafted by the president of the Supreme Jaᶜfari court in 1994 and reedited in 2010, which collects and explains rules related to personal status matters in Jaᶜfari law, appears to be essential, although not binding on judges. The Jaᶜfari courts also refer to the doctrine of the most renowned *fuqahā'* (Islamic jurists) of the times.

Finally, regarding the Druze community, the personal status of its members is governed by the Law of 24 February 1948 (hereafter referred to as the 'Druze Personal Status Law' or 'Druze Law'), which has codified the customs and traditions of the Druze in personal status matters,[19] and in a subsidiary way by the Hanafi legal doctrine in the matters not regulated by the latter.[20]

As a result of the abovementioned sources of law, case law appears to form an important source of law in matters of personal status. Regrettably, in the absence of regular and permanent publication of the rulings issued by religious courts, the researcher is often left to conduct a door-to-door enquiry at the various religious courts.[21]

---

14 Decree No. 46/2011 of 1 October 2011 (Sunni Family Law).

15 Article 36 Sunni Family Law.

16 Article 38 Sunni Family Law.

17 Furthermore, consistent with the Shiᶜi *fiqh* that considers '*ijtihād*' as one of the sources of the law, the door is open to interpretation of Islamic rules, allowing these rules to be adapted to evolving circumstances, provided that the '*mujtahid*' is recognized by the majority of scholars (*ᶜumūm al-ulamā'*) as a '*marjaᶜ*', i.e. a reputed and respected authority whose interpretation is therefore leading.

18 Niᶜma 2010.

19 The law applicable to Druze is often very specific compared to Islamic law. To take a few examples from marriage and inheritance law, it does not authorize polygamy or repudiation, and does not limit the free will of a testator by providing for reserved inheritors' shares in the deceased's estate.

20 Article 171 Druze Personal Status Law.

21 In this regard, the authors wish to express their gratitude to all the Sunni, Jaᶜfari and Druze judges who provided the research team with significant explanations and supporting documentation. The authors also express their deep appreciation to the civil judges, civil servants, directors and representatives of residential care institutions, managers and members of associations, and all other individuals interviewed for the purposes of this report.

7.1.3 Sources of Islamic Law with Regard to Filiation and Child Protection

Although the family is widely recognized as the key unit of Lebanese society, and is praised for having prevented its collapse in the aftermath of the civil war (1975–1990), it should be noted that the Lebanese Constitution does not dedicate a single provision to the family, neither within its body nor in its Preamble. This is but a clear indication of the fact that, for Lebanese constituents, families are not the direct concern of the state but rather pertain to the various religious communities and their personal status laws.

Being part of personal status, the establishment of filiation and the parental rights and obligations therein fall within the scope of religious laws and are subject to the jurisdiction of religious courts.

In light of the relative brevity of codified rules designed to govern matters of filiation and child protection, Shar^c^i judges have generally based their rulings on the predominant Hanafi (for Sunnis) and Ja^c^fari (for Shiites) schools of law. In this respect, despite some differences between the two schools, Sunni and Ja^c^fari rules often coincide. Therefore, together they can be considered to form Islamic law in Lebanon, and they only constitute two different schools of interpretation, which makes it possible to study them together by referring to relevant divergences when necessary. The same method will be followed as regards Druze law.

7.1.4 Interference of Civil Law and Civil Courts' Jurisdiction

Religious jurisdiction is not exclusive in matters of filiation. Firstly, one must bear in mind that the registers of births, marriages and deaths are directly administered by civil servants and adjudicated by civil judges pursuant to the Law of 7 December 1951 on state registers,[22] the provisions of which may interfere with religious jurisdiction regarding the acknowledgment of filiation, as will be seen in more detail below. Secondly, civil courts also intervene by implementing civil law provisions on the protection of the child's assets and supervision of the guardian's actions, as well as in cases of illegitimate or unknown filiation (given the fact that the jurisdiction of religious courts is generally restricted to cases of legitimate filiation, i.e. arising from marriage). Thirdly, Law No. 422/2002 of 6 June 2002 on Juvenile Protection gives the juvenile state courts grounds to order protection measures when a child is deemed to be in danger, whatever the status of this child may be.

---

[22] This law has been subject to numerous amendments, the last of which occurred through Law No. 203/1993 of 2 March 1993.

This law is one of the outcomes of Lebanon's ratification of the UN Convention on the Rights of the Child.

7.1.5 *Impact of the UN Convention on the Rights of the Child (CRC)*

Lebanon ratified the Convention on the Rights of the Child (CRC)[23] on 14 May 1991 and did not stipulate any reservation thereto. The principle of the best interests of the child is therefore, through the ratification of the CRC, explicitly recognized in the Lebanese legal system. And clearly, the ratification of the CRC has had an impact on the institutional and legal framework pertaining to children's issues in Lebanon.

On the institutional level, in 1994 the state created the Higher Council of Childhood, the purpose of which is to implement the Convention in Lebanon and oversee its proper application under the authority of the Ministry of Social Affairs, as well as to create a framework of cooperation between non-governmental organisations and the public sector to offer protective and rehabilitative social services on behalf of child care and development. However, the work of governmental institutions and NGOs remains hampered by limited human resources and funding, as well as insufficient implementation of the relevant laws. It is, more deplorably, impeded by the lack of comprehensive civil law and the absence of state organisations that would accurately respond to the problems of parentless children and children without permanent caretakers, as we will explore in detail in Sect. 7.4 of this chapter.

On the legal level, the ratification of the CRC – combined with societal pressures, lobbying by non-governmental organisations, and the efforts of human rights activists – has heavily influenced the policies and agendas of Lebanese lawmakers and pushed them to enact a series of laws pertaining to the child's interests and protection in various fields such as child labour, criminal law, access to health, education and social security. More importantly for our purposes, the Lebanese Parliament has adopted Law No. 422/2002 of 6 June 2002 on Juvenile Protection as mentioned above. This law addresses the situations of children who are threatened or at risk and is seen as one of the most significant improvements in child protection in Lebanon.[24] Directing juvenile judges to base their decisions on the children's best interests, the law grants them the mandate to issue protective orders and introduces the concept of foster care; it remains, however, insufficient in respect to alternative care, as will be shown in Sect. 7.4 below.

---

23 Lebanon also ratified the optional protocol on the Sale of Children, Child Prostitution and Child Pornography through Law No. 414/2002 of 5 June 2002.

24 See the comprehensive field study in UNICEF 2012.

This chapter aims to explore the legal means used to protect parentless children in Lebanon as articulated in the domestic law applicable to Muslim and Druze citizens, in view of the legal practice and courts' interpretation and in the context of Lebanon's social and religious particularities. In order to understand how those means of protection function, it is important first to assess how filiation operates and identify the categories of children that might face legal and social problems in cases where their filiation is somehow defective or where their biological parents are absent. Accordingly, this paper will first address the rules related to the establishment of filiation (*nasab*). It will then complete the picture by examining the status of children who are not covered by this legitimate filiation scheme. Finally it will explore the existing legal and social schemes that aim to protect parentless children in Lebanon, whether these children are deprived of filiation or of permanent caretakers.

7.2 The Establishment of Filiation

7.2.1 Establishing Filiation by Law

In Islamic law, filiation (*nasab*) is, as a principle, established through the blood relationship between the child and his/her validly wedded parents. However, a strict and rigid application of this principle would have left many children without filiation. Islamic *fuqahā'* have hence developed many rules and fictions that moderate the rigidity of the principle. Lebanese laws and customs regulating filiation reflect these rules, as we shall see below.

7.2.1.1 Children Born into a Valid Marriage

Nasab under Islamic law in Lebanon results from a blood relationship between the child and his/her validly married parents.[25] It thus requires double evidence: the birth of the child to a wedded woman, resulting from intercourse with her husband. While the filiation of the child to the mother is established by her giving birth to the child, paternal filiation is established through marriage to the woman who gave birth to the child and operates on the basis of a legal presumption of paternity. This clear distinction between the child's affiliation to the mother and to the father is a keystone of Islamic legal doctrine.

[25] Articles 332, 333 and 350 Qadri Pasha Code; Article 318 Guide to Ja^{c}fari Justice.

Maternity

Unlike paternal filiation, the establishment of maternal filiation results from a material fact that is easy to observe, which is the fact of a woman giving birth to a child. Evidence of this fact is needed when a child brings a claim against his father and/or mother to establish his or her filiation (*ithbāt al-nasab*). It is also needed to allow the child or his/her mother to establish *nasab* in cases where the birth and the identity of the child are disputed, for example, by the woman's husband or by the husband's heirs.

In the Islamic law applicable in Lebanon, the child's birth may be proven, in accordance with the evidentiary rules provided for under Islamic law, by any of the means of proof admitted before the Sharᶜi judges (*bayyina sharᶜiyya*) and enumerated at Article 91 of the Law on Sharᶜi Courts, i.e. judicial or out-of-court oral or written acknowledgment, testimony, presumptions, oaths, experts' opinions, or the findings of the judge.

Regarding testimonial evidence specifically, the requirements vary under Hanafi law depending on whether the child whose maternity is disputed is born during the marriage or after its dissolution. In the first case, the proof of the child's birth and identity may be established by the testimony of a single Muslim woman.[26] If the marriage has been dissolved by an irrevocable divorce or by death, and the birth is disputed by the man or his heirs, or the pregnancy was not apparent, the proof of the birth requires the testimony of two men or the testimony of a man and two women, while the proof of the child's identity requires the testimony of a single Muslim woman.[27] Jaᶜfari law requires the 'full' evidence in both cases, i.e. the testimony of four women, or of two men, or of a man and two women.[28] As for the law applicable to the Druze sect, it requires the testimony of the midwife or woman present at the time of the birth, and discards the distinctions made by the Hanafi doctrine in this respect.[29]

In any event, such means of evidence and notably testimonial rules have lost much of their significance since the promulgation of the Law on civil status registers of 7 December 1951. This state law applicable to all citizens regardless of their religious affiliation sets the requirements for the recording of births in the civil status registers. The birth of a child is therefore proved in Lebanon by the registration and issuance of the birth certificate – which includes the name of the child's mother – as required by Articles 11 to 14 of the Law of 7 December 1951. The registration of the birth on state registers is not, however, definitive and peremptory proof of filiation; it can be overturned by contrary evidence. Pursuant to Article 12 of the law, disputes relating to personal status registration fall under the jurisdiction

---

26 Article 348 Qadri Pasha Code; al-Ibiyānī 1911, p 505.

27 Article 349 Qadri Pasha Code; al-Ibiyānī 1911, p 506.

28 See Gannagé 2003, no. 263, p 27.

29 Article 142 Druze Personal Status Law.

of civil courts; consequently, religious courts dealing with filiation claims do not have authority over matters related to registration on state registers.

Although the evidentiary rules provided for under Islamic law lost importance as mentioned above, they have regained some significance in recent years in view of the large number of people fleeing the Syrian conflict to Lebanon, and the subsequent large number of births that occurred among these displaced communities without any form of state registration.

Finally, it should be noted that the rules related to proof of motherhood might be reassessed in view of modern assisted reproductive technologies. Specifically, in the case of egg donation, it will be important to determine whether motherhood should be recognized for the woman who donated the egg or the woman who gave birth to the child. While Sunni scholars consider the woman who carried and gave birth to the child to be the legal mother of the child, modern Shiᶜi scholars have given divergent opinions.[30] For the moment, though, as *firāsh* remains the general principle establishing filiation in Islamic doctrine, it is clear that the woman who carries and gives birth to the child is considered his or her legal mother irrespective of any genetic issues arising from assisted reproductive technology.

Presumption of Paternity

With respect to paternity, *nasab* operates on the basis of the well-known principle of the 'child of the marital bed' (*al-walad li-ṣāḥib al-firāsh*'[31]). Accordingly, a child conceived during the marriage will be linked to the mother's husband, with the child being exempted from bringing any further proof other than his or her maternal filiation.

The legal presumption of paternity is based on two conditions. It requires, first, the existence of a valid marriage, and thus of legitimate intercourse. Generally marriage is proven by a marriage certificate. Yet, more challenging is the proof of informal customary marriage (*nikāḥ ᶜurfī*), a marriage that is not registered with state authorities.[32] While the non-registration of a marriage clearly does not affect the validity of the marriage itself, children born into such marriages might face difficulties in proving the marriage of their parents and therefore their filiation. In this event, the marriage will be proven by the testimony of the witnesses or the *mukhtār* of the city or the village where the couple resides.[33] In such cases, a double

---

30 See Clarke 2009, pp 116–140.

31 Which can be translated literally as 'the child belongs to whom the marital bed belongs to'.

32 These marriages (also called *fātiḥa* marriages as the short Quranic verse is recited to characterize the union of the spouses) sometimes remain deliberately unregistered, for various reasons such as a divorced woman's desire to keep custody of her children (which she might otherwise lose by remarrying under Islamic law) or a husband's desire to hide a polygamous marriage from his first wife.

33 Interview of Judge Mohammad Kanaan, President of the High Sharᶜi Jaᶜfari Court of Beirut, by Chamseddine B and Haroun M, 15 May 2017.

claim will be initiated before the court: one to certify the marriage (*ithbāt al-zawāj*), and one subsequently to establish filiation (*ithbāt al-nasab*). Regarding intercourse, it does not need further proof as marital community implies the occurrence of marital intercourse. If, however, such marital community was not established at the time of the child's conception, such as in the case of the husband's absence (long-distance trip, imprisonment, etc.), the presumption does not apply.[34]

The second requirement for the presumption to operate is the child's birth within a certain timeframe in accordance with the legal period of conception based on the duration of pregnancy. Islamic legal doctrine in Lebanon is unanimous in setting the duration of pregnancy at a minimum of six months,[35] while the maximum duration of pregnancy in Ja^c^fari *fiqh* is either nine months[36] or one year,[37] and in Druze law a maximum of 300 days.[38] In contrast, Hanafi *fiqh* fictionally extends the pregnancy period to up to two years under the notion of the sleeping embryo.[39] This fictitious rule is, obviously, designed to uphold paternal *nasab* in the child's best interests. It also applies to the mother's ex-husband under the condition that she has not remarried within that period.

The presumption of paternity is not specific to Islamic law, and can be found in most legal systems;[40] however, 'Islamic law gives it an exceptional power',[41] making it very difficult to discard it. In fact, the husband cannot deny paternity of his wife's child unless he proves her adultery either through testimony (with stringent requirements) or through the legal procedure of *li^c^ān* (imprecation or anathema). *Li^c^ān* is a formal denial of paternity through a mutual oath-swearing procedure,[42] which leads to the dissolution of the marriage by the courts and the disownment of the child, who is hence deprived of paternal filiation. That being said, *li^c^ān* can only be performed within specific and brief time limits after the birth, namely during the days preceding or following the birth within the customary period for congratulations.[43] If the father is absent, the time limit begins from the

34 See, for example, Article 144 Druze Personal Status Law.

35 See e.g. al-Ibiyānī 1911, pp 483–484; Maghniyya 1961, Article 71 Section 1. Same (180 days): Article 137 Druze Personal Status Law.

36 Maghniyya 1961, Article 71 Section 1 and notes 1 and 2, p 50.

37 Article 320 Guide to Ja^c^fari Justice, which also specifies that the calculation is made on the basis of the lunar month.

38 Article 137 Druze Personal Status Law.

39 See Mūsā 1958, no. 491.

40 See in Roman Law the presumption *Pater is est quem juste nuptiae demonstrant.*

41 Bilani 1963, p 118.

42 *Li^c^ān* is a legal procedure that has become obsolete, and that occurs when a man accuses his wife of adultery and does not provide four witnesses to prove it. The judge invites the husband in that case to take the special oath of anathema; if the wife denies the accusation, she is invited to take the same oath. The ensuing divorce pronounced by the court allows the husband's oath to prevail.

43 See Article 335 Qadri Pasha Code; Article 321 Guide to Ja^c^fari Justice; Article 139 Druze Personal Status Law (within a month of the birth).

moment the birth comes to his knowledge. Furthermore, disownment is not possible after the express or tacit acknowledgment of paternity by the father, or after a court ruling establishing the paternity of the mother's husband, or after the birth of a stillborn child.[44]

7.2.1.2 Children Born into an Invalid Marriage *(zawāj fāsid)*

The presumption of paternity also applies to children born into an invalid marriage (*zawāj fāsid*),[45] provided the birth occurred within the legal timeframe, with the concession that the minimum period of six months is set both for Sunni and Shi^{c}i doctrine at the date of the marriage's consummation and not the date of its celebration.[46]

The marriage is considered *fāsid*, for example, when it was concluded under coercion, or by a person lacking the capacity to marry, or despite the existence of marriage obstacles.[47] Sunni doctrine also considers *mut^{c}a* and *muwaqqat* (temporary) marriages[48] as well as marriages concluded in the absence of witnesses as void.[49]

7.2.1.3 Children Born under Dubious Circumstances

If the birth of the child does not occur within the time limit determined by the law,[50] the presumption of paternity does not apply and *nasab* is not established.[51] In this event, *nasab* will nevertheless be established under Sunni[52] and Druze[53] law if the husband acknowledges the child.

[44] Al-Ibiyānī 1911, pp 486, 487, 488; Articles 321, 322, 340 Guide to Ja^{c}fari Justice; Article 140 Druze Personal Status Law.

[45] In *fāsid* marriages, the husband and wife must separate immediately and the marriage has to be dissolved. The procedure of *li^{c}ān* cannot intervene in this case, because it requires the existence of a valid marriage.

[46] See al-Ibiyānī 1911, p 495.

[47] Articles 57, 52 and 54 Ottoman Family Code.

[48] Article 55 Ottoman Family Code.

[49] Article 56 Ottoman Family Code.

[50] See above, section "Presumption of Paternity".

[51] Article 318 Guide to Ja^{c}fari Justice; Article 138 Druze Personal Status Law. See, on refusing to establish *nasab* as the child is born from *zinā*: Shar^{c}i Sunni Court of Tyr, 14 September 1994 (unpublished); High Shar^{c}i Sunni Court of Beirut, 18 March 2009, cited in Maḥmūd 2013, no. 37, p 135f, with commentary.

[52] Article 333 Qadri Pasha Code.

[53] Article 138 Druze Personal Status Law.

7.2.1.4 Children Born into Temporary Marriages

Temporary marriage (*nikāḥ muwaqqat*) is a marriage abiding by all the substantive and formal conditions required, but concluded for a set period of time. A specific type of temporary marriage, the *nikāḥ al-mut^{c}a* (literally meaning 'marriage of pleasure'), is deemed valid under Ja^{c}fari law.[54] Article 55 of the Ottoman Family Code considers both of these marriages to be *fāsid* marriages that must be dissolved.

In any event, children born into such temporary marriages are considered legitimate with an established *nasab* to both parents, as enjoyed by children born into permanent marriages. The problem that these children may encounter in practice concerns the proof of their parents' temporary marriage, given that such marriages are often met with social disapproval and thus not registered. These problems, however, are not specific to temporary marriages, but can occur with all unregistered marriages (see above, section "Presumption of Paternity").

7.2.1.5 Children Born into a Presumed Marriage *(al-wạt' bi-shubha)*

The Qadri Pasha Code refers in Article 342 to the child conceived under erroneous cohabitation (*al-wạt' bi-shubha*). Erroneous cohabitation can be defined as intercourse which is neither intentional nor adulterous, and which occurs outside a valid or *fāsid* marriage. Accordingly, children born to parents who erroneously believed that they were married at the time of sexual intercourse are considered to be the children of any of their parents who were mistaken about the existence of the marriage or the identity of the spouse, or about the legitimacy of the intercourse.

In this respect, the courts give decisive importance to the parents' good faith and sincere beliefs, as the child's parents should not have been aware of the illicit nature of the intercourse.[55] This illustrates the judges' efforts to bring illegitimate relationships, when possible, into the scheme of legitimate filiation.

Pursuant to Article 343 of the Qadri Pasha Code, a child conceived during erroneous cohabitation needs still to be acknowledged to establish *nasab*. Thus, under Hanafi law such filiation is established by acknowledgment and not by *firāsh*. On the contrary, Article 324 of the *Guide to Ja^{c}fari Justice* specifies that if a man engaged in sexual intercourse with a person whom he believed to be his wife, filiation is established under the presumption of *firāsh*.

---

[54] Bilani 1963, p 107, note 98.

[55] See al-Ibiyānī 1911, p 497.

7.2.2 Establishing Filiation by Private Autonomy: The Acknowledgment of Filiation

Apart from the presumption of paternity within a valid marriage or other Islamic proof as mentioned above, *nasab* can also be established by private autonomy, that is, through the acknowledgment (*iqrār*) of paternity or maternity. Here too, Lebanese laws and customs regulating filiation reflect traditional Islamic rules.[56]

7.2.2.1 Definition of *iqrār bi-l-nasab*

Acknowledgment (*iqrār*) is a means of evidence of filiation.[57] When validly made, it entails all the consequences of filiation: the acknowledged child will benefit from the same rights, including inheritance rights, and will be bound by the same duties, such as *nafaqa* (maintenance) obligations and submission to the father's *wilāya*, as those of a legitimate child. Acknowledgment is based on the proverb 'the declaration of the sound-minded about himself is taken to be true'. Consequently, 'if an adult couple of sound mind states that they are married and that a certain person is their child, this is taken to be true'.[58] What matters is the certainty of the acknowledgment made by free consent by an individual who possesses legal capacity and soundness of mind. In accordance with this evidentiary rule, Sharᶜī courts often issue decisions establishing the existence of the marriage (*ithbāt al-zawāj*) on the basis of the declaration of the parents of the child and thereby establishing the child's filiation (*ithbāt al-nasab*).[59]

---

[56] For instance, under Article 334 of the Guide to Jaᶜfari Justice, *nasab* can be proven through *iqrār*, *bayyina* (means of evidence) or even *shiyāᶜ* ('widespread knowledge' or 'what is widely known', i.e. when everybody takes it for a fact that this person is the father or mother of that child). While the word *bayyina* refers to the general means of evidence admitted under Article 91 of the Law on Sharᶜi Courts – that is, judicial or out-of-court oral or written acknowledgment, testimony, presumptions, oaths, expert opinions, or the findings of the judge – it is understood in practice that, with regards to the establishment of filiation, it mainly refers to testimonial evidence.

[57] See Article 350 Qadri Pasha Code; Article 337 Guide to Jaᶜfari Justice.

[58] Interview of Judge Mohammad Moughnieh (Sharᶜi Jaᶜfari Court of Tyr) by Aziz J-M and Sabbagh N, 25 May 2017.

[59] Sharᶜi Sunni Court of Shtaura, 19 October 2015 (unpublished); Sharᶜi Jaᶜfari Court of Jbaᶜ (Nabatiyyeh district, Southern Lebanon), case no. 41/2017, 25 April 2018 (unpublished). In this last case, the court established the *nasab* of a woman to her Shiᶜi validly wedded parents, at the acknowledger's and the acknowledged's request, in quite specific circumstances as the woman had been adopted by a French couple in the fifties after having been abandoned to a Christian orphanage at her birth; the court considered that under Articles 177, 91 and 249 of the Law on Sharᶜi Courts, the acknowledgment made by a sound-minded person is valid (*iqrār al-ᶜāqil ᶜalā nafsihi jā'iz*).

7.2.2.2 Conditions of *iqrār bi-l-nasab*

In addition to the general conditions related to legal capacity and free consent,[60] acknowledgment of filiation is subject to three specific conditions.[61] First, the acknowledgment must occur with regards to facts or circumstances that make the filiation possible, such as an age difference between the acknowledger and the acknowledged child that would allow for the possibility of parenthood, and the possibility for the 'father' and 'mother' to have had legitimate intercourse. Second, the child must accept the acknowledgment if he or she has reached puberty or the age of discernment (i.e. seven years old). This requirement aims to prevent any abuse by a person who would acknowledge a child for her own profit. Third, and most importantly, the acknowledgment must be legally authorized; in this regard the legal provisions explicitly outlaw the acknowledgment of a child whose filiation to another person is established or presumed or the acknowledgment of a child who was conceived out of wedlock.

This specifically raises the issue of the acknowledgment of a child by his or her unmarried biological parents. In Islamic law, this acknowledgment would not be possible, as sexual intercourse outside marriage cannot lead to the establishment of filiation. In practice, however, it may be possible for a person's illegitimate biological child to be acknowledged by this person provided this illegitimate status is not known, with the concept of *shubha* (doubt) driving judges to rule in favour of the children's filiation. As Ahmed Fekry Ibrahim indicated in Chap. 1 of this book, this situation arose for children born out of wedlock in the premodern period: 'In this case, parents commonly claimed they were married, albeit without providing evidence. At the very least, they might have avoided discussing how the child came about at all, given that most jurists (except for Mālikīs) did not consider pregnancy itself as evidence of fornication out of wedlock'.[62]

Conversely, as the existence of a biological relationship between the acknowledger and the child is not required for the acknowledgment to be valid, acknowledgment has in practice often served to establish *nasab* between persons who are not bound by any biological links, in particular between a married couple and a child of unknown filiation or a foundling.[63] This flexible approach to the acknowledgment of children, which does not require proof of paternity, has therefore allowed foundlings and abandoned children to be provided with a family life.

Consequently, acknowledgment of *nasab* may lead, in practice, to bringing into the mould of filiation either the biological child of a couple, provided the status of the child is not known (thus bypassing in practice the prohibition of filiation to a

60 Article 92 para 1 Law on Sharᶜi Courts.

61 Al-Ibiyānī 1911, p 507; Articles 336 and 341 Guide to Jaᶜfari Justice. On acknowledgment legal requirements, also see Bilani 1963, p 117.

62 See Sect. 1.3.4, p XX.

63 Al-Khatīb 1962, p 52, cited by Ṣāghiyya 1999, p 439.

child born out of wedlock), or children of unknown filiation and foundlings (thus bypassing in practice the formal prohibition of adoption).

7.2.3 Role of Scientific Evidence

While Islamic laws on personal status accept various means of proof of *nasab*, including legal presumptions, they do not specifically address scientific methods such as DNA screening or medical tests to determine sterility. It was the courts who first ruled on the admissibility of such evidence that is provided for by scientific progress.

Sunni courts have clearly refused to order or admit DNA tests as evidence for establishing or refuting *nasab*.[64] By contrast, Jaᶜfari courts have taken DNA results into account in filiation claims. Ruling on an *istiftā'*,[65] renowned Shiᶜi scholars have stated that 'objective scientific tests such as DNA tests that give undoubtedly true results are taken as final even when in contradiction with the rest of the proofs presented'.[66] Similarly, Druze courts admit DNA tests and consider them to be semi-categorical proof (*shibh qaṭᶜī*).[67]

However, analysis of the existing legal framework reveals that in cases of disputed paternity, recourse to medical testing has a different value for married and unmarried parents. DNA tests are ordered or admitted when the existence of a marriage has already been proven. Thus, scientific methods such as DNA tests seem to be admitted only to confirm *nasab* in instances where the circumstances surrounding the birth of the child are dubious. Furthermore, research also revealed that

---

64 High Sharᶜi Sunni Court of Beirut, 18 March 2009; see also High Sharᶜi Sunni Court of Beirut, 5 May 1999, both cited in Maḥmūd 2013, no. 37, p 135f, with commentary. In this respect, some of the interviewed judges maintained that it is not possible to take such tests into consideration without an explicit amendment of the law (interview of Judge Abdul Rahman Moghrabi (High Sharᶜi Sunni Court of Beirut) by Mehanna M, 1 June 2017), while others called for DNA tests to be admitted in cases of the establishment of *nasab*, especially in view of the large number of *iqrār* proceedings related to unregistered births amongst the Syrian displaced population in Lebanon (interview of Judge Mohammad Nokkari, President of the Sharᶜi Sunni Court of Shtaura, by Najm MC, 8 May 2017).

65 Request for *fatwā*, by virtue of which the applicant asks the *faqīh*'s opinion on a legal issue he or she is facing.

66 See, for example, ruling on *istiftā'*, Sayyed Ali Al-Husseini Al-Sistani, 23 March 2000, provided by Judge Mohammad Moughnieh (Sharᶜi Jaᶜfari Court of Tyr). During one of the interviews conducted, the President of the Jaᶜfari court of Beirut, though indicating that few judges order DNA tests, asserted that the judges may rely on such tests, provided the procedure is monitored by the court: the DNA sampling is done in front of judges, the analysis is done by certified laboratories and doctors, and the result is given to the court (interview of Judge Mohammad Kanaan, President of the High Sharᶜi Jaᶜfari Court of Beirut, by Chamseddine B and Haroun M, 15 May 2017).

67 Interview of Judge Fouad Hamdan (Druze High Court of Appeal of Beirut) by Karamé L, June 2017.

such tests will not be ordered or admitted if the presumption of paternity applies. No instance was encountered where DNA tests have served to overrule the legal presumption of paternity. This is not surprising given the force of this presumption in Islamic law and the judges' motivation to preserve paternal *nasab* in the child's best interests. A court could nevertheless order DNA tests in connection with a father challenging the paternity of the child born to his wife, usually through the procedure of *li*ᶜ*ān*; in such cases the court may additionally rely on DNA tests if it has reasons to suspect the husband's untruthfulness.

Finally, Lebanese Muslim courts are not ready either to consider DNA evidence to establish paternity outside of a marriage or at least to declare that biological paternity entails an obligation to the child's maintenance (without establishing paternal filiation and the consequences thereof, such as naming the child after the father and mutual inheritance).[68]

7.3 Status of Children of Defective or Unknown Filiation

Defective or unknown filiation is rarely discussed in Muslim literature, as is the legal status of children born out of wedlock. This has to do with the fact that the jurisdiction of religious courts is restricted to filiation claims arising from (valid or void) marriages only.[69] With the exception of cases of erroneous cohabitation, courts do not hear filiation cases of children born out of wedlock or children of unknown filiation or foundlings.[70] Indeed, filiation and parental care matters before religious courts generally arise in the context of disputed marriage or *nasab*, or in the context of married couples who separate or divorce. Specifically, a father's responsibility arises only where *nasab* has been previously established. Accordingly, children of defective or unknown filiation face very harsh legal consequences on both the legal and social levels.

---

[68] Such a decision would be similar to the 'action à fins de subsides' (Article 342 of the French Civil Code), by virtue of which the defendant is sued for the sole purpose of contributing to the maintenance of the child, without establishing any paternal filiation. The level of evidence required for the success of such a claim is, of course, much lower than that required for establishing paternity, as it is sufficient to prove that the defendant had sexual intercourse with the child's mother during the legal period of conception.

[69] Indeed, the Sharᶜi courts' jurisdiction covers '*nasab*' claims under Article 17(6) of the Law on Sharᶜi Courts.

[70] Nonetheless, one finds reference to these children in the rules of *nasab* and mainly in the ones governing acknowledgment.

7.3.1 *Children Born out of Wedlock* (walad al-zinā)

A child born out of wedlock is a child born to unmarried parents, sometimes also called *walad al-zinā*. In a broad sense, *zinā* is sexual intercourse between a man and a woman who are not married to each other, and who are not mistaken about this fact. In a narrower sense, it designates intercourse between a man and a woman who are not married to each other while at least one of them is married to another person; in this latter case, adulterous intercourse may even be subject to criminal sanctions under Article 487 of the Lebanese Criminal Code.

The status of children born out of wedlock is very unfavourable in Islamic Lebanese law. As seen in Sect. 7.1 above, *nasab* cannot be established, and the defective status of such child cannot be remedied either by subsequent acknowledgment or through the marriage of the biological parents. For example, under Article 332 of the *Guide to Ja*ᶜ*fari Justice*, the biological father cannot establish the filiation of a child born of adultery, even should he marry the mother while she is pregnant.

The child's unfavourable status is intended to discourage illicit non-marital relationships, which are viewed as a disturbance to the social order and a violation of good morals. Yet it entails extremely harmful effects on the child, as he or she lacks rights towards his or her biological parents in terms of care, protection, maintenance and inheritance. This harsh status does not, however, exclude the existence of a legal relationship between the child and his or her mother. Whereas Lebanese Islamic law rejects the filiation of such a child to his or her biological father, it recognizes the filiation of a child to his or her mother.

7.3.1.1 The Relationship of a Child Born out of Wedlock to his/her Biological Father

As a general rule, a child born from a non-marital relationship will have no legal relationship to his or her biological father. In other words, *nasab* cannot be established between them by any means.

By denying the existence of the paternal link, the law deprives the child of the rights a legitimate child enjoys, including the right to the name and the nationality of the father, the right to enjoy the father's protection and care, the right to maintenance and support, and inheritance rights.

However, the Law of 7 December 1951 on state registers has attenuated the consequences of this rule. Article 15 of the 1951 Law allows the father (or the mother) of a child born out of wedlock to 'acknowledge' the child. The effects of such acknowledgment are, however, limited to the registration of the child on state registers under the name of his or her father. In other words, while this state registration will provide the child with a name, a lineage and an identity card, it does not establish *nasab* and therefore does not confer upon the child any right to his or her father's protection and care in terms of maintenance and education, or any inheritance rights to the father's estate.[71]

7.3.1.2 Maternal Filiation to a Child Born out of Wedlock

Whereas filiation cannot be established between a child born out of wedlock and his or her biological father, maternity of this child can be established and will produce some but not all of the consequences of *nasab.* A child will always have a legal link to the woman who has given birth to him/her. The mother has, however, to voluntarily acknowledge the child. Such acknowledgment is not subject to any formal conditions, and should not be confused with the acknowledgment of filiation described in Sect. 7.2.2 above. Conversely, the child may not petition legally for maternal filiation.

The establishment of maternity between a mother and her child born out of wedlock has rather significant consequences, although they are still limited compared to filiation. Although Lebanese citizenship is exclusively transmitted through the father,[72] a child born out of wedlock may acquire Lebanese citizenship where the maternity of his or her Lebanese mother is established.[73] The mother owes the child maintenance and has to care for him or her; the child has the right to bear the mother's family name.[74] Inheritance rights arise between them, provided there are no other legal heirs. The right to inheritance does not, however, extend to the mother's relatives,[75] who have no legal relation to the child.

This situation is rather burdensome to the child's mother and possibly her family. The Lebanese Criminal Code punishes child abandonment or neglect (Articles 498–501) as well as abortion (Articles 539–545). Hence, an unmarried woman who becomes pregnant can be prosecuted for seeking an abortion, or for abandoning or neglecting her child; if she decides to keep and raise the child, she is still left alone with no or limited legal remedy under Lebanese Islamic law. Whereas biological paternity as such does not impose legal and financial duties on

[71] Inheritance matters for the Muslim communities fall indeed under the jurisdiction of Muslim courts who apply the Islamic inheritance rules, and thus will not recognize inheritance rights to children whose *nasab* has not been established in accordance with the Islamic applicable rules.

[72] Article 1(1) Decree No. 15/1925 of 19 January 1925 completed and amended, notably, by the Law of 11 January 1960.

[73] Article 2 Decree No. 15/1925, by virtue of which the illegitimate child shall have the Lebanese nationality of the parent with whom filiation has first been established. In practice, the General Security operates thorough investigations to make sure that the father is unknown.

[74] This is the consequence of the mother's declaration upon the registration of the birth under Article 15 of the Law of 7 December 1951 on civil status registers.

[75] Gannagé 2003, no. 265, p 27.

the father, biological maternity determines the mother's duties to her child. Furthermore, both the mother and the child (but not the father, who can remain unnamed or unknown) are very likely to become victims of social stigmatisation.

7.3.2 Children of Unknown Filiation/Foundlings

Where neither paternal nor maternal filiation can be established, the child will be treated as being of unknown filiation (*majhūl al-nasab*) and sometimes referred to as a foundling (*laqīṭ*). In fact, these two statuses are not quite identical. A child of unknown filiation is a child whose parents are not legally identified. A foundling is a child found in a public space – most often abandoned – and whose filiation is unknown. The legal status of children of unknown filiation and foundlings is not expressly regulated in Lebanese Islamic law. Their status must therefore be derived from civil law.

There are no available data on the number of abandoned children, though the media often report on cases of foundlings.[76] When an abandoned child is found, the competent authorities (i.e. the district attorney or the juvenile judge, depending on the circumstances) decide on a first and last name, and have them registered on the state registers under a fictitious register number and under fictitious parents' names, in accordance with the institution to which the child was abandoned, or in accordance with the neighbourhood in which the child was found. If found in a Christian neighbourhood or in front of or close to a church, the child is usually given a Christian name and placed in a Christian faith-based residential care institution, and vice versa in the case of a Muslim neighbourhood.[77]

It should be noted further that up until the early 1990s, the illegitimate status of the child (*mawlūd ghayr sharᶜī*) was indicated on the child's identity card and on the civil status extract (*ikhrāj qayd*) delivered by the state registrars. This was highly prejudicial to the child given the social stigmatisation of children of unknown or illegitimate descent. The civil status extracts are indeed required for various procedures and formalities such as school registration or employment applications. Fortunately, since the entry in force of Law No. 541/1996 of 24 July 1996,[78] this has been forbidden. The civil status registrars and personal status

---

[76] See, for reporting on such a case while this article was undergoing the editing process: Liban, un nouveau-né retrouvé abandonné dans une benne à ordure, L'Orient - Le Jour, 7 September 2018.

[77] In certain circumstances, where the region in which the child is found is 'religiously mixed', the child has been attributed the religion of the district attorney (!), see Ṣāghiyya 1999, p 436.

[78] Law amending Article 18 of the Decree No. 2851 of 2 December 1924 on the regulation and organisation of civil status registers.

officers are only allowed to provide such information through certificates delivered upon the request of the concerned person or the competent courts and for valid reasons. A reminder about this law, which was in fact one of the outcomes of the Lebanon's ratification of the CRC in 1991, has been recently included in a circular addressed to the civil status registrars.[79]

Although children of unknown filiation and foundlings are placed in residential care institutions, as is the case for orphans who do not have relatives available to care for them, they must be differentiated from orphans, who are children whose parents are known but dead. In both situations, though, they require the same protection within the social welfare system and institutions.

Whereas Christian children can be adopted in Lebanon according to their own religious rules, Muslim children come under the general prohibition of adoption in Islamic law.[80] However, informal or indirect 'adoptions' are sometimes disguised through acknowledgment, where the conditions of the latter are met. For example, the finder of a child may validly acknowledge *nasab* given the fact that the biological link with the child need not be proven. Other informal or indirect 'adoptions' can also occur when the parents manage to register the child as theirs, in which case the Shar^c^i judge cannot from his own motion challenge the filiation registered in the state registers.[81]

The protection of these children will be addressed in more detail in the fourth and last section below.

---

[79] The Circular No. 7/2 issued on 15 January 2018 by the General Director of the Personal Status Department at the Ministry of Interior, ordered the civil status registrars (i) to abide by Article 18 of the Decree 2851/1924 as amended by the Law No. 541/1996, and thus to abstain from inserting the phrase 'illegitimate child' (*mawlūd ghayr sharᶜī*) on all civil status documents, namely the identity card, the individual civil status extract and the family civil status extract; (ii) to replace it instead with the phrase 'not valid for inheritance proceedings' (*ghayr ṣāliḥ li-muᶜāmalāt al-irth*); and (iii) to restrict the use of the phrase 'illegitimate child' to the section related to comments, and this only at the request of the judicial authorities in pending inheritance lawsuits or at the request of the administration. The mention of inheritance proceedings is to be understood in view of the legal discrimination between legitimate and illegitimate children in inheritance rights; in fact such discrimination makes it necessary to characterize the legitimate or illegitimate nature of the filiation, in order to allocate the deceased's estate.

[80] The Quranic prohibition is traditionally founded on verses Q.33:4: 'Nor has He made those whom you claim as sons your sons' and Q.33:5: 'Call them after their fathers, and if you do not know their fathers, then they are your brethren in religion and your clients'.

[81] See for example *istiftā'*, Judge Mohammad Moughnieh (Sharᶜi Jaᶜfari Court of Tyr), 31 January 2016: the judge 'has no power to question the legal documents in the absence of an opposing party'.

7.4 Protection of Children without Filiation or Permanent Caretakers

7.4.1 General Legal Schemes of Protection and Care

In the absence of a law regulating children's alternative care in Lebanon, the legal measures in place for parentless children find their sources in an array of different legal provisions and customary practices. Children's alternative care is thus negotiated within a pluralistic legal system, in which formal and informal laws intertwine and intersect.

On the one hand, given that personal status laws organize and regulate children's custody (*ḥaḍāna*) and guardianship (*wilāya* and *wiṣāya*[82]), religious courts have jurisdiction to resolve disputes over a child's custody and guardianship in the case of parents' death or unfitness.[83] This implies, of course, that the child's *nasab* has been established in the first place, and excludes cases related to children of unknown descent or foundlings, or children born out of wedlock. The personal status laws are indeed centred on the family model, which requires filiation, and do not regulate the personal status of children without filiation, including abandoned, orphaned, or foundling children. While these laws proclaim the prohibition of adoption, they do not address the issue of substitute care for parentless children and specifically do not contain provisions on *kafāla*.

On the other hand, and in parallel to the jurisdiction of religious courts, the civil juvenile judge has jurisdiction to intervene in situations where the child, whatever his or her status may be, is deemed to be in danger. The juvenile judge issues protection orders that could constitute, in certain situations, alternative care measures.

In addition to these formal procedures, customary practices can also be identified. In fact, the absence of a national law regulating children's alternative care, in addition to strong family bonds within the Lebanese society, has allowed the existence of informal practices. These practices include placing the child directly within his or her larger family (kinship care), or within residential care institutions (which are in fact private and most often faith-based institutions, partially funded by the state), or – although this very rarely occurs – within a foster family (i.e. within a family other than the child's family). The absence of a regulating law and the lack of state monitoring have also facilitated the amplification of illegal practices, which are commonly described as disguised 'adoptions'.

The complexity of this legal landscape is reflected in the difficulty of any attempted research on the topic. Even when rules are codified, the case law remains inconsistent: judges (both religious and civil) might issue decisions that are formally not in line with the law in cases where the literal application of the law goes

---

[82] See El-Husseini Begdache 2008; Moukarzel Hechaimé 2008.

[83] On this issue, see Najm 2017, pp 152–159.

against the child's interests. Furthermore, the interpretation of the child's interests varies among the courts. The fact that court rulings are not subject to systematic publication, and thus are not easily accessible, limits the analysis of case law to the relatively few rulings made available and to interviews with judges.

As per a study published by UNICEF Lebanon in 2012, 2.8% of children between 0 and 17 years old have lost one or both of their parents, with less than 1% living with non-biological parents.[84] These numbers indicate the general tendency to keep children within their biological families. However, there are no nationally available statistics determining the number of children placed within their larger family or within foster families. The lack of studies regarding the recurrence of informal measures is a serious limitation of this research.

Keeping in mind the limits above, and in order to understand alternative care schemes that aim to respond to the needs of parentless Muslim and Druze children in Lebanon, to which this fourth and last part is dedicated, we will first briefly address the prohibited adoption of Muslim children and the substitute practices it has given rise to, namely informal or disguised 'adoptions' occurring in the shadow of law; we will then concentrate on the formal alternative care measures that can be ordered by the religious courts or by the juvenile judges, and lastly explore the various types of informal alternative care practices.

For the purpose of this report, formal or official alternative care shall designate all types of care decided through a court order, whereas informal or unofficial alternative care shall cover all situations where alternative care measures are decided within the family or the private sphere, allowing the child to be taken care of by relatives or friends or placed in residential care institutions outside any judicial order.

7.4.2 The Prohibition of Adoption of Muslim Children: The Law and the Practice

There is no unified civil law addressing adoption for all Lebanese people. In fact, only laws governing the personal status for Christian communities regulate and allow for adoptions, while Muslim children are subject to the general prohibition of adoption under Islamic law. However, Muslim-born children have been involved in adoptions decided by ecclesiastical courts or by civil courts when these children were abandoned at Christian orphanages – mainly at the Saint Vincent de Paul orphanage – where they have been given fictive Christian names and ultimately been legally adopted by Lebanese or foreign couples.[85] Furthermore, one should not ignore the occurrence of informal or disguised 'adoptions' in Lebanon, in

[84] UNICEF 2012, p 32.

[85] This appears, for instance, in the abovementioned decision of the Shar^{c}i Ja^{c}fari Court of Jba^{c} (Nabatiyyeh district, Southern Lebanon), case no. 41/2017, 25 April 2018 (unpublished).

particular through acknowledgment, but also through workarounds of the legal framework. Registration of a newborn child under the name of the parents-to-be instead of the biological mother is one example, generally involving the subsequent remuneration of both the biological mother and the hospital's doctor and administration.[86] Single mothers are, in particular, encouraged to give up their children to wealthy couples, with this arrangement being most often finalized before the birth of the child.[87] During the Lebanese civil war, relatives would also register a child under their own name if the child's father had died before the child was born or when the child was still very young; this was usually done through a counterfeit birth certificate. In one of the interviews conducted, a Sharᶜi judge informed us that these procedures still occur nowadays.[88]

7.4.3 Formal Alternative Care (riᶜāya badīla rasmiyya)

When parents have died or are unfit to take care of their child, the religious courts will order alternative care measures in accordance with their rules. In addition, when the juvenile judge deems a child to be in danger and issues a protection order to safeguard the child's safety, such an order may consist of an alternative care measure. Yet it is important to note that in practice – and save for very rare and limited circumstances – none of these schemes actually entail the placement of the child into a new home, be it temporarily until the parents' hindrance is overcome or permanently in terms of the establishment of a new parent-child relationship.

7.4.3.1 Alternative Care in Religious Courts' Practice

The placement of a Muslim orphaned child or a child with unfit parents is regulated under personal status laws and customary rules applicable to Muslims. It is important to bear in mind, however, that the majority of cases involving deceased

---

86 Allouche 2015.

87 It should be noted in this regard that parents face criminal charges if they abandon their children (Articles 498-500 Criminal Code), or give them up to another person even for adoption purposes in return for money or other gain (Article 500 bis Criminal Code). For the description of two recent cases pertaining to the illegal adoption of children born in Lebanon, see Frangieh 2018, p 12. In both cases the investigating judges (respectively the Investigative Judge in Mount Lebanon and the Indictment Chamber in Beirut) characterized the adoptions as a human trafficking felony under Article 586(1) of the Criminal Code and referred the birth mother, as a partner in the perpetration of this felony, for trial before the Criminal Court. In one of the cases the child's mother was also charged with the misdemeanour of giving up a minor for gain (Article 500 bis of the Criminal Code). The commentary criticizes the decisions for charging the mothers with primary liability for human trafficking, or at least liability equal to that of the wealthy adoptive families to which the children were given and the middlemen and doctors who exploited the mothers' vulnerability.

88 Interview of Judge Mohammad Moughnieh (Sharᶜi Jaᶜfari Court of Tyr) by Aziz J-M and Sabbagh N, 25 May 2017.

parents (and, to a lesser extent, unfit parents) often do not reach religious courts and are resolved informally within the family. Thus, social practices are not necessarily in line with the regulations described below and the description of the law only partially accounts for the range of domestic extrajudicial arrangements practiced within Lebanese families.

In the event of the death or unfitness of the custodial parent, personal status laws regulate the placement of the child with the other parent or with a relative.[89] Interestingly, the laws have emphasized the importance of keeping the child within his or her family environment, including in cases where both parents have died or are unfit to care for the child. Generally, children are placed with their grandparents or the next available and fit relative according to a pre-established order. The courts may also order the placement of the child in a residential care institution,[90] even if our research did not reveal such rulings. On the contrary, in one of the cases reviewed, the judge discussed whether the children should be placed in a residential care institution given that both parents were unfit and concluded that the situation of these institutions might be more harmful for the children, and thus decided to keep them with their family.[91]

7.4.3.2 Alternative Care in Juvenile Judges' Practice

Lebanon's ratification of the CRC and its adherence to the standard of the child's best interests have had a serious impact on child protection in the Lebanese legal system. Illustrative here is the adoption of Law No. 422/2002 of 6 June 2002 regarding the Protection of Juvenile Delinquents or Juveniles in Danger. In order to support the implementation of the provisions of the law, the Ministry of Justice mandated a specialized agency, the Union for the Protection of Juveniles in Lebanon (UPEL), to provide services for these categories of children. Most importantly for our purpose, this child protection law gives the juvenile state court legal grounds to intervene and take protective measures if a child is in a situation of danger.

Jurisdiction of the Juvenile Judge

A child is deemed to be in danger or at risk under Article 25 of the law if he or she is exposed to exploitation or is threatened in his/her health, safety, morality or

[89] Najm 2017. With regard to the parents' unfitness, personal status laws provide little explanation of the 'unfitness' criterion, which has paved the way to various court interpretations.

[90] Article 19 of the Sunni Family Law states that, in the absence of an available custodian, the judge shall choose whomever he deems fit from among the child's relatives or others, or decide to place the child in an Islamic Sunni institution.

[91] See for example: Shar^{c}i Sunni Court of Beirut, 13 May 2010 (unpublished); Interview of Judge Fouad Hamdan (Druze High Court of Appeal of Beirut) by Karamé L, June 2017.

upbringing; is a victim of sexual abuse or physical violence; or is found begging or vagabonding. Article 26 of the Law gives the juvenile judges the right to take the needed measures (protective measures, supervised freedom measures or corrective measures, depending on the circumstances of the case), upon the petition of the minor child or one of his/her parents or guardians or persons responsible for him/her, or upon the petition of the social assistant or the public prosecutor, or upon received information.[92] Juvenile judges can also take such decisions on their own motion in urgent matters. Article 26 directs them to take into consideration the best interests of the child when assessing the need to order any of these measures.[93]

Protective Measures Ordered by Juvenile Judges

Pursuant to Article 27 of the law, the juvenile judges shall do their best to keep the children within 'their natural environments'. This means that the child has to be kept, whenever possible, with a family member. In the absence of a family member who has a good ability to raise the child, the law allows the placement of the at-risk child in a 'trustworthy family' (thus introducing the concept of a foster family) or a 'social or health institution'. However, as frequently observed, the law 'does not regulate how the placement of children in alternative care is assessed, determined, monitored, supported and managed according to their best interests and in compliance with the UN Guidelines on Alternative Care'.[94]

Interviews with juvenile judges and a review of their decisions have shown that, similarly to religious courts, juvenile judges prioritize keeping the child within his or her natural family environment. When both of the child's parents are unknown or deceased or unfit, juvenile judges first seek to find out if a relative of the child is willing and fit to take care of him or her. In this case, the juvenile judge is not bound by the order set by personal status laws. The only criterion followed is the child's best interest. Where the child does not have family or caretakers, or in cases where the family is unfit to take care of the child, the child would be placed in a residential care institution or a protection centre.[95] It is to be noted that juvenile judges have issued, albeit in rare cases, court orders placing the child with a host or foster family. In this regard, the child's age may have a very important influence on the juvenile judge's decision. In general, children who are old enough are placed in an institution, whereas newborn children tend rather to be placed in a foster family.[96]

[92] In some cases, juvenile judges have intervened upon knowing of a situation of abuse from a TV show as indicated by Roland Chartouni, Juvenile Judge of Mount Lebanon, Shartūnī 2016.

[93] Khamīs and Al-ᶜArīdī 2011.

[94] Save the Children Lebanon 2016, p 89.

[95] Such cases include homelessness, violence, neglect, abandonment, etc. The Union for the Protection of Juveniles (UPEL) follows up on the issue to determine if the child should stay in the institution or if he or she is safe to return home.

[96] Interview of Mrs. Dima Dib, Juvenile Judge of North Lebanon (Tripoli), by Abdo N and Markbaoui J, 20 May 2017.

However, it is unclear how such decisions are implemented and followed up, and whether judges have applied them to Muslim children.[97] It is interesting to note in this respect that according to some of the Shar^{c}i judges interviewed, only Muslim children of unknown filiation or foundlings could be placed within foster families.[98]

7.4.4 *Informal Alternative Care* (ri^{c}āya badīla ghayr rasmiyya)

As mentioned above, the legal void in regulating children's alternative care in Lebanon has led to informal implementation of alternative care practices that occur mostly outside of court-mandated processes. As important as such practices are in filling the legal gap in the matter, they are also alarming as they lack governmental oversight, especially in making sure that a placement measure is in the child's best interest. This section will discuss the measures undertaken by families and communities. Such measures are often rooted in social practices, traditions and cultural norms and may overlap with formal measures in certain situations. In what follows, we will detail two mechanisms, namely residential care (which is actually a semi-formal mechanism) and *kafāla*. It is important to note that although not detailed in this section, kinship care tends to be very frequent in Lebanon given the existence of strong family bonds. This also applies to foster care, but to a much lesser extent. However, no statistics or figures have been found on the percentage or occurrence of such practices as they have never been surveyed or mapped.

7.4.4.1 Out-of-Court Placement in Residential Care Institutions

At first glance it would seem strange to include residential care amongst the informal alternative care mechanisms. Yet such a categorisation is justified by the means of access to these institutions as well as by their hybrid legal status – as private institutions whose activities are partly funded by the state – which makes them providers of formal and informal care.

For the sake of this research, three major residential care institutions were visited for interview purposes, which are affiliated with the largest Muslim groups in the country (Sunni[99] and Shi^{c}i[100]) and with the Druze community.[101]

---

97 Rabāḥ 2012, pp 130–131.

98 Interview of Judge Mohammad Moghrabi (High Shar^{c}i Sunni Court of Beirut) by Mehanna M, 1 June 2017.

99 Dar al-Aytam al-Islamiyya, Mu'assasat al-Ri^{c}aya al-Ijtima^{c}iyya fi Lubnan (Islamic Orphanage, the Social Welfare Institutions).

100 Jam^{c}iyyat al-Mabarrat al-Khayriyya (Al-Mabarrat Foundation, Lebanon).

101 Beit al-Yateem al-Durzi (The Druze Orphanage, Lebanon-Druze Orphans and Charitable Organisation).

History and Legal Status of Residential Care Institutions in Lebanon

There are no public or state-owned residential care institutions in Lebanon. In order to implement the public service of children's protection, the state enters into contracts with existing private (including faith-based) institutions. In fact, the Ministry of Social Affairs (MoSA) contributes to the children's financial support within the institution.[102] In 2016, 24,106 children were placed in residential care institutions (of various sectarian affiliations and all over the country),[103] among them 19,143 children of between 4 and 15 years old.

The relationship of the state to care institutions has a long history. During the Ottoman Empire and the *mutasarrifiyya* era, the concept of social welfare was limited to donations given to the poor by princes and affluent families. It was not until the French mandate that the first laws regulating the situation of orphans were enacted by Decree no. 3110 issued on 10 May 1925. Pursuant to this decree, the state was obligated to assist children of which both parents were dead and children of which one parent was dead and the other unfit to provide for them[104] by housing them in public (Article 3) or alternatively in private orphanages (Article 9). This decree illustrates the state's initial willingness to afford legal protection to parentless children by establishing state-owned orphanages.

Upon the independence of the Lebanese state in 1943, social policies were, however, limited to the allocation of financial aid to private orphanages. Some sources consider this allocation to have taken into consideration the sectarian

---

[102] There are currently three categories of institutions that are under contract with the Ministry of Social Affairs: (1) Child social welfare institutions (known as '*riᶜāya ᶜādiyya*', literally meaning ordinary social welfare). This welfare is currently provided by more than a hundred institutions (across all of Lebanon and all sectarian affiliations) and is limited to children of Lebanese paternal or maternal descent (however, this identity/nationality requirement might be discarded for orphans by judicial decision). The highest number of children funded by the MoSA is in this first category. (2) Institutions for the protection of children in danger (*ḥimāyat al-aḥdāth*). This category is relatively recent (2004) as it is one of the outcomes of the Law No. 422/2002. Children are admitted to these institutions regardless of any criteria of identity, nationality or religion as this social welfare is related to the endangered children. There are currently 14 *ḥimāya* associations under contract with the MoSA (4 associations admitting over-night *riᶜāya* and 10 associations limited to a daily *riᶜāya*), which is a very low number to face the emergency situations of children in danger, especially given the high increase in the latter as a result of the Syrian displaced population in Lebanon since 2011. (3) Specialized social welfare institutions (homeless people, women victims of violence with their children, unmarried women with their children, drug addicts, AIDS patients, prison victims of violence and torture…).

These three categories of institutions correspond to the three sections of the social welfare department at the MoSA: the social welfare section, the juvenile protection section and the specialized care section.

[103] Ministry of Social Affairs, Table of Care Social Welfare Institutions under Contract with the Ministry of Social Affairs for the year 2016, issued and provided by the Ministry of Social Affairs.

[104] Kanaᶜān 2008, p 32.

repartition of Lebanon.[105] As significantly revealed by Mrs. Neamat Kanaan, former general director of the Ministry of Social Affairs, the state's attempt to regulate alternative care was hampered by the pressure of social actors, most of them sectarian, who feared the intrusion of public authorities into their field of action.[106] By the end of the Lebanese civil war in 1990, despite the fact that a Ministry of Social Affairs had been founded[107] and notwithstanding major prerogatives to set development strategies, no significant measure had been taken up with regard to establishing or promoting state care institutions. To date, the government does not provide, or very rarely provides, direct social services; rather, it has outsourced responsibility for child welfare and protection services to a number of civil society organisations.

Admission to Residential Care Institutions: Formal and Informal Processes

Although children can be admitted to residential care institutions through a court order – either a ruling issued by a religious court in the case of the parent's unfitness or death and the unavailability of a caretaker or a protection order issued by the juvenile judge, as we have seen above (in which case the process gains a layer of formality) – such court orders are not required for the placement of children in residential care institutions. The child can indeed be admitted to the institution (directly or through MoSA or the Social Development Centres of the Higher Council of Childhood) at the request of the child's parents (if they exist) or other members of his or her family[108] or the Union for the Protection of Juveniles in Lebanon (UPEL) or an NGO dealing with childhood protection. This process is relatively simple, and could be considered informal, as the state organs and particularly the judiciary do not intervene, or do not necessarily intervene, in the child's admission.

Every institution has its own criteria for admitting children.[109] However, poverty and family disintegration are clearly identified as the two main grounds for

---

105 Kanaᶜān 2008, p 43. See also Sibai 2014. The paper indicates that of 197 institutions that entered into a contract with the Ministry of Social Affairs in 2013, 120 are religious institutions.

106 Kanaᶜān 2008, p 51.

107 Law No. 212/1993.

108 Fieldwork has also shown that some children have been admitted to residential care institutions upon the referral of neighbours (e.g. in cases where the children were left alone at home).

109 For instance, Al-Mabarrat does not admit foundlings but may admit children of defective filiation. It should be pointed out that there is, formally, no religious criterion for admission to the residential care institutions. However, and given the absence of state institutions, families and judges tend to place children in a faith-based institution affiliated to the religious sect to which the child belongs. For example, Sunni children are referred to Dar al-Aytam al-Islamiyya, while Shiᶜa children are referred to Al-Mabarrat al-Khayriyya and Druze to the Druze Orphanage.

admission to residential care institutions.[110] In fact, official statistics have shown that around 90% of children placed in residential care institutions are not orphans or more generally parentless children, but rather children from poor families unable to care for them.[111] This practice of institutionalising children for social and economic reasons is not recent; since the mid-nineteenth century and the arrival of foreign missionaries, children from poor families have been placed in residential institutions. The deterioration of the socio-economic situation in Lebanon after the civil war (1975–1990), and moreover during the current decade with the impact of the Syrian crisis, has significantly amplified the practice.[112]

Although this poverty-based admission responds to a serious need within low-income families, it remains particularly alarming as it violates the children's right to remain within their natural family environment, and it has been criticized extensively by the United Nations Committee for the Rights of the Child.[113] Children whose parents are not absent or unfit (and who thus do not require alternative care) are indeed placed in residential care institutions in order to receive state support for education and relief, while this issue could be better addressed through a state policy of poverty alleviation measures targeting the families in order to maintain the children in their family environment or to reintegrate those who have been unnecessarily enrolled in residential institutions.

It is to be noted in this regard that residential care providers have all emphasized the importance of child-family contact and described their endeavours to maintain contact between the child and his or her family, as they are aware that 'the family

[110] Interviews of Mrs. Nada Fawaz (Director of the Social Welfare Department, Ministry of Social Affairs) by Najm MC, May 2017 and of Mrs. Samar Hariri (Director of Dar al-Aytam al-Islamiyya) by Sabbagh N, Markaoui J, and Moubarak L, 11 May 2017. Other criteria such as the parents' sickness or drug use have also been mentioned. Interview of Mrs. Joumana Diab (responsible for the Alternative Care Centre for Juvenile Protection at Jam^{c}iyyat al-Mabarrat al-Khayriyya) by Karamé L, June 2017.

[111] Consultation and Research Institute 2006. See also Save the Children Lebanon 2016, p 90: 'The Social Welfare Department of MOSA used to apply institutionalisation as an alternative to parental care through residential contractual agreements with NGOs that manage institutions. It previously targeted children who were orphaned, neglected, and those belonging to families suffering difficult circumstances like divorce, abandonment, disability, or the imprisonment of one or both parents. In response to deteriorating economic conditions in Lebanon, MOSA created a new category eligible for institutionalisation for children experiencing a "decrease in income and the deterioration of the economic situation of the family" (State Party Report on the UNCRC, 2004)'.

[112] Social Welfare Department – MoSA (2015), Draft State National Periodic 4th and 5th Report, HCC, Beirut.

[113] UN Committee on the Rights of the Child 2006, para 44(a). See also UN Committee on the Rights of the Child 2002, para 36.

cannot be replaced'.[114] Although the government acknowledges the serious need to develop and support family-based care schemes, the current trend is still to contract institutional care to civil society organisations, including faith-based organisations, and to invest substantial resources in the increasing number of institutions for children. Over the decades this predominant form of alternative care 'has become rooted within an entrenched socio-political system that would be difficult to dismantle due to its powerful constituencies'.[115]

Supervision of Residential Care Institutions

Residential care institutions are officially under the supervision of the MoSA. However, in recent years, a number of legal practitioners, social workers and NGOs have questioned the effectiveness of such state monitoring.[116] As a matter of fact, the situation of children in residential care institutions is not well known. The available research does not provide information on the children themselves or the standards that are applied within the institutions. Even though interviewed representatives from both residential care institutions and the MoSA assured the interviewers that semi-annual reports are required and that periodic assessment and supervision visits to residential care institutions are operated by MoSA's inspectors and social workers, many remain vocal about the need for stricter supervision mechanisms.[117] In its 2016 report to the Committee on the Rights of the Child, the Lebanese state acknowledged that its contractual relationship with these institutions 'is not subject to systematic or scientific control based on specific and transparent criteria'.[118] For example, the social workers mandated by the Ministry of Social Affairs do not have a unified and specific 'cahier de charges' (specification of requirements). In addition, some institutions abide by strict internal observation mechanisms and have employed highly qualified social workers and psychologists, whereas others are very far from meeting international standards in this respect.

It is to be noted that judges themselves have sometimes been reluctant to place children within residential care institutions given the poor living conditions in a

---

[114] Interview of Mrs. Samar Hariri (Director of Dar al-Aytam al-Islamiyya) by Sabbagh N, Markaoui J, and Moubarak L, 11 May 2017, who added: 'We can never provide the child with the affection and tenderness that he or she would receive within a family'. During the interview with Mrs. Joumana Diab (Responsible for the Alternative Care Centre for Juvenile Protection at Jam^{c}iyyat al-Mabarrat al-Khayriyya) by Karamé L, June 2017, we were also told that the institution focuses on child-family contact by specifically demanding a weekly meeting between the child and his family, and in certain cases by looking for the child's family to ensure that such contact is maintained.

[115] Save the Children Lebanon 2016, p 94.

[116] Sibai 2014.

[117] Interview of Mrs. Iqbal Doughan, specialized family lawyer, by Kallab W and Saad C, 18 April 2017, in which she stated that 'the care in those associations is not always satisfactory and the government's oversight is insufficient'.

[118] UN Committee on the Rights of the Child 2016, para 43.

large number of these institutions.[119] In some orphanages, children have reported malnutrition, sexual abuse and violence; however, despite media attention, civil society claims that no serious investigation has been conducted and the supervision of orphanages is still not sufficient.[120]

As for children who are placed in institutions that are not under contractual agreements with the MoSA, there are no available statistics or information on their number or situation, as they lack any sort of government monitoring.

7.4.4.2 The Practice of Islamic *kafāla*

Kafāla or *takafful* is a traditional Islamic procedure in which citizens undertook to care for children through an arrangement contracted with the child's mother, the child's legal guardian or the state. If the mother was alive, the stepfather (the mother's new husband) would very often bind himself to care for the child. In any event, *kafāla* did not create filiation between the *kāfil* (the person taking care of the child) and the child (*makfūl*).

Kafāla is codified neither in civil laws nor in the personal status laws applicable in Lebanon. It remains, however, a common social and religious practice amongst Muslims, which consists of providing a child, who is usually (but not necessarily) an orphan, with a regular payment covering his or her living and education expenses. The child remains with his or her family and is raised by his own parents or relatives, while the *kāfil* volunteers to support the child financially through a periodic allowance.

A *kafāla* could also be provided for a child living in a residential care institution.[121] Each institution has a different scheme for *kafāla* with varying amounts. The *kafāla* can be comprehensive and include full financial coverage of the child (ranging between 1,500 and 1,800 USD per year). It could also consist of a partial financial support determined by the *kāfil*. The *kāfil* is also encouraged to visit the child inside the institution in order to provide the child with moral and emotional support. However, the child is to remain in the residential care institution and not reside with the *kāfil*. All the Shar^{c}i judges interviewed in the course of this research insisted that the *kafāla* does not entail the placement of the child with the *kāfil*. Islamic rules generally exclude placing a child with a foster family, i.e. with

[119] Shar^{c}i Sunni Court of Beirut, 13 May 2010 (unpublished), in which the court stated that the child's best interest would be to be kept away from both parents and thus to be placed within an alternative care institution; however, the court then mentioned that negative experiences with such institutions in Lebanon made the court reconsider its decision and decide instead to keep the children with their father; interview of Judge Fouad Hamdan (Druze High Court of Appeal of Beirut) by Karamé L, June 2017.

[120] See for example Allouche 2014. See also Allouche 2016.

[121] According to the state's periodic reports to the UN Committee on the Rights of the Child, there are a large number of institutions that are applying the *kafāla* system; however, there are no statistics available on the number of children supported through *kafāla*.

non-blood relatives, as they would not be *muḥarram* to the child. This religious impediment – though it has not been properly investigated, and could even be challenged given that many Muslim countries have implemented family-fostering programmes for children – would probably explain why fostering non-relative children is still not common or accepted in Lebanese Muslim society.

Interviews with representatives of two residential care institutions confirmed this approach. While the *kafāla* system is operative within the institutions, the child is never allowed to accompany the *kāfil* outside the institution's premises. This might occur only in extremely rare situations and under the supervision and accompaniment of a social worker, with the child coming back to the institution on the same day.[122]

However, it has come to our attention that *Dar al-Aytam al-Islamiyya* adopts a *kafāla* system that includes the placement of the child in the *kāfil*'s family. In such a case, the *kafāla* system is not mere sponsorship, but rather becomes a form of alternative care that is comparable to foster care. This scheme occurs specifically for children of unknown filiation who are under one year old. The conditions of maintaining or revoking this sort of *kafāla* when the child reaches an older age are, however, unclear. This institution has a *Kafāla* committee formed of seven members, who are chosen from among the institution's board of directors. The committee meets the *kāfil*'s family and investigates their social and financial status to make sure that they can satisfy the child's needs. The *kāfil*'s family must be Muslim and living in Lebanon. The committee also investigates the *kāfil*'s motives and requests official documents such as the family status record, abstracts of judicial records, etc. Upon this meeting, the committee issues a decision accepting or refusing the *kafāla*; however, the director of the institution indicated that she has not encountered any refusals in the cases she has handled so far.[123] Certainly, such a foster-care step is to be encouraged as it leads to inserting the child into a family environment. However, the process remains problematic. The placement of the child with the *kāfil*'s family is indeed determined by a private institution that mostly operates on donation-based funding, outside the intervention of the court or any other public organ. In this sense, social workers fear that children are being placed within homes of affluent families who remunerate the institution financially. In fact, while Lebanese Islamic law prohibits full adoption, it does not rule out other forms of private or institutional foster care for parentless children.

An alternative could be the issuance of a law that institutionalizes *kafāla* as a family-based alternative care solution for parentless Muslim children by granting the *kāfil* full parental authority over the child. Such a law can build on the Islamic tradition that exhorts believers to provide for the care of orphans, and on the growing endorsement of *kafāla* in the Muslim world as an ethical response to

[122] Interview of Mrs. Joumana Diab (Responsible for the Alternative Care Centre for Juvenile Protection at Jamᶜiyyat al-Mabarrat al-Khayriyya) by Karamé L, June 2017.

[123] Interview of Mrs. Samar Hariri (Director of Dar al-Aytam al-Islamiyya) by Sabbagh N, Markaoui J, and Moubarak L, 11 May 2017.

children being deprived of their biological parents. The proposed law can also build on the international human rights language of the best interests of the child. Article 20 of the UNCRC recognizes the *kafāla* institution as an alternative form of protection together with adoption and fostering (though they are not identical, particularly in terms of custody and inheritance subsequent to the death of the *kāfil*). This private-care scheme would therefore come in line with the UN standards, as there is widespread agreement among professionals in children's care that children's safety and well-being would be better insured if they were placed in an alternative family rather than in a residential care institution. Financial considerations would also argue for this solution.[124]

With respect to its content, the suggested law should clearly outline the state's official procedure for the awarding of parentless children's care to *kāfil* families, and especially the means of investigating their reliability to ascertain that children would be properly cared for. It should also determine the rights and responsibilities of the *kāfil* in terms of parental care and maintenance, as well as other issues such as marriage hindrances. The law should also provide for children of unknown filiation to take the surname of the *kāfil*.[125] Such a change of name does not constitute filiation, nor does it spark the registration of the child in the guardian's family register, let alone give rise to inheritance rights. In everyday life, however, it would make relations with the authorities easier, as the *makfūl* child's paperwork would carry the name of the adult responsible for him or her and, more importantly, it would increase the child's feeling of belonging to the *kāfil*'s family.

7.5 Conclusion

Nasab results from one of two schemes for Muslim and Druze children in Lebanon. First and foremost, it arises from the blood relationship between a child and his or her validly wedded parents; this is the only religiously based mechanism for establishing filiation. In parallel, though, legal rules and court practice often remedy situations affected by legal deficiencies (children whose parents' marriage is uncertain, children born outside the timeframe required for the presumption of legitimate paternity, children born outside a valid marriage, etc.) to establish filiation. One of the simplest mechanisms in this respect is the acknowledgment of

[124] In a study published in 2006, the economist Kamal Hamdan argued that the cost incurred for a child in a foster family is much lower than the cost incurred by the state when the child is placed in an institution. See Consultation and Research Institute 2006; see also Sibai 2014.

[125] Such a provision would appear to stand in contradiction to the dominant interpretation of Islamic jurisprudence, which forbids the child to take the guardian's family name on the basis of Quranic verse 33:4–5 'Call them by their fathers' names, for that shall be more pleasing to God'. However, this contradiction could easily be overcome, as it should be noted that in the time of the Quran's revelation there were no surnames in use; individuals were instead called by their given name and their father's given name.

paternity or maternity, which entails all of the consequences of filiation. Acknowledgment clearly serves as a pragmatic tool to facilitate paternity and private care of children, mitigating the harsh consequences of out of wedlock births, of the prohibition of adoption and of the absence of regulated alternatives to adoption. In any event, all of the legal remedies for defective status operate within the scheme of *nasab*, allowing children to enjoy all rights arising from filiation.

Children of defective, unknown or illegitimate descent, on the other side, are left with a much less favourable status and face harsh legal and social consequences. For example, children born out of wedlock cannot establish their filiation towards their father, and are thus deprived of parental rights such as maintenance and inheritance. The law only provides these children with a minimum of legal security. This is revealed, for example, in the possibility for the unmarried mother to establish maternity through acknowledgment; the effect of this is, however, limited. The Law of 7 December 1951 also provides the child with a name and an identity card if the father registers the birth at the state registers, although this does not establish *nasab* – and therefore does not establish any parental rights and obligations – between the child and his or her father.

Where children have no permanent reliable caretakers, they are not left without protection, either. Various schemes exist which seek to provide a minimum of legal security and financial support. One major deficiency of the Lebanese protection system is, however, the lack of state policies and statutory laws regulating children's alternative care. Consequently, the legal measures that exist for parentless children find their sources in an array of different laws and customary practices.

On the one hand, personal status laws organize and regulate children's custody and guardianship in the event of parents' death or unfitness, and religious courts have jurisdiction to take alternative care measures in this situation. On the other hand, civil juvenile judges have jurisdiction to intervene in situations where the child is deemed to be in danger by issuing protection orders that could constitute, in certain situations, alternative care measures. In all such cases, Muslim and Druze courts as well as juvenile judges prioritize keeping the child within the larger family (kinship). Yet, in the absence of family members or caretakers, it is important to note that – save for very rare and limited circumstances such as for newborn children – none of these schemes actually entail the placement of the child into a foster family, whether temporarily until the parents' hindrance is overcome or permanently in terms of the establishment of a new parent-child relationship. Even when the child is placed within a foster family, the analysis of the existing legal framework and practice reveals that caretakers, whether appointed by religious courts or by juvenile judges, will primarily assume the role of custodian (*ḥāḍin*) rather than being granted full parental authority and thus unlimited rights of guardianship (*wilāya*). While Christian parentless children may be adopted in Lebanon, Muslim children may not, and no functionally equivalent options have emerged.

Most importantly, the lack of an inclusive law regulating children's alternative care has, in addition to the strong family bonds existing within the Lebanese society, allowed for the implementation of informal or customary practices that are decided within the family or the private sphere absent any judicial or administrative order. These practices include placing the child directly into kinship care, or in residential private care institutions funded by the state, or – although this rarely occurs – in a foster family. As important as such practices are in filling the legal gap in the matter, they are also problematic as they occur outside of officially mandated processes and lack permanent governmental oversight, especially in making sure that a placement measure is made for the child's best interests. This is all the more regrettable given that the family's poverty has been clearly identified as one of the main grounds for admission of children to residential care institutions. Although this placement responds to a serious need of low-income families, it is particularly alarming as it violates the children's right to remain within their natural family environment. Child development specialists are unanimous in acknowledging that residential care institutions, in particular those which host a very large number of children, fail to meet children's needs in terms of affection and social integration.

This is particularly important given the fact that acknowledgment, as seen above, can only apply to children of unknown filiation. For children whose *nasab* cannot be legally established, such as children born out of wedlock, *kafāla* would constitute an appropriate alternative private care solution if it could create a functionally equivalent parent-child relationship through the better integration of the *makfūl* child into the *kāfil*'s family.

Though *kafāla* does not entirely fulfil the best interests of the child in terms of alternative care, as it does not allow for the establishment of filiation with the subsequent rights to name and inheritance, it may, however, if clearly framed by statutory law, offer a more appropriate model of care than the current institutional model and a functional equivalent to adoption for Muslim parentless children in Lebanon, enabling these children to be provided with a family life. It would offer an acceptable reconciliation of traditional Islamic discourse with the modern conceptions of the needs and best interests of the child. There is a real prospect for the Muslim religious authorities in Lebanon to contribute to a positive structural change in children's alternative care by pushing for the adoption of such a law, thus contributing to the urgently needed decrease in the number of children in residential care institutions.

In conclusion, given the lack of state regulation of alternative care, and specifically of family-based alternative care, and the absence of state-regulated residential care institutions in accordance with international standards, the legal and social protection of parentless children in Lebanon remains insufficient and is clearly not in line with the UN Guidelines for Alternative Care of Children. What is needed, therefore, is the adoption of a unified state law whereby parentless children would be under the protection of the state in children's homes that would provide for their care and support until an adoptive or a foster family is found, under the permanent oversight of qualified inspectors and social workers. Alternatively, a solution could be sought through the issuance of a law on *kafāla* that would allow a functionally equivalent family-based model. It is, indeed, primarily the duty of the state to ensure proper care and maintenance for children in need, and to ensure that those who do not have a family can still have a better life. Compared to the current situation, there is still a long way to go.

Acknowledgments The authors wish to thank the team of students at the CEDROMA for their research help in the field study: Nathalie Sabbagh, Lynn Moubarak, Jean Maroun Aziz, Wassim Kallab, Nour Zein, Cynthia Saad, Jad Markbaoui, Nihal Abdo, Bouchra Chamseddine and May Haroun. They also express their appreciation to the Council of Scientific Research at Saint Joseph University of Beirut, which has provided funding for portions of this research.

References

Al-Bīlānī B (1997) Qawānīn al-Aḥwāl al-Shakhṣiyya fī Lubnān [The Personal Status Laws in Lebanon], 5th edn. Dār al-^{c}Ilm li-l-Malāyīn, Beirut.

Al-Ibiyānī MZ (1911) Sharḥ al-Aḥkām al-Shar^{c}iyya fī al-Aḥwāl al-Shakhṣiyya [Explanation of Shar^{c}ī Rules in Matters of Personal Status], vol II, 2006 edn. Al-Ḥalabī, Beirut.

Al-Khatīb A (1962) Al-Aḥwāl al-Shakhṣiyya [The Personal Status]. Dār Maktabat al-Ḥayāt, Beirut.

Allouche Z (2014) Betraying Tarek Mallah and Children of Alternative Care: Time for State and Care Institutions to Act. Legal Agenda, issue number 21, 23 October 2014, p 10.

Allouche Z (2015) Illegal Adoption in Lebanon: Mechanisms and Consequences. Legal Agenda, issue number 24, 20 January 2015, p 10.

Allouche Z (2016) The Colonialism of Care: A Critical Approach to the Lebanese Experience. Legal Agenda, issue number 37, 16 September 2016, pp 18–19.

Bilani B (1963) Droit musulman. In: Catala P, Gervais A (eds) Le droit libanais, vol I. LGDJ, Paris, pp 98–126.

Clarke M (2009) Islam and New Kinship: Reproductive Technology and the Shariah in Lebanon. Berghahn Books, New York and Oxford.

Clarke M (2014) Shari^{c}a Courts and Muslim Family Law in Lebanon. In: Giunchi E (ed) Adjudicating Family Law in Muslim Courts. Routledge, New York, pp 32–47.

Consultation and Research Institute (2006) Situational Analysis Study on Children Deprived of Family Care in Lebanon. Ministry of Social Affairs and UNICEF, Beirut.

El-Husseini Begdache R (2008) L'enfant en droit musulman au Liban. In: Khaïat L, Marchal C (eds) L'enfant en droit musulman (Afrique, Moyen-Orient), Actes du colloque du 14 janvier 2008. SLC, Paris, pp 165–188.

Frangieh Gh (2018) Illegal Adoption: Is the birth mother a perpetrator or a victim of human trafficking? Legal Agenda, issue number 56, July 2018, p 12.

Gannagé P (2003) Jurisclasseur de droit comparé, Liban, fascicule n°2 (Mariage, Filiation). LexisNexis, Paris.

Kana^{c}ān N (2008) Al-^{c}Amal al-Ijtimā^{c}ī fī Lubnān [Social Work in Lebanon]. Ra^{c}īdī, Beirut.

Karamé L (forthcoming) Custody under legal pluralism: Children as silenced victims, LLM School of Oriental and African Studies, University of London.

Khamīs F, Al-^{c}Arīdī F (2011) Ḥimāyat al-Aḥdāth al-Mu^{c}arraḍīn li-l-Khaṭar [Protecting Children in Danger in Light of the Law and Case Law in Lebanon], 2nd edn. Friedrich-Ebert-Stiftung, Beirut.

Maghniyya MJ (1961) Al-Fuṣūl al-Shar^{c}iyya [Shar^{c}ī Provisions]. Al-Maktaba al-Ahliyya li-l-Ṭab^{c} wa-l-Tarjama wa-l-Ta'līf wa-l-Nashr, n.p.

Mahmassani M, Messarra I (1970) Statut personnel: Textes en vigueur au Liban. In: Bilani B, Decocq A (eds) Documents Huvelin. Faculté de droit et des sciences économiques, Université Saint-Joseph, Beirut (in French and Arabic).

Maḥmūd ᶜA Al-S M (2013) Majmūᶜat Ijtihād al-Qaḍā' wa-l-Fiqh al-Sharᶜiyyīn [Collection of Sharᶜī Case Law and Fiqh]. Al-Mu'assasa al-Ḥadītha li-l-Kitāb, Tripoli.
Moukarzel Hechaimé A (2008) Liban: l'enfant dans une famille brisée. In: Khaïat L, Marchal C (eds) L'enfant en droit musulman (Afrique, Moyen-Orient), Actes du colloque du 14 janvier 2008. SLC, Paris, pp 351–356.
Mūsā MY (1958) Aḥkām al-Aḥwāl al-Shakhṣiyya fī al-Fiqh al-Islāmī [The Rules of Personal Status in Muslim Law]. Dār al-Kitāb al-ᶜArabī, Cairo.
Najm MC (2017) Lebanon. In: Yassari N, Möller L-M, Gallala-Arndt I (eds) Parental Care and the Best Interests of the Child in Muslim Countries. T.M.C. Asser Press, The Hague, pp 145–168.
Niᶜma ᶜA (2010) Dalīl al-Qaḍā' al-Jaᶜfarī [Guide to Jaᶜfari Justice]. Dār al-Balāgha, Ghobeiry.
Rabāḥ Gh (n.d.) Dirāsa Ḥawla al-Jawānib al-Qānūniyya li-Awḍāᶜ Aṭfāl al-Shawāriᶜ fī Lubnān [Study on the Legal Aspects of Street Children in Lebanon]. Higher Council for Childhood, Arab Council for Childhood and Development, UNESCO. http://std.atfalouna.gov.lb/Files/dockids1.doc. Accessed 17 December 2018.
Rabāḥ Gh (2012) Ḥuqūq wa-Qaḍā' al-Aḥdāth [Juvenile Rights and Juvenile Jurisdiction]. Manshūrāt al-Ḥalabī al-Ḥuqūqiyya, Beirut.
Ṣāghiyya N (1999) Al-Qaḍā' aw al-Ḥaqq bi-ᶜAdāla Afḍal [Judiciary or the Right to a Better Justice]. In: Al-Qaḍā' al-Lubnānī: Binā' al-Sulṭa wa-Taṭwīr al-Mu'assasāt [The Lebanese Judiciary: Building Judicial Power and Reforming the Institutions], Lebanese Centre for Policy Studies, Beirut.
Save the Children Lebanon (2016) Child Rights Situation Analysis – Lebanon. www.thinktriangle.net/wp-content/uploads/2017/01/Save-the-Childrens-Child-Rights-Situation-Analysis-CRSA-Report-Lebanon-.pdf. Accessed 17 December 2018.
Shartūnī R (2016) Al-Qāḍī al-Madanī al-Lubnānī wa-l-Aḥwāl al-Shakhṣiyya: Ḥimāyat al-Qāṣir [The Lebanese Civil Judge and the Personal Status: the Child's Protection], Conference given at the Faculty of Law and Political Science at Saint Joseph University of Beirut, 5 December 2016.
Sibai N (2014) The Poor of Lebanon, Orphans in the Custody of Sectarian Institutions. Legal Agenda, issue number 14, 4 March 2014, pp 6–7.
Sterry W, Abcarius N (translators) (1914) Code of Mohammedan Personal Law According to the Hanafite School by Mohammed Kadri Pasha. Spottiswode & Co. Ltd., London.
UN Committee on the Rights of the Child (2002) Twenty-ninth session, Consideration of reports submitted by States parties under article 44 of the Convention, Concluding observations of the Committee on the Rights of the Child: Lebanon, 21 March 2002, CRC/C/15/Add.169. www.refworld.org/docid/3df5887b4.html. Accessed 28 January 2019.
UN Committee on the Rights of the Child (2006) Forty-second session, Consideration of reports submitted by States parties under article 44 of the Convention, Concluding observations of the Committee on the Rights of the Child: Lebanon, 8 June 2006, CRC/C/LBN/CO/3. www.refworld.org/docid/45377ee70.html. Accessed 28 January 2019.
UN Committee on the Rights of the Child (2016) Consideration of reports submitted by States parties under article 44 of the Convention, Fourth and fifth periodic reports of States parties due in 2013: Lebanon, 19 July 2016, CRC/C/LBN/4-5. www.refworld.org/docid/57f3cad24.html. Accessed 28 January 2019.
UNICEF (2012) Strengthening the Child Protection System in Lebanon, Challenges and Opportunities. UNICEF, Beirut.

Marie-Claude Najm is a professor at the Faculty of Law and Political Science of Saint Joseph University of Beirut, Lebanon, where she is president of the Department of Private Law and director of the Centre of Legal Studies and Research for the Arab World (CEDROMA), and a visiting professor at Panthéon-Sorbonne University (Paris I) and Panthéon-Assas University (Paris II). Her focal field of research is private international law, specifically concentrating on family and successions law. Born in Beirut, she studied law in Paris and Beirut and holds a Ph.D. from

Panthéon-Assas University (Paris II), and she is an Agrégée des Facultés françaises de droit. Her main publications include *Principes directeurs du droit international privé et conflit de civilisations. Relations entre systèmes laïques et systèmes religieux* (Dalloz, 2005); "La Cour de cassation française et la répudiation musulmane, une décennie après l'entrée en vigueur des réformes du droit de la famille au Maroc et en Algérie," Journal de droit international, 2015; "The Enforcement of Foreign Judgments in Lebanese Private International Law," Yearbook of Private International Law 2015/2016; "Lebanon," in Basedow/Rühl/Ferrari/De Miguel (eds.), *Encyclopedia of Private International Law* (Edward Elgar Publishing, 2017).

Myriam Mehanna is a lawyer affiliated with the Beirut Bar and a researcher at The Legal Agenda, a Beirut-based NGO and research center. She holds a bachelor's degree in private law from the Faculty of Law and Political Science at Saint Joseph University of Beirut, and a Ph.D. in law from the University of Panthéon-Assas (Paris 2). Since 2015, she has been a lecturer in private law at the Faculty of Law and Political Science of Saint Joseph University of Beirut. Currently, her research is primarily focused on the independence of the judiciary in Lebanon and the Arab world. She has been a primary contributor to the draft law on judicial reform and the organization of the judiciary which is currently being discussed in the Lebanese Parliament.

Lama Karamé is a lawyer affiliated with the Beirut Bar and a researcher at The Legal Agenda, a Beirut-based NGO and research center. She holds a bachelor's degree in public law from the Faculty of Law and Political Science at Saint Joseph University of Beirut and a bachelor's degree in sociology from the Lebanese University, as well as an LL.M. in law, culture and society from the School of Oriental and African Studies at the University of London. Prior to completing her masters, she was a visiting scholar at Columbia Law School in New York, where she focused her research on the role of legal professions in promoting public interest law. She is currently contributing to the litigation of various human rights cases before Lebanese courts, as well as conducting research on the intersectionality of law and society.

Chapter 8
Malaysia

Azizah Mohd

Contents

Abstract Filiation (*nasab*) under Islamic law generally refers to lineage or descent from a marriage relationship, be it maternal or paternal. Nevertheless, a mere maternal lineage without marriage may not confer *nasab* to a child. Therefore, paternal lineage is very significant in a child's life as it safeguards the status conferred upon the child through its father within a family. Adoption, on the other hand, can be understood as taking the child of another into a person's custody and care as one's own child. Adoption thus changes the status of the child from the child of one person to the child of another person and confers *nasab* to the child

Azizah Mohd is associate professor at Ahmad Ibrahim Kulliyyah of Laws, International Islamic University Malaysia.

A. Mohd (✉)
Ahmad Ibrahim Kulliyyah of Laws, International Islamic University Malaysia, Jalan Gombak, 53100 Kuala Lumpur, Malaysia
e-mail: azizahmohd@iium.edu.my

N. Yassari et al. (eds.), *Filiation and the Protection of Parentless Children*, https://doi.org/10.1007/978-94-6265-311-5_8

through the child's adoptive father, or parent. In Islam, this kind of adoption is known as '*tabanni*' and is prohibited. On the other hand, Islamic law recognizes and encourages foster parenting so as to provide help and assistance to children in need of protection, without affecting the status of the child. In this spirit, adoption law in Malaysia was enacted with the aim of catering to a multiracial society and taking into account both religious and cultural limitations. Thus, in Malaysia the law on adoption is regulated in two Acts: (i) the Registration of Adoptions Act 1952, governing both Muslims and non-Muslims and (ii) the Adoption Act 1952, governing only non-Muslims. This paper explores the practice and law of filiation and adoption as governing Muslims in Malaysia. It examines the legal provisions and seeks to assess whether the law provides for a balanced approach in line with Islamic law while at the same time providing means and alternatives for child protection especially for parentless children.

Keywords Filiation (*nasab*) · Adoption (*tabanni*) · Fostering · Malaysian law · Registration of Adoptions Act 1952 · Islamic Family Law (Federal Territories) Act 1984

8.1 Introduction

Filiation (*nasab*) for Muslims in Malaysia is based on Islamic jurisprudence. It is primarily established by a valid marriage (*'aqd*) and therefore differs from a civil law approach whereby adoption is also recognized as a way to establish filiation. Under Islamic law, adoption (*tabanni*) does not create *nasab*. At the same time, as a multi-religious country, Malaysia generally recognizes both adoption and foster parenting (*kafalah*) as legal tools for integrating parentless children into new families. The UNCRC 1989 also acknowledges adoption and foster placement as means to protect children who are deprived of a family environment.[1] Both adoption and foster placement have been long practised and for many different reasons, these including childlessness, the endeavour to help the poor or needy relatives and the desire to provide protection and a family environment to abandoned children or children without filiation.

In 2015, the Ministry of Women, Family and Community Development (Malaysian Social Welfare Department) Adoption Statistics reported 1,354 cases of applications for adoption through the National Registration Department of Malaysia and 573 cases of application through the courts.[2] There were additionally a total of 1,144 applications for foster care.[3] Statistics recorded by the National Registration Department of Malaysia in 2015 revealed 5,389 registrations of legal adoption

[1] See United Nations Convention on the Rights of the Child 1989 (UNCRC), Article 20(3).

[2] Jabatan Kebajikan Malaysia 2015.

[3] Kementerian Pembangunan Wanita, Keluarga dan Masyarakat (n.d.).

throughout the year among Malays, Chinese and Indians.[4] Disregarding the potential for even more unrecorded adoptions and foster care cases, these numbers are encouraging.

8.1.1 Sources of Law: The Laws on Filiation Governing Muslims in Malaysia

Malaysia consists of thirteen states and is a multiracial and multi-religious Muslim-majority country. The population includes Malays, Chinese, Indians, natives of Sabah and Sarawak and aborigines, amounting to a total population of about 31 million people.[5] Even though Islam is the religion of the Federation,[6] other religions are freely practised. The Malaysian legal system is characterized by legal dualism, with Islamic law governing Muslims and civil law governing both Muslims and non-Muslims. There are also statutes that govern only the non-Muslims, like the Adoption Act 1952.[7] Administration of the law occurs both at the federal and state levels.[8] The power to enact laws for the whole Federation is vested with the federal government whilst states can enact laws only with regard to state matters.[9] For example, the power to enact laws on matters dealing with Islamic law is entrusted to the state as set out in the Federal Constitution in item 1 of the State List, with this power including matters relating to adoption involving Muslims.[10]

Islamic law, especially matters relating to personal law, including the law relating to *nasab*, applies only to Muslims and is administered by the federal states, with each of the thirteen states having their own state enactment competence. The laws dealing with *nasab* are the 'Islamic Family Law Enactments' of each state, which concur to a great extent.[11] For the purpose of this report, reference will be specifically made to the Islamic Family (Federal Territories) Act 1984 (IFLA) since

[4] Jabatan Pendaftaran Negara 2015.

[5] Department of Statistics Malaysia, Official Portal, www.dosm.gov.my (accessed 5 July 2017).

[6] See Federal Constitution of Malaysia, Article 3.

[7] Act 257.

[8] Ibrahim 2000, p 37.

[9] See Federal Constitution of Malaysia, part VI, Article 73.

[10] See Federal Constitution of Malaysia, List II, State List, Ninth Schedule, (Article 95B) (1)(a).

[11] For the purpose of this chapter, except where it is seen as relevant and appropriate to cite specifically to particular State Enactments, reference will be made only to the IFLA as its provisions are quite similar to and representative of State Enactments. The IFLA is the pioneer Act governing Muslims in Malaysia. The IFLA is applicable to Kuala Lumpur, Labuan and Putrajaya. See Islamic Family Law (Federal Territories) Act 1984, Act 303, s. 1(1). See also Ali Mohamed 2004.

it is the pioneer Act[12] on which all other states have based their Islamic family law provisions.

The provisions of the IFLA are based on the Shari'ah. Additionally, in case of legal lacuna in the IFLA, the court is to refer to and apply Hukum Syarak[13] in its original form.[14] The IFLA defines *nasab* as 'descent based on lawful blood relationship'.[15] As regards the establishment of filiation, the IFLA provides for two main mechanisms: birth into a valid marriage and acknowledgement (*al-iqrar*). It is important to note that filiation between a child and its mother is recognized in the IFLA regardless of whether the child is the product of a valid marriage or an unlawful sexual relationship. This can be deduced from the provisions on maintenance and custody for children born out of wedlock. Here, the IFLA imposes on the mother a duty to maintain such children (other than children resulting from rape).[16] Also, custody rights in respect of these children belong exclusively to the mother and her relations.[17]

8.1.2 Jurisdiction of the Courts

Since Malaysia practices a dual legal system, the administration of the laws, i.e. the court structure, is also twofold: namely the civil courts and the Syariah courts. Civil courts deal with cases relating to both Muslims and non-Muslims while Syariah courts deal only with cases relating to Muslims. By virtue of article 121(1A) of the Federal Constitution, the civil courts, including the high courts and subordinate courts, have no jurisdiction in any matter in which the Syariah courts have jurisdiction.[18] It follows that the Syariah courts administer Islamic law, but they are limited to family law and succession law matters as regards Muslim parties[19] and to Shari'ah offences.[20] As the Syariah courts are established by their respective state and federal laws, a Syariah court will have jurisdiction over a Muslim who is

---

[12] Act 303.

[13] Hukum Syarak is defined in the IFLA as Islamic law according to the Shafi'i, Maliki, Hanafi or Hanbali *madhhab*. See Islamic Family Law (Federal Territories) Act 1984, s. 2, A1261.

[14] See Islamic Family Law (Federal Territories) Act 1984, s. 134A(2).

[15] See Islamic Family Law (Federal Territories) Act 1984, s. 2. See also, for example, Islamic Family Law (State of Selangor) Enactment 2003, no. 2, s. 2; Islamic Family Law (State of Malacca) Enactment 2002, no. 12, s. 2; Islamic Family Law (State of Pulau Pinang) Enactment 2004, no. 5, s. 2.

[16] See Islamic Family Law (Federal Territories) Act 1984, s. 80.

[17] Islamic Family Law (Federal Territories) Act 1984, s. 85. See also the case of *Mohamad Ariff bin Ali v Siti Nor Aslinah Lim Li Ming*, [2017] 4 ShLR 75.

[18] See Federal Constitution of Malaysia, Article 121(1A), see also Ibrahim 2000, pp 41–43.

[19] See Federal Constitution of Malaysia, Ninth Schedule, List II State List.

[20] See Shuaib 2003, p 27.

residing in the respective state or federal territorial jurisdiction.[21] The jurisdiction of Syariah courts is provided under the Administration of Islamic Law Act (for federal territories) and the Administration of Islamic Law Enactment (for states other than federal territories) along with the Syariah Court Act (for federal territories) and the Syariah Court Enactments in the states.[22] For example, as regards the jurisdiction of Syariah courts in the Federal Territories, a Syariah high court has jurisdiction throughout the Federal Territories and is to be presided over by a Syariah judge.[23] Concerning subject matter, the Administration of Islamic Law (Federal Territories) Act 1994 states that the Syariah high court has, inter alia, criminal jurisdiction over any offence committed by a Muslim and punishable under the Enactment or the Islamic Family Law (Federal Territories) Act 1984 as well as criminal jurisdiction over any other currently applicable written law prescribing offences against any precepts of the religion of Islam. By contrast, in terms of its civil jurisdiction, the Syariah high court is to hear and determine all actions and proceedings in which all the parties are Muslims and which relate to betrothal, marriage, legitimacy, maintenance, custody of infants etc.[24]

Accordingly, any matter relating to filiation and the status of a Muslim child is under the jurisdiction of the Syariah court and is to be dealt with by the Syariah high court.

8.2 The Establishment of Filiation

8.2.1 Establishing Filiation by Law

8.2.1.1 Filiation Through a Valid Marriage

The maternity of a child is not an issue and *nasab* to the mother – in the strict sense of biological ancestry – is established through childbirth. Statutory provisions on *nasab* thus regulate only paternity. A child is considered to have *nasab* from the father if born at least six months after the conclusion of the marriage and not later than four (lunar) years after its dissolution.[25] This rule is in line with the views of

---

[21] Shuaib 2003, p 29.

[22] See Ibrahim 2000, p 228.

[23] Administration of Islamic Law (Federal Territories) Act 1994, s. 46(1).

[24] Administration of Islamic Law (Federal Territories) Act 1994, s. 46(2).

[25] Islamic Family Law (Federal Territories) Act 1984, s. 110: 'Where a child is born to a woman who is married to a man more than six qamariah months from the date of the marriage or within four qamariah years after dissolution of the marriage either by the death of the man or by divorce, the woman not having remarried, the nasab or paternity of the child is established in the man, but the man may, by way of li'an or imprecation, disavow or disclaim the child before the Court.'

the Shafi'i school of law[26] and is similar in all states.[27] In Perlis and Kedah the maximum gestation period after the dissolution of a marriage had previously been limited to one year.[28] This provision was, however, amended and standardized by virtue of the IFLA after the effort to harmonize State Enactment provisions.[29]

Issues of legitimacy and birth in connection with a marriage are generally raised in cases where the father refuses to either take care of his child or provide maintenance. The Syariah courts generally presume the legitimacy of the child based on the general principles of (1) birth of the child no less than six months after the conclusion of the marriage and (2) sexual intercourse having taken place or the husband having been able to consummate the marriage.[30]

In the 2013 case of *Zafrin Zulhilmi bin Pauzi v Noor Aini bt Nasron*,[31] the child whose paternity was in question was born on 3 September 2010 while the marriage between the applicant (the father) and the respondent (the mother) had been solemnized on 16 April 2010, i.e. only 4 months and 24 days prior to the birth of the child. Despite the fact that the child was born less than six months after the conclusion of the marriage, the court held that paternity of the child could be ascribed to the applicant as he had not stated/claimed that the child was conceived out of wedlock when the case had arisen. Consequently, the Registrar of Births and Death Terengganu could register the child as the daughter of the applicant. However, the court also held that in this specific case, i.e. a case where the child was born less than six months after the conclusion of marriage, the girl in question will not have any succession rights nor will her father be her marriage guardian.

In other cases, however, the Syariah court reversed that decision and rejected the paternal *nasab* of children born earlier than six months after the conclusion of the marriage. In *Maryam Nurisa binti Othman v Huzairin bin Basir*,[32] the daughter was born only a month after the conclusion of the marriage, and both parents conceded that the child had been conceived prior to marriage. The court held that the girl could not be ascribed to her biological father.[33] Finally, in the recent case of *Mohamad Ariff bin Ali v Siti Nor Aslinah Lim Li Ming*,[34] the Syariah high court held

---

[26] See Abu Zahra (1957), pp 386–387.

[27] See, for example, Islamic Family Law (State of Selangor) Enactment 2003, no. 2, s. 111; Islamic Family Law (State of Malacca) Enactment 2002, no. 12, s. 111; Islamic Family Law (State of Pulau Pinang) Enactment 2004, no. 5, s. 111.

[28] See Administration of Islamic Family Law (State of Perlis) Enactment 1992, s. 109 & 110. See also Islamic Family Law (Kedah) Enactment 1979, s. 99 & 100.

[29] See Islamic Family Law (Perlis) Enactment 2006, no. 7, s. 111.

[30] See *Wan Azmi v Nik Salwani* [1990] 9 JH (2) 192; *Salim v Masiah* [1976] 2 JH (2) 296; *Hj Ghazali v Asmah* (1977) 1 JH 81; *Norzaini binti Alias v Mohamad Sharif bin Mohamad Taib* (2003) 16 JH (2) 101; *Wan Khairil bin Wan Azmi v Farah Nurliliana bt Jauhari* [2011] 2 ShLR 1.

[31] [2013] 2 ShLR 39.

[32] (2011) 33 JH(2) 227.

[33] A similar position was adopted in *Rosliza Mustafa v Wan Mohd Kamil Abd Ghani* [2008] 1 CLJ (Sya) 253 and *Mohd Faizol bin Zainal v Suhaila bt Yusoff* [2014] 2 ShLR 83.

[34] [2017] 4 ShLR 75.

that custody of a child born only three months after the conclusion of the marriage appertained exclusively to the mother and her relatives.

On the other side of the range, under s. 112 of the Islamic Family Law (Federal Territories) Act 1984, s. 112, if a divorced woman has not remarried and has completed her period of *'iddah* and subsequently delivers a child, the paternity of the child will be attributed to the ex-husband of the mother if the child is born less than four lunar years from the date of the separation. Where that period is exceeded, the child will be attributed to the ex-husband of the mother only where he or his relatives acknowledge paternity of the child.[35] In *Fatimah binti Abdullah and Anor v Mat Zin bin Kassim*,[36] for example, the court held that a child born one year after its parents' divorce was legitimate considering that the plaintiff and the defendant had sexual intercourse during the marriage and that the child was born later than six months after the intercourse occurring in the marriage relationship. In the same vein, in *Ismail v Kalam*,[37] the court held that a child born more than four years after the divorce could not be considered legitimate as this period exceeds the maximum gestation period as provided by Hukum Syarak and the provisions of Islamic law.

8.2.1.2 Status of a Child Born from Shubhah Intercourse

Shubhah intercourse is defined in the IFLA 1984 as intercourse performed under the erroneous impression that the marriage was valid or as intercourse by mistake and includes any intercourse not punishable by *hadd* in Islam.[38] This basically means that, where a marriage was held to be invalid (*fasid*) by the court due to non-fulfilment of marriage conditions, sexual intercourse between the spouses will be considered *shubhah* if the parties believed that their marriage was valid. Accordingly, a child born from *shubhah* intercourse will be attributed to its father if it is born within the legal timeframe governing the general presumption of paternity, i.e. at least six months and no longer than four years after sexual intercourse.[39] This situation can be best illustrated in the case of *Nagira Begum bte E Mohamed v Rajul Ali*,[40] where the marriage of the plaintiff to her husband was held to be invalid as it did not fulfil all the necessary conditions, particularly the requirement for the 'bride' to be in the *'iddah*[41] period. The court cited from the book *Mu'jam al-wasit*, which defines the word *shubhah* as 'a matter that is unclear as to whether it is permissible or prohibited and whether it is right or wrong.' Therefore, the court further ruled

---

[35] Islamic Family Law (Federal Territories) Act 1984, s. 111.

[36] (2001) 14 JH (2) 225.

[37] (1995) 10 JH 41.

[38] Islamic Family Law (Federal Territories) Act 1984, s. 2.

[39] Islamic Family Law (Federal Territories) Act 1984, s. 113.

[40] [2006] 3 ShLR 117.

[41] *'Iddah* refers to the waiting period of a woman due to divorce or separation from the husband or due to the death of the husband.

that the sexual relationship between the plaintiff and her husband was '*shubhah* intercourse' as they believed that their marriage was valid and that the child born from such relationship was considered legitimate. In the recent case of *Abd Halim bin Md Hashim v Azila bt Ramli or Ismail*,[42] a marriage was held to be *fasid* due to non-fulfilment of the requirement of a guardian (*wali*) in the marriage *'aqd*. As the parties believed in the validity of their marriage, the sexual relationship that took place between the spouses was considered *shubhah* and, as a result, all their three children born from the marriage were held to be legitimate. The court referred to, inter alia, the work *Al-Fiqh al-Islami wa-Adillatuhu* by Wahbah al-Zuhayli, according to which the paternity of a child born in a *fasid* marriage is similar to that of a child born in a valid marriage. This is a precautionary measure to safeguard the child's paternity.

As *shubhah* intercourse requires the spouses to believe in the validity of their marriage, in *Re Mohd Fairus bin Othman & Ita Wijaya binti Ismail*,[43] the court rejected the plaintiff's application to be ascribed paternity of his biological child as both spouses were aware of the fact that their marriage did not comply with the legal procedures in Malaysia. These kinds of marriages – called syndicate marriages – are defective as they do not follow the proper procedure for marriage. They are normally performed by an unauthorized person and are especially meant to avoid the proper marriage procedure. Against this background, the judgment of the court can also be understood as a ruling made to protect the interest of the Muslim community and to discourage this kind of marriage.

8.2.2 Establishing Filiation by Private Autonomy: Acknowledgement of Filiation

8.2.2.1 Acknowledgement of Paternity

The IFLA provides for the acknowledgement (*al-iqrar*) of *nasab*. Under section 114 IFLA, a man can acknowledge another person either expressly or implicitly as his child, thereby establishing *nasab*.[44] For the acknowledgement to be valid, eight conditions must be met. Firstly, paternity of the child must not already be established in relation to anyone else.[45] Secondly, the ages of the man and the child must be such as to make *nasab* factually possible.[46] In other words, their age gap must clearly show that they could be father and son/daughter.[47] Thirdly, a

[42] [2017] 2 ShLR 57.

[43] (2009) 28 JH (2) 203, [2010] 1 CLJ (Sya) 126.

[44] For further reading see Mohd 2006.

[45] Islamic Family Law (Federal Territories) Act 1984, s. 114(a) and s. 115(c).

[46] Islamic Family Law (Federal Territories) Act 1984, s. 114(b).

[47] Islamic Family Law (Federal Territories) Act 1984, s. 115(b).

mumayyiz child, i.e. a child who has reached the age of discernment, must accept the acknowledgement.[48] Fourthly, marriage between the man and the mother of the child must have been legally permissible at the time of conception.[49] Thus, when at the time of conception the person claiming to be the father of the child was legally prevented from marrying the mother, an acknowledgement is not possible.[50] Fifthly, the acknowledgement must explicitly state that the child is the legitimate child of the man.[51] Sixthly, the man must have contractual capacity,[52] i.e. be a sane person that has reached the age of puberty. Seventhly, the acknowledgement must also be with the distinct intention of conferring the status of legitimacy;[53] as this is in fact the purpose of acknowledgement and acknowledgement must not, for example, be because the child is a rich person and the father wishes to inherit from him. Finally, for the acknowledgement to be valid it must be definite[54] and aim to create *nasab*.[55]

The IFLA further provides that the presumption of paternity arising from acknowledgement may be rebutted only by one of the following: firstly, a disclaimer on the part of the person acknowledged; secondly, by proof of such proximity of age or seniority of the acknowledged as would render the alleged relationship physically impossible; thirdly, by proof that the acknowledged is in fact the child of some other person; and finally by proof that the mother of the acknowledged could not possibly have been the lawful wife of the acknowledging man at the time when the acknowledged child would have been conceived.[56]

8.2.2.2 Acknowledgement by a Woman in Her *'iddah* Period

The IFLA further provides for several other situations of acknowledgement with regard to the mother. Thus, *nasab* may also be established through the acknowledgement of a married or divorced woman while in her *'iddah*.[57] This being said, the husband of the mother will not be attributed paternity as well unless he confirms her acknowledgement or she backs it with other evidence.[58]

48 Islamic Family Law (Federal Territories) Act 1984, s. 114(c) and s. 115(a).

49 Islamic Family Law (Federal Territories) Act 1984, s. 114(d).

50 Islamic Family Law (Federal Territories) Act 1984, s. 115(d).

51 Islamic Family Law (Federal Territories) Act 1984, s. 114(e).

52 Islamic Family Law (Federal Territories) Act 1984, s. 114(f).

53 Islamic Family Law (Federal Territories) Act 1984, s. 114(g).

54 Here, 'definite' may imply that the acknowledgement is very clear and cannot give any meaning other than that to confer the status of legitimacy on the child acknowledged.

55 Islamic Family Law (Federal Territories) Act 1984, s. 114(h).

56 Islamic Family Law (Federal Territories) Act 1984, s. 115.

57 *'iddah* refers to a certain waiting period for a woman after she is divorced or separated from the husband or in the event of the death of the husband.

58 Islamic Family Law (Federal Territories) Act 1984, s. 116.

8.2.2.3 A Child or another Person's Acknowledgement of Someone as Mother or Father

Acknowledgement of paternity can also work in the other direction: the IFLA contains provisions on a child or adult's acknowledgment of another person as his or her mother or father. Such acknowledgment requires the acceptance of the potential parent. The acknowledgment will create *nasab* provided that the person consents to it and the age gap is such as to make the relationship possible.[59] Finally, the IFLA also provides for the acknowledgement of other kinship relations (*al-iqrar bi al-nasab 'ala al-ghayr*). Again such acknowledgment requires the acceptance of the other person.[60] Once an acknowledgement has been made in respect of paternity/maternity or kinship, it is irrevocable.[61]

8.2.3 Proof of Paternity Through Blood Tests and DNA Screening

Nowadays, the paternity of a child can also be proved through DNA and blood tests. Contemporary Muslim scholar 'Abd al-Karim Zaydan contends that if it is established medically that the blood of the child matches the blood of the father or the mother, this represents reliable circumstantial evidence to prove a blood relationship between the child and the parents.[62] However Zaydan does not further discuss the basis for his view more than pointing to the discussions on the permissibility of relying on the characteristics of breastmilk in determining paternity as discussed in the classical book of Hanbali scholar al-Bahuti, '*Kashshaf al-Qina'*.'

DNA tests are generally admissible under the Syariah Court Evidence (Federal Territories) Act 1997 as a type of circumstantial evidence in the determination of *nasab*.[63] These tests may not, however, be referred to in order to establish paternity of the child outside the conditions set out under section 110–119 of the IFLA as discussed above. Therefore, a DNA test may not establish the *nasab* of a child born out of wedlock.

So far, there are no reported cases where DNA screening was used to prove the paternity of an illegitimate child. There is however an interesting case that highlights

---

59 Islamic Family Law (Federal Territories) Act 1984, s. 117.

60 Islamic Family Law (Federal Territories) Act 1984, s. 118. Thus, in *Husin bin Mamat & Two Others v Bustaman bin Ali* (2001) 14 JH (1) 101, the plaintiff claimed that the deceased was his mother. As the mother was dead, the sister of the deceased woman acknowledged the plaintiff as her nephew. The court found that the conditions for a valid acknowledgement were fulfilled and therefore confirmed the acknowledgement.

61 Islamic Family Law (Federal Territories) Act 1984, s. 119. For further reading, see Mohd Zin et al. 2016, pp 299–318.

62 See Zaydan (n.d.), p 414.

63 See Syariah Court Evidence (Federal Territories) Act 1997, s. 33.

the relationship between Islamic evidence law and DNA testing, the Brunei case of *Mohammad Ismail bin Hj Abu Bakar v Hajah Rosita or Nurul Asyiqin bt Hj Lakat*.[64] In that case, the child was born seven months after the dissolution of her parents' marriage. The ex-husband denied paternity of the child. The court advised the parties to undergo a DNA screening, the results of which showed that the child was not biologically related to the father. The court, however, held that since the child was born within the period of four years after the dissolution of the marriage, the only way to deny *nasab* was through the procedure of *li'an* (imprecation). The father decided to perform *li'an*, and the court ordered the parties to take the respective oaths. After both parties took the oath, the court made an order affirming that the plaintiff was not the biological father of the child. This case shows that a DNA test alone is not considered conclusive proof for determining or excluding *nasab* but mere corroborative evidence or a supportive procedure.

8.2.4 **Fatwas** ***on Filiation***

Besides federal statutory provisions there are *fatwas* issued by the Fatwa Committee of Islamic Religious Affairs Malaysia. This committee was established in early 1970 under Article 11 of the Regulation of the National Council for Islamic Religious Affairs Malaysia.[65] Once published in the Official Gazette these *fatwas* become legally binding and have to be accepted by the courts.[66] Also, *fatwas* bind only the residents of the state in which they have been published.

As matters of religion are under the jurisdiction of the state, all *fatwas* issued by the National Fatwa Committee may be adopted as a *fatwa* by any state with or without any modification.[67]

In the meeting of 27 July 2004 the Fatwa Committee of the National Council for Islamic Religious Affairs Malaysia discussed and agreed on several matters relating to illegitimate children. Pursuant to the decision in the 64th meeting of that committee, the issued *fatwa* defined an illegitimate child and the consequences of illegitimacy as follows:

(i) A child born out of wedlock whether as a result of adultery or rape where *shubhah* does not apply
(ii) A child born less than six months and two seconds (*lahzah*) based on the lunar calendar from the date of the (last) marital sexual intercourse (*tamkin*).
(iii) Such child cannot be attributed to the biological father or to anybody who declares himself to be the father of the child. Therefore, the child and the

---

64 [2009] 3 ShLR 84.

65 For a discussion on *fatwas* see Ibrahim et al. 2016, pp 2235–2238; see also Ibrahim and Mohd 2017, pp 69–84.

66 See Administration of Islamic Law (Federal Territories) Act 1993, Act 505, s. 34(3) and (4). For a detailed account on *fatwas* in Malaysia, see Ibrahim et al. 2016, pp 2235–2238.

67 See Ibrahim and Mohd 2017, pp 70–71.

putative father have no right to inherit from one another and are not *mahram* nor can they be guardians for one another.[68]

The above *fatwa* reiterates almost literally the provisions of the IFLA. It explicitly spells out, however, that an acknowledgement made by the biological father is not effective if the child falls within the two categories mentioned above. Similar *fatwas* have been issued in other states, such as Selangor, Negeri Sembilan and Sarawak.[69]

In contrast, a *fatwa* issued by the Perlis Fatwa Committee in the state of Perlis takes a more lenient view on *nasab*. The *fatwa* held that a child born less than six months after the conclusion of marriage could be attributed to the mother's husband, unless he denied paternity.[70] This is the only state *fatwa* that contradicts the *fatwa* issued by the National Fatwa Committee as well as the provisions of the laws of other State Enactments.[71] As this *fatwa* was published in the Official Gazette on 17 January 2013,[72] it is effective as a binding *fatwa* in the State of Perlis as provided for by the Administration of Islamic Law Enactment (State of Perlis) 2006.[73]

To date, there is one reported case in line with this *fatwa*. In *A Child & Ors v Jabatan Pendaftaran Negara & Ors*,[74] the appeal court granted the appeal of the biological father seeking to confer his name upon a child born less than six months after conclusion of marriage. This decision naturally caused some controversy as it was contrary to the Islamic law provisions of other State Enactments,[75] such as in Selangor, Malacca and Negeri Sembilan, as well as the IFLA[76] which set a time frame of birth not earlier than six months after the conclusion of marriage. Furthermore, the above case was tried by the civil courts, whereas jurisdiction to

[68] See decision of the National Fatwa Committee meeting, no. 64, 27 July 2004. See also JAKIM 2015, p 206.

[69] See Dari Meja Mufti, Bayan Linnas Siri Ke-106 (n.d.) Isu Penamaan 'bin/binti Abdullah' kepada anak tidak sah taraf oleh Mahkamah Rayuan, www.muftiwp.gov.my/index.php/ms-my/perkhidmatan/bayan-linnas/1714-bayan-linnas-siri-ke-106-isu-penamaan-bin-binti-abdullah-kepada-anak-tidak-sah-taraf-oleh-mahkamah-rayuan (accessed 15 January 2018).

[70] See Zainul Abidin (n.d.).

[71] See footnote 25 as discussed above. See also Islamic Family Law Enactment (Perlis) 2006, no. 7, s. 111.

[72] See the statement of the *mufti* of Perlis in Utusan Online, Jangan Hukum Anak bin Abdullah, 11 June 2017, www.utusan.com.my/rencana/utama/jangan-hukum-anak-bin-abdullah-1.491951 (accessed 15 January 2018).

[73] Enactment no. 4, s. 48(6).

[74] [2017] 4 MLJ 440.

[75] See, for example, the statement of the *mufti* of Perak, Tan Sri Harussani Zakaria, Boleh menjurus menghalalkan zina, kata mufti, Malaysia Kini, 31 July 2017, www.malaysiakini.com/news/390369 (accessed 15 January 2018).

[76] See Islamic Family Law (State of Selangor) Enactment no. 2 of 2003, s. 111; Islamic Family Law (State of Malacca) Enactment no. 12 of 2002, s. 111; Islamic Family Law (State of Negeri Sembilan) Enactment no. 11 of 2003, s. 111; Islamic Family Law (Federal Territories) Act 1984, s. 110.

determine cases relating to the *nasab* of Muslims lies with the Syariah courts.[77] In fact, after the amendment of the Article 121(1A) of the Federal Constitution of Malaysia, civil courts have no jurisdiction in any matters that fall under the jurisdiction of the Syariah courts.[78] According to one commentator, this case exposes quite clearly the ambiguities in Malaysia's legal system. Notwithstanding the fact, that there is no unanimous view among Malaysian scholars on whether a child born outside the legal framework, i.e. a child conceived out of wedlock, can take his father's name,[79] some parts of the Muslim community consider this decision as a challenge to Islam as the official religion of the state, and by extension an 'insult to the religion'.[80]

8.3 Adoption in Malaysia

8.3.1 Customary Adoptions

Since long before the introduction of statutory law governing adoption, it has been practised according to the customary laws of the various peoples in Malaysia.[81] For instance, in the Malay community, a couple could take on a child from their relative or friend under a mutual agreement among themselves. While the couple would claim that the child had become their child, the legal links between the child and its biological parents were never disrupted. A girl would, for example, still need the consent of her biological father for her first marriage as he remained her marriage guardian. Similarly, she would have to observe the rules of social interaction with her adoptive parents and siblings, especially if her adoptive parents were not her blood relatives and therefore not related to her to the prohibited degree of marriage.[82] Although this situation is a disadvantage for her integration in the nucleus of her new family, it preserves her original lineage and at the same time gives the adoptive family the opportunity to provide her with full assistance in a very special manner.

In 1951, customary adoption was recognized under the law in *Jainah binti Semah v Mansor bin Iman Mat & Anor.*[83] There, the plaintiff and her husband had taken on the daughter of the husband's brother and raised her since her birth. When

---

[77] See Federal Constitution of Malaysia, Ninth schedule, List II, State List.

[78] See discussion on jurisdiction of the courts above.

[79] See www.thestar.com.my/opinion/columnists/reflecting-on-the-law/2017/08/03/constitutional-view-on-bin-abdullah-case-islam-is-like-a-mansion-with-many-rooms-and-diversity-aboun/ (accessed 29 November 2018).

[80] Khairul Anuar 2017.

[81] For further reading, see Taylor 1970, pp 134–143. See also Suhor 2008, pp 2–10.

[82] See Majid 1999, p 218.

[83] [1951] MLJ 62.

the child was eleven years old, her adoptive father died; subsequently, the child, who lived with her adopted mother, was taken away by her biological father. One of the main questions to be decided was whether this customary adoption amounted to a legal adoption, i.e. an adoption recognized under Malaysian law. Legal adoptions are accomplished upon a court order giving the child the same status as the biological child of the adoptive parents. The court held that customary adoption was recognized in the personal law of Pahang Malays, and as the child had been taken on by a married couple, the adoptive mother would ordinarily be entitled to the custody of the child where the adoptive father has died.

A similar situation applies in the Chinese community, which also recognizes customary adoption consistent with Chinese custom. In *Tan Kui Lim & Anor v Lai Sin Fah*,[84] for example, the court held that the adoption of a maternal grandson as a son by a maternal grandparent was contrary to Chinese customary law and thus invalid. Conversely, in *Re Theow Seng Yeap; Thow Chow Goon & Anor v Khar Kar Chooi & Anor*,[85] the biological parents of an infant who had been given up for adoption according to Chinese custom sought return of the child as they had changed their minds two years after the customary adoption. The adoptive parents applied for a legal adoption, but the biological parents withheld consent. The court held that the biological parents' withholding consent was not unreasonable as there were no grounds whereby the adoptive parents should be preferred over them from the point of view of the welfare of the infant. The court reasoned that it would defeat the objective of the legislature that all adoptions be in accordance with the statutory law if the courts were to recognize customary (*de facto*) adoption as a ground for dispensing with parental consent. This decision shows that customary adoption is recognized in Malaysia although no formal registration under the law takes place. This kind of adoption is also known as a *de facto* adoption.[86]

8.3.2 **De facto** *Adoptions and Fostering*

A *de facto* adoption is not defined under the law. In general, a *de facto* adoption denotes an informal adoption before it is registered under the Registration of Adoptions Act 1952 (RAA).[87] A *de facto* adoption can be an adoption that is arranged informally among the biological parents and the adoptive parents and later registered by virtue of the RAA under the National Registration Department of Malaysia (NRD) after the conditions of registration are fulfilled. A *de facto* adoption can also be done through the Department of Social Welfare Malaysia

[84] [1980] 1 MLJ 222.

[85] [1989] 3 MLJ 482.

[86] See Registration of Adoptions Act 1952, s. 6. See also Majid 1999, p 218.

[87] Act 253.

(DOSW).[88] The DOSW is an agency under the National Unity and Social Development Ministry that directly manages adoption. It is one of the most people-oriented of government departments and it participated in nation building even before an independent Malaysian state came into being in 1963. The department was started in 1946 by the British Military Administration to address social needs subsequent to the Second World War.[89] The DOSW organizes adoptions and fostering, especially of children in the children's homes or welfare homes that host abandoned and abused children as well as children from poor families and orphans.[90] The Director General of the DOSW is mandated to allow for a child's adoption or fostering by suitable applicants in order to enable such a child to live in a family environment instead of in a welfare home.[91] To prevent child trafficking[92] and to protect the children involved, the law restricts any advertisements which could incite a parent to give up a child for adoption as well as any advertisements showing the desire of a person to adopt or the desire of an entity (other than the DOSW) to facilitate the adoption of a child.[93] Also for this reason, any application for adoption will be heard and determined in chambers unless the judge or a court orders otherwise.[94]

If the *de facto* adoption is processed by the DOSW, the applicants have to notify the competent person, termed the protector,[95] within one week from the date of taking custody of the child. On receiving notice, the protector will investigate the matter and see whether the person is qualified to become the custodian of the child, in accord with the best interests of the child. If the protector is satisfied that it is in the best interests of the child to stay with the applicant, the child will be surrendered to the applicant on terms and conditions such as to provide the child with love and affection. If these conditions are not met the child will be taken away and placed in a safe location. Failure to give such notice will subject the person to a fine not exceeding ten thousand ringgit or to five years imprisonment or to both.[96]

Other than through the DOSW, children, especially those who are parentless, can also be taken in for fostering or adoption by non-governmental organizations

---

88 Act 253. See Suhor 2008, p 47.

89 See Jabatan Kebajikan Masyarakat Malaysia 1996, pp 1–3.

90 See Jabatan Kebajikan Masyarakat (n.d.), p 1.

91 Child Act 2001, s. 30(1e). See also Majid 1999, p 237.

92 See Majid 1999, p 237.

93 Any person who contravenes this section is subject to punishment of imprisonment for six months or a fine of two hundred and fifty ringgit or to both, see Adoption Act 1952, s. 26.

94 See Adoption Rules 1955, rule 12, see also *TPC v ABU* [1983] 2 MLJ 79.

95 A protector is defined under the Child Act 2001 as the Director General of Social Welfare; the Deputy Director General of Social Welfare; a Divisional Director of Social Welfare, Social Welfare Department of Malaysia; the State Director of Social Welfare of each state; and any Social Welfare Officer appointed under section 8 of the Child Act 2001.

96 Child Act 2001, s. 35(1–7). With regard to the power of the protector to require the child, pursuant to section 35 of the Act, to be produced before him, see s. 37.

(NGOs) like OrphanCare,[97] KEWAJA[98] and the Children's Protection Society.[99] The need for NGOs has grown considerably in light of the increase in child abandonment cases.[100] This allows the greater public to get involved in the protection of parentless children by applying through those channels to foster and perhaps adopt a child.

Just what amounts to a *de facto* adoption has been defined in the leading case of *Tang Kong Meng v Zainon bte Md Zain*.[101] In this case, the plaintiff was the biological father of a girl born out of wedlock who was adopted by the defendant and registered under the Registration of Adoptions Act 1952 (RAA). The plaintiff disputed the validity of the registration of the adoption. While the adoptive parent did have physical custody of the girl for more than the required two years before making the application for adoption, maintenance had been paid by the biological mother. Therefore, the registration for adoption was held void *ab initio* as the requirement of paying maintenance for at least two years had not been fulfilled. The court emphasized that a person seeking a *de facto* adoption must have physical custody inclusive of paying for maintenance for a certain period of time,[102] and the law requires it to be two years continuously.[103]

A *de facto* adoption can also encompass a foster relation.[104] Although fostering is not adoption, it gives the foster parents *de facto* control over the child.[105] Currently, there is no specific legislation governing fostering in Malaysia, except for several laws relating to child protection in general, the main law being the Child Act 2001 (CA 2001).[106] This Act is of general application and governs both Muslims and non-Muslims.[107] The CA 2001 defines 'foster parent' as a person who is taking care of the child but is not a parent or relative of the child.[108] Basically, fostering as experienced in Malaysia is based on the practice of the DOSW and amounts to the placement of a child in the care, custody and control of foster parents for a period of two years or until the child reaches the age of eighteen years, whichever comes first.[109]

---

[97] OrphanCare 2011.

[98] Kem Modal Insan KEWAJA (n.d.).

[99] Children's Protection Society Penang (n.d.).

[100] Pak 2010.

[101] [1995] 3 MLJ 408.

[102] See *Tang Kong Meng v Zainon bte Md Zain* [1995] 3 MLJ 408, p 414.

[103] See Registration of Adoptions Act 1952, s. 6.

[104] For further reading, see Mohd and A Kadir 2014, pp 295–308.

[105] For further details, see Khoo 1984, p xxviii.

[106] Act 611.

[107] See Child Act 2001, s. 1.

[108] Child Act 2001, s. 2.

[109] The information is obtained based on an interview conducted with Mr Nizam Kassim, Assistant Director, Children's Division, Social Welfare Department of Malaysia, on 23 February 2011. See also Child Act 2001, s. 30.

8.3.3 Statutory Adoptions

Legal sources regulating legal adoption are found both at the federal level as part of the civil law as well as at state level as part of Islamic law. To suit both Muslims and non-Muslims, there are two statutes on adoption, namely the Registration of Adoptions Act 1952 (RAA)[110] and the Adoptions Act 1952 (AA).[111] These Acts regulate (i) adoptions involving Muslims and non-Muslims and (ii) the legal recognition of adoptions achieved either by registration under the RAA or by an order of the court under the AA.[112] For the purpose of this chapter, discussion will focus only on the Registration of Adoptions Act 1952 as it governs the adoption of Muslim children in Malaysia.

8.3.3.1 Registration of Adoptions Act 1952 (RAA)

The RAA has general application to both Muslims and non-Muslims, but only in West Malaysia.[113] Thus, the RAA requires that the adopted child and the adoptive parents be ordinarily resident in West Malaysia.[114] In practice, this requirement prohibits anyone other than those who reside in West Malaysia from adopting a child, regardless of the applicants themselves being West Malaysians. The RAA is general in nature and applicable to the adoption of all children, including an abandoned child. It has to be noted that, in addition to other requirements, for the purpose of registration, the applicant has to enclose either the birth certificate of the child if it was born in Malaysia or the child's traveling document if it was born outside Malaysia.[115] In the case of an abandoned child who has no birth certificate, the adoptive parents must fill out Form JPN AA 01, provide all relevant documents required for adoption[116] and make application in the registration office where the applicant resides.[117]

The RAA regulates the registration of *de facto* adoptions, including customary adoptions.[118] Under the RAA, any child adopted by Muslims or non-Muslims must be registered. However, the failure to register an adoption will not affect the validity

[110] Act 257.

[111] Act 253.

[112] For further details see Mohd 2012, pp 79–89.

[113] See s. 1. The law applicable in Sabah is the Adoption Ordinance 1960 (no. 23 of 1960), while in Sarawak it is the Adoption Ordinance (Cap 910) of the Laws of Sarawak 1958.

[114] Registration of Adoptions Act 1952, s. 10(3).

[115] See Abd Ghafar 2002, p 10.

[116] Registration of Adoptions Act 1952, s. 6(1).

[117] See Abd Ghafar 2002, p 11.

[118] See Majid 1999, p 218. The whole objective of the Act seems to be allowing for *de facto* adoptions. See comments by James Foong J in *Tang Kong Meng v Zainon bte Md Zain* [1995] 3 MLJ 408, p 414.

of an adoption if all other requirements are met.[119] The Act provides for a Registrar General who is in charge of and supervises all adoption registers and who must keep a register in a specific form as provided in the Second Schedule. He is under the duty to enter the particulars to be registered and to record all proceedings in respect of the registration of adoptions, including the identity of the adopted child, the name of the person adopting it, the name of the person, if any, consenting to the adoption and all evidence taken by him in any such proceeding under this Act.[120] The RAA further provides that if the Registrar is not satisfied of the truth of any statement made to him, he may refuse to register the adoption, or if he requires evidence with regard to any particulars that need to be registered, he may postpone registration and call for any further evidence that he thinks necessary. The Registrar is required to record his reasons for any such refusal or postponement.[121]

8.3.3.2 Conditions and Procedures for Adoption

Age

The RAA sets certain requirements regarding the age difference between the adoptive parent and the adopted child. For a valid adoption under the RAA, the adopted child must be under eighteen years of age, while the adoptive parents must be at least twenty-five years of age or at least eighteen years older than the adopted child. The latter requirement applies only where the adoptive parents are not relatives of the child. If one of the adoptive parents is a relative, the prospective parent must be at least twenty-one years old.[122]

Consent

Further, the consent of the biological parents (where known) is required for an adoption to be valid. Where the biological parents are unknown, the Registrar has the power to dispense with such consent if he is satisfied that it is just and equitable and the adoption is for the welfare of the child.[123]

A *de facto* adoption can be proved by presenting the written consent of either the biological parents or, in the case of a child born out of wedlock, its mother; in the

---

[119] Registration of Adoptions Act 1952, s. 11. See also Majid 1999, p 222.

[120] Registration of Adoptions Act 1952, ss. 3–5.

[121] Registration of Adoptions Act 1952, s. 10(1).

[122] Registration of Adoptions Act 1952, s. 10(2)(a), (b) and (c).

[123] Registration of Adoptions Act 1952, s. 6(1)(b). See also the case *Tang Kong Meng v Zainon bte Mohd Zain & Anor* [1995] 3 MLJ, 408, where consent of the illegitimate father was dispensed with and consent of the mother alone was acceptable.

case of abandoned children, a letter from the court or the DOSW is sufficient.[124] The law also requires that the biological parents or one of the biological parents or, in absence of the parents, the guardian of the child appear before the Registrar and express consent to the adoption.[125] Consent for adoption was an issue raised particularly in *Tan Kong Meng v Zainon bte Md Zain & Anor.*[126] In that case, the father had not consented to the adoption. The court, however, held that it sufficed that the biological mother had consented as she had continuously visited the child and paid for its maintenance.[127]

In *Sean O'Casey Patterson v Chan Hoong Poh & Ors,*[128] the adoptive parents had registered an adoption under the RAA based on the birth mother's written consent. At the time of adoption, the child's birth father was identified as 'Bart' on the birth certificate. The actual biological father, the appellant in this case, was an American citizen who requested that the adoption be declared null and void. He asked that the high court both declare him to be the biological father of the child and rectify the birth certificate. In discussing whether the biological father's consent was necessary for the registration of the adoption under the RAA, the federal court held that at the time of the adoption, the appellant was not known to be the child's birth father. His consent was thus irrelevant since it was only after the adoption was completed and subsequent to a DNA test that he was confirmed to be the child's birth father.

Procedure

In order to determine the suitability of the adoptive parents, the National Registration Department (NRD) will conduct interviews, having in particular the best interests and welfare of the child in mind. Both the applicants and the child are required to attend these interview proceedings.[129] The parties and witnesses who give evidence before the Registrar are bound to speak the truth and in the event of providing false evidence are liable under Chapter XI of the Penal Code.[130] The Registrar is responsible for making sure that the supporting documents and the statements given during the interview proceeding are consistent. He is also obliged to monitor the interaction of the child with the applicants.[131] Particular caution is to be exercised when abandoned children are involved. Here a report from the DOSW

[124] Registration of Adoptions Act 1952, s. 6(a). See also Abd Ghafar 2002, p 11.

[125] Registration of Adoptions Act 1952, s. 6(b).

[126] [1995] 3 MLJ 408.

[127] See *Tang Kong Meng v Zainon bte Mohd Zain & Anor* [1995] 3 MLJ, 408. See also Registration of Adoptions Act 1952, s. 6(1). For further details, please read Buang 1995.

[128] [2011] 4 MLJ 137.

[129] See Registration of Adoptions Act 1952, s. 6(1)(a).

[130] Registration of Adoptions Act 1952 s. 8(1) and (2). See also Penal Code, Chapter XI.

[131] See Abd Ghafar 2002, p 13.

is required to support the application. If satisfied, the Registrar approves the application and the applicant is required to pay a registration fee of thirty ringgit, which is a quite reasonable fee.[132] It has to be noted that strict compliance with the interview procedure is necessary; otherwise the application may be either postponed until further evidence is presented or rejected.[133]

Upon the registration of an adoption in accordance with section 6 RAA, a certified copy of the entry in the register signed by the Registrar is to be delivered or sent to the person or spouses who applied for such registration; additionally, a certified copy of the entry in the register is to be sent to the Registrar General, with all such certified copies constituting the adoption register of the Registrar General.[134]

Effect of Adoption

The registration of an adoption under the RAA is proof of a *de facto* adoption and awards the adoptive parents the right to custody over the child. The registration does not, however, create *nasab* between the adoptive parents and the child. Such a child has no right to inherit from its adoptive parents. The adoptive parents may however bequeath in the child's favour. For instance, in *Re Loh Toh Met, (Decd), Kong Lai Fong & Ors v Loh Peng Heng*,[135] the deceased had adopted a number of children, one of which was done under the Registration of Adoptions Ordinance 1952 (which is equivalent to the RAA) and the others in accordance with Chinese custom. Despite the registration, the child did not possess any rights of inheritance as the registration did not entitle it to such rights. Similarly, the definition of 'child' was confined to an adopted child under the AA.[136]

In terms of social interaction within the adoptive family, the adopted child is treated as a stranger and certain moral values required by Islamic law must be observed.[137] It follows that the RAA does not prohibit a single parent from adopting a child of a different sex. However, it is questionable whether this practice should be discouraged as it might cause social problems when the child grows up.[138]

Registration of a *de facto* adoption is, however, crucial as it confers benefits on the child as regards access to education, application for an identity card and a

---

[132] Registration of Adoptions Act 1952, s. 6(1).

[133] Registration of Adoptions Act 1952, s. 10(1).

[134] Registration of Adoptions Act 1952, s. 7(1).

[135] [1961] MLJ 234.

[136] See the case *Yeap Chan Aik v Yeap Chan Hoe & Ors* (2000) 1 MLJ 78.

[137] See Mohd Wahie 1997, p 11. For further details on the rights of an adopted child, see Mohd 2011.

[138] See Mohd Wahie 1997, p 19.

passport[139] and, more importantly, Malaysian nationality. Thus, the adoptive parents may apply for Malaysian citizenship on behalf of the child as the nationality of a person normally follows the nationality of that person's legal parents.[140] The citizenship of an adopted child is normally registered in the certificate of adoption. The registration also serves to establish an income tax deduction for the adoptive parent.[141]

8.3.4 Adoption Under the Islamic Family Law (Federal Territories) Act 1984 (the IFLA)

The Islamic law that is set forth in Malaysia's individual State Enactments does not include any specific provisions on adoption. The same holds true for the IFLA. Although the law is very extensive on child-related issues, no single provision covers adoption and foster care.[142] Instead, matters pertaining to adoption in Malaysia are handled and managed by the government. With the availability of the RAA, legislators might have felt it unnecessary to have an Act specifically dealing with Islamic adoption that governs Muslims.

However, there seems to be confusion regarding the application of the statutes on adoption i.e. the RAA and the AA. In *Abdul Shaik bin Md Ibrahim & Anor v Hussein bin Ibrahim & ors*,[143] the plaintiff's child, who was later successfully registered under the RAA, was given into adoption on the condition that the defendants would return the child to the plaintiff should the defendants have a child of their own. However, when after five years the defendants indeed had a child, they refused to return the adopted child. The plaintiffs applied for an order declaring the registration of adoption to be null and void. The defendants, in turn, sought dismissal of the application on the ground that the claim fell under the jurisdiction of the Syariah Court as both parties were Muslims. Despite the fact that the adoption had been registered, the court ruled that the adoption was null and void after having incorrectly construed section 31 of the AA as being equally applicable to adoption under the RAA.[144]

Although the IFLA and the Islamic law enactments are silent on matters relating to adoption and foster care, there is a provision under the IFLA which prescribes the duty of a person to maintain a child who is accepted as a member of the family.[145]

---

[139] See Mohd Wahie 1997, p 11.

[140] See Abd Ghafar 2002, pp 20 and 21.

[141] See Abd Ghafar 2002, pp 20 and 21.

[142] See Islamic Family Law (Federal Territories) Act 1984, Act 303, ss. 81–87. See also Daud 2002, p 10.

[143] [1999] 5 MLJ 618.

[144] Section 31 of the AA provides that it does not apply to Muslims.

[145] Islamic Family Law (Federal Territories) Act 1984, s. 78.

This provision requires that a child who is adopted or fostered by a person be deemed a family member and be regarded as the person's own child with respect to the duty of maintenance. Therefore, the adopting or fostering person is responsible for that child. This is regardless of the fact that the act of adoption or fostering does not confer *nasab* to the child. The application of this law can be seen in *Rosnah v. Ibrahim*,[146] where the Syariah Court decided that the adopted child was entitled to maintenance from the adoptive father after the adoptive parents divorced. In that case, the child had been only one day old when he was given over into the care of its adoptive parents.

Meanwhile, in *Aminah bt Ahmad v Zaharah bt Sharif & Ors*[147] the Syariah Court recognized the adoptive mother's duty to maintain her two adopted children after the death of her husband (the adoptive father). In this case, after her husband's death the adoptive mother filed a claim in relation to jointly acquired property that was a part of her deceased husband's estate. The court took cognizance that the adoptive mother would be responsible for continuing to raise the two adopted children and held that she was entitled to half of the jointly acquired property since she had such heavy responsibilities to carry out.

8.4 Conclusion

The Malaysian State Enactments which govern Muslims as regards the issue of *nasab* operate within the framework of Islamic law. The majority views of Muslim jurists, in particular of the Shafi'i school of law, are followed by all states with the exception of the state of Perlis, where the *fatwa* on the establishment of a child's legitimacy and filiation to the father is based on a minority view. This affects to a certain extent the decisions of the courts, something which could be clearly seen in the previously discussed cases of *Zafrin Zulhilmi bin Pauzi v Noor Aini bt Nasron*[148] and *A Child & Ors v Jabatan Pendaftaran Negara & Ors.*[149] Nevertheless, such cases occur very rarely. In all other states, the Syariah Courts apply the provisions of their respective State Enactment based on the majority view of Muslim jurists.

As regards adoption, there are a variety of options. While the laws seem to be adequate to allow for adoptions involving both Muslims and non-Muslims in Malaysia, adoption is recognized only at the national level. In other words, there are no provisions on inter-state adoption. Some time ago, a suggestion was made to

---

146 (1979) 1 JH (2) 94.

147 [2008] 3 ShLR 56.

148 [2013] 2 ShLR 39.

149 [2017] 4 MLJ 440.

have a single Act governing adoptions for all Muslims.[150] The proposal was discussed in a Workshop on Adoption, but it is unknown whether it was ultimately brought before Parliament. It was suggested in the workshop that the Act should cover the inheritance rights of an adopted child; the rights and responsibilities of adoptive parents in terms of the child's maintenance, custody, education and upbringing; and rules on social interaction between the adopted child and the adoptive family. Additionally, it also has been proposed that the new Act should encourage the suckling (*rada'ah*) of an adopted child as an alternative to legalizing the relationship between the adopted child and the adoptive family.[151] Other than suckling, it was also proposed that the new Act should discuss and elaborate the means of distributing property, including bequests (*wasiyyah*) or gifts (*hibah*) made to the adopted child and the adoptive family.[152]

It was further suggested that the Islamic Family Law Enactments in each state in Malaysia need to be amended in terms of jurisdiction and the judicial guidelines on custody matters involving an adopted child. It has been argued that a special fund must be established to meet the needs of adopted children – who are typically from various backgrounds – so that they can be brought up by qualified and dedicated people.[153]

References

Abd Ghafar K (2002) Prosedur pengambilan anak angkat dan realitinya di Malaysia. In Seminar on Bengkel Hak dan Kedudukan Anak Angkat Mengikut Syariah dan Perundangan Malaysia, Jabatan Agama Islam Wilayah Persekutuan, 15 June 2002 (n.p.).

Abu Zahra M (1957) Al-Ahwal al-Shakhsiyya, Dar al-Fikr al-'Arabi (n.p.).

Al-Bukhari (n.d.) (Translated by Khan MM) Sahih al-Bukhari, vol 8. Kazi Publication, Lahore.

Ali Mohamed AA (2004) The Annotated Statutes of Malaysia, Islamic Family Law (Federal Territories) Act 1984, Act 303. Malayan Law Journal, Kelana Jaya.

Bengkel Hak Dan Kedudukan Anak Angkat Mengikut Syariah Dan Perundangan Malaysia (2002) Workshop organized by Hawa Negeri Selangor, Nazri and Nazri Associates Sdn. Bhd., Mass Magazine and YADIM.

Buang S (1995) Adoption, a little bundle of heartache, case comment on the Alvina adoption case, Malaysian Law News 16–19.

Children's Protection Society Penang (n.d.) Who we are. www.cpspg.org.my/webpages/who.html. Accessed 27 January 2011.

Curzon LB (n.d.) A Dictionary of Law, 2nd edn. Pitman Publishing, London.

[150] See Bengkel Hak Dan Kedudukan Anak Angkat Mengikut Syariah Dan Perundangan Malaysia 2002.

[151] This is because suckling will give to the child the status of a natural child, with the exception of the issues of inheritance and marriage guardianship, see Daud 2002, p 12.

[152] See Daud 2002, p 12.

[153] Daud 2002, p 13.

Daud AB (2002) Keutamaan hak jagaan anak angkat: Panduan dan penyelesaian mengikut perundangan di Malaysia in bengkel hak dan kedudukan anak angkat mengikut Syariah dan perundangan Malaysia, Mass Magazine and YADIM.
Ibrahim A (2000) The administration of Islamic law in Malaysia. IKIM, Kuala Lumpur.
Ibrahim B et al. (2016) An appraisal on the administration of fatwa in Malaysia. Advanced Science Letters 22(9):2235–2238.
Ibrahim B, Mohd A (2017) Maslahah based *fatwa* on issues relating to wealth in Malaysian contexts. Journal of Islamic Law Review 13(1):69–84.
Jabatan Kebajikan Malaysia (2015) Buku JKM 2015. www.jkm.gov.my/jkm/uploads/files/penerbitan/Buku%20JKM%202015%E2%80%A2Final.pdf. Accessed 28 March 2017.
Jabatan Kebajikan Masyarakat (n.d.) Panduan pelanggan, Proses permohonan anak angkat / anak pelihara. (n.p.) Kuala Lumpur.
Jabatan Kebajikan Masyarakat Malaysia (1996) 50 tahun Jabatan Kebajikan Masyarakat Malaysia (n.p.).
Jabatan Pendaftaran Negara (2015) Laporan Tahunan 2015. www.jpn.gov.my/wp-content/uploads/LaporanTahunan2015-WEB.pdf. Accessed 30 March 2017.
JAKIM (2015) Kompilasi Pandangan Hukum, Muzakarah Jawatankuasa Fatwa Majlis Kebangsaan Bagi Hal Ehwal Ugama Islam Malaysia, Jabatan Kemajuan Islam Malaysia, Putrajaya. www.islam.gov.my/images/ePenerbitan/KOMPILASI_MUZAKARAH_MKI_2016.pdf. Accessed 29 November 2018.
Kem Modal Insan KEWAJA (n.d.) Maklumat Ringkas KEWAJA. www.scribd.com/doc/19757913/MAKLUMAT-RINGKAS-KEWAJA. Accessed 25 July 2017.
Kementerian Pembangunan Wanita, Keluarga dan Masyarakat (n.d.) Statistik Permohonan Anak Pelihara. www.data.gov.my/data/ms_MY/dataset/statistik-permohonan-anak-pelihara. Accessed 28 March 2017.
Khairul Anuar K (2017) Children's Rights, Illegitimacy and the Rule of Law in Malaysia, Oxford Human Rights Hub, 1 September 2017. http://ohrh.law.ox.ac.uk/childrens-rights-illegitimacy-and-the-rule-of-law-in-malaysia/. Accessed 19 July 2018.
Khoo OS (1984) Parent – Child law in Singapore. Butterworths, Singapore.
Majid MK (1999) Family law in Malaysia. Malayan Law Journal, Kuala Lumpur.
Mohd A (2006) Legitimacy of a child through acknowledgement (*al-iqrar*) under Islamic law: the extent to which acknowledgement establishes paternity of an illegitimate child. Shariah Law Reports (ShLR), July – September.
Mohd A (2011) Protection of rights of adopted children in relation to duties of adoptive parents under the law in Malaysia. Journal of Adoption Quarterly 14(4):229–245.
Mohd A (2012) Adoption as a means of child protection: the law and practice in Malaysia. Asia Pacific Journal of Social Work and Development 22(1–2):79–89.
Mohd A, A Kadir N (2014) Children foster care law and practice: what Malaysia can learn from foster care (*ihtidhan*) in Jordan. IIUM Law Journal 22(2):295–308.
Mohd Wahie N (1997) Pemeliharaan anak angkat, satu panduan. MKKM, Kuala Lumpur.
Mohd Zin N et al. (2016) Islamic Family Law in Malaysia. Thomson Reuters Malaysia Sdn Bhd, Kuala Lumpur.
OrphanCare (2011) OrphanCare Baby Hatch. www.orphancare.org.my/index.php/baby-hatches. Accessed 1 February 2011.
Pak J (2010) Growing problem of abandoned babies in Malaysia. BBC News, 21 August 2010. www.bbc.co.uk/news/world-asia-pacific-11050427. Accessed 5 April 2011.
Shuaib FS (2003) Powers and Jurisdiction of Syariah Courts in Malaysia. Malayan Law Journal, Kuala Lumpur.
Suhor S (2008) Anak angkat dan undang-undang. Dewan Bahasa dan Pustaka, Kuala Lumpur.
Taylor EN (1970) The customary law of Rembau. In: Hooker MB (ed) Reading the Malay Adat laws. Univ. Press, Singapore.
Zainul Abidin MA (n.d.) Minda Tajdid, 'Menasabkan Anak Kepada Suami Ibu Sekalipun Perkahwinan Kurang Dari Enam Bulan'. http://drmaza.com/home/?p=488. Accessed 15 January 2018.

Zaydan 'A al-K (n.d.) Al-Mufassal fi Ahkam al-Mar'a wa-l-Bayt al-Muslim fi al-Shari'a al-Islamiyya, vol 9. Mu'assasat al-Risalat (n.p.).

Azizah Mohd is associate professor at the Ahmad Ibrahim Kulliyyah of Laws at the International Islamic University Malaysia. At present, she is teaching Islamic family law and Usul al-Fiqh. She specializes in Islamic family law and the protection of children's rights in Islam, especially the law on illegitimate and abandoned children. She was the coordinator for IIUM Legal Clinic at Ahmad Ibrahim Kulliyyah of Laws from 2013 to 2017. She obtained her Ph.D. from the same university. Her dissertation primarily examines rules relating to foundlings (laqit) under Islamic law and the law in Malaysia. The first book authored by her is *Protection and Adoption of Abandoned Children in Malaysia: A Comparative Overview with Islamic Law* (2008). She co-authored her latest book, *Islamic Family Law in Malaysia* (2016). She has written a number of articles on issues relating to women's rights, children's rights and child protection as well as the means of protecting children through adoption, foster care and breastfeeding.

Chapter 9
Morocco

Katherine E. Hoffman

Contents

Abstract This chapter considers laws and social realities determining the status of the Moroccan child born inside or outside of marriage. It considers first, the legal grounds for filiation and second, the legal framework for guardianship of parentless (abandoned or orphaned) children. In both the legal and social approaches to these two issues, there are several constants over time, especially the strong – but not absolute – influence of Maliki jurisprudence. Proposed reforms in the deeply conservative fields of family and guardianship laws indicate that judges are not only considering the 2011 Moroccan Constitution, the 2004 Family Code (Moudawana) and the 2002 *kafala* (guardianship) law, but also the United Nations Convention on the Rights of the Child and its concept of the best interests of the child. I argue that in regards to *kafala* guardianships, which are handled under contract law rather than

Katherine E. Hoffman is associate professor of Anthropology, director of the Middle East and North African Studies Program, and faculty member in the Legal Studies Program at Northwestern University.

K. E. Hoffman (✉)
Department of Anthropology, Northwestern University, 1810 Hinman Ave., Evanston IL 60208, USA
e-mail: khoffman@northwestern.edu

N. Yassari et al. (eds.), *Filiation and the Protection of Parentless Children*, https://doi.org/10.1007/978-94-6265-311-5_9

family law in Morocco, the state occupies an ambivalent position, mandating replacement care at the level expected of biological parents while denying the child the rights and responsibilities of biological children. Recent cases in the Moroccan courts question longstanding conservative approaches to gender as well as family, raising the possibility of female-headed families (not only households) by issuing family booklets to women, and increasing calls to recognize biological paternity as entailing responsibilities otherwise only expected of fathers with paternal filiation through marriage.

Keywords Morocco · Adoption · Family · Family law · Islamic guardianship · Private international law

9.1 Introduction

In Morocco, there are both religiously inspired and secular national and international legal tools that frame the legal filiation of children and the state or private care of relinquished (abandoned) children who are deprived of filiation or parental care, or both. The 2004 Moroccan Family Code (commonly called the Moudawana, Ar. *mudawwanat al-usra*)[1] largely follows Maliki jurisprudence and governs marriage, descent, custody, and other matters related to the legally recognized family, including rights of women. The Family Code does not govern the legal status or rights of children without filiation; its Article 149 states that 'adoption has no legal value' and does not entail the rights afforded by filiation. The legal rights of children come under Articles 32 and 34 of the 2011 Moroccan Constitution with general principles about the rights of all children, 'regardless of family status'. A 2002 law pertaining specifically to *kafala* (Islamic guardianship) governs legal guardianship with parental authority for parentless children, which is a contractual arrangement between a provincial Royal Prosecutor and private individuals. In recent years, judges have referred to the international legal tool of the 1989 United Nations Convention on the Rights of the Child, signed by Morocco in 1990 and ratified by the Moroccan Parliament in 1993. Finally, in their interpretations of these sources as pertaining to contested filiation or guardianship, judges make

[1] This chapter calls this legal tool by its conventional translation, the Family Code (Ar. *mudawwanat al-usra*) even though it is a personal status code for all Moroccans regardless of their conditions of birth. Moroccan law considers personal status to be grounded in relations of the biological, legal family. This code is also commonly perceived to be the key to women's rights in Morocco, but as Žvan Elliott has argued, its rights pertain only to married or previously married women, and not to never-married women (colloquially referred to as 'girls' (Ar. *banat* or *anisat*) because of the presumed virgin status of unmarried women). The normative and rights-bearing woman in Morocco is therefore a married woman and a mother who parents within the institution of marriage. This unstated qualification excludes a significant portion of Moroccan urban and rural dwellers. See Žvan Elliott 2015.

recourse to interpretations of Maliki Islamic jurisprudence as well as existing state laws.

As this chapter will explain, the legal grounds for establishing filiation differ according to the marital status of the biological parents. In cases of disputed paternity, medical testing (to match DNA or determine sterility) to establish or dispute paternity has a different value for married and unmarried parents. There is no question that the 'legitimate' marital family is at the centre of Moroccan society, and the Constitution states as much in its Article 32. Children outside this context continue to suffer from stigma and social exclusion. However, civil society has increasingly drawn attention to the problem of children who do not fit the norm, whether abandoned children housed in hospitals and group homes, street children, or young girls from the countryside 'hired' by upper-middle-class households to work as domestic help in exchange for lodging and low wages. Among these children outside the norm, relinquished children specifically constitute 'surplus bodies in a political and symbolic economy of modernity'; preserving the biological-legal family, from which these children are excluded, is a matter of 'public order'.[2]

In this chapter, I challenge the predominance of what is colloquially called 'blood' (Ar. *damm*) – biological lineage – as the central link between child and parent in Moroccan law and society.[3] I do this in two ways. First, I examine filiation as the result of the legal contract of marriage, rather than blood, generously bounded in law as a period exceeding the duration of a marital contract, and the gestation period as legally permitted to surpass the length established by medical science. Second, I argue that in regards to children without established filiation, the *kafala* contract of replacement care purports not to create a new family relationship, yet it entrusts the guardian parent to be, as the standard *kafala* contract states, a 'father to his son.'[4] The ambivalence of this *de facto* but non-*de jure* family inheres to the *kafala* institution whether the guardians reside in Morocco itself or instead in the transnational sphere.[5] The normative expectations of paternal sentiment and protection, and maternal care towards the child, are inscribed in the *kafala* law, and conform to the treatment of orphans in religious texts that seem to have inspired the *kafala* law even though this law falls outside the purview of family law and within the purview of Moroccan contracts and obligations. State institutions, I argue, only ambivalently uphold the family/non-family distinction that is otherwise so forcefully defended in Moroccan law and in the personal status law applied to *makful* children in some European states, especially France.[6]

---

[2] Bargach 2002, pp 6 and 68.

[3] See Geertz 1979 for an example of the view that biological ties necessarily lead to the closest affective bonds between caretaker and child.

[4] This language is gendered as male regardless of the gender of the contracting guardian(s) or the *makful* child.

[5] Kiestra 2014 argues that the ECHR makes clear that the existence of *de facto* family life does not obligate member states to recognize these domestic units as 'families'.

[6] The European Court of Human Rights (ECHR) upheld France's right not to transform a *kafala* relationship into adoption when presented with *Harroudj v. France* in 2012, noting that there was

This chapter argues as well that in the adjudication of both filiation and guardianship, two forces introduced from outside – international human rights law and medical testing – present challenges to the legal certainties contained in Moroccan law.[7] More specifically, some judges recently have incorporated into their decisions concern with the best interests of the child (as advocated by the 1989 United Nations Convention on the Rights of the Child, which Morocco has signed and ratified), and consideration of DNA and sterility testing under some circumstances, but not others, to establish or disprove paternity.

Regardless of the legal parameters of these various forms of family and care for children in Morocco, it is worth noting that a description of law only partially accounts for the range of domestic arrangements practiced by Moroccans. A variety of long-standing and fluid cultural practices permit and perpetuate the extrajudicial exchange of children between biological parents and non-biological adults. This occurs in 'requested adoptions' when 'patrons' in a relationship of authority request a child from established couples who hierarchically can be seen as clients, especially when these married couples appear to have 'extra' or 'available' children.[8] Such transfers of children can be willing or unwilling, but function socially as part of relations of reciprocity, with children as buffers against old age and infirmity. These children then represent the 'acknowledgement of debts and obligations' between biological and 'adopting' parents.[9] This is a form of intentional family-making that is declining with the decreased fertility rate in both urban and rural areas over the last few decades. Transfers of children may instead involve couples who register an abandoned child born out of wedlock as their 'own' in the husband's family booklet,[10] creating a legal fiction through documents originally intended to confirm a pre-textual biological reality. In the first is an exchange of children whose transfer of parental authority typically is not registered or codified in texts; in the second is a surreptitious 'adoption' through registration of children who may discover their personal status later in life when they need identity papers, or when they face the estate division of one of their parents and learn from 'adoptive' siblings and relatives that they are not equal to blood siblings before the law. If in contrast the legal claim to these children is successfully concealed, the child has all the filial privileges and responsibilities of a biological child. Through such fluid kinship practices, we can see that the management of children, household composition, labour, care, and affect are only incompletely and contingently shaped by the national and international laws intended to regulate the family unit that the 2011 Moroccan Constitution considers the bedrock of society.

---

no consensus among European states as to how to treat this institution. See *Harroudj v. France*, European Court of Human Rights (Fifth Section), Case No. 43631/09, 4 October 2012, http://hudoc.echr.coe.int/sites/eng/pages/search.aspx?i=001-113819 (accessed 8 July 2015). See also the ECHR's treatment of a notarial *kafala* in *Chbihi Loudoudi et al. v. Belgium*, European Court of Human Rights (Fifth Section), Case No. 52265/10, 25 August 2010, http://hudoc.echr.coe.int/sites/eng/pages/search.aspx?i=001-113819 (accessed 28 July 2017).

[7] See An-Na'im 1990, 2010 and Syed 1998 on the compatibility of human rights law and Islam.

[8] Fioole 2015.

[9] Fioole 2015, p 260.

[10] Bargach 2002.

9.2 Filiation

The Moroccan Family Code of 5 February 2004 in its Book 3 stipulates maternal and paternal filiation. Filiation may be 'legitimate' (Ar. *nasab shar^{c}i*) or 'illegitimate' (Ar. *nasab ghayr shar^{c}i*).[11] Filiation to both parents stems from the conjugal bed, and this includes a child born up to six months after the conclusion of the marriage contract (if there had been the opportunity for sexual intercourse before the contract's conclusion), whether that contract was valid or 'defective', and up to one year after the couple separates or the husband dies. The marital period is generously interpreted by courts, when brought to their attention, as including the engagement period during which both parties intend to marry and in which there may be 'sexual relations by error'. The engagement no longer (since 2004) requires the consent of the woman's father or other male representative (*wali*), although culturally this is still preferred.[12]

Maternal filiation is always through birth (Article 147).[13] It has the same effects (e.g. mutual inheritance) regardless of the birth mother's marital status and the cause of her pregnancy (consensual sexual relations or rape).[14]

Paternal filiation is more complex, since paternity is inherently speculative without genetic confirmation. According to Article 151 of the Family Code, 'Paternity is established by presumption and may only be refuted by judicial decision.' In Morocco, filiation is automatically assigned to the husband of the birth mother when the marriage is registered with state authorities. When the child is born outside of this recognized marriage, paternal filiation can be established in three ways. The first is declaration of paternity, as in many customary (*fatiha*) marriages. When the couple is engaged but the marriage is not yet finalized, a child born of sexual relations between the partners still has paternal filiation. Paternal filiation allows the child to take the father's surname, inherit, and obtain maintenance in the case of a divorce, and requires the observance of marriage prohibitions. The principle of legitimate paternal filiation within a widely conceived scope of

---

[11] In contrast, filiation in Algeria may only be 'legitimate'. I put these terms in quotation marks because of the strong moralizing tone, despite their technical function in jurisprudence.

[12] The 2004 Family Code eliminated the need for a *wali* to legitimate a marriage, but still permits it. In many families, it is still preferred to have parental consent before marriage so as to avoid problems later if a troubled marriage leads a wife to return to her parental home and require protection from her husband. See Žvan Elliot 2015.

[13] Surrogacy is outlawed and not practiced in Morocco; in situations of surrogacy outside of Morocco, countries differ as to whether maternal filiation is assigned to the progenitor (contributor of the egg, who may be the surrogate mother or the intended mother entrusting the surrogate mother), or instead the woman who carries the fetus and gives birth to the child.

[14] Until 2014, the penal code allowed a rapist to avoid conviction if he married his victim. The widely publicized suicide of 16-year-old Amina Filali in 2012, who drank rat poison after being forced to marry her rapist, brought attention to this law. The suicide provoked widespread outrage and calls to dissolve the law. In response, in 2014, Article 475 was eliminated so that a family could no longer force a raped daughter to marry her rapist so as to avoid family shame, which was in practice the context for such marriages after rape.

marriage has been affirmed at least 18 times by the Moroccan High Court since 1962, with eight of these cases in 2009 alone.[15] These High Court cases have established that a pregnancy that began after the engagement entails paternal filiation, even when the child is born as soon as three months after the marriage ceremony was concluded.[16] In some instances, courts have requested no marriage deed when the father declared that the child was conceived during the engagement period.[17] As one judge remarked to me in a case of customary marriage that involved the birth of a child, if the couple was engaged to be married and had good intentions, 'Why make things harder for them?'[18]

The second means to establish paternity outside of marriage is through court order. Yet even when paternity is established, conventionally, no rights accrue to the child if the parents are not at least engaged to be married. This is what makes a Tangier family court decision in January 2017 so unusual, and potentially ground-breaking, as I describe later in this chapter.

The third way for a man to establish paternity is by simply claiming it for a child who has no filiation at any time prior to the man's death. This claim may be accepted by judicial decision if it is feasible, if the man is of sound mind, and so long as the child does not refute this paternity if he or she is of legal majority (12 years old). If the child is a minor, s/he may contest the man's paternity upon reaching majority.

Regardless of the much-debated matter of whether and how paternity can be established for children born outside of marriage, Moroccan law forbids the paternal filiation of a child born outside marriage (whether registered or customary) when the mother is known. This is the fate of children born to mothers in fleeting and/or socially unrecognized sexual relationships and to sex workers. A single case from 1982 considered by the High Court established that a child born of unmarried partners is a child of adultery and cannot have paternal filiation even when the father has acknowledged the child as his own. No other case involving birth outside of marriage was heard by the High Court between 1982 and 2009. This principle was reconfirmed with the 2017 appeals court in Tangier.

Article 154 of the Family Code delimits the temporal boundary of paternity presumed by the conjugal bed *(al-firash)* and the length of possible gestation. Paternity is assigned to the mother's husband if the birth occurs at least six months after 'valid' (Ar. *shar^{c}i*) or 'invalid' (Ar. *ghayr shar^{c}i*) marriage, provided the opportunity for sexual relations existed. In the case of separation, divorce, or death, paternity is also presumed to align with the ex-husband if the child is born within one year of the couple's separation. The reader may note the latitude in the

[15] In 1957, the newly independent Morocco established the Supreme Court as the country's highest court. Since October 2001, this Court has been called the Cour de cassation. This paper uses the term High Court for them both.

[16] Morocco, Cass. 25 March 2009 no. 546/2/1/2009.

[17] Morocco, Cass. 25 April 2009 no. 576/2/1/2007.

[18] Judge quoted in Hoffman 2015, p 44.

Moroccan legal time frame, implicitly accommodating the possibility of post-marital (that is, extramarital) sex with either the ex-husband or another man, even though both forms of 'sexual relations by error' are prohibited in the Moroccan penal code (Articles 490 and 491). Additionally, the assignment of paternity to the ex-husband up to one year after divorce can be interpreted as an implicit understanding that sexual relations may endure between former spouses, even if forbidden by law. The provision may also ease the suffering of a child who results from the mother's extramarital relations with a man other than the ex-spouse as the marriage dissolved. Explicitly, the time frame adheres to the 'sleeping fetus' theory or 'maximum length of pregnancy allowed under Islamic law.'[19] This theory holds that a fetus may be present but dormant in a married woman, meaning the pregnancy only reveals itself months after conception. From a purely functionalist perspective, the sleeping fetus theory has been analysed by scholars as a long-standing social accommodation to resolve the problem of children born outside of marriage who otherwise would lack paternity and paternal filiation and suffer stigma as a result.[20]

The provision allowing paternity to be established between engaged but not married partners was a significant change in the 2004 Family Code. This paternity is allowed if the marriage had been agreed to by the partners but had not yet taken place because of a *force majeure.* Sexual relations 'by error' refers to the situation in which a couple is engaged subsequent to a request for marriage and affirmative response, but for reasons of *force majeure* the marriage itself does not take place. Conception during the engagement is called *shubha* and allows the mother to claim her fiancé as the biological and legal father provided they indeed marry eventually.[21] This means that a child conceived during the engagement period still has filiation through the biological father even though the latter is not legally married to the birth mother. The engaged man and woman must agree that the pregnancy is the result of their actions; if the man refutes this, a paternity test may be ordered by the court. The judicial decision is final. Filiation through this kind of 'defective' marriage has the same effects as filiation through legitimate marriage. *Shubha* has been viewed unfavourably among some male and female judges who see it as encouraging promiscuity.[22] It is clearly a legal accommodation to benefit the child (and biological mother) regardless of the circumstances of his or her conception, and to reduce the number of 'illegitimate' (Ar. *ghayr sharᶜi*) children in Morocco.

This expansion of the legal limits of the period of marriage is only an issue because Moroccan law allows for sexual relations only within marriage. A sexual relationship outside of marriage, even when mutually consenting, is called *zina.*

[19] Miller 2006.

[20] The maximum time frame for the manifestation of this pregnancy is defined in the major schools of Islamic jurisprudence, ranging from two years for the Hanafis to up to five to seven years for the Malikis of North Africa. See Rezig 2004, p 161 and Miller 2006.

[21] See discussion of *shubha* and its innovative usage in the 2004 Family Code in Sonneveld 2017.

[22] See Sonneveld 2017.

Those accused of *zina* can be sanctioned in the Penal Code to one to twelve months' imprisonment in the case of fornication (Article 490), and one to two years' imprisonment in the event the fornication is adulterous. Charges of adultery are supposed to originate with an individual party rather than the state. With adultery, the offended spouse must issue a complaint to the court in order for the charge to be prosecuted if the alleged offender resides in Morocco. If the offended spouse resides outside Morocco, the alleged offender can be prosecuted in absentia (Article 491).[23] Required evidence to support an accusation of adultery must include two witnesses to the adulterous act, an almost impossible condition to fulfil. Sources differ as to the frequency with which claims of adultery are filed, but the practice of outlawing consensual sexual relations between adults elicits widespread disapproval both outside and inside the Muslim world. The watchdog group Freedom House claims that adultery cases are 'rarely' prosecuted in Morocco. In contrast, a report by the Moroccan periodical *Maroc Hebdo* stated that the Moroccan Democratic League for Women's Rights (LDDF) claims that accusations by men against their wives are prosecuted more frequently, and a husband's word is believed more often than that of a wife, even without the two witnesses to *flagrant délit* or admission of the adulterous spouse.[24] Human Rights Watch has likewise critiqued aggressive police intrusions into personal affairs, as police have engaged in planned actions to 'catch' women in extramarital relations, even staging evidence to photograph, then referring the evidence to the offender's spouse. Moreover, men suspected of participating in extra-marital sexual relations have been put under police surveillance and can be tried for facilitating prostitution, a separate crime under penal law. In this manner, the police have allegedly targeted male critics of the Moroccan regime, including journalists. According to Human Rights Watch, such criminalization of sexual relations between consenting adults is a violation of the right to privacy guaranteed under the International Covenant on Civil and Political Rights (ICCPR), which entered into force in Morocco in 1979 after ratification.[25] Regardless of the outcome of these relations for adults themselves, the status of any children born of these consenting relationships is undoubtedly fragile, only one of the reasons that the Moroccan Human Rights Association (AMDH) has called (unsuccessfully) for the decriminalization of consensual, extramarital sexual relations between adults. Such calls have been to no avail to this point.

However, two recent developments may suggest future directions for change in the way Moroccan courts handle extramarital relations and the filiation of the child born of these relations. First, we may note that the Moroccan Penal Code contains violations for several related activities: sexual relations outside of marriage (Article 490), abandonment of a child (Section 459), and abortion (Article 449 section I chapter VIII). These seemingly contradictory laws mean that an unmarried woman who becomes pregnant can be prosecuted for seeking an abortion; for giving birth

23 Sonneveld 2017, p 133.

24 See Izdinne 2011, also cited in Immigration and Refugee Board of Canada 2013.

25 See Human Rights Watch 2015.

to and keeping her child, thereby admitting to illicit sexual relations; or for instead abandoning her child. In sum, anything a mother does with a fetus or child conceived outside of wedlock or engagement is criminally punishable. Increasingly, the penal code is not applied to unmarried mothers who keep or relinquish their child, arguably because of the growing moral weight of the concept of the best interests of the child as enshrined in the UNCRC, which is taken seriously by many Moroccan judges as a guiding principle in matters related to children.[26] While the social stigma remains on both the unmarried mother and her child (but not on the biological father, who goes unnamed), increasingly authorities focus on the child's prospects and needs rather than the criminal acts of the child's biological parents. In the associative sector, NGOs endeavour to make it more feasible, socially and financially, for unmarried women to keep and raise their children without spousal or family support.[27] Yet for many women, family pressure makes keeping a baby conceived outside marriage an impossible solution, especially as it renders it unlikely that the mother will be able to marry given the strong cultural preference for virgins and, even among divorced women, a preference for childless women. There are certainly many exceptions to these culturally dominant orientations towards family and marriage.

Children born to parents in customary (Ar. *ᶜurfi*) marriages (also called 'informal' or *fatiha* marriages after the short Quranic verse recited to mark the marital union)[28] have only recently been able to gain full filiation rights, at least if the parents registered their customary marriage after the 2004 Family Code, for instance during the campaign conducted by the Ministry of Justice beginning in 2010.[29] This marriage registration campaign was instigated by the 2004 Family Code, which stated that customary marriages could be registered for up to five years beyond the application of the new code. The deadline was subsequently extended at least twice, but it still did not prevent new customary marriages.[30] In some instances, children born in more longstanding customary marriages whose filiation was socially recognized (through parents' cohabitation, for instance) have been able to apply and thus secure rights to a Moroccan identity card for themselves and their children. But without legally established marriage and filiation, other rights can be denied, particularly when the individual cannot count on an acquaintance or intercessor (Ar. *wusta*) smoothing the process. These include the right to a passport, inheritance, joint bank accounts, and representation for a parent's personal business or other matter.

26 Sonneveld 2017 notes in her fieldwork with judges that judges tended to consider the best interests of the child in deliberations over paternity cases involving unmarried woman, as did the judges in my conversations with them in southern Morocco between 2009 and 2013.

27 The best-known one here is Aicha Chenna's Association that works across the country, Solidarité Feminine. Lesser-known associations benefitting women and representing them in legal affairs exist in numerous regions throughout the country and in the major Moroccan cities.

28 Sonneveld 2017, p 135.

29 See Hoffman 2015.

30 See Sonneveld 2017.

Discrimination against the child born outside of marriage is inscribed in the family civil status booklet and birth certificate. The child without paternal filiation will have the mother's surname rather than that of the father, thus giving the child a legal identity previously unavailable to them. This provision was introduced only in 2004, although it was managed differently in the country's municipalities and provinces; some provinces require approval from the woman's male siblings to give the mother's surname to her child, whereas in others, authorities consult no one (including the mother herself). Establishing the child's paternity could be a subsequent procedure; in the meanwhile, the child would be eligible at least for state services such as schooling and health care. A child with legitimate paternal filiation shares the father's surname only, as typically Moroccan women do not change their surname upon marriage, so that parents retain different surnames throughout their lives regardless of marital status. On the birth certificate, in the place of the biological father's name, the clerk or administrator inscribes a masculine given name starting with Abd- (Abdallah being the most common). There is no fictive father's surname, and there are no names from the biological father's own filiation in the space provided for the father's name (e.g. Abdallah son of Moussa son of Hmed). If the mother relinquishes the child, the child's surname may be chosen arbitrarily by orphanage officials or civil servants, rather than using the biological mother's surname; there is variation in this practice as well. The birth certificate and subsequent extracts from it (used for school registration, medical care, employment, etc.) will announce the lack of a father's surname and distinguish the child from one born of legally recognized parents. As such, the naming practice for children constitutes a visible discrimination. It is arguably an improvement over the procedure formerly in place in which the entry for the father's name was left entirely blank and the mention *walad/bint zina* (Ar. child of adultery) noted in the margin.

A court ruling in November 2017 allowed a single mother, for the first time, to procure a family booklet in her own name, and therefore inscribe her child's name in it.[31] The plaintiff had turned to the Moroccan courts because Moroccan consular authorities in Spain, where she resided, denied her request for a family booklet on the grounds that mothers are not entitled to this booklet. The plaintiff had requested the family booklet in order to register her child born of an unnamed father, as this was part of her petition for a family reunification visa for her child. The Moroccan consulate in Spain literally interpreted the civil status law in its Article 23 which lists individuals eligible for a family booklet, including the 'Moroccan husband registered in civil status records,' as it contains no mention of mothers without husbands. The judicial decision authorizing the plaintiff to a family booklet in her name, according to judge Anass Sadoun, was based on Article 231 of the Family Code that says that in the absence of a father, a mother who is past the age of majority is the family representative. The judge also considered Article 54 of the

[31] See AEH 2017; Al-Mufakkira al-Qanuniyya 2017. Bargach suggests that the case may have been successful, and legitimate, because it was brought against Moroccan authorities abroad rather than a domestic Moroccan administration (personal correspondence February 2018).

Family Code, which requires the state to 'take the necessary adequate measures to protect children, and for guaranteeing and preserving their rights according to the law.' This article allows women who are current or divorced wives, or legal representatives, only a notarized copy. However, the legal precedent the case established was widely applauded by women's rights activists and advocates for single mothers and their children without paternal filiation. Previously, only men could establish family booklets, and this meant that children born outside wedlock with no paternal filiation were not inscribed in any family booklet at all. Their births were recorded in the municipal register, which then served as the basis for subsequent requests for birth certificate extracts.[32]

There are some calls in Morocco for greater flexibility in the recognition of biological paternity (as distinguished from paternal filiation *nasab*) for the child born outside of marriage. Here is an issue where the Quranic injunction to 'call them by their fathers' names' (sura 33:5) aligns with the UNCRC Article 7 stating that every child has a right to know his or her identity and parents. Key to this call is advocacy for the expansion of the use of DNA tests outside of marriage. However, up until 2016, DNA tests were allowed in Moroccan courts as evidence almost exclusively in the event that a husband challenged his paternity of a child born to his wife or ex-wife. Usually, this renunciation of paternity was in response to the mother's request for compensation.[33] In each of these cases, however, the High Court first considered the dates of the couple's separation and the child's birth. A child born up to one year after the couple's separation has paternal filiation through the mother's ex-husband, according to Articles 153 and 154 of the Third Chapter of the 2004 Family Code. That article demonstrates the presumption that conjugal relations will exist within a marriage, so long as there is cohabitation and the husband is not sterile. Those exceptional conditions of lack of cohabitation or sterility, however, must be proven to the court by the husband in order for the court to consider his disavowal of paternity. When the birth falls within the dates of what the law considers a legal marriage, the child has paternal filiation through the mother's husband at the time of conception. Medical expertise in high court rulings can only be considered when ordered by the court (Article 159). There were only four cases of this up to 2009; in two cases, the testing involved the establishment of the husband's sterility. In two others, the 'expertise' involved the husband's verbal accusation of his wife's infidelity through the oath of renouncement *li^c^an* (Fr.

---

[32] The Minister of Family Affairs, Bassima Hakkaoui, recently called on legislators to require DNA testing to establish paternal responsibility for children born outside of wedlock, stating that the tests were necessary so that 'every child will have a father, or at least to identify the person responsible for his conception.' See Id Hajji 2017.

[33] In Al Zerda's court in Tangier, the lump payment in this case was called *nafaqa al-tifl* or *nafaqa al-awlad,* terms commonly used for court-ordered child support. Elsewhere, the payment requested of the biological father was called compensation, particularly as it referred to the Code of Contracts and the harm the biological father caused the mother in impregnating her. For the former, see Al-Sahra' 2017.

serment d'anathème).[34] However, the only time a medical test took priority in a judicial ruling in the High Court was when the test proved the husband's sterility. In the absence of proof of sterility, the law of the marital bed (*al-firash*) prevails.

There is little information available on the filiation of children born to one Moroccan parent and one non-Moroccan parent outside of marriage, but there are three notable cases I will summarize here. The Family Code states that it applies to Moroccans (unless Jewish law is relevant) even should they hold another citizenship, and to relationships between Moroccan citizens when one of the parties is Muslim, as well as relationships where one of the parties is Moroccan. In a first case heard by the High Court in 1961, a Moroccan woman first pleaded to the Rabat appeals court for child support and compensation for the children she bore while with a French man to whom she was not married. The appeals court upheld the request for support from the biological father. In 1962, the French man appealed to the Supreme Court, arguing that the appeals court had established an 'illicit obligation' and thus violated Articles 62 and 403 of the Moroccan Code of Obligations and Contracts, since the penal code in its Article 490 outlaws adulterous relationships. In the end, the French man was required to pay reparations to the Moroccan woman by the French courts, citing Article 342 of the French Civil Code established by law on 15 July 1955.[35] In the second case, the Moroccan High Court in 1983 heard a case of extra-marital paternal filiation from a Moroccan man who claimed paternity of a child born outside of marriage. The Moroccan court denied the request for filiation on the grounds that 'Islamic law' established the grounds for filiation rather than the Law of Obligations and Contracts.[36] The third case involved both French and Moroccan courts. The plaintiff brought a case to the appeals court in El Jadida in 2003 requesting support for her daughter born seven months after her ex-husband repudiated her. Between 2001 and 2003, she had already received an increase in the child support payment. However, the French court of Mulhouse had established in 2000, subsequent to a DNA test, that the man was not the child's father. When the mother requested an increase in 2003, her ex-husband appealed to the Moroccan High Court. He claimed that the Court of Appeal's decision violated Article 11 of the French-Moroccan Convention, which forbids contradictory judicial decisions. The Moroccan High Court responded that the French tribunal's decision is contrary to Articles 76 and 89 of the 1957 Moudawana that cannot be overridden by French law. On that basis, the ex-husband's case was rejected, and thus his filiation to the daughter of his ex-wife was upheld.[37]

---

[34] The foundation of this Quranic institution is found in sura 24:6–9 for repudiation by a husband of his wife for adultery in the absence of witnesses. *Li^can* is used specifically for legal divorce on the grounds of adultery (*zina*) without formal, legal proof (i.e. witnesses). It is sometimes translated as 'mutual repudiation,' 'renouncement,' or 'marriage dissolution,' but none of these English translations captures the specific circumstance, moreover as it is used to refute paternity. See Oxford Islamic Studies Online (n.d.).

[35] Article 342, al. 2 French Civil Code, as amended by the Law of 15 July 1955.

[36] Morocco, Cass. 30 March 1983 no. 54758. On the modern state's use of 'Islamic law', see Rosen 2000.

[37] Morocco, Cour Suprême 30 December 2004 no. R656.

A recent case involves the use of DNA in the establishment of paternity (Ar. *ubuwwa*), paternal filiation (Ar. *nasab*), and child support/maternal compensation outside of marriage. This unprecedented use of a DNA test emerged from a family court case in Tangier in January 2017 that was overturned at the appeals level in November 2017 and is, as of 2018, headed to the High Court. It is the first case in Morocco in which a court has considered DNA evidence to establish paternity outside of marriage, as well as paternal responsibility for the child's maintenance, even when paternal filiation was not established. The case is notable as well in that the lower court, at least, acknowledged that biological paternity entails financial responsibility for a child, yet without declaring filiation rights to the child (including naming after the father and mutual inheritance). The case unfolded in the following way:

In 2016, a judge in family court in Tangier accepted a paternity declaration for a child born to an unmarried woman. The judge sentenced the biological father, after a positive DNA test from the Medical Laboratory of the Royal Gendarmerie in Rabat, to compensation (100,000 MAD, around 9400 euros) that represented a portion of the child's maintenance by the mother, who kept her child. The reasoning for this was that the child's upbringing weighed on the mother, in practice and in law, rather than the father. However, the man had been sentenced to two months of jail for corruption of an unmarried girl. The mother then sued the man for compensation when the man tested positive for the child's paternity. The judges responsible for this decision were represented by Judge Mohammed Al Zerda, Head of the Family Court in Tangier, who has granted video interviews to explain the court's reasoning. He claimed that 'the state strives to protect these children and all children equally, regardless of their family situation,' basing his interpretation on Article 32 of the Moroccan Constitution that 'assures one equal juridical protection and one equal social and moral consideration to all children, regardless of their familial situation.' Al Zerda also referred to the UNCRC's Article 7, the child's right to know his or her identity and to have a name and a nationality at all times. Furthermore, Al Zerda invoked the 1996 European Convention on the Exercise of Children's Rights, and Quranic verse 33:5.[38] Upon review by the appeals court, the Tangier family court judgment was overturned, with an appeals court reasoning that differed sharply from that of the lower family court. The appeals decision referred exclusively to the bounds of paternal filiation (Ar. *nasab*) delineated in the Moudawana, in contrast with the first instance decision of the family court. The family court, in recognizing the man's paternity as proven by DNA, referred not to the Moroccan Family Code, but instead to the UNCRC and its concept of the best interest of the child.[39] The stipulated monetary fine clearly would not begin to cover maintenance costs for the child until her adulthood. Yet in principle this was a

[38] See video interview with Al Zerda in Arabic regarding his court's decision, Qudri 2017.

[39] For coverage of this court case in French, see Verdier 2017. In Arabic, see Ait Musa 2017 and Lakhdar 2017a, b. English sources are scarcer, but a summary of the January case ruling can be found at Lahsini 2017.

significant ruling, for it legally recognized the man as the child's biological father and declared him (at least theoretically) responsible for the child, even if he was not required to give his surname to the child.

In this case, we should note the crucial distinction between paternity (*ubuwwa*) and filiation (*nasab*) in terms of rights and responsibilities. Indeed, there was a parsing of these two forms of affiliation in the lower court ruling, but not in the appeals court ruling. For the appeals court, the fact of biological paternity does not require a man to assume responsibility for or even associate himself with the child if that child is born to a woman other than his wife. From a human rights perspective, the appeals decision is clearly discriminatory against the child born outside of wedlock, and unfair towards the woman who alone will bear the cost of raising the child. The lower court ruling, in contrast, appears to place paternity in the panoply of children's rights, whereas filiation is a right bestowed by the state on the children of married parents. In that respect, a child appears to have no 'human right' to filiation (and its associated legal rights), or to maintenance by the biological father, but she or he may have the right to know the identities of biological parents, and have these recognized by the state through its courts. From a historical cultural perspective, we might keep in mind that filiation was once considered a privilege for the father, since parents counted on children to care for them in old age or illness. It is only more recently that parentage for the child outside wedlock has been reconfigured as a burden and responsibility. Denying a biological father what was once considered the privilege, not the burden, of paternal filiation could be construed as a sanction for his actions (meaning, refuting the filiation condemned the man for engaging in sexual relations outside of marriage).[40] The shift in the social meaning of children from providers to charges is a major social transformation in Morocco and one with which law has not kept pace. Widespread media attention to the groundbreaking lower court decision, and its dramatic overturning by the appeals court which removed consideration of international law, has elicited broad debate and calls to revise Moroccan laws around filiation.

The laws of filiation and the requirement of marriage for the establishment of paternal filiation demonstrate that legal association, through marriage, is more important than blood in fatherhood, while blood suffices for motherhood. The social problem remains given the number of children with unregistered paternal filiation. A recent study found that there are 210,000 children without a registered father in Morocco, including 44,211 births outside marriage in the greater Casablanca area alone between 2004 and 2014.[41] Another study found that 6480 children were born outside of marriage in 2008 in Morocco.[42] A 2002 study found that 83% of abandoned children were found under the age of three months, with 61% found just

[40] See Kutty 2015.

[41] According to a study by La Ligue Marocaine pour la Protection de l'Enfance and UNICEF 2010. For these statistics and a general discussion of the Tangier 2017 case, see Zine 2018.

[42] Zine 2018.

after birth.[43] For the children of non-marital unions, when the mother does not want to or cannot raise her child, the institution of *kafala* is the best possible solution available for the care of these children under Moroccan law.[44] This is because according to Article 149 of the Family Code, adoption has no legal value and does not result in the effects of legitimate filiation. Awarding *tanzil* as a part (usually one-third) of inheritance to a child one raises is a common and recommended financial precaution for *kafil* parents, but it does not establish filiation to the *makful* child: '"gratitude adoption" (*jaza*) or "testamentary adoption" (*tanzil*) cannot establish paternal filiation, and are subject to the terms of the will.' The following section considers the care and legal status of children who lack any filiation, lack paternal filiation, or otherwise lack parental care.

9.3 Relinquished Children and Kafala Guardianships

9.3.1 Legal Frameworks and Social Realities

The legal framework for Islamic guardianship (*kafala*), and the problem of parentless children in Morocco, are both receiving increasing attention in civil society debates. Non-governmental associations, lawyers, psychologists, and child advocates working with abandoned children and the structures that accommodate them based in both Morocco and Europe have increased calls for legal reform around *kafala* and the status of children without birth filiation, and raised awareness around the need for measures to remedy the problem and care adequately for these children. It is widely recognized that there are multiple facets to address simultaneously: for birth mothers, decriminalization of pregnancy outside of marriage, and public awareness campaigns to discourage child abandonment; for single mothers, financial and social assistance to help them raise their children themselves, including job training and placement, and childcare; increasing public awareness about the benefits and availability of guardianship and fostering to retain abandoned children in Morocco rather than having them go into families abroad; efforts to recruit potential families and provide training and support services to them to ensure

[43] Iraqi 2002, also cited in Barraud 2010.

[44] The UNCRC in 1990 first introduced many individuals in non-Muslim countries to *kafala* as an alternative for parentless children when adoption was not allowed by a signatory state. Article 20 of the UNCRC lists *kafala* alongside adoption and fostering without equating them or ranking their relative merits. Some courts have presumed that this international legal tool renders the different forms of protection equivalent simply by their juxtaposition. Yet a close look at the protections entailed suggests they are not identical, particularly in terms of custody and inheritance subsequent to the death of the *kafil* parent/guardian, and access to rights constrained to officially recognized family members (e.g. hospital visitation rights restricted to immediate family). The fact remains that the mention of *kafala* in this international convention has led to its widespread recognition in international private law and to a greater acceptance of this institution as a form of care for parentless children born in countries using Muslim personal status law. See Assim and Sloth-Nielsen 2014.

appropriate matching between parentless children and prospective families; and finally, increased training to provide *kafil* parents with the help they need to meet the challenges of their *makful* children, particularly when they have special needs and/or early histories of trauma and/or abuse. Most of these efforts remain in the planning stages, and their advocates seek partners in the government and private sectors to help fund this work in the non-governmental sector. Meanwhile, advocates for child welfare call on politicians to revise existing laws and introduce new ones that can increase the integration of *makful* children into both their *kafil* families and society more generally, and to decrease the stigma associated with *makful* children's legal status.[45] Within the grassroots organizations advocating for children's rights and placement in families, civil society actors build on both the growing endorsement of *kafala* by religious scholars in Morocco and elsewhere in the Muslim world as the best solution for parentless children, and the international human rights language of the best interests of the child. Central to these efforts are an emphasis on empathy rather than disdain as an ethical Muslim response to children in need, and a lauding of Moroccan *kafil* parents as living examples of the compassion required to raise children deprived of their biological parents.

Since the Moroccan Family Code is only intended to apply to families, and families require filiation, the Code does not contain legal guidance for the personal status of children without paternal filiation, including most importantly abandoned, orphaned, or foundling children. It only mentions that adoption has no legal effect in Morocco, but does not mention replacement care for parentless children.[46] The explicit legal silence in Moroccan law around abandoned children is deafening;

45 Most recently, a conference organized by the Plateforme Droits de l'Enfant (CDE Maroc) and the European Union on 25 January 2018 at the Académie du Royaume du Maroc in Rabat was called 'Je veux mes droits, pas la charité! Séminaire sur les procédures de la Kafala' ('I want my rights, not charity! Seminar on the Kafala procedure'). It brought together speakers and audience participants from all of these professional domains and addressed the issues noted here.

46 This is in contrast to the Algerian personal status law that covers both filiation and *kafala* guardianship, and explicitly prohibits adoption (*al-tabanni*), which the Moroccan law stops short of doing. Scholars have noted that the widespread Muslim prohibition of adoption as we know it today, or at least suspicion of adoption, was shared by Judaism and Christianity. European states only began permitting adoption in the 19th c. with the codification of their civil codes, and largely with the purpose of transferring inheritance and the male patronym. Adoption in Greek and Roman society was of adults for the purpose of transferring inheritance or continuity of economic interests, but not of protecting and raising minors without parents, the latter of whom were typically considered a threat to the biological, 'legitimate' family and, in later periods, as a deformation of God's will which manifested in pregnancy within marriage. See for instance Rezig 2004. Some Muslim scholars and jurists have argued that the prohibition or lack of acknowledgement of adoption does not have solid grounding in the Islamic sources, which can be interpreted differently in themselves, and even more so when custom, which is a component of Islamic jurisprudence, is taken into consideration. See Libson 1997 on the role of custom in Islamic law. However, these challenges to the ban on adoption largely come from outside the countries influenced by the Maliki school of jurisprudence. See for instance Kutty 2015 and Suleiman 2017 and Muslim Women's Shura Council 2011 for critiques of the dominant interpretation of Islamic sources as unequivocally opposing adoption, and for arguments in favour of adoption so long as it is revealed to the child. See also Sonbol 1995.

only the 2002 law on *kafala* addresses their lot, and only within the framework of guardianship.

Younger parentless children and babies live in children's wards at urban and provincial (state) hospitals and at orphanages. Children ages 7–18 are then sent to group or institutional housing run by NGOs such as Ousraty and Association Bayti in Casablanca, or group homes, such as those managed by the international SOS Villages NGOs, or locally governed boarding hostels known as *khayriyat*. Some parentless children end up living on the street and falling outside the purview of state or private protection, and these are among the children that associations such as Bayti try to reach. For younger children and babies, orphanages and group homes may receive state funding or instead operate with cash and in-kind donations (mostly nappies, formula, and foodstuffs), both domestic and international, as well as volunteers. Two legal instruments delineate the rights of the child and the responsibilities of the state to provide protection for parentless children: the 2011 Moroccan Constitution and the UNCRC, which Morocco ratified in 1993. There is widespread agreement among professionals and laypeople in Morocco that the best protection for parentless children is guardianship by a *kafil* parent or parents, and the *kafala* institution is recognized as an alternative form of protection in Article 20 of the UNCRC. There is also increased pressure on the Moroccan state to provide equal opportunities for children deprived of their birth families given critiques launched by the UNCRC commission of efforts exerted by the Moroccan state, so as to improve specific measures that impede equal treatment of Moroccan citizens born outside of marriage.

The *kafala* as it exists today is a form of Islamic guardianship that exists in two forms: judicial *kafala* contracted in family courts, and notarial *kafala* signed in the presence of a notary (*ᶜadul*). The former is increasingly practiced and is the form required for the guardianship of children formerly housed in collective institutions, whereas the notarial form is more commonly contracted between birth mothers and extended family members to confer parental authority and permit children to benefit from educational or medical advantages in a location away from their birth mother or parents. Judicial *kafala* was first organized publicly in a 1993 proposed law intended to standardize its practice and most importantly to recognize officially the existence of 'abandoned children'[47] and increase their legal visibility. Prior to this, *kafala* was regulated through a series of circulars.[48] *Kafala* only received a decree for the law's application in 2002 after a decade during which it was a recognized principle without a legal reality with a codified process. Article 2 of the 2002 law describes the *kafala* as 'the commitment to undertake the protection, education, and upkeep of an abandoned child as would a father for his son.'

[47] Bargach 2001 calls the 'adopted child' 'in historical terms, a recent category.' Children deprived of their parents (the 'surplus of children') in earlier historical periods were absorbed into childless households or families that already had biological children. See also Barraud 2010 on the importance of the recognition of this demographic.

[48] See Bargach 2001.

This emphasis on a family-like 'gift of care'[49] – despite the absolute prohibition on the succession and filiation available to marital children – does nothing to encourage qualified adults to petition to be guardians, particularly if they believe that their religion forbids adoption, yet they cannot fathom raising a child without considering the child as their own. This care relationship therefore cannot be a legal family relationship, even though it is supposed to be a social and affective relationship of care between adults and children. That is, there is an insistence on the absence of filiation when it comes to abandoned children and foundlings, given that these children are nonetheless constrained to trace lineage through biological parents. This then presents a challenge to the process of 'kinning'[50] – the rendering of a child as embedded in kin relations – which is necessary in order for any child to embed himself or herself within webs of family that both protect them and make them socially legible to others. Moreover, this ambivalence around family and rejection of filiation for relinquished children raises challenges for the transnational attachment of relinquished children to caregivers in the diaspora. This is particularly true in the case of France, the former power over the Moroccan Protectorate from 1912–1956, and Spain, the two countries with the most families formed through Moroccan *kafala*, as I describe below.[51]

The *kafala* system of guardianship or sponsorship permits a parentless child to integrate into the household of the guardian (m. *kafil*/f. *kafila*) until the age of maturity for the child (m. *makful*/f. *makfula*; 18 years old for boys, marriage or economic independence for girls).[52] It does not permit the establishment of filiation or inheritance rights. The *kafala* arrangement is found in Morocco's Law of Contracts and Obligations, as I discuss below, but has longstanding roots in local custom around the secret or overt 'adoptions' of foundlings or of extended kin.[53] Notwithstanding that the *kafala* is supported today by legal personnel and laypeople as rooted in Islamic law, the central legal sources of Islamic jurisprudence (the Quran and hadith) do not mention, let alone prescribe a state institution resembling contemporary Moroccan *kafala* for the care of parentless children.

According to local understandings within Morocco, *kafala* is adamantly not adoption (Ar. *tabanni*). But at the same time, the legal distinction is one that is not

---

49 The phrase comes from Bargach 2002.

50 See Howell 2006.

51 See van Loon 2010 and Alidadi and Foblets 2012 on the role of religion in private international law regarding minors in the transnational sphere.

52 The gender difference in the termination point of the *kafala* contract is similar to that of the period of maintenance required of parents towards children, for instance after divorce, as stipulated in Chapter III Section I of the 2004 Family Code, except that for legitimate children, the age is capped at 25 for sons who pursue their education. Similarly, in both documents the custodian is responsible for maintenance of the handicapped child unable to earn a living independently.

53 Bargach 2001, p 81 notes that, since the *kafala* is not considered part of family law/statute and instead is a contract, 'the fuqaha clearly see kafala as a commercial transaction even while it is inscribed in a rather humane domain. One is indeed buying a place in paradise by engaging herself to the physical upkeep of an orphan or foundling. It is therefore similar to a business transaction.'

necessarily practiced in families contracting *kafala*. Even some court personnel informally refer to *kafala* as *tabanni*.[54] The legal connotations of *tabanni*, 'making a person into one's son', are largely insufficient for those who wish to offer care to a child as surrogate parents. Colloquially, Moroccans use the term *trebbi* for the practice of 'raising' (caring for, guiding, taking in) a child. Moroccans do not usually refer to the *kafala* institution explicitly in describing their relationship to their *makful* child; instead they say, 'I am raising (*kanrebbi*) him or her.' In many households, the child and parent(s) use kinship terms to refer to each other: son, daughter, mother, father. The lack of legal filiation does not override the familial sentiment that emerges from their *de facto* family life. Culturally, the motivation for these families is to raise them, not to acquire an heir to land or wealth as motivated Roman adoptive fathers, for instance. The fact that guardianship is open to single women (but not single men) as well as couples, in a cultural context in which parenting is highly gendered, suggests that the state values the ability to care for and nurture children, as this is culturally associated with women.

Contemporary legal practices obfuscate the firm distinction between biological families and families formed through *kafala*. For instance, following on Algeria's 1992 Executive Order allowing a *makful* child of unknown filiation to assume the *kafil* father's surname, Moroccan law now allows for the *kafil* parent to petition the King to replace the *kafil* child's official surname with the *kafil* parent's surname (if contracted by a couple) or the *kafil* mother's surname (if contracted by an unmarried woman). In its application, this ruling has not required that the surname be Arab, as is usually required when assigning a surname (for instance, to a relinquished child of unknown paternal filiation). This provision was justified in the best interests of the child, since sharing a surname between adult and child has been argued to increase the psychological well-being of the child and ease social integration.[55] The name change does not constitute filiation or registration of the child in the guardian's family booklet, which remains prohibited, and it does not allow for the inheritance rights that would accompany filiation. In everyday life, however, it increases the perceived sense of cohesion between *kafil* and *makful*, and the child's sense of belonging on par with any biological children. It clearly facilitates

[54] Personal observation in Moroccan family courts, 2013.

[55] Despite the dominant interpretation of Islamic jurisprudence that changing a child's surname is forbidden, it is crucial to note that in the time of the revelation of Quranic sura 33:4-5 – widely interpreted as forbidding the child to take the guardian's family name ('Call them by their fathers' names, for that shall be more pleasing to God …') – there were no surnames in use. Instead, an individual was called by given name ibn father's given name, e.g. Zayd ibn Mohammed reverted to Zayd ibn Haritha when the Prophet declared his adopted son was not in truth his son, and that thereby the prohibitions on marriage to one's son's ex-spouse did not apply to him, rendering Zayd's ex-wife licit to him. This was then confirmed in sura 33:40: 'Mohammed was never the father of one of your men, but the messenger of God and the last of his prophets.' Rezig 2004, p 153 notes that certain *fuqaha'* said that 'human reason precludes having two fathers, just as a person cannot have two hearts.' Some have argued that taking on a parent's family name in this way is similar to a woman assuming her husband's name at marriage, and that it constitutes a descriptor (*nisba*) more than a surname (*kunya*). See Suleiman 2017 and Kutty 2015.

interactions with authorities, as well, when the *makful* child's paperwork carries the name of the adult responsible for him or her.

Even if the relationship between *kafil* and *makful* is not one that constitutes family (Ar. *al-usra/al-^{c}a'ila*), a *makful* child can become *mahram* (forbidden) as with a biological child born within marriage, and also become a milk sibling of the *kafil*'s children if the *kafila* mother breastfeeds the *makful* child at least five times during the first two years of the child's life.[56] The 2002 *kafala* law explicitly states that the *kafil* is charged with 'raising, protecting, and educating the *makful* child as a father to his son', and this phrasing is used in the *kafala* contract drawn up by the responsible judge and signed by him and the *kafil* parent(s). The notion of family that operates colloquially is through care and protection in the household, and sharing meals. In the indigenous Moroccan Tamazight ('Berber') language, the *takat* means both biological 'family' and 'hearth', as in the French term *foyer*. Legally in Morocco, however, sharing maternal milk can help bring the status of a parentless child into alignment with that of a biological child born within a marriage.

The 2004 Family Code article stating that the effects of adoption are void differs from the Algerian Family Code that claims that adoption (Ar. *tabanni*) is prohibited in both *shari^{c}a* and Algerian positive law (Family Code Article 46).[57] The cultural and religious emphasis on the family as the central social institution in Morocco – an orientation stated explicitly in the 2011 Moroccan Constitution[58] – and the predominance in particular of adult women in the Family Code[59] leads to an

[56] Importantly to many devout Muslims weighing their ability to bring an unrelated child into their home, the child who is *mahram* does not need to veil (if a girl) or be veiled in front of (if a boy). This question is the most pervasive one in on-line forums on *kafala* and its practical implications for modesty in the home. As some legal scholars have emphasized, modesty should be practiced in all Muslim families anyway, and it is common for women to wear headscarves when male extended family members (such as cousins) come to visit, so it is not a radical departure from custom for modesty practices to be observed among the core family members as well. The Family Code Chapter 1, Article 38 states that: 'Impediments to marriage resulting from kinship by breastfeeding are the same as those prohibited through blood kinship and kinship by marriage. Only the breastfed child – not his or her brothers and sisters – is considered the child of the woman who breastfeeds him or her and of her husband. Breastfeeding is only an impediment to marriage if it occurred during the first two years of the child's life.' For this reason, some *kafila* mothers promote the production of breast milk and encourage their young *makful* child to breastfeed, thereby integrating the child more fully into the family with the prohibition on marriage that otherwise only exists between related immediate family members. One can imagine that this lessens fears of sexual activity within the household as well. For more on milk siblings, see Ensel 2002, p 93.

[57] Unlike Morocco's Family Code that excludes *kafala*, Algeria's Family Code includes the provision on *kafala* in Articles 116 to 125.

[58] Article 32 of the 2011 Moroccan Constitution begins, 'The family, founded on the legal ties of marriage, is the basic unit of society.' English translation provided by Constituteproject.org.

[59] See Žvan Elliot 2015 for a sustained critique of the Moudawana as centred on the married woman-mother, erasing the unmarried, childless woman from policy considerations despite the growing number of educated, never-married, childless women now in their 30s, 40s, and 50s.

in-between relationship for *kafil* guardians to their *makful* wards, despite the affective bonds that result from co-habitation and care. Nonetheless, the 2011 Moroccan Constitution guarantees the protection and rights of all children 'regardless of their family situation,'[60] in parallel with Article 2 of the UNCRC as inspired by the Universal Declaration of Human Rights.[61] In Morocco, the social shame associated with childbearing out of wedlock – the primary reason for the abandonment of children in Morocco (5377 children in 2013, 5274 children in 2009)[62] – and even its illegality in the penal code (which is rarely enforced given that it counters the best interests of the child) means that in society more generally, abandoned children, too, are taken as evidence of social breakdown. This makes children born of non-marital sexual relations the source and carriers of stigma not easily taken on by prospective *kafil* parents, and helps explain why some *kafil* parents find illicit ways to register the child as their biological child, even going so far as to hide the child's origins from him or her.[63]

9.3.2 Finding Parents for Parentless Children

A person or married couple interested in taking on the role of guardian must take the initiative to commence the *kafala* procedure by contacting or visiting provincial orphanages, hospital children's wings housing parentless children, or associations with ties to the social workers who match waiting babies or children to potential guardians. The administrative and legal processes that await prospective parents are simultaneously structured and idiosyncratic, subject to the discretion of judges and social workers whose requirements and orientations can differ considerably among provinces and towns. The 2002 law on *kafala* outlines the state's official procedure for declaring a child abandoned and establishing its care, while outlining responsibilities of the *kafil* parent(s). Yet in practice the process lacks transparency and is more politically charged than it need be, leading to a situation where certain judges issue large numbers of *kafala* (e.g. in Meknes and Tangier with reputable

[60] Article 32 Moroccan Constitution 2011.

[61] UDHR Article 25: 'All children, whether born in or out of wedlock, shall enjoy the same social protection.'

[62] This is according to the former Minister of Justice, Mustafa Ramid, in 2014. The association INSAF reported that in 2010, 24 of the 153 babies born out of wedlock each day are abandoned, or around 16% of these children, see Medias24 2014. INSAF has elsewhere reported that between 2003 and 2009, there were 210,000 children born outside marriage, or 30,000 annually, see Verdier 2017.

[63] See Bargach 2002 for a rich ethnographic account of social stigma and the ways in which stigma and marginalization, as well as integration, are lived by *makful* children and caretaker adults in *kafala* relationships. She details as well deviation from lawful practices such as secret 'adoptions' through the unauthorized inscription of abandoned babies into caretakers' civil registries. Some of these arrangements were the result of agreements between biological mothers and wealthy couples or women, sometimes finalized before the child's birth.

orphanages, engaged directors, and connections to adoption agencies abroad) whereas judges in other provinces rarely do so at all. Despite established procedures, there is considerable room for both favouritism and discrimination towards prospective *kafil* parents.

Moroccan Law 15-01 concerning the supervision (Fr. *prise en charge*) of abandoned children was adopted on 13 June 2002 and led to Royal dahir 1-02-172 for implementation. This document outlines which children may be considered 'abandoned' (*muhmil*). They may be born to unknown parents, or to an unknown father and a known mother who of her own volition relinquished the child. The child may have deceased parents, no relatives willing to raise the child, or parents who are unable to fulfil the child's subsistence needs. Alternatively, the child may have parents who do not fulfil their responsibility to ensure the child is raised with 'good behaviour', or who neglect the child.

The law further requires that anyone who encounters a foundling must provide aid as needed and bring the child to the authorities (police or gendarme station) in the area where the child was found. Anyone who does not do so is subject to penal sanctions.[64] The Crown Prosecutor (Fr. *procureur du roi*, Ar. *wakil al-malik*) in the Family Court will proceed and assume responsibility for the child and place him or her in an appropriate facility while investigating the child's situation. He will also endeavour to register the child's birth in the civil registry, as any person with an interest in a child may undertake this registration, not only immediate kin. The ensuing investigation attempts to discern whether the child was abandoned. If no parents or biological relatives are found, the prosecutor advertises the child's existence in local courts and public spaces, with a name and possibly a photograph, calling for the parents to reclaim the child. This announcement stays posted for three months, after which time the prosecutor can pronounce the child officially abandoned. The abandonment decision is delivered to the provincial Guardianship Judge (Fr. *juge des tutelles*, Ar. *qadi al-wisaya*) as well as to any person who has already requested guardianship of the child. The child is then placed either with a couple or a single woman who wishes to undertake guardianship for that child, provisionally caring for the child. If no *kafil* is immediately available, the child is placed in a governmental unit such as the children's ward of a hospital, with an organization approved for the protection of children, or in another institution that can tend to the child's needs, at the discretion of the Crown Prosecutor. During this period, the guardianship judge remains the legal representative of the child.

The officials and organizations charged with the protection of abandoned children do not advertise for prospective guardians; there are no public service campaigns urging Moroccans to take in a child, and no online registries of 'waiting children' similar to those available for adoption to some Western countries. In many institutions housing abandoned children, adults must solicit permission to see the waiting babies and children. Prospective *kafil*s tend to visit the institutions,

---

[64] Article 431 of dahir 1-59-413 amended the Penal Code, with a sanction of imprisonment from three months to five years and/or a fine of 200 to 1000 dirhams.

especially hospitals and orphanages, where these available children are housed, and seek an eligible child before beginning the process of applying for *kafala* with the social worker. However, in the case of the children's section of many hospitals and housing facilities, not all of the children in residence are available for guardianship. These children often do not have a recognized father, but there remains a biological mother who has declared that she is temporarily unable to care for her child and thus handed over her child(ren) for safekeeping for an undefined period without officially relinquishing them. Some children have mothers in prison; others have mothers who are sex workers, substance abusers, or simply too poor to pay for formula when they find themselves unable to provide breast milk. Some biological mothers intend to return when the child is weaned or when they have earned enough money, informed their families, or managed their addiction. Of those biological mothers, only a few actually take back their children, according to social workers in these institutions. Other biological mothers are unmarried and hiding their child from their family; in some cases, the women place their children provisionally in these institutions while working up the courage and the financial means to either explain their situation to their families so as to be accepted back into their home or else leave their families for another part of Morocco where they can raise their child without their family knowing. Biological mothers often have a sister, aunt, cousin, or friend in an urban area who facilitates these moves. Intentions often clash with abilities, however, leading a good number of these institutionalized children into a legal and affective limbo, unavailable for the close care afforded by a guardianship and at risk of developing attachment disorders and traumas related to the uncertainty and neglect endemic to all such institutions.[65]

These institutions are on the whole understaffed, crowded, and insufficiently funded. While the caloric needs of the resident children may be mostly met, the children's diet tends to consist of staples dominated by starches (barley or wheat porridge, bread, rice, lentils). Beyond nutrition, key needs for these young children are not met: babies' and children's need for play, exploration, physical and intellectual stimulation, verbal exchange, encouragement, and loving touch. Personnel tend to be untrained or undertrained, and paid a meagre wage. Some resident children have already demonstrated a physical or mental handicap or a developmental delay due to the lack of stimulation that exacerbates with time spent in the institution. The risk of a condition called institutional autism (due to the way it manifests in the child) is high in Moroccan orphanages and hospitals because of stress, neglect, and chronic fear. The incidence of Autism Spectrum Disorder in young children in Moroccan orphanages and institutions appears to be high, based on parental reports and observations by social workers. The only illness for which institutionalized children are regularly screened is the HIV virus, and the results of this test are conveyed to prospective *kafil* parents. Other illnesses with potential

[65] Descriptions of conditions on the ground in institutions and courthouses are based on personal observations and open-ended interviews with staff personnel, social workers, occupational therapists, relinquishing mothers, prospective guardians, and laypeople over a 10-month period in southern Morocco, from December 2012 to September 2013.

long-reaching consequences, such as chronic ear infections and malnourishment remain unacknowledged and untreated. Lead poisoning is rampant. ADHD and SPD (sensory processing disorder) are common outcomes of these living conditions, even if they were not present in children through genetic transmission. The most prevalent cause of death in these institutions, however, is the lack of intimate human, physical contact that feeds a baby's brain, nurtures its hormonal system, and allows its immune system to develop. Without these, mental illness often sets in as well. A potentially fatal decline in health from lack of nurturing often results in what is medically characterized as failure to thrive.

According to the 2002 *kafala* law, in the event that more than one couple requests a *kafala* for the same child, priority is given either to a childless Moroccan couple or the applicant(s) with the greatest documented ability to provide for the child's needs.[66] In practice, there are far too few prospective *kafil*s, particularly for boys, for sibling sets, for special needs children, and for children older than babies. The vast majority of applicants request a healthy baby, with a preference for girls over boys (the wait list for girls in many provinces can exceed one or two years and is prohibitive for many couples and single women, most of whom end up requesting a baby boy[67]). There is some attempt to keep siblings together, but this is not a legal requirement. Depending on the practices in place in the institution, prospective parents either select from the available children presented to them, or accept or refuse children proposed by the institution's social worker. Typically potential guardians spend time with the baby or child in the institution, and they visit multiple times during the period when the authorizations and background checks are pending. Some prospective parents are quick to choose 'their' child based on first sight of the baby and often worry that the baby will go to another waiting parent. Other prospective parents take longer to assess the potential bond with the baby or child proposed to them, visiting often, holding and playing with the child until they believe an affective bond can develop. The prospective guardian then confirms interest in the child or sibling set to the social worker, and petitions the family court for preliminary custody while awaiting the final guardianship decision.

66 See Article 10 of the *kafala* law of 2002.

67 Conversations with prospective parents and social workers in 2012–2013 indicated that girls were generally viewed as more adaptable and likely to fit in to families formed through *kafala*, and that they were kinder than boys. Bargach 2002 has noted that boys are suspected of being more susceptible to rejection of their adoptive parents, more aggressive and violent. Personal communication with *kafil* parents in France has suggested that in a minority of cases, girls taken in *kafala* and brought abroad are treated more as maids than as daughters, and we can suspect this it true within Morocco as well, even more so given that there is even less oversight by authorities after the child leaves the institution.

9.3.3 *Jurisdiction: Family Court*

The regional family courts (Ar. *mahakim al-usra*) primarily treat divorce and custody cases, but they also handle *kafala* cases. Here again we see an ambivalent demarcation between family types, as *kafala* does not legally create families, but the processes leading up to it – the establishment of the child's status as abandoned, and the verification through background checks of the prospective *kafil*s' suitability as substitute caregivers – all take place in the family courts. Petitioners lodge requests with the court scribe directly or through a lawyer. Requests do not require a lawyer, but as with all court matters, the requests must use particular wording that is familiar to the public scribes who usually work inexpensively from desks outside and adjacent to family courthouses. These scribes formulate petitions to the court using conventional legal formulas in Standard Arabic that are not readily known to the Moroccan layperson without legal training or experience in family court matters.

Kafala is considered a contract between the Royal Prosecutor for child welfare in each province, on the one hand, and the *kafil* parent or parents on the other. The judge officially charged with children's affairs is responsible for ensuring the best interests of the child are respected for all abandoned children. In reality, this judge only tends to encounter children for whom prospective parents propose to engage a *kafala*. That is, he or she[68] is only actively engaged in assisting institutionalized children when they have the potential to emerge from the state care the judge is originally tasked with overseeing – not at potentially earlier crucial moments when an outside advocate is needed to ensure care for a special needs child, for instance.

9.3.4 *Evaluating the Prospective* Kafil(a) *Guardian(s)*

The basic requirements for *kafil*s are that they be Muslim, of sound health and mind, socially and morally upright, with sufficient financial resources to raise a child, and that they not have been convicted of crimes or immorality towards children, and not be in a legal dispute with the child or his or her biological parents. If the applicants are a couple, they must be married (and, by implication, of different sexes). Single women applicants, but not single men, fulfilling these conditions are also eligible as prospective *kafil*s.[69]

---

[68] Morocco authorized women to pass the exams to become judges in the 1960s, but their numbers were minimal until recent years. As of 2015, around 1000 of the country's 4000 judges were women, a substantial increase that still falls short of the 50% parity set forth in the Moroccan Constitution.

[69] Article 9 of the 2002 *Kafala* law.

Before a judge can grant a *kafala* request, the suitability of prospective *kafil*s must be investigated. The prospective single *kafila*[70] (or the married couple) submits a petition to the Guardianship Judge along with the required documents. These may vary somewhat among provinces and judges, but generally documents requested with a *kafala* petition are proof of employment and salary, bank statements, medical certificate of good health and absence of contagious disease, and, for non-Moroccans, additional documents: a certificate of faith or of conversion to Islam, and a home study or other authorization for guardianship conducted in the country of intended residence (Moroccan nationals residing in Morocco or abroad are presumed to be Muslim). At that point, the Guardianship Judge launches four investigations in the province of residence of the prospective *kafil* parent: the Ministry of Religious Affairs, which requires an interview to assess the faith and familiarity of the applicant(s) with Islam; a social worker from the local governmental unit charged with child welfare, which assesses the living conditions of the applicant(s) through a home study; the Ministry of the Interior, which assures a clean police record for the applicant(s); and an authorization by a local authority (which again usually entails a personal interview with a high-ranking official in the location of the applicant's official residence, such as a mayor). Depending on the responsible judge, these investigations can be merely perfunctory, or can instead be drawn-out and laborious, particularly if the investigations raise red flags as to an applicant's suitability or competence. Sealed reports are delivered to the custodial judge, who evaluates them and calls in the applicant for a court date. If the applicant is found to be eligible for *kafala*, the request for provisional guardianship can be issued immediately by the judge, after which the applicant takes the child home (if living in Morocco).[71] If the child has not yet been officially abandoned, this is the point at which the official call for the child's biological relatives is posted in the provincial courthouse. While waiting the three months before the abandonment decree, the petitioner may be able to begin caring for the child, at the judge's discretion. The petitioner then awaits the court date for the final decree of *kafala*. Once this is secured, if the petitioner resides outside of Morocco, the court must issue another authorization to remove the child from Morocco for permanent residence abroad. This is the point at which many *kafalas* have been blocked since the 2012 Ramid circular cautioning against sending *makful* children outside of Morocco, as I describe below. Once this authorization is issued, *kafil* parents can apply for the emigration paperwork required by the country of residence, usually a visa.

[70] Barraud 2013 notes that ironically the change in *kafala* laws in both Morocco and Algeria to permit single women to contract creates a new category of 'single mothers' legitimated by the state, in contrast to the low status of the single biological mothers of these children.

[71] Some judges approve temporary custody of the child by the adult applicant, with the final *kafala* contract issued only after approval subsequent to the investigations.

9.3.5 *Rights and Responsibilities of the* Kafil *Parent*

The Family Code in Articles 229–231 stipulates that the court-appointed guardian is the legal representative of the minor child. While the Family Code concerns families, who, it claims in its preamble, are the cornerstone of Moroccan society, the provisions would seem to hold as well for children with guardians who are outside the framework of the family, for these articles primarily establish the guardian's legal status before elaborating on that person's responsibility for managing the minor's financial affairs. We might suspect that in the case of abandoned children, such considerations should be moot. But Article 235 of the Family Code claims the guardian is responsible for the 'personal affairs of the ward, including religious orientation, training, and preparation for life, and shall also assume the daily management of the ward's property.' The *kafala* law also stipulates that the guardian is responsible for any crime or injury perpetrated by the *makful* child.

In other respects, the family formed through *kafala* differs from the biological, marital family. Most importantly for many *kafil* parents, there is an abiding anxiety because of the potential reversibility of the *kafala* contract. While judges and social workers claim that it rarely happens, it is at least theoretically possible for the judge to terminate the *kafala* if the biological mother requests that the child be restored to her. The revocability of the *kafala* contract is the feature that distinguishes it most sharply from adoption, which is not reversible. This pushes some guardians to pursue adoption if they live in Europe, or secret registration of the child in the family booklet if they live in Morocco. Article 29 of the 2002 *kafala* law provides that the [biological] 'parents' of the *makful* child 'can resume the custody of their child' if the reasons for abandonment cease to exist, yet in practice this can only be done by judicial decision. Presumably, this would include changes in the biological mother's situation such as steady income, elimination of addiction, and/or the dissolution of any other impediment to the biological mother's custody. If the child has attained the 'age of discernment' (12 years old), the judge also theoretically considers the child's wishes to either return to the birth family (or more realistically, the birth mother) or stay with the guardian(s), and decides according to the 'best interests of the child', which after age 12 includes the child's desires. According to local court authorities in the south of Morocco, as well as French lawyers who have handled *kafala* cases, this scenario rarely transpires. Abandoning mothers almost never return to reclaim their biological children in Morocco, and judges rarely look favourably upon returning biological mothers who have abandoned their children, when given the choice between revoking or sustaining the *kafil* parent's custody, so long as there is no evidence of mistreatment by the *kafil* parent(s).

Yet an adult who contracts a *kafala* cannot change their mind and refuse responsibility for the child. Relatedly, if a couple that has contracted a *kafala* separates or divorces, the wife or husband may request that the judge render the *kafala* in his or her name only, or make another arrangement as necessary and in the child's interest. The judge can ensure as well that the child has visitation rights from the ex-spouse without custody after separation. In this respect, the *kafala* parties are again subject to the same laws as the legal [biological] family, where the same guidelines exist for the custody and visitation of minor children after a divorce. Indeed, it is notable that the *kafala* law contains footnotes referring to the 1958 Moudawana law 70-03 concerning custody and visitation after divorce. The law holds that in the event the *kafala* is withdrawn by the Guardianship Judge, the judge names a guardian, whether a person or an organization. There has been only one case that reached the High Court in which a *kafil* parent withdrew consent for the guardianship after separation from his wife. Yet the court ruled that a *kafala* obligation could not be annulled by a guardian, and the man was responsible for maintenance of the child, who remained in the custody of his ex-wife.[72]

Despite similarities in responsibilities between biological and *kafala* families, there are important rights denied to the *makful* child. The Family Code's Article 54 states that '[Legitimate] children have the right to the following care from their [biological] parents:

1. Protection of their lives and health from conception until they come of legal age;
2. Ensuring respect of their identity and its preservation, particularly their name, nationality and registration in the civil status record;
3. Paternity, custodial care and financial maintenance in conformity with the provisions of the third book of this Moudawana.'

The Family Code here makes explicit the importance of naming and identity as central to the individual's legitimacy, yet for children without filiation, these protections are not ensured. We might note, however, that a revision to the Moroccan civil code now permits *kafil* parents to petition the Palace for a surname change for their child, a process called *concordance des noms* (Ar. *mutabaqa*).[73]

9.3.6 Effects of the **Makful** *Status on the Relinquished Child*

Moroccan law says little about the effects of the *makful* status on the child's development or life changes other than delineating the rights that are *not* afforded to him or her, namely the rights of filiation and inheritance. Once the Guardianship Judge establishes the *kafala*, the mention of *kafala* and the name(s) of the guardian (s) are written into the margins of the child's birth entry in the civil registry. According to Article 21 of the 2002 law, the *kafala* must not be mentioned on any copies of birth certificate deeds delivered to either the guardian or the child. In

[72] Morocco, Cour Suprême 14 January 2004 no. S15.

[73] Interestingly, the French-language administrative website for the Government of Morocco has an explanation of the process of attributing names to children of unknown parentage or children whose fathers are unknown, but there is no mention of this on the Arabic-language version of the same website, see www.service-public.ma.

practice, this prohibition is not uniformly respected, and thus *kafil* parents may indeed have civil register or birth certificate copies with mention of the *kafala* parent(s)' name(s) as well as biological filiation, if known. We can turn to ethnography to understand something about the effects of the *makful* status on the child, but can summarize in brief that these range from devastating to barely noticeable, largely depending on the wider *kafil* family's acceptance of the child and the adults' attitude towards raising a child of unknown filiation, as well as such factors as early trauma or abuse prior to relinquishment. Here we see where culture and religion coexist uneasily, and where cultural disdain for parentless children, for instance, can lead to the *makful*'s questioning of his or her self-worth, leading to sometimes debilitating depression or anxiety,[74] and also potentially to attachment disorder resulting from disrupted attachment between the child and the primary caregiver (usually the biological mother) or caregivers (including siblings and the extended family).

Returning to the religious underpinnings of the *kafala* contract, we can see the abiding concern with marriage prohibitions between parties in this contract. Since the *makful* child is not related to the *kafil* parent(s), there is no inherent marriage prohibition. While there are no available statistics on the prevalence of such marriages, it is hard to envision them culturally in Morocco because such a union would be socially taboo, even if not religiously or legally prohibited. Additionally, there is no marriage prohibition between the *makful* child and the biological children of the *kafil* parent(s). This possibility perhaps underlies the preoccupation of participants in some online *kafil* parents' groups with modesty and the obligation of veiling in the presence of an unrelated member of the opposite sex. That is, some parties involved in *kafala* insist that a *kafil* mother and daughters should cover their heads even at home when a male *makful* child shares the family space, and vice-versa. This would mean a reversal of the common cultural practice in Morocco in which a woman or girl removes her headscarf when at home with members of the family, if she wears one outside the home. If a *kafil* mother believes she needs to veil in front of the boy she is raising, or her biological daughter must do so for the woman's *makful* son, we see that this contract does not transform the individuals into family members, as does adoption in other countries.

9.3.7 Transnational **Kafala** *of the Moroccan Child*

Under Moroccan law, the *kafala* of a Moroccan child is transportable across national boundaries. Article 24 of the 2002 *kafala* law states that the *kafil* parent(s) may take the *makful* child out of Morocco to reside permanently with the *kafil*(s) if so authorized by the guardianship judge and if this move is 'in the best interests of the child.' It has generally been determined internationally, and in Moroccan law,

[74] See Bargach 2002.

that it is in the best interest of the child to reside with the adult(s) judicially invested with parental authority. The authorizing Moroccan judge is then requested to send a copy of the *kafala* contract to the Moroccan consular authorities in the country of residence to ensure verification that the *kafil* parent is indeed upholding the goals of the contract (maintenance, protection, education, and ensuring the child's health and well-being). The standard procedure is then supposed to be that the consular officer reports back to the guardianship judge on the *kafil* parent's compliance with the contract's terms. It is unclear how frequently this kind of reporting is required; consulates have uneven access to reports and inconsistent procedures. Even within Morocco itself, it is widely known that after the *kafala* is finalized, there are rarely official check-ins with the *kafil* parent(s) or oversight. This is widely decried by civil society actors as a problem that needs to be resolved to ensure the child's well-being.

There has long been significant judicial discretion in the designation of *kafala* contracts, yet inequality in the review of requests by applicants residing abroad has been exacerbated since an August 2012 circular issued by the former Minister of Justice Mustafa Ramid. The Ramid circular warned provincial judges to be wary of foreigners and foreign residents who request *kafala*s for parentless children in their jurisdictions. This warning appeared motivated not only by a general suspicion among Islamist politicians of Westerners' motives; it emerged after widespread media reporting of accusations of proselytizing by Europeans who ran an orphanage in the High Atlas mountain region. That orphanage was closed and its directors expelled from Morocco, but it evoked a latent suspicion that dated back to the French Protectorate period, when confirmed reports of French proselytizing in neighbouring Algeria made Moroccans presume that the Christianization of Moroccan youth impended, although this never came to pass. The orphanage incident provoked widespread outrage, although it did not lead to a higher number of Moroccans clamouring for custody of those children. The Ramid Circular effectively brought the *kafala*s issued to foreign parents to a halt, and brought about the requirement that foreigners be resident in Morocco for periods judged necessary by individual judges. Spanish *kafala*s were the first to be reissued in 2013 after assurances by the Spanish government that it would oversee the Islamic religious education of Moroccan children brought to Spain. A similar agreement was never reached with other Western countries, but gradually tensions eased, although they did not disappear. The circular was never formulated into a proposed law, debated, or brought to a vote in the Parliament, despite Islamist politicians' calls to establish a law prohibiting foreigners from contracting *kafala*. Around a quarter of *kafala*s prior to that point were issued to foreigners or to MREs (*marocains résidents à l'étranger*, or Moroccan emigrants), and it was eventually (although not originally) clarified that the MREs were not intended to be the target of this directive. *Kafala*s that were being processed at that point were essentially frozen, while prospective *kafil*s attempted to find solutions to the new requirement that the *kafil* reside in Morocco for at least two years. The suspicion that surrounds foreigners' desires to become *kafil*s persists in spite of the growing numbers of parentless Moroccan children and the insufficient numbers of willing and authorized guardians within Morocco to raise these children.

For those *makful* children who join their guardians in European countries or in North America, significant legal differences govern the international private law applied to them and the entities they constitute or do not constitute together.[75] Most important to *kafil* parents who reside in the West is the question of whether their state laws permit them to transform the Moroccan *kafala* contract into an adoption, which is widely considered the highest form of child protection. Among European countries, Belgium, Switzerland, Italy, England, and the Netherlands permit the law of the guardians' residence to govern this matter, meaning that adoption of the *makful* child is permitted right away, so long as the *kafala* was contracted in court and the child is of unknown filiation.[76] If filiation is known, permission from the biological mother must precede adoption. 'Simple adoption' (Fr. *adoption simple*) is permitted in France for children for whom maternal filiation is known. France, the former Protectorate power, has been the most conservative country in regards to state law on adoption, at least since 2001 when an article of the Civil Code was amended to prohibit the adoption of any child 'whose personal law prohibits it.'[77] Without mentioning *kafala* or interpretations of Islamic law outright, the 2001 French law that modified Articles 370–373 of the Civil Code clearly concerned North Africans, and it was designed to end the judicial conversion of Moroccan *kafala* contracts into French adoptions. The international legal tools that are supposed to guide private international law considerations (especially the UNCRC and the Hague Convention, but also various bilateral accords between Morocco and European states) serve as inspiration but do not definitely delimit the ways in which this regime of care is managed outside of Morocco. In its immigration law, France specifically claims that the existence of a *kafala* relationship cannot be used as a justification for emigration, but that the best interests of the child hold that children should stay with their legal guardian, and that judicial decisions issued abroad are respected in French courts. *Kafil* parents residing in France with their *makful* children have developed a practice that, while not explicitly advocated in French law, has become standard practice: they wait three years[78] for the child to be eligible for French citizenship, and then with the child naturalized as French, and with the approval of a committee of concerned adults (usually family and friends of the guardian(s)), the *kafil*s petition for simple or full

[75] See Lixinski 2013 on international legal pluralism narratives and Oubrou 2009 on the 'legal abyss' in which guardians in transnational *kafala* arrangements find themselves.

[76] See Verhellen 2013 and Nishitani 2014 on state laws that refer to the guardian's country of residence as establishing the form of law used, as in Belgium, rather than original personal status law, as in France. Murat 2009 argues that this constitutes discrimination on the basis of birth origin.

[77] See Le Boursicot 2006 and 2010 regarding the non-translatability of 'social kinship' into 'blood kinship' in France.

[78] The period was five years until revised in March 2016. Civil society actors and some politicians had been advocating for two years.

adoption of the *makful* child.[79] Although this seems to be the most widely adopted solution for most *kafils* in France, the issue remains a burning one because of the French government's insistence that prohibiting adoption for *makful* minors is simply respecting the foreign court and the religious law of sovereign states. This justification is supported by some jurists, whereas other legal scholars and family rights advocates insist that the *kafala*, although mentioned in Article 20 of the UNCRC, is not the fullest protection available to children in countries that recognize adoption, even if *kafala* is the most complete protection available to parentless children within Morocco itself.[80]

9.4 Conclusion

While Moroccan law contains provisions for the establishment of filiation and an institution to care for relinquished children through substitute parental care, both filiation and *kafala* are topics of legal and social debate in contemporary Morocco. For filiation, increasingly there is an awareness of the difference between paternity (Ar. *ubuwwa*) and filiation (Ar. *nasab*). Each of these potentially afford rights to the child in question, but the distinction between them pits medical science and international human rights principles against dominant interpretations of Maliki jurisprudence, with Moroccan judges left to interpret the relevant legal instruments. The UNCRC wields significant influence not only on legal institutions and laws, but also on emerging understandings of collective human rights that pertain to all individuals inside and outside Morocco, regardless of faith. In this respect, there is widespread disagreement in civil society and in some corners of the judicial system, with state-specific laws that counter either ethical common sense or international standards in the rights of the child. This chapter has touched on some of the laws and practices around children that prevail in Morocco today, as well as providing some elements to understand the contemporary debates that are playing out in Moroccan courts and the public sphere.

Acknowledgements This paper benefitted from research assistance by Madeline Ewbank, Isabelle Laskero, and Mathilde Karekezi. Funding for portions of this research was provided by the Institute for Advanced Study in Lyon (the Collegium) and by the Northwestern University Office of Undergraduate Research. Earlier iterations of the project benefitted from discussion with members of the Max Planck Working Group on Child Law and Collegium fellows. I wish to thank in particular the Social and Political Dynamics of Private Life working group of the Max Weber Center, Université de Lyon 2, and especially Gaelle Clavandier and Isabelle Sayn. Exchanges with Jamila Bargach undergird my inquiry and analysis. All errors remain my own.

---

[79] Simple adoption is additive, so filiation is established to the *kafil*(s) while the original biological filiation, whether known or unknown, is retained. Plenary ('full') adoption replaces original filiation with the adoptive filiation and severs all ties to the original parent(s), when known.

[80] See Hoffman (forthcoming 2019) for a fuller discussion of transnational families through *kafala* in France and in the United States.

References

AEH (2017) Livret de famille: nouvelle décision judiciaire en faveur d'une mère célibataire. Medias24, 4 December 2017. www.medias24.com/MAROC/DROIT/178696-Justice-Une-mere-celibataire-admise-a-recevoir-le-livret-de-famille.html. Accessed 1 February 2018

Ait Musa ^{c}A (2017) Isti'nafiyyat Tanja Tulghi Hukman Qada bi-'al-I^{c}tiraf bi-Bunuwat al-Tifl' min ^{c}Alaqa ghayr Shar^{c}iyya [Tangier Appeal Annuls Ruling That 'Recognized the Paternity of the Child' from an Illegitimate Relationship]. Al-Sahra', 10 October 2017. https://assahraa.ma/web/2017/139704. Accessed 2 February 2018

Alidadi K, Foblets M-C (2012) Framing Multicultural Challenges in Freedom of Religion Terms: Limitations of Minimal Human Rights for Managing Religious Diversity in Europe. Netherlands Quarterly of Human Rights 30(4):460–488

Al-Mufakkira al-Qanuniyya (2017) Al-Qada' al-Maghribi Yuqirru Haqq Umm ^{c}Aziba fi al-Husul ^{c}ala Daftar ^{c}A'ili [Moroccan Judiciary Recognizes the Right of a Single Mother to Obtain a Family Booklet]. Al-Mufakkira al-Qanuniyya/Legal Agenda, 4 December 2017. http://legal-agenda.com/article.php?id=4084. Accessed 3 February 2018

Al-Sahra' (2017) Asdarathu Mahkamat al-Usra bi-Tanja ma^{c}a Ta^{c}wid li-Fa'idat al-Umm: Awwal Hukm fi al-Maghrib bi-Bunuwat Tifla min ^{c}Alaqa Kharij Itar al-Zawaj li-l-Ab [Family Court in Tangier Issues Ruling with Compensation for Mother's Benefit: The First Ruling in Morocco in Paternity of Child Born Out of Wedlock to Father]. Al-Sahra', 24 February 2017. www.assahraa.ma/journal/2017/203545. Accessed 13 February 2018

An-Na'im AA (1990) Toward an Islamic Reformation: Civil Liberties, Human Rights and International Law. Syracuse University Press, Syracuse, NY

An-Na'im AA (2010) The Compatibility Dialectic: Mediating the Legitimate Coexistence of Islamic Law and State Law. The Modern Law Review 73(1):1–29

Assim U, Sloth-Nielsen J (2014) Islamic kafalah as an alternative care option for children deprived of a family environment. African Human Rights Law Journal 14:322–345

Badel M, Pujolar O (2009) Kafala et droits sociaux. Droit de la famille 1:25–30

Baderin M (2001a) Establishing Areas of Common Ground between Islamic Law and International Human Rights. International Journal of Human Rights 5(2):72–113

Baderin M. (2001b) A Macroscopic Analysis of the Practice of Muslim State Parties to International Human Rights Treaties: Conflict or Congruence? Human Rights Law Review 1 (2):265–303

Bargach J (2001) Personalizing It. In: Faubion J (ed) Ethics of Kinship. Rowman and Littlefield, Lanham MD, pp 71–97

Bargach J (2002) Orphans of Islam: Family, Abandonment, and Secret Adoption in Morocco. Rowman and Littlefield, Lanham MD

Barraud E (2010) La filiation légitime à l'épreuve des mutations sociales au Maghreb. Droit et cultures 59:255–282

Barraud E (2013) L'adoption entre France et Maghreb: de Terre et de Sang. Editions Non Lieu, Paris

Bollée S (2013) La conformité à la Convention européenne des droits de l'homme de l'interdiction d'adopter un enfant recueilli en kafala. Revue trimestrielle des droits de l'homme 717–724

Coulson NJ (1969) Conflicts and Tensions in Islamic Jurisprudence. University of Chicago Press, Chicago

Dahiri M (2016) Morocco. In: Nieto Morales C (ed) Comparative Intervention with Minors in Different Countries. Editorial Dykinson, Madrid

Detrick S (ed) (1992) The United Nations Convention on the Rights of the Child: A Guide to the '*Travaux Préparatoires*'. Martinus Nijhoff Publishers, Dordrecht et al.

Di Noto R (2011) Le droit au respect de la vie privée et familiale, nouveau paradigme en droit international privé des personnes? In: Alleweldt R, Callsen R, Dupendant J (eds) Human Rights Abuses in the Contemporary World. Peter Lang, New York, pp 145–168

Donders Y (2013) Cultural Pluralism in International Human Rights Law. In: Vrdoljak AF (ed) The Cultural Dimension of Human Rights. Oxford University Press, Oxford, pp 205–239
Duca R (2014) Family Reunification: the Case of Muslim Migrant Children in Europe. Athens Journal of Social Sciences (April) 111–120
Emon AM (2016) Codification and Islamic Law: The Ideology Behind a Tragic Narrative. Middle East Law and Governance 8:275–309
Ensel R (2002) Colactation and fictive kinship as rites of incorporation and reversal in Morocco. Journal of North African Studies 7(4):83–96
Fetzer J, Soper C (2005) Muslims and the State in Britain, France, and Germany. Cambridge University Press, Cambridge
Fioole JCCM (2015) Give me your child: adoption practices in a small Moroccan town. Journal of North African Studies 20(2):247–264
Fricero N (2012) Respect du droit à la vie familiale en dépit du refus d'adoption: CEDH, 5e sect., 4 Oct. 2012, n° 43631/09, Harroudj c. France. Procédures: Revue Mensuelle commentaires 16–18
Geertz H (1979) The Meanings of Family Ties. In: Geertz C, Geertz H, Rosen L (eds) Meaning and Order in Moroccan Society: Three Essays in Cultural Analysis. Cambridge University Press, Cambridge, pp 315–391
Goody J (1969) Adoption in Cross-Cultural Perspective. Comparative Studies in Society and History 1(11):55–78
Gouzes G (2001) Pour une éthique de l'adoption internationale. Rapport au Premier ministre. La Documentation française, Paris
Hallaq WB (2009) Shari`a: Theory, Practice, Transformations. Cambridge University Press, Cambridge
Hammje P (2012) L'interdiction d'adoption face aux droits fondamentaux. Recueil Dalloz 43:2947–2951
Hervieu N (2012) L'adoption internationale aux prises avec la kafala sous le regard européen. Lettre 'Actualités Droits-Libertés' du CREDOF, 8 October 2012
Hoekema AJ, van Rossum WM (2010) Empirical conflict rules in Dutch legal cases of cultural diversity. In: Foblets M-C et al (eds) Cultural Diversity and the Law: State Responses from Around the World. Bruylant, Brussels, pp 851–888
Hoffman KE (2015) Pratiques juridiques et idéologies langagières dans un tribunal non officiellement multilingue. Anthropologie et Sociétés 39(3):29–50
Hoffman KE (forthcoming 2019) Famille, filiation, et foi: le traitement judiciaire de la tutelle islamique (*kafala*) en France et aux Etats-Unis. In: Fillod-Chabaud A, Odasso L (eds) La famille et la nation: Pour une sociologie juridique des migrations et des circulations familiales. Presses universitaires de Rennes
Howell S (2006) The Kinning of Foreigners: Transnational Adoption in a Global Perspective. Berghahn Books, New York
Human Rights Watch (2015) Morocco: Prison Terms for Adultery. Unfair trial of Activist, Friend. www.hrw.org/news/2015/06/02/morocco-prison-terms-adultery. Accessed 9 February 2018
Hunter-Henin M (2006) Droit des personnes et droits de l'homme: combinaison ou confrontation? Revue critique de droit international privé 4:743–775
Hussin I (2007) The Pursuit of the Perak Regalia: Islam, Law, and the Politics of Authority in the Colonial State. Law & Social Inquiry 32(3):759–788
Id Hajji L (2017) Bassima Hakkaoui en faveur d'un test ADN obligatoire de paternité. Medias24, 20 December 2017. www.medias24.com/MAROC/SOCIETE/179109-Bassima-Hakkaoui-en-faveur-d-un-test-ADN-obligatoire-de-paternite.html. Accessed 6 February 2018
Immigration and Refugee Board of Canada (2013) Morocco: Application of adultery laws, in particular, of Article 490 of the Penal Code and of the articles that follow it; treatment by family members and in-laws of people who commit adultery (2010-August 2013), 9 September 2013. www.refworld.org/docid/53732b014.html. Accessed 1 February 2018.
Iraqi Z (2002) L'enfant abandonné. Thèse de doctorat de médecine, Université Mohammed V, faculté de médecine et de pharmacie de Rabat

Izdinne M (2011) Adultère: le dernier tabou. MarocHebdo, 16 March 2011

Kiestra LR (2014) The Impact of the European Convention on Human Rights on Private International Law. T.M.C. Asser Press, The Hague

Kutty F (2015) Islamic 'Adoptions': Kafalah, Raadah, Istilhaq and the Best Interests of the Child. In: Ballard RL et al. (eds) The Intercountry Adoption Debate: Dialogues Across Disciplines. Cambridge Scholars Publishing, Newcastle upon Tyne, pp 526–563

La Ligue Marocaine pour la Protection de l'Enfance, UNICEF (2010) Enfance abandonnée au Maroc: Ampleur, état des lieux juridique et social, prise en charge, vécus. www.unicef.org/morocco/french/2010-Etude_Enfance_abandon_UNICEF-LMPE.pdf. Accessed 9 February 2018

Lahsini C (2017) Historic First in Morocco: Justice Recognizes Natural Filiation. Morocco World News, 22 February 2017. www.moroccoworldnews.com/2017/02/209083/historic-first-moroccan-justice-recognized-natural-filiation. Accessed 2 February 2018

Lakhdar Y (2017a) Hukm Qada'i Yamnahu 'Umman ^{c}Azibatan' al-Haqq fi Hiyazat Kunnash al-Hala al-Madaniyya [Court Ruling Grants 'Single Mother' the Right to Acquire a Civil Status Booklet]. Hespress, 6 December 2017. www.hespress.com/societe/373699.html. Accessed 2 February 2018

Lakhdar Y (2017b) Qissat al-Umm al-^{c}Aziba bi-Tanja.. Wa^{c}d bi-Zawaj wa-Ightisab wa-'Haqq' Yatabakhkharu [The story of the single mother in Tangier … Promised Marriage, Rape and 'Right' Evaporates]. Hespress, 16 October 2017. www.hespress.com/societe/368036.html. Accessed 1 February 2018

Le Boursicot M-C (2006) Les enfants recueillis en Kafala par des ressortissants français. Journal du droit des jeunes 10(260):46–49

Le Boursicot M-C (2010) La *Kafâla* ou recueil légal des mineurs en droit musulman: une adoption sans filiation. Droit et cultures 59:283–302

Libson G (1997) On the Development of Custom as a Source of Law in Islamic Law: *Al-rujū^{c}u ilā al-^{c}urfi aḥadu al-qawā^{c}idi al-khamsi allatī yatabannā ^{c}alayhā al-fiqhu*. Islamic Law and Society 4(2):131–155

Lixinski L (2013) Narratives of the International Legal Order and Why They Matter. Erasmus Law Review 1:2–5

Medias24 (2014) 5377 enfants légalement abandonnés au Maroc en 2013. Medias24, 15 October 2014. www.medias24.com/SOCIETE/15069-5.377-enfants-legalement-abandonnes-au-Maroc-en-2013.html. Accessed 12 February 2018

Miller SG (2006) Sleeping Fetus: Overview. In: Joseph S (ed) Encyclopedia of Women & Islamic Cultures, vol III. Brill, Leiden and Boston, pp 421–424

Murat P (2009) Le refus de la transformation en adoption. Droit de la famille 1:37–41

Muslim Women's Shura Council (2011) Adoption and the Care of Orphan Children: Islam and the Best Interests of the Child. American Society for Muslim Advancement. https://bettercarenetwork.org/library/the-continuum-of-care/adoption-and-kafala/adoption-and-the-care-of-orphan-children-islam-and-the-best-interests-of-the-child. Accessed 12 February 2018

Nishitani Y (2014) Global Citizens and Family Relations. Erasmus Law Review 3:134–146

Oubrou T (2009) La kafala et la sharia. Droit de la famille 1:10–16

Oxford Islamic Studies Online (n.d.) Lian. www.oxfordislamicstudies.com/article/opr/t125/e1345. Accessed 30 January 2018

Qudri S (2017) Bi-l-Fidiyu: Qadi bi-Tanja Yakshifu ^{c}an Hukmihi Manaha al-Ubuwa li-Tifl min Umm ^{c}Aziba [Video: Judge in Tangier Makes Known His Ruling to Allow Paternity for a Child Born to a Single Mother]. Le360, 24 February 2017. http://m.le360.ma/ar/societe/102979. Accessed 1 February 2018

Rezig M (2004) Les aspirations conflictuelles du droit de l'adoption: Etude Comparative. Arab Law Quarterly 19(1/4):147–168

Rosen L (2000) The Justice of Islam: Comparative Perspectives on Islamic Law and Society. Oxford University Press, Oxford

Sonbol A (1995) Adoption in Islamic Society: A Historical Survey. Children in the Muslim Middle East. University of Texas Press, Austin

Sonneveld N (2017) Seeking Portia and the Duke: Male and Female Judges Dispensing Justice in Paternity Cases in Morocco. In: Sonneveld N, Lindbekk M (eds) Women Judges in the Muslim World: A Comparative Study of Discourse and Practice. Brill, Leiden, pp 123–152

Suleiman O (2017) Adoption and Fostering: Fiqh of Islam. Presentation. Yaqeen Institute for Islamic Research, Irving, TX, 17 May 2017

Syed S (1998) The impact of Islamic law on the implementation of the Convention on the Rights of the Child: The plight of non-marital children under Shari'a. International Journal of Children's Rights 6(4):359–393

van Loon H (2010) The Accommodation of Religious Laws in Cross-Border Situations: The Contribution of the Hague Conference on Private International Law. Cuadernos de Derecho Transnacional 2(1):261–267

Verdier M (2017) Le Maroc reconnait la paternité d'un enfant née hors mariage. La Croix, 24 February 2017. www.la-croix.com/Monde/Afrique/Le-Maroc-reconnait-paternite-dune-enfant-hors-mariage-2017-02-24-1200827205. Accessed 12 February 2018

Verhellen J (2013) Lost in Nationality: Private International Law and Cultural Diversity. In: Foblets M-C, Yassari N (eds) Legal Approaches to Cultural Diversity. Martinus Nijhoff Publishers, Leiden/Boston, pp 521–572

Zine G (2018) Enfants nés hors-mariage, 200 000 bombes à retardement. Dîn Wa Dunia, 8 February 2018. http://dinwadunia.ladepeche.ma/enfants-nes-hors-mariage. Accessed 12 February 2018

Žvan Elliot K (2015) Modernizing Patriarchy: the Politics of Women's Rights in Morocco. University of Texas Press, Austin

Katherine E. Hoffman is associate professor of Anthropology at Northwestern University, Evanston, IL (United States). She is a linguistic, sociocultural, and legal anthropologist, who specializes in the relationship between expressive culture, ethnicity, law, history, and political economy. Her research explores this nexus primarily in North Africa, and especially Morocco, from the late 19th century to the present, particularly as it has been shaped by the processes of French colonialism, anti-imperialism, nationalism, and postnationalism. Her most recent research looks at the transnational migration of Muslim children to Europe and the United States, whether through adoption or war, and especially the regimes of care available to abandoned and orphaned Muslim children taken into kafala arrangements (Islamic guardianship). Among others, she has been awarded fellowships from the Institute for Advanced Study in Lyon (the Collegium de Lyon), the American Council of Learned Societies' Charles A. Ryskamp Research Fellowship and a National Endowment for the Humanities Faculty Fellowship. She has served on the editorial boards of the Oxford Bibliographies in Anthropology, the Journal of Linguistic Anthropology and American Anthropologist.

Chapter 10
Pakistan

Ayesha Shahid and Isfandyar Ali Khan

Contents

Ayesha Shahid is Senior Lecturer in Law at Coventry University, United Kingdom.

Isfandyar Ali Khan is currently Senior Partner of S&K Partnership, a law and policy consulting firm in Peshawar, Pakistan.

A. Shahid (✉)
Coventry University, Coventry, UK
e-mail: ayesha.shahid@coventry.ac.uk

I. A. Khan (✉)
S&K Partnership, Peshawar, Pakistan
e-mail: isfandyaralikhan@yahoo.co.uk

N. Yassari et al. (eds.), *Filiation and the Protection of Parentless Children*, https://doi.org/10.1007/978-94-6265-311-5_10

Abstract In Pakistan, the *Qanun-e-Shahadat* Order 1984 deals with the issue of establishing filiation (*nasab*). It lays down a minimum and maximum period of gestation. However, there is no specific legislation regarding acknowledgement (*iqrar*), proof (*bayyina*), or the use of scientific methods such as DNA testing for determining the filiation of a child. The law also does not make a clear distinction between a valid and an irregular marriage. In this chapter it is argued that the courts in Pakistan have played an important role in establishing the filiation of a child and have adopted a more progressive approach to save the mother and the child from the stigma of illegitimacy. In the absence of specific legislation, the courts in Pakistan have recognized that an irregular marriage featuring sexual intercourse has the semblance of marriage such as to constitute legal proof establishing filiation. In 2010, consequent to the 18th Constitutional Amendment, legislative and administrative competence as well as financial authority on child rights issues has been devolved to the provincial legislative assemblies. As a result, in the province of Punjab laws such as the Child Protection and Welfare Act 2010 (CPWA 2010); the Punjab Destitute and Neglected Children Act 2004 (PDNCA 2004); and the Employment of Children Act 1991 (ECA 1991) have been enacted to provide protection to orphaned children, abandoned children or foundlings (*laqit*), and street children. Besides these pieces of legislation, issues relating to the custody and guardianship (*vilayat*) of children are covered by the Guardians and Wards Act 1890 (GWA 1890), federal-level legislation enacted and implemented throughout Pakistan. Although adoption in its strict Western sense is not allowed in Pakistan, the GWA 1890 makes provision for an individual to obtain legal guardianship of a child.

Keywords Pakistan · Filiation · Foundlings · Children's rights · Adoption

10.1 Introduction

10.1.1 Sources of Law

The 1973 Constitution of the Islamic Republic of Pakistan acknowledges in its Principles of Policy the protection of marriage, family, mothers, and children. Under Article 35 of the 1973 Constitution, the State is under an obligation to 'protect … the mother and the child'. However, contrary to what is stated in the Constitution, Pakistani laws do not afford a sufficient protection against the ill-treatment of children. Article 37 of the 1973 Constitution lays down commitments for promoting social justice and eradication of social evils. This includes the State's obligation to 'remove illiteracy and provide free and compulsory secondary education within minimum possible period' and 'make provision for securing just and humane conditions of work, ensuring that children and women are not employed in vocations unsuited to their age or sex, and for maternity benefits for women in employment'.[1] This is further strengthened by the inviolability of the privacy of the home, which is a fundamental right under Article 14 of the 1973 Constitution. These provisions support parental guidance through the institution of marriage and the strengthening of the family as the primary unit of the social system, within the inviolable right of privacy of the home. Article 227 of the Constitution also lays down that Islamic law is a main source for Pakistani law. Thus, Pakistani law follows Islamic principles of law in matters relating to filiation and determining the filiation of a child.

Besides the provisions in the Constitution, there are other pieces of legislation that deal with child rights issues. The most significant development in this respect has been the passage of the 18th Constitutional Amendment to the Constitution of Pakistan in 2010. Consequent to this Amendment, legislative and administrative competence as well as financial authority on child rights issues has been devolved to the provincial legislative assemblies and provincial governments.[2] In the province of Khyber Pakhtunkhwa (KP), the Child Protection and Welfare Act 2010 (CPWA 2010) has been enacted. The KP government has also established a Child Protection and Welfare Commission (CPWC), while in the provinces of Sindh and Punjab the Sindh Child Protection Authority Act 2011 (SCPAA 2011), the Punjab Destitute and Neglected Children Act 2004 (PDNCA 2004), and the Employment of Children Act 1991 (ECA 1991) have been enacted.[3]

Substantive family law matters relating to marriage, divorce, etc. are dealt with under the Muslim Family Law Ordinance 1961 (MFLO 1961), the Dissolution of

[1] Articles 37(b) and (e) of the Constitution of the Islamic Republic of Pakistan.

[2] The federal government can therefore now legislate on child-related issues only in relation to federal territories and those areas not forming part of a province. However, under Article 142 of the Constitution, legislative competence in relation to criminal law, procedure, and evidence still lies concurrently with the federal Parliament and provincial assemblies. Legislation affecting the child and child rights in these areas, therefore, can be and still is made through federal law.

[3] In 2010, KP promulgated the Child Protection and Welfare Act 2010 (CPWA 2010), which provides mechanisms at local and provincial levels for the welfare and protection of children at risk. It is based on the principle of the best interests of the child. In 2011, KP also promulgated the KP Borstal Institutions Act 2011 (BIA 2011), under which separate detention places will be established for juvenile convicts for their basic education and their mental, moral and psychological development. The province of Sindh has promulgated the Sindh Child Protection Authority Act (SCPAA) 2011, through which an authority has been constituted which will monitor and ensure implementation of the child-protection-related provisions under the Convention in the province. The law seeks to establish district level child-protection institutions. In 2011, the Remand Home Rules were also announced by the government of Sindh. The Remand Home is a place of temporary custody for child inmates where they are provided with care. In 2013, the Sindh Assembly passed the Sindh Right of Children to Free and Compulsory Education Act 2013. Also in the same year, the province of Balouchistan promulgated the Balouchistan Compulsory and Free Education Ordinance 2013.

Muslim Marriages Act 1939 (DMMA 1939), the Child Marriage Restraint Act 1929[4] (CMRA 1929), and the Shariat Application Act 1937,[5] whereas issues relating to custody and guardianship are covered by the Guardians and Wards Act 1890[6] (GWA 1890). The Majority Act 1875 (No. IX) determines when a minor attains the age of majority. Under this Act the age of eighteen years has been fixed as the age of majority.[7] However, the age of minority is extended to the completion of the age of twenty-one years in two situations: first, when a guardian (of the person or property, or both) of a minor has been appointed before the minor child attains the age of eighteen years and, second, when the property of the minor is under the superintendence of a court of wards. The origin of these pieces of legislation can be traced back to the Anglo-Mohammadan law introduced by the British colonizers in the Indian sub-continent. While framing laws for the Muslims in India, the British relied specifically on the commentaries *Hidayah* and *Fatawa-i-Alamgiri*, which were based on the

[4] The Child Marriage Restraint Act 1929 (CMRA) was a norm-setting legal document as the framers of the Act, bearing in mind prevailing societal norms, did not invalidate child marriage. However, under the Act the father or guardian may be punished for contracting their children into such marriages. In 2009 a private member bill to amend the CMRA was tabled in the National Assembly, the Child Marriage Restraint (Amendment) Bill 2009. It seeks to 'remove the gender disparity in age' of marriage of males and females, among other provisions, and set eighteen years as the minimum age of marriage for both. It has also proposed to raise the punishment for violations from one month to two years and the fine from one thousand to one hundred thousand rupees. Once the age of marriage for females is raised to eighteen years under the CMR (Amendment) Bill, amendments will be required in the option of puberty provision in the Dissolution of Muslim Marriages Act 1939 so as to provide effective relief to the victims of under-age marriages.

[5] The second piece of legislation that Pakistan inherited from pre-partition India was the Shariat Application Act 1937. The Shariat Application Act laid down that in Muslim family matters the rule of decision would be Muslim personal law. A substantial portion of personal law, therefore, remained un-codified and subject to interpretation by the courts. After the creation of Pakistan, the first legislative attempt made by the Punjab Legislative Assembly, which passed the New West Punjab Muslim Personal Law (Shariat) Application Act (IX of 1948), enlarged the scope of personal law to questions relating to succession, including succession to agricultural land (whereas the previous Act applied only to intestate succession). However, these changes were not welcomed in all parts of the country as men were still not willing to give women their share in property. As a result, to deprive women of their inheritance rights, amendments were made to the same Act in the Province of Sindh, and the following words were deleted from sec 2 of the Shariat Application Act: 'save questions relating to agricultural land and other than charitable institutions and charitable and religious endowments'.

[6] This Act sets out the framework for the court's consideration of custody disputes. The objectives of the Guardians and Wards Act 1890 are to promote the interests of children to make sure that the child will not suffer any discrimination or disadvantage because of the marital status of his or her parents.

[7] However, the Majority Act 1875 laid down an exception to the rule in section 2(a), which states that its provisions will not affect 'the capacity of any person to act in the following matters (namely), marriage, dower, divorce and adoption' under their personal law.

teachings of the Hanafi school of thought. These commentaries were followed as a final and unquestionable authority in family matters.

In addition to these pieces of legislation in Pakistan, the supremacy of the *Shari'a* as the supreme law of Pakistan was affirmed under the Enforcement of Shariat Act 1991, which states that all statutory law is to be interpreted in the light of the *Shari'a* and that all Muslim citizens of Pakistan are to observe the *Shari'a* and act accordingly. The Preamble of the Act clearly states that it is obligatory for all Muslims to follow the injunctions of the Qur'an and Sunnah to regulate and order their lives in complete submission to Divine law. Section 20 of the Act states that notwithstanding anything contained in the Act, the rights of women as guaranteed by the Constitution are not affected. An important provision of the Act is section 15, which requires the state to take steps to set up a funding body (*Bait-ul-Mal*) for providing assistance to the poor, needy, helpless, handicapped, invalids, widows, orphans, and the destitute.

In Pakistan the two key pieces of legislation that deal with establishing the filiation of a child are the *Qanun-e-Shahadat* Order 1984 (which replaced the Evidence Act 1872)[8] and the Offence of *Qadhf* (Enforcement of *Hudood*) Ordinance 1979. The *Qanun-e-Shahadat* Order 1984 was meant to consolidate the law of evidence so as to bring it in conformity with the injunctions of Islam as laid down in the Qur'an and Sunnah.[9] It introduced changes to the law as it relates to the presumption of legitimacy. Under section 128 of the *Qanun-e-Shahadat* Order 1984, birth during marriage is conclusive proof of the legitimacy of a child.[10] It lays down rules that a child born during a valid marriage – if not born before the expiry of six lunar months from the date of marriage – or within two years after its dissolution, and whose mother has remained unmarried, will be considered as a 'legitimate' child. Legitimacy will not be established if the husband refuses to accept the child or if the child is born more than six lunar months after the

[8] Section 112 of the Evidence Act 1872 dealt with the issue of the legitimacy of the child, and it provided that a child born during a valid marriage or within 280 days after dissolution of a marriage would be legitimate, except where it was proved that the husband and the wife had no access to each other. Section 112 of the Evidence Act 1872 created a presumption of legitimacy applicable to the offspring of all married couples in India irrespective of their personal law. It laid down that a child would be deemed to be legitimate if it was born either (1) 'during the continuance of a valid marriage' between its parents or (2) 'within 280 days after its dissolution, the mother remaining unmarried.'

[9] Sabreen 2013, p 25.

[10] *Qanun-e-Shahadat* Order 1984 section 128: (1) The fact that any person was born during the continuance of a valid marriage between his mother and any man and not earlier, that the expiration of six lunar months from the date of the marriage or within two years after its dissolution, the mother remaining unmarried, shall be conclusive proof that he is the legitimate child of that man, unless – (a) the husband had refused, or refuses, to own the child; or (b) the child was born after the expiration of six lunar months from the date on which the woman had accepted that the period of iddat had come to an end. (2) Nothing contained in clause (1) shall apply to a non-Muslim if it is inconsistent with his faith.

expiration of the waiting period as accepted by the woman. The important points of this legislation are the determination of minimum and maximum periods of gestation.

The second piece of legislation is the Offence of *Qadhf* Ordinance, under which a child may be disowned by imprecation (*lian*). Section 14 of the Ordinance lays down the procedure for taking an oath if the husband accuses the wife of committing adultery (*zina*). In addition, at the international level Pakistan has ratified the UN Convention on the Rights of the Child and specifically the Optional Protocol to the Convention on the Rights of the Child on the sale of children, child prostitution and child pornography (2011). In the light of Pakistan's international obligations, there is a strong need to provide a more conducive environment for the protection of the rights of children in the country.

10.1.2 Jurisdiction of the Courts

A 'Family Court' is constituted in Pakistan under section 2(b) of the West Pakistan Family Courts Act 1964 (FCA 1964). The jurisdiction of the family court is prescribed under Part I of the Schedule and is subject to the provisions of MFLO 1961 and the Conciliation Courts Ordinance 1961 (CCO 1961).[11] A family court has exclusive jurisdiction to entertain, hear, and adjudicate upon the matters mentioned in the schedule, and it is a civil court. The family courts have inquisitional jurisdiction under a special procedure, including an obligation to discover the possibilities of amicable settlement. Section 10(3) of the FCA 1964 reads: 'At the pre-trial stage, the Court shall ascertain the points at issue between the parties and attempt to effect a compromise or reconciliation between the parties, if this be possible.' Under section 14 of the Family Court Rules, in-camera proceedings can also be conducted, and the court has the power to direct that all or any part of the proceedings be held in camera. This may also be done upon request of both parties.

Provincial governments are empowered to establish one or more family courts in each district and appoint a judge for each court. A family court is bound to dispose of the case within six months from the date on which proceedings were instituted. If the case is not concluded within the six-month timeframe, any party can make an

[11] Under section Sec 5(2) FCA, family courts have exclusive jurisdiction in the following matters: (a) Dissolution of marriage including *Khula*; (b) Dower; (c) Maintenance; (d) Restitution of conjugal rights; (e) Custody of children and the visitation rights of parents to meet them; (f) Jactitation of marriage; (g) Dowry; (h) Personal property and belongings of the wife; (i) Guardianship; (j) Offences specified in Part II of the Schedule, where one of the spouses is victim of an offence committed by the other.

application to the High Court for necessary direction in this regard.[12] Under Rule 7 (a) of the Family Courts Rules 1965, suits relating to custody and guardianship of children are instituted, heard, and decided by the court of the district judge. The district judge may also transfer the case to a senior civil judge (first class) or to additional civil judges. In *Muhammad Zaffar Khan v Mst. Shehnaz Bibi*, the Karachi High Court suggested to the government of Sindh that

> the word 'Civil Judge' [in section 4 of the Family Courts Act 1964] includes 'Second Class as well as Third Class Judges' ... who serve as Family Judges. As Constitutional jurisdiction is invoked in large number of cases against the orders of Family Courts, therefore, such cases in the Trial [Family] Court should be dealt with by Senior and more experienced Judges as compared to the Second or Third Class Civil Judges.[13]

However, neither the High Court nor the legislature has enforced this suggestion and family cases are being heard by all categories of civil judges.[14] It is also pertinent to mention that through an amendment in 1994, section 3 of the FCA prescribes that at least one female judge is to be appointed in each district upon the request of the provincial government and in consultation with the High Court. The government can appoint more female judges if necessary. The Federal Shariat court in *Ansar Burney v Federation of Pakistan* held that appointing female judges is not un-Islamic. The court relied on the Islamic legal maxim 'What is not prohibited by the Holy Qur'an and Sunnah is permitted' and the burden of proof about anything being prohibited is on the person who claims it to be so.[15]

In order to be appointed as a judge of a family court a person has to be qualified to be appointed as a district judge, an additional district judge, or a civil judge. The law does not state that the judge has to be a Muslim; the emphasis is rather on the role and functions of the judge. Recently, the Family Courts (Amendment) Act 2015 has made some amendments to the Family Courts Act 1964. Section 20 of the Family Courts (Amendment) Act 2015 has extended the jurisdiction of family courts. Under this section a family court is to be deemed as the judicial magistrate of the first class for taking cognizance and trial of any offence under the Code of Criminal Procedure 1898 (V of 1898), the Muslim Family Laws Ordinance 1961 (VIII of 1961), and the Child Marriage Restraint Act 1929 (XIX of 1929). Previously the jurisdiction of the court as 'judicial magistrate of first class' was restricted to maintenance disputes under section 488 of the Code of Criminal Procedure 1898 (Cr.PC).[16]

---

[12] Proviso to s 12A of the FCA, as amended by the amending Ordinance 2002.

[13] [1996] CLC 94.

[14] Munir 2006.

[15] PLD 1983 Federal Shariat Court 73, p 93.

[16] The previous section 20 stated that the government may invest any judge of a family court with powers of magistrate first class to make order for maintenance under section 488 of the Code of Criminal Procedure 1898.

10.2 The Establishment of Filiation

10.2.1 Establishing Filiation by Law: Application of the Principle of the Conjugal Bed (**firash**) *by the Pakistani Courts*

The Courts in Pakistan follow the principle of the 'conjugal bed' or 'the child follows the bed' (*firash*), and it serves to establish conclusive proof unless evidence to the contrary is produced. This principle gives rise to a presumption of legitimacy that the child belongs to the husband of the mother, and there is no need for acknowledgement or evidence of paternity if the existence of the conjugal bed is proved. This presumption of paternity is so strong that in cases where a child is born at least six months from the date of marriage and within two years of dissolution of marriage by death or by divorce, a simple denial of paternity on the part of the husband will not deprive the child of filiation (*nasab*). It is interesting to note that the courts also take into account the custom of the area where the father resides; thus, for instance, the father must disown the child at the time of the birth or at the time of making preparations for the arrival of the child or, if he is absent, when he comes to know about the birth. The application of the principle of *firash* by the judiciary is clearly illustrated in *Khizar Hayat v. Additional District Judge, Kabirwala*. In this case the Lahore High Court held that a child born within two years of the dissolution of marriage will be considered as legitimate provided the mother has not remarried during this period and if paternity is not denied by the father.[17]

Notwithstanding these rules, courts have deviated from the classical Islamic rule and held that a child born within six months of the marriage is legitimate if acknowledged by the husband, as in the *Hamida Begum v. Murad Begum* case before the Supreme Court of Pakistan.[18] The Supreme Court observed that according to the Hanafi school of thought, a child born in wedlock is of his parents even if the husband had no access to the wife.

Establishing *nasab* is one of the fundamental rights of the child, as rights relating to inheritance, maintenance, guardianship, and family name are dependent on its existence. One of the key factors in determining *nasab* is the legitimacy of the child. Under Islamic law a child is considered to be legitimate if born/conceived in a valid (*sahih*) marriage, or by acknowledgement (*iqrar*) if born/conceived in an irregular marriage, or by other means of evidence. If a child is born within a valid marriage, legal kinship is established with the parents and their families.

In Pakistani law, the establishment of legitimacy has no effect on the establishment of maternity. For a child, whether born into or outside of a marriage, maternity is always established. The Lahore High Court in the *Roshni Desai v.*

[17] PLD 2010 Lahore 422.

[18] PLD 1975 Supreme Court 674.

Jahanzeb Niazi[19] case had held that an illegitimate child belongs only to the mother while it has no relation with the father, such as inheritance, maintenance, or guardianship rights. An illegitimate child will inherit only from her mother, and custody of the child can be given to the mother and maternal relatives.[20]

10.2.1.1 The Evidence Act 1872

Before the promulgation of the *Qanun-e-Shahadat* Order 1984, the Evidence Act 1872 enacted by the British colonizers in the Indian subcontinent was followed. Section 112 of the Evidence Act 1872 provided that a child born during a valid marriage or within 280 days after the dissolution of a marriage would be legitimate, except where it was proved that the husband and the wife had no access to each other.

The Evidence Act 1872 had, however, an adverse effect on the provisions of Muslim personal law regarding the legitimacy of the child and the period of gestation, as illustrated in *Muhammad Allahdad v. Muhammad Ismail.*[21] In this case, the father of Allahdad Khan, a Sunni, died leaving behind two sons and three daughters. Allahdad filed a suit to be declared the eldest son of the deceased and therefore was entitled to a two-sevenths share in the estate. The defence in this case was that the plaintiff was only the stepson of the deceased. The plaintiff contended that even if he failed to prove that he was the son of the deceased, he had been acknowledged as his son on several occasions. Justice Syed Mahmood of the High Court of Allahabad held that the plaintiff had established himself as the legitimate son of the deceased and was therefore entitled to succeed him. However his Lordship left the question open whether section 112 of the Evidence Act 1872 had the effect of superseding the contrary provisions of Muslim personal law.

Nearly half a century later, the High Court of Allahabad in *Sibt Muhammad v. Muhammad case*[22] held that the Evidence Act superseded Muslim law and that section 112 of the Evidence Act 1872 did apply to Muslims, thereby overriding the corresponding provisions of Muslim personal law. The court held that had it 'been intended that the provisions of Section 112 should not apply to Muhammadans we should certainly expect to find a clear proviso to this effect'. The Lahore High Court in *Mst. Rahim Bibi v. Chiragh Din and Ghulam Mohy-ud-Din v. Khizar* adopted the same view.[23]

However, Muslim scholars in the Indian subcontinent expressed their concerns regarding the applicability of section 112 to Muslims. Kashi Prasad Saksena, while commenting on the application of section 112 of the Evidence Act to Muslims,

[19] PLD 2011 Lahore 423.

[20] PLD 2011 Lahore 424.

[21] 10 All. 1880 289, 339.

[22] 48 All. 1926 625.

[23] 10 Lah. 1929 470, 114 I.C. 495.

states: 'It is probable that Sir Fitz James Stephen drafted this section without giving sufficient thought to the Muslim law of legitimacy. Whatever be the reason, the Muslim law of legitimacy constitutes substantive law and as such cannot be superseded by section 112 of the Evidence Act'.[24] Tahir Mahmood states that it is not known whether the framers of the Evidence Act took notice of the contrary provisions of Muslim personal law and had the intention of abrogating them by the implications of the new provisions drafted by them.[25] Similarly, Ameer Ali was of the opinion that section 112, which embodied English law, could not be held to supersede contrary rules of Muslim law by implication.[26]

The application of section 112 of the Evidence Act 1872 became particularly problematic in cases of irregular Muslim marriages. The Evidence Act 1872 only referred to valid and void marriages and did not recognize the irregular marriage category as defined under Muslim personal law. It was almost 100 years later, in 1962, when the High Court of Lahore in *Abdul Ghani v. Taleh Bibi*[27] once again revived the Muslim law and held that where the parties to a disputed case of legitimacy were Muslims, the rules of Muslim personal law and not section 112 of the Evidence Act would be applicable.[28] The High Court further held that the 'repeal of section 2 of the Evidence Act 1872 (which stated that all contrary laws would be deemed to be abrogated) by the Repealing Act of 1938 had the effect of reviving the Muslim law'.[29]

10.2.1.2 Qanun-e-Shahadat *Order 1984*

As section 112 of the Evidence Act did not provide for a minimum and maximum period of gestation and was contrary to the provisions of Muslim personal law, it was declared un-Islamic, and in 1984 it was finally replaced by the *Qanun-e-Shahadat* Order 1984.[30] Section 128 of the *Qanun-e-Shahadat* Order

---

[24] Saksena 1972, p 135.

[25] Mahmood 1972.

[26] As cited in Fyzee 2005, p 182.

[27] PLD 1962 (West Pakistan) Lahore 531.

[28] The brief facts of the case are that in the year 1953, Abdul Ghani and others, appellants in the case, had filed a suit in the court of Senior Civil Judge Lyallpur to seek a declaration that they were the owners of the land in dispute, as Mst. Taleh Bibi, who had been entitled to it on the death of Allah Baksh, had relinquished her claim in their favour. They alleged that Mst. Taleh had filed a suit for the recovery of rent against them and, therefore, they were compelled to file a suit to establish their title. Their main ground of challenge was that Mst. Taleh Bibi was born within six months of the date of marriage of her mother, Mst. Aishan Bibi, with Allah Bakhsh, and that she was therefore not the legitimate daughter of the latter. The court, among other issues, determined the issue of legitimacy of Mst. Taleh Bibi and stated that she is to be presumed the legitimate daughter of Allah Bakhsh.

[29] PLD 1962 (West Pakistan) Lahore 531.

[30] Sabreen 2013, p 28.

1984 is in accordance with the rules of the Hanafi school of thought. Hanafis concede a gestation period of up to two years between conception and birth of a child. A child born not less than six months after the conclusion of a valid marriage is conclusive proof of the child's legitimacy unless evidence to the contrary is produced. Section 128 of the Order thus sets a minimum period of pregnancy of six months and a maximum of two years from the date of dissolution of marriage. However, it does not make any distinction between valid and irregular marriages and is silent on the issue of legitimacy of a child born in an irregular marriage.

This gap has been filled by the courts, who consider children born of an irregular marriage as legitimate. In *Lt-Col. Muhammad Yusuf, Commissioner Quetta Division v. Syed Ali Nawaz Gardezi*, the court held that 'a child born of a marriage subsequently declared void is legitimate, provided the parties believed in good faith that there was no impediment to their marriage. If at a later stage it is found that there was such an impediment, the marriage will be considered null and void, but the children born of such a marriage will be legitimate'.[31] This clearly suggests that the law should be reformed to include irregular marriages and that children born in irregular marriages should be recognized as legitimate by operation of law.

In *Malik Jiand Khan v Province of Sindh*, the court considered the issue of an alleged marriage, the proof of marriage by indirect evidence, and the effect of acknowledgement of a child. It was stated that, according to Muslim law, for a child to be legitimate it must be the offspring of a man and his wife or of a man and his slave. It was further stated that the term 'wife' necessarily connotes marriage, but as a marriage could be constituted without any ceremonial event, the existence of marriage in a particular case would be an open question. But 'where direct proof was not available, indirect proof would suffice. A way of providing indirect proof would be by acknowledgement of legitimacy in favour of a son'.

In a more recent case, *Ghazala Tehsin Zohra v Mehr Ghulam Dastagir*,[32] the Supreme Court held that the legislative intent and rationale behind extending the gestation period to a term of up to two years under section 128 of the *Qanun-e-Shahadat* Order 1984 was to avoid controversy in matters of *nasab*. The court further held that '[t]he Article is couched in a language which is protective of societal cohesion and the values of the community … classical Islamic Law, which is the inspiration behind the *Qanun-e-Shahadat* Order (though not incorporated fully) and was referred to by learned counsel for the appellant, also adheres to the same rationale and is driven by the same societal imperative'. The Court further held that 'it is also worth taking time to reflect on the belief in our tradition that on the Day of Judgment, the children of Adam will be called out by their mother's name … the Divine Being has, in His infinite wisdom and mercy, taken care to

[31] PLD 1963 Lahore 141.

[32] PLD 2015 Supreme Court 327.

ensure that even on a day when all personal secrets shall be laid bare the secrets about paternity shall not delved into or diverged.' In *Waqar Ahmad v Nomina Akhtar*, the Peshawar High Court held that as the child was born after six months of marriage, the child is a legitimate child under section 128 of the *Qanun-e-Shahadat* Order 1984.[33] The honourable judge further held that 'both, father and mother of the child in the absence of any evidence in rebuttal are held to have indulged in continuous coitus and she conceived the child from the petitioner [;] thus, being his lawful father, the petitioner is bound to maintain the child under the law'.

It is evident from the above-mentioned cases that the judges have taken a proactive approach to establishing paternity of the child. The judges avoid administering DNA tests in paternity disputes due to the statutory conclusive presumption in favour of legitimacy. This judicial approach has primarily been shaped by Article 128 of the *Qanun-e-Shahadat* Order 1984, which does not allow for the introduction of any piece of evidence meant to destabilize the presumptive legitimacy.[34] One can thus argue that by excluding DNA evidence in paternity cases the judges have given preference to the collective interest of society over an individual's interest. The judges have used both religious and societal context in looking at the negative impact of rejecting paternity and are generally reluctant to declare a child as illegitimate. Therefore every effort is made to save the child and the mother from the stigma of illegitimacy and to establish the *nasab* of the child, in order to safeguard the child's rights to inheritance, maintenance, and guardianship.

10.2.1.3 Lian (*Imprecation*)

Another important piece of legislation related to the legitimacy of the child and *nasab* is the Offence of *Qadhf* (Enforcement of Hudood) Ordinance 1979. Under this law a child may be disowned by imprecation (*lian*). *Lian* is a procedure in consonance with Islamic law and embodied in section 14 of the Ordinance, which states that a husband who accuses his wife of adultery has to take an oath in court regarding his accusation. After the completion of this procedure, the marriage is dissolved and no appeal against the dissolution is allowed. In cases where *nasab* is being disputed, Pakistani courts have to consider the effect of *lian*. In *Muhammad Riaz v. Asia Perveen*, the Court held that the father (petitioner) had raised false imputations of un-chastity against his wife and caused immeasurable humiliation and misery to his son by attempting to disown him to avoid maintenance payment. The court followed the principle of 'the conjugal bed' and accepted a medical report presented by the mother that proved the paternity of the child as well as a report of the chairman of the union council.

---

[33] PLD 2010 Peshawar 10.

[34] Cheema 2016, p 6.

10.2.2 Establishing Filiation by Private Autonomy: Acknowledgement of Filiation

The law is silent on the issue of acknowledgement of *nasab*, and it was the Pakistani courts that developed the principle of acknowledgement of paternity. Accordingly, through acknowledgement legitimacy is awarded to a child born prior to marriage, as eloquently elaborated by the Privy Council in Sadiq Hussain Khan's case.[35] The Privy Council held that the doctrine of acknowledgement of paternity is based on the continuous cohabitation of a man and a woman for a long period of time coupled with the acknowledgement of the father, thereby raising the presumption that the father was married to the mother of the acknowledged child and, further, a presumption of lawful marriage.[36] In *Bibi Amu v. Mst. Asiat and others*, the Karachi High Court held that if there is no direct proof of marriage the status of legitimacy will be presumed from acknowledgement or treatment of the child as his child by the father.[37] In *Sher Afzal v. Shamin Firdaus* the court held that if the father admits that the relationship is not adulterous and treats the minor as his child, this will amount to an acknowledgement of paternity.[38] Further in *Asadullah Khan v. Abdul Hamid*, the High Court held that if the parents are separated but not divorced and there is no proof of a lack of access, a child born during that period is considered legitimate.[39] Finally, in *Munir Ahmad v Muhammad Saddique* the courts expressed the opinion that direct proof of legitimacy is not needed as it can be inferred from circumstances.[40]

The cases discussed above show that although the law is silent on the issue of acknowledgement of paternity, the courts have taken a liberal approach on the basis of the Islamic principle of acknowledgement to establish filiation. Again, one can see that the courts are generally reluctant to stigmatize a child and declare it illegitimate, and therefore every effort is made in favour of the child's legitimacy.

10.2.3 Establishing Paternity through a DNA Test

Although establishing paternity through DNA screening has been recognized by the courts, they are reluctant to apply this method as, due to the lack of scientific facilities, the possibility of error in conducting such tests is great. As a consequence,

---

[35] AIR 1916 Privy Council 27.

[36] See, for example, Ghulam Muhammad v. Muhammad Hussain, PLD 1978 Lahore 478, where the Lahore High Court held that where there is continuous cohabitation by the alleged parents and the father acknowledges the child, legitimacy of the child is established.

[37] PLD 1958 Karachi 420.

[38] PLD 1980 Supreme Court 228.

[39] PLD 1967 BJ 1.

[40] MLD 2005 Lahore 364.

the doctrine of the conjugal bed still prevails over establishing paternity through DNA screening. This is exemplified in the case of *Muhammad Arhad v Sughran Bibi and Others*, a Constitutional petition heard by the Lahore High Court. In that case, the petitioner had initially challenged the existence of *nasab* before the family court, claiming that the respondent did not perform her matrimonial obligations during the first month of the marriage and then left for Saudi Arabia after this month. The learned judge of the family court rejected the petitioner's application based on the results of a DNA test supporting a determination of *nasab*. The High Court, however, impugned the family court's reliance on the DNA test. Instead the court held that there was no evidence that the child was born after the divorce nor that the respondent had been committing adultery. The sole purpose of disowning the child was to avoid the liability to maintain the child. By referring to the writings of Islamic scholars, the court further held that evidence provided by a woman would be sufficient to prove parentage of a child.[41] For these reasons, the court was able to rule against the petitioner without relying on the DNA test.

In *Khizar Hayat v. Additional District Judge, Kabirwala* the Lahore High Court considered the knowledge of birth by the father and the entry of the child's name in the family tree by a local administrator, who was responsible for recording births, to be sufficient proof of acknowledgement.[42] The court said that a birth certificate, being a public document, is acceptable as proof and a presumption of truth is attached to it. The court further observed that it has become a common practice that in the event of a breakdown of marriage, extreme hatred develops between the spouses and due to this hatred fathers often refuse to acknowledge the child for the reason of either evading maintenance or depriving the child of an inheritance. The court held that this trend is not only damaging but also very dangerous for society and in such a situation a request for a DNA test is not proper. The court also expressed its concern regarding the accuracy of DNA tests in Pakistan due to the lack of sufficient training and the competence of the medical staff conducting such tests. The court finally held that an error in conducting the test could result in the child's being labelled as illegitimate and would thereby fail to fulfil the requirements of justice; moreover, it could jeopardize the child's future.

In a more recent case – *Muhammad Ashiq VS. Rani Bibi* – the learned judge of the Lahore High Court accepted the method of DNA testing as a 'valid criteria' for ascertaining *nasab*. In this case, the request for conducting a DNA test was made by the respondent wife, who herself with her child had undergone a DNA test but the petitioner father never did.[43] The child was born two months after the divorce. The court held that on the basis of Islamic principle of gestation period the child was legitimate. This case suggests that the judges allow a DNA test only in cases where they are certain about the validity of the marriage and the legitimacy of the child.

[41] Sections 146–149 of Majmooa-e-Qawaneen-e-Islam edited by Dr. Tanzeel-ur-Rehman as cited in Mohammad Arshad v Sughran Bibi, PLD 2008 Lahore 302.

[42] PLD 2010 Lahore 422.

[43] PLD 2016 Lahore 242.

The aforementioned judgments illustrate that although the courts in Pakistan recognize DNA testing as a valid scientific method for ascertaining the paternity of a child and establishing *nasab*, they are still hesitant about it. The courts are of the view that the conducting of DNA tests should not be allowed as a matter of routine and attending circumstances must be taken into consideration. The two main reasons for not going down the route of a DNA test are, firstly, the non-reliability of the test results due to the lack of proper laboratory equipment and training of the medical staff in Pakistan; and, secondly, a DNA test could lead to declaring a child as an illegitimate child. These cases also show that the courts are conscious of the fact that insistent requests by fathers to conduct a DNA test or insistent refusals to acknowledge the child as their own are very much linked to the issue of providing maintenance to the mother and the child.

10.3 Status of Children of Defective or Unknown Filiation

10.3.1 Children Born Out of Wedlock

10.3.1.1 Status of Such Children

In Pakistan the population of children and adolescents, ages zero to nineteen, is estimated to be around 82.05 million, which is projected to increase to 86 million in 2020.[44] Since the country's inception, the various governments in Pakistan have always subscribed to the view that the best care and protection for children can be provided by parents within the family institution. Therefore, all laws and judicial practices discourage any actions that lead to a breakup of families and that would deprive children of parental protection and care. However, there are still many instances where children need protection: Children born out of wedlock or children of culturally unaccepted or illicit relationships are often abandoned by their mothers/parents, usually in unattended areas on roadside pavements, garbage heaps, and streams.[45] A child born out of wedlock is considered as illegitimate (*najaiz*) and does not have any legal relationship with its father. Ali has argued that the issue of inheritance could be dealt with by following the Islamic injunction of abiding by one's duty to one's (foster) relations and by making a conscious effort to make a gift (*hiba*) to the child or by making a will of up to one-third of the foster parent's property.[46]

---

[44] Pakistan Economic Survey 2010–2011, Economic Adviser's Wing, Finance Division, Government of Pakistan, Islamabad.

[45] In Gilgit-Baltistan such children are called 'Nalbu' (illegitimate children) and are thrown into a water stream (*Nullah*) to meet their fate of death. One of those water streams in Skardu in the Northern area of Gilgit-Baltistan is known as 'Nalbu' (meaning the water stream of illegitimate children), labelled after the way it is utilized, that is to get rid of illegitimate children.

[46] Ali 2007, p 156.

As it stands today, however, there is no comprehensive legislation imposing obligations on the father to protect and care for their biological children. There is some reference to an illegitimate child in section 488 of the Criminal Procedure Code (Cr.PC 1898), according to which a father is responsible for providing maintenance to the mother and the child, whether legitimate or illegitimate.[47] This section was, however, omitted under the Federal Laws (Revision and Declaration) Ordinance XXVII of 1981 during the military dictatorship of General Zia ul Haq, when he took upon himself the process of an Islamization of laws in Pakistan. Unfortunately, no alternative legislation was introduced to protect the interests of illegitimate children. The rejection of such children is, however, against the very spirit of Islam, as the protection of children belongs to the essence of Islamic teachings.[48] It is thus the duty of the lawmakers to frame laws that protect the rights of children to a name, identity, property and inheritance, sponsorship in a family, healthcare, and education as well as laws that protect them from physical and moral humiliation.

It is interesting to note that the courts in Pakistan have taken a proactive approach towards compensating victims of rape and children born as a result of rape.[49] In 2015, the Lahore High Court in *Nadeem Masood v The State*[50] imposed an obligation upon the rapist under sections 544-A and 545 of the Cr.PC 1898 to make compensation to the child for the 'mental anguish and psychological damage' caused by his actions as well as to the mother who was raped. The court ordered the appellant, Nadeem Masood, to pay Rs. 1,000,000 to his illegitimate daughter born as a result of a rape for which he was convicted under section 376 of Pakistan Penal Code 1860.[51] By issuing such an order, the Lahore High Court invoked the right of appellate courts to order that compensation be paid under sections 544-A and 545 of the Cr.PC 1898. The payment of compensation did not legitimize the child, but it did render some financial support to the mother for maintenance of the child. The appellate court held that '[a] child has an undeniable right of life [that has] to be protected by the biological parents and the State … [the] right extends to children

[47] Section 488 Cr.PC states: (1) If any person having sufficient means neglects or refuses to maintain his wife or his legitimate or illegitimate child unable to maintain itself, … a Magistrate of the first class may, upon proof of such neglect or refusal, order such person to make a monthly allowance for the maintenance of his wife or such child, at such monthly rate, not exceeding four hundred rupees in the whole, as such Magistrate thinks fit and to pay the same to such person as the Magistrate from time to time directs. (2) Such allowance shall be payable from the date of the order, or if so ordered from the date of the application for maintenance.

[48] The Qur'an in Sura al-Fatir, verse 17, lays down the principle: 'No bearer of burdens can bear the burden of another,' which means that an illegitimate child in Islam bears no stigma for the sin of one or both parents.

[49] For further details see Ahmed 2015.

[50] PLD 2015 Lahore 4524; Criminal appeal No. 2066 of 2012.

[51] Pursuant to section 375 (v) of the PPC, a man is said to commit rape when he has sexual intercourse with a woman when she is less than sixteen years of age. This qualifies as rape irrespective of whether the woman gave her consent to sexual intercourse.

born as a result of rape and cannot be repudiated due to the unfortunate circumstances of their birth that they had no sway over'.[52]

Although there had been previous cases where the appellate courts ordered compensation for the victims of rape or for their heirs,[53] this case represents the first time that a child born from the act of rape has been compensated. Children born as a result of rape have never been considered to suffer from 'mental anguish and psychological damage', and thus have never been specifically compensated by the Pakistani Courts before. In this respect, the *Nadeem Masood* case is a landmark judgment that has not only recognized the right of the child to be compensated but also acknowledged the psychological trauma that a child goes through in such cases. This judgment is also significant in the sense that the court has concluded that under sections 544 and 545 of the Cr.PC, an appellate court can issue an order in favour of a child conceived as a 'result of the crime committed by the accused'.[54]

Further, an analysis of section 545 of Cr.PC 1898 makes it clear that court-ordered compensation is not restricted to the victim or her legal heirs but can be extended to 'any person' who has suffered from 'mental anguish or psychological damage caused by the offense'.[55] Furthermore, section 544-A(5) of Cr.PC vests in appellate courts the right to modify judgments regarding the compensation payable to all eligible parties. Thus, the appellate court can use these provisions to modify the trial court's judgment and order compensation to be paid to the child born due to rape.[56]

However, illegitimate and abandoned children still suffer discrimination. In an unreported case the Federal Shariat Court of Pakistan, while defending an illegitimate child's right to claim maintenance from the biological father, held that making the father pay maintenance does not amount to establishing *nasab*; rather, it only holds the father financially responsible for his actions.[57] The court considered it unfair to make the mother responsible for all needs of the child and not the father. However, this approach has not been followed by other courts.

---

52 PLD 2015 Lahore 4524; Criminal appeal No. 2066 of 2012 (n 1) para [14].

53 In *Mokha v Zulfiqar* PLJ 1978, Supreme Court 19 section 544(A) was declared as a 'mandatory provision' and the appellant was ordered to pay compensation to the legal heirs of the deceased since the trial court had failed to give any such directive. Similarly in *Muhammad Shakeel v The State* SCMR 2006 SC 1791, the fine imposed by the trial court was converted into compensation under section 544(A) that was awarded to the legal heirs of the deceased. In *Muhammad Younis v The State* 2002 SCMR 1308, compensation ordered for legal heirs was increased by the appellate court from Rs. 70,000 to Rs. 250,000 in the spirit of truly upholding the principles of equity and justice. In *Shehzad Ahmed alias Mithu v The State*, PCrLJ 2005 Federal Shariat Court 1316, the accused was asked to deposit compensation in the form of instalments as he did not have the means to pay all of it at once.

54 PLD 2015 Lahore 4524; Criminal appeal No. 2066 of 2012 para [15].

55 Criminal appeal No. 2066 of 2012 para [16].

56 Ahmed 2015.

57 As cited in Sabreen 2013, p 28.

10.3.1.2 Legislative Provisions at Provincial Level to Protect Children Born Out of Wedlock and Destitute Children

As children's rights have now become a provincial matter, in two provinces in Pakistan some laws have been enacted where we do find indirect reference to children born out of wedlock, e.g. the children of prostitutes and abandoned children, under the category of neglected or destitute children. As such, in section 3 (1) of the Punjab Destitute and Neglected Children Act 2004 (PDNCA 2004), the first piece of legislation enacted on that matter, there is a definition of destitute and neglected child, including children born out of wedlock and abandoned children.[58] Under section 20 of the PDNCA 2004, the court may entrust the custody of a child to an institution or to a suitable person until the child attains the age of eighteen years, or in exceptional cases custody could be awarded for a shorter period. Such person or institution have to execute a bond (with or without sureties) when undertaking the responsibility for the care, education, and well-being of the child. Under this section the court may order submission of periodical reports to the court by an authorized officer as to the welfare of the child. At the same time the court may issue an order to produce the child before the court in order to assure itself that the child is being properly looked after. The PDCNA 2004 also imposes punishment if the child is kept in contravention of the provisions of the Act. A person can be imprisoned for up to three years or be subject to a fine of up to fifty thousand rupees or both.[59]

Similar to the PDNCA 2004, the Khyber Pakhtunkhwa province also enacted a Child Protection and Welfare Act in 2010 (CPWA 2010). Under section 2 of the CPWA 2010, a 'child' is defined in conformity with Article 1 of the UN Convention on the Rights of the Child 1989 (UNCRC) as a natural person who has not attained the age of eighteen years. This act as well uses 'the best interests of child' as a basic principle in taking actions concerning children.

---

[58] The Act defines a destitute or neglected child as a child who: (i) is found begging; or (ii) is found without having any home or settled place of abode and without any ostensible means of subsistence; or (iii) has a parent or guardian who is unfit or incapacitated to exercise control over the child; or (iv) lives in brothel or with a prostitute or frequently visits any place being used for the purpose of prostitution or is found to associate with any prostitute or any other person who leads an immoral or depraved life; or (v) is being or is likely to be abused or exploited for immoral or illegal purpose or unconscionable gain; or (vi) is beyond the parental control; or (vii) has lost his parents or one of the parents and has no adequate source of income; or (viii) is victim of an offence punishable under this Act or any other law for the time being in force and his parent or guardian is convicted or accused for the commission of such offence; or (ix) is at risk owing to disability or child labour; or (x) is imprisoned with the mother or is born in a jail; or (xi) is abandoned by the parents or guardian.

[59] For instance, where the person in charge of the custody of the child wilfully assaults, ill-treats, neglects or abandons the child or exposes the child to or causes or procures the child for assault, ill-treatment, neglect, or abandonment, or exposes the child to not having or negligently fails to provide adequate food, clothes, medical aid, or lodging, that person will be subject to imprisonment.

The CPWA 2010 provides a comprehensive definition of a 'child at risk', which also includes orphaned and abandoned children and children born out of wedlock.[60] One of the positive outcomes of these changes is that child beggars on the street are no longer considered vagrants or offenders but are considered as children at risk who require complete protection and care through child protection systems and units. Under the CPWA 2010, a Child Welfare Commission has been appointed to improve the registration of birth rules and procedures.[61] Section 20 of the CPWA stipulates that upon information or receipt of complaint, a child protection officer in charge of the case management of children in need of protection is to initiate an inquiry into alleged violence and abuse of children. It is the responsibility of the child protection officer to produce the child before the court within twenty-four hours in order to establish the child's legal status. The court may then remove a child who is the victim of parental or family abuse from parental custody and provide a legal caretaker and/or an alternative protective service, i.e. a child protection institution.

This Act is certainly an improvement upon the previous legislation as it has extended the scope of the term child by including a range of children who need care and protection as offered by the State and society.

10.3.2 Children of Unknown Filiation, Foundlings and Registration of Births

Pakistan recognizes the registration of children at birth as a fundamental right. The legal obligation to register children at birth is provided by the Births, Deaths and Marriages Registration Act 1886, the Cantonment Act 1924, the National

[60] Section 2(e) states that 'child at risk' means a child in need of protection who; (i) is at risk, including an orphan, child with disabilities, child of migrant workers, child working and or living on the street, child in conflict with the law and child living in extreme poverty; (ii) is found begging; or (iii) is found without having any home or settled place of abode or without any ostensible means of subsistence; or (iv) has a parent or guardian who is unfit or incapacitated to exercise control over the child; or (v) lives in a brothel or with a prostitute or frequently visits any place being used for the purpose of prostitution or is found to associate with any prostitute or any other person who leads an immoral or depraved life; or (vi) is being or is likely to be abused or exploited for immoral or illegal purposes or gain; or (vii) is beyond the parental control; or (viii) is imprisoned with the mother or born in jail; (ix) has lost his parents or one of the parents and has no adequate source of income; or (x) is victim of an offence punishable under this Act or any other law for the time being in force and his parent or guardian is convicted or accused for the commission of such offence; or (xi) is left abandoned by his parent or parents as the case may be, which will include a child born out of wedlock and left abandoned by his parent.

[61] Section 4(k) of the CPWA gives powers to the Child Protection Welfare Commission to 'improve rules and procedures concerning compulsory birth registration and registration of children without birth documents including registration of an abandoned child with the State filling for his parentage'.

Registration Act 1973, the National Data Registration Authority Ordinance 2000 and the Local Government Ordinance 2001.

Under section 9(1) of the National Database Registration Ordinance 2000, the authority is bound to register every citizen of Pakistan, inside or outside the country, who has attained the age of eighteen years.[62] This Ordinance also includes normative provisions regarding civil registration of children and stipulates the registration of the child by his/her guardian/parent not later than one month after his/her birth. The National Database Registration Authority (NADRA) is responsible for the registration process and for issuing the Child Registration Certificate, also known as 'Form B'. This certificate, or Form B, is legal proof of a person's date of birth, parentage, and place of birth.

Until recently NADRA was not issuing any such 'Form B' to children whose filiation was unknown or that were abandoned by their parents (*lawaris*). 'Father'/ 'husband'/or 'unknown' are the only three choices available for the child's birth registration. There was no column for 'guardian' in the registration form, and if a child could not be named after their father or someone's husband, they were registered as unknown (*na-maloom*). As a result children without known filiation could not get themselves registered with NADRA and were unable to get a Computerised National Identity Card (CNIC); and thus they were being deprived of their fundamental right to be citizens of Pakistan. This affected not only orphaned and abandoned children but also children who were legally adopted by single women.

Under the new policy, it is mandatory that the orphanage in question is registered with NADRA, and the orphanage is to provide the CNIC of the guardian. In case of unknown filiation, the orphanage is to provide an affidavit stating the supposed names of parents. NADRA will issue a CNIC to children with unknown filiation residing in registered orphanages. In this way such children will not be deprived of their fundamental right to identity upon reaching eighteen years of age.

In situations involving an unmarried guardian, where the court orders adoption of a child in favour of unmarried male/female, NADRA will process such cases for the issuance of a CNIC on the production of the original court order. As the NADRA data structure does not support proceedings initiated by an unmarried applicant, necessary amendments in the existing data capturing system will have to be introduced.

---

[62] Section 9(1) Every citizen in or out of Pakistan who has attained the age of eighteen years shall get himself and a parent or guardian of every citizen who has not attained that age shall, not later than one month after the birth of such citizen, get such citizen registered in accordance with the provisions of this Ordinance: Provided that the Authority may, on case-to-case basis, extend the period for registration of a citizen who has not attained the age of eighteen years: Provided further that all such citizens who stand validly registered under any law immediately before the commencement of this Ordinance shall be deemed to have been registered under this Ordinance and their registration shall, subject to sections 17, 18 and 30 remain valid till the expiry of two years from the commencement of this Ordinance, or such time as may be notified by the Federal Government, or till such time as such citizen is registered afresh as hereinafter provided, whichever is earlier.

In Human Rights Case No. 22607-S of 2011, dated 29 May 2014, the Supreme Court of Pakistan acknowledged the policy of NADRA for the registration of orphan children. The policy provides for the mechanism of registering grown-up children as well as the registration of babies. This policy was taken on board when the Senate of Pakistan (Pakistan's upper house of the parliament) was considering the Unattended Orphans (Rehabilitation and Welfare) Bill 2016 in its meeting of the Business Advisory Committee, held on 19 May 2016; the Bill was being drafted and enacted for the Islamabad Capital Territory. According to the statement of objects and reasons presented by the then minister-in-charge, the bill was introduced because:

> The un-attended orphans and unknown parentage children in Pakistan are facing many problems. Our society is also facing problems due to non-provision of facilities like education, health and security of life to such children. They may involve in crimes and other social evils. The legislation to protect the rights and provision of facilities to such children and welfare schemes for them has not been launched so far. After proper legislation and providing said facilities to such children, society can succeed to make them respectable and useful citizens. This legislation is very important and requirement of the day.

Unfortunately, the proposed bill was not prioritized by the government and for multiple reasons lapsed at the National Assembly of Pakistan (Lower House) despite having been passed by the senate of Pakistan. However, the government of Pakistan has initiated programmes for the registration of orphans and abandoned children with the help of UNICEF as well as other NGOs, government agencies, and local union councils. Measures for registration of birth have been taken at various provincial levels.[63]

---

[63] In KP, the Department of Local Government has been working with UNICEF and NADRA to take measures for birth registration. In this regard, birth registration is being done by a computerized local union data system. In Balouchistan, a steering committee has been set up for birth registration under the chairmanship of the Secretary Local Government to encourage birth registration. The Child Protection Wing of the Federally Administered Tribal Areas (FATA) Secretariat considers birth registration one of the most important issues; therefore, in association and with the support from the political administration of FATA, NADRA has introduced a program for birth registration of children in FATA regions. In 2010, the local government in Azad Jammu and Kashmir (AJK) in collaboration with NADRA launched a project on birth registration. The National Commission for Child Welfare and Development (NCCWD) has drafted the Child Protection Policy (CPP) for ICT, which includes provisions for the improvement of rules and procedures related to compulsory birth registration and registration of all children without birth documents. Additionally, the KP CPWA 2010 (section 4(k)) gives powers to the Child Protection Welfare Commission to 'improve rules and procedures concerning compulsory birth registration and registration of children without birth documents including registration of an abandoned child with the State filling for his parentage'. In Sindh, KP, Balouchistan, Punjab, Islamabad, AJK and Gilgit-Baltistan, NADRA and local governments have in association with UNICEF organized consultations for the promotion of birth registration. UNICEF has developed a communication strategy and a nationwide campaign launched in 2012 to support the review of normative and regulatory provisions for cooperation between local governments and NADRA for birth registration, and an action plan is being applied in twenty-two districts.

10.4 General Legal Schemes of Protection and Care

10.4.1 Procedure for Guardianship of Children Born Out of Wedlock and Foundlings

Although the prohibition on *adoption* in its Western sense is explicit and foster placement is not recognized in Pakistan under any law,[64] there are certain informal arrangements by which childless Pakistani couples can take on children.[65] The term '*laiy palak*' is often used for adopted children. In most of the cases childless couples agree with their siblings to take on their nieces or nephews. In some cases, boys were adopted by couples who had only daughters.[66] These 'adoptions' are conducted on an informal basis with the mutual consent of both natural and adoptive parents and are not necessarily endorsed by court orders. Besides their own relatives, orphans (*yateem*) and foundlings (*laqit* or *lawaris*) are also 'adopted' by childless couples. In Pakistan 'adoption' is a form of guardianship under which a child is placed in the care of a competent family by judicial decree while ensuring the child's knowledge of his or her filiation. The GWA 1890 makes provision for an individual to obtain legal guardianship of a child. This can be done in conjunction with the State, but it is more common that an orphanage or a third party is involved.

The applicants have to seek a guardianship order in respect of the child (orphan or foundling) from a guardian's court. If a child is abandoned in a hospital or medical clinic, as a first step the hospital will make an application to the deputy commissioner of that area, who will assess the application. The assessment takes the form of a home study report accompanied by the usual references and an assessment of the applicants' eligibility and suitability to provide a home environment likely to safeguard the welfare of the child. If approved, the child is then transferred from an orphanage to their care, and they will be vested with custody and guardianship rights. If the child's parents are known to the authorities, and the applicants wish to 'adopt', then all parties will have to enter into an irrevocable, bilateral, intra-familial agreement in writing in which the birth parent/s clearly waive any right to reclaim the child. To adopt a child from the orphanage the applicants have to seek a guardianship certificate from the court.

[64] Ali and Khan 2017, p 320.

[65] Ali and Khan 2017, p 320.

[66] There are no official statistics available, but there is anecdotal evidence which shows various forms of informal adoptions.

10.4.1.1 Appointment of Guardians by the Courts

Guardianship orders are granted under the provision of section 7 of the GWA 1890.[67] Any person, including a relative or friend, interested in becoming a guardian can apply to the court under the provisions of the GWA 1890.[68] The procedure for such an application is stated in section 10 of the GWA 1890, and no order should be made unless notice of the application is given to persons interested in the minor. During the court proceedings, the district court exercises parental jurisdiction over the child. The court is also empowered to award temporary custody and order protection of the person and property of the minor during the maintenance of the case.

The welfare of the minor is always taken into consideration by the courts when appointing a guardian.[69] The court considers factors such as the age, sex, and religion of the child, the character and capacity of the proposed guardian, and the guardian's closeness to the child. The court also has to consider the wishes, if any, of the deceased parents and any existing or previous relations of the proposed guardian with the minor or his or her property. The GWA 1890 also lays down that if the child is old enough to form an intelligent preference, then such preference should also be considered by the court when appointing a guardian.[70]

10.4.1.2 Rights and Duties of the Guardian or Adoptive Parents

Statutory law does not specifically lay down rules regarding the rights and obligations of those who assume responsibility for children born out of wedlock and foundlings. However, under the GWA 1890 a guardian is responsible for ensuring that the minor is supported, fed, housed, clothed, and educated in a manner suitable

---

[67] Section 7 Power of the Court to make order as to guardianship. (1) Where the Court is satisfied that it is for the welfare of a minor that order should be made: (a) appointing a guardian of his person or property, or both; or (b) declaring a person to be such a guardian, the Court may make an order accordingly. (2) An order under this Section shall imply the removal of any guardian who has not been appointed by will or other instrument or appointed or declared by the Court. (3) Where a guardian has been appointed by will or other instrument, or appointed or declared by the Court, an order under this Section appointing or declaring another person to be guardian in his stead shall not be made until the powers of the guardian appointed or declared as aforesaid have ceased under the provisions of this Act.

[68] Section 8 Persons entitled to apply for order. An order shall not be made under the last foregoing Section except on the application of: (a) the person desirous of being, or claiming to be, the guardian of the minor; or (b) any relative or friend of the minor; or (c) the Collector of the District or other local area within which the minor ordinarily resides or in which he has property; or (d) the Collector having authority with respect to the class to which the minor belongs.

[69] Sections 7, 8, 9, and 10 Guardians and Wards Act 1890.

[70] Section 17 Guardians and Wards Act 1890.

to his or her position in life, and to the fortune which he or she is likely to enjoy upon attaining the age of majority. The guardian appointed by the court is entitled to such allowance as the court thinks fit for the minor's care and for the effort that he or she expends while undertaking the duties. The allowance can be paid out of the property of the ward.

A guardian appointed by the district court with the court's permission cannot remove the ward from the limits of the court's jurisdiction. The permission can be special or general and can be specified in the court order. Illegal removal of a ward from the court's jurisdiction is punishable by a fine not exceeding Rs. 1000 or by a jail term of up to six months. It was held in *Rabia Khatun v Azizuddin and others* that 'an adoptive father taking … the position of de-facto guardian of an adopted child is regarded as guardian de-jure and [the] rule of making [a] gift of property in favour of such child is the same as in the case of [a] gift by [the] real father/mother to his/her son/daughter'.[71] The court in this case followed the Islamic principle of making a gift where the guardian can make a gift of his property to the adopted child. Later, in the *Mariam Bibi* case, the Lahore High Court also followed the same principle and laid down the rule that 'adoption … does not give the adopted child a right to inherit the estate of the adoptive parents; nor does it deprive him or her from inheriting the estate of the real parents. However, the adoptive parents have the option of writing up to one-third of their estate for their adopted child'.[72]

10.4.1.3 Revocation of Guardianship

The family court has the jurisdiction to revoke guardianship on the application of any interested person or on its own motion, and it may remove a guardian appointed or declared by it, or even a guardian appointed by will. Reasons for a revocation of guardianship could be an abuse of trust, failure and incapacity to perform the duties of trust, ill-treatment or neglecting the child/ward, including other grounds as stated in section 39 of the Guardians and Wards Act 1890.[73]

A guardian may also apply to the court to be discharged from the responsibility of being a guardian. A person also ceases to be a guardian in the case of his or her death; upon the ward reaching majority; upon a female ward's marriage to a husband who is not unfit to be her guardian; or upon the court itself assuming superintendence of the minor.

---

[71] PLD 1965 Supreme Court 665.

[72] PLD 2015 Lahore 336.

[73] Other grounds include contumacious disregard of any of the GWA's provisions or of any court orders; conviction of an offence implying a defect of character, having an interest adverse to the faithful performance of his duties, ceasing to reside within the local limits of the court's jurisdiction and bankruptcy or insolvency in the case of a guardian of property.

10.4.2 *Divorce of the Adoptive Parents and the Best Interests of the Child*

In cases where adoptive parents have divorced, the courts have followed the 'best interests of the child' principle in giving custody of the adopted child to one of the adoptive parents. In *Mst. Irfana Shaheen v Abid Waheed*[74] the Lahore High Court ordered the recovery of the minor girl from the custody of her adoptive father and awarded custody to the petitioner mother. As to the facts of the case, Abid Waheed had married the petitioner in 1992. The spouses, being issueless, approached a social institution run under the control of the Social Welfare Department, Government of the Punjab, and adopted a girl aged about one month. Subsequently, the relations between the spouses became strained, and the respondent husband ousted the petitioner wife from the house together with the minor. The petitioner, having taken shelter in the house of her parents, filed suit for dissolution of marriage. The suit was decreed by the learned judge of the family court at Kahuta (vide judgment dated 5 December 2000) and marriage was dissolved on the ground of *khula*. The mother later sought custody of the minor, who was allegedly forcibly abducted from her by the respondent on dissolution of marriage and who was, despite repeated requests, not returned to the petitioner. The mother now claimed the girl on the basis that after the dissolution of the marriage the man – not being the biological father of the child – would have no special or preferential right over a female relative so as to retain custody of the minor child. The court in this case held that 'the female partner in adoption had accepted her duty and responsibility of [the] upbringing of the child with motherly love and affection and such responsibility could not be discharged by the male partner … therefore the adoptive mother will exclusively be entitled to custody of the female child'.[75] The court further held that the welfare of the child would similarly demand that the minor girl should remain in the custody of the female partner to the adoption.

10.4.3 *Constructive Guardianship and the Fiduciary Relationship of a Guardian to a Ward*

Under section 20 of the GWA 1890, a guardian stands in a fiduciary relation to the ward and must not make any profit out of his office.[76] In the case of *Mariam Bibi through Abida Parveen v Naseer Ahmad and 2 others*,[77] the question before the

[74] PLD 2002 Lahore 283.

[75] PLD 2002 Lahore 285.

[76] A fiduciary relation means that a person is in a position of trust, or occupies a position of power and confidence with respect to another, such that this person was obliged by various rules of law to act solely in the interest of the other, whose rights he had to protect.

[77] PLD 2015 Lahore 336.

Lahore High Court was whether the husband/adoptive father was compelled to pay maintenance allowance for a minor who had been adopted during the time of his and the adoptive mother's marriage. By using the doctrine of 'constructive guardianship', the court held that the adoptive father must provide for the maintenance of the adopted child. It continued that per the concept of adoption in Islam, the wife could not claim maintenance from the husband for a minor who had no milk-relationship with the adoptive mother; however, from the perspective of the concept of 'constructive guardianship', the petitioner/adoptive mother was under the GWA 1890 entitled to claim a maintenance allowance for such an adopted minor. The court observed that 'if adoptive parents voluntarily undertake to perform the noble task of taking care of a minor, they not only create a relationship of trust with the minor but also assume the role and status of "constructive guardian" of a minor'.[78] The trust and constructive guardianship also created a fiduciary obligation/relationship between the adopted parents and the minor. In the present case, the minor was adopted by the parents and remained with the adoptive parents for a considerable period of time, and the husband/respondent had admitted that the minor was adopted and presented her as his daughter before the public-at-large. The court held that the respondent/husband was therefore obligated to pay a maintenance allowance for his adopted daughter. The impugned orders were set aside, and the constitutional petition was allowed.

10.4.4 Foreign Adoptions

Pakistan is not a signatory to the 1993 Hague Convention on Protection of Children and Cooperation in Respect of Intercountry Adoption and is therefore not a Hague Convention country. However, the movement of children across international borders for the purpose of adoption is generally allowed in Pakistan. It is possible for prospective adopters to adopt a child residing in Pakistan as long as the procedures of both the countries are adhered to and the eligibility requirements of both countries are met. Such adoptions include children born out of wedlock and foundlings. In most cases the 'born out of wedlock' children and foundlings who are subject to adoption come from orphanages or private child welfare institutions. Adopting parents have to obtain legal custody of the child by applying for guardianship in a civil/family court in Pakistan under the provisions of the GWA 1890. The procedure for such application is stated in section 10 of the GWA 1890. After obtaining a guardianship decree from the court, adopting parents will have to obtain a 'Form B', also called a Child Registration Certificate, from the offices of the NADRA and get a CNIC number issued for the baby. Once adopting parents have received this, they can apply for a Pakistani passport for the child. Parents who

[78] PLD 2015 Lahore 337.

reside overseas can apply for a National Identity Card for Overseas Pakistanis (NICOP) for their child.

It is also essential that adoptive parents must be Muslims, if applying as a couple they must be married for at least three years, and at least one of the prospective adoptive parents must be of Pakistani origin. Christian prospective adoptive parents will only be considered if the child was from a Christian family. Single prospective adoptive parents are accepted, although in practice it can be hard to achieve a placement.[79]

In the recent case of *Ms Zahra Bhola and Shelina Saleh Mohammed*,[80] where the parties sought permission to adopt two infant babies from the CEENA Child Welfare Centre Gilgit-Baltistan, the Appellate Supreme Court of Gilgit-Baltistan addressed two specific issues: firstly, the precise question of whether the guardian court judges in Gilgit-Baltistan had jurisdiction to issue a guardianship certificate for a deserted child that would allow a non-Pakistani citizen to take custody of the child beyond the territorial jurisdiction of the court; and, secondly, whether a Muslim or a non-Muslim foreigner could be given custody of a Muslim or non-Muslim child without the intervention of any official agencies of the government of Gilgit-Baltistan and the government of Pakistan.[81] The court held that:

> The Guardian Courts in Gilgit-Baltistan in their respective jurisdiction may exercise power under GWA 1890, but may not appoint a person as Guardian of a Child in the Custody of an Orphanage Centre, who is not otherwise entitled to Guardianship of the Child. The adoption and appointment of adoptive parents as Guardian of a Child with the consent of natural parents/Guardian is permissible but a stranger to a parentless child in custody of Orphanage Center or a child whose parentage is not known cannot be appointed as Guardian without the permission of Home Department, Government of Gilgit-Baltistan.

The Court further held that the adopted child cannot be taken outside of the jurisdiction of the court in Gilgit-Baltistan without the special permission of the court, nor can such a child be taken out of the country without prior permission of the Ministry of Interior for the government of Pakistan.

The appellate court held that the orphanage centre must follow the procedure under the Control of Orphanage Act 1958 to create a guardianship certificate in the

[79] IAC 2016.

[80] SMC No. 12/2010.

[81] Gilgit-Baltistan, formerly known as the Northern Areas, is the northernmost administrative territory in Pakistan. According to the UNSC Resolution of 1947, the territory is part of the disputed Kashmir region. In 2009, it was granted limited autonomy and renamed to Gilgit-Baltistan via the Self-Governance Order signed by Pakistan's president Asif Ali Zardari, which also aimed to empower the people of Gilgit-Baltistan. The order granted self-rule to the people of Gilgit-Baltistan, by creating an elected Gilgit-Baltistan legislative assembly and a Gilgit-Baltistan council. Gilgit-Baltistan thus gained a *de facto* province-like status without constitutionally becoming a part of Pakistan. Currently, Gilgit-Baltistan is neither a province nor a state. It has a semi-provincial status. However, real power rests with the governor and not with the chief minister or the elected assembly. The Pakistani government has rejected Gilgit-Baltistani calls for integration with Pakistan on the grounds that it would jeopardize its demands that the whole Kashmir issue be resolved according to UN resolutions.

name of the natural or adoptive parents, as the case may be; in the case of unknown filiation of a child this is to be done in a common Muslim name and the orphanage centre may obtain registration accordingly from NADRA on the basis of a guardianship certificate to be issued by the court of competent jurisdiction. A guardianship certificate will not be issued for a parentless child without proper verification of the antecedents of the person seeking guardianship, and NADRA authorities may register the child on the basis of the guardianship certificate.

The appellate court in this case laid down the rules regulating record-keeping by the orphanages. The honourable judge held that the orphanage centre must immediately inform the Home Department of the government of Gilgit-Baltistan upon taking a child and must maintain the records of all children in the custody of the orphanage centre under the authority of the Home Department. The appellate court also laid down the rule that the orphanage centre should not accept the custody of a child of unknown filiation without obtaining undertakings regarding the origin of the child as given by the person who brings the child to an orphanage centre. Finally, the appellate court also clearly stated that an adopted child cannot be transferred from one country to another without prior notification to NADRA authorities and also to the relevant governmental agency of the country of the adoptive parents.

This judgment is significant as the court not only clearly interpreted the various provisions of the law but also sought the views of different Muslim sects in Gilgit-Baltistan as to the concept of adoption and the right of an adopted child in Islam. It also decided the case on the basis of the opinions expressed by official agencies in Saudi Arabia and as found in the *Fatwas* of renowned *Ulemas* with reference to Surah Al-Ahzab in the Qur'an. This case suggests that in the absence of specific legislation the courts in Pakistan take into account a range of sources, including the Qur'an, Sunnah, and the expert opinions of Islamic scholars.

In another case, a childless couple living in the US were allowed to adopt a child in Pakistan. The petitioners in this case were issued a guardianship certificate with regard to the parentless child adopted by them.[82] The court in this case emphasized the significance of adoption, holding that

> a deserted parentless child has got the full right to be adopted by genuine adoptive parents who can provide the facility of good up-bringing, good education and fruitful life. Any individual who can be in a good financial position to provide the facility to a child should be encouraged instead of creating hurdles and problems or discouragements.[83]

The court further observed that encouraging adoption of children by couples will relieve the burden on orphanages and welfare institutions as it can lead to genuine, sound individuals sharing the burden of providing home, shelter, education etc. to needy children so as to make them honourable members of the society.

[82] Dr. Shahid Iqbal v Public at Large and Another Respondent C.P.L.A. No. 10 of 2013.

[83] Dr. Shahid Iqbal v Public at Large and Another Respondent C.P.L.A. No. 10 of 2013.

However, in recent years some countries have imposed a ban on child adoptions from Pakistan, and Canada is one such country. In July 2013 the Canadian government imposed a ban on the grounds that Pakistan had no legal equivalent matching Canada's rules on the transfer of parenting responsibilities. Pakistani law prohibits adoption, instead recognizing a form of guardianship called *kafalah*; therefore, such adoption placements would violate Canada's obligations under the Hague Convention on Protection of Children and Co-operation in Respect of Intercountry Adoption. This decision of the Canadian government has left in limbo many prospective would-be-parents who were in the process of adopting children from Pakistan.

10.4.5 Other Institutional Measures for the Protection of Destitute Children and Children Without Filiation

Under various laws, alternative care institutions have been set up for children at risk or children needing care and protection. A National Child Protection Centre (NCPC) was set up in 2007 to provide temporary shelter to child survivors of violence as well as to homeless, street, and runaway children. It also provides psychological counselling and social, legal, and medical assistance and helps in the rehabilitation, reunification, and reintegration of these children. The NCCWD, the CSOs and other stakeholders evaluate the existing care policies for the care institutions on a regular basis. All concerned government departments receive detailed reviews of the alternative care institutions on a monthly, quarterly, bi-annual, and annual basis.[84]

In each province different types of child care institutions have been set up and governed by different sets of laws. For example, orphanages are set up by the Orphanage Act 1976, and in KP child protection institutions are set up under CPWA 2010. However, some of the new institutions need to be brought under the law, such as the Police Child Protection Centres in Peshawar and Quetta and the NCPC in Islamabad.

Orphanages and welfare homes have been set up also by non-governmental organizations and by private individuals. Such institutions and individuals include

[84] All alternative care institutions are established in accordance with laws, rules, and regulations and are regularly monitored by the relevant departments and CSOs. Monitoring teams highlight issues of governance and the quality of facilities for redressal. In KP, under the CPWA, there has been improvement in monitoring and coordination. Between October 2009 and November 2012, a total of 335 child protection committees were formed in eight districts to monitor and respond to cases of protection. They have also held regular awareness raising and coordination meetings with the line departments at the district level. By November 2012, a total of thirty-six district coordination meetings (DCMs) had been conducted in the Peshawar, Mardan, Swabi, Buner, Kohat, Charsadda, and Abbottabad districts.

the Edhi Foundation, Anjuman Kashana-e-Itfal-o-Naunehal, SOS Children's Village of Pakistan, the Ansar Burney Trust, Hope, Didar Karim, and the Cenna Welfare Organization to name a few. These institutions rehabilitate lost, runaway, and kidnapped children as well as children who are victims of violence. It may be noted that these institutions are considered to be 'last resort' arrangements as State and society consider that a child should live in a family environment. A '*Jhoola* Scheme' has been introduced by these welfare institutions, which encourages leaving newly born children in a cradle adjoining the office buildings of these institutions rather than simply abandoning them on garbage heaps and roadsides. These unclaimed children are afterwards handed over to desiring new parents. According to a report of the Edhi Foundation, 20,000 abandoned babies have been saved by putting *Jhoola* (cradles) in front of Edhi's offices/centres.

Similarly, in the province of Punjab under the PDNCA, Child Protection Welfare Boards (CPWBs) have been established in seven cities. For the period 2008–2011, the CPWBs under 'the Socio Economic Development of Destitute & Neglected Children's Families' project rehabilitated 10,250 destitute and neglected children's families, addressed the socio-economic needs of families, and developed the capabilities of the most vulnerable families and persons with disabilities.[85]

Alongside legislative enactments and institutional setups, other measures taken by the provincial governments include training sessions for staff working at the various institutions that rescue, protect, rehabilitate, and reunify children with their families. These sessions are being conducted across the country by government departments with the help of CSOs and United Nations agencies.

Unfortunately, despite these measures alternative care for abandoned and illegitimate children is still grossly inadequate and very poor.[86] There is a great deal of concern regarding the treatment of children in both public and private sector institutions. Abandoned children usually end up on the streets, and few are accommodated in these welfare institutions. Social biases and prejudices against such children are still prevalent, and little has been done to change the general perception of such children.[87]

The lack of statistical data is another issue that requires the government's serious attention. In its concluding observations on the fifth periodic report submitted by Pakistan, the UN Committee on the Rights of the Child has also raised the issue of providing data (disaggregated by age, sex, type of disability, geographical location, and ethnic origin) on the number of children abandoned by their families.[88]

---

85 The Punjab Social Welfare Department has established model institutions, like Negehban and Chaman, to provide institutional care to the marginalized sections of society. In the reporting period, these institutions have provided services to 13,021 children and families.

86 Kalanauri (n.d.).

87 Kalanauri (n.d.), p 5.

88 List of Issues, Seventy-Second Session, Item four of the provisional agenda.

10.5 Conclusion

In the absence of clear and specific legislation dealing with the issue of establishing filiation, the courts in Pakistan have played a significant role in setting out rules regarding *nasab* and in particular the filiation of children born out of wedlock. The judges have in the process used their discretionary powers to widen the scope of legitimacy and to establish *nasab*. The approach of the judiciary in Pakistan has been to protect the interests of children born out of wedlock, to hold their fathers responsible, and to prevent fathers from severing their blood relationship with their natural children. Pakistani courts have taken a lenient approach to avoid declaring children as illegitimate particularly in irregular marriages, where the offspring are recognized as legitimate.

Since the *Qanun-e-Shahadat* Order 1984 does not distinguish between regular and irregular marriages, it is suggested here that irregular marriages should be included in section 128 of the *Qanun-e-Shahadat* Order, as under Hanafi law children born into an irregular marriage are considered legitimate. Moreover, clear rules should be laid down in relation to inheritance and the maintenance of children born in irregular marriages.

Last but not least, some legislative and institutional measures have been taken at the provincial level to provide protection to orphans, children born out of wedlock, and destitute children, yet there is room for further improvement. There is a need to set up support mechanisms for abandoned children and to improve the living conditions in orphanages, especially the State-run ones. The efficiency of existing institutions should be improved by allocating more financial, technical, and human resources and by regularly scrutinizing how those resources are being used for the benefit and welfare of children.

References

Ahmed OS (2015) Compensation Payable by Convicted Rapists to Their Illegitimate Children. LUMS Law Journal vol. 2. https://sahsol.lums.edu.pk/law-journal/compensation-payable-convicted-rapists-their-illegitimate-children. Accessed 25 October 2018.

Ali SS (2007) A Comparative Perspective of the Convention on the Rights of the Child and the Principles of Islamic Law: Law Reform and Children's Rights in Muslim Jurisdictions. In: UNICEF (ed) Protecting the World's Children: Impact of the Convention on the Rights of the Child in Diverse Legal Systems. Cambridge University Press, Cambridge, pp 142–208.

Ali SS, Khan SS (2017) Evolving Conceptions of Children's Rights: Some Reflections on Muslim States' Engagement with the UN Convention on the Rights of the Child. In: Yassari N et al. (eds) Parental Care and the Best Interests of the Child in Muslim Countries. T.M.C. Asser Press, The Hague, pp 285–324.

Cheema SA (2016) DNA Evidence in Pakistani Courts: An Analysis. LUMS Law Journal vol 3. https://sahsol.lums.edu.pk/law-journal/dna-evidence-pakistani-courts-analysis. Accessed 6 December 2018.

Fyzee AAA (2005) Outlines of Muhammadan Law, 5th edn. Oxford University Press, New Delhi.

IAC (2016) Brief Guide – April 2016, The Islamic Republic of Pakistan. www.icacentre.org.uk/media/1125/the-islamic-republic-of-pakistan.pdf. Accessed 6 December 2018.

Kalanauri ZI (n.d.) Islamic Law and Adoption in Pakistan. http://zklawassociates.com/wp-content/uploads/2012/03/ISLAMIC-LAW-AND-ADOPTION.pdf. Accessed 25 October 2018.

Mahmood T (1972) Presumption of Legitimacy under the Evidence Act: A Century of Action and Reaction. Journal of the Indian Law Institute (Special Issue) 78–89.

Munir MA (2006) Family Courts in Pakistan: In Search of 'Better Remedies' for Women and Children. LAWASIA Journal. http://ssrn.com/abstract=1922837. Accessed 26 October 2018.

Sabreen M (2013) Parentage: A Comparative Study of Islamic and Pakistani Law. Frontiers of Legal Research 1(2):21–36.

Saksena KP (1972) Need for a Code of Muslim Law. In: Tahir Mahmood (ed) Islamic Law in Modern India. I.L.I., New Delhi, pp 133–137.

Ayesha Shahid is senior lecturer in law at Coventry University in the United Kingdom. Her research interests are broadly in the area of international human rights law (gender, migration and informal labor) and Islamic family law (post-divorce maintenance rights for Muslim women, child rights and Islamic family law in the West). Her monograph *Silent Voices, Untold Stories: Women Domestic Workers in Pakistan and their Struggle for Empowerment* was published by Oxford University Press in 2010. She has recently edited a book on the history of international law and Islam with Prof. Ignacio De La Rasilla, *International Law and Islam: Historical Explorations* (Brill 2018). She is also the associate editor of the *Asian Yearbook of International Human Rights and Humanitarian Law* (Brill). She has carried out a number of research projects for the Asia Foundation, the International Labour Organization, the Human Rights Commission of Pakistan, the Higher Education Commission of Pakistan and the Max Planck Institute for Comparative and International Private Law. She was awarded a research fellowship in 2016–17 by the Max Planck Institute to conduct research on Muslim women's rights to post-divorce maintenance in Pakistan and Iran. She also received the Warwick Postgraduate Research Fellowship Award in 2002 and the International Research Fellowship Award of the Center for Human Rights at Columbia University in 2000 and 2002.

Isfandyar Ali Khan is currently senior partner of S&K Partnership, a law and policy consulting firm in Peshawar, Pakistan, and has been supporting an international consulting firm in alternative dispute resolution (ADR)/community-based dispute resolution (CBDR) project management in Khyber Pakhtunkhwa (KP) province in Pakistan for the past two years. For over five years, he was associated with the alternate dispute resolution project of IFC/World Bank Group as a project officer and was instrumental in supporting the development of the Karachi Centre for Dispute Resolution (now known as the National Centre for Dispute Resolution) and the launch of mediation practices in Lahore, Punjab province. He is currently serving as provincial vice-president (KP) of the Pakistan Mediators Association. Prior to joining IFC in 2008, he worked as a project coordinator for UNDP in Vientiane, Laos (2006/07) and a young professional officer at UNDP Islamabad in Pakistan (2005/06). He has worked with Aurat Publication and Information Services Foundation (2005) in Peshawar and at the law firm Afridi, Shah and Minallah in Peshawar (2003–2005). He has a strong interest in dispute settlement, rule of law, democracy, governance, access to justice, human and child rights, investment climate, and environmental issues.

Chapter 11
Saudi Arabia

Dominik Krell

Contents

Abstract Saudi Arabia's religious foundations shape the legal discourse on filiation (*nasab*) and the care of children in need. Saudi judges have to be trained in Islamic jurisprudence (*fiqh*) and, due to the absence of a codified law, they refer directly to the primary sources of Islamic law and *fiqh* books in their judgements. On some legal questions, as I show in this chapter, Saudi jurists depart from mainstream Islamic law in order to protect *nasab* or grant *nasab* to children who otherwise would be without a legal father. Leading Saudi scholars have extended the Islamic ruling on orphans to foundlings and children without filiation and thereby allowed foster care for various children in need. Foster care, however, does not lead to a full child-parent relationship. In order to be eligible for foster care, a

Dominik Krell is a research associate within the Research Group 'Changes in God's Law – An Inner Islamic Comparison of Family and Succession Law' at the Max Planck Institute for Comparative and International Private Law, Hamburg.

D. Krell (✉)
Max Planck Institute for Comparative and International Private Law, Mittelweg 187, 20148 Hamburg, Germany
e-mail: krell@mpipriv.de

N. Yassari et al. (eds.), *Filiation and the Protection of Parentless Children*, https://doi.org/10.1007/978-94-6265-311-5_11

member of the potential foster family is advised to breastfeed the child to create milk kinship. However, milk kinship does not entitle foster children to inheritance and maintenance rights even though they legally become members of the foster family. The generous help of the Saudi government compensates for the foster children's lack of financial rights.

Keywords Saudi Arabia · Filiation · Children born out of wedlock · Foundlings · Maximum time of pregnancy in Islam · DNA tests

11.1 Introduction

11.1.1 The Importance of Genealogy

Despite significant social and economic transformations during the last century, the bond between the rulers of the al-Sa^c^ūd family and the community of Islamic scholars (*^c^ulamā'*) continues to shape the Saudi state and its legal system. Notwithstanding the Islamic scholars' general scepticism towards tribal[1] belonging and especially notions of tribal supremacy,[2] genealogy has long played a key role in Saudi Arabia, not only in politics but also in social organisation. Today, even as the Saudi state administers the life of its citizens, genealogy remains the key facet of Saudi identity. As Sebastian Maisel, a scholar of tribal identity in Saudi Arabia puts it: 'The large majority of Saudi citizens define their identity first by bloodlines and then geographically'.[3] The importance of tribal descent is reflected in a booming interest in the study of family genealogies. During the last half century, Saudis have written thousands of books and articles in order to prove and document their families' tribal lineages.[4] Hence, *nasab* not only constitutes the foundation for certain legal rights and duties, but is crucial for an individual's position in society. Having 'good' *nasab* can be a huge advantage in business as well as family life.

In addition, the legal importance of filiation cannot be overstated. It is filiation that entitles a child to maintenance from their father and qualifies them as an inheritor. The allocation of paternity can also affect the child's future marriage since some Saudi scholars argue that the requirement of wedding adequacy (*kafā'a*) also extends to *nasab*.[5] The social expectation that women should not marry men with 'lower' *nasab* is thereby transformed into a legal norm. Even though the absence of

---

[1] Due to its evolutionary connotations, the concept of tribe and tribal identities is discussed critically by social anthropologists. See for the discussion and more references Maisel 2014.

[2] Since it is believed that the members of the Muslim community are equal before God, discrimination based on tribal belonging is generally rejected.

[3] Maisel 2014, p 103.

[4] Samin 2015, p 2.

[5] Al-Daqaylān 1425/2004, p 139.

what is considered to be proper *nasab* does not necessarily lead to a void (*bāṭil*) marriage, the bride and her marriage guardian (*walī*) can demand the dissolution (*faskh*) of the marriage by a court if it turns out after the marriage that the husband had lied and is in fact not of adequate descent.[6]

11.1.2 The Saudi Legal System

The foundation of the Saudi legal system is Islamic law. Officially, the Quran and the Sunna of the Prophet Muḥammad serve as the constitution of the Saudi state.[7]

Even though Islamic law is believed to be all-encompassing, the Saudi monarchs can issue royal decrees and thereby regulate some areas of the law. These codified rules are not called laws (*qawānīn*, sing. *qānūn*), but statutes (*anẓima*, sing. *niẓām*), since God is believed to be the only lawgiver. Lower-ranked regulations (*lā'iḥāt*) address further procedures such as the implementation of the statutes. Both statutes and regulations are enacted by decision of the king, the councils of ministers, individual ministers or other government officials.

These statutes and regulations address areas that can be regulated by the king according to the concept of *siyāsa sharᶜiyya*.[8] *Siyāsa sharᶜiyya* can be translated as 'governance in the name of the sacred law'.[9] The main idea is that once rulers correctly observe Islamic law, their political decisions will not be in conflict with it.[10] *Siyāsa sharᶜiyya* entails a complex separation of powers between the *ᶜulamā'* and the king, through which every party is assigned distinct functions.[11] For example, the registration of civil status is considered to fall into the realm of the state and can therefore be regulated by the king, but how a marriage is concluded is almost entirely left to the interpretation of Islamic scholars.

According to the idea of *siyāsa sharᶜiyya*, the king has no immediate power over the courts and their interpretation of Islamic law. However, the king can control the judicial procedure and the structure of the courts. In the course of the last twenty years, the Saudi kings have increasingly used these competences to build a judicial

---

[6] Al-Daqaylān 1425/2004, p 139. Although highly controversial, it is still possible to file for divorce on the basis of lack of wedding adequacy through the Ministry of Justice's online system.

[7] See Article 1 of the Basic Statute (*niẓām al-asāsī li-l-ḥukm 1412/1991*). The statute is available on the website of the Bureau of Experts at the Council of Ministers: www.boe.gov.sa/ViewStaticPage.aspx?lang=2&PageID=25.

[8] Generally, the ruler can only address questions for which there is no 'text' (*naṣṣ*) in the revelation. The meaning of this, however, continues to be heavily disputed. See Vogel 2000, p 174. The concept of *siyāsa sharᶜiyya* was mainly developed in the post-classical period by Ibn Taymiyyah (d. 728/1328), see Anjum 2012.

[9] See Johansen 2008.

[10] Bramsen 2010, p 158.

[11] The short description here cannot do justice to the complexity of the concept. See for more details Vogel 2000, Chaps. 5–8.

system that can face the demands of a modern state. In 1421/2000, an extensive code of procedure was released with the aim of making court procedures more transparent.[12] In 1428/2007, a different court structure was introduced by the new Statute of the Judiciary.[13] As a result, specialised family courts opened in the major cities. These specialised courts now hear all cases related to family law, including paternity disputes. In smaller cities, however, a single judge with unlimited jurisdiction still prevails. Furthermore, the 1428/2007 reform increased the number of appellate courts (*maḥākim al-isti'nāf*) and introduced a High Court (*al-maḥkama al-ᶜulyā*).[14]

Apart from legal and administrative procedure, royal decrees generally do not address family law itself. Instead, the courts refer to Islamic jurisprudence (*fiqh*). Hence, from the courts' perspective, there is no such thing as 'Saudi family law', but only supra-state, universally applicable Islamic law.[15] From the first centuries of Islam onwards, several different schools (*madhāhib*) of Islamic jurisprudence have emerged. Today the most important schools of Sunni law in Saudi Arabia are the *ḥanbalī*, the *mālikī*, the *ḥanafī* and the *shāfiᶜī* school, although views advanced by the formally extinct *ẓāhirī* school are regaining some influence, particularly in Saudi family law.

Saudi scholars are traditionally hostile towards following (*taqlīd*) a particular school of Islamic jurisprudence. One of the leading Islamic authorities in Saudi Arabia, the Permanent Committee for Research and Legal Opinion (*al-lajna al-dā'ima li-l-buḥūth wa-l-iftā'*) has emphasised that scholars are not to follow a single school of Islamic jurisprudence.[16] Laypeople, on the contrary, are free to orientate themselves according to a legal school.[17]

Furthermore, the committee opposes restricting scholars to the four major schools of jurisprudence.[18] Instead, they should choose the preferable (*rājiḥ*) opinion only according to the proofs (*adilla*) in the Quran and Sunna. Judges regularly refer to Ibn Taymiyya (d. 728/1328) and his disciple Ibn al-Qayyim (d. 751/1350), two medieval scholars from the post-classical period who often deviate from the prevailing opinions in the four major schools.[19]

As will be shown, the idea of independent Islamic judicial reasoning (*ijtihād*) is very present among judges. At least some senior judges see themselves as able to

[12] *Niẓām al-murāfaᶜāt al-sharᶜiyya* 1421/2000, printed in La China and Alotaibi 2010.

[13] *Niẓām al-qaḍā'* 1428/2007. The statute is available on the website of the Ministry of Justice: www.moj.gov.sa/Documents/Regulations/pdf/06.pdf.

[14] See Mathieu 2008.

[15] However, laypeople do speak of a Saudi family '*qānūn*', a term that is used for 'law' in other Arab jurisdictions. This expression is also used by professionals in areas of the law that have been addressed to a large extent by royal decrees, such as administrative law and labour law.

[16] See for example Al-Dawīsh 1424/2003, vol 5, p 42. The committee is a branch of the Council of Senior Scholars (*hay'at kibār al-ᶜulamā'*).

[17] Al-Dawīsh 1424/2003, vol 5, p 29.

[18] Al-Dawīsh 1424/2003, vol 5, p 42.

[19] See Melchert 2013, pp 146–161.

perform *ijtihād*.[20] Applicants for a position as a judge must hold a degree in *fiqh* und its methodology (*uṣūl al-fiqh*) from one of Saudi Arabia's universities.[21] Many judges publish on questions of Islamic jurisprudence and some are regular guests on the kingdom's many religious talk shows.

In practice, courts consistently follow the legal consensus (*ijmā*ᶜ) on a ruling, as long as the consensus is not disputed, and they often agree on similar positions in disputed legal questions.[22] The prevailing practice of the courts (*al-ma*ᶜ*mūl bi-hi*) in disputed questions is to some extent binding for the judges, and the appelate courts ensure that the first-instance courts follow the prevailing practice. A judge is only allowed to deviate from the prevailing practice of the court when he convincingly argues that another opinion is preferable due to the circumstances of the individual case.[23]

The prevailing practice originates from circular letters to the courts issued by the High Court (*al-maḥkama al-*ᶜ*ulyā*) or the Supreme Judicial Council (*majlis al-a*ᶜ*lā li-l-qaḍā'*) and from legal opinions of the Council of Senior Scholars (*hay'at kibār al-*ᶜ*ulamā'*) or respected Saudi scholars like the former Grand Mufti and Chief of the Judiciary (*ra'īs al-qaḍā'*) Muḥammad bin Ibrāhīm Āl al-Shaykh (d. 1389/1969). The prevailing practice, however, can also stem from influential research articles by high-ranking judges or researchers.

11.2 The Establishment of Filiation

11.2.1 Establishing Filiation Through Marriage

11.2.1.1 The General System of Filiation

According to all schools of Islamic jurisprudence, *nasab* is first and foremost established through a valid marriage.[24] The Saudi courts also share this view. The courts generally cite an account (*ḥadīth*) of the prophet Muhammad, according to which he decided 'The child is attributed to the marital bed (*firāsh*)',[25] and once a valid marriage has been concluded and can be proven, the child will automatically be affiliated to the mother's husband.

---

[20] See for example Fawzān 1430/2010, p 209.

[21] Article 31 of the Statute of the Judiciary (*niẓām al-qaḍā'1428/2007*). Graduates from other universities have to sit an additional exam in order to qualify for judgeship. Vogel argues that Saudi universities aim to train ᶜ*ulamā'* that are capable of high degrees of *ijtihād*, see Vogel 2000, p 79.

[22] The consensus (*ijmā*ᶜ) of the Islamic community is the third of the main sources of Islamic law besides the Quran and the Sunna of the Prophet Muhammad.

[23] Āl Khunayn 1433/2012, vol 1, p 15.

[24] Abū Jayb 1984, vol 2, p 1049.

[25] Al-Bukhārī 1423/2002, p 1686 (no. 6818).

Marriages can generally be concluded without any involvement of the state or religious scholars. Although marriages have to be registered, the registration itself does not affect the validity of the marriage.[26]

In practice, the most important requirements for a valid marriage are the consent of the bride's guardian (*walī*), normally her father, and the presence of two male witnesses.[27] Unmarried couples sometimes claim to have married in secret when the woman gets pregnant. In this case, neither the involvement of the *walī* nor the presence of the witnesses can be proven. Some scholars see a marriage without the *walī* as a defective (*fāsid*) marriage that still has legal effect until its obligatory dissolution.[28] The child is thus affiliated to the man that claimed to have married the mother. Others consider such a marriage to be void (*bāṭil*).[29] This, however, does not mean that a child from this marriage is considered illegitimate. Islamic scholars have developed the concept of 'sexual intercourse in uncertainty' (*al-waṭ' bi-shubha*). Once the parents have had the intention to marry, the children are affiliated to the would-be husband. For example, Muḥammad bin Ibrāhīm Āl al-Shaykh was asked by a woman who had married in London without her father and without two male witnesses about the validity of her marriage.[30] Muḥammad bin Ibrāhīm replied that her marriage was not valid because of the absence of the marriage guardian and the required witnesses. However, he assured the couple that the children that resulted from the marriage are legitimate and have to be affiliated to the husband, since they were fathered through 'sexual intercourse in uncertainty'.[31]

Whether the husband is in fact the biological father of the child does not matter. One court decision from Jeddah, for example, quoted the medieval scholar Ibn Daqīq al-ᶜĪd (d. 702/1302), who emphasized that a child has to be attributed to the husband (*ṣāḥib al-firāsh*) even if they stem from illicit intercourse (*waṭ' muḥarram*).[32] A biological relationship is thus not seen as the key element of paternity.

11.2.1.2 The Maximum Length of Pregnancy

Questions of paternity are often raised after a divorce or the death of the husband. Therefore, legal assumptions about the maximum and minimum length of

---

[26] Al-Shaᶜbī 1424/2003, p 11.

[27] According to Ibn ᶜUthaymīn, two female witnesses and one male witness are not acceptable. See Ibn ᶜUthaymīn 1428/2007, vol 12, p 97.

[28] See for example Ibn ᶜUthaymīn 1428/2007, vol 12, p 70.

[29] See for example Al-Dawīsh 1424/2003, vol 18, p 141. However, the terminology is often used ambiguously.

[30] Female witnesses were, however, present when the marriage was concluded.

[31] Ibn Qāsim 1399/1979, vol 10, p 91.

[32] Ibn Daqīq al-ᶜĪd 1372/1953, vol 2, p 220; Jeddah General Court, decision no. 3432937 (9.2.1434/23.12.2012).

pregnancy play a key role in paternity disputes. Pre-modern scholars agreed that the minimum length of pregnancy is six months.[33] Since this is more or less in accordance with the findings of modern medicine, contemporary Saudi scholars agree with the opinion of their predecessors without further discussion.[34]

The maximum length of pregnancy, however, continues to be heavily debated. Pre-modern scholars had suggested timeframes that clearly contradict the findings of modern medicine. Although early scholars generally recognized that an ordinary pregnancy lasts around nine months, they argued that this timeframe can be exceeded in unusual cases. Due to the absence of any revelation in the Quran or the Sunna of the Prophet Muhammad,[35] most scholars turned to what they or others observed in life.[36] As a result, their opinions differed immensely.

The Ḥanafīs held that the maximum time of pregnancy is two years.[37] The Shāfiᶜīs[38] and Ḥanbalīs tended towards four years,[39] and according to Mālik, the founder of the eponymous legal school, a woman can be pregnant for up to five years.[40]

This leaves many contemporary scholars troubled. On the one hand, they generally trust modern medicine, especially when Muslim doctors explain its findings, but on the other hand, even scholars who are critical of the legal schools respect the opinions of influential early scholars. Whereas probably the majority of contemporary scholars outside Saudi Arabia agree that a woman cannot be pregnant for more than one year due to the findings of modern medicine, many famous Saudi scholars disagree.

Some, like Ṣāliḥ al-Fawzān, a current member of the Permanent Committee for Research and Legal Opinion, follow the classic *ḥanbalī* opinion. Al-Fawzān holds that when a woman is divorced and bears a child no later than four years after the divorce, the child is attributed to the husband.[41] However, many authoritative Saudi scholars go one step further and put no maximum limit on pregnancy. Ibn ᶜUthaymīn (d. 1421/2001), one of the leading Saudi scholars of the twentieth century, wrote: 'According to the school[42] (*madhhab*) a child that is born more than four years [after the death of the testator] does generally not inherit. [But] the correct [opinion] is that it inherits if no sexual intercourse has taken place after the death of the testator, because the time of pregnancy can exceed four years, as it

---

33 Ibn Mundhir 1420/1999, p 122.

34 See for example Ibn Bāz 1425/2004, vol 22, p 179.

35 There is, however, a *ḥadīth* of ᶜĀ'isha, the wife of the Prophet, according to which she said that a woman can be pregnant for a maximum of two years, see Ibn Qudāma 1417/1997, vol 11, p 232.

36 See for example Al-Bahūtī 1403/1983, vol 5, p 414.

37 Ibn Qudāma 1417/1997, vol 11, p 232; thereby, the Ḥanafīs follow ᶜĀ'isha's opinion.

38 Al-Ramlī 1424/2003, vol 7, p 112.

39 Al-Bahūtī 1403/1983, vol 5, p 414.

40 Ibn Rushd 1415/1994, vol 3, p 219.

41 Al-Fawzān Ṣ 1423/2002, vol 2, p 416.

42 He most likely refers to the *ḥanbalī* school of law.

happens'.[43] He then quotes Ibn al-Qayyim, who argued that no limit can be set, because there is no revelation about the maximum length of pregnancy.[44]

Muḥammad bin Ibrāhīm Āl al-Shaykh maintained that earlier scholars did not claim that the time limit proves paternity in any case, but merely says that it is possible that a child born in this timeframe is the child of the husband. He demands that if a time limit is placed on pregnancy, it has to be reliable in order to have legal certainty.[45] According to him, the justification (*ta^c^līl*) for the four-year limit in the *ḥanbalī* school is that this was the longest pregnancy ever observed (*akthar mā wujida*). However, Muḥammad bin Ibrāhīm argued that pregnancies can exceed four years and that it has been observed that a pregnancy took fourteen years and the child was then born with his full teeth.[46]

A 1430/2009 article in *al-^c^Adl*, the widely circulated journal of the Ministry of Justice, agrees that there is generally no fixed length of pregnancy in Islamic law, because of the silence of the revelation in this question. However, in the case of the inheritance rights of a child born to the wife of a deceased man, which requires the wife to be pregnant at the time of the husband's death, the opinions of the medical specialists (*ahl al-ikhtiṣāṣ*) should be preferred. Their opinions, the author ^c^Abd al-^c^Azīz al-Ghāmdī argues, rest on modern knowledge (*al-^c^ilm al-ḥadīth*), whereas the medieval *fiqh* scholars had to rely on lies or misinterpreted fake pregnancies.[47]

Al-Ghāmdī writes that many Saudi judges have informed him that in cases of inheritance, the length of pregnancy regularly does not exceed nine months.[48] The judges' concern for this question demonstrates the uncertainty surrounding the length of pregnancy that is present in the contemporary Saudi legal discourse. In his article, al-Ghāmdī advises the judges to demand a medical certificate in inheritance cases to scientifically prove that the wife was already pregnant at the time of her husband's death in order to avoid the recognition of fake pregnancies.[49]

The vice president of the family court in Riyadh, ^c^Abd Allāh al-Rashūd confirmed that according to the Code of Civil Procedure, the judges now have to refer to medical experts in order to determine the length of a pregnancy.[50] In paternity disputes the judges have to demand a detailed report from a hospital.[51]

Ḥamd al-Khuḍayrī, however, a renowned senior judge from the appellate court in Riyadh, holds that pregnancies can exceed the time limit set by modern medicine.

---

43 Ibn ^c^Uthaymīn 1404/1983, p 102.

44 See Ibn al-Qayyim 1426/2005, p 146.

45 Ibn Qāsim 1399/1979, vol 11, p 151.

46 Ibn Qāsim 1399/1979, vol 11, p 151. Other scholars, like the former Grand Mufti Ibn Bāz (d. 1999), agree without further explanation. See Ibn Bāz 1409/1989, p 99.

47 Al-Ghāmdī states that according to modern medicine a pregnancy can exceed nine months in rare cases; however, not by more than two months. Al-Ghāmdī 1430/2009, p 221.

48 Al-Ghāmdī 1430/2009, p 221.

49 Al-Ghāmdī 1430/2009, p 224.

50 Interview with ^c^Abd Allāh al-Rashūd in the family court in Riyadh, 9 August 2018.

51 Interview with ^c^Abd Allāh al-Rashūd in the family court in Riyadh, 9 August 2018.

Medical knowledge, he argued, is still developing and changes over time. It could be that in a few years Western medicine would discover that women can be pregnant for more than one year in rare cases. Accordingly, in a couple of cases, he has judged that pregnancies lasted for several years.[52]

In a similar way, a judge in Mecca decided an inheritance case in 1429/2008. The plaintiff, a woman, claimed that one year before the death of her husband, she started suffering from bleeding and pain in her belly. Since the pain continued after the death of her husband, the woman went to the hospital. The doctors, according to her statement, diagnosed a fibroid in her uterus, but the woman decided not to let the doctors remove it. Many months later, so she told the judge, she started to feel movements in her belly and went to the hospital again. This time, the doctors told her that she was seventh month pregnant. She then gave birth to a boy, almost two and a half years after her husband's death. In court, she demanded to determine the filiation of the child and to add the child to the husband's inheritance document (*ḥaṣr al-waratha*). The deceased husband had fathered eight other children. All of them confirmed their mother's story. Two of the sons further testified and acknowledged that the new-born was their brother and the son of their deceased father.

In his ruling, the judge argued that the Islamic scholars (*ahl al-^{c}ilm*) decided that if two men of moral integrity from the group of inheritors witnessed that they had another common inheritor (*wārith mushārik*), this person was affiliated to the deceased and shared the inheritance.[53] The judge then went on to note that the time between the death of the husband and the birth of the boy was less than the maximum length of pregnancy according to the preferred (*rājiḥ*) opinion of the Islamic scholars, and decided that the new-born was the son of the deceased and would inherit from him.[54]

The case exemplifies the complex interplay between rules of inheritance and the more general rules of filiation. Even though he refers to medieval scholars, the judge's argument is not solely based on their view of the maximum length of pregnancy, but also on the idea that inheritors can decide for themselves if they want to share the inheritance with another potential inheritor or not.

Many judges told me that cases regarding the maximum length of pregnancy are very rare. In general, paternity disputes are uncommon, since Saudi courts do not hear them unless financial rights resulting directly from paternity are claimed.[55] The jurists generally give more value to the stability of the family than to the biological

---

[52] Interview with Ḥamd al-Khuḍayrī in the appellate court in Riyadh, 29 July 2018.

[53] Mecca General Court, decision no. 11/29/16 (14.3.1429/22.3.2008). The judge quoted Ibn Qudāma's book 'Al-Mughnī', see Ibn Qudāma 1417/1997, vol 7, p 322, and strengthened his argument by referring to al-Mardāwī's book 'Al-Inṣāf', see Al-Mardāwī 1417/1997, vol 7, p 341, which states that, at least in the *ḥanbalī* school, there is no dispute in this matter.

[54] The judge again quoted Ibn Qudāma, see Ibn Qudāma 1417/1997, vol 9, p 180. According to Ibn Qudāma, the preferred opinion is that a woman can be pregnant for four years; however, the judge himself did not refer to a set limit.

[55] Markaz al-Buḥūth 1438/2017, p 194.

realities. By not admitting paternity disputes, they try to encourage people not to question their family relationships.

11.2.1.3 Admissibility of Scientific Evidence

Since a biological relationship is not seen as the key element of paternity, Saudi courts do not recognize DNA tests as a way to establish filiation to a man other than the husband. In the decision from Jeddah mentioned previously, the judge referred to the ruling of the 'scholars' (*ᶜulamā'*) not to allow DNA tests as a way to prove paternity if the mother of the child is married, since the marriage (*firāsh*) is in any case the stronger proof.[56] Moreover, the judge stated that a DNA test cannot be used to negate already established paternity.[57]

However, men are allowed to negate paternity through the Quranic *liᶜān* procedure. In *liᶜān*, the husband testifies four times that the child in question is not his child. The fifth time, he swears that the curse of God will be on him if he is lying. The wife, on the other hand, has to testify four times that her husband is lying. The fifth time she swears that God's wrath will be on her if he is telling the truth. As a result, the marriage is irrevocably dissolved and the child is no longer affiliated to the husband. Due to the grave allegations and the explicit references to God, *liᶜān* is generally handled with care.

In one of the rare published decisions containing *liᶜān*, a Saudi court directly referred to the Quranic verse six in Sūrat al-Nūr that states: 'And those who accuse their wives [of adultery] and have no witnesses except themselves – then the witness of one of them [shall be] four testimonies [swearing] by Allah that indeed, he is of the truthful.'[58]

Since there is no fixed time limit to the proclamation of *liᶜān*, the negation of paternity is even possible once the parents have separated.[59] However, the Supreme Judicial Council decided that the right to *liᶜān* can be forfeited with time.[60]

The position of Saudi judges regarding the use of DNA tests during the *liᶜān* process remains unclear. It is mostly held that a DNA test does not influence *liᶜān* at all, but it is also discussed that a positive DNA test can uphold filiation despite the *liᶜān* by the husband.[61]

However, there is evidence that DNA tests are ordered by judges before the husband proclaims *liᶜān*. A judge at the court in Riyadh, for example, was

---

56 Jeddah General Court, decision no. 3432937 (9.2.1434/23.12.2012).

57 Jeddah General Court, decision no. 3432937 (9.2.1434/23.12.2012); the judge referred to a decision of the Islamic Fiqh Academy (*al-majmaᶜ al-fiqhī al-islāmī*).

58 Riyadh General Court, decision no. 7/193 (17.4.1416/13.9.1995). The subsequent verses in the Quran then address the procedure of *liᶜān*.

59 Riyadh General Court, decision no. 7/193 (17.4.1416/13.9.1995).

60 Markaz al-Buḥūth 1438/2017, p 193.

61 See Al-Suwaylim 1429/2008, p 151.

confronted with the husband's wish to proclaim *liᶜān*. He then ruled that the father and the child first had to carry out a DNA test. Since the DNA test proved that the child was biologically related to him, the husband refrained from pursuing *liᶜān*.[62]

11.2.1.4 Acknowledgement

Filiation can further be established through acknowledgment (*iqrār*). As we have seen in the cited inheritance case, two inheritors can create filiation between their brother and their deceased father by acknowledgment. However, more commonly it is the father who acknowledges a child as his son or daughter.

For the acknowledgement to be valid, the child must be of unknown filiation (*majhūl al-nasab*).[63] A child is of unknown filiation when the child's father is unknown. If, for example, the father is known, but has died, the acknowledgement is considered an adoption (*tabannī*). Adoption is seen as completely forbidden due to several clear statements about it in the Quran and the Sunna.[64]

Furthermore, the acknowledger must be mentally sane and the age difference between the child and the acknowledger must make it biologically possible for the acknowledger to have fathered the child.[65] The acknowledgement only has to be confirmed by the acknowledged child if he or she is already legally capable of doing so.[66]

In practice, acknowledgements seem to happen mostly in cases in which the parents had concluded the marriage without registering it. This occurs often in Mecca, where many Saudis marry foreign women without going through the registration procedure.[67]

The acknowledgement does not have to be formal. The Supreme Judicial Council decided in 1415/1994 that when a man had acted as marriage guardian for a girl or had added a child to his civil register, this would be sufficient to prove his paternity.[68]

11.2.1.5 Testimony and *qiyāfa*

However, if paternity is disputed between the parents, filiation can also be established with the help of other forms of proof. In such cases, the judicial demands for proof are loose, since Saudi courts generally aim to establish filiation. For example,

---

[62] The case is described by Al-Suwaylim 1429/2008, p 155.

[63] Ibn ᶜUthaymīn 1428/2007, vol 15, p 500.

[64] Al-Dawīsh 1424/2003, vol 20, p 344.

[65] Al-Suwaylim 1429/2008, p 98.

[66] Ibn ᶜUthaymīn 1428/2007, vol 15, p 499.

[67] Al-Ḥarbī 2014.

[68] Markaz al-Buḥūth 1438/2017, p 192.

in one judgement, the judge wrote that filiation is proven with the lowermost probability.[69] Islamic law, the judge goes on, aspires (*yatashawwaf*) to affiliate a child to a father.[70] Several Saudi judges told me that this general idea guides their judgements in all questions related to paternity.

The plaintiff, usually the mother of the child, can demand that the judge admits two male witnesses who testify that the person in question is the child's father or that he has already acknowledged paternity outside of court.[71] As a result, the child is affiliated to the father, even if he still denies paternity.

According to a widely used book on judicial procedure before Saudi courts by Ḥamd al-Khuḍayrī, *qiyāfa* will take place if the plaintiff cannot present any witnesses.[72] *Qiyāfa* is a process whereby two people are affiliated to each other due to their physical appearance. Several similar-looking people have to gather in the same place, including the child and the potential father. An appointed person, the *qā'if*, has to rightly conclude through the physical appearance alone that the child and the potential father are related. If the *qā'if* is successful, the filiation of the child to the potential father is proven.[73]

It is unclear to what extent *qiyāfa* is actually practiced in contemporary Saudi Arabia. Al-Khuḍayrī said that he himself has used *qiyāfa* several times and that it was a regular practice of Saudi courts. However, he emphasized that paternity disputes were very rare and therefore it was very difficult to evaluate to what extent it was used.[74] Other judges are much more critical. The appellate judge Muḥammad Jār Allāh from Riyadh, for example, explained that he has never heard of *qiyāfa* actually taking place in Saudi Arabia.[75]

In addition to *qiyāfa*, a judge can arrange a DNA test. Like in the case of *qiyāfa*, a DNA test cannot be taken if witnesses are admitted, since, similarly to an existing valid marriage, a positive DNA test cannot overrule the witnesses' testimony.[76] If two male witnesses testify that someone is the child's father, the child will be affiliated to the defendant even if the DNA test shows no biological relationship.

---

69 Mecca General Court, decision no. 34234804 (7.6.1434/18.4.2013).

70 The judge referred to the *ḥanbalī* jurist Ibn Qudāma (d. 1223), see Ibn Qudāma 1417/1997, vol 8, p 374.

71 Al-Khuḍayrī (n.d.), p 125.

72 Al-Khuḍayrī (n.d.), p 125.

73 Al-Khuḍayrī (n.d.), p 125.

74 Interview with Ḥamd al-Khuḍayrī in the appellate court in Riyadh, 29 July 2018.

75 Interview with Muḥammad Jār Allāh in the appellate court in Riyadh, 29 July 2018.

76 Al-Khuḍayrī (n.d.), p 126.

11.2.2 Establishing Filiation Outside of a Valid Marriage

Extramarital sex (*zinā*) is considered a major crime in Saudi Arabia. For a married person, the Quranic punishment (*ḥadd*) is death, whereas an unmarried person is punished with 100 lashes.[77] However, the only way to prove *zinā*, according to the majority of the Islamic schools of law, is the testimony of four male Muslims who witnessed the sexual intercourse or heard the accused acknowledge it.[78] Saudi scholars, however, also tend to accept the pregnancy of an unmarried woman as proof of *zinā*.[79] For example, in one tragic case in Mecca, an Indonesian woman entered a hospital suffering from abdominal pain. She had been pregnant and had tried to abort the child, but the abortion failed and the foetus started to rot in her belly. The hospital alarmed the police and she was put to trial by the public prosecutor on the charge of *zinā*.[80]

Hospitals and other governmental or non-governmental institutions, as well as licensed doctors and midwives, are obliged to record every birth that occurs on their premises. The records have to include the parents' full name, religion and nationality, and have to be presented to the authorities by the end of every month.[81] Furthermore, Saudi judges tend to also accept DNA tests, analyses of the clothes of suspects and other forms of evidence in order to prove *zinā*.[82]

However, the Quranic punishment is generally not applied when there is any doubt about the guilt of the accused.[83] The claim that the woman had been married at the time of conception, even if she cannot prove it, can raise enough doubt to escape the Quranic punishment. Yet this does not mean that there is no sentence, since Saudi courts then apply the non-Quranic punishment of *taᶜzīr*. This non-Quranic punishment can be imposed even if there is doubt and can also lead to severe sentences. The Indonesian woman, for example, claimed to have been married; however, she could not provide any proof. The judge referred to *taᶜzīr* and sentenced the woman to one year in prison and one hundred lashes.[84]

As we have seen, a child of a married woman resulting from *zinā* is attributed to the husband even if it is known that he is not the biological father. If the mother, however, was not married at the time of the child's conception, the rulings of Islamic scholars differ about the affiliation of the child to their biological father.

The four major schools of Islamic law agree that a child born out of wedlock cannot be affiliated to the biological father if the mother was not married. This opinion is mainly based on the mentioned prophetic account that 'the child is

---

77 See for example Ibn Bāz 1425/2004, vol 12, p 402.

78 Al-Zuḥaylī 1418/1997, vol 7, pp 5371–5372.

79 See for example Ibn ᶜUthaymīn 1428/2007, vol 14, pp 274–277.

80 Mecca General Court, decision no. 33437000 (25.10.1434/1.9.2013).

81 Article 44 of the Statute of Civil Status (*niẓām al-aḥwāl al-madaniyya 1407/1986*).

82 Al-Khuḍayrī (n.d.), p 37.

83 Al-Bahūtī 1425/2004, p 411.

84 Mecca General Court, decision no. 33437000 (25.10.1434/1.9.2013).

attributed to the marital bed (*firāsh*) and the fornicator gets [nothing but] the stone'.[85]

This opinion is also popular in Saudi Arabia. For example, the Permanent Committee for Research and Legal Opinion and the former Grand Muftis Muḥammad bin Ibrāhīm and Ibn Bāz (d. 1420/1999) argued that a child who results from an illicit relationship can under no circumstances be affiliated to the biological father.[86] As a consequence, the child has no legal connection to their biological father and is thus not allowed to take the father's name, nor are they entitled to financial support (*nafaqa*).[87]

However, other widely respected scholars, especially Ibn Taymiyya and his student Ibn al-Qayyim, held the opinion that a child born out of wedlock can nevertheless be affiliated to the biological father.[88] They argued that the aforementioned hadith only applies to a married woman. In the case of an unmarried woman, there is no restriction against affiliating the child to the biological father. Furthermore, ᶜUmar bin al-Khaṭṭāb is said to have attributed a child of unknown filiation to their biological father.[89]

The way a Saudi court handles this question depends largely on the judge. In 1422/2001, the appeals court (*maḥkamat al-isti'nāf*) in Riyadh decided that courts have to follow the first opinion stating that a child born out of wedlock cannot be affiliated to the biological father.[90] However, ᶜAdnān al-Daqaylān, a judge at the court in Dammam, wrote in 1425/2004 in al-ᶜAdl, the influential journal of the Ministry of Justice, that when a first instance court, contrary to the appeals court's decision, decides to affiliate a child to their biological father, his judgement cannot be revoked, since one *ijtihād* cannot change another *ijtihād*.[91]

Another article in the same journal three years later argued against the appeals court decision, claiming that the preferable opinion for the judges to follow is that the child born out of wedlock has to be affiliated to the biological father.[92] In 1435/2013, the newly established High Court (*al-maḥkama al-ᶜulyā*) issued a decision regarding the question of the legal status of a child that was fathered before the conclusion of the marriage. The High Court ruled that the judges have to decide

---

[85] Al-Bukhārī 1423/2002, p 1686 (no. 6818).

[86] Al-Dawīsh 1424/2003, vol 20, p 389; Ibn Bāz 1425/2004, vol 12, p 402; Ibn Qāsim 1399/1979, vol 11, p 146. This opinion is also shared by Ibn ᶜUthaymīn. See Ibn ᶜUthaymīn 1428/2007, vol 13, p 439.

[87] However, marriage hindrances between the father and the child are created.

[88] Ibn Taymiyya 1432/2011, vol 16, p 73; Ibn al-Qayyim 1416/1996, vol 5, p 426. This view is sometimes also attributed to Abū Ḥanīfa, the founder of the eponymous legal school.

[89] Ibn Taymiyya 1432/2011, vol 16, p 73.

[90] Al-Daqaylān 1425/2004, p 138.

[91] Al-Daqaylān 1425/2004, p 138, Islamic law is traditionally hostile to judicial appeal. A basic principle (*qāᶜida*) of Islamic law states that a judgement by one judge cannot be revoked by another judge due to a different stance on a legal question (*al-ijtihād lā yunqaḍu bi-mithlihi*).

[92] Al-Fawzān ᶜA 1427/2006, p 176.

which opinion to follow on a case-by-case basis, considering the particularities of each case.[93]

Judge al-Khuḍayrī asserted that the courts today would in practice affiliate children born out of wedlock to their biological fathers. However, the judiciary would avoid communicating this openly to the Saudi public in order to promote and uphold correct moral behaviour.[94]

11.3 Protection of Children Without Filiation or Permanent Caretakers

11.3.1 The General Legal Schemes of Protection and Care

Different terms are used to describe children without filiation. In the Saudi context, a foundling (*laqīṭ*) is understood to be a child who does not have any known relative to take custody of them and, at least according to the common understanding, has been left on the street, in front of a mosque or in another public space.[95] The Saudi social welfare system uses the expression 'children of unknown parents' (*majhūl al-abawayn*)[96] synonymously, and defines them as children born inside the kingdom to unidentified parents.[97]

Another term that is commonly used in Saudi legal discourse is children of unknown filiation (*majhūl al-nasab*). This term can either mean that both parents are unknown, or just the father, but it is mostly used as a synonym for 'foundling'.[98]

An orphan (*yatīm*), on the other hand, is considered to be a pre-pubescent child who has lost their father or both of their parents, for example in an accident. However, their descent is known and the child may still have other relatives.[99]

Provisions on foster care can be found in the Regulations Regarding Children in Need.[100] These are, however, only applied if there are no relatives who can assume the role of caretaker.

[93] Decision of the High Court no. 12/M (10.5.1435/12.3.2014); the marriage of the couple after committing *zinā* does not have any influence on the status of the child, see for example the fatwa by Ibn ᶜUthaymīn, printed in Al-Musnad 1414/1994, vol 3, p 370.

[94] Interview with Ḥamd al-Khuḍayrī in the appellate court in Riyadh, 29 July 2018.

[95] Al-Miḥaymīd 1428/2007, p 244; see also Al-Bahūtī 1403/1983, vol 4, p 226.

[96] Al-Dughaythir 1437/2016, p 1.

[97] Article 1 of the Regulations Regarding Children in Need (*al-lā'iḥa li-l-aṭfāl al-muḥtājūn li-l-riᶜāya*).

[98] See for example Al-Dawīsh 1424/2003, vol 11, p 264.

[99] See for example Ibn Bāz 1425/2004, vol 14, p 329.

[100] *Al-lā'iḥa li-l-aṭfāl al-muḥtājūn li-l-riᶜāya*, enacted by decision no. 5 of the Minister of Work and Social Affairs on 13.5.1395/24.5.1975. The regulations can be found on the online platform eastlaws.com.

11.3.2 Relatives as Alternative Caretakers

As long as the child's relatives are known, they are responsible for the care of the child. Provided that the mother is alive and capable of caring for the child and the child is younger than seven, she is given custody of the child. After the age of seven, the rulings of the courts differ according to the judge's understanding of the best interests of the child. Saudi courts generally allocate custody according to their understanding of the best interests of the child.[101]

If both the father and the mother have died or disappeared and the child still has known relatives, they have to take care of the child. Saudi courts generally see custody as a right of the child.[102] This means that for the custodian, custody is both a right and an obligation. A potential custodian can refuse to take custody of a child only if there is another relative willing and able to take care of the child. Saudi courts usually follow the *ḥanbalī* order of custodians. If the mother is incapable of caring for the child, her mother, the maternal grandmother of the child, is expected to take the child into her custody. When the grandmother is also unable to provide care, the father and his female relatives are expected to exercise custody.

If the father is dead or missing, the question of guardianship arises. In Islamic law, the guardian is responsible for the child's financial matters and their education According to the prevailing opinion in the legal schools, only men from the father's side can be guardians of a child. The exact order of guardians, however, is disputed among Saudi judges. A circular letter by the Supreme Judicial Council to the courts states two possible opinions for the judges to follow.[103] The common (*mashhūr)* opinion, the council writes, is that the paternal grandfather succeeds the father in the order of guardians, followed by his trustee (*waṣī*). If the trustee is unknown or incapable, then the judge serves as the guardian of the child. The second opinion is that the grandfather will follow the father in the order of guardians, but the judge can decide to take over the guardianship in order to protect the child.[104]

If the father and his family are unknown, the General Commission for Guardianship over the Funds of Minors and the Like[105] administers the property of minors.[106] The commission's powers in administering the property are, however, limited. For example, the commission is generally not allowed to buy any

---

[101] Markaz al-Buḥūth 1438/2017, p 197.

[102] Al-Miḥaymīd 1428/2007, p 244.

[103] Circular letter no. 84/1/T, 24.5.1403/9.3.1983, printed in Al-Ṣā'igh 1431/2010, p 30.

[104] Circular letter no. 84/1/T, 24.5.1403/9.3.1983, printed in Al-Ṣā'igh 1431/2010, p 30. The Supreme Judicial Council urges the judges to follow one of these opinions in order to unify court procedure with that of the administration.

[105] *Al-hay'a al-^{c}āmma li-l-wilāya ^{c}alā amwāl al-qāṣirīn wa-man fī ḥukmihim.*

[106] Article 2.1 of the Statute of the General Commission for Guardianship over the Funds of Minors and the Like (*niẓām al-hay'a al-^{c}āmma li-l-wilāya ^{c}alā amwāl al-qāṣirīn wa-man fī ḥukmihim 1427/2006*), enacted by royal decree no. 17/M. The statute is available on the website of the Bureau of Experts at the Council of Ministers: www.boe.gov.sa/ViewSystemDetails.aspx?lang=ar&SystemID=130&VersionID=159 (accessed 11 September 2018).

properties, movables or securities or to establish, take part in or acquire companies with the property of the child.[107] The commission's guardianship ends when the minor has reached the age of legal maturity (*rushd*) as long as the court does not see a need to prolong the guardianship.[108] There is no fixed age for legal maturity in Saudi Arabia. A court must decide about the legal maturity of a person individually according to the rules of Islamic law.[109]

11.3.3 The Role of the Saudi Welfare System

According to Islamic law, it is the father who has to provide financially for his children. Therefore, children without a known or living father can face financial adversity.

Saudi Arabia's extensive social welfare programme includes financial help for children of dead, missing or unknown fathers. The Saudi Statute of Social Welfare[110] lists orphans, children of an unknown father or unknown parents and children of a father that has been missing for more than six months as potential recipients of social welfare.[111]

The statute entitles orphans and other beneficiaries to receive generous monthly social welfare payments for their living expenses.[112] However, social welfare is only paid until the child's eighteenth birthday. Once the child reaches the age of 18, they lose their right to social welfare as long as there are no other reasons for entitlement to further payments. Furthermore, there is a generous education programme for children who have no parents or whose parents are unknown. The children also receive financial assistance for their schooling.[113]

---

107 Article 2.1 of the Statute of the General Commission for Guardianship over the Funds of Minors and the Like.

108 Article 32.1 of the Statute of the General Commission for Guardianship over the Funds of Minors and the Like.

109 See for the detailed rules Al-Miḥaymīd 1422/2001, pp 189–193.

110 *Niẓām al-ḍamān al-ijtimāʿī 1427/2006*, enacted by royal decree no. 45/M. The statute is available on the website of the Bureau of Experts at the Council of Ministers: www.boe.gov.sa/ViewSystemDetails.aspx?lang=ar&SystemID=187&VersionID=202#search1 (accessed 11 September 2018).

111 Article 1.5 of the Statute of Social Welfare; Article 2/1 of the executive regulations (*al-lā'iḥa al-tanfīdhiyya*) of the Statute of Social Welfare. The statute defines 'orphan' (*yatīm*) more narrowly than most Islamic scholars. According to Article 1.5 of the statute, an orphan is a male or female person who has lost his father, has not yet reached the age of 18, and has neither family able to care for him nor any source of income to provide for his living expenses.

112 Article 3.1 of the Statute of Social Welfare.

113 According to the website of the Ministry of Work and Social Affairs, http://sd.mlsd.gov.sa/ar/print/node/618 (accessed 22 June 2017).

11.3.4 Foundlings

11.3.4.1 The Legal Procedures Concerning a Foundling

In recent years, the number of new-born children found on the streets or in front of mosques has been steadily rising in the kingdom. The reasons for this seem to be manifold. In public discourse, foundlings are often considered to stem from illicit relationships and therefore are especially subjected to social discrimination. However, other factors, especially the poverty among some sections of Saudi society and particularly among the foreign workforce, also seem to lead to parents' decision to abandon their children.[114]

In the Statute of Civil Status, the Saudi administration has regulated the steps that have to be undertaken when a child is found.[115] Everyone who encounters a new-born foundling is obliged to immediately inform the nearest police department. At the police department, a detailed report has to be filed, which includes the place where the child was found, the appearance of the child, and other information that could lead to the identification of their parents.

The finder can request to remain anonymous.[116] However, if the finder wishes to take care of the child, he is free to do so as long as the Ministry of Social Affairs considers him capable of providing care. If the finder does not want to take care of the child, they must be handed over to an officially approved institution or a capable individual. Throughout this process, the Ministry of Social Affairs is responsible for any issues regarding the care of these children.[117]

11.3.4.2 The Registration and Naming of a Foundling

The institution that has committed itself to take care of the child is obliged to register the child.[118] Regardless of their appearance, the child will be registered in the civil register as a Saudi citizen.[119] The authorities then have to issue a birth certificate. The certificate does not state that the child is a foundling.[120]

---

114 Āl Kulayb 1432/2011, pp 2–3.

115 *Niẓām al-aḥwāl al-madaniyya 1407/1986*, enacted by royal decree 7/M. The statute is available on the website of the Bureau of Experts at the Council of Ministers: https://boe.gov.sa/ViewSystemDetails.aspx?lang=ar&SystemID=228&VersionID=33 (accessed 11 September 2018).

116 Article 39 of the Statute of Civil Status.

117 Al-Miḥaymīd 1428/2007, p 242; see also Article 3 of the Regulations Regarding Children in Need.

118 Article 40 of the Statute of Civil Status.

119 No. 106 of the implementing regulations (*al-lā'iḥa al-tanfīdhiyya*) of the Code of Civil Status. The implementing regulations are available on the website of the Ministry of the Interior: www.moi.gov.sa/ (accessed 9 September 2018).

120 Article 40 of the Statute of Civil Status.

Naming plays a key role in avoiding possible discrimination against the child. The Ministry of Social Affairs is responsible for giving the child a suitable name.[121] Naming in general is restricted, since it has to follow Islamic law.[122] The name of the foundling has to be a common name and has to follow the traditional Arab naming system in that it must consist of four names (*ism rubāᶜī*).[123]

The foster family or the orphanage can ask the ministry for permission to name the child themselves; however, the child can under no circumstances be named after them, since Islamic law, it is argued, explicitly prohibits taking the name and filiation of someone other than the legal father.[124] The foster family or the ministry can choose a first name for the child, but cannot assign a name for their father and grandfather. The Supreme Judicial Council has decided that children without a known father should be called either the son or daughter of ᶜAbd Allāh or ᶜAbd al-Raḥmān. Both names literally mean 'servant of God'. The council argues that since every man is a servant of God, the unknown father of the child can in any case be called that.[125]

11.3.4.3 The Nationality of a Foundling

Another important issue regarding discrimination against foundlings is the awarding of nationality. According to Article 7 of the Saudi Nationality Statute,[126] normally only children born to a Saudi father are given Saudi nationality. But the same article also stipulates that all children of unknown parents that are born inside Saudi Arabia receive Saudi nationality. It is assumed that children that are found in the kingdom were also born in it, as long as it is not proven otherwise.[127] As a result, the vast majority of foundlings become Saudi citizens and are thereby entitled to generous welfare payments and free education.

---

121 Al-Dughaythir 1437/2016, p 7; see also Al-Dawīsh 1424/2003, vol 11, p 264.

122 Article 45 of the Statute of Civil Status. The Permanent Committee for Research and Legal Opinion is responsible for deciding which names are in accordance with the rulings of Islamic law. See no. 114 of the implementing regulations (*al-lā'iḥa al-tanfīdhiyya*) of the Statute of Civil Status.

123 Al-Miḥaymīd 1435/2014a, p 364.

124 Articles 11 and 12 of the Regulations Regarding Children in Need; Al-Miḥaymīd 1427/2006, pp 233–234.

125 Decision no. 6331 (26.2.1395/10.3.1975), printed in Al-Miḥaymīd 1435/2014b, p 380.

126 *Niẓām al-jinsiyya al-saᶜūdiyya 1374/1954*, enacted by decision no. 4 (25.1.1374/23.9.1954) of the Council of Ministers. The statute is available on the website of the Bureau of Experts at the Council of Ministers: www.boe.gov.sa/printsystem.aspx?lang=ar&systemid=223&versionid=25 (accessed 1 October 2018).

127 Article 7 of the Statute on Saudi Nationality.

11.3.4.4 The Conditions for Foster Care

The day-to-day care of a foundling can be carried out by a foster family or a government-supervised Saudi institution.[128] Potential families can apply for foster care (*iḥtiḍān*) and thereby commit themselves to care for a child full-time. Although state institutions have long taken care of children in need, the idea that the state and NGOs administer a system in order to hand over foundlings to foster families is a relatively new development.

In 1998, the Permanent Committee for Research and Legal Opinion released an influential fatwa stating that children of unknown filiation fall under the Prophetic ruling on orphans. The committee stated that care for a child of unknown filiation, like for an orphan, leads to religious reward (*ajr*). Children of unknown filiation would even need more care than orphans, since they, unlike most orphans, have no known relatives.[129]

However, the committee also imposed limitations on the care of children of unknown descent. Under no circumstances could those children be affiliated to the foster families, and they are therefore not permitted to be added to the family documents.[130]

Furthermore, the committee pointed to the major problems that arise in their opinion when the child reaches the age of legal capacity (*sinn al-rushd*).[131] In the view of the committee, it is then legally forbidden for the child to see family members of the opposite sex unveiled or spend time alone with them. Therefore, the committee proposed that milk kinship be actively established between the child and the foster family in order to create an enduring bond between them.[132] According to Islamic law, kinship can be created not only through shared blood, but also through shared milk. If a child is breastfed five[133] times within the first two years of their life by a woman that is not their mother, the child will become related to the woman and her kin.[134]

Milk-kinship creates the same bond as kinship by blood, except inheritance rights and the right to maintenance.[135] However, the foster parents can grant the foster child up to a third of the estate by will (*waṣiyya*). At least legally, the child becomes a member of the foster family.[136] Family members of the opposite sex and

---

[128] Al-Miḥaymīd 1428/2007, pp 239, 242.

[129] Al-Dawīsh 1424/2003, vol 14, p 255.

[130] Al-Dawīsh 1424/2003, vol 14, p 255.

[131] The Committee's use of the term *sinn al-rushd* is surprising. Islamic jurists generally see puberty (*sinn al-bulūgh*) as the critical age.

[132] Al-Dawīsh 1424/2003, vol 14, p 255.

[133] The schools of Islamic law do not agree in this matter; however, five times seems to be the prevailing opinion in Saudi Arabia.

[134] Al-Miḥaymīd 1435/2014a, p 364.

[135] There are also further differences with regard to criminal law. See Ibn ᶜUthaymīn 1428/2007, vol 13, p 442.

[136] Ibn ᶜUthaymīn 1428/2007, vol 13, p 422.

the foster child are allowed to see each other unveiled and spend time together alone even after puberty.[137] If the woman who wishes to care for a foundling is not lactating at the time when she receives the foster child, her sisters or other female family members can breastfeed the child. The created milk kinship then extends to the foster family.

According to the Minister of Social Affairs, the capability of the potential foster family to create milk kinship is an important condition for the fosterage.[138] The Widād Foundation, the first Saudi NGO that explicitly focuses on the care of children without filiation, quotes the committee's decision and states that they demand the creation of milk kinship in order to enable a 'normal life' (*ḥayāt ṭabīᶜiyya*) for the child.[139]

According to the regulations regarding children in need, foster families have to fulfil several conditions.[140] The most remarkable condition is that there should not be any obvious difference in skin colour between the child and the foster family.[141] Moreover, the potential foster family must consist of two spouses who are both Saudi nationals. However, if necessary, a single woman can also be accepted as caretaker for the child.[142] Single men are not eligible for foster care. Whether married or not, the woman must not be older than 50 years in order to be physically able to take care of the child and there should not be more than three children under six years old in the family.[143] A medical test must furthermore be conducted in order to prove that no one in the foster family suffers from communicable or infectious diseases. The good character and manners of the family have to be assured and a 'social examination' has to prove the capability of the foster family to take care of the child.[144]

Uncodified Islamic law moreover demands that the foster parents be Muslims.[145] More specific rulings, for example about what happens when two or more people encounter a foundling at the same time, are also derived from uncodified Islamic law and therefore subject to the judge's *ijtihād*.[146]

The supervising function of the ministry does not end with the selection of the foster family. The family is obliged to present a medical examination of the child every six months. In special cases the ministry can ask for a monthly

---

137 Ibn ᶜUthaymīn 1428/2007, vol 13, p 441.

138 Interview in the newspaper 'al-ḥayāt' (4 July 2014), available online: http://alhayat.com/Articles/3377818 (accessed 14 July 2017).

139 See their website www.wedad.org (accessed 14 July 2017).

140 Al-Miḥaymīd 1428/2007, p 243.

141 Article 13 of the Regulations Regarding Children in Need.

142 Unfortunately, 'necessity' is not further defined in the regulations.

143 Article 13 of the Regulations Regarding Children in Need.

144 Article 10 of the Regulations Regarding Children in Need.

145 Al-Miḥaymīd 1428/2007, p 239.

146 Al-Miḥaymīd 1428/2007, pp 240–242.

examination.[147] If the ministry comes to the conclusion that the foster family is unfit to care for the child, the ministry can end the fosterage and look for another family or institution that is able to do so.[148] For the time of the fosterage, the guardianship remains with the judge.

11.3.4.5 Financial Assistance for Foster Families

The Saudi government offers generous financial help for foster families, starting with the arrival of the child.[149] The families receive a monthly payment that depends on the age of the foster child.[150] Once the period of custody has ended, foster families get an extra payment of 20,000 Riyal for each child they took care of.[151] The fosterage generally ends when the child has reached the age of legal capacity (*sinn al-rushd*). However, the fosterage can continue if the child has not yet completed their education or if they suffer from impairments that justify further care.[152]

The child cannot make any claims against the foster family on the basis of the regulations on foster care, and vice versa. The fosterage constitutes a non-permanent bond between the foster family and the child. Once the foster agreement has ended, only the bond of milk kinship connects the foster family with the child.

11.4 Conclusion

Saudi jurists understand filiation as a matter of men's private autonomy, whereby biology is not of key importance. Men can decide whether they accept children born to their wives or they can negate them through *liᶜān*. Through acknowledgement, they can add a child of unknown descent to their lineage.

Although DNA tests are thus generally rejected as means to establish or negate filiation, they are nevertheless slowly becoming more important, most interestingly as a method to avoid the negative implications of *liᶜān*.

The Saudi approach to Islamic law opens up some ways to protect children that are otherwise condemned in Islamic law. The general acceptance of minority views

---

147 Article 13 of the Regulations Regarding Children in Need.

148 Article 12(g) of the Regulations Regarding Children in Need.

149 Article 16 of the Regulations Regarding Children in Need.

150 According to the website of the Ministry of Work and Social Affairs, the foster family receives 2,000 Riyal monthly for every child that is under six. Foster families that take care of a child that is six years or older are payed 3,000 Riyal monthly. See http://sd.mlsd.gov.sa/ar/print/node/618 (accessed 22 June 2017).

151 Article 16 of the Regulations Regarding Children in Need.

152 Article 12(b) of the Regulations Regarding Children in Need.

and the high degree of judicial independency enable judges to affiliate children stemming from illegitimate relationships to their biological father when the mother is unmarried – a view that is rejected by the major schools of Islamic jurisprudence. The idea that a woman can be pregnant for far more than a year can empower divorced or widowed women to successfully claim that their former husband is the father of an otherwise illegitimate child.

Care for children of unknown filiation reflects both Saudi Arabia's religious foundations and its oil wealth. The strict emphasis on the rules of Islamic law bans some important ways of protecting children in need, most importantly adoption. However, when the Permanent Committee for Research and Legal Opinion extended the religious command to care for orphans to children of unknown filiation, this was a powerful call for the care for such children. The Committee thereby legitimised foster care religiously and promised religious reward for it. The Islamic concept of milk kinship is used in a creative way to integrate foster children into their foster families without, however, entitling them to inheritance or maintenance.

Saudi Arabia's oil wealth allows the government to provide generous financial assistance to every family that decides to take care of a child of unknown filiation. The Saudi government thereby ensures that families can fulfil the Prophetic command in practice.

Acknowledgements I would like to thank the King Faisal Center for Research and Islamic Studies in Riyadh for their support during my fieldwork in Saudi Arabia. A special thanks to Majed bin Khunein and Sarah al-Dajani for introducing me into the Saudi legal community.

References

Abū Jayb S (1984) Mawsū^{c}at al-Ijmā^{c} fī al-Fiqh al-Islāmī, 2 vols. Dār al-Fikr, Damascus.

Āl Khunayn ^{c}A (1421/2000) Muqābila ma^{c}a Ṣāḥib al-Faḍīla al-Shaykh ^{c}Abd Allāh bin Muḥammad bin Sa^{c}d Āl Khunayn. Al-Majalla no. 1086 (6–12 Ramaḍān 1421/3–9 December 2000).

Āl Khunayn ^{c}A (1433/2012) Al-Kāshif fī Sharḥ Niẓām al-Murāfa^{c}āt al-Shar^{c}iyya, 2 vols. Dār Ibn Farḥūn, Riyadh.

Āl Kulayb ^{c}A (1432/2011) Kafālat al-Laqīṭ wa-Atharuhā fī al-Wiqāya min al-Jarīma. Unpublished master's thesis, Nauss University.

Al-Bahūtī M (1403/1983) Kashshāf al-Qinā^{c} ^{c}an Matn al-Iqnā^{c}, 6 vols. ^{c}Ālam al-Kutub, Riyadh.

Al-Bahūtī M (1425/2004) Al-Rawḍ al-Murbi^{c}. Dār al-Ḥadīth, Cairo.

Al-Bukhārī ^{c}A (1423/2002) Ṣaḥīḥ al-Bukhārī. Dār Ibn Kathīr, Damascus.

Al-Daqaylān ^{c}A (1425/2004) Nasab Walad al-Zinā. Majallat al-^{c}Adl 22:123–139.

Al-Dawīsh A (ed) (1424/2003) Fatāwā al-Lajna al-Dā'ima li-l-Buḥūth wa-l-Iftā', 23 vols. Dār Mu'ayyid, Riyadh.

Al-Dughaythir ^{c}A (1428/2007) Ḥujjiyyat al-Sawābiq al-Qaḍā'iyya. Majallat al-^{c}Adl 34:174–200.

Al-Dughaythir ^{c}A (1437/2016) Al-Aṭfāl al-Luqaṭā': Ḥuqūquhum wa-^{c}Ināyat al-Mamlaka al-^{c}Arabiyya al-Sa^{c}ūdiyya (n.p.).

Al-Fawzān ^{c}A (1427/2006) Ḥukm Istibrā' al-Zāniyya wa-Istilḥāq Walad al-Zinā. Majallat al-^{c}Adl 30:126–176.

Al-Fawzān Ṣ (1423/2002) Al-Mulakhkhaṣ al-Fiqhī, 2 vols. Dār al-^{c}Āṣima, Riyadh.
Al-Ghāmdī ^{c}A (1430/2009) Aqall Muddat al-Ḥaml wa-Aktharuha bayna al-Fiqh wa-l-Ṭibb. Majallat al-^{c}Adl 43:200–224.
Al-Ḥarbī N (2014) 1853 Qaḍiyya 'Ithbāt Bunūwa' bi-l-Maḥākim. Al-Waṭan, 26 October 2014. www.alwatan.com.sa/Nation/News_Detail.aspx?ArticleID=203929&CategoryID=3. Accessed 22 August 2017.
Al-Khuḍayrī Ḥ (n.d.) Al-Ijrā'āt al-Qaḍā'iyya. Self-published, Riyadh.
Al-Mardāwī ^{c}A (1417/1997) Al-Inṣāf, 12 vols. Dār al-Kutub al-^{c}Ilmiyya, Beirut.
Al-Miḥaymīd N (1422/2001) Ijrā'āt Qaḍā'iyya: Ithbāt Bulūgh al-Qāṣir. Majallat al-^{c}Adl 20:189–193.
Al-Miḥaymīd N (1427/2006) Ijrā'āt Qaḍā'iyya: Tasmiyat al-Laqīṭ. Majallat al-^{c}Adl 32:232–236.
Al-Miḥaymīd N (1428/2007) Ijrā'āt Qaḍā'iyya: Ḥaḍānat al-Laqīṭ. Majallat al-^{c}Adl 33:238–244.
Al-Miḥaymīd N (1435/2014a) Ijrā'āt Qaḍā'iyya: al-Ijrā'āt al-Muttaba^{c}a bi-Ithbāt al-Nasab wa-l-Qarāba. Majallat al-^{c}Adl 64:358–364.
Al-Miḥaymīd N (1435/2014b) Ijrā'āt Qaḍā'iyya: al-Ta'ṣīl al-Niẓāmī li-Ithbāt al-Nasab wa-l-Qarāba. Majallat al-^{c}Adl 65:378–382.
Al-Musnad M (1414/1994) Fatāwā Islāmiyya, 4 vols. Dār al-Waṭan, Riyadh.
Al-Ramlī Sh (1424/2003) Nihāyat al-Muḥtāj, 8 vols. Dār Kutub al-^{c}Ilmiyya, Beirut.
Al-Ṣā'igh M (1431/2010) Ḥuqūq al-Ṭifl al-Qaḍā'iyya 'Fiqhan wa-Niẓāman'. Wizārat al-^{c}Adl, Riyadh.
Al-Sha^{c}bī ^{c}A (1424/2003) Al-Ma'dhūn al-Shar^{c}ī wa-Wājibātuhu al-Shar^{c}iyya wa-l-Niẓāmiyya fī al-Mamlaka al-^{c}Arabiyya al-Sa^{c}ūdiyya. Majallat al-^{c}Adl 20:10–66.
Al-Suwaylim B (1429/2008) Al-Baṣma al-Wirāthiyya wa-Atharuhā fī al-Nasab. Majallat al-^{c}Adl 38:82–166.
Al-Zuḥaylī W (1418/1997) Al-Fiqh al-Islāmī wa-Adillatuhu, 11 vols. Dār al-Fikr, Damascus.
Anjum O (2012) Politics, Law and Community in Islamic Thought: The Taymiyyan Moment. Cambridge University Press, Cambridge.
Bramsen D (2010) Divine Law and Human Understanding – The Idea of Shari^{c}a in Saudi Arabia. In: Nielsen J, Christoffersen L (eds) Shari^{c}a As Discourse: Legal Traditions and the Encounter with Europe. Ashgate, Farnham, pp 157–178.
Fawzān M (1430/2010) Al-Tanẓīm al-Qaḍā'ī al-Jadīd fī al-Mamlaka al-^{c}Arabiyya as-Sa^{c}ūdiyya. Maktabat al-Qānūn wa-l-Iqtiṣād, Riyadh.
Ibn al-Qayyim (1416/1996) Zād al-Ma'ād fī Hadī Khayr al-'Ibād, 6 vols. Maktabat al-Manār al-Islāmiyya, Kuwait.
Ibn al-Qayyim (1426/2005) Tuḥfat al-Mawdūd bi-Aḥkām al-Mawlūd. Dār al-Kutub al-^{c}Ilmiyya, Beirut.
Ibn Bāz ^{c}A (1409/1989) Matn al-Raḥbiya wa-l-Fawā'id al-Jaliyya fī al-Mabāḥith al-Farḍiyya. Al-Idāra al-^{c}Āmma li-l-Ṭab^{c}a wa-l-Tarjama, Riyadh.
Ibn Bāz ^{c}A (1425/2004) Majmū^{c}at al-Fatāwā wa-Maqālāt Mutanawwi^{c}a, 24 vols. Dār al-Qāsim, Riyadh.
Ibn Daqīq al-^{c}Īd T (1372/1953) Iḥkām al-Aḥkām Sharḥ ^{c}Umdat al-Aḥkām, 2 vols. Al-Maṭba^{c}a al-Sunna al-Muḥammadiyya, Cairo.
Ibn Mundhir A (1420/1999) Al-Ijmā^{c}. Maktabat Makka al-Thaqāfiyya, Mecca.
Ibn Qāsim M (ed) (1399/1979) Fatāwā wa-Rasā'il Samāḥat al-Shaykh Muḥammad bin Ibrāhīm Āl al-Shaykh, 13 vols. Maṭba^{c}at al-Ḥukūma bi-Makka al-Mukarrama, Mecca.
Ibn Qudāma M (1417/1997) Al-Mughnī, 15 vols. Dār ^{c}Ālam al-Kutub, Riyadh.
Ibn Rushd M (1415/1994) Bidāyat al-Mujtahid, 4 vols. Maktabat Ibn Taymiyya, Cairo.
Ibn Taymiyya T (1432/2011) Majmū^{c}at al-Fatāwa, 20 vols. Dār Ibn Ḥazm, Beirut.
Ibn ^{c}Uthaymīn M (1404/1983) Tashīl al-Farā'iḍ. Dār al-Ṭayba, Riyadh.
Ibn ^{c}Uthaymīn M (1428/2007) Al-Sharḥ al-Mumti^{c} ^{c}alā Zād al-Mustaqni^{c}, 15 vols. Dār Ibn al-Jawzī, Dammam.
Johansen B (2008) A Perfect Law in an Imperfect Society: Ibn Taymiyya's Concept of 'Governance in the Name of the Sacred Law'. In: Bearman P, Heinrichs W and Weiss B (eds) The Law Applied: Contextualizing the Islamic Shari^{c}a. I.B. Tauris, London, pp 259–294.

La China S, Alotaibi M (2010) La legge sul processo civile dell'Arabia Saudita. Giuffrè Editore, Milan.
Maisel S (2014) The New Rise of Tribalism in Saudi Arabia. Nomadic Peoples 18(2):100–122.
Markaz al-Buḥūth (1438/2017) Al-Mabādi' wa-l-Qarārāt al-Ṣādira min al-Hay'a al-Qaḍā'iyya al-ᶜUlyā wa-l-Hay'a al-Dā'ima wa-l-ᶜĀmma bi-Majlis al-Qaḍā' al-ᶜĀlā wa-l-Maḥkama al-ᶜUlyā min ᶜĀm 1391 ilā ᶜĀm 1437. Markaz al-Buḥūth, Riyadh.
Mathieu M (2008) Le nouveau système judiciaire de l'Arabie Saoudite – Un exemple d'adaption de la *Chari'a* au monde moderne. Revue internationale de droit comparé 60(2):447–459.
Melchert C (2013) The Relation of Ibn Taymiyya and Ibn Qayyim al-Jawziyya to the Ḥanbalī School of Law. In: Krawietz B, Tamer G (eds) Islamic Theology, Philosophy and Law: Debating Ibn Taymiyya and Ibn Qayyim al-Jawziyya. De Gruyter, Berlin.
Samin N (2015) Of Sand or Soil: Genealogy and Tribal Belonging in Saudi Arabia. Princeton University Press, Princeton.
Vogel F (2000) Islamic Law and Legal System: Studies of Saudi Arabia. Brill, Leiden.

Dominik Krell is a research associate at the Max Planck Institute for Comparative and International Private Law in Hamburg and a doctoral candidate at the University of Hamburg. His research focuses on the way Islamic law is applied by Saudi Arabian courts. He studied German law, contemporary legal history and legal theory at Humboldt-Universität zu Berlin. In addition to his legal training, he holds a bachelor's degree in history and culture of the Middle East from Freie Universität Berlin and an MSc in social anthropology from Oxford University. In April-May and July-August 2018, he was a visiting fellow at the King Faisal Center for Research and Islamic Studies in Riyadh, Saudi Arabia.

Chapter 12
Tunisia

Souhayma Ben Achour

Contents

Abstract This study seeks to analyze the Tunisian legal rules that govern filiation and the child's relationship with his or her family, as well as the status and protection of parentless children. In line with Islamic doctrine, the Tunisian Personal

Souhayma Ben Achour is a professor of private law at the Faculty of Law and Political Science at Université de Tunis El Manar.

S. Ben Achour (✉)
Faculté de Droit et des Sciences Politiques, Université de Tunis El Manar,
Campus universitaire El Manar, 2092 Tunis, Tunisia
e-mail: benachoursouhayma@ymail.com

N. Yassari et al. (eds.), *Filiation and the Protection of Parentless Children*, https://doi.org/10.1007/978-94-6265-311-5_12

Status Code of 1956 only recognized the general notion of *nasab* or legitimate filiation, and made no room for natural filiation. The recognition of out-of-wedlock filiation depended on the courts' interpretation of the provisions of the Personal Status Code. It was only with the adoption of the law of October 28, 1998, that natural filiation was clearly introduced into Tunisian law. This law allowed for the establishment of natural filiation by various means, including DNA testing. Thus, Tunisian family law recognizes two distinct types of biological filiation today: legitimate filiation or filiation resulting from marriage, which is subject to the provisions of the Personal Status Code, and natural filiation or filiation outside marriage, which is governed by the law of October 28, 1998. Tunisian law also guarantees a substitute family to the child through two main institutions – *kafala* and adoption – which were introduced by the law of March 4, 1958. *Kafala* is an institution drawn from Islamic law. It does not break the child's relationship with his or her family of origin and does not create a relationship of filiation between the child and the *kafil*, which is in line with the meaning of this concept in Islam. However, the admission of adoption makes Tunisia unique in the Arab Muslim world. The adopted child is fully equated with the legitimate child. In addition to *kafala* and adoption, Tunisian law ensures the child temporary protection through family placement, which was instituted by the law of November 21, 1967. Family placement occurs most often as a temporary solution pending the implementation of *kafala* or adoption.

Keywords Tunisia · Legitimate filiation · *nasab* · *firash* · Presumption of paternity · *iqrar* · Paternity recognition · Paternal natural filiation · Maternal natural filiation · DNA test · Cohabitation · Paternity disownment · *kafala* · Adoption · *tabbani* · Substitute family · Family placement

12.1 Introduction

12.1.1 General Overview of Tunisian Family Law

Tunisian family law holds a special place in the Arab Muslim world. Just a few months after Tunisia gained independence, its legislature chose to establish a new social model. On August 13, 1956, an innovative Personal Status Code that deviates from the traditional remedies of Islamic law was promulgated.[1] The Code prohibited polygamy and made it a criminal offense, abolished the institution of the matrimonial guardian, and required the consent of both spouses for marriage. The Code also prohibited repudiation and prescribed the judicial dissolution of marriage on equal grounds.

[1] Decree of August 13, 1956, Promulgating the Personal Status Code, Official Gazette no. 104 of December 28, 1956, pp 1742–1751.

Upon its promulgation, the Code was widely praised in Western countries. Its reforms were described as 'revolutionary' and 'audacious,'[2] and the Code was perceived as heralding the first signs of an Arab spring.[3] In the Arab Muslim world, however, the Code was not welcomed with the same enthusiasm. In Tunisia, it was negatively perceived by the conservative segment of the population. Trying to accommodate this broad swathe of the public, the political discourse thus sought to link the Code to *ijtihad* by grounding it in an innovative reading of the religious texts. Ahmed Mestiri, then the Minister of Justice, explained in the press releases accompanying the promulgation of the Code that its prescriptions were drawn from Islamic law and did not contradict the Qur'anic text. Similarly, President Bourguiba repeatedly stated that the Code had not marginalized religion, and that its content was, to the contrary, a return 'to the pure sources of Islam.'[4]

The reforms were then pursued in small incremental steps. The Law of August 1, 1957, Regulating Civil Status[5] transformed the marriage contract into a solemn act. The law of June 3, 1966,[6] amended the Personal Status Code by repealing the order of custody devolution that directly derived from the Maliki rite, and made the child's interest the sole criterion for awarding custody. The reforms of 1981[7] and 1993[8] gave the mother certain prerogatives of guardianship.

The rules governing the child's relationship with his or her family are part of this general movement to modernize Tunisian family law.[9] Specifically, the law of March 4, 1958,[10] broke with Islamic doctrine by authorizing adoption, making of this institution a privileged mode of protecting parentless children. More recently, the law of October 28, 1998, opened the path for the establishment of natural filiation by allowing paternity to be proved on the basis of genetic testing and outside any marriage bond.[11] Both laws considerably deviate from the traditional restrictions of Islamic law.

---

[2] Ben Achour 1992; Colomer 1957, p 114.

[3] Benoist-Méchin 1959.

[4] Bostanji 2009, no. 1, p 11; Fregosi 2004, pp 78–99.

[5] Law No. 57-3 of August 1, 1957, Regulating Civil Status, Official Gazette no. 2 and 3 of July 30 and August 2, 1957, pp 10–14.

[6] Law No. 66-49 of June 3, 1966, Amending the Personal Status Code, Official Gazette no. 24 of June 3, 1966, p 880.

[7] Law No. 81-7 of February 18, 1981, Amending Certain Articles of the Personal Status Code, Official Gazette no. 11 of February 20, 1981, pp 334–335.

[8] Law No. 93-74 of July 12, 1993, Amending Certain Articles of the Personal Status Code, Official Gazette no. 53 of July 20, 1993, pp 1004–1005.

[9] Ben Achour 2008, pp 279–311.

[10] Law No. 58-27 of March 4, 1958, on Public Guardianship, Informal Guardianship (*kafala*) and Adoption, Official Gazette no. 19 of March 7, 1958, pp 236–237.

[11] Law No. 98-75 of October 28, 1998, Concerning the Assigning of a Patronymic Name to Abandoned Children or Children of Unknown Paternity, Official Gazette no. 87 of October 30, 1998, p 2119.

12.1.2 The Sources of Law

In Tunisian domestic law, there are four main bodies of rules that regulate the relationship of a child to his or her family: Articles 68–75 of the Personal Status Code promulgated on August 13, 1956, which govern legitimate filiation (*nasab*); the Law of March 4, 1958, on Public Guardianship, Informal Guardianship (*kafala*) and Adoption;[12] the Law of November 21, 1967, on Family Placement;[13] and the Law of October 28, 1998, Concerning the Assigning of a Patronymic Name to Abandoned Children or Children of Unknown Paternity.[14] In addition to these statutes, case law is a source of great importance in Tunisian family law. The Tunisian courts have indeed played an important role in the interpretation of legal provisions that often have lacunae or are unclear.

With regard to international sources, the United Nations Convention on the Rights of the Child of November 20, 1989, should be mentioned.[15] This Convention clearly recognizes the right of the child to a family. According to the preamble of the Convention, the signatory States acknowledge 'that the child, for the full and harmonious development of his or her personality, should grow up in a family environment, in an atmosphere of happiness, love and understanding.' Article 7 of the Convention admits that the child has 'as far as possible, the right to know and be cared for by his or her parents.' The text thus enshrines the right of the child to be raised in his or her family of origin. Article 20 of the Convention ultimately recognizes the right of the child to a replacement family, by providing that 'a child temporarily or permanently deprived of his or her family environment, or in whose own best interests cannot be allowed to remain in this environment, shall be entitled to special protection and assistance provided by the State.' The text adds that the States Parties should provide alternative care for this child in accordance with their national law. Such alternative care, according to the same text, 'could include, inter alia, foster placement, kafalah of Islamic law, adoption or if necessary placement in suitable institutions for the care of children. When

---

[12] Law No. 58-27 of March 4, 1958. In this regard, the present report will focus on informal guardianship (*kafala*) and adoption as means of alternative family care. Public guardianship as an institutional mode of alternative care will not be specifically addressed. In fact, Law No. 58-27 of March 4, 1958, does not give a definition of public guardianship, but it provides that the found or abandoned child will be placed under the guardianship of the state, and it designates the public guardian which can be, notably, the director of the hospital or the orphanage or the nursery, or the director of the rehabilitation center or the children's home, in the event the child has been placed in such institutions, or the governor in other cases.

[13] Law No. 67-47 of November 21, 1967, on Family Placement, Official Gazette no. 49 of November 21–24, 1967, p 1446.

[14] Law No. 98-75 of October 28, 1998.

[15] Law No. 91-92 of November 29, 1991, Ratifying the United Nations Convention on the Rights of the Child, Official Gazette no. 82 of December 3, 1991, p 1890. The Convention was published by Decree No. 91-1865 of December 10, 1991, Official Gazette no. 84 of December 10, 1991, pp 1946–1952.

considering solutions, due regard shall be paid to the desirability of continuity in a child's upbringing and to the child's ethnic, religious, cultural and linguistic background.'

12.1.3 The Competent Courts

The Tunisian judicial system has been totally unified since 1957. Unlike many Arab Muslim countries, Tunisia does not have religious courts ruling on family law.[16] Matters relating to family law fall within the jurisdiction of the tribunal of first instance, which is the ordinary court in civil matters.[17] In accordance with the general rules, judgments issued by the tribunal of first instance may be appealed before the Court of Appeal, and judgments issued by the Court of Appeal may be subject to cassation review before the Court of Cassation. Some questions are specifically assigned to the cantonal tribunal. For example, the cantonal judge is competent to rule on adoption.[18] Judgments given by the cantonal tribunal may be appealed before the tribunal of first instance.

12.2 Legitimate Filiation or *nasab* (Filiation in Marriage)

The Tunisian Personal Status Code does not use the concept of legitimate filiation.[19] It uses the Islamic notion of *nasab*, which corresponds to the 'direct family relationship between a man and a child introducing the latter into the agnatic line,'[20] and does not regulate legitimate maternal filiation.

12.2.1 The Establishment of nasab

Legitimate paternal filiation or *nasab* can be established according to Article 68 of the Personal Status Code by three means: 'cohabitation, the acknowledgment of the father or the testimony of two or more honorable persons.' The text is directly drawn from classical Islamic law.

16 Mezghani 1991, no. 170-205; Parisot 2013; Tobich 2008.

17 Article 40 Code of Civil and Commercial Procedure, Official Gazette no. 59 of November 27 and December 1, 1959, pp 1325–1336, and Official Gazette no. 60 of December 4, 1959, pp 1399–1411.

18 Article 13 Law No. 58-27 of March 4, 1958.

19 On the Tunisian law of filiation: Ben Halima 1976; Ben Halima 2001, pp 459–480; Ben Halima 2003, no. 16, pp 19–37; Ben Fadhel 2005, pp 683–716; Bouguerra 1977–1978; Pruvost 1977.

20 Meziou 2013, no. 203.

12.2.1.1 Cohabitation

The word 'cohabitation,' which is the French translation of the Personal Status Code for the Arabic term *firash* or bed, aims at designating marriage. In fact, the term cohabitation does not correctly reflect the term *firash*. *Firash* is not simply cohabitation, nor is it marriage. It covers, according to classical Islamic law, any lawful relationship that the child's father entertains with the child's mother.[21]

The legitimate father of a child born in the context of marriage is the husband of the child's mother. This is the presumption *pater is est quem nuptiae demonstrant*, which is the legal presumption concerning the biological period of conception. The starting point for the presumption of paternity is not clearly established because of a contradiction between two different provisions of the law. On the one hand, Article 71 of the Personal Status Code makes this presumption operative from the date of the conclusion of the marriage, by providing that the presumption of paternity covers 'the child born to a married woman, six months or more after the conclusion of the marriage.' On the other hand, Article 22 of the same Code establishes the presumption only if the marriage is consummated. The consummation of marriage is a concept inspired by Islamic law, which means the existence of sexual relations between the spouses. Article 22, however, corresponds more to the biological truth, since an important period may separate the date of the marriage's conclusion from that of its consummation.

The presumption of paternity ends, pursuant to Article 69 of the Personal Status Code, one year after the husband's death or after a divorce. Thus, a child born to a married woman within one year after a divorce or the husband's death remains covered by the presumption of paternity. The solution is quite logical in the case of death because it is an event that occurs with certainty and can be determined accurately. However, it may seem unrealistic in the case of divorce, since a long period of time may elapse between the separation of the spouses and the pronouncement of the divorce.

It should be noted, finally, that the presumption of paternity is operative 'irrespective of the validity or invalidity of marriage' according to Article 71 of the Personal Status Code. This solution is confirmed by Article 22 of the Code, which expressly provides for the establishment of filiation among the effects of a void marriage. The cause of the nullity of the marriage, whether the lack of a substantive or of a formal requirement for the marriage's validity, does not matter. The concept of the void marriage has often led to the conferring of legitimate filiation upon children who were, in reality, natural children.

[21] On this issue, Meziou 2013, no. 206.

12.2.1.2 Acknowledgment *(iqrar)*

In addition to marriage, legitimate filiation can be proved by acknowledgment (*iqrar*), which means recognition of paternity. Filiation established by acknowledgment is, in principle, legitimate filiation. It is thus conceived as a means to corroborate a relationship between the parents in the context of a null marriage by strengthening the presumption of paternity.[22] This stems from a constant jurisprudence according to which 'the acknowledgment provided for under Article 68 of the Personal Status Code is based on the existence of a marriage relationship, even should this marriage be null, and not based on the existence of a mere cohabitation relationship;' therefore 'the decision that establishes the filiation of a child to a man on the basis of a mere acknowledgment by the latter of intimate relations with the mother and of the child's paternity should be overruled.'[23]

12.2.1.3 Testimony

Legitimate filiation may be proved by the testimony of two or more honorable persons. The Personal Status Code regulates neither the form nor the content of the testimony. Similarly to acknowledgment, the testimony can be conceived as a means to corroborate the existence of a marriage. This particularly stems from a decision of the Court of Cassation, according to which witnesses must prove the existence of a lawful relationship between parents, constituted on the basis of a valid marriage, or even on the basis of a marriage that is null because it has not been celebrated in the required authentic form.[24]

12.2.2 The Revocation of **nasab**

Legitimate filiation established according to the provisions of Article 68 of the Personal Status Code may be broken. Two legal provisions regulate the breakdown of legitimate filiation: Article 69 and Article 75 of the Personal Status Code.

Article 69 of the Code provides that 'filiation is not established in the event of the disavowal of a child of a married woman whose lack of cohabitation with the husband has been proved, or of a child born one year after the husband's absence or death or after the date of divorce.' This action is not reserved to the husband. In a

---

22 It will be seen that acknowledgment has also served, in case law, to establish natural filiation, irrespective of any marriage.

23 Cass. civ., May 15, 1984, no. 9976, Bulletin des arrêts de la Cour de cassation (Chambres civiles) (hereinafter: Bull.) 1984, I, p 198.

24 Cass. civ., May 7, 1996, no. 49-089, Bull. 1996, II, p 231.

decision of June 13, 1989, the Court of Cassation admitted the use of this action by the mother, by the child or by the heirs.[25]

The action provided for by Article 75 of the Personal Status Code is, however, reserved to the husband. This article provides that 'if the husband denies being the father of a child conceived or born during the marriage, the contested filiation will be broken only by a court decision.' The same provision allows the use of 'all the modes of evidence provided for under the law.' Courts have admitted several means to break filiation, including blood tests.[26]

12.3 Natural Filiation (Filiation Outside Marriage)

Prior to the law of October 28, 1998, natural filiation was not clearly recognized in Tunisian law. It depended on the court's interpretation of the provisions of the Personal Status Code. By allowing the establishment of natural filiation, the law of October 28, 1998 has profoundly transformed the law of filiation.

12.3.1 Filiation Outside Marriage in the Personal Status Code

The Personal Status Code did not directly address natural filiation. However, it dealt with it indirectly, from the perspective of inheritance. Article 152 of the Code provides that 'the child of adultery (*walad al-zina*) shall inherit only from his mother and her parents. The mother and her parents will have, alone, inheritance rights in the succession of the said child.' This text excludes the child of adultery from inheriting from his or her father.

In line with Islamic law, the Personal Status Code did not regulate natural paternal filiation. In fact, the question of whether natural paternal filiation was recognized under Tunisian law depended on the interpretation to be given to Article 68 of the Personal Status Code. Indeed, the main issue was to know whether filiation could be proved outside of 'cohabitation,' that is, marriage. In fact, this implied determining the role of acknowledgment and testimony, in relation to marriage, as a means to prove filiation. Could these two ways of establishing filiation be considered to be linked to marriage and to serve only to consolidate it, especially when the marriage was void, or were they to be considered autonomous ways to establish filiation?

---

[25] Cass. civ., June 13, 1989, no. 21419, Bull. 1989, I, p 292.

[26] Cour d'appel Tunis, June 2, 1992, no. 93630 (unpublished), reported by Meziou 2013, no. 291; Cass. civ., January 26, 1993, no. 27777, Bull. 1993, p 283.

Tunisian case law is not settled on the question of whether acknowledgment alone could constitute a means of establishing filiation irrespective of any marital relationship. Five stages in the evolution of the jurisprudence of the Court of Cassation can be distinguished. In the years following the independence of the Tunisian state, the Court of Cassation conferred a probative value upon acknowledgement regardless of marriage, stating that the father's acknowledgment is sufficient to establish filiation and that proof of marriage is not necessary to that effect.[27] In a second stage, the Court of Cassation adopted a more traditional solution: in a decision of May 15, 1984, it held that 'the acknowledgment provided for under Article 68 of the Personal Status Code is based on the existence of a marriage relationship, even should this marriage be null, and not based on the existence of a mere cohabitation relationship,' adding that 'the decision that establishes the filiation of a child to a man on the basis of mere acknowledgment by the latter of intimate relations with the mother and of the child's paternity should be overruled.'[28] After returning to its first position,[29] the Court of Cassation reconsidered it and again adopted a restrictive reading of Article 68 of the Code: it stated, in a decision of May 13, 1997, that 'Article 68 of the Personal Status Code does not allow for establishing the filiation of a child born of an adulterous relationship' and that 'the three means of evidence enumerated in this article can be used only to prove the filiation of a child born from a legitimate marital union even should one of the substantive or formal requirements of marriage be lacking.'[30] The last shift was a decision issued on April 13, 2006, by the Court of Cassation, which states that 'each of the means of evidence set out in Article 68 of the Personal Status Code constitutes sufficient proof of filiation, without any other condition, the text using the conjunction "or," which means the possibility of a choice.'[31] On the basis of this interpretation of Article 68, the Court of Cassation conferred inheritance rights in the estate of his father upon a child of adultery.

The establishment of natural filiation thus depended on random and questionable means of proof. It is only with a certain leniency towards the natural child that some court decisions have been able to recognize natural filiation on the basis of the father's acknowledgment or on the basis of testimony. Nevertheless, neither of these two means of proof make it possible to establish filiation in a way that is certain and unquestionable.

---

[27] Cass. civ., December 5, 1963, no. 2000, cited by Ben Attar 1963–1965, p 28.

[28] Cass. civ., May 15, 1984, no. 9976, Bull. 1984, I, p 198.

[29] Cass. civ., June 13, 1989, no. 21419, Bull. 1989, I, p 292, stating that the procedures for establishing filiation provided for by the legislature are distinct from one another and that if the legislature had intended to tie the acknowledgment to the existence of a conjugal relationship, it would have mentioned cohabitation (or marriage), the presumption of paternity being sufficient to establish filiation.

[30] Cass. civ., May 13, 1997, no. 56315, Revue tunisienne de droit 2001, p 141, with case note by Ben Halima.

[31] Cass. civ., April 13, 2006, no. 7332, Bull. 2006, p 229.

It should be noted in this regard that testimonial evidence is less valuable than acknowledgement as a means of establishing filiation. A few first-instance decisions have definitely admitted the establishment of filiation on the basis of testimony, but the Court of Cassation has always shown open hostility towards this means of establishing filiation, by considering that it could only be used to prove the existence of a lawful relationship, that is, a marriage.[32] In view of the quasi-systematic refusal by the Court of Cassation to accept testimony as a means of establishing filiation outside marriage, the establishment of out-of-wedlock filiation was ultimately dependent on the father's desire, through the acknowledgment of paternity.

12.3.2 Filiation Outside Marriage in the Law of October 28, 1998

Mastering the technique of DNA testing has deeply transformed Tunisian filiation law. By making it possible to access the biological truth, genetic tests allow the filiation of a child to be established with certainty. The Tunisian legislature is sensitive to the situation of the natural child, and could not remain indifferent to the impact of this technique on filiation issues. On October 28, 1998, the legislature promulgated an innovative law that, although timidly titled 'Law Concerning the Assigning of a Patronymic Name to Abandoned Children or Children of Unknown Paternity,'[33] in fact opens the path to the establishment of natural filiation under Tunisian law.[34]

12.3.2.1 The Meaning of the Law of October 28, 1998

The law of October 28, 1998, allows the establishment of paternal natural filiation and maternal natural filiation.

The Establishment of Paternal Natural Filiation

Article 3 of the law of October 28, 1998, states that the party concerned, the father, the mother or the public prosecutor can request from the relevant first instance tribunal that the father's patronymic name be assigned to a child of unknown

[32] See, in particular, Cass. civ., January 6, 1981, no. 4339, Revue de jurisprudence et de législation 1981, no. 2, p 61; Cass. civ., June 2, 1992, no. 26431, Bull. 1992, p 183; Cass. civ., November 18, 1996, no. 43-354, Bull. 1996, II, p 225; Cass. civ., November 26, 1996, no. 51-346, Bull. 1996, II, p 228; Cass. civ., May 7, 1996, no. 49-089, Bull. 1996, II, p 231.

[33] Law No. 98-75 of October 28, 1998.

[34] On this law, Ben Achour 2013b, pp 71–90; Ben Halima 2000, pp 245–269; Mezghani 2005, pp 651–682; Ben Tardaiet-Ghamersa 2004, pp 179–205.

paternity whose paternity is proved by acknowledgment, testimony or genetic analysis. Contrary to what its title might suggest, the 1998 law does not deal solely with the assigning of the patronymic name. Its real object is, in fact, to allow for the establishment of natural paternal filiation.[35] It is, as Ali Mezghani notes, 'to attach a child to his or her father first, and to provide him or her with a name afterwards. The patronymic name indicates filiation. It is the consequence or the effect. It is obvious but it needs to be demonstrated since the law is written in reverse. The law prescribes that the child be assigned the name of the man who has been established to be his or her father.'[36]

It should be noted, in this respect, that the hostility shown by some court decisions to the establishment of natural filiation was not solely due to legal, sociological and cultural motives, but also to scientific ones. Before the advent of DNA testing, it was sometimes impossible to access the biological truth. The admission of natural filiation by the legislature is, therefore, not only the result of societal evolution and change in mentalities; it is largely based on the biological certainty that DNA testing allows for.

However, the courts remained divided as to the meaning of the law of October 28, 1998. While certain decisions, taking the full measure of the wording and especially of the spirit of the new law, allowed for the establishment of out-of-wedlock paternal filiation,[37] several decisions issued by first instance tribunals have very seriously reduced the law's input by merely assigning a patronymic name to the child born out of wedlock without establishing his or her filiation.[38] The Court of Cassation has approved this last trend. Specifically, in a decision of May 11, 2001, it stated that 'the law of October 28, 1998 makes it possible to assign the father's patronymic name to the child whose filiation is proved by acknowledgment, testimony or DNA testing. This issue does not relate to the establishment of filiation or the proof of paternity.'[39]

In addition, the question arose as to what consequences the father's refusal to submit to DNA testing should have. In its original version, the law of October 28, 1998, remained silent on this sensitive issue, leaving it to the judge to fill the gap. Courts have split on this matter. In a decision issued on November 16, 2000,[40] the Court of Cassation ruled that the father's refusal to submit to a DNA test cannot be considered acknowledgment of paternity within the meaning of Article 429 of

---

35 In this sense, Ben Halima 2000, p 245; Mezghani 2005, p 658.

36 Mezghani 2005, p 658.

37 Tribunal de première instance (hereinafter: TPI) Tunis, May 10, 1999, no. 29308; TPI Tunis, November 22, 1999, no. 31846 (both unpublished).

38 In this sense, TPI Sfax, June 11, 1999, no. 41164; TPI Tunis, June 21, 1999, no. 29840; TPI Tunis, December 6, 1999, no. 31968; TPI Sousse, February 29, 2000, no. 40376 (all unpublished). On this issue, Abdelkader 2001.

39 Cass. civ., May 11, 2001, no. 6719, Bull. 2001, p 331. In the same sense, Cass. civ., November 16, 2000, no. 4182/2000, Revue tunisienne de droit 2001, p 169, with case note by Charfeddine.

40 Cass. civ., November 16, 2000, no. 4182/2000, Revue tunisienne de droit 2001, p 169, with case note by Charfeddine.

the Code of Obligations and Contracts.[41] In another decision on October 12, 2001,[42] it held the opposite position.

The new para 3 of Article 3 bis of the 1998 law, which was added by the law of July 7, 2003,[43] attempts to solve the issue. This provision allows the court, 'in the event of refusal to comply with the order prescribing genetic analysis,' to rule on the basis of 'numerous, consistent, serious and precise presumptions.' The idea underlining this rule is that the refusal to submit to genetic analysis presumes an implicit acknowledgment of paternity. This was decided by the Court of Cassation in a ruling of October 8, 2004,[44] in which it states that 'the law of October 28, 1998, is intended to protect children who have been abandoned or are of unknown paternity' and that 'the refusal of the father to undergo genetic analysis constitutes an implicit acknowledgment of his daughter's filiation as established in paragraph 3 of Article 3 bis of the aforementioned law, the tribunal having ruled on the case on the basis of numerous, consistent, serious and precise presumptions at its disposal.' The solution is repeated in a decision of March 2, 2006, in which the Court of Cassation clearly states that 'the refusal of the father to submit to DNA testing constitutes an implicit acknowledgment of his paternity.'[45]

The Establishment of Maternal Natural Filiation

In addition to natural paternal filiation, the law of October 28, 1998, makes it possible to establish natural maternal filiation. Paragraph 2 of Article 3 bis of this law allows the person concerned, the father, the mother or the public prosecutor to request from the competent first instance tribunal 'that the mother be subjected to genetic analysis to prove that she is the mother of the person whose filiation is unknown'. As is the case is for the father, the court may rule on the basis of numerous, consistent, serious and precise presumptions in the event that the mother refuses to submit to the DNA test.

The mother's submission to DNA testing is of practical interest, especially when the child has been abandoned at birth. This test makes it possible to identify the mother with certainty and to establish the biological link between her and the child.

---

[41] Article 429 of the Code of Obligations and Contracts states that 'judicial acknowledgment may result from the silence of the party when, formally invited by the judge to provide explanations as to the question addressed to it, this party persists in not answering and does not request a deadline for doing so,' Code of Obligations and Contracts of December 15, 1906, Official Gazette no. 100 of December 15, 1906.

[42] Cass. civ., October 12, 2001, no. 2001-10020, Revue tunisienne de droit 2001, p 169, with case note by Charfeddine.

[43] Law No. 2003-51 of July 7, 2003, Amending and Completing the Law No. 98-75 of October 28, 1998, Concerning the Assigning of a Patronymic Name to Abandoned Children or Children of Unknown Paternity, Official Gazette no. 54 of July 8, 2003, pp 2259–2260.

[44] Cass. civ., October 8, 2004, no. 2494 (unpublished).

[45] Cass. civ., March 2, 2006, no. 7799, Bull. 2006, p 279.

However, the establishment of natural maternal filiation must not affect the mother's ability to give birth anonymously. For various reasons, it is sometimes preferable for the origin of the child to be kept unknown. It is up to the judge to decide, according to the best interests of the child, whether or not to subject the mother to genetic testing.

12.3.2.2 The Implementation of the Action Initiated by the Law of October 28, 1998

There are three main restrictions on the use of genetic evidence in the context of the action initiated by the law of October 28, 1998: the action is solely reserved to abandoned children or children of unknown paternity; it can only be used within a judicial framework; and it can only be exercised by certain persons restrictively determined by the law.

Beneficiaries of the Action: Children Without Filiation

Action to seek natural paternity or maternity is reserved to abandoned children and children of unknown paternity. In the first case, it concerns children whose paternal and maternal filiation are unknown, and in the second, children whose paternal filiation is not established.

This action is not open to the adopted child since his or her filiation is established with regard to the adopter. 'Affective'[46] filiation thus outweighs the biological truth. There is no point in disturbing the tranquility of a family built solely on legal ties. However, the revocation of adoption, which the Court of Cassation has authorized, could legitimately be believed to allow for the use of DNA testing.[47] The revocation of adoption has the effect of breaking the bond of adoptive filiation. The child may therefore, in some cases, be deprived of filiation.

The action instituted by the law of October 28, 1998, is also not open to legitimate children, except in the context of the judicial proceedings provided for in Article 75 of the Personal Status Code.[48] The exclusion of the adopted child and the legitimate child from the scope of the 1998 law thus makes it possible to preserve the peace of families.

---

[46] Mechri 2002, p 213.

[47] On this question: Béjaoui 1994; Bel Hadj Yahia 1979, pp 83–104; Ben Halima 1996, p 171.

[48] Article 75 of the Personal Status Code provides that 'if the husband denies being the father of a child conceived or born during the marriage, the contested filiation shall be severed only by a court decision. All the modes of proof provided for in this matter by the law are admitted.'

The Judicial Framework of the Action

Secondly, DNA testing can only be used in a judicial context. This limit is intended to preserve the peace of families. There are several reasons why a person might seek genetic testing outside of any judicial framework. These may include seeking to gather certain evidence before taking legal action, pressuring or blackmailing a family member, or disinheriting a natural child.

The Capacity to Exercise the Action

Only four persons are eligible to seek genetic evidence: the person concerned, the father, the mother and the representative of the public prosecutor. This list is therefore exhaustive, not indicative.[49]

The possibility for the person concerned to request DNA testing is based on the child's fundamental right to know his or her origins, a right enshrined in the United Nations Convention of November 20, 1989.[50] If the person concerned has reached the age of majority, he or she will directly exercise the action opened by the law of October 28, 1998. If he or she is a minor, he or she will be represented by his or her mother or father. However, the representation of the minor child by his or her mother or father does not seem to be of great practical interest since the latter can exercise, on the child's behalf, the action instituted by the law of October 28, 1998. If neither parent is known, the child can be represented by his or her guardian.[51] However, the exercise of such an action by the guardian encounters a practical obstacle, given that no parent is known and the guardian would not be able to identify the alleged father; it is indeed one of the parents, most often the mother, who designates the person on whom the test will be performed.

The possibility for the father to request the use of DNA testing to prove his paternity may, at first glance, seem odd. Indeed, nothing prevents the father from registering the newborn child under his name at the civil registry office, since the civil registry officer does not require a marriage certificate to be submitted at the birth of the child. One can, however, conceive of cases in which the father, doubting his paternity upon the birth of the child, seeks the use of DNA testing to

---

[49] Article 3 bis, paras 2 and 3 Law No. 98-75 of October 28, 1998.

[50] Article 7 of the Convention provides that 'the child shall be registered immediately after birth and shall have the right from birth to a name, the right to acquire a nationality and, as far as possible, the right to know and be cared for by his or her parents.'

[51] Even if Law No. 98-75 of October 28, 1998, does not expressly provide for it, the child whose parents are both unknown may be represented by the public guardian to exercise the action provided for by the law. According to Article 2 Law No. 58-27 of March 4, 1958, on Public Guardianship, Informal Guardianship (*kafala*) and Adoption, the public guardian has the same rights and obligations vis-à-vis the ward than as those of the father and mother.

be certain that he is the child's father.[52] The law also allows the father to request the use of DNA testing to prove natural maternity.

In practice, it is primarily the mother who requests the use of genetic evidence in court to establish natural paternal filiation. This possibility for the mother to prove the natural paternity of her child is one of the major contributions of the law of October 28, 1998. By giving the mother the right to establish paternal filiation in court, the law of 1998 allows her to override the mere will of the father. In addition, to facilitate the mother's task, the law did not require her to be the custodian or the guardian of her child. On the other hand, it may seem strange to grant the mother the right to request a DNA test to prove her maternity. However, one could imagine a case in which the mother has abandoned her child and then, feeling remorseful, seeks to find the child. The DNA test performed on her and the child supposed to be hers would establish with certainty the biological link between them.

Finally, the 1998 law allows the representative of the public prosecutor's office to request genetic analysis in court. This possibility raises the question of how the public prosecutor's office could become aware of situations of abandoned children or children of unknown paternity. The answer to this question could be found in Article 26 of the Code of Criminal Procedure, which places the public prosecutor, as the representative of the public prosecutor's office before the tribunal of first instance, in charge of 'recording all offenses ..., receiving denunciations made to him by public agents and individuals and receiving complaints from injured parties.' The public prosecutor is thus able to discover criminal acts that may be at the origin of situations of abandoned children or of unknown paternity.[53] However, the action taken by the public prosecutor's office must be in the best interests of the child. It must not result in the disclosure of natural paternity or maternity where this undermines the best interests of the child. It is indeed with the aim of protecting the child that the law of October 28, 1998, allowed the use of DNA testing.

12.4 Adoption

Islamic law clearly prohibits adoption. This prohibition results from two known Qur'anic verses[54] and is explained in particular by the fact that it undermines the equilibrium of the agnatic family that is based on blood relations.[55] Indeed, it blurs

---

52 Ben Tardaiet-Ghamersa 2004, p 179.

53 Ben Tardaiet-Ghamersa 2004, p 179.

54 The ban is from the Confederates Sura 33, verse 4: '... nor has He [Allah] made your adopted sons your sons.' Verse 5: 'Call them [your adopted sons] by [the names of] their fathers: that is juster in the sight of Allah' (The Holy Qur-ān: English translation of the meanings and Commentary (1990) (Translated by Ali Y) King Fahd Holy Qur-ān Printing Complex, Medina).

55 It is not sufficient to explain the prohibition of adoption through the factual circumstances surrounding the Prophet's desire to marry the repudiated ex-wife of his adopted son Zeid. On this question, Pruvost 1977, p 402.

the natural links of filiation by creating artificial links of filiation and disrupts inheritance rules designed to protect families who are related by blood.

With the exception of Tunisia, all Arab Muslim countries prohibit adoption. Deciding to break with tradition in order to better address the problem of abandoned children, the Tunisian legislature authorized adoption from the first years of independence with the law of March 4, 1958, on public guardianship, *kafala* (informal guardianship) and adoption.[56] However, the law regulated the conditions and effects of adoption in a rather imprecise way, and remained silent on the important issue of the revocation of adoption.

12.4.1 The Conditions for the Formation of Adoption

12.4.1.1 Substantive Conditions

The conditions required by the legislature for adoption can be divided into two categories. Some aim to provide the child with a satisfying moral and material environment. Article 9 of the law of March 4, 1958, requires the adopter to be 'a person of the age of majority, of either sex … and enjoying full civil capacity … of good moral character, with a healthy body and mind, and able to support the needs of the adopted person.'

Other conditions aim to bring the adoptive family 'closer' to the legitimate family based on the bonds of marriage. Thus the legislature requires, in Article 9 of the law, that the adopter be married. When only one person requests the adoption, it is necessary that the consent of the spouse be given. The judge may, however, exempt the widowed or divorced adopter from the marriage requirement if the best interests of the child require this. In this event, the adoption remains in the context of the legitimate family since the adopter has been married fora certain period of his life; the marriage dissolved by divorce or death allows the adopted child to be covered by the legitimacy previously acquired. However, it seems that, despite this possibility provided by the law, adoption is rarely granted to a widowed or divorced person.[57] In order for adoption to be granted to a widowed or divorced person, a bond must already have been established between that person and the child. This is the case, for example, when the child has been placed with a married couple and one of them dies before the adoption is pronounced; to ensure continuity in the child's life, the adoption may be granted to the surviving spouse.

Finally, in order to create a bond that is similar to the biological bond between parents and their legitimate child, the law requires an age difference of at least 15

---

56 On this law, Pruvost 1973, pp 141–149. On the difference between adoption and *kafala*, Ben Achour 2013a, pp 19–32.

57 A recent judgment dated August 28, 2018 by the Cantonal Tribunal of Tunis (Journal La Presse, August 29, 2018) authorized, for the first time, the adoption of a child (disabled) by a single woman.

years between the adopter and the adoptee. Such a requirement is waived when the adoptee is the child of the adopter's spouse.

12.4.1.2 Formal Conditions

The creation of the adoption relationship is subject to two phases: a preparatory phase and a judicial phase.

With regard to the preparatory phase, candidates for adoption must first submit a request to the Ministry of Social Affairs. An investigation of the prospective candidates is then conducted to assess their ability to provide the child with good moral and material conditions. If the investigation results in a favorable opinion, the child may be placed with the family. A social worker is then charged with carrying out several checks. If the social worker gives a favorable opinion, the judicial phase is triggered.[58]

The second phase involves the judicial authority. According to Article 13 of the law, the adoption 'is established by a judgment rendered by the cantonal judge sitting in chambers in the presence of the adopter, his spouse, the father and mother of the adoptee, or the administrative authority vested with the public guardianship, or the informal guardian.'

12.4.2 The Effects of Adoption

12.4.2.1 Effects on the Family of Origin

The Tunisian legislature did not provide for adoption to sever ties with the family of origin.[59] However, notwithstanding the silence of the law, we can consider that there is a breakdown of the links between the adoptee and his or her family of origin under Tunisian law. Indeed, the very extensive patrimonial and extra-patrimonial effects that adoption produces with regard to the adoptive family make it possible to consider that links with the family of origin have been severed, and that the links with the adoptive family replace them.

Some of the adoptee's links with his or her family of origin are, however, not totally severed. There are three reasons for this. First, for obvious religious, moral, ethical and biological reasons, the matrimonial impediments persist between the adoptee and his or her family of origin.[60] Second, a record of the filiation of origin

---

[58] Béjaoui-Attar 2003, no. 16, pp 79–101.

[59] Other laws have been much clearer on the issue. For example, Article 356 of the French Civil Code provides that full adoption 'confers on the child a filiation which replaces his or her filiation of origin. The adoptee ceases to belong to the family by blood.'

[60] Article 15, para 3 Law No. 58-27 of March 4, 1958.

is kept in the civil registry archives, as well as in the archives of the INPE (National Institute of Child Protection) in cases in which the child had been entrusted to the INPE before his or her adoption. An original civil status record, mentioning the child's original name, is in fact kept by these services. A copy of this original deed is also attached to the adoption judgment and given to the adoptive parents. Finally, the fact that the Court of Cassation has admitted the possibility of revoking adoption suggests that the ties between the family of origin and the adopted child are not completely severed.

12.4.2.2 Effects on the Adoptive Family

With respect to the adoptive family, adoption produces the same patrimonial and extra-patrimonial effects as legitimate filiation. This is clear from Article 15 of the law of March 4, 1958, pursuant to which 'the adoptee has the same rights and the same obligations as a legitimate child. The adopter has vis-à-vis the adoptee the same rights as the law grants to legitimate parents and the same obligations as it imposes on them.'

Patrimonial Effects

Adoption has two main patrimonial effects: maintenance and inheritance. The maintenance obligation includes 'food, clothing, housing, education, and all that is considered necessary for existence, according to usage and custom,' pursuant to Article 50 of the Personal Status Code. The adopter has a maintenance obligation towards the child. The adopted child's right to maintenance extends beyond the age of majority as it is governed by the same legal regime as the legitimate child's right to maintenance.[61] The adopted child's right to maintenance extends to persons other than the adoptive parents, in accordance with Article 43 of the Personal Status Code. This article, which concerns the legitimate child and which applies to the adopted child through Article 15 of the law of March 4, 1958, provides that 'descendants, to whatever degree they belong, have the right to maintenance.' In the event of the parents' disappearance, the adopted child, like the legitimate child, can thus claim maintenance, for example, from his or her grandfather.

As the adopted child is assimilated to the legitimate child, he or she may succeed his or her adoptive family under the same conditions. Similarly, the members of the adoptive family may succeed the adopted child under the same conditions as in a legitimate family.

---

[61] Article 46 of the Personal Status Code provides that 'children shall continue to be served until they reach the age of majority, or beyond that age, until the end of the age of majority or the end of their studies, provided that they do not exceed the age of 25 years. The girl continues to be entitled to maintenance as long as she has no resources or is not taken in charge by her husband.'

Extra-Patrimonial Effects

Adoption has three main effects on the adoptive family: the assigning of the name, of guardianship and of custody.

Regarding the assigning of the name, Article 14 of the law clearly states that the adoptee takes the name of the adopter. This implicitly means that the name of the adopter replaces the name of the family of origin if the latter is known. The name of the adopter is included in the adoptee's civil status register; the name of the biological father disappears.

Adoption leads to the assigning of guardianship to the adoptive parents. Adoptive parents exercise guardianship under the same conditions as legitimate parents by application of Article 15 of the law of March 4, 1958. The rules relating to the guardianship of the legitimate child, which apply to the adoptive child, are laid down in Article 154 of the Personal Status Code. The adoptive father thus becomes the child's guardian, and in the event of death or incapacity, the mother becomes the child's guardian.

Finally, the rules relating to the custody of the child, contained in Articles 54 et seq. of the Personal Status Code, apply in the event of adoption.

12.4.3 The Termination of the Adoption Relationship

The law of March 4, 1958, has gaps, as it does not address the important issue of the revocation of adoption.[62] In other legal systems, the issue has been clearly regulated; for instance, Article 349 of the French Civil Code provides that 'adoption is irrevocable.'

The Tunisian judges had to fill this regrettable gap left by the legislature. The first instance judges were initially divided on the matter. Relying on Article 13 para 3 of the 1958 law, which provides that the adoption judgment is final, several decisions issued by the courts have considered adoption to be irrevocable.[63] Other decisions, on the other hand, held that adoption was revocable,[64] considering that the term 'definitive,' used in Article 13 of the Law, related only to the procedural aspect of the judgment and not to the merits, in the sense that it could only be challenged by extraordinary remedies such as cassation and third-party opposition; adoption could, however, be challenged and revoked.

---

[62] On the issue of the revocation of adoption, Barhoumi-Néji 2007–2008, p 411; Béjaoui 1994; Bel Hadj Yahia 1979, pp 83–104.

[63] TPI Tunis, April 17, 1978, no. 57554; TPI Monastir, February 1, 1985, no. 4064; TPI Monastir, May 19, 1989, no. 6126; Cour d'appel Monastir, December 21, 1991, no. 557 (all unpublished), cited by Béjaoui-Attar 2003, pp 98, 99.

[64] Cour d'appel Monastir, December 9, 1987, no. 319; TPI Tunis, October 19, 1989, no. 5813; TPI Kairouan, March 6, 1989, no. 20973 (all unpublished), cited by Barhoumi-Néji 2007–2008, p 411.

The Court of Cassation endorsed this second trend. In a first decision issued on April 2, 1991,[65] it recognized the possibility of breaking the adoptive bond by accepting the third-party opposition formed by one of the parties. This position was confirmed in a second decision of March 23, 1993,[66] in which the court considered that adoption has a mixed contractual and judicial nature, and that by applying the principle of parallelism of forms, adoption is concluded and dissolved in the same way, that is, on the basis of a declaration of intent certified by the judge. To declare the adoption revocable, the Court of Cassation also based its decision on the interests of the child. It considered that the interests of the child are the basis for the constitution of the adoption relationship and that such interest should also justify its possible revocation.

The first instance judges, however, showed some resistance to the Court of Cassation. Several decisions following the judgment of March 23, 1993, considered adoption to be irrevocable. This was the case in a judgment of the Court of Appeal of Sousse of May 5, 1993,[67] and in two judgments of the Tribunal of First Instance of Monastir dated October 21, 1999,[68] and February 10, 2000.[69]

The possibility of revoking adoption, as admitted by the courts, weakens it and brings it closer to the institution of *kafala*. Indeed, if adoption can be broken, it corresponds more to a method of moral and material care of the child than to a filiation relationship. Adoption, once established, should no longer depend on the will of the parties. If the interests of the child so require, for example in cases of child abuse, other legal means will help to keep the child away from the adoptive family. All the measures provided for by the Child Protection Code[70] can indeed be implemented.

12.5 Kafala *(Informal Guardianship)*

Named informal guardianship by the law of March 4, 1958, *kafala* is an institution derived from Islamic law that constitutes a mode of protection for children deprived of families. Article 3 of the law defines *kafala* as the act by which an adult person, enjoying full civil capacity, or an assistance organization takes charge of a minor child by taking custody of him or her and by meeting his or her needs. Tunisian law

[65] Cass. civ., April 2, 1991, no. 27008 (unpublished), cited by Barhoumi-Néji 2007–2008, p 461.

[66] Cass. civ., March 23, 1993, no. 295, Bull. 1993, p 290.

[67] Ben Halima 1996, p 171.

[68] TPI Monastir, October 21, 1999, no. 12574 (unpublished), reproduced by Barhoumi-Néji 2007–2008, p 397.

[69] TPI Monastir, February 10, 2000, no. 12824 (unpublished), reproduced by Barhoumi-Néji 2007–2008, p 405.

[70] Law No. 95-92 of November 9, 1995, Relative to the Publication of the Child Protection Code, Official Gazette no. 90 of 1995, p 2095.

devotes only four articles to *kafala*. There are gaps in these articles' governance of the conditions and effects of *kafala*.

12.5.1 The Conditions for kafala

The creation of the *kafala* bond is subject to substantive and formal conditions. The substantive conditions are provided for in Article 3, which only requires that the informal guardian (*kafil*) be a physical adult person enjoying full civil capacity; the law does not specify any substantive condition as to age or to the existence of a marriage bond. Furthermore, the *kafil* need not be a physical person; it may be an 'assistance organization.' The *kafil* must be able to provide for the child's needs.

Concerning the formal conditions, *kafala*, like adoption, goes through a double phase, preparatory and judicial. The preparatory phase takes place under the same conditions as those described above for adoption.[71] However, the judicial phase is subject to different conditions than those set for adoption. In the case of *kafala*, the cantonal judge only approves a contract signed before a notary public between, on one hand, the informal guardian (*kafil*), and on the other hand, the parents of the child, or one of them if the other is unknown or deceased, or the public guardian.[72] Thus, *kafala* results from a simple contract approved by the judge, while adoption results from a judicial decision. Notwithstanding this difference, the judge has the option, in either case, to refuse to approve the *kafala* or to pronounce the adoption.

12.5.2 The Effects of kafala

12.5.2.1 Effects on the Family of Origin

Unlike adoption, *kafala* does not break the bond between the *makful*, i.e. the child protected by the institution of *kafala*, and the family of origin. This is clear from Article 6 of the law of March 4, 1958, which provides that 'the ward retains all the rights arising from his or her filiation, and in particular his or her name and inheritance rights.' Article 6 confirms the idea that *kafala* does not create a filiation relationship, and that it merely constitutes a means of moral and material support of the child.

---

[71] Béjaoui-Attar 2003, pp 79–101.

[72] Article 3 Law No. 58-27 of March 4, 1958.

12.5.2.2 Effects on the Replacement Family

First, *kafala* entails patrimonial effects on the replacement family. It puts the *kafil* in charge of providing for the material needs of the child.[73] Such a maintenance obligation ends when the child reaches the age of majority since *kafala* itself ends when the child reaches the age of majority in accordance with Article 7 of the law of March 4, 1958. This is a significant difference from adoption.[74] The right of the *makful* to the maintenance obligation weighs only on the *kafil*, and does not extend to other family members, in particular to the grandparents. No provision in the law of March 4, 1958, provides that the maintenance obligation vis-à-vis the *makful* is subject to the rules governing the maintenance obligation toward the legitimate child. This point is also a significant difference from adoption.[75]

In addition, there is no reciprocal right to inheritance between the *makful* and the *kafil* family. The *makful* cannot inherit from the *kafil*, and retains his or her inheritance rights with regard to his or her family of origin as clearly stated in Article 6 of the law of March 4, 1958. Similarly, the *kafil*, as well as his or her family, does not inherit from the *makful*. It is, however, possible to circumvent the inheritance rules to allow the child to collect some, if not all, of the property that belongs to the *kafil*, by using a will or a donation.[76]

Regarding non-patrimonial effects of *kafala*, the effects on name, guardianship and guardianship will be examined. The *makful* does not take the name of the *kafil*. Article 6 of the law of March 4, 1958, provides clearly that the ward keeps the name of his or her family of origin. Such a solution can be understood in the case of a child whose parents of origin are known. But it may seem inadequate when the family of origin is not known. What, indeed, is the advantage of keeping the fictitious name assigned to the ward by the public guardian?[77] In cases in which the

---

[73] Article 3 Law No. 58-27 of March 4, 1958.

[74] See section "Patrimonial Effects".

[75] See section "Patrimonial Effects".

[76] Such a possibility is clearly provided for by Moroccan Law No. 15-01 of June 13, 2002, on the Care of Abandoned Children, Official Gazette no. 5036 of September 5, 2002, pp 914–918. Article 23 of this law clearly allows the person providing *kafala* 'to make the child cared for the beneficiary of a donation, a will, a *tanzil* or a charity.'

[77] The public guardian is required to assign a patronymic name to the child of unknown parents. This obligation results today from the Law No. 98-75 of October 28, 1998.

child's original family is not known, it seems better to change his or her name in order to give him or her the *kafil*'s name.[78]

Kafala has no effect on legal guardianship. Guardianship belongs to the child's legal father if *kafala* has been concluded with him. It belongs to the public institution – that is to say, essentially the INPE – in the event that the child has been entrusted to the *kafil* by this institution.[79] The rules relating to the guardianship of the legitimate child, contained in Articles 54 et seq. of the Personal Status Code, apply to the *kafala*, by reference to Article 5 of the law of March 4, 1958.

12.6 Family Placement

Governed by the law of November 21, 1967,[80] family placement is a form of family protection for the child; it may be short-term or long-term.

12.6.1 Short-Term Family Placement

Short-term placement occurs in two ways. First, family placement can be a step prior to establishing *kafala* or adoption.[81] The child is thus placed in the family that will subsequently become his or her adoptive family or his or her *kafila* family. In this case, family placement appears to be an 'experimental stage' that measures the family's ability to welcome the child and the child's integration into the family.

---

[78] This is the solution provided by Algerian law. Indeed, Decree-Law No. 92-24 of January 13, 1992, Completing the Decree No. 71-157 of June 3, 1971, on the Change of Name, Official Gazette no. 05 of January 22, 1992, p 113, provides that if the minor child admitted by *kafala* is of unknown paternity, he or she may change his or her name to match that of the *kafil*. The request for a change of name is made by the guardian of the *makful*. This possibility of assigning the name of the *kafil* to the *makful* brings *kafala* closer to adoption, and makes it practically 'disguised adoption under *kafala*.' The assimilation between *kafala* and adoption remains limited, however, as the possibility of assigning the *kafil*'s family name to the *makful* only applies to children born to an unknown father.

[79] The solution is different in other legal systems. For instance, pursuant to Article 17 of the Moroccan Law No. 15-01 of June 13, 2002, the guardianship judge designates the person in charge of the *kafala* as a dative tutor, that is to say, judicial guardian of the child. Algerian law goes even further, since guardianship exercised over the *makful* child by the *kafil* is not judicial guardianship, but legal guardianship. This is clearly the result of Article 121 of the Algerian Family Code, according to which 'the legal reception confers on the beneficiary legal guardianship,' Law No. 84-11 of June 9, 1984, on the Family Code, Official Gazette no. 24 of June 12, 1984, pp 612–625. *Kafala* in Algerian and Moroccan legislation therefore grants the *kafil* more rights toward the *makful* than in Tunisian legislation.

[80] Law No. 67-47 of November 21, 1967.

[81] See Sects. 12.4.1 and 12.5.1.

Second, short-term family placement can be provided by 'professional families' who welcome children into their homes. The family with whom the child is placed receives material compensation (about 100 dinars a month) as well as help in kind (diapers, clothes, baby formula, etc.) in order to enable them to provide for the child's needs.[82] Family placement therefore appears to be an 'arrangement' between the state and some low-income families: the state gives them material assistance, and these families in return provide care for the child, thus relieving the burden on the public authorities. At present, about 300 children under the guardianship of INPE are placed in host families. The duration of placement in these 'professional families' varies according to the situation. Family placement can be a short- or medium-term solution, pending the return of the child to his or her family of origin or the establishment of *kafala* or adoption. The child spends a few weeks or months with the host family before returning to his or her family of origin, or before the establishment of the *kafala* or adoption with another family.

12.6.2 Long-Term Family Placement

Family placement can last for several years. In this case, it will constitute a longer-term solution when the child's situation neither allows the child to return to his or her mother, in particular because of difficulties that the latter faces, nor allows for the establishment of *kafala* or adoption. This is, unfortunately, often the situation of disabled children, as Tunisian families who request *kafala* or adoption generally claim to 'require' a child in good health. To this extent, family placement seems to be a last resort where no more satisfactory solution has been found.

12.7 Conclusion

Tunisian law holds a special place in the Muslim world. Without totally rejecting the rules of Islamic law, it has in many ways departed from such rules and has significantly strengthened consideration of the interests of the child. Indeed, the Personal Status Code remained faithful to Islamic law and took up the traditional solutions of the Maliki rite by adopting the notion of *nasab*, which corresponds to legitimate paternal filiation. The rules governing the establishment and termination of legitimate filiation quite faithfully reproduce those of Islamic law.

As for natural filiation, the Code ignores it. An important trend in case law attempted to make room for the establishment of natural filiation by providing a flexible reading of the rules enshrined in the Personal Status Code. However, a different and contrasting trend refused to recognize filiation outside marriage. The

[82] Article 2 Law No. 67-47 of November 21, 1967.

situation of the child born out of wedlock thus remained uncertain and depended on the courts' interpretation of the law. Fortunately, the law of October 28, 1998, put an end to judicial hesitation by allowing natural filiation to be proven through various means, in particular through DNA testing. This law marks an important turning point in Tunisian filiation law, because it makes it possible to base filiation on the biological truth and to disconnect it from marriage.

Tunisian law is also notable for authorizing adoption despite the latter's prohibition in Islamic law. Indeed, the law of March 4, 1958, offers children without family support protection that can fit into the traditional Islamic *kafala* framework or into the more modern adoption framework.

References

Abdelkader A (2001) La filiation paternelle d'après la loi du 28 octobre 1998. Unpublished DEA thesis, Faculté des sciences juridiques, politiques et sociales de Tunis.

Barhoumi-Néji M (2007–2008) Al-Tabanni [Adoption]. Unpublished thesis, Faculté de droit et des sciences politiques de Tunis.

Béjaoui I (1994) La révocation de l'adoption. Unpublished DEA thesis, Faculté de droit de Tunis.

Béjaoui-Attar I (2003) L'intérêt de l'enfant, fondement de l'adoption en droit tunisien. Actualités juridiques tunisiennes 16:79–101.

Bel Hadj Yahia B (1979) La révocation de l'adoption en droit tunisien. Revue tunisienne de droit 83–104.

Ben Achour S (2008) Le statut de l'enfant en droit tunisien. In: Khaïat L, Marchal C (eds) L'enfant en droit musulman (Afrique, Moyen-Orient), Actes du colloque du 14 janvier 2008. Société de législation comparée, Paris, pp 279–311.

Ben Achour S (2013a) L'adoption et la *kafalah*: quelles différences en droit? In: Regards croisés sur l'adoption, actes de la journée d'études organisée à la Faculté des sciences juridiques, politiques et sociales de Tunis, le 24 mai 2012, avec le soutien de la Fondation Hanss Seidel, Tunis, pp 19–33.

Ben Achour S (2013b) Le droit tunisien de la filiation à l'épreuve du progrès biologique. In: Ben Achour S, Chedly L (eds) La diversité dans le droit, Mélanges offerts à la Doyenne Kalthoum Meziou-Dourai. Centre de Publication Universitaire, La Manouba, pp 69–90.

Ben Achour Y (1992) Une révolution par le droit? Bourguiba et le Code du statut personnel. In: Ben Achour Y (ed) Politique, religion et droit dans le monde arabe. Cérès-CERP, Tunis, pp 203–225.

Ben Attar R (1963–1965) La filiation dans le Code du statut personnel tunisien. Revue tunisienne de droit 25–29.

Ben Fadhel O (2005) Unité du statut de la filiation en droit tunisien. In: Zine M et al. (eds) Mouvements du droit contemporain, Mélanges offerts au Professeur Sassi Ben Halima. Centre de Publication Universitaire, Tunis, pp 683–716.

Ben Halima S (1976) La filiation paternelle légitime en droit tunisien. Unpublished thesis, Faculté de droit et des sciences politiques de Tunis.

Ben Halima S (1996) Hal Yajuzu al-Ruju^c fi al-Tabanni? [Can Adoption Be Revoked?]. Revue tunisienne de droit/Al-Majalla al-Qanuniyya al-Tunisiyya 176–199.

Ben Halima S (2000) Ithbat al-Bunuwwa Hasaba Ahkam al-Qanun al-Mu'arrakh fi 28 Uktubar 1998 [The Establishment of Natural Filiation According to the Law of October 28, 1998]. In: Ayari C et al. (eds) Mélanges en l'honneur de Habib Ayadi. Centre de Publication Universitaire, Tunis, pp 245–269.

Ben Halima S (2001) La filiation naturelle en droit tunisien. In: Mélanges en l'honneur de Mohamed Charfi. Centre de Publication Universitaire, Tunis, pp 459–480.
Ben Halima S (2003) La filiation en droit tunisien. Actualités juridiques tunisiennes 16:19–37.
Ben Tardaiet-Ghamersa M (2004) La preuve génétique de la paternité à travers la loi n° 98-75 du 28 octobre 1998 relative à l'attribution d'un nom patronymique aux enfants abandonnés ou de fili tion inconnue, telle que modifiée par la loi n° 2003-51 du 7 juillet 2003. Revue tunisienne de droit 179–205.
Benoist-Méchin J (1959) Un printemps arabe. Albin Michel, Paris.
Bostanji S (2009) Turbulences dans l'application judicaire du Code tunisien du statut personnel: le conflit de référentiels dans l'œuvre prétorienne. Revue internationale de droit comparé 61(1): 7–47.
Bouguerra M (1977–1978) Ithbat Nasab Ibn al-Khatibayn [The Establishment of the Filiation of the Child of the Betrothed]. Unpublished DES thesis, Faculté de droit de Tunis.
Colomer A (1957) Le Code du statut personnel tunisien. Librairie Ferraris, Algiers.
Fregosi F (2004) Bourguiba et la régulation institutionnelle de l'Islam: les contours audacieux d'un gallicanisme politique à la tunisienne. In: Camau M, Geisser V (eds) Habib Bourguiba, la trace et l'héritage. Karthala, Paris, pp 78–99.
Mechri F (2002) L'enfant, objet et sujet d'affection. CPU-Publisud, Tunis.
Mezghani A (1991) Droit International Privé, Etats Nouveaux et Relations Privées Internationales, Cérès-CERP, Tunis.
Mezghani A (2005) Le droit tunisien reconnaît ses enfants naturels. In: Zine M et al. (eds) Mouvements du droit contemporain, Mélanges offerts au professeur Sassi Ben Halima. Centre de Publication Universitaire, Tunis, pp 651–682.
Meziou K (2013) Tunisie – Droit civil, Droit de la famille. Droit comparé, fasc. 20/Notarial Répertoire, Législation comparée, fasc. 1. In: Labic J (ed) Jurisclasseur droit comparé, vol IV. LexisNexis, Paris.
Pruvost L (1973) L'enfant abandonné : bilan de législation tunisienne. Revue IBLA 131:141–149.
Pruvost L (1977) L'établissement de la filiation en droit tunisien. Unpublished thesis, Université de Paris II.
Parisot V (2013) Les conflits internes de lois. Thesis, Université de Paris I, Panthéon-Sorbonne, vol II. IRJS Editions, Paris.
Tobich F (2008) Les statuts personnels dans les Pays Arabes: de l'éclatement à l'harmonisation. Presses universitaires d'Aix-Marseille, Aix-en-Provence.

Souhayma Ben Achour is professor of private law at the Faculty of Law and Political Science at Université de Tunis El Manar. She holds a DEA in private international law from the Université Panthéon-Assas in Paris and a DEA in private law from the Université Robert Schuman in Strasbourg. In 2003, she completed her Ph.D. in law at the Université de Tunis Carthage. She has held various teaching positions in private law at universities in Tunisia, and has published widely on issues of family and succession law in private international law and the impact of religion on Tunisian private international law. More recently, her research has also focused on migration trends to and from Tunisia.

Chapter 13
United Arab Emirates

Lena-Maria Möller

Contents

Abstract The Emirati Code of Personal Status of 2005 recognizes four grounds for establishing filiation (*nasab*): a valid marriage (usually circumscribed as '*firāsh*'), acknowledgment (*iqrār*), proof (*bayyina*), and scientific methods (*ṭuruq ʿilmiyya*). At the same time, these options are all limited by additional requirements that need to be fulfilled for a full parent-child relationship to emerge. Should both paternal and maternal filiation not be established, the child will be treated as '*majhūl al-nasab*', i.e. of unknown filiation, with such a child sometimes also being referred to as a foundling (*laqīṭ*). Foundlings or abandoned children are a growing societal problem in the United Arab Emirates. They are protected by the state insofar as they are automatically awarded citizenship, thereby having access to the far-reaching governmental benefits available only to nationals. Nonetheless, these benefits have

Lena-Maria Möller is a senior research fellow within the Research Group 'Changes in God's Law – An Inner Islamic Comparison of Family and Succession Law' at the Max Planck Institute for Comparative and International Private Law, Hamburg.

L.-M. Möller (✉)
Max Planck Institute for Comparative and International Private Law,
Mittelweg 187, 20148 Hamburg, Germany
e-mail: moeller@mpipriv.de

N. Yassari et al. (eds.), *Filiation and the Protection of Parentless Children*, https://doi.org/10.1007/978-94-6265-311-5_13

not solved the issue entirely, as foundlings and children of unknown filiation are still in need of a permanent caretaker. It is for this reason that the Emirati legislature passed the federal Foster Care Act of 2012, which comprehensively regulates questions regarding the protection of children without filiation. This specialized legislation has unified (i) the procedure for awarding and revoking foster care, (ii) the requirements for potential caretakers, and (iii) the rights and duties of caretakers; further, it allows for both married couples and single females over the age of thirty to foster children. Yet an analysis of the existing legal framework reveals that caretakers will primarily assume the role of custodian (*ḥāḍin*) rather than being granted full parental authority, including unlimited rights of guardianship (*wilāya*).

Keywords United Arab Emirates · *nasab* · *iqrār* · DNA test · *riʿāyat al-aṭfāl majhūlī al-nasab* · Foundling (*laqīṭ*) · Foster care · Single female caretakers

13.1 Introduction

Emirati family law has experienced significant changes within the last decade and a half. While adjudication in matters of Muslim personal status was previously based on traditional Islamic legal doctrine, in 2005 the United Arab Emirates for the first time introduced a code which comprehensively covered questions of marriage, divorce and custody as well as inheritance.[1] Moreover, in the years following the introduction of the country's first personal status code, further legislation was enacted in the area of family law as well as on related issues, including foster care. The most important piece of legislation in this regard is the 2012 Federal Act on Care (*riʿāya*) for Children of Unknown Filiation (*aṭfāl majhūlī al-nasab*).[2]

The Code of Personal Status is largely inspired by Sunni Maliki legal doctrine, which has historically reigned supreme, given that the ruling families of the two largest emirates, Abu Dhabi and Dubai, adhere to the Maliki school of legal thought.[3] Where the code remains silent on an issue, courts are therefore required to resort to Maliki legal doctrine first and to Hanbali law (the country's second most dominant school of legal thought) second.[4] In theory, the Code of Personal Status mandatorily applies to all (Muslim) citizens, while foreigners may opt to have the

[1] Federal Code of Personal Status no. 28 of 2005, Official Gazette no. 439 of November 30, 2015 (hereafter: Code of Personal Status); see also Möller 2016.

[2] Federal Law on Care for Children of Unknown Filiation no. 1 of 2012, Official Gazette no. 537 of June 7, 2012 (hereafter: Foster Care Act).

[3] See for example Dubai Court of Cassation, appeal no. 23/2005 of May 22, 2006 (on file with author) and Federal High Court, appeal no. 555/26 of September 12, 2005 (on file with author), both explicitly referencing the supreme position of Maliki law in the United Arab Emirates.

[4] Article 2(3) Code of Personal Status; Shafiʿi legal doctrine comes third and Hanafi legal doctrine last.

code applied to their personal status affairs.[5] In reality, given the multinational demographic setting of the United Arab Emirates,[6] a multitude of family law regimes are being applied (formally or informally), largely depending on both the nationality and the religious affiliation of the parties.

Upon reaching independence in 1971, the United Arab Emirates established a judicial system which, in addition to civil and criminal courts, also featured personal status courts (sing. *maḥkamat al-aḥwāl al-shakhṣiyya*) primarily adjudicating in matters related to Muslim family and succession law (regardless of sectarian affiliation).[7] Judgments in personal status cases can be appealed before the respective chamber of the appeal courts and the courts of cassation of those emirates that have an independent judicial system (i.e. Abu Dhabi, Dubai and Ras al-Khaimah) or before the Federal High Court for the remaining four emirates.[8] The country's personal status courts are competent to hear cases relating to both filiation and foster care arrangements. In the latter case, the courts are crucial in providing the necessary documents to integrate a child into his or her foster family more permanently, such as certificates regarding custody and appointed guardianship (*wiṣāya*), as will be discussed in due course.

This country report will first and foremost cover the legislative framework governing the establishment of filiation (*nasab*) as well as protective measures for children lacking filiation and/or permanent caretakers as articulated in the domestic law applicable to Muslims citizens. This analysis of Emirati law will be carried out against the background of the country's social particularities as well as legal practice and the courts' interpretation of *nasab* and foster-care relationships.

13.2 The Establishment of Filiation

13.2.1 Establishing Filiation by Law

According to Emirati family law, maternal filiation is established through a woman giving birth to a child.[9] Hence, whoever bears the child will be considered his or her mother regardless of genetic questions raised by modern artificial reproduction

---

[5] Article 1(2) Code of Personal Status; theoretically, the code applies to non-Muslim citizens only insofar as their religious affiliation does not hold its own set of laws governing matters of personal status. In reality, however, virtually all Emirati citizens are Muslim.

[6] According to the latest census of 2010, the United Arab Emirates' total population numbers 8,264,070, of whom only 947,997 are national citizens, see United Arab Emirates National Bureau of Statistics, www.uaestatistics.gov.ae/ReportPDF/Population%20Estimates%202006%20-%202010.pdf (accessed June 6, 2017).

[7] Al Tamimi 2003, pp 9–18; Möller 2015, pp 81–82, 86–87.

[8] Ras al-Khaimah does not have a Court of Cassation; the final appellate court is the emirate's Appeal Court.

[9] Article 90(3) Code of Personal Status.

technologies such as egg donation. This rule further implies that maternal filiation will not be influenced by a mother's marital status. In contrast, paternity is first and foremost established through a valid marriage to the woman bearing the child.[10] This clear distinction between maternal and paternal filiation and the principle of '*al-walad li-l-firāsh*', namely that 'the child belongs to the marital bed', mark a cornerstone of traditional Islamic legal doctrine on the parent-child relationship and were incorporated by the Emirati legislature upon the codification of family law in 2005.

13.2.1.1 Presumption of Paternity

The Code of Personal Status defines the shortest and the longest potential duration of a pregnancy.[11] Accordingly, for paternal filiation to be established within a valid marriage, it is required that the child be born not less than 180 days after the marriage was concluded and not more than 365 days after the marriage was dissolved (through divorce or death of the husband).[12] Even though a period of 365 days clearly exceeds the potential duration of any pregnancy and cannot be justified on the basis of medical science, there is no explicit mention of the pre-modern Islamic legal concept of the 'sleeping embryo' (*al-rāqid*) in the current Code of Personal Status. The Explanatory Memorandum to the code elaborates on the varying opinions among Sunni schools of legal thought without giving any particular preference to the Maliki position (up to five years as part of the sleeping embryo doctrine according to the Explanatory Memorandum). Instead, the legislature has chosen a compromise between scientific knowledge and Islamic legal doctrine (developed in the absence of precise medical tests and making allowances for the importance of a child's *nasab*) and, as stated by the Explanatory Memorandum, has also paid attention to the legislative choices of other Arab-Muslim countries.[13]

Generally, paternal filiation cannot arise from a void marriage. According to the Code of Personal Status, a marriage can be valid (*saḥīḥ*) or invalid (*ghayr ṣaḥīḥ*), whereby the latter category comprises two types of invalidity, defective (*fāsid*) and void (*bāṭil*).[14] Prior to their consummation (*qabl al-dukhūl*), both a defective and a

[10] Article 90(1) Code of Personal Status.

[11] Article 91 Code of Personal Status.

[12] See also Abu Dhabi Court of Cassation, appeal no. 12/2009 of February 25, 2009 (on file with author); Abū Rakhiyya and Al-Jabūrī 2010, p 281; Maʿhad al-Tadrīb al-Dirāsāt al-Qaḍāʾiyya (2010) Al-Mudhakkira al-Īḍāḥiyya li-Qānūn al-Aḥwāl al-Shakhṣiyya [Explanatory Memorandum to the Code of Personal Status], Abu Dhabi, notes to Article 90 (hereafter: Explanatory Memorandum).

[13] Explanatory Memorandum, notes to Article 91; see also Abū Rakhiyya and Al-Jabūrī 2010, pp 279–280.

[14] Article 57 Code of Personal Status.

void marriage do not give rise to any legal consequences, including *nasab* (only as regards the child's father, of course). Following consummation, however, a defective marriage will result in the establishment of a child's paternal filiation.[15] By contrast, should the marriage be *bāṭil*, even consummation will not remedy its invalidity, with the consequence that children born into a void marriage will have no legal relation to their father unless the code stipulates otherwise.[16] The latter is the case only where a marriage is *bāṭil* because it was concluded without the involvement of the woman's marriage guardian (*walī*). While such a marriage is considered void under Emirati family law, children born into the union will have paternal filiation.[17] However, the couple itself will nonetheless be deemed without legal relation.[18]

As opposed to a marriage which is clearly void, a presumed marriage, i.e. a nonexistent marriage which the parties wrongly believe to have been concluded properly or a void marriage in instances where the parties are unaware of their union's invalidity,[19] gives rise to paternal filiation. In these cases, *nasab* is established through the concept of '*al-waṭ' bi-shubha*'.[20] *Al-waṭ' bi-shubha* originates in pre-modern Islamic legal doctrine and can be regarded as a 'safety net' in family law as well as criminal law in the sense that extramarital sexual relations could not be prosecuted as *zinā'* (adultery) if the parties were unaware of their intercourse being illicit. In addition, children born into such an illicit union are protected as regards their paternal affiliation and as regards further rights arising from such filiation.[21]

13.2.1.2 Evidentiary Proceedings

Apart from the above-mentioned legal presumption of paternity, the Code of Personal Status describes additional mechanisms that may prove paternity whenever *firāsh* and *waṭ' bi-shubha* are not evident, or even where they are disputed. The most common instance of these evidentiary proceedings coming into play would be that of an informal marriage.

---

15 Article 60(2) Code of Personal Status.

16 Article 61(2) Code of Personal Status.

17 Article 39 Code of Personal Status; see also Abu Dhabi Court of Cassation, appeal no. 524/2008 of November 19, 2008 (on file with author).

18 See also Dubai Court of Cassation, appeal no. 35/2007 of March 4, 2008 (on file with author).

19 For the different categories of presumption/doubt (*shubha*) see Explanatory Memorandum, notes to Article 90; see also Dubai Court of Cassation, appeal no. 89/2007 of November 20, 2007 (on file with author) in which the marriage between a Muslim man and a Hindu woman was declared void while paternal *nasab* for their mutual son was upheld due to the husband's lack of knowledge about his wife's true religious affiliation.

20 Article 90(2) Code of Personal Status.

21 See further Sect. 13.3.1 below.

The Socio-Legal Context: Informal *misyār* Marriages

Informal marriages, at least in theory, give rise to the same rights as formal marriages registered with the relevant state authorities. While the Emirati legislature generally requires marriages to be registered,[22] its non-registration or conclusion outside of the court will not affect the validity of the marriage itself. Indeed, for a long time it was common practice to register a marriage officially only once children were born into the union and upon the father requesting that a 'family book' (*khulāṣat qayd*) be issued for him, his spouse and his offspring. Nowadays, as the family book is one of the documents that are crucial for accessing the often far-reaching governmental benefits available to newlyweds, registration of marriage has become more widespread.[23] Thus, in the United Arab Emirates, as well as in the overall Gulf region, it is mostly the marriages known as 'travelling marriages' or *misyār* marriages which remain unregistered.

Misyār marriages are concluded for various reasons, including divorced women's desire to retain custody of their children (which, under Emirati family law, they might lose upon remarrying[24]) and polygamous unions that are to be hidden from the first wife. These marriages are characterized by their conclusion without any involvement of state authorities and often by the spouses continuing to live separately and by the wife waiving her right to maintenance.[25] As outlined above, should a *misyār* marriage be concluded without the attendance of witnesses, it will be *fāsid* under Emirati law, so that its consummation will nonetheless lead to the establishment of paternal filiation. Should the marriage be concluded without the *walī*'s consent or knowledge, the marriage will be *bāṭil*, but children will similarly attain *nasab*. Therefore, the issue in *misyār* marriages in the United Arab Emirates concerns not so much the child's general right to *nasab* arising from such a secret union, but rather the mother's ability to prove in court that a marriage has in fact been concluded should the father deny paternity or any involvement with the child's mother. It is in these cases in particular that the aforementioned legal presumptions of paternity will not automatically come into effect and that a child's paternal filiation has to be proven.

Scientific Methods (*ṭuruq ʿilmiyya*)

The Code of Personal Status distinguishes between proof (*bayyina*) and scientific methods (*ṭuruq ʿilmiyya*).[26] The latter essentially comprises DNA testing (circumscribed as '*al-faḥawaṣāt al-jīniyya wa-l-baṣamāt al-wirāthiyya*') and can be

[22] Article 27(1) Code of Personal Status.

[23] Möller 2015, pp 161–164.

[24] Article 144(1) Code of Personal Status.

[25] See generally Arabi 2001, pp 147–167; Hasso 2009, pp 211–222; Al-Nasr 2011, pp 43–57.

[26] Article 89 Code of Personal Status.

ordered only where the existence of a marriage has been proven first.[27] The Explanatory Memorandum clearly states that the provisions on proving paternity through scientific methods have been linked to the existence of *firāsh* 'in order to prevent the manipulation of proof of filiation and make it absolutely impossible to prove this relationship by medical examination [only].'[28] This approach has been confirmed in legal practice. For example, in a case before the Dubai Court of Cassation in 2007, a mother's application to establish paternal filiation (which was denied by the alleged father) through the use of scientific methods was turned down since the woman was unable to prove that she had been married (at least informally) to the defendant. As a result, and particularly without the prior establishment of *firāsh* or *waṭ' bi-shubha*, the court would not agree to order a DNA test to verify that biological filiation existed between the child and the defendant.[29]

Until now, both the Emirati legislature and the judiciary seem eager to avoid any conflict that may arise from proving paternity outside a valid marriage, including the question of a child's rights vis-à-vis his or her biological father. Similarly, the only instance of a court-ordered DNA test being explicitly envisioned in the Code of Personal Status is in connection with a father denying paternity of his wife's child, usually through the procedure of *li'ān*.[30] Accordingly, in such cases, the court may additionally rely on scientific methods.[31] Given that the procedure of *li'ān*, originating in traditional Islamic legal doctrine, generally allows a father to deny the paternity of a child born to his wife simply by taking an oath (without having to present further evidence), it is likely that the court would order a DNA test only where it strongly suspects the claimant's dishonesty. A similar approach has been taken in Jordan and Saudi Arabia where, according to the country reports in this volume, a DNA test can be ordered prior to a *li'ān* proceeding with the result that courts will not allow the mother's husband to conduct *li'ān* once the DNA test proves that he is in fact the child's biological father.

But even in cases where a prior examination has revealed that a child was not the alleged father's biological offspring, courts have been hesitant to admit legal actions for annulment of paternity (*nafī al-nasab*). In August 2010, for example, the Abu Dhabi Court of Cassation ruled against a man's motion to revoke his son's paternal filiation after blood samples and DNA testing had revealed that they were not biologically related. At that time, the child was already eight years old and the case had been pending in different courts for nearly four years. Finally, the Court of Cassation upheld paternity based primarily on the fact that the child was born into a valid marriage between the claimant and his former wife. The court confirmed that a valid marriage was the strongest proof of *nasab* and that annulment of paternity

[27] Article 89 Code of Personal Status, see also Explanatory Memorandum, notes to Article 89.

[28] Explanatory Memorandum, notes to Article 89; see also Abū Zayd 2016, p 127.

[29] Dubai Court of Cassation, appeal no. 105/2007 of December 4, 2007, cited in Abū Zayd 2016, pp 127–128.

[30] Articles 96–97 Emirati Code of Personal Status.

[31] Article 97(5) Emirati Code of Personal Status.

(through means other than a *li'ān* proceeding) was not admissible if filiation was already established through *firāsh*.[32] Likewise, in April 2012, the Abu Dhabi Court of Cassation again confirmed the inadmissibility of scientific evidence if *nasab* had already been established through Islamic (*shar'ī*) and/or legal (*qānūnī*) presumptions of paternity.[33] The court thereby confirmed an earlier judgment issued by the Abu Dhabi Court of Appeal and turned down the first-instance family court's decision to revoke a four-year-old girl's paternal *nasab* based on DNA test results.[34] In both cases, biological evidence did not in any way alter the court's appraisal. The judgments therefore appear to have been motivated primarily by considerations regarding the child's best interests and the overall importance of preserving paternal *nasab*.[35]

In sum, instances of a court either ordering or admitting a DNA test in a family law proceeding are extremely rare. Neither can such a test be ordered if no marriage has been established nor will it be admitted if a presumption of paternity already prevails. The inclusion of scientific methods seems to be of rhetorical value in the first place without their strength of evidence having much impact on legal practice.

Proof (*bayyina*)

In addition to scientific methods, the Code of Personal Status recognizes other means of evidence which are described as proof/*bayyina*. According to the Explanatory Memorandum, the category of *bayyina* encompasses all kinds of Islamically valid evidence ('*al-bayyina al-shar'iyya wa hiya kull mā yubayyinu al-ḥaqq wa yuẓhiruhu*').[36] In particular, this definition describes evidence given by two male Muslims or one male and two female Muslims as to the fact that a child is the son or daughter of someone.[37] What remains unclear, however, is whether such testimony will be admitted exclusively to prove the existence of an informal/unregistered marriage and thereby the legal relationship between a child and his or her parents, or whether *bayyina* may also serve the sole purpose of proving the biological (but not legal) filiation in the absence of a marriage. Given the strict rules

---

[32] Abu Dhabi Court of Cassation, appeal no. 797/2010 of August 25, 2010 (on file with author).

[33] Abu Dhabi Court of Cassation, appeal no. 99, 104/2012 of April 11, 2012, cited in Abū Zayd 2016, pp 129–130.

[34] Abū Zayd 2016, p 129.

[35] In a similar vein, the Abu Dhabi Court of Cassation also turned down a man's request for DNA testing to potentially negate biological filiation between him and his child merely because he had already missed the rather short deadline for initiating a *li'ān* proceeding (one month according to the Code of Personal Status), see Abu Dhabi Court of Cassation, appeal no. 300/2011 of May 18, 2011 (on file with author). The court thereby upheld the child's *nasab* and showed no interest in substituting denial of paternity through the procedure of *li'ān* with scientific means of proof.

[36] Explanatory Memorandum, notes to Article 89.

[37] Abū Rakhiyya and Al-Jabūrī 2010, p 284; see also Abu Dhabi Court of Cassation, appeal no. 156/2009 of June 3, 2009 (on file with author).

on recognition, as will be discussed below, it can, however, be assumed that *bayyina* may not serve to prove the biological filiation of a child born out of wedlock.

13.2.2 Establishing Filiation by Private Autonomy: Acknowledgment of Filiation

Apart from the presumption of paternity within a valid marriage, proof, and scientific methods, *nasab* can also be established by private autonomy, i.e. by either a man or woman acknowledging that a child is theirs.[38] At first glance, acknowledgment (*iqrār*) seems to open up far-reaching possibilities of establishing filiation for children born under dubious circumstances. In reality, however, the Emirati legislature has limited the option of creating *nasab* by acknowledgment, especially by excluding cases in which the acknowledged child (*al-muqarr lahu*) was conceived out of wedlock (*min al-zinā'*).[39]

Iqrār creates a binding and permanent legal relationship between the child and the acknowledging person (*al-muqarr*).[40] This means that the acknowledging person, in general, will not be allowed to retract his or her acknowledgment. Should the acknowledgment nevertheless be revoked, it will only be of limited consequence for the acknowledged child in the sense that, for example, the child will continue to inherit from the acknowledging person, but not vice versa.[41]

Conditions for a valid acknowledgment include that the child is of unknown filiation (*majhūl al-nasab*),[42] that the acknowledging person is an adult of sound

---

38 Articles 89, 92–95 Code of Personal Status.

39 Article 92 Code of Personal Status.

40 Explanatory Memorandum, notes to Article 92.

41 Abdallah Kaleeb, Attorney General and Chief of Civil Prosecution in Dubai, in an interview with the Emirati newspaper 'Al-Imārāt al-Yawm' of October 12, 2012 (see Salūm 2012).

42 Article 92(1)(a) Code of Personal Status; see also Dubai Court of Cassation, appeal no. 31/2005 of October 3, 2005 (on file with author), which revoked a man's *iqrār* pronounced with regard to two boys once the court had established that the boys' *nasab* was in fact known. In this rather curious case, an Emirati citizen had originally acknowledged two boys. At a later stage, he filed a case before the Dubai family court in order to revoke his *iqrār*, claiming that one of the boys was in fact his sister's son (born to her husband who holds Iranian citizenship) and that the other was his stepbrother (or half-brother from the same mother, the term '*akhūhu ghayr al-shaqīq*' is ambiguous here). The man argued that he had only provided the two with *nasab* in order to allow for them to work for the Emirati armed forces (which would have clearly been impossible for his nephew given that, due to his Iranian father, he did not hold Emirati citizenship). While the first instance family court turned down the man's request, the competent appeal court revoked his *iqrār*, a ruling which the acknowledged sons appealed before the Dubai Court of Cassation. The court, however, confirmed the earlier judgment issued by the Appeal Court and argued that a major prerequisite of *iqrār* was that the acknowledged child is of unknown filiation, which did not hold true for the two boys whose fathers were known and cited by name in the judgment.

mind (‘*bālighan ʿāqilan mukhtāran*’), and that the age difference between the acknowledging person and the child is such that the acknowledgment seems plausible (‘*yuḥtamalu ṣidq al-iqrār*’).[43] Finally, if the acknowledged person is not a child, but an adult, he or she needs to consent to the acknowledgment.[44] These four requirements apply to all forms of *iqrār*, whether initiated by a woman (as the child's mother-to-be) or a man (as the child's father-to-be). They are complemented by special regulations governing acknowledgment by either a woman or a man as well as ‘reverse acknowledgment’ by an adult who declares that someone is his or her father or mother.

Acknowledgment of paternity is described as ‘*istilḥāq*’ and can only be pronounced by the father himself and, in theory, only as long as the child has not been conceived out of wedlock.[45] Contrary to this general rule, however, in 2012 Dubai's Court of Cassation did accept an acknowledgment of paternity for a child born into a valid marriage less than six months after the marriage had been concluded. The court opined that the statutory minimum duration of a pregnancy could be disregarded if all other conditions of a valid *iqrār* were fulfilled.[46] This judgment is particularly interesting as *istilḥāq* is considered a special form of *iqrār* and constitutes acknowledgment of paternity in the technical sense of the word: In contrast to a regular *iqrār*, which does not necessarily create a legal relationship to other members of the family (such as brotherhood or cousinage), *istilḥāq* gives rise to all legal rights and duties established by paternal filiation.[47] Interestingly enough, the Code of Personal Status explicitly states that *istilḥāq* cannot be performed by the grandfather-to-be.[48]

Should a married woman or a woman in her waiting period (*ʿidda*) acknowledge a child as her own, her *iqrār* will not automatically create paternal filiation between the child and her husband unless the husband consents or *bayyina* is presented.[49] Similarly, ‘reverse acknowledgment’ by an adult who declared that someone is his or her father or mother is valid only if the acknowledged parent consents or if proof regarding the legal relationship between the two is given.[50] It can be assumed that the term ‘*bayyina*’ in this context again refers to all kinds of Islamically valid evidence, as mentioned above. In general, a close reading of the rules governing *iqrār* confirms that Emirati law considers *bayyina* to be stronger evidence of filiation than what is potentially established through *iqrār*.[51] Therefore, *bayyina* can

[43] Article 92(1)(b), (c) Code of Personal Status.

[44] Article 92(1)(d) Code of Personal Status.

[45] Article 92(2) Code of Personal Status.

[46] Judgment reported in Salūm 2012.

[47] Explanatory Memorandum, notes to Article 92.

[48] Article 92(2) Code of Personal Status.

[49] Article 93 Code of Personal Status.

[50] Article 94 Code of Personal Status.

[51] See also Abū Rakhiyya and Al-Jabūrī 2010, p 285.

not only invalidate *iqrār*, it can also serve to establish *nasab* through acknowledgment where the other party does not consent.

Finally, it should be noted that the rules on *iqrār* are explicitly designed to provide children of unknown filiation with *nasab*. Children whose filiation is known or children who are assumed to have been born out of wedlock thus remain significantly more vulnerable.

13.3 Status of Children of Defective or Unknown Filiation

13.3.1 Children Born Out of Wedlock

The Code of Personal Status does not explicitly discuss the legal status of children born outside a (valid) marriage. Nonetheless, in those articles regulating *nasab* – especially concerning the recognition of a child, as discussed above – reference is sometimes made to the concept of '*walad al-zinā*'', i.e. a child born out of wedlock. In addition, it is implied throughout the code that a father's rights and duties only come into effect if *nasab* has been established.

In cases in which paternity has not been established through legal presumptions, evidence, or acknowledgment, the child will still have maternal *nasab* if the woman who bore the child is known. However, significant legal rights, such as a name, may be denied to him or her due to the lack of paternal filiation. This is in part because Emirati law remains almost silent on the question of how to acquire a family name. Instead, the Emirati Civil Code merely states that each person has a first name (*ism*) and a family name (*laqab*) and that a person's name is 'added' to 'his' children's names ('*yulḥaqu laqabuhu bi-asmāʾi awlādihi*').[52] This rule is reiterated in Law no. 18 of 2009, governing the registration of births and deaths.[53] The general understanding is that children will automatically acquire their father's family name, and Emirati law does not grant spouses the right to choose their children's future last name. It can be assumed, however, that children born out of wedlock will be registered under their mother's family names and may potentially have their maternal grandfather's first name added to their own.[54]

Emirati nationality law, in contrast, recognizes situations in which a mother gives birth to a child whose father is unknown, or at least not married to the mother,

52 Article 80 Emirati Civil Code, Official Gazette no. 158 of December 29, 1985 as amended by Law no. 1 of 1987.

53 Federal Law on the Registration of Births and Deaths no. 18 of 2009, Official Gazette no. 503 of January 13, 2010.

54 See also Al Khan 2013.

such that *nasab* can be established. In these cases, the child will nonetheless acquire Emirati citizenship through his or her mother.[55]

Finally, without paternal *nasab*, no financial rights in respect of the biological father, such as maintenance and inheritance, can be asserted. The child will, however, inherit from his or her mother's family as long as maternal *nasab* has been established through birth. It can further be assumed that maintenance responsibilities will fall upon the maternal male relatives of the child, especially in cases in which the mother is needy.

13.3.2 Children of Unknown Filiation/Foundlings

Should neither paternal nor maternal filiation be established, the child will be treated as '*majhūl al-nasab*', i.e. of unknown filiation, with such children sometimes also being referred to as foundlings (sing. *laqīṭ*). Foundlings or abandoned children are a growing societal problem in the United Arab Emirates.[56] This is partly due to the country's criminal law system, which prohibits sexual relations outside a valid marriage and frequently punishes mothers who give birth out of wedlock.[57] It is commonly presumed that many of the children who have been abandoned are the offspring of migrant workers, maids and household staff, individuals whose families abroad depend on their employment in the United Arab Emirates and who are among the most vulnerable in terms of legal support and protection.[58]

Children of unknown filiation and foundlings are protected by the state insofar as they are automatically awarded citizenship,[59] thereby having access to the far-reaching financial benefits available only to nationals. Yet these benefits did not solve the issue entirely and further legislative intervention was necessary to provide foundlings and children of unknown filiation with a caretaker. As a result, in 2012, the Emirati legislature passed the Foster Care Act, which from that point forward was supposed to regulate the protection of children without filiation.

---

55 Article 2(c), (d) Federal Law on Nationality and Passports no. 17 of 1972, Official Gazette no. 7 of November 28, 1972 as amended by Law no. 10 of 1975 (hereafter: Federal Law on Nationality and Passports).

56 Kakande 2014; Hanif 2014; Mursī et al. (n.d.); National Editorial 2014; Nereim 2012b.

57 Fischer 2015; National Editorial 2014; Za'za' 2013.

58 Fischer 2015; Hanif 2014; National Editorial 2014.

59 Article 2(e) Federal Law on Nationality and Passports. According to the article, a child born inside the United Arab Emirates to unknown parents will be considered a citizen as a matter of law. A foundling will be considered as having been born in the country unless proved to be otherwise.

13.4 Protection of Children Without Filiation or Permanent Caretakers

13.4.1 General Legal Schemes of Protection and Care

Although the Code of Personal Status remains silent on the issue, it is generally agreed that full adoption (*tabannī*) is prohibited for Muslim citizens of the United Arab Emirates.[60] Prior to the enactment of the Foster Care Act in 2012, protection of abandoned children and orphans fell under the authority of each individual emirate. While Sharjah had a single piece of legislation in place since 1985 that comprehensively governed the placement of children in foster families, other emirates did not enact specialized regulations detailing foster care.[61] Two centers, one in Sharjah and one in Al-Ain, operate as 'orphanages' (essentially caretaking facilities for abandoned children) and have programs aimed at placing minors in foster families.[62] From 2008 to 2012, a hospital in Dubai ran a similar program.[63] In 2013, the emirate of Dubai established a new system to take over this task. Through what is known as the 'Embrace program' (*barnāmaj iḥtiḍān*), professional foster mothers raise up to six children in the family-style environment offered by their own home.[64] Moreover, the Foster Care Act of 2012 has unified the procedure of foster care as well as the requirements for potential caretakers and their rights and duties. Since 2014, a ministerial decree has complemented the act and detailed practical questions regarding the awarding and revocation of foster care in the United Arab Emirates.[65]

[60] Abū Rakhiyya and Al-Jabūrī 2010, pp 286–287, see also the information provided online by the Emirati government, https://government.ae/ar-ae/information-and-services/social-affairs/adoption-in-the-uae (accessed June 29, 2017).

[61] Al Khan 2013; Nereim 2012a; for Sharjah's foster care program in particular, see also Mursī et al. (n.d.).

[62] Nereim 2013; Nereim 2012b. These orphanages are divided by age and gender, whereby girls up to the age of eighteen are housed with male children up to the age of eight. Boys between nine and eighteen are housed in a separate facility. Girls may continue to reside in the facility after they have turned eighteen until they marry, see Article 8(d) Executive Regulations for Federal Law on Care for Children of Unknown Filiation no. 1 of 2012 (for a full reference, see n. 65 below).

[63] Al Khan 2013.

[64] Government of Dubai, Community Development Authority, www.cda.gov.ae/ar/socialcare/childrenandyouth/pages/embrace_a_child.aspx (accessed June 28, 2017). Upon establishing the Embrace program, authorities also called upon families who had taken in foundlings informally to come forward and register the children and thereby legalize their status without fear of legal repercussions, see Issa 2013; Mursī et al. (n.d.).

[65] Ministerial Decree no. 368 of 2014 on the Executive Regulations for Federal Law on Care for Children of Unknown Filiation no. 1 of 2012, Official Gazette no. 567 of July 24, 2014 (hereafter: Executive Regulations).

13.4.2 *The Emirati Foster Care Act of 2012*

13.4.2.1 Terminology and Scope of Application

The Foster Care Act defines the term ‘*ṭifl majhūl al-nasab*’ as a (minor) child of unknown parents found in the United Arab Emirates.[66] It can therefore be concluded that the act only covers care for foundlings and that orphans (sing. *yatīm*), i.e. children with known filiation whose parents have passed away, or children whose parents are not available as caretakers for other reasons, cannot be cared for through the Foster Care Act.

According to the Foster Care Act, married couples as well as single women may foster a child. Potential foster families and single female caretakers are respectively defined as ‘*al-usra al-ḥāḍina*’ or ‘*al-ḥāḍina*’, i.e. the family or the person entrusted with the custody of a child (of unknown filiation).[67] They have to be Emirati Muslims permanently residing inside the United Arab Emirates.[68] Foreign residents of the United Arab Emirates may not foster. Depending on their nationality, however, they may adopt children from abroad under the laws of their home country.[69]

13.4.2.2 Procedure for the Award of *riʿāyat al-aṭfāl*

All procedures envisioned by the Foster Care Act are overseen by the Ministry for Social Affairs. In addition, each emirate has a specialized committee charged with the practical execution of the act.[70]

Anyone who finds a child must inform the nearest police station and must hand over the child immediately. The child will then be sent to a medical center for examination and the competent doctor will assess the child’s age. In addition, the public prosecutor will be notified regarding the circumstances under which the child was found (including the location, date and time, name, occupation, and address of the person who found the child), after which the child will be transferred to one of

[66] Article 1 Foster Care Act.

[67] Article 1 Foster Care Act.

[68] Article 10(1) Foster Care Act; Article 13 of the newly enacted Ministerial Decree no. 52 of 2018 on the Executive Regulations for Federal Law on Children’s Rights no. 3 of 2016 (commonly referred to as ‘Wadeema’s Law’) merely states that the foster family and the foster child must share the same religion, see Muḥammad 2018. It must be assumed, however, that abandoned children of unknown filiation found in the United Arab Emirates will generally be considered Muslim.

[69] See https://government.ae/ar-ae/information-and-services/social-affairs/adoption-in-the-uae (accessed June 29, 2017). In 2013 the emirate of Sharjah discussed allowing foreign residents to foster children in exceptional cases, see Nereim 2013. It remains unclear what has become of the initiative created by the emirate’s social services.

[70] Articles 4, 7 Foster Care Act.

the country's orphanages. According to the Foster Care Act, it is at the orphanage that a fictitious quadrinomial name (i.e. first names and a last name according to Emirati Civil Code and Law no. 18 of 2009 on the Registration of Births and Deaths) will be chosen for the child and that the child will be registered with the state authorities.[71]

At the start of the foster care process, the family's social and psychological condition will be assessed through interviews and visits. A comprehensive study on the family is then submitted to the relevant committee in order to decide on the family's eligibility to foster. Following their acceptance, a first meeting between the family and the child will be held, after which a 'transition plan' is drawn up for the child to move in with his or her new foster family. After a trial period of six months, during which time the relevant authorities will cooperate closely with the family, the foster care arrangement is finalized.[72] It may then last until the child attains majority at the age of twenty-one.[73]

13.4.2.3 Revocation of *riʿāyat al-aṭfāl*

Foster children are monitored periodically through visits and phone calls in order to ensure the child's welfare and adaptation to the new family environment. Regular support by the responsible authorities is also designed to sort out difficulties, including social, psychological and health issues that are faced by both the child and the foster family.[74] Should the competent social worker establish that physical and mental harm is being caused to the foster child and that the foster family is neglecting their obligations towards the minor, foster care can be withdrawn from them.[75] In addition, and without prejudice to any more severe penalties provided for in other laws, the act envisions penalties for foster families who have caused serious harm to their foster child or who have gravely violated or neglected their responsibilities towards the competent authorities involved.[76] More specifically, any person who contravenes any of the provisions detailed in the Foster Care Act will

[71] Article 3 Foster Care Act. Details regarding this procedure can be found in Articles 3, 14 Executive Regulations, for the child's name and registration procedure see also 13.4.2.6 below.

[72] Article 9 Foster Care Act. Details regarding this procedure can be found in Articles 11, 13 Executive Regulations. See also Government of Dubai, Community Development Authority, www.cda.gov.ae/ar/socialcare/childrenandyouth/pages/embrace_a_child.aspx (accessed June 28, 2017).

[73] Article 85(2) Emirati Civil Code sets the age of majority at twenty-one lunar years (approximately twenty solar years and four month). Surprisingly though, many public services, the country's orphanages in particular, limit their services once children have turned eighteen, see n. 62 above.

[74] Articles 8(3), 13, 14(1) Foster Care Act. Details regarding this procedure can be found in Articles 15–17 Executive Regulations. See also Issa 2013.

[75] Article 14(2), (3) Foster Care Act. Details regarding the potential withdrawal of foster care can be found in Articles 21, 22 Executive Regulations.

[76] Article 14(3) Foster Care Act; see also Article 23 Executive Regulations.

be subject to imprisonment and a fine of not less than 10,000 AED and not more than 100,000 AED, or to one of these two penalties.[77]

If the child dies while under the care of the foster family, the relevant authorities must be notified immediately.[78] Should one the fostering spouses die or should they separate, the authorities may agree to the continuation of foster care by one of them.[79] Interestingly enough, while the act does not allow single men to foster children initially, it does not automatically withdraw custody from them should their wife die or should there be a divorce. Where a single female caretaker passes away, one or more of her relatives may continue fostering the child if they fulfil the general requirements of the act and if the authorities approve.[80] Finally, the foster care arrangement will be terminated whenever its reasons cease to exist, i.e. especially if a child's filiation can be established and relatives (or even the child's parents) have been found.[81]

13.4.2.4 Eligibility of the Caretaker and the Child

While both married couples and single women may foster a child, the requirements for each category of caretakers differ slightly. The minimum age for spouses who wish to foster is twenty-five, while single female caretakers must be at least thirty years old.[82] As mentioned above, in order to foster, families and single women have to be Emirati Muslims permanently residing inside the United Arab Emirates.[83] Moreover, they must be free of infectious diseases and psychological or mental disorders, which must be proven by submitting an official medical report.[84] Persons willing to foster should also be able to financially support family members and the new foster child.[85] The emirate of Dubai, for example, has set the minimum monthly income for potential foster families at 10,300 AED (around 2,100 US$).[86] Finally, potential foster parents must not have a criminal record.[87]

The child, as discussed above,[88] has to be of unknown filiation.[89] Hence, children of known filiation but without permanent caretakers cannot be placed in a

[77] Article 22 Foster Care Act.

[78] Article 16(1) Foster Care Act.

[79] Article 16(2) Foster Care Act.

[80] Article 16(3) Foster Care Act.

[81] Articles 17, 18 Foster Care Act.

[82] Articles 10(2), 11 Foster Care Act.

[83] Article 10(1) Foster Care Act.

[84] Article 10(4) Foster Care Act.

[85] Article 10(5) Foster Care Act.

[86] Issa 2013.

[87] Article 10(3) Foster Care Act.

[88] See 13.4.2.1.

[89] See also Article 9 Executive Regulations.

foster home through the process envisioned in the act. As regards parentless children of local families, it can be assumed that they will be cared for within the extended family (by aunts, uncles, or grandparents), while the majority of foreign children will likely be brought back to their country of origin should their parents pass away or be absent for other reasons. Nevertheless, this naturally leaves a small number of children without extended family or the option to be relocated back to their country of origin, and it is unclear how they will be taken care of other than through the country's public orphanages.

13.4.2.5 Rights and Duties of the Caretaker

The Foster Care Act defines the caretaker's main duty as the proper upbringing (*tarbiyya ṣāliḥa*) of the child as well as attending to his or her development, health and education.[90] These duties are in accord with the overall aim of the act, which is to provide medical, psychological, social, and educational care to children of unknown filiation, to guarantee their rights and liberties, and to safeguard their best interests and protect them from abuse or neglect, as well as to provide them with a good social and religious (Islamic) upbringing.[91]

Foster parents are obliged to inform the competent authorities of any potential changes in their home address should they change their place of residence.[92] This implies that they are generally free to relocate with the child. However, it must be assumed that this only applies to relocation within the United Arab Emirates given that one of the requirements to serve as a foster family is to reside within the country.[93] Moreover, foster parents may not place the child with another family unless this has been approved in advance,[94] and they must not terminate their foster care without giving prior notice to the relevant authorities.[95] Additionally, every year the caretaker must provide a medical report on the health status of the foster child.[96] Finally, the Foster Care Act clearly states that all costs of foster care must be financed by the caretaker. The foster parents may neither demand reimbursement from the state nor claim it from the child's own assets.[97]

Foster families are called upon to inform and educate the child about his or her background and the overall family situation. This should be done in accordance

---

[90] Article 10(6) Foster Care Act.

[91] Article 2 Foster Care Act.

[92] Article 12(1) Foster Care Act; see also Article 20(1) Executive Regulations.

[93] See 13.4.2.1.

[94] Article 12(2) Foster Care Act.

[95] Article 12(3) Foster Care Act.

[96] Article 12(4) Foster Care Act.

[97] Article 15 Foster Care Act.

with the age and developmental stage of the child. At any rate, the child should not be left completely unaware of his or her family history.[98]

13.4.2.6 Other Legal Issues Concerning *riʿāyat al-aṭfāl*

The definition of the caretakers' role and their duties towards the child demonstrates that the core of *riʿāyat al-aṭfāl*, as envisioned in the Foster Care Act, is custody (*ḥaḍāna*) rather than guardianship (*wilāya*). At the same time, none of the relevant laws explicitly state who the *walī* of a foundling should be. According to one employee of the Embrace program at Dubai's Community Development Authority, *wilāya* continues to lie with the state (represented by the competent authorities) even if the child resides with his or her foster family more permanently. However, the foster father will usually be granted *wiṣāya* (i.e. appointed guardianship) by court order so that foster parents are able to oversee and manage the child's day-to-day affairs such as enrolling him or her in a school of their choice.[99] The court order (*ḥujjat wiṣāya*) can outline and limit the appointed guardian's powers and responsibilities.[100] Should a single woman foster a child, she could theoretically serve as the child's appointed guardian too, as Emirati law does not bar women from becoming *waṣī*.[101] As an alternative – with the preference for awarding guardianship to males still being evident in legal practice – *wiṣāya* could also be given to the single female caretaker's own father.

The Foster Care Act remains silent on the question of the inheritance rights of the foster child vis-à-vis the foster parents and vice versa. Given the sensitivity of the issue, it can be supposed that no such rights exist unless spelled out clearly in the relevant laws. The absence of inheritance rights was also confirmed by Dubai's Community Development Authority.[102] Foster parents are, however, free to bequeath a part of their assets to their foster child by will within the limits of testamentary succession as detailed in the Emirati Code of Personal Status. Hence, they could theoretically bequeath up to one-third of their estate to their foster child.[103] In addition, it has been reported that foster parents often register land in the child's name.[104]

What has been regulated in detail by the Foster Care Act is the question of the name. As mentioned above, the abandoned child's name will be chosen by the

[98] Article 12(4) Foster Care Act; Article 20(4) Executive Regulations.

[99] Personal interview with psychologist working for the Embrace program (*barnāmaj iḥtiḍān*) at Dubai's Community Development Authority, interviewed on March 26, 2018.

[100] Article 216 Code of Personal Status.

[101] Article 217 Code of Personal Status.

[102] Personal interview with psychologist working for the Embrace program (*barnāmaj iḥtiḍān*) at Dubai's Community Development Authority, interviewed on March 26, 2018.

[103] Article 243 Code of Personal Status.

[104] Personal interview with psychologist working for the Embrace program (*barnāmaj iḥtiḍān*) at Dubai's Community Development Authority, interviewed on March 26, 2018.

orphanage, and the child will not carry his or her foster family's last name. Interestingly enough, however, the act's accompanying Executive Regulations make it very clear that the chosen name should in no way indicate that the child is of unknown filiation. Moreover, the name should correspond with the religious and national environment.[105]

Finally, religious considerations have influenced questions surrounding foster care arrangements in the majority-Muslim country. The most sensitive issues in this regard are the existence (or non-existence) of marriage impediments between biological children and foster children and the matters of veiling and gender segregation. Apparently, it is the thorny nature of these issues which in part explains why orphanages find it more difficult to place baby boys in foster families.[106] On more than one instance, Islamic scholar Ahmed Al Haddad, head of Dubai's fatwa department and the emirate's Grand Mufti, has addressed these topics. He has confirmed that biological children and foster children generally may marry one another (this theoretically also applies to foster children and their foster parents) and that, from a religious standpoint, rules on gender segregation and veiling apply among foster family members. Al Haddad's solution to this concern is to create milk kinship (*raḍāʿ*) between the child and his or her foster parents by either having the foster mother breastfeed the child or having the mother's sister, daughter, or sister-in-law do so.[107] Milk kinship is a legal fiction rooted in pre-modern Islamic doctrine, which creates marriage impediments. While Al Haddad's position may be of concern to some Emiratis, others do not see themselves bound by these religious considerations. The Foster Care Act itself remains completely silent on the issue.

13.5 Conclusion

Emirati family law recognizes four grounds for establishing filiation (*nasab*): (i) a valid marriage (usually circumscribed as '*firāsh*') or at least *waṭʾ bi-shubha*, (ii) acknowledgment (*iqrār*), (iii) proof (*bayyina*), and (iv) scientific methods (*ṭuruq ʿilmiyya*). At the same time, these options are all limited by different additional requirements that need to be fulfilled for a full parent-child relationship to emerge. For example, biological evidence can never overrule a legal presumption of paternity, and scientific methods to determine paternity will not be admitted in court should *firāsh* have not been proven first. As such, mere biological filiation outside the legal categories of marriage, *waṭʾ bi-shubha*, or acknowledgment does not yet exist in the United Arab Emirates.

---

105 Article 3(5) Executive Regulations. Additional information on the registration procedure for foundlings in the United Arab Emirates can be found in Article 10 Ministerial Decree no. 44 of 2011 on the Executive Regulations for Federal Law on the Registration of Births and Deaths no. 18 of 2009, Official Gazette no. 520 of March 31, 2011.

106 Nereim 2012b.

107 Al Khan Nereim 2013; Nereim 2012b. For a similar discussion, see also Mursī et al. (n.d.).

Whenever neither paternal nor maternal filiation is established, the child will be treated as '*majhūl al-nasab*', i.e. of unknown filiation; sometimes, these children are also referred to as foundlings (sing. *laqīṭ*). While foundlings or abandoned children are protected by the state insofar as they are automatically awarded citizenship (and thus have access to the far-reaching governmental benefits available only to nationals), their legal status and need for protection has become a growing social issue in the United Arab Emirates, demanding legislative intervention.

Until recently, only Sharjah possessed a single piece of legislation governing the placement of children in foster families, while other emirates had not enacted any specialized regulations governing questions of foster care. As a consequence, in 2012, the federal legislature enacted the Foster Care Act, which regulates questions regarding the protection of children without filiation or permanent caretakers. This specialized legislation has unified (i) the procedure for awarding and revoking foster care, (ii) the requirements for potential caretakers, and (iii) the rights and duties of caretakers; further, it allows married couples as well as single females over the age of thirty to act as foster parents. The act defines the term '*ṭifl majhūl al-nasab*' as a (minor) child of unknown parents found in the United Arab Emirates. This definition suggests that the act covers care only for foundlings, and that orphans or children whose parents are not available as caretakers for other reasons cannot be cared for through the system envisioned in the Foster Care Act.

Finally, an analysis of the existing legal framework reveals that caretakers will primarily assume the role of custodian (*ḥāḍin/a*) of their foster child. They are not automatically given full parental authority, including rights of *wilāya*. In addition, important questions, such as those regarding marriage restrictions between (foster) family members as well as the mutual inheritance rights of the foster child and the foster parents, are not addressed explicitly in the relevant legislation.

References

Abū Rakhiyya M, Al-Jabūrī AM (2010) Fiqh al-Zawāj wa-l-Ṭalāq wa-mā ʿalayhi al-ʿAmal fī Qānūn al-Aḥwāl al-Shakhṣiyya al-Imārātī [The Islamic law of marriage and divorce and its implementation in the Emirati Code of Personal Status], 2nd edn. Maktabat al-Jāmiʿa, Sharjah.

Abū Zayd M (2016) Ḥulūl Qānūniyya li-Ishkāliyāt wa-Tasāʾulāt ʿAmaliyya fī Mawādd Qānūn al-Aḥwāl al-Shakhṣiyya al-Imārātī [Legal solution to practical problems and questions in the rules of the Emirati Code of Personal Status]. Maʿhad Dubayy al-Qaḍāʾī, Dubai.

Al Khan MN (2013) Grand Mufti urges Emiratis to foster children abandoned in the UAE. The National of May 6, 2013. www.thenational.ae/news/uae-news/grand-mufti-urges-emiratis-to-foster-children-abandoned-in-the-uae. Accessed June 27, 2017.

Al-Nasr TJ (2011) Gulf Cooperation Council (GCC) Women and Misyar Marriage. Evolution and Progress in the Arabian Gulf. Journal of International Women's Studies 12(3):43–57.

Al Tamimi E (2003) Practical Guide to Litigation and Arbitration in the United Arab Emirates. Kluwer Law International, The Hague et al.

Arabi O (2001) The Itinerary of Fatwā: Ambulant Marriage (al-Zawāj al-Misyār), or Grass Roots Law-making in Saudi Arabia of the 1990s. In: Arabi O (ed) Studies in Modern Islamic Jurisprudence, Kluwer Law International, The Hague et al., pp 147–167.

Fischer A (2015) Adopting orphans and breaking taboos in Dubai. Al Jazeera online of March 6, 2015. www.aljazeera.com/news/2015/03/adopting-orphans-breaking-taboos-dubai-150302080741099.html. Accessed June 27, 2017.

Hanif N (2014) Alert over increase in abandoned newborns in the UAE. The National of March 30, 2014. www.thenational.ae/uae/health/alert-over-increase-in-abandoned-newborns-in-the-uae. Accessed June 21, 2017.

Hasso FS (2009) Shifting Practices and Identities, Nontraditional Relationships among Sunni Muslim Egyptians and Emiratis. In: Cuno KM, Desai M (eds) Family, Gender, and Law in a Globalizing Middle East and South Asia, Syracuse University Press, Syracuse, pp 211–222.

Issa W (2013) Dubai unveils new fostering rules for care of abandoned children. The National of April 3, 2013. www.thenational.ae/news/uae-news/dubai-unveils-new-fostering-rules-for-care-of-abandoned-children. Accessed June 28, 2017.

Kakande Y (2014) Three abandoned babies in Sharjah within a week. The National of March 5, 2014. www.thenational.ae/uae/three-abandoned-babies-in-sharjah-within-a-week. Accessed June 21, 2017.

Möller L-M (2015) Die Golfstaaten auf dem Weg zu einem modernen Recht für die Familie? Mohr Siebeck, Tübingen.

Möller L-M (2016) Struggling for a modern family law: A Khaleeji perspective. In: Yassari N (ed) Changing God's Law: The dynamics of Middle Eastern family law, Routledge, London/New York, pp 83–112.

Muḥammad M (2018) Muḥammad bin Rāshid Yaṣdiru al-Lā'iḥa al-Tanfīdhiyya li-Qānūn 'Wadīma' [Mohammed bin Rashid promulgates the Executive Regulations to 'Wadeema's law']. Al-Bayān of December 17, 2018. www.albayan.ae/across-the-uae/news-and-reports/2018-12-17-1.3436958. Accessed January 7, 2019.

Mursī A, Al-Nuʿaymī A, Al-Ḥamūdī M (n.d.) Majhūlū al-Nasab: bayna Aḥḍān al-Dawla wa-Qaswat al-Mujtamaʿ [Unknown filiation: between the embrace of the state and the cruelty of society]. Al-Ittiḥād. www.alittihad.ae/investigations_details.php?id=139&pid=1. Accessed June 28, 2017.

National Editorial (2014) Solution needed to baby abandonment in the UAE. The National of January 13, 2014. www.thenational.ae/thenationalconversation/editorial/solution-needed-to-baby-abandonment-in-the-uae. Accessed June 21, 2017.

Nereim V (2012a) Emirati mother bonds with child from Sharjah foster home. The National of July 30, 2012. www.thenational.ae/news/uae-news/emirati-mother-bonds-with-child-from-sharjah-foster-home. Accessed June 27, 2017.

Nereim V (2012b) Homes hard to find in UAE for abandoned baby boys. The National of September 19, 2012. www.thenational.ae/news/uae-news/homes-hard-to-find-in-uae-for-abandoned-baby-boys. Accessed June 27, 2017.

Nereim V (2013) Will expats be allowed to foster in UAE as Sharjah examines rule change? The National of March 13, 2013. www.thenational.ae/news/uae-news/will-expats-be-allowed-to-foster-in-uae-as-sharjah-examines-rule-change. Accessed June 28, 2017.

Salūm R (2012) Maḥkamat al-Tamyīz: al-Iqrār Yuthbitu al-Nasab bi-Sharṭ allā Yujāfī al-Manṭiq [Court of Cassation: acknowledgment proves filiation unless it defies logic]. Al-Imārāt al-Yawm of October 12, 2012. www.emaratalyoum.com/local-section/accidents/2012-10-12-1.518789. Accessed June 27, 2017.

Za'za' B (2013) Unmarried Dubai couple deny endangering life of illegitimate child. Gulf News of May 8, 2013. http://gulfnews.com/news/uae/courts/unmarried-dubai-couple-deny-endangering-life-of-illegitimate-child-1.1180462. Accessed June 21, 2017.

Lena-Maria Möller is a senior research fellow at the Max Planck Institute for Comparative and International Private Law in Hamburg, Germany. Holding an M.A. in Middle East studies and a Ph.D. in law, she has taught and researched in the area of Islamic law, with a particular focus on Muslim family law, as well as in comparative and private international law. She has held teaching positions at the University of Hamburg, the University of Augsburg and, most recently, the University of Münster, where she served as visiting professor of Islamic law. She is the author of *Die Golfstaaten auf dem Weg zu einem modernen Recht für die Familie?* (Mohr Siebeck 2015) and a co-editor of *Parental Care and the Best Interests of the Child in Muslim Countries* (T.M.C. Asser Press 2017). Her articles have been published in journals including Hawwa (Journal of Women of the Middle East and the Islamic World), Journal of Private International Law and The American Journal of Comparative Law, and she is a contributor to *Brill's Encyclopedia of Law and Religion* and the *Encyclopedia of Women and Islamic Cultures*.

Chapter 14
The Recognition and Enforcement of Foreign Filiation Judgments in Arab Countries

Béligh Elbalti

Contents

Béligh Elbalti is associate professor at the Graduate School of Law and Politics at Osaka University.

Abbreviations used in this chapter: Bull. Civ. = Bulletin Civil de la Cour de Cassation – Civil; CA = Court of Appeal; CCCP = Code of Civil and Commercial Procedure; CCP = Code of Civil Procedure; CFI = Court of First Instance; COC = Code of Obligations and Contracts; CPIL = Code of Private International Law; EA = Execution Act; EFCJA = Enforcement of Foreign Court Judgments Act; EFJA = Enforcement of Foreign Judgments Act; FC = Family Code; PIL = Private international law; PSC = Personal Status Code; RJL = Revue de la jurisprudence et de la législation/Majallat al-Qaḍāʾ wa-l-Tashrīʿ; RSC = Review of the Supreme Court/Majallat al-Maḥkamat al-ʿUlyā; RTD = Revue tunisienne de droit/Al-Majallat al-Tūnisiyya li-l-Qānūn; SC = Supreme Court; UAE = United Arab Emirates.

B. Elbalti (✉)
Graduate School of Law and Politics, Osaka University, 1-6, Machikaneyama, Toyonaka, Osaka 560-0043, Japan
e-mail: be-elbalti@law.osaka-u.ac.jp; benkei.tun@gmail.com

N. Yassari et al. (eds.), *Filiation and the Protection of Parentless Children*, https://doi.org/10.1007/978-94-6265-311-5_14

Abstract The purpose of this chapter is to provide a general overview of the recognition and enforcement of foreign judgments in matters relating to filiation. 'Filiation' is understood here in a broad sense. It covers in-wedlock, out-of-wedlock and adoptive filiations. The chapter reviews a number of cases relating to the recognition and enforcement of foreign filiation judgments reported in certain Arab countries, namely, Morocco, Tunisia and Lebanon. It discusses the likelihood of the reception of foreign filiation judgments in other Arab countries based on the general treatment of the matter in legal literature. The issue is also analysed in its general context of cross-border family dispute resolution in order to gain insight on the fate of foreign filiation judgments in Arab countries. The analysis reveals the existence of two opposing approaches to this issue. The first approach can be characterized as conservative as it remains faithful to the traditional domestic rules and religious values. It tends to be followed when foreign judgments are rendered in countries where the legal system is assumed to be fundamentally different from the national legal system. To this effect, it relies significantly on the public policy mechanism of PIL. The second approach relies more on a case-by-case approach that aims to accommodate family law regulation to modern needs.

Keywords In-wedlock filiation · Out-of-wedlock filiation · Adoption · Recognition and enforcement of foreign judgments · Public policy · Islamic Sharia

14.1 Introduction

This chapter deals with the recognition and enforcement of foreign judgments relating to the establishment of filiation in Arab countries. The analysis here will be limited to national domestic rules to the exclusion of international conventions.[1] In addition, since 'recognition' and 'enforcement' are subject to the same regime and conditions,[2] focus here will be placed on the 'enforcement' of foreign judgments unless otherwise indicated.[3]

[1] Almost all Arab jurisdictions have their own network of bilateral conventions dealing with foreign judgments. Arab countries have also concluded a number of regional conventions. For a detailed list, see Elbalti 2018, pp 220–221. However, reference to such conventions will be made only when necessary.

[2] The recognition and enforcement of foreign judgments refers to the effects that foreign judgments can enjoy in States other than their State of origin. Recognition of foreign judgments means that matters already decided by a foreign court should be treated as conclusive, thus precluding the re-litigation of the claims anew. Enforcement, on the other hand, refers to the use of coercive powers in order to compel the judgment debtor to comply with the judgment.

[3] The recognition of a foreign judgment usually depends on its enforcement in Arab countries. The situation is slightly different in Lebanon and Tunisia due to the legislative acceptance of 'recognition' at least as far as the *res judicata* effect of personal status judgments is concerned. For Lebanon (Article 1012 CCP), see Gannagé 2010, no. 35; Najm 2015/2016, p 467. In Tunisia, the question is unclear (compare Article 482 COC with Articles 13, 14 and 16 CPIL) and

'Filiation' (*nasab* or *bunuwwa*) is understood here in a broad sense as a generic concept that covers all types of filiation unless otherwise indicated. Thus, it includes filiation by blood – which can in Arab legal terminology be either 'legitimate' (filiation of a child born in wedlock) or 'illegitimate/natural' (filiation of a child born out of wedlock) – and adoptive filiation (filiation by legal fiction).[4] For the purpose of this chapter, Arab countries refer to the twenty-two States that form the League of Arab States.[5] Except for a few countries whose laws have not been accessible to the author,[6] the law and practice relating to the establishment of filiation in Arab States will be examined here. A special focus will be placed on three countries, namely Morocco, Tunisia and Lebanon, given that reported cases on the enforcement of foreign filiation judgments are available in these countries. As for other Arab countries, to the extent of the case law reports and databases consulted by the author, there are unfortunately no reported cases on the issue.[7] It should also be noted from the outset that the research on this topic has been undertaken within the limits of the available and accessible information. The fact that court decisions are not regularly reported in most Arab countries makes it difficult to trace the evolution of case law in these countries.

The question to be examined here is whether foreign filiation judgments can be given effect in Arab jurisdictions and, if yes, under what conditions. Since the law of filiation in Arab jurisdictions is highly influenced by religious principles and values, it is interesting to examine whether the preference under domestic law for one type of filiation (i.e. in-wedlock filiation) and the hostility towards other types

contradictory judgments exist. However, there is a tendency in the courts' practice to accept the *de jure* effect of foreign judgments even in the absence of an exequatur judgment. See for example in matters of custody of children born out of wedlock, the judgment of the Sousse CFI no. 1692 of 4 July 2011 (unpublished, on file with author).

[4] The use of terminology in Arabic literature is not always clear. The terms *nasab* and *bunuwwa* are often used interchangeably to mean 'filiation' as a generic concept that covers all types of filiation. In this case, the necessary distinctions will be made by adding distinctive terms: 'legitimate' for filiation in wedlock (*nasab sharʿī/bunuwwa sharʿiyya*); 'illegitimate' (*nasab ghayr sharʿī/bunuwwa ghayr sharʿiyya*) or 'natural' (*nasab ṭabīʿī/bunuwwa ṭabīʿiyya*) for filiation out of wedlock; and 'adoptive' (*nasab* or *bunuwwa bi-tabannī*) for filiation by adoption. However, in the legal terminology as inherited from Islamic jurisprudence (*fiqh*), *nasab* is used to refer to 'legitimate filiation' i.e. fatherhood in marriage in the sense that *nasab* will not be conferred nor recognized for children when their birth out of wedlock is established or asserted. In this sense, *bunuwwa* may be used as a broader concept than *nasab* i.e. as a generic concept covering both *nasab* ('legitimate filiation') and 'illegitimate' filiation (see for example, Articles 142, 144 and 148 of the Moroccan FC). *Bunuwwa* can also be used in a restrictive way to mean 'illegitimate' or 'natural' filiation only; this use is frequent in Tunisian legal literature.

[5] These are (in alphabetical order): Algeria, Bahrain, Djibouti, Egypt, Iraq, Jordan, Kuwait, Lebanon, Libya, Mauritania, Morocco, Oman, Palestine, Qatar, Saudi Arabia, Somalia, Sudan, Syria, Tunisia, Union of Comoros, United Arab Emirates and Yemen. Not included in this study is the law of other Islamic countries, such as Indonesia, Iran or Turkey.

[6] Namely, Djibouti, Somalia, Sudan and the Union of Comoros.

[7] There are, however, numerous reported cases on cross-border maintenance or custody.

of filiation (out-of-wedlock and adoptive filiation) and their legal effects influence the resolution of cross-border filiation disputes.

This chapter is organized as follows. Section 14.2 provides a general overview of the enforcement systems in place in Arab jurisdictions for the reception of foreign judgments and their peculiarities. Section 14.3 focuses on the enforcement of foreign filiation judgments. Some reported cases from Morocco, Tunisia and Lebanon will be first reviewed and analysed. Thereafter, the legal literature of other Arab countries where case law is not available will be reviewed. Section 14.4 places the enforcement of foreign filiation judgments in its general context of cross-border personal status dispute resolution in order to identify general approaches and tendencies in Arab jurisdictions. Finally, Sect. 14.5 will draw some concluding remarks.

14.2 The Enforcement of Foreign Judgments: A General Overview

14.2.1 Domestic Sources and Scope of Application

All Arab jurisdictions have statutory rules on the enforcement of foreign judgments. In the majority of Arab States, rules governing the effect of foreign judgments have been included in their respective Codes of Civil Procedure.[8] In other jurisdictions, provisions relating to foreign judgments have been included either in a special statute called 'Execution Act'[9] or in special legislation on the enforcement of foreign judgments.[10] In some other jurisdictions, in addition to the general rules of enforcement, which have either been included in the Code of Civil Procedure or in a special statute, special rules on enforcement have been enacted in separate statutes.[11] Finally, only Tunisia has a comprehensive PIL code, which includes a

[8] Algeria (Code of Civil and Administrative Procedure of 2008, Articles 605–608); Bahrain (CCCP of 1971, Articles 252–255); Egypt (CCP of 1968, Articles 296–301); Lebanon (CCP of 1983, Articles 1009–1024); Kuwait (CCCP of 1980, Articles 199–203); Libya (CCCP of 1953, Articles 405–411); Mauritania (Code of Civil, Commercial and Administrative Procedure of 1999, Articles 303–304); Oman (CCCP of 2002, Articles 352–355); Qatar (CCCP of 1990, Articles 379–383); Sudan (CCP of 1983, Articles 288–290); Syria (CCP of 2016, Articles 308–313); UAE (CCP of 1992, Articles 235–238) and Yemen (Code of Civil Procedure and Enforcement of 2002, Articles 491–497).

[9] Saudi Arabia (EA No. 53 of 2012, Articles 11–14) and Palestine (EA No. 23 of 2005, Articles 36–39).

[10] Iraq (EFCJA No. 30 of 1928) and Jordan (EFJA No. 8 of 1952).

[11] This is the case in Morocco, where, in addition to the general rules found in the CCP of 1974 (Articles 430–432), a special rule on the enforcement of foreign divorces and dissolution (*faskh*) of marriages is found in the FC (Article 28 FC). The same holds true for Jordan where, in addition to the general enforcement rules found in the EFJA No. 8 of 1952, special rules of enforcement before the Sharia courts have been enacted in law No. 10 of 2013.

chapter on the enforcement of foreign judgments, although some other provisions can be found elsewhere.[12]

It should be noted that Arab legal systems do not differentiate between foreign monetary judgments and non-monetary judgments, especially those rendered in family and personal status matters, for the purpose of enforcement. Therefore, the same rules apply regardless of the matter on which the foreign judgment is issued, including judgments ruling on filiation. Iraq, however, is a notable exception, as the Iraqi EFCJA No. 30 of 1928 limits enforcement to judgments on debts or definite sums of money (Article 6(c)), thus *a priori* excluding from its scope of application judgments rendered in family matters not including a monetary valuation (such as rulings on divorce or filiation).[13] A similar restriction is found in the Jordanian EFJA No. 8 of 1952.[14] However, Jordanian courts have affirmed the application of the 1952 EFJA to judgments rendered in family matters. The enforceability of such judgments was later officially permitted in the Sharia [Court] Execution Law (*Qānūn al-Tanfīdh al-Shar'ī*) No. 10 of 2013 (Article 2). This includes the enforcement of non-monetary judgments, such as rulings on affiliation (*ḍamm*), custody (*ḥaḍāna*) and visitation (*ru'ya wa-ziyāra*).[15]

14.2.2 General Requirements

As stated above, the enforcement regime is generally applicable to judgments rendered in civil and commercial matters[16] as well as in family matters. The conditions for enforcement of foreign judgments in Arab countries can be grouped into three categories: the first category includes conditions that are expressly stated in all Arab legislation. This category encompasses (1) the condition of finality; (2) the jurisdiction of the foreign court and (3) non-violation of public policy. The second category includes conditions that are largely shared and expressly mentioned in the

[12] See for example Article 443 COC on the evidentiary weight of foreign judgments and Article 482 COC on their *res judicata* effect.

[13] However, the Act applies when the enforcement of the foreign judgment is subject to international conventions. See decision of the Federal Supreme Court no. 286/2017 of 17 October 2017, excerpt available at www.hjc.iq/qview.2389/ (accessed 15 February 2019). Otherwise, the regularity of the foreign judgment will be examined in the context of a new action during which the foreign judgment will be confirmed (*taṣdīq*) if it is deemed to be, *inter alia*, in conformity with the local legislation, namely the Iraqi FC.

[14] Scholars are divided on the issue. For an affirmative view, Al-Haddāwī 2017, pp 285–287. *Contra* Al-Dāwudī 2013, p 350.

[15] See the explanatory note on this law available at www.jpm.jo/index.php?type=leg_respon&id=234 (accessed 15 February 2019). This does not, however, include agreements acknowledged by the foreign court. See decision of the Jordanian Sharia Supreme Court no. 24-2017/18 of 14 June 2017 (on file with author). But see *contra*, the decision of the Jordanian Supreme Court no. 3281/2005 of 20 December 2005 (on file with author).

[16] See Elbalti 2018, pp 218 et seqq.; Bremer 2016–2017, pp 37 et seqq.; Bremer 2018, pp 109 et seqq.

law of many but not all Arab countries. This category includes the conditions of (4) proper service,[17] (5) the right of defense;[18] (6) the absence of conflicting judgments[19] and (7) reciprocity.[20] The third and last category includes conditions that are found in only few Arab legislative acts. This category includes (8) the absence of fraud[21] and (9) control of the applied law.[22] Only Oman and Sudan expressly subject the enforcement of foreign judgments to all the conditions stated above. Finally, review on the merits is prohibited as a matter of principle in all jurisdictions.[23]

These requirements apply also to the enforcement of foreign filiation judgments. However, despite the apparent uniformity, the standards upon which some of these conditions are based differ in the various Arab jurisdictions.[24] In addition, among all the enforcement requirements, public policy plays a very important role, and it is not an overstatement to say that it is the cornerstone of the enforcement regime in Arab countries.[25] The salient feature of the enforcement of foreign personal status judgments in Arab jurisdictions is indeed the frequent interference of public policy in the name of religious values. Certainly, taking religious values into consideration in the assessment of public policy in family law matters is not unique to Arab countries. However, what characterizes public policy in Arab countries, in general, is the excessive reach of this notion. This is because the fundamental morals and values underlying the Arab legal systems also include the body of inherited traditional tenets, the respect for which should be absolute as a matter of principle. Therefore, in the sensitive field of family law, which is highly permeable to religious values and principles, public policy might become an insurmountable hurdle to the reception of foreign judgments in general and foreign filiation judgments in

---

[17] Algeria, Morocco, Tunisia and Palestine are exceptions. The condition is, however, usually examined within the framework of procedural public policy.

[18] Algeria and Palestine are exceptions, but the condition is covered by procedural public policy.

[19] Iraq, Jordan and Morocco are exceptions, but the condition is covered by public policy.

[20] Algeria and Morocco are exceptions.

[21] Fraud is an independent requirement in Iraq, Jordan, Oman and Sudan. In Lebanon, fraud justifies a review of the foreign judgment on the merits. In Tunisia, fraud may act as an independent ground for non-recognition despite the absence of a statutory provision. See for example, CA Tunis no. 22715 of 22 February 2006 (unpublished), reported in Chedly and Ghazouani 2008, p 263.

[22] Applicable in Oman (Article 352 CCPC) and Sudan (Article 288 CCP).

[23] However, it is permissible in Lebanon, but only in limited situations (Article 015 CCP). Interestingly, despite the prohibition, it is not uncommon that Arab courts review the merits of the foreign judgment under the cover of public policy. For a representative example from Morocco, see the Moroccan SC no. 188 of 30 March 2005 (on file with author) in which the court examined the content of a foreign divorce judgment in the light of the Moroccan FC and declared, upon such examination, that the foreign judgment was not inconsistent with the Moroccan domestic law of divorce and was therefore not in violation of Moroccan public policy.

[24] See Elbalti 2018, pp 223 et seqq.

[25] However, on the specifically weak nature of public policy in Lebanon due to the existence of different religious communities having contradictory family law regulations, see Najm 2015/2016, p 472.

particular. This is particularly true when the judgment is rendered in a country where the family law system is deemed as fundamentally different from the family law system existing in Arab jurisdictions.[26]

14.3 The Enforcement of Foreign Filiation Judgments

14.3.1 Review of the Reported Cases from Morocco, Tunisia and Lebanon

Generally speaking, the attitude of Arab courts towards foreign filiation judgments differs largely according to the country and according to the matter in question (adoption, out-of-wedlock filiation, acknowledgement or disavowal of paternity via DNA blood tests etc.). A reading of the reported cases indicates the existence of three categories of cases. The first category includes cases where the enforcement of foreign filiation judgments was rejected in the name of public policy and non-conformity with religious principles, notably Islamic Sharia (Sect. 14.3.1.1). The second category covers cases where the enforcement of filiation judgments was allowed but with certain reservations (Sect. 14.3.1.2). The third category features cases where the enforcement was allowed without major difficulties (Sect. 14.3.1.3).

14.3.1.1 Rejection of Foreign Filiation Judgments

The reported cases within this category deal with adoption and the rebuttal of legitimate filiation.

Adoption

In Morocco, the Rabat Court of Appeal (CA) refused in 2004 to enforce the alimony element of a foreign divorce judgment on the ground that the payment of the alimony was ordered in favour of an adopted child and therefore contrary to public policy.[27] The case concerns an exequatur action regarding a French divorce judgment initiated by a woman against her ex-husband (seemingly Moroccan nationals). In addition to declaring the divorce, the foreign judgment fixed the child alimony amount to be borne by the ex-husband. The first instance court refused to grant exequatur for the divorce judgment as a whole after examining the

[26] See Sect. 14.4.

[27] Decision of the Rabat CA (Morocco) no. 81 of 26 April 2004, file no. 147/2002/10 (unpublished), reported in Loukili 2012, pp 154–155.

compatibility of the grounds on which the divorce was declared under the lens of Moroccan public policy. On appeal, the arguments of the parties focused on the compatibility of the foreign divorce with Moroccan law and Islamic Sharia. The husband argued that the divorce judgment, including the alimony, should not be enforced for the following reasons: (1) his wife abducted 'their daughter' and took her away from him without his permission; (2) the alimony amount was fixed on the basis of a different standard of living and (3) it was unfair for the appellant to be deprived of his daughter and be obliged to pay alimony at the same time.[28] Based on an indication in the foreign judgment that the daughter was adopted, the CA refused to grant exequatur for the alimony component, declaring that the French judgment ordering the payment of alimony to the adopted daughter was 'contrary to public policy and the rules of Islamic Sharia, which forbids adoption and does not grant it any legal effect'.

In Tunisia, the Tunis Court of First Instance (CFI) decided in 2000 that a foreign judgment pronouncing the adoption of a Tunisian child by a foreigner was against public policy because, *inter alia*, the adopter was not Muslim.[29] The case concerns an exequatur action of an Austrian adoption judgment. The facts of the case and the reason why the action was initiated are unclear.[30] The court first pointed out, as it appeared from the Austrian judgment, that the case concerned the adoption of a Tunisian child (the adoptee) by an Austrian (the adopter). The court then inferred from Tunisian law on adoption, which mentions only the possibility of Tunisians adopting foreign children,[31] that Tunisian law did not allow the adoption of Tunisian children by foreigners and that the rules of this law were of a public policy nature. The court concluded by stating that 'the Austrian judgment whose enforcement is being sought … is contrary to Tunisian public policy *notably* since there is no evidence in the records of the case showing that the adopter has converted to Islam' (emphasis added).[32]

In a different case decided in 1999, the Tunis CFI also refused to enforce a foreign adoption judgment on the ground that adoption by a single person was against public policy.[33] The case concerned an exequatur action regarding a French judgment that pronounced the adoption of a Tunisian girl by a single French

[28] The facts of the case are based on the overview provided by Zeidguy 2007, pp 265–267.

[29] Judgment of the Tunis CFI no. 34256 of 26 June 2000 (unpublished), reported in Chedly and Ghazouani 2008, p 239. For critical comments on this decision, see Bostanji 2003, pp 155 et seq. For a supportive opinion, see Boukhari 2011, p 136.

[30] The author failed to obtain a copy of the judgment. The overview here is based on what has been reported in Tunisian legal literature.

[31] According to Article 10(2) of Law No. 58-27 of 4 March 1958 Concerning Public Guardianship, Unofficial Guardianship (*kafāla*) and Adoption, 'Tunisians can adopt foreign [children]'.

[32] See, however, the contradicting Tunisian judgments on this issue in the field of choice of law, *infra* Sect. 14.3.2.

[33] Judgment of the Tunis CFI no. 30070 of 28 June 1999 (unpublished), reported in Ben Achour 2017, p 119.

woman. The court rejected the case, considering that uniparental adoptions were contrary to Tunisian public policy since Tunisian law does not allow adoption by single adopters.[34]

In Lebanon, the Mount Lebanon CA refused in 1987 to enforce a foreign adoption judgment on the ground that full adoptions entailing a complete break with the biological family were against public policy.[35] The case concerns an exequatur action on the adoption of an abandoned and handicapped Lebanese child that was pronounced in Belgium. The child was already in Belgium at the time of the adoption, where he obtained the Belgian nationality. The biological Lebanese parents of the child, who were Maronite Christians, agreed to the full adoption. The exequatur proceeding was initiated by the biological father in order to remove the name of his child from his family register.[36] The Mount Lebanon CA[37] rejected the exequatur claim on the ground that the personal status law of Catholic communities did not allow a complete and irrevocable break of filiation with the biological parents. The court took into consideration the local religious law, which allows only 'simple' adoption, i.e. adoption that does not terminate the filiation link between the adoptee and the biological parents.[38]

Rebuttal of Legitimate Filiation

The refusal to grant recognition and enforcement of foreign filiation judgments on public policy grounds can also be seen in matters of a rebuttal of legitimate *nasab* based on DNA blood tests. This was decided, for example, in a ruling of the Plenary Chamber of the Moroccan SC in 2004.[39] The case concerned an action brought by a Moroccan woman against her ex-husband, seeking, *inter alia*, the payment of alimony to her child. The child was born a couple of months after the divorce of the couple, and therefore her filiation was covered by the legitimacy presumption under Moroccan law. The ex-husband applied for the dismissal of the claim. He argued that his ex-wife had already brought the same action before French courts and that

---

[34] See Article 9(1) of the 1958 law, *supra* note 31. However, Paragraph (3) exempts divorced or widowed adopters from the marriage requirement, taking into consideration the best interests of the child.

[35] Decision of the Mont Lebanon CA of 10 June 1987 (unpublished). For a critical analysis of this decision, see Najm 1996–1997, pp 194–199.

[36] The overview is based on Najm 1996–1997, pp 165 et seqq.

[37] Requests for exequatur need to be filed before the Civil CA in Lebanon. See Najm 2015/2016, p 468.

[38] See Najjar 1989, p 655.

[39] Decision of the Plenary Chamber of the Supreme Court (*Qaḍā' al-Majlis al-A'lā*) no. 658 of 30 December 2004 (on file with author), cited in Loukili 2012, pp 154–155.

the claim was rejected as it had been established on the basis of DNA blood tests ordered by the court that he was not the biological father of the child. The first instance court (CFI) and the court of appeal rejected his argument and ruled in favour of the ex-wife. According to the CFI, the French judgment that, on the basis of DNA blood tests, rejected the paternity legally established in accordance with Moroccan law violated 'Moroccan law and Islamic Sharia'. In addition, the lower courts considered that the legitimate *nasab* of the daughter could be refuted only in accord with the procedure admitted under Islamic law, that is *li'ān* (mutual imprecation or cursing). The decision was upheld on appeal.[40] The respondent eventually appealed to the Supreme Court. He contested the decision of the lower courts, arguing, *inter alia*, that (1) his defense was based on a final and binding judgment rendered on the basis of serious medical analyses establishing that the child was not his daughter; (2) the Franco-Moroccan Convention of 1981 on judicial assistance in family matters was applicable[41] and (3) the recourse to DNA blood tests was not contrary to Moroccan law and Islamic Sharia. However, the Supreme Court rejected these arguments. It upheld the appealed decision, which reasoned that the legitimate *nasab* of the child as established according to Moroccan law could not be rebutted by a foreign judgment relying on DNA blood tests. The Supreme Court also agreed with the stance of the CA according to which the father should have followed the *li'ān* procedure if he wished to disavow his paternity.[42]

14.3.1.2 Enforcement of Foreign Filiation Judgements with Reservations

The cases reported here show that the traditional hostility towards impermissible forms of filiations as well as their consequences can to a certain extent be alleviated. However, what is interesting here is that the courts dealing with the cases were eager to justify their judgments in a way that suggests that the solution would have been different, and that the foreign filiation judgments would have been refused enforcement, had the circumstances of the case been different.

---

[40] The summary of the case is based on Zaher 2009, p 79.

[41] The Convention Concerning the Status of Persons and Family and Judicial Cooperation of 10 August 1981. The convention, by way of reference to Articles 16 and 17 of the 1957 Franco-Moroccan Convention on Judicial Assistance in Civil and Commercial Matters, recognizes the *de jure* effect of judgments rendered by the courts of the contracting States (Article 7).

[42] The SC also rejected the argument based on the applicability of the Franco-Moroccan 1981 Convention, concluding that the case was governed by Moroccan law applicable as a matter of public policy. In the court's view, such an application was allowed by the convention itself (Article 4). For a critical analysis of this decision, see Zaher 2009, pp 83 et seq.

Attribution of Patronymic Name

In Tunisia, the Supreme Court in 2001 granted exequatur in connection with an Italian judgment attributing a patronymic name (family name) to a child on the basis of an acknowledgement of fatherhood (*ubuwwa*). The facts of the case are unclear,[43] but it appears that an exequatur action regarding the Italian judgment was initiated against the father, who, in meantime, had initiated a separate action for the disavowal of *nasab* (paternity).[44] The decision granting exequatur was contested before the SC presumably because the foreign judgment was contrary to public policy since it would lead to establishing *nasab* (legitimate filiation). The court rejected the argument. It stated instead that the foreign judgment was in conformity with Tunisian public policy since, under Tunisian law (see Sect. 14.3.2.2), a patronymic name could be attributed to a child if it is established via acknowledgement or testimony or by genetic tests showing that the concerned person is the father the child. Subsequently, the court added that the allocation of a patronymic name does not establish *nasab*, but only biological fatherhood (*ubuwwa*). The court continued by stating that *nasab* and *ubuwwa* are interrelated but not identical since the establishment of *nasab* may necessitate the establishment of *ubuwwa* whereas the establishment of the latter does not necessarily lead to the establishment of the former. The reason, according to court, lies in the fact that the purposes, the method of ascertainment and the legal consequences of the two notions are different. The court concluded that the action for disavowal of *nasab* brought by the father had no impact on granting exequatur to a foreign judgment relating to the establishment of *ubuwwa*.[45]

Rights of an Adulterine Child

The Lebanese SC decided in 2007 that a foreign judgment allowing an adulterine child represented by his mother to request an inventory of his deceased married father's estate (located abroad) was not contrary to public policy.[46] The case concerns an exequatur request regarding a French non-contentious judgment awarded to the French mother of an adulterine child that was brought in her capacity as legal guardian, the judgment conferring to the mother the right to request an inventory of Monaco-based assets owned by the child's deceased father (a Lebanese citizen). The father, who died in Monaco, acknowledged the child at his birth and registered him as an 'illegitimate child' in his family register. The

[43] The summary of the case is based on an excerpt of the judgment published in Chedly and Ghazouani 2008, pp 239–240.

[44] The term '*nasab*' is used in the judgment. On the issue of terminology, see *supra* note 4.

[45] Decision of the Tunisian SC no. 5480 of 1 March 2001 (unpublished), reported in Chedly and Ghazouani 2008, pp 239–240.

[46] Decision of the Lebanese SC no. 81 of 31 May 2007, Al-ʿAdl no. 4 of 2007, p 1702 (on file with author).

adoptive daughter of the deceased opposed the application for exequatur regarding the French decision before the Beirut CA. The CA declared the judgment unenforceable for inconsistency with Lebanese public policy. According to the court, there was a close relation between the inventory order and the status of the adulterine child as an heir of the deceased, and it was doubtful that the child be considered as an heir in light of the law governing non-Muslim inheritance (Article 31 of the law of 23 June 1959), which deprives an 'adulterine' child of any right in his married father's estate. The mother appealed to the Supreme Court. Different issues were raised before the Lebanese regulatory court. These include, *inter alia*, (1) the jurisdiction of the French court that exercised jurisdiction based on the nationality of the plaintiff,[47] (2) reciprocity[48] and (3) the judgment's consistency with public policy.

With regard to (3), it was argued that the French judgment granting the request of an inventory necessarily entails the recognition of an heir-status in the adulterine child. However, according to the Lebanese law governing non-Muslim inheritance,[49] adulterine children are excluded from succession from their fathers since the purpose of this rule is to preserve the peace, security and unity of the Lebanese family. The court rejected this argument. For the Regulatory Court, the concern of preserving the peace, security and unity of the Lebanese family was no longer relevant in this case since the deceased had acknowledged the child without any objection of the other members of his family, including his adoptive daughter. Hence, the court added, the question *in casu* concerns the monetary aspect of the exclusion rule, and this question, although important, is subject to conciliation, settlement and waiver. The court then concluded that the French protective order did not confer succession rights to the child over property located in Lebanon but simply allowed him to investigate the assets left by his father in preparation of any action to be taken later.

---

[47] The court considered that the indirect jurisdiction of the French rendering court can be accepted even if is based on the nationality of the plaintiff. According to the court, the rule rejecting nationality as an appropriate ground for indirect jurisdiction applies only to contentious judgments to the exclusion of non-contentious judgments.

[48] The court considered that what matters in establishing reciprocity is the likelihood of enforcing Lebanese judgments and not the special treatment that those judgments would face under specific recognition requirements of the rendering State.

[49] Although the law does not apply to the Muslim and the Druze communities and despite the fact that the title of the law suggests that it is of religious nature, Lebanese scholars consider that this law is 'civil' law applied by 'civil' and not 'religious' courts. See Gannagé 2010, no. 13. But from the same author admitting the 'religious' influence on this law in matters of filiation, see Gannagé 2001, p 865.

14.3.1.3 Enforcement of Foreign Filiation Judgments Without Substantial Difficulties

Two cases from Tunisia are illustrative of this category of cases. The first case decided by the Tunis CFI relates to the enforcement of a French judgment invalidating the acknowledgement of an out-of-wedlock child (*bunuwwa*) made by a Tunisian father in France.[50] In this case, an exequatur action was brought by a French mother against her Tunisian partner. The Tunisian decision itself is silent about the factual context of the dispute. However, as it was related by commentators,[51] the couple had cohabited in France. The child born from that relationship was acknowledged by the father as his child. Later, the mother initiated a legal action, arguing that the acknowledgement of the father was contrary to the biological reality of the filiation. During the proceeding, the father took the child and went back to Tunis. Thereafter, and based on certain medical analyses done on the mother in the absence of the father, the court confirmed the non-paternity of the father. The mother sought enforcement of the judgment in Tunisia. The Tunis CFI indicated that the father did not appear, although he was duly served, and that he did not oppose exequatur. The court then admitted the action; without undertaking any close examination whether all the enforcement requirements were met, the court stated that the foreign judgment could be declared enforceable, especially because it had become irrevocable (*force de la chose jugée*) under French law.

The second case is a more recent one decided by the Tunisian Supreme Court in 2018.[52] It concerns an exequatur action regarding a Libyan judgment which had established the *nasab* (legitimate filiation) of a child to his father. Both the CFI and the CA approved enforcement of the Libyan judgment. The father appealed to the SC, arguing, *inter alia*, that the lower courts wrongly considered that the establishment of filiation was based on the legal presumption of *firāsh* (the marital bed) whereas the Libyan court had reached its conclusion based on an acknowledgement of *nasab*; a *nasab* that he had in fact never admitted. The representative of the child responded by stating that the father's argument entailed a prohibited *révision au fond* and that the Libyan judgment was in conformity with Tunisian public policy in the sense that the establishment of *nasab* was not only based on the registered acknowledgement of the father but also on the legal presumption of *firāsh*. The SC agreed with this reasoning. It found that the arguments of the father were related to the determination of the facts as assessed by the foreign court whereas the review of the enforcing court must be limited to an examination of whether the foreign judgment satisfied the Tunisian requirements for enforcement.

---

[50] Decision of the Tunis CFI no. 72380 of 29 November 1982, RTD 1984, p 105, with a case note by Kotrane.

[51] Ibid.

[52] Decision of the Tunisian SC no. 50867 of 29 March 2018 (unpublished, on file with author). The nationality of the parties is not clear, but it seems that they are all Tunisian nationals.

14.3.2 Comments and Analyses

Comments on the above-reported cases will proceed by country.

14.3.2.1 Morocco

The treatment of foreign filiation judgments in Morocco is consistent with the general Islamic prohibition of adoption as incorporated in Moroccan domestic legislation.[53] The prohibition extends to cross-border cases involving Moroccan nationals (Article 2 FC). The case reported above shows that the prohibition could be invoked *ex officio* by the court although the parties did not contest the validity of the adoption. The justification of the court focused on the Islamic prohibition and failed to take into consideration the interests of the child. As a result of the judgment, the child was deprived of important financial support. This decision is in line with an old reported case decided in 1962 by the Casablanca CFI. In that case, the court refused in the name of public policy and Islamic Sharia to enforce a foreign judgment ordering a Moroccan Muslim father to pay maintenance to his biological child following the foreign court's having established, on application of the national law of the child, an out-of-wedlock filiation.[54]

With regard to the second case concerning the rebuttal of legitimate filiation, it is possible to consider that the outcome of the decision is consistent with the best interests of the child in maintaining the 'legitimate' character of his filiation, taking into consideration the vulnerable status of children born out of wedlock in Arab countries. However, such a reading remains speculative. The court did not engage in any concrete analyses nor did it make any reference to the implications of the decision on the status of the child. In addition, the general factual context in which the case was decided barely reflects any advantages falling to the child. Indeed, even if the mother was successful in her maintenance claim against the father, the Moroccan judgment had little chance, if any, of being enforced in France – the place of residence of the father – because of its inconsistency with a prior French judgment. Moreover, maintaining a fictitious 'legitimate' filiation could prove to be very harmful to the child since the father would continue to refuse to acknowledge any paternity with the child on the basis of the foreign judgment. In fact, this decision shows that acknowledgement and disavowal of paternity as established by a foreign court in contradiction with the accepted Islamic-based Moroccan rules are

[53] Article 149 of the Moroccan FC: 'Adoption has no legal value and does not result in any of the effects of legitimate filiation.'

[54] Decision of the Casablanca CFI of 23 November 1962, cited in Sarehane 2013, no. 118. However, the same author mentioned, in the field of choice of law, a decision of the Moroccan Supreme Court in which it rejected the claim of the mother to establish the natural filiation of the child to his biological father but nevertheless recognized certain effects in terms of maintenance under the law applicable to the case, Sarehane 2013, no. 117. See also Loukili 2012, p 158, fn. 78.

unlikely to be recognized in Morocco. This confirms the idea that what mattered for the court was the protection of the pre-established religious order.[55]

14.3.2.2 Tunisia

The attitude of the Tunisian court in the cases reported above regarding foreign adoptions might seem quite surprising. Tunisia has indeed departed from traditional Islamic rules and allows adoption in spite of the firmly undisputed religious prohibition. The case shows that the acceptance of adoption does not necessarily mean that foreign adoption judgments can be enforced without difficulty, especially when a Tunisian child is adopted by a foreigner (presumably a non-Muslim). In addition, the existence of a law on adoption should not overlook the vivid reactions that this very law has produced. For some authors, the fact that adoption is permitted under Tunisian law in violation of the Islamic prohibition does not open the door for non-Muslims to adopt Tunisian (Muslim) children.[56] In some purely domestic cases, Tunisian courts did refer to the traditional prohibition to justify the revocation of an adoption[57] or to overtly criticize the solution of the legislature.[58] The future of the institution also might depend on the political developments in the country.[59]

---

[55] In the same vein, the Supreme Court affirmed in 2005 the validity of the acknowledgement because it was made in accordance with Islamic principles, although it was established that the children were born out of wedlock as the result of an illegitimate relationship between the Moroccan father and the French mother. See decision of the Supreme Court no. 142 of 9 March 2005, cited in Loukili 2012, pp 144–145. This decision shows that the strict compliance with the methods for establishing filiation as recognized under Islamic law matters more than the outcome of such an application. Therefore, these methods can be applied to produce a child-friendly outcome if the traditional rules are respected.

[56] See Al-Jandalī 2011, p 561, fn. 1, invoking the best interests of the child and his right to be raised in his cultural environment as a justification against the adoption of Tunisian children by non-Muslims foreigners. See also Boukhari 2011, p 148, for whom the intervention of public policy in the matter of adoption is justified by the need to protect the personal status of the child by prohibiting adoption of (Muslim) Tunisian children by (non-Muslim) foreigners.

[57] For example, the decision of Sousse CFI no. 2074 of 5 May 1993, RTD 1996, pp 171 et seqq., with a case note by Ben Ḥalīma, reproduced in Ben Ḥalīma 2012, p 1118. See also the decision of the Tunisian SC no. 295 of 23 March 1999, in which the court declared that 'adoption remains in the mind of the majority religiously prohibited from the point of view of Islamic law although it is legally permitted.' (unpublished), reported in Al-Jandalī 2011, pp 538–539.

[58] See the decision of the Kairouan CFI no. 20973 of 6 March 1989 (unpublished), reported in Al-Jandalī 2011, pp 536–538, considering that the prohibition of adoption is based on undisputed religious texts and the consensus of legal scholars despite the legislative intervention.

[59] On the recurring intense debate – especially after the 2011 Revolution – regarding the abolition of adoption in Tunisia due to its running counter to undisputed Sharia principles, see Afif Jaidi 2014. A former Minister of Justice (M. Noureddine Bhiri) from the Islamist party (Ennahdha) indicated in an interview given to a Qatari newspaper on 19 April 2012 in his capacity as member of the government that Tunisian family law as a whole was in conformity with Islamic prescriptions *except for adoption* (emphasis added). When he was asked about the possibility of a

Second, the possibility of allowing the adoption of Tunisian children by foreigners is still an unsettled issue in Tunisia, as the second case clearly shows. One might be doubtful here whether the real reason behind the refusal to recognize the French adoption was, as indicated, the single status of the adoptor[60] or whether it was, in fact, the disparity of religion between the adoptive French mother (presumably non-Muslim) and the child.[61] Still, this may be contradicted by (i) another reported decision granting exequatur for a French adoption decision regarding a Tunisian girl (seemingly an adult[62]) residing in Tunisia who was adopted by a French citizen, stating that the foreign adoption was not against public policy[63] or (ii) the existence of a number of reported cases in which Tunisian judges awarded the adoption of Tunisian children to mixed Tunisian-foreign couples.[64] This has led some scholars to contend that foreigners can adopt Tunisian children and that Tunisian judges no longer require that the adopter be a Muslim in order to allow the adoption to take place.[65] Others affirm that 'religion *no longer has any significance* in the awarding of adoption' in Tunisia (emphasis added).[66] However, for three reasons it seems too hasty to make such an assertion. First, the Islamic element is not completely absent in the cases awarding adoptions to mixed couples.[67] Second, Tunisian case law is unpredictable with regard to the place of Islamic rules in the

reform of Tunisian family law, he simply mentioned that the Tunisian people have other priorities. The interview, which is still posted on the official website of the Ministry of Justice, is available at www.e-justice.tn/index.php?id=1125 (accessed 5 January 2019).

[60] See the decision of the Cantonal Court of Tunis no. 12639 of 12 July 2018 (unpublished, on file with author), affirming the adoption of a child by a single unmarried Tunisian mother. The judge deciding the case based his decision on the best interests of the child (the need for care, the critical health condition of the child) and the spirit of the Tunisian adoption law, which aims at protecting children, to overcome the legal marriage requirement.

[61] Cf. Boukhari 2011, pp 146, 148.

[62] It is not clear whether the girl had reached the age of majority at the time of the adoption or not. However, the case is presented in literature as an adult adoption case.

[63] Judgment of the Tunis CFI no. 9985 of 5 November 1999 (unpublished), reported in Ben Achour 2017, pp 119–120, who agreed with the decision stating that adoption of adults was unknown in Tunisia. However, this opinion seems to be oblivious of the Tunisian SC's decision no. 57743 of 22 April 1997, Bull. Civ. part 1 of 1997, p 273, in which the court considered that the adoption of an adult is not permitted because under Tunisian law, the requirement that the adoptee should be a minor who has not reached the age of twenty is a matter of public policy. Accordingly, the court overturned the decision of the lower court, which had allowed the adoption by a Tunisian woman of a 32-year-old woman according to her birth certificate as delivered by the General Consulate of Abu Dhabi.

[64] See in particular the study based on the examination of 100 decisions rendered by the Cantonal Court of Tunis made by the judge Ghazouani 2013, pp 389 et seqq.

[65] See Ghazouani 2013, pp 389 et seq.; Ben Cheikh 2016, pp 217 et seqq.

[66] See Yassari 2015, p 947.

[67] All the cases concern the adoption of Tunisian children (presumed to be Muslims) made by mixed couples that include a Tunisian partner (and therefore presumed to be Muslim). See however, Būshamāwī 2009, p 12, in which the author mentions three unpublished court decisions in which adoption was approved for foreign (presumably non-Muslim) couples without requiring any certificate of conversion to Islam.

Tunisian legal system, given the existence of contradictory decisions even at the level of the Supreme Court itself.[68] Finally, all the above-mentioned decisions have been issued by the lower courts in the judicial system. Therefore, this promising tendency needs to be confirmed by higher courts, especially the Supreme Court.[69] Nonetheless, the dynamics of the Tunisian society indicate the existence of an undeniable movement towards more equality and less discrimination based on religious creed,[70] although the resistance to that movement from the conservative segment of society should not be ignored or underestimated.[71]

As is largely known, with regard to the establishment or disavowal of out-of-wedlock filiation, Tunisian law allows the establishment of biological parentage (*bunuwwa*).[72] However, the 1982 judgment reported here was rendered before the entry into force of the law. In fact, it is very difficult to assess the implications this case entails. As it was rightfully pointed out, the court could have considered that the acknowledgement of the father covered the 'illegitimacy' of the filiation.[73] The interests of the child also could have served to preserve his 'legitimate' filiation as duly established under Tunisian law.[74] In addition, the court did not examine any of the enforcement requirements, neither those admitted under Tunisian law nor those included in the Franco-Tunisian bilateral convention on judicial assistance that was applicable to the case.[75] Therefore, it is unclear what this case says about the enforcement of foreign filiation judgments in Tunisia. This explains the reason why it is rarely cited or discussed in legal literature.[76]

---

[68] The fact that court decisions are not regularly published complicates matters further.

[69] According to the Ghazouani himself, 'it is still premature to affirm that the ... Court ... has completely abandoned the religious impediment to adoption', and the trend he has detected needs to be confirmed, Ghazouani 2013, p 405.

[70] Recent major developments include (1) the abolishment of the *circulaire* prohibiting Tunisian women from marrying non-Muslims by the *circulaire* of the Ministry of Justice no. 164 of 8 September 2017; (2) the presidential initiative on equality and individual freedoms, which resulted in a 'truly revolutionary' report that courageously tackles all the problematic issue of the incompatibilities and the incoherencies found in the Tunisian legal system in connection with the newly adopted Tunisian Constitution and the human rights conventions concluded by Tunisia (the Colibe Report), see the report available at http://legal-agenda.com/uploads/Rapport-COLIBE.pdf (accessed 24 February 2019). Finally, (3) the announcement of the legal reform of the PSC to modify the Islamic succession rules in the current law so as to achieve more equality-compliant and non-discriminatory rules. See the law proposal on the reform of succession law in Tunisia adopted by the Ministerial Council on 23 November 2018 (on file with author).

[71] Reactions to these developments often resulted in protests and calls to fight to preserve and maintain the 'Islamic' identity of Tunisian society.

[72] See Law No. 98-75 of 28 October 1998 Regarding the Allocation of a Patronymic Family Name to Abandoned Children and Those of Unknown Parentage, amended by Law No. 2003-51 of 7 July 2003, allowing for the biological paternity of adulterine children to be legally established.

[73] See Kotrane, *supra* note 50, p 112.

[74] Ibid.

[75] See the critical assessment of this decision by Kotrane, ibid.

[76] See for example, Ben Achour 2017, p 122.

As for the second case, the caution taken by the court in explaining the non-conformity of the Italian decision with public policy deserves attention. It is indeed in line with the tendency in court practice[77] to distinguish *bunuwwa* (parentage) from *nasab* (legitimate filiation) in the sense that only marriage (either valid or voidable) can confer *nasab* with its full effects, including succession rights.[78] This distinction has been endorsed by the legislature itself. During the parliamentary debates on both the 1998 Law on the Allocation of a Patronymic Family Name and its 2003 reform, the government clearly indicated that the purpose of the law was simply to provide 'a minimum protection' to children of unknown parentage, and that these limited solutions of the law were 'better than nothing'.[79] Therefore, one can legitimately wonder whether a foreign judgment establishing illegitimate filiation (*bunuwwa*) with full effect, including succession rights, would ever be recognized in Tunisia.[80]

This uncertainty can best be illustrated by a case involving a choice-of-law issue in which the consequences of the 'non-legitimacy' of the filiation of a child was raised as an incidental question in a succession case. The case concerned the exclusion of a child born out of wedlock from the succession of his biological father, who had acknowledged the child before his death. The standing of the representative of the child (his mother) to claim any succession rights was contested by the other heirs of the father. On a first appeal to the SC, the regulatory court observed that 'acknowledgement of the father does not render the child legitimate in the absence of marriage (*firāsh*)' and that 'the child whose filiation is acknowledged by his father in the absence of marriage between his father and his mother is an adulterine child who inherits only from his mother according to Article 152 PSC and according to the Law No. 98-75 of 18 October 1998 Regarding the Allocation of a Patronymic Name to Abandoned Children and Those of Unknown Parentage. Accordingly, the acknowledgement of filiation confers to the child the right to alimony, care and custody … without conferring succession rights on him'.[81]

The same court, however, changed its position on the very same case upon a second appeal.[82] It first considered that the filiation (*bunuwwa*) of the child should be established in accordance with the law that is more favourable to the child

[77] It should be noted that case law on the issue of establishing *nasab* in the absence of marriage is inconsistent at best. See notes below.

[78] The distinction has important legal implications. See the Tunisian SC decision – in a case involving a choice-of-law issue – no. 18400/18709 of 2 July 2008 (unpublished, on file with author).

[79] See the parliamentary debates on the 1998 law and its 2003 amendment available at www.legislation.tn/ (accessed 15 February 2019).

[80] Compare the opinion based on this very same judgment, according to which 'the right of each child to establish his/her filiation seems to be of public order'. Benjemia et al. 2012, p 220.

[81] Ibid.

[82] The decision of the Tunisian SC no. 38151/37494 of 19 October 2009, Bull. Civ. 2009, p 317. See comments on this case by Ketata in Ketata and Belhadj 2013, p 192.

(Article 52 CPIL) – which was, in this case, Swiss law – without distinguishing between (*bunuwwa shar'iyya*) and 'natural filiation' (*bunuwwa ṭabīʿiyya*).[83] The court then declared that the distinction between *bunuwwa sharʿiyya* and *bunuwwa ṭabīʿiyya* argued by the appellants was not relevant since under Tunisian law *nasab* could be established by acknowledgement (*iqrār*) independently of *firāsh* (marital bed). The court concluded that Swiss law, which allows the establishment of natural filiation inclusive of succession rights for an illegitimate child, was not contrary to Tunisian public policy. It then stated in a *dictum* that the Tunisian legal system, which allows illegitimate children to identify their biological father, has been moving towards the recognition of *bunuwwa ṭabīʿiyya* despite the absence of any express legal provision to that effect. This is certainly an important and unprecedented move by the SC. However, it seems early to characterize this judgment as a '*revirement de jurisprudence*' as the principle of the ruling needs to be confirmed and approved by subsequent decisions of lower courts and hopefully the SC itself.[84]

Finally, the 2018 decision shows how foreign filiation judgments can be accepted in the enforcing State's legal system without any tension or hesitation. The refusal of the SC to engage in any investigation of the facts determined by the foreign court should be highly appreciated.

14.3.2.3 Lebanon

In Lebanon as well, Lebanese courts have refused to enforce a foreign adoption on the ground that its effect could not be reconciled with the law of the concerned religious community. Lebanese scholars have explained the outcome of this case in different ways. According to one opinion, the Mount Lebanon CA rejected the exequatur request based on public policy.[85] For others, who pointed out that the CA did not expressly refer to public policy, enforcement was refused because the foreign judge failed to apply the national law of the adoptee, i.e. the religious law of the community to which he was affiliated.[86] However, both views agree that the decision reflects a concern to satisfy the fundamental requirements of religious law in Lebanon. The court ruling has been open to criticism as it failed to take into consideration the interests of the adopted child in the case.[87]

As for the case concerning the adulterine child's succession rights, and despite the undeniable liberal attitude of the Lebanese Supreme Court, one cannot help but wonder whether the outcome would have been different had the foreign legal order

---

[83] The terminology here is the one used by the court.

[84] See the Colibe Report, *supra* note 70, pp 189 et seqq., suggesting the abolition of all distinctions between children with regard to the circumstances of birth. Unfortunately, the proposal was not adopted.

[85] Gannagé 2010, no. 41.

[86] Najm 1996–1997, p 195.

[87] In the same sense, Najjar 1989, p 655.

ruled on the succession rights of the adulterine child over property located in Lebanon.[88] The court seems to have been very cautious in this respect. It pointed out that the foreign judgment had no impact on inheritance rights although this has been doubted by some authors.[89]

14.3.3 The Enforcement of Foreign Filiation Judgments in Other Arab Jurisdictions

The issue of the enforcement of foreign filiation judgments has been straightforwardly tackled in only a few Arab jurisdictions, namely Morocco, Tunisia and Lebanon. In other Arab jurisdictions, and in the absence of reported cases,[90] the question of the enforceability of foreign filiation judgments needs to be examined on the basis of academic writings on the subject.[91]

In this respect, and unlike with choice of law,[92] it should be mentioned from the outset that the issue of the enforcement of foreign filiation judgments has rarely been specifically addressed in Arab legal literature.[93] Usually, the issue of

[88] In the field of choice of law, see the decision of the Mount Lebanon CFI of 29 January 1991, Al-ʿAdl 1990–1991, p 262, and Gannagé 2001, p 865, in which the court excluded the application of the Brazilian law applicable to the adulterine filiation of a Brazilian child because, in application of Brazilian law, the child would have been conferred succession rights equal to those conferred to legitimate children.

[89] For a critical analysis of this decision, see the comment of M-C Najm in Al-ʿAdl no. 1 of 2008, pp 186 et seqq. Finally, in a decision rendered in 2011, the Lebanese SC recognized a succession right of the child, but limited to 12.5% of the estate as an 'illegitimate child' compared to 87.5% for his adopted sister as a 'legitimate child', Lebanese SC no. 56 of 21 June 2011 (unpublished, on file with author). The decision was ultimately refused enforcement in France on the ground of public policy because of its discriminatory character towards 'illegitimate children', Paris CA no. 14/15527 of 16 December 2015, Revue de planification patrimoniale belge et internationale no. 2 of 2016, p 185, with a case note by Van Boxstael, pp 199 et seqq.

[90] Needless to say, the absence of reported cases does not necessarily mean that such cases do not actually exist.

[91] For the sake of brevity, the author will cite only to sources that are representative of the law in the majority of Arab jurisdictions. Two general characteristics of these sources deserve to be highlighted. First, in the overwhelming majority of cases, especially those written in Arabic, the content does not substantially differ. Second, almost all of these writings are based on early works of Egyptian scholars and abundantly cite, for the sake of convenience, early French case law. On the 'verbose' character of legal writing in Egypt that can be transposed to the majority of Arab countries, see Berger 2002.

[92] It is possible to come across a number of articles dealing with various aspects of choice of law in matters of adoption, *nasab*, establishment of filiation, etc. These articles are often written in Arabic and published in local law reviews.

[93] In a matter of adoption, however, see Najm 1996–1997.

enforcement is discussed in general terms without distinguishing personal status judgments from civil and commercial judgments. Therefore, in many Arab PIL textbooks, the presentation of the enforcement system is limited to a general outline of the basic notions and requirements. Even public policy is presented in a general manner that does not take into account the specificity of this requirement in the Arab enforcement system in general or in its application by local courts.[94] However, it is not uncommon to read in the same textbooks, especially in the part relating to public policy as regards the choice of law, that foreign norms which contradict Islamic Sharia rules and principles should be considered as contrary to public policy.[95] The examples that are usually given are those of adoption, out-of-wedlock filiation (and their effect, including maintenance and succession rights), interfaith marriages or successions.

Many other scholars clearly indicate that foreign judgments rendered in violation of Islamic Sharia rules and principles should be refused enforcement. Such indication can be found in the legal literature coming from almost all Arab countries. The recurrent examples often given include the following: a foreign judgment declaring the validity of a marriage between a Muslim woman with a non-Muslim man or obliging a Muslim wife to cohabitate with a non-Muslim husband;[96] a foreign judgment assigning the custody of a Muslim child to his/her non-Muslim mother;[97] a foreign judgment ordering the payment of maintenance to an adopted child or a child born out of wedlock.[98]

---

[94] See El Chazli 2013/2014, p 403, pointing out how difficult it is to 'describe, or even predict, the content of public policy' in Egypt. In the present author's view, this opinion largely applies also to other Arab countries.

[95] See for example Al-Dāwudī 2013, pp 352–353 on public policy in the field of the enforcement of foreign judgments, and pp 239 et seqq. on public policy in the field of choice of law.

[96] It is undisputed in the overwhelming majority of Arab countries that interfaith marriages between non-Muslim men and Muslim women are null and void. See for example the case decided in the field of choice of law by the Dubai SC appeal no. 51 of 21 October 2008 (on file with author), invalidating a marriage between a British-Turkish Muslim woman and her British husband who refused to convert to Islam. Tunisia is the exception, see *supra* note 70, although, in practice, some mayors would refuse to conclude a marriage between Tunisian women and non-Muslim foreigners without their being presented a certificate of conversion to Islam. See Bobin 2018.

[97] See however the decision of the Egyptian SC which allowed the enforcement of a French judgment assigning custody of the child to his mother, decision no. 200/66 of 14 May 2005 (unpublished, on file with author), rendered in application of the French-Egyptian bilateral Convention on Judicial Assistance of 15 March 1982. Compare this with the decision of the Tunisian SC no. 7286 of 2 March 2001, RJL no. 1 of 2002, p 183, concerning the enforcement of a Belgian judgment awarding the custody of one of the children of the divorced couple to his Danish mother domiciled in Belgium, and with the SC's contradictory and questionable earlier judgment in the very same case no. 69523 of 4 January 1999, RJL no. 1 of 2002, p 167. On both judgments, see the comment of M Ghazouani, RTD 2001, p 201 (in Arabic).

[98] See the reported cases from Morocco provided above.

14.4 The Enforcement of Foreign Filiation Judgments Within the General Context of Cross-Border Personal Status Dispute Resolution

In the author's view, it is very difficult to grasp the complexity and the peculiarity of the enforcement of filiation judgments without placing the issue in its general context, i.e. the enforcement of foreign personal status judgments and the PIL resolution of cross-border personal status disputes.[99] In this respect, the existence of opposing approaches deserves to be highlighted.

The first approach is conservative and aims to preserve domestic laws and values. Most Arab countries follow this approach. Yet, here it is possible to distinguish two parallel tendencies. On the one hand, there is a tendency which consists in the accommodation, whenever possible, of general religious principles in a way that serves the interests of the weaker parties (usually women and children) and aims at avoiding unfair results. Many cases show how Arab judges are sensitive to the factual details of the cases in a way that prevents the perversion of religious rules and principles to serve the illegitimate interests of one party, usually males. In this respect, the Emirati SC has, for example, considered unfounded the request made by a Muslim Austrian-Egyptian to declare his marriage to a Christian Austrian woman inconsistent with Sharia principles. In this case, the marriage was concluded in Austria, the place of residence of the parties at the time of the marriage, but without the presence of the legal tutor (*walī*) of the woman as Sharia law requires. The court pointed out that 'any Sharia-based rule (*ḥukm sharʿī*) derived from an explicit provision of the law (*naṣṣ ṣarīḥ*) whose authenticity is beyond doubt and whose meaning is indisputable (*qaṭʿī al-thubūt wa-l-dalāla*) is considered as part of public policy'. However, in opposition to the lower courts, it upheld the validity of the marriage not only because it was valid under the common national law of the parties (i.e. Austrian law), but also because it considered it valid under the national law of the husband, i.e. Egyptian law based on Hanafi doctrines, which under certain conditions allows women to marry without a tutor.[100] Thus the court ruled that the conclusion of a marriage in the absence of a *walī* did not contravene the undisputed Sharia rules (*al-aḥkām al-qaṭʿiyya li-l-sharīʿa al-islāmiyya*).[101]

---

[99] This section does not aim to provide a comprehensive review of the issue. In a much more modest way, it tries to highlight some aspects of the dynamics of cross-border family dispute resolution in Arab countries.

[100] This case is interesting because the Court applied foreign laws *ex officio* despite the fact that the husband pleaded the application of Emirati law, knowing that Emirati case law has always treated foreign law as a fact that needs to be pleaded and its content ascertained by the party arguing for its application; otherwise Emirati law applies in family matters as well. See Article 1 of the Emirati PSC. Compare with the Dubai SC appeal no. 51 of 21 October 2008, *supra* note 96.

[101] Dubai SC decision no. 206, appeal no. 36 of 2008 of 23 September 2008 (on file with author). Similarly, the Omani SC rejected an action instituted by a father, filed in his capacity as legal tutor, seeking to declare void a marriage that his daughter concluded without his permission. The couple, which lost their patience due to the unjustified refusal of the father to accept the groom, eloped to Egypt where they

A similar tendency can be seen in some cases relating to the assignment or modification of custody or the enforcement of foreign custody judgments. In a number of cases – where the claim was not supported by good reasons or risked being contrary to the interests of the child – courts have rejected an action to revoke the custody of the mother because she lives with the children in a different country in a way that prevents the father from exercising his *wilāya* (guardianship) prerogatives.[102] The common justification is that mother should be given priority in respect of custody because she is presumed to be a better caregiver than the father.[103] Maintenance cases also reveal a certain desire of Arab judges to secure financial support for children.[104]

On the other hand, there is also a parallel tendency under which any 'serious' deviation from the pre-established religious rules and principles is not acceptable. Accordingly, the contravention of any Sharia-based rule derived from an explicit text whose authenticity is beyond doubt and whose meaning is indisputable will be deemed as contrary to public policy and will entail either the exclusion of the foreign applicable law or the refusal to enforce foreign judgments. The courts will even go further so as to 'assume' that laws and judgments of non-Muslim countries are, in principle, fundamentally different and therefore against public policy.[105] This tendency can have serious implications, and it can be far-reaching as well. It may, for instance, bear upon judgments from other Arab countries whose domestic

concluded their marriage. The court characterized the presence and acceptance of the *walī* as an issue of formal validity subject to the law of the place of conclusion of the act, in this case Egyptian law as influenced by Hanafi doctrines, which under certain conditions allows the conclusion of a marriage without the presence of the legal tutor. See decision of the Omani SC no. 40 of 8 October 2005, appeal no. 2005/35 (unpublished, on file with author).

102 See Egyptian SC decision no. 200/66 of 14 May 2005 and Tunisian SC no. 7286 of 2 March 2001, *supra* note 97.

103 See Bahraini Supreme Court decision no. 8 of 17 June 2017 (unpublished, on file with author). In this case. The court quashed the order made by the lower courts requiring a Bahraini wife to move with her children to the domicile of the husband located in Egypt (or else lose the custody of her children). In this case, the Supreme Court considered that the conditions for a safe and sound custody environment were not satisfied to justify the relocation order.

104 See for example the decision of the Jordanian Supreme Court no. 2004.3582 of 20 February 2005 (unpublished, on file with author). The case concerned an action brought by a grandmother of a child, in her capacity as custodian, for the enforcement of a Kuwaiti judgment on maintenance. See also the decision of the Algerian Supreme Court no. 355718 of 12 April 2006, RSC no. 1 of 2006, p 477. The case concerns an exequatur action regarding a French judgment declaring the divorce of two Algerians (Muslims) residing in France, assigning the custody of the children to the mother and ordering the father to pay maintenance. The father opposed the exequatur, arguing, *inter alia*, that the order to pay maintenance (*nafaqa*) on a monthly basis even after the expiration of the waiting period (*ʿidda*) was contrary to Algerian law. The court rejected the arguments, stating that the order to pay a monthly wage (*ujra shahriyya*) to the custodian of the children did not constitute a violation of fundamental rules of Algerian law.

105 On this tendency under Moroccan law, see Loukili 2012, pp 152 et seqq.

family law has considerably deviated from the traditional path.[106] It may also affect cases involving only foreign nationals if one of the parties is Muslim. This tendency has been widely described and was criticized in some earlier legal literature.[107] However, the situation does not seem to have changed since then.[108] In other words, it is not uncommon that the mere involvement of a Muslim party in the dispute, even a foreign party, will trigger the application of domestic law which is either based on or inspired by Islamic rules and principles regardless of the law normally applicable according to the forum's choice-of-law rules.[109] This situation

[106] See the decision of the Supreme Court of Algeria no. 0773081 of 13 November 2013, RSC no. 2 of 2014, p 256. The case concerns an exequatur action regarding a Tunisian judgment declaring the divorce of the spouses (nationality unclear) for disobedience (*nushūz*) and conferring custody of the child to the husband. Exequatur was refused on the ground that it was inconsistent with a prior Algerian judgment. However, the court also pointed out that the Tunisian judgment could not be enforced as it was inconsistent with the established general principles on disobedience and with Algerian rules on custody, namely Articles 64 and 65 FC, which set out the priorities in awarding custody as inspired by Islamic principles. In a different case from Tunisia, a Tunisian woman who had been adopted by a Libyan woman brought an action to revoke her adoption on the ground that such adoption was not recognized in Libya based on the Islamic prohibition of adoption, see Tunis CFI no. 3917 of 19 November 1991, RJL no. 10 of 1992, p 131.

[107] Many examples from different Arab countries have already been related in literature. See for example Elgeddawy 1971, pp 151–171; Charfi 1988, pp 410–431; Déprez 1990, pp 102–41.

[108] See for Egypt: Berger 2002, pp 555 et seqq.; Abdel Wahab 2012, pp 71 et seqq.; El Chazli 2013/2014, pp 403–405. For Morocco: see Loukili 2012, pp 138 et seqq.; see also Gannagé 2013, pp 80 et seqq.

[109] This is often referred to as the privilege of religion. See, references *supra* note 107. For an explicit application of this principle in a case where it was decided that family law was of mandatory application if one of the parties to the dispute was Muslim, because the legislative rules were based on undisputed sources the authenticity of which were beyond any doubt as they were detailed in the Qur'an, see the decision of the Supreme Court of Qatar of 10 November 2015 (appeal no. 264 of 2015, on file with author). In this case, the Supreme Court indicated that in the connecting factor in determining the governing law in family disputes was 'religion' and therefore the national family legislation should apply to all Muslims. In another case from Kuwait, it was decided that the divorce of a converted Muslim woman from her Christian husband (both Lebanese nationals) married in the Maronite Church should be governed by Kuwaiti law instead of the national law of the husband in application of the conflicts rules on divorce. *In casu*, the law normally applicable (here Lebanese law of the concerned Christian community of the spouses) was excluded for its contradiction to public policy because, for the court, a Muslim woman cannot be subject to any other law except Sharia law. See the decision of the Kuwaiti Supreme Court of 4 March 2007 (appeal no. 315 of 2005, on file with author) and the Dubai SC judgment appeal no. 51 of 21 October 2008, *supra* note 96.

can still be seen in recently reported cases in some Arab countries in relation to either the revocation of custody,[110] the validity of marriage and its impact on filiation,[111] *ṭalāq* divorce[112] or *taṭlīq* divorce.[113]

The second approach is modern and more sensitive to recent developments in the field of PIL and more focused on ensuring a smooth coordination of different legal systems. This is the approach followed in Tunisia despite a lingering adherence to traditional Islamic principles.[114] In the field of cross-border filiation dispute

---

110 Decision of the Emirati Federal SC of 10 April 2004 (appeal no. 193 of the 24th judicial year 2004, on file with author). In this case, a non-Muslim mother domiciled in England, to whom an English judgment conferred custody of the child, brought an action before the Abu Dhabi Sharia Court against the Muslim father, who had left England and settled in the UAE for work. The mother asserted her priority right in the custody of the child and requested that the child be handed over to her on the basis of the English judgment. The Emirati Federal SC rejected her claim as contrary to Sharia law. In this case, the father expressed his concerns regarding the religious upbringing of his daughter since her non-Muslim mother took the child to church and drank wine.

111 See the Dubai SC no. 236 of 21 October 2008, *supra* note 96 (after declaring an interfaith marriage between a Muslim woman and a non-Muslim man who refused to convert to Islam as null and void, the court considered that the filiation of their child could be established only with regard to her mother).

112 See the decision of the Emirati Federal SC of 12 June 2007 (appeal no. 365 of the 27th judicial year, on file with author) (affirmation of a *ṭalāq* divorce pronounced by a British husband against his British wife in which the application of English law as the national law of the husband was rejected as contrary to public policy and Sharia law on the ground that English law 'deprives husbands of their right to effectuate *ṭalāq*').

113 See the Bahraini SC decision no. 54/2016 of 12 April 2017 (unpublished, on file with author) (a *taṭlīq* divorce action brought by the wife against her non-Muslim British husband based on English law, but as a consequence of a declaration of Islamic faith made by the husband during the proceeding, the divorce was ordered on application of Bahraini family law without any reference to choice of law).

114 There is abundant literature on the influence of Islamic principles on the Tunisian legal system and the consequences this entails. See for example in the field of PIL, Bostanji 2009a or in the field of family law, Bostanji 2009b.

resolution, this approach results in taking the interests of children more concretely into consideration by allowing adoption and by facilitating the establishment of filiation.[115] It can be also be detected even in cases where one of the parties tries to take advantage of the systematic consequences of the traditional rules.[116]

14.5 Conclusion

This report has attempted to provide a general overview of the recognition and enforcement of foreign filiation judgments in Arab countries. The reported cases found in certain Arab jurisdictions show the existence of opposing approaches. One approach considers a judgment to be contrary to public policy if it is inconsistent with domestic principles and the underlying religious values, sometimes even when such values contradict the modern legislation of the forum State (such as in Tunisia). However, there is also another approach that attempts to fit a concrete consideration of the interests of the child within the general legal framework permeated by religious values. Interestingly, case law from Tunisia and Lebanon

[115] This particular attention to the best interests of the child can be seen especially in the conflict-of-law resolution of cross-border filiation disputes, see the Tunisian SC's decision no. 38151/37494 of 19 October 2009, *supra* note 82; see also the Tunis CFI judgment no. 1525 of 4 March 2006 (unpublished), reported in Chedly and Ghazouani 2008, p 641 (establishment of the filiation of a child born out of wedlock by favouring the application of Tunisian law (the national law of the father and the law of his domicile) instead of Libyan law (the law of the domicile of the child)). See also the Tunis CFI's decision no. 41373 of 26 November 2002 (unpublished), reported in Chedly and Ghazouani 2008, p 641 (establishment of the filiation of a child born in Tunisia in an action brought by an Algerian mother against her Algerian husband; all parties were domiciled in Tunisia. The court decided to apply Tunisian law [law of the domicile of the child and the father] and not Algerian law [law of nationality of the father and the child], considering that Tunisian law is more favourable to the establishment of filiation.).

[116] The decision of the Sousse CFI no. 1692 of 4 July 2011, *supra* note 3, deserves to be highlighted. The case concerned an action on the allocation of custody of two children born out of wedlock in Luxembourg. The Tunisian father acknowledged that the children were born out of wedlock, and he explained before the court that he had to return to Tunisia with the children because their mother (a Luxembourg citizen) started living with another man and neglected her children. The social worker assigned by the court determined, in accord with the father's arguments, that custody should be awarded to the father on the ground that the best interests of the children consisted in their being raised in an Islamic environment. The defendant contested the jurisdiction of Tunisian court on the ground that the Luxembourg court had already decided the case and granted her the guardianship of the children. The court found that the foreign judgment should be recognized. It pointed out that the 'sudden return' of the father with the children to Tunisia constituted a fraud as to jurisdiction in order to obtain their custody. See also the Tunis CFI, summary judgment no. 42028 of 25 September 2014 (unpublished, on file with author). That case is a summary action invalidating an interdiction order prohibiting the removal of a Tunisian child from Tunisian territory; the order was addressed to a French mother who had come to Tunisia to recover a child that had been abducted by the father. The judge deciding the case first recognized the French judgment assigning guardianship of the child to the mother before declaring the interdiction invalid.

indicates that courts are tending to be less conservative. This can be explained either by the special lawmaking policy in Tunisia or by the special features of the Lebanese legal system as a multi-confessional State without a predominant or State religion.

The general context of cross-border dispute resolution relating to family matters, in general, and to filiation, in particular, demonstrates that the conservative approach is still practised in many Arab jurisdictions. However, the parallel tendencies identified in many Arab jurisdictions are very interesting to analyse. This shows that efforts to accommodate traditional family law with modern needs can have certain implications for cross-border family disputes. It also shows that behind the static and immutable rules often codified in modern legislation, a more complex reality exists that deserves a closer investigation based mainly on case law. But, in the author's views, this flexibility in accommodating fundamental principles is consistent with the general traditional tendencies in Sharia law.[117] The law of filiation can best illustrate this. Indeed, the strict and uncompromising prohibitions of adoption and out-of-wedlock filiation are met with far-reaching flexibility so as to make room for doubtful situations within the traditional prohibitions and avoid infringing upon the principles underlying the prohibitions.[118] This can be easily seen in cross-border family dispute resolutions. The accommodating tendency runs parallel to a firm tendency rejecting any compromise over pre-established religious

[117] Muslim scholars have developed over the centuries various technics that allow them to mitigate the restrictive and absolute nature of Sharia rules while affirming the validity of traditional assumptions. One of the most notable examples is the *takhayyur* or *talfīq* (i.e. selection and fabrication respectively). This technique consists in the combination of different legal opinions from different schools to achieve a specific result. On these concepts, see Ibrahim (n.d.); Layish 2000. Another important example is the *ḥiyal* (sing. *ḥīla*), i.e. legal tricks (evasions or stratagem) that consist in recourse to Sharia-compliant methods to circumvent the Sharia-based prohibitions and achieve the desired result (see Schacht 1986). These techniques show the concern of Muslim scholars to adhere to the traditional religious assumptions (sometimes in a fictitious way) while departing from them to accommodate Muslim society to its changing conditions. They should not, however, be used to demolish the traditional religious presumptions nor to declare legal (*ḥalāl* or *mubāḥ* [permitted]) what is religiously illegal, forbidden or prohibited (*ḥarām*) or vice versa (see the Preamble of the Moroccan FC in which King Mohamed VI declares that he could not 'as Commander of the Faithful (*amīr al-mu'minīn*) permit what God has forbidden and forbid what God has permitted'). This may explain why the Tunisian example of prohibiting polygamy and allowing adoption, which were based on the *neo-ijtihād*, i.e. reinterpretation of religious sources, has simply never been followed in other Arab countries, where instead some clinical accommodations have been made within the traditional framework of reasoning and without reversing the legal presumptions.

[118] This can be exemplified by the classical doctrines of the 'sleeping embryo' (*al-janīn al-rāqid*) and *nikāḥ shubha* (mistaken sexual intercourse) or by the hidden adoptions achieved by acknowledging children of unknown parentage. This has led scholars to draw the general principle according to which '*al-shar' yatashawwafu li-ithbāt al-nasab*' (Sharia [irresistibly] yearns to establish *nasab* [legitimate filiation]). The principle sometimes works against the will of the father or the 'legitimate' heirs who might want to avoid some legal obligations by contesting the *nasab* of a child. On this basis, legitimate filiation can be established as long as the illegal nature of the relationship is not revealed or ascertained.

precepts, even if detrimental to the interests of the child. This tendency becomes unduly excessive when such refusal is based on the assumption that non-Muslim family laws are fundamentally different from Muslim-based family laws and therefore contrary to public policy without examining *in concreto* whether such an assumption is founded or not. In this respect, PIL in Arab countries – which is largely based on old models dating back to the first half of the 20th century – deserves to be thoroughly reconsidered.[119]

References

Abdel Wahab MS (2012) L'ordre public en droit international privé égyptien de la famille. In: Bernard-Maugiron N, Dupret B (eds) Ordre public et droit musulman de la famille. Bruylant, Brussels, pp 71–95.

Afif Jaidi M (2014) Adoption in Tunisia: Turning Back the Clock on a Legal Achievement. The Legal Agenda, 16 October 2014. http://legal-agenda.com/en/article.php?id=657&folder=articles&lang=en. Accessed 5 January 2019.

Al-Dāwudī Ghʿ A (2013) Al-Qānūn al-Duwalī al-Khāṣṣ: Tanāzuʿ al-Qawānīn, Tanāzuʿ al-Ikhtiṣāṣ al-Qaḍāʾī, Tanfīdh al-Aḥkām al-Ajnabiyya – Dirāsa Muqārana [Private International Law: Conflict of Laws, Conflict of International Judicial Jurisdiction, the Enforcement of Foreign Judgments – A Comparative Analysis], 2nd edn. Dār al-Thaqāfa li-l-Nashr wa-l-Tawzīʿ, Amman.

Al-Haddāwī H (2017) Al-Qānūn al-Duwalī al-Khāṣṣ: Tanāzuʿ al-Qawānīn, al-Mabādiʾ al-ʿĀmma wa-l-Ḥulūl al-Waḍʿiyya fī al-Qānūn al-Urdunnī – Dirāsa Muqārana [Private International Law: Conflict of Laws, General Principles and Positive Solutions in Jordanian Law – A Comparative Analysis], 7th edn. Dār al-Thaqāfa li-l-Nashr wa-l-Tawzīʿ, Amman.

Al-Jandalī Ḥ (2011) Qānūn al-Aḥwāl al-Shakhṣiyya al-Tūnisī wa-ʿAlāqatuhu bi-l-Sharīʿa al-Islāmiyya [Tunisian Personal Status Law and its Relation with Islamic Sharia]. Manshūrāt Majmaʿ al-Aṭrash li-l-Kitāb al-Mukhtaṣṣ, Tunis.

Ben Achour S (2017) La réception des décisions étrangères dans l'ordre juridique tunisien. Centre de publications universitaires, Tunis.

Ben Cheikh W (2016) L'intérêt de l'enfant et l'adoption internationale: Etude des conflits de lois en droit tunisien. In: Ben Achour S, Ben Jémia M (eds) Droit fondamentaux et droit international privé, Journées Mohamed Charfi de droit international privé les 10 et 11 avril 2015. La Maison du Livre, Tunis, pp 217–230.

Ben Ḥalīma S (2012) Majmūʿat Taʿālīq ʿalā Qarārāt fī Māddat al-Aḥwāl al-Shakhṣiyya [Collection of Comments on Judgments Rendered in Personal Status Matters]. Markaz al-Nashr al-Jāmiʿī, Tunis.

Benjemia M, Ben Achour S, Bellamine M (2012) L'ordre public en droit international public tunisien de la famille. In: Bernard-Maugiron N, Dupret B (eds) Ordre public et droit musulman de la famille. Bruylant, Brussels, pp 197–238.

Berger MS (2002) Conflicts Law and Public Policy in Egyptian Family Law: Islamic Law through the Backdoor. The American Journal of Comparative Law 50:555–594.

[119] The political instability in many Arab countries is not a convincing argument for not reconsidering the foundations of the PIL systems in these countries, as is clearly shown by the legislative activity in this field in many Arab countries, encompassing recent reforms and codifications. However, this legislative activity has a limited impact as, apart from Tunisia, it has consisted of putting old wine in new bottles.

Bobin F (2018) Inside Tunisia's Battle over Inter-Religious Marriages. Worldcrunch, 15 September 2018. www.worldcrunch.com/world-affairs/inside-tunisia39s-battle-over-inter-religious-marriages. Accessed 5 January 2019.
Bostanji S (2003) L'émergence d'un statut privilégié de l'enfant en droit international privé tunisien. Actualités Juridiques Tunisiennes 16:125–158.
Bostanji S (2009a) Les survivances du communautarisme dans l'application judiciaire du droit international privé tunisien. Revue critique de droit international privé 2:251–274.
Bostanji S (2009b) Turbulences dans l'application judiciaire du Code tunisien du statut personnel: le conflit de référentiels dans l'œuvre prétorienne. Revue internationale de droit comparé 61 (1):7–47.
Boukhari R (2011) L'adoption internationale vue à travers le prisme de la loi tunisienne du 4 mars 1958. Revue juridique Thémis 45(1):115–148.
Bremer N (2016–2017) Seeking Recognition and Enforcement of Foreign Court Judgments and Arbitral Awards in the GCC Countries. McGill Journal of Dispute Resolution 3:37–65.
Bremer N (2018) Seeking Recognition and Enforcement of Foreign Court Judgments and Arbitral Awards in Egypt and the Mashriq Countries. Journal of Dispute Resolution 1:109–142.
Būshamāwī D al-J (2009) Tabannī al-Ajnabī fī al-Qānūn al-Tūnisī [Adoption of Foreigners in Tunisian Law]. Infos Juridiques/Al-Akhbār al-Qānūniyya 64/65:12–13.
Charfi M (1988) L'influence de la religion dans le droit international privé des pays musulmans. In: Académie de droit international de la Haye (ed) Recueil des cours 1987/III, vol 203. Martinus Nijhoff Publishers, Dordrecht et al., pp 321–454.
Chedly L, Ghazouani M (2008) Majallat al-Qānūn al-Duwalī al-Khāṣṣ Mu'allaq 'alayhā [Code of Private International Law Annotated]. Markaz al-Dirāsāt al-Qānūniyya wa-l-Qaḍa'iyya, Tunis.
Déprez J (1990) Droit international privé et conflits de civilisations: Aspects méthodologiques – Les relations entre systèmes d'Europe occidentale et systèmes islamiques en matière de statut personnel. In: Académie de droit international de la Haye (ed) Recueil des cours 1988/IV, vol 211. Martinus Nijhoff Publishers, Dordrecht et al., pp 9–372.
El Chazli K (2013/2014) Recognition and Enforcement of Foreign Judgments in Egypt. In: Bonomi A, Romano GP (eds) Yearbook of Private International Law 15:387–409.
Elbalti B (2018) The Recognition of Foreign Judgments as a Tool of Economic Integration: Views from Middle Eastern and Arab Gulf Countries. In: Sooksripaisarnkit P, Garimella SR (eds) China's One Belt One Road Initiative and Private International Law. Routledge, Abingdon and New York, pp 218–234.
Elgeddawy AK (1971) Relations entre systèmes confessionnel et laïque en droit international privé. Dalloz, Paris.
Gannagé L (2013) Les méthodes du droit international privé à l'épreuve des conflits de cultures. Martinus Nijhoff, The Hague.
Gannagé P (2001) Chronique de jurisprudence libanaise. Journal du droit international 3:865–882.
Gannagé P (2010) Liban – Droit International privé. Droit comparé, fasc. 60/Notarial Répertoire, Législation comparée, fasc. 5. In: Labic J (ed) Jurisclasseur droit comparé, vol III. LexisNexis, Paris.
Ghazouani M (2013) Cent jugements d'adoption internationale – Eclairages sur la pratique du Tribunal Cantonal de Tunis. In: Ben Achour S, Chedly L (eds) La diversité dans le droit, Mélanges offerts à la Doyenne Kalthoum Meziou-Dourai. Centre de Publication Universitaire, La Manouba, pp 389–422.
Ibrahim AF (n.d.) Talfīq/Takhayyur. Oxford Islamic Studies Online. www.oxfordislamicstudies.com/article/opr/t349/e0082?_hi=4&_pos=64. Accessed 18 March 2018.
Ketata F, Belhadj S (2013) La Jurisprudence du droit international privé. In: Annuaire de jurisprudence tunisienne. Publications de l'Ecole Doctorale de la Faculté de droit de Sfax, Sfax, pp 165–203.
Layish A (2000) Talfīḳ. In: Bearman PJ et al. (eds) The Encyclopaedia of Islam, vol X, new edn. Brill, Leiden, p 161.

Loukili M (2012) L'ordre public en droit international privé marocain de la famille. In: Bernard-Maugiron N, Dupret B (eds) Ordre public et droit musulman de la famille. Bruylant, Brussels, pp 127–159.
Najjar I (1989) Chronique de droit privé libanais. Revue trimestrielle de droit civil 88:651–669.
Najm M-C (1996–1997) L'adoption en droit international privé – Etude comparative du cas d'adoption d'un enfant libanais par un Français. Proche-Orient, Études Juridiques 49–50:123–221.
Najm M-C (2015/2016) The Enforcement of Foreign Judgments in Lebanese Private International Law. In: Bonomi A, Romano GP (eds) Yearbook of Private International Law 17:463–475.
Sarehane F (2013) Maroc – Conflits de lois, Conflits de juridictions. Droit comparé, fasc. 60/ Notarial Répertoire, Législation comparée, fasc. 4. In: Labic J (ed) Jurisclasseur droit comparé, vol III. LexisNexis, Paris.
Schacht J (1986) Ḥiyal. In: Lewis B et al. (eds) The Encyclopaedia of Islam, vol III. Brill, Leiden, pp 510–513.
Yassari N (2015) Adding by Choice: Adoption and Functional Equivalents in Islamic and Middle Eastern Law. The American Journal of Comparative Law 63:927–962.
Zaher K (2009) Conflit de civilisations et droit international privé. L'Harmattan, Paris.
Zeidguy R (2007) Analyse de la jurisprudence. In: Benradi M et al. (eds) Le code de la famille – Perceptions et pratique judiciaire. Friedrich Ebert Stiftung, n.p., pp 217–271.

Béligh Elbalti has been an associate professor at the Graduate School of Law and Politics at Osaka University since April 2017. He teaches Japanese law, comparative law and private international law, among other subjects. He holds one LL.M. from Tunisia (2008) and another from Japan (2011). He earned his Doctor of Law degree at the Graduate School of Law at Kyoto University in 2014. He is the author of a number of scholarly articles and case notes, notably in the field of private international law (international jurisdiction, the recognition and enforcement of foreign judgments and choice of law).

Chapter 15
Synopsis

Nadjma Yassari and Lena-Maria Möller

Contents

Keywords *nasab* · Filiation · Legal presumptions · Scientific evidence · DNA testing · Adoption · Foster care

15.1 Introduction

This volume's overarching themes are *nasab*, the (partial) absence thereof, and legal structures to remedy such a deficiency as well as its social implications. Outside the narrow realm of law, translating *nasab* as merely 'filiation' would not capture its significance in both premodern and contemporary Muslim societies. Rather, *nasab* is equally used to describe a person's lineage or descent, and thereby his or her general belonging within society.[1] Being the proper legal child of someone, carrying one's father's name, and inheriting from him carries weight in Muslim societies and forms an important pillar of personal identity. Thus, while every person has, at least theoretically, both maternal and paternal *nasab*, it is the

[1] Mohammadi 2016, pp 53–55.

N. Yassari · L.-M. Möller (✉)
Max Planck Institute for Comparative and International Private Law, Mittelweg 187, 20148 Hamburg, Germany
e-mail: moeller@mpipriv.de

N. Yassari
e-mail: yassari@mpipriv.de

N. Yassari et al. (eds.), *Filiation and the Protection of Parentless Children*, https://doi.org/10.1007/978-94-6265-311-5_15

latter which the discussion usually circles around, and it is a lack of *nasab* which results in children being legally disadvantaged.

This first category of 'parentless' (or 'fatherless') children is at the center of our inquiry, together with those children deprived of permanent caretakers due to the passing away of their parents or their parents' inability to care for them for various reasons. The analysis therefore probes the extent to which premodern Islamic legal doctrine and contemporary Muslim family law regimes have developed structures which safeguard the care and protection of these parentless children, and, by extension, whether social family structure have emerged to complement those already established by operation of law and/or by biological facts.

Based on ample examples contained in the collected reports comprising this volume, this short comparative exercise aims at shedding some light on the legal, biological, and social frameworks within which families in contemporary Muslim jurisdictions live and operate today.

15.2 The Legal Family

Across the world's legal systems, and for many centuries, a child's legal status has been predominantly determined in relation to his or her wedded parents.[2] The notion of children's filiation first and foremost arising from and depending on their parents' marital status has similarly formed the main pillar of legal family structures in contemporary Muslim jurisdictions; it epitomizes the premodern Islamic juristic maxim of '*al-walad li-l-firāsh*' (i.e. 'the child belongs to the conjugal/marital bed'). In addition, all jurisdictions covered in this volume require a minimum duration of the marriage (usually six months) for paternal *nasab* to be established by birth. The implementation of this time frame reflects a desire to increase the probability that the child is not only born into, but actually conceived in the said marriage. In this regard contemporary Muslim legislatures diverge from other jurisdictions around the globe, in which the mere existence of a marriage at the time of birth – if only for a split second prior to it – results in the married couple being considered their offspring's legitimate parents. Nonetheless, in Islamically inspired legal systems too, the designation of the husband of the mother as her children's father remains a (rebuttable) legal presumption that is not subject to further biological scrutiny.

In consequence, only children born to a married couple within certain time limits will automatically acquire *nasab* with regard to both their parents. By way of contrast, children born under more doubtful circumstances, i.e. because the validity of their parents' marriage is uncertain, will face serious legal and social challenges. They do not automatically become part of a legal family with two parents, and their *nasab* is established through their mother's side only. The centrality of the marital status of the parents is one of the salient features of the diverse family law regimes

[2] Stoljar 1973, Sect. 15.

discussed in this volume. Nonetheless, both premodern Islamic legal doctrine and contemporary Muslim jurisdictions uphold the possibility of remedying the legally disadvantaged status of children born under dubious circumstances or out of wedlock. As far as the first category of children is concerned, the law employs legal fictions, such as the 'sleeping embryo' (*al-rāqid*), which artificially extends the gestation period, or the concept of '*al-waṭ' bi-shubha*', through which the good faith belief of the biological parents that they were married suffices to establish paternal and maternal filiation of their offspring.

In addition, the concept of acknowledgment or '*iqrār al-nasab*' offers an opportunity to include children into the realm of a legal family. While generally everyone, including women, may acknowledge a child of unknown filiation (*majhūl al-nasab*) as their own, the most common form of *iqrār* is that which gives rise to paternal filiation. The country reports collected herein illustrate the different degrees and ends to which *iqrār* is being used, from 'secret adoptions' to the acknowledgment of biological children born under dubious circumstances. Nonetheless, *iqrār* remains an institution difficult to grasp fully. While its conditions seem rather lenient, the ways and ends to which *iqrār* is actually used in relation to the establishment of filiation remain ambiguous. While all jurisdictions formally reject the acknowledgement of children (notoriously) born out of wedlock, in some instances (unmarried) mothers have forced the biological father to register the child under his name, even if this did not imply the establishment of paternal *nasab*.

Muslim jurisdictions therefore oscillate between two possibly conflicting interests: One is to safeguard the institution of marriage as the only acceptable realm to conceive children and raise them; the second is to ensure that as many children as possible have an established *nasab* to both parents. These interests also explain the very narrow legal options to disavow *nasab* once it has been established by legal presumption. In fact, the principle of *firāsh* is the strongest proof of filiation and may not be challenged by either biological facts or scientific evidence. It may be refuted only by a procedure called *li'ān*, which requires the husband to formally accuse his wife of adultery and take an oath that the child is not his offspring, a procedure that is hardly ever reported in the case law of any of the countries under review. At the same time, and despite the prominent position of legal presumptions for establishing filiation, the question remains if and how biology matters and possibly impacts the concept of *nasab*.

15.3 The Biological Family

Generally, the principle of *firāsh* is a legal fiction that attributes paternity to the husband of the child's mother. Biology matters to that extent that the presumption works in line with a medically plausible time frame; childbirth within a minimum of six months after the conclusion of the marriage means, *inter alia*, increasing the likelihood of the husband having actually fathered the child. Nonetheless, the biological reality is not a *condition de fond* for the attribution of paternity.

Maternity, on the other hand, has always been and remains a matter of biology. This is true for all schools of Muslim legal thought, which, until very recently, have unanimously agreed that the woman who carries the child to term – i.e. the gestational mother – is the legal mother. However, with the emergence of new artificial reproduction technologies, ideas are evolving. Whereas Sunni scholars still retain the basic principle of the gestational mother being the legal mother, modern Shiite scholars have given priority to the owner of the gamete in the event the gestational and genetic mother diverge. Thus, in surrogacy cases for example, maternity is attributed to the genetic and not the gestational mother.[3]

In Sunni legal doctrine, biological considerations vis-à-vis maternity apply also to children born out of wedlock. Such children will always have a legal mother, as they will always be legally attributed to the woman who gave birth to them. In Shiite law, even when it comes to maternal *nasab*, the legality of birth remains a greater good than the biological fact; accordingly, a child born out of wedlock will have no filiation to his or her biological mother unless she acknowledges the child, as illustrated in Gleave's contribution to this volume. At the same time, Shiite scholars too place importance on biology, for instance when it comes to marriage impediments between a man and his biological daughter born out of wedlock.

In premodern legal doctrine, one point of entry for biological considerations into the issue of *nasab* was the concept of physiognomy (*qiyāfa*/*qāfa*), a practice retained from pre-Islamic times to settle paternity disputes. While some schools of Muslim legal thought have theoretically upheld the option of proving paternity by physiognomy, Ibrahim's chapter in this volume demonstrates that most Muslim scholars opted for a system which 'privileged legal presumptions over biological investigations'. In consequence, *qiyāfa* was never able to overrule the *firāsh* principle. This hierarchy of evidence in premodern paternity disputes can be seen as the conceptual starting point for contemporary jurists and legislatures' perspectives on DNA testing (and other means of scientific evidence).

DNA testing is currently being discussed in most jurisdictions, it is explicitly referenced in the statutory law of many jurisdictions, and it has generally become a common aspect of contestation in paternity disputes. However, the possibility to order a DNA test or to have such results considered in court proceedings remains limited. A first constraint present in all countries under review is that a DNA test alone is not sufficient to establish *nasab*. Secondly, where paternity has been established on the basis of the principle of *firāsh*, it cannot be refuted through a DNA test alone.[4] In other words, biological reality has no weight where a legal presumption is clearly established.

Thus, a first observation is that DNA tests always need specific circumstances or certain additional features to become operative. Accordingly, DNA tests – and

[3] Clarke 2009, pp 116–140.

[4] See, for instance, the country reports on Iran, Lebanon, Pakistan, Saudi Arabia, and United Arab Emirates, which detail that DNA tests have not been admitted in court for the sole purpose of the mother's husband denying paternity established by *firāsh*.

scientific evidence in general – may be introduced in instances where *nasab* is somehow jeopardized, for example because the marriage of the parents is defective or its date of conclusion unclear. Similarly, where the child could be attributed (by *firāsh*) to more than one man, scientific evidence can be used to clarify the contesting paternity claims without the immediate risk of stripping a child of his or her rights vis-à-vis a father altogether.[5] Further, DNA tests may be used when paternity is denied through the process of *li'ān*, as courts do occasionally resort to DNA testing prior to granting *li'ān*.[6]

A second observation is that DNA tests may not be used to establish *nasab* where *nasab* is impermissible. This applies in particular to children born out of wedlock. As mentioned above, none of the eleven jurisdictions covered in this volume recognize paternal *nasab* based solely on biological facts. Marriage still reigns supreme in all countries, and it is not foreseen that couples will have extramarital children. In consequence, the legal system does not offer any way to create *nasab* by proving biological descent alone. Establishing biological descent through a DNA test may however unfold certain legal effects, including not only the duty of the father to care financially for the child and to register the child with state authorities in order to have identification documents issued, but also the right of the child to know who his or her father is and in some cases to carry his or her father's family name. These rights and duties are mainly the outcome of case law and illustrate the awareness of judges in attending to the needs of the child and thereby partially relieving him or her from bearing the costs of a very narrow understanding of legitimacy of birth.

The third observation relates to terminology, as the admission of scientific evidence in paternity disputes and the subsequent creation of a legal relation between the father and the child have generated new legal terms in some jurisdictions. In Morocco, for instance, while *nasab* is still used to designate filiation according to Islamic legal doctrine, the expression '*ubūwa*', a more neutral term for paternity, is employed when referring to the relationship between a biological father and his child. In the same vein, whenever *nasab* is to be established, the term to describe this procedure is '*ithbāt al-nasab*', i.e. filiation ascertained through established means of evidence. However, where biological descent is at stake, the term used by the Algerian Court of Cassation, for example, is '*ilḥāq al-nasab*',

---

5 This is the case, for example, where a child is born less than one year following a divorce and more than six months after the conclusion of a new marriage (thereby having two potential legal fathers). In this regard, see the country report on Jordan illustrating how, where a child has two potential legal fathers, courts have resorted to a consideration of scientific evidence (at least when all concerned parties demanded clarification regarding the biological reality) to answer the ensuing question of whose *nasab* a child holds and – as a consequence – who will carry the parental responsibility attached to filiation.

6 This is the case in, *inter alia*, Jordan, Saudi Arabia, and the United Arab Emirates, where a potential father's request for *li'ān* may not be heard should a prior DNA test reveal that he is the biological father of the child in question. In Pakistan, courts haven even annulled a *li'ān* already pronounced after scientific evidence revealed that the claimant was in fact the child's biological father.

possibly to highlight that this kind of relation is solely based on scientific proof. The terminological differentiation points to the appearance of another class, possibly a 'second-class category' of *nasab* having unspecified legal implications.

Notwithstanding these multiple limitations and constraints placed on scientific evidence vis-à-vis legal filiation, these developments are also indicative of the evolution and emergence of factual familial communities, thereby inviting the question whether a social definition of family is emerging in contemporary Muslim societies.

15.4 The Social Family

The perhaps most common form of a social family set-up is the so-called 'patchwork family', where relatives and non-relatives (in particular, stepparents and stepchildren) form a common household. Such patchwork families exist in various forms in most Muslim jurisdictions, with their numbers having increased lately due to more recent family law reforms which have allowed either divorced parent to retain custody of his or her children after remarriage.[7] Yet, while patchwork families are built on the basis of the collapse of two family units, in some instances the family breakdown is such that a reconstruction is not possible. If parents have been stripped of their parental rights because of their own deficiencies, or whenever children have been abandoned or their parents have predeceased them, alternative arrangements must become operative to protect and care for the left-behind children.

All jurisdictions under review have dealt with these issues, and all have devised some schemes for alternative caretaking. While their legal implications as well as their labels and practical relevance diverge, they have led to the creation of familial communities based on social bonds, thus connecting persons who share neither legal nor biological lineage. It is thus worth investigating whether a social definition of parenthood is emerging in Muslim jurisdictions and societies. Such an endeavor is even more appealing against the background of the general rejection of the concept of adoption by Islamic jurisprudence, both in Sunni and Shiite legal doctrine.[8] With due respect to the differences of each jurisdiction, four categories of alternative caretaking schemes can be broadly distinguished:

First, the complete incorporation of a child into a new family – what one would label full adoption under a mainstream definition – is an option currently available only under Tunisian law.[9] The parent-child relationship created by Tunisian Law No. 58-27 of 4 March 1958 is entitled '*tabannī*' in Arabic and displays all the legal effects of a full adoption, including the creation of parental care and authority,

[7] Cf. Möller 2016, pp 483, 486; Yassari et al. 2017, 341.

[8] On the background of this rejection, cf. Yassari 2015.

[9] Prior to independence this option was available in Algeria too.

reciprocal inheritance rights, and the right to carry the adoptive parent's surname. In Malaysia too, Muslim parents may adopt a child, albeit with certain shortcomings: While an adoption can be registered by Muslims, no comprehensive legal framework has been established which would govern all its aspects, including the rights and duties of the adoptive parents. There thus remains a void regarding the implications of such an arrangement which is left to the courts to fill.

The second category comprises legal schemes allowing for the wide-ranging incorporation of a child into a new home. Interestingly, none of the examined jurisdictions has used the legal term of *tabannī* to designate these structures. Instead, legislatures have been careful to resort to new terminology.[10] Likewise, the corresponding regulations have often been 'hidden' in separate or unrelated legislative acts, possibly to dilute the impression of a full-fledged accommodation of adoption in their legal systems.[11] The respective statutes describe the effects of the arrangements in some detail, essentially awarding the new caretakers all relevant rights and duties arising from *nasab*. These include full parental care and authority (i.e. custody, *ḥaḍāna*, and guardianship, *wilāya*) resulting in full legal representation without state interference, a recommendation or a duty of the new caretakers to erect an irrevocable will to bequeath to the child up to one-third of their property prior to the placement of the child into the new home to account for the lack of intestate inheritance rights of the child vis-à-vis the new parents, and the right of the child to carry the caretaker's family name.[12] Finally, and most importantly, the statutes are silent on an automatic termination of the caretaking arrangement and, by extension, the legal relationship between the child and the caretakers. As a result, a permanent social family bond is being established assuring robust legal protection for the child. Thus, while from their own domestic perspective these schemes do not establish *nasab* and do not result in a full parent-child relationship, they undoubtedly constitute functional equivalents to adoption given the family units they recognize.[13]

The third category comprises structures that (only) provide for the temporary caretaking of parentless children and could therefore be labelled 'foster care arrangements'.[14] Under those schemes, the custody of a child is generally awarded to new caretakers, while the court or the competent authorities retain guardianship

---

[10] For example, the term *sarparastī* is used in Iran, *ḍamm* in Iraq, and *kafāla* in Algeria.

[11] Such being the case in Iran and Iraq.

[12] See the country reports on Iraq, Algeria, and Iran. Under Iranian *sarparastī*, even a child with known *nasab* may carry his or her caretakers' family name, but the child's original name must be recorded by the competent authorities.

[13] Cf. Yassari 2015.

[14] The terms used to denote these structures are diverse, such as *iḥtiḍān* in Jordan and Saudi Arabia, *ri'āyat al-aṭfāl majhūlī al-nasab* in the United Arab Emirates, and *kafāla* in Morocco and Tunisia.

and oversight authority.[15] While under some of these structures the child may carry the caretaker's surname, in particular when the child is of unknown *nasab*, no compulsory inheritance arrangement has to be made nor is any financial deposit in favor of the ward demanded. Finally, the legal relationship ends (at the latest) automatically with the child coming of age. To facilitate everyday life within the new familial community, and since no marriage restrictions exist between the child and the foster family, the creation of a milk kinship is advised.[16]

Finally, forming the fourth category, only two out of the eleven jurisdictions covered in this volume, namely Lebanon and Pakistan, have no formalized legal framework for the placement of parentless children into new homes. In Lebanon, foundlings, orphans, and children of unfit caretakers are mostly cared for in residential care institutions. Secret adoptions (through *iqrār*, i.e. acknowledgement of *nasab*) are practiced informally, and in very rare cases judges have consented to non-relatives fostering a child, yet no legal basis for this practice exists. In Pakistan, fostering and adoption (including cross-border cases) take place within the framework of the Guardians and Ward Act of 1890, whereby the potential foster family will be awarded guardianship and custody through court order.

While the different structures that have been established to care for and protect parentless children in the eleven countries under review in this volume differ as regards their legal implications, they have led to the creation of alternative family bonds based on the will of the participants to build a community closely resembling that of parents and their legal and/or biological children.

15.5 Conclusion and Outlook

A strict legal regime governing filiation naturally disadvantages those children who do not fit the narrow category of being conceived and born in wedlock. Premodern Islamic legal doctrine has remedied these children's status through various concepts, including that of *iqrār*, by which children can be acknowledged and thereby acquire the status of the acknowledger's legal child. Contemporary Muslim jurisdictions have maintained this option. At the same time, most likely in an attempt to deter unmarried couples from having extramarital children, many legal regimes have excluded children born out of wedlock from such a remedy, at least formally. Therefore, from the legislature's perspective, *iqrār* is primarily devised to solidify a doubtful kinship relation and to provide for foundlings and children of unknown filiation.

---

[15] In some countries, foster parents may be designated as appointed guardians (Sing. *waṣī*) by court order, see, for instance, the country reports on Morocco, Jordan, Saudi Arabia, and the United Arab Emirates.

[16] In Saudi Arabia, creating a milk kinship has become a *de facto* requirement.

In consequence, a very cautious stance has also been taken towards scientific evidence and biological descent. While modern technologies haven been woven into the religiously grounded family law regimes, their application and recognition in court proceedings is under debate and differs significantly from country to country as well as from court to court. To have scientific evidence negate established social and normative orders seems, at least for now, unthinkable in the eleven Muslim jurisdictions under review.

While the position towards biological parenthood without legal ties is strict, social families are emerging and provide parentless children with a home and family environment. At the same time, these new communities do create difficulties for legal and social systems that abide by a single familial leitmotif: the conception of children in a valid marriage. Undoubtedly, broad-scale social acceptance of these new communities remains a long way off. On the bright side however, the legal structures discussed in this volume also bear witness to state legislation that has begun to (better) address the situation of parentless children. Filiation and the question of who forms a family are presently very much in motion.

References

Clarke M (2009) Islam and New Kinship – Reproductive Technology and the Shariah in Lebanon. Berghahn Books, New York and Oxford.

Mohammadi A (2016) The Ambiguity of Maternal Filiation (nasab) in Early and Medieval Islam. The Graduate Journal of Harvard Divinity School 11:52–68.

Möller L-M (2016) Improving Women's Rights Through Children's Rights? The Reform of Custody Laws in Contemporary Muslim Jurisdictions. In: Jänterä-Jareborg M, Tigroudja H (eds) Women's Human Rights and the Elimination of Discrimination/Les droits des femmes et l'élimination de la discrimination. Brill, Leiden and Boston, pp 465–489.

Stoljar SJ (1973) Children, Parents and Guardians. In: Drobnig U et al. (eds) International Encyclopedia of Comparative Law Online. http://dx.doi.org/10.1163/2589-4021_IECO_COM_040701. Accessed 12 October 2018.

Yassari N (2015) Adding by Choice: Adoption and Functional Equivalents in Islamic and Middle Eastern Law. Am J Comp L 63:927–962.

Yassari N, Möller L-M and Gallala-Arndt I (2017) Synopsis. In: Yassari N, Möller L-M and Gallala-Arndt I (eds) Parental Care and the Best Interests of the Child in Muslim Countries. T.M.C. Asser Press, The Hague, pp 325–353.

Nadjma Yassari is a senior research fellow at the Max Planck Institute for Comparative and International Private Law in Hamburg, Germany, where she heads the Department for the Laws of Islamic Countries. Since April 2009, she has led the Research Group "Changes in God's Law – An Inner Islamic Comparison of Family and Succession Laws." Her main fields of research are national and private international law of Islamic countries, particularly the Arab Middle East, Iran, Afghanistan and Pakistan, with a special focus on family and successions law. In her monograph *Die Brautgabe im Familienvermögensrecht – Innerislamischer Rechtsvergleich und Integration in das deutsche Recht* (Mohr Siebeck 2014), she considers the function of the dower within the marital property law regimes of pre-modern Islamic law, contemporary Muslim jurisdictions and German law. Born on 6 March 1971 in Tehran, Iran, she studied law in Vienna, Paris and London. She holds an LL.M. from the School of Oriental and African Studies at the University of London and an LL.D. from the University of Innsbruck in Austria. In 2000/2001, she spent a year at the faculty of languages of the University of Damascus in Syria. In 2016, she was awarded a post-doctoral degree (Habilitation) from the University of Hamburg.

Lena-Maria Möller is a senior research fellow at the Max Planck Institute for Comparative and International Private Law in Hamburg, Germany. Holding an M.A. in Middle East studies and a Ph.D. in law, she has taught and researched in the area of Islamic law, with a particular focus on Muslim family law, as well as in comparative and private international law. She has held teaching positions at the University of Hamburg, the University of Augsburg and, most recently, the University of Münster, where she served as visiting professor of Islamic law. She is the author of *Die Golfstaaten auf dem Weg zu einem modernen Recht für die Familie?* (Mohr Siebeck 2015) and a co-editor of *Parental Care and the Best Interests of the Child in Muslim Countries* (T.M.C. Asser Press 2017). Her articles have been published in journals including Hawwa (Journal of Women of the Middle East and the Islamic World), Journal of Private International Law and The American Journal of Comparative Law, and she is a contributor to *Brill's Encyclopedia of Law and Religion* and the *Encyclopedia of Women and Islamic Cultures*.

Kolibri 360 GmbH
Ferdinand-Jühlke-Straße 7
99095 Erfurt, Deutschland
produktsicherheit@kolibri360.de